The
TENNESSEE
CIVIL WAR
VETERANS
QUESTIONNAIRES

VOLUME ONE
Federal Soldiers (Acuff–Wood)
Confederate Soldiers (Abbott–Byrne)

Compiled by
Gustavus W. Dyer & John Trotwood Moore

Editors: Colleen Morse Elliott (Mrs. O. L.) &
Louise Armstrong Moxley (Mrs. R. L.)

Publisher: The Rev. Silas Emmett Lucas, Jr.

SOUTHERN HISTORICAL PRESS, INC.

P.O. Box 738

Easley, South Carolina 29641-0738

ISBN 0-89308-216-3
ISBN 0-89308-221-X (The Set)

Library of Congress Catalog Card No. 85-50211

PREFACE

It is an unusual event when historians discover that kindred spirits pursued eyewitnesses to significant events, asked them penetrating questions, and recorded their answers. By the twentieth century, dozens of students of American history actively sought to persuade Southern whites and blacks to describe their antebellum lives. Well known to contemporary scholars are the autobiographies and interviews of ex-slaves recorded in the twentieth century. With the exception of the pioneering work of Fred Bailey, little use has been made of a parallel set of autobiographical sources on the lives of antebellum whites: the questionnaires completed by more than 1,600 Tennessee Civil War veterans between 1915 and 1922.

A remarkably well-conceived project, the collection of the questionnaires created a body of unique documents providing a window into the Old South that will yield rich insights. Comparable in many ways to George Rawick's collection of the WPA interviews of ex-slaves, the publication of the stories of the veterans is an event students of the Old South and the Civil War will applaud. The stories of the veterans add life to the social contours often drawn heavily from statistics. They bring us close to the pains and pleasures of war, labor, class relationships, education, and the place of slavery in antebellum society. Genealogical detail is abundant. The range of questions asked is so that the stories contain data of interest to practically all students of the Old South.

We can only hope that the publication of these stories will encourage scholars to search for comparable collections in other states. Given the interest of journalists and historians in Confederate veterans in the last decades of the nineteenth and the early years of the twentieth century, Tennessee could not have been alone in its systematic attempt to record the stories of Civil War veterans.

The publication of the Tennessee volumes marks the beginning of a renaissance in Southern studies based on sources historians have long yearned to examine. There could have been no better beginning than these magisterial works.

John W. Blassingame
Yale University

FOREWORD

In 1914 and 1915, questionnaire forms were sent to all known living Tennessee Civil War Veterans by Dr. Gus Dyer, who was then serving as Archivist of Tennessee. This form is shown as Form No. 1 in the text of this book and did not include questions No. 45 and No. 46 as did the later questionnaire. In 1920, Mr. John Trotwood Moore, Director of the Tennessee Historical Commission, sent a revised form which covered essentially the same data and is shown as Form No. 2 in the text, but included No. 45 and No. 46.

All the completed forms were returned by 1922 and contain such information as date and place of birth; date and place of enlistment; war service, including descriptions of battles, prison life and hospital experiences; rosters of the Company of which the veteran was a member; comments on the economic and social status of the veteran; opinions on slavery; genealogical data; educational and religious data; his and his father's occupation both before and after the war, and many incidental facts. The veterans were encouraged to write fully of their experiences and to give as much family history as they remembered. Many of them included additional pages of material, newspaper clippings, book pages of published information from the *Veteran*, and an occasional photograph.

These interviewed veterans came from all social classes, and their answers varied from short and barely literate annals of the poor farmer to perceptive assessments of pre-war social conditions and detailed autobiographies of well-educated sons of planters, artisans and merchants. This cross-section of human experience makes the material useful to historians (for whose purposes it was created), as well as to the genealogist pursuing information about lives of specific ancestors.

In transcribing this material from the microfilm copy, the editors found some errors in the names applied to the file folders which contain the veteran forms. These have been noted in the text with corrections. No effort has been made to correct the spelling, grammar, lack of punctuation, etc. — the material has been copied just as the veteran wrote. Some of the writing was not clear: certain letters were difficult to decipher, and places were blurred or otherwise unreadable. Notation has been made so that researchers may go back to the original film and read it for themselves. We have made every effort to include all the important data written by the veteran unless it was a duplication of previous answers and this was then deleted. We recommend viewing the microfilm for the pleasure of reading this material for handwriting content and to see the reproduction of photographs. These records contain a wealth of information and are housed in the Manuscripts Section of the Tennessee State Library and Archives.

Colleen Morse Elliott
Louise Armstrong Moxley
Fort Worth, TX   1985

PUBLISHER'S PREFACE

The publisher wishes to express his appreciation to the many people who have had a part in helping to make the publication of the *Tennessee Civil War Veterans Questionnaires* a reality.

First, I would like to express my sincere appreciation to the staff of the Tennessee State Library and Archives, and especially to Mrs. Jean B. Waggener who so kindly arranged for me to obtain microfilm copies of these Questionnaires. Also, I would like to thank Miss Kendall J. Cram, currently director of the Tennessee State Library, for her invaluable assistance and advice on other Tennessee projects we at Southern Historical Press have undertaken. The two people who warrant the highest praise for assisting in this project are Colleen Morse Elliott (Mrs. O. L.) and Louise Armstrong Moxley (Mrs. Robert L.), both of Fort Worth, Texas, who are the editors of this project. Hundreds of selfless hours were given by these two ladies, and several others who assisted them at times, in the transcribing of this material from the microfilm, and then typing it camera ready for the printer.

I would also like to express my appreciation to Fred Bailey, Associate Professor of History at Abilene Christian University, who, by accident, I discovered was one of the two knowledgeable authorities on these Questionnaires, and who, at this writing, has a recently published article[1] and a forthcoming book, concerning a sociological analysis of the Tennessee Civil War Veterans Questionnaires. Dr. Bailey so kindly wrote the excellent Introduction to the *Tennessee Civil War Veterans Questionnaires*, plus a short blurb for our advertising brochure.

Finally, my thanks also go to the other authority on these Questionnaires, Dr. John W. Blassingame, Chairman of the Department of Afro-American Studies and Editor in Chief of the Frederick Douglas Papers of Yale University, who so generously wrote a Preface to these volumes, in addition to a blurb for our advertising brochure.

The Rev. Silas Emmett Lucas, Jr.
Publisher
Ash Wednesday, 1985

---

[1] Fred Bailey, "Class and Tennessee's Confederate Generations," *Journal of Southern History*, Vol. LI, No. 1 (February 1985), pp. 31–60.

INTRODUCTION

Nearly six decades after the last Rebel soldier surrendered, Civil War passions still echoed throughout Tennessee. To be sure, the great leaders were now dead. Such Unionists as Senator Andrew Johnson, Congressman T.A.R. Nelson, and parson-editor-Governor William G. Brownlow rested beneath their monuments comforted that they had vanquished the Confederate cause. Secessionist Governor Isham G. Harris was reconciled to the Federal Union and had gone on to his reward after a long — though undistinguished — career in the United States Senate. The Southern commanders — Braxton Bragg, Joseph E. Johnston, and John B. Hood — had contributed their memoirs, assuring posterity that their actions were strategically valid and morally justified. Politicians and generals made peace with the past. At their passing a generation of historians took up the cause, refighting the Civil War as partisans of the North or the South. These scholars largely ignored the thousands of surviving veterans who still lived. Tennessee was a happy exception. Between 1915 and 1922, the state granted to its common soldiers the opportunity to respond to the Tennessee Civil War Veterans Questionnaires and to share their perceptions of the Old South, the Civil War, and the postbellum world.

The 1,650 respondents to the Tennessee Civil War Veterans Questionnaires were painfully conscious that they were the last remnants of that generation that knew firsthand both the Old and the New South. Seeing "the ranks of the gray become thinner day by day," wrote Benjamin Hagnewood, "serves to remind me that I . . . must soon lay aside this mortal coil." More despondent, Henry Dunavant described a celebration of Robert E. Lee's birthday in 1922. "I was the only old confederate there," he sadly remembered, "and felt so *lonesome* that I was sorry I went." These aging Rebels yearned to relate their stories.

Each of the questionnaires constituted a short, uniform autobiography of a Civil War veteran. It requested from each old soldier a discussion of his antebellum lifestyle: How much land did his family own, did his family have slaves, what kind of house did his family occupy and how many rooms did it have, what kind of activities were engaged in by his father and his mother, what type of work did he do as a boy, and how much education did he receive? This was followed by a series of questions soliciting the veterans' opinions concerning social class relations: Did white men respect manual labor; was there a friendly feeling between slave owners and non-slave owners, or were they antagonistic; was slave ownership a factor in politics; and were there opportunities for a poor man to advance economically? The men were then encouraged to relate their Civil War experiences. They were specifically asked to name their regiments, tell when and where they enlisted, and recount their first battle. This was followed by an invitation to discuss briefly their military engagements, their camp life, and, if relevant, their experiences in hospitals or in prisons. The questionnaires concluded with a request that each veteran write a short sketch of his life since the Civil War stating his occupation, where he lived, his church relation, and whether he held a civic office. In 1915, William E. Orr added at the end of his correspondence the inscription: "I hope you will be able to read what I have written and appropriate at leas[t] a part of it to the History of our beloved South-land." Seven years later, the barely literate Isaac Griffith finished his contribution and then prayed that he might "Live to Read a True Hisary of the Old South."

The Civil War Veterans Questionnaires were collected by two notable archivists at the Tennessee State Library — Gustavus W. Dyer and John Trotwood Moore. Dyer developed the questionnaires during his brief tenure there from 1913 to 1915. Moore, who held the same post from 1919 to 1929, gathered the vast majority of the responses. Their efforts resulted in a rich collection which makes it possible to compare the lifestyles and social attitudes of poor whites, plain folks, and planters.

Dyer was best remembered as an eccentric Vanderbilt University professor. Those who knew him in his last years recalled a rugged individualist, given to peculiarities of dress and to strong conservative views. Despite his later eccentricities, the younger Dyer was a scholar with merit. While working on his doctorate in sociology at the University of Chicago in 1905, he published a small, controversial volume entitled *Democracy in the South Before the Civil War*. The book's last chapter was a harbinger of Dyer's future interest in Tennessee soldiers. It was based upon his oral interviews with 25 ex-Confederates from the Virginia counties of Henry, Franklin, Pittsylvania, and Bedford. Talking with these men during the summer of 1902, he solicited responses to 19 questions dealing with the subject's occupations, land and slave ownerships, and perceptions of social class relations. Thirteen years later, he would improve and expand these questions and send them out to Tennessee's Civil War veterans.

Dyer's concern for Tennessee's Confederate soldiers developed during his short tenure as the director of the state archives in Nashville. On March 15, 1915, he sent out the first of the Civil War Veterans Questionnaires. "As a student and teacher of history," he explained in his cover letter, "I am convinced . . . that the leading history [*sic*] of the United States grossly misrepresents conditions in the Old South . . . The true history of the South is yet to be written." He then urged the veterans to make "a real contribution to the land you love, and to the cause for which you have made many sacrifices." Before more than a handful responded, Dyer's job was terminated and the project aborted.

Seven years later the quest for "a true history of the Old South" was taken up by John Trotwood Moore. A more stable scholar than Dyer, Moore brought to the position the positive attributes of strong passions, deep curiosity, and considerable energy. Just when and under what circumstances Moore discovered Dyer's questionnaires is uncertain, but Moore quickly saw their value and began to collect the vast majority of the responses. A member of Tennessee's Confederate pension board, he had ready access to their files, and he supplemented this information with advertised appeals to Tennessee soldiers in the *Confederate Veteran* (March and April 1922) and with intensive follow-ups on additional names supplied by the aged men in their questionnaires. He probably succeeded in reaching the majority of the state's living soldiers. Writing to Moore, William Harkleroad of Sullivan County noted that he knew "Several veterans around here but think all of them have filled out blanks"; Richard Howell of Hardeman County observed that "all those . . . I know have received blanks like this one"; and James M. Jones of Fayette County reported that "most [old soldiers] I know of have recd letters from you." Little wonder that one ex-Confederate's daughter could express to Moore the confidence "that we have the right man in the right place. We are sure Tennesseans will be grateful for the store of information you have laid up for them."

Genealogists, professional historians, and Civil War buffs will find this "store of information" to be a gold mine, opening up not only the "facts" of the past, but also the passions and the humanity of the Civil War participants. Each questionnaire reveals the respondent's personality. The soldiers took seriously their opportunity to tell about their lives and demonstrated a tremendous diversity of outlook. From the planters in their magnificent mansions, to the plain folk in their humble cabins, to the poor in their dreadful hovels, Tennesseans saw the Old South in many different ways. This superb collection, made possible by the labors of Gustavus W. Dyer and John Trotwood Moore, has remained until recently the single most important untapped resource for understanding the social history of the nineteenth-century South.

Fred A. Bailey
Associate Professor of History
Abilene Christian University

CIVIL WAR QUESTIONNAIRES

(FORM NO. 1)

The chief purpose of the following questions is to bring out facts that will be of service in writing a true history of the Old South. Such a history has not yet been written. By answering these questions you will make a valuable contribution to the history of your State.

1. State your full name and present Post Office address:

2. State your age now:

3. In what State and county were you born?:

4. In what State and county were you living when you enlisted in the service of the Confederacy, or of the Federal Government?:

5. What was your occupation before the war?:

6. What was the occupation of your father?:

7. If you owned land or other property at the opening of the war, state what kind of property you owned, and state the value of your property as near as you can:

8. Did you or your parents own slaves? If so, how many?:

9. If your parents owned land, state about how many acres:

10. State as near as you can the value of all the property owned by your parents, including land, when the war opened:

11. What kind of house did your parents occupy? State whether it was a log house or frame house or built of other materials, and state the number of rooms it had:

12. As a boy and young man, state what kind of work you did. If you worked on a farm, state to what extent you plowed, worked with a hoe, and did other kinds of similar work:

13. State clearly what kind of work your father did, and what the duties of your mother were. State all the kinds of work done in the house as well as you can remember — that is, cooking, spinning, weaving, etc.

14. Did your parents keep any servants? If so, how many?:

15. How was honest toil — as plowing, hauling and other sorts of honest work of this class — regarded in your community? Was such work considered respectable and honorable?:

16. Did the white men in your community generally engage in such work?:

17. To what extent were there white men in your community leading lives of idleness and having others do their work for them?:

18. Did the men who owned slaves mingle freely with those who did not own slaves, or did slaveholders in any way show by their actions that they felt themselves better than respectable, honorable men who did not own slaves?:

19. At the churches, at the schools, at public gatherings in general, did slaveholders and non-slaveholders mingle on a footing of equality?:

20. Was there a friendly feeling between slaveholders and non-slaveholders in your community, or were they antagonistic to each other?:

21. In a political contest in which one candidate owned slaves and the other did not, did the fact that one candidate owned slaves help him in winning the contest?

22. Were the opportunities good in your community for a poor young man — honest and industrious — to save up enough to buy a small farm or go in business for himself?:

23. Were poor, honest, industrious young men, who were ambitious to make something of themselves, encouraged or discouraged by slaveholders?:

24. What kind of school or schools did you attend?:

25. About how long did you go to school altogether?:

26. How far was it to the nearest school?:

27. What school or schools were in operation in your neighborhood?:

28. Was the school in your community private or public?:

29. About how many months in the year did it run?:

30. Did the boys and girls in your community attend school pretty regularly?:

31. Was the teacher of the school you attended a man or a woman?:

32. In what year and month and at what place did you enlist in the Confederate or of the Federal Government?:

33. State the name of your regiment, and state the names of as many members of your company as you remember:

34. After enlistment, where was your company sent first?:

35. How long after your enlistment before your company engaged in battle?:

36. What was the first battle you engaged in?:

37. State in your own way your experience in the war from this time on until the close. State where you went after the first battle — what you did, what other battles you engaged in, how long they lasted, what the results were; state how you lived in camp, how you were clothed, how you slept, what you had to eat, how you were exposed to cold, hunger and disease. If you were in the hospital or in prison, state your experience here:

38. When and where were you discharged?:

39. Tell something of your trip home:

40. What kind of work did you take up when you came back home?:

41. Give a sketch of your life since the close of the Civil War, stating what kind of business you have engaged in, where you have lived, your church relations, etc. If you have held an office or offices, state what it was. You may state here any other facts connected with your life and experience which has not been brought out by the questions:

42. Give the full name of your father: _____; born _____ at _____; in the county of: _____ state of: _____. He lived at _____. Give also any particulars concerning him, as official position, war services, etc.; books written by, etc.

43. Maiden name in full of your mother: _____; She was the daughter of _____(full name)_____ and his wife _____(full name)_____, who lived at _____.

44. Remarks on ancestry. Give here any and all facts possible in reference to your parents, grandparents, great-grandparents, etc., not included in the foregoing, as where they lived, office held, Revolutionary or other war services; what country the family came from to America; where first settled, county and state; always giving full names (if possible) and never referring to an ancestor simply as such without giving the name. It is desirable to include every fact possible and to that end the full and exact record from old Bibles should be appended on separate sheets of this size, thus preserving the facts from loss:

45. Give the names of all the members of your Company you can remember: (If you know where the Roster is to be had, please make special note of this.)

46. Give here the NAME and POST OFFICE ADDRESS of living Veterans of the Civil War, whether members of your company or not.

    NAME   POST OFFICE   STATE

(FORM NO. 2)

In case the space following any question is not sufficient for your answer, you may write your answer on a separate piece of paper. But when this is done, be sure to put the number of the question on the paper on which the answer is written, and number the paper on which you write your answer.

Read all the questions before you answer any of them. After answering the questions given, if you desire to make additional statements, I would be glad for you to add just as much as you desire.

1. State your full name and present post office address:

2. State your age now:

3. In what State and county were you born?

4. Were you a Confederate or Federal soldier?

5. Name of your Company?

6. What was the occupation of your father?

7. Give full name of your father: _____;
   born at _____; in the County of _____;
   State of _____; He lived at _____;
   Give also any particulars concerning him, as official position, war services, etc.; books written by him, etc.:

8. Maiden name in full of your mother: _____;
   she was the daughter of: _____(full name)_____
   and his wife: _____(full name)_____;
   who lived at: _____.

9. Remarks on ancestry. Give here any and all facts possible in reference to your parents, grandparents, great-grandparents, etc., not included in the foregoing as where they lived, offices held, Revolutionary or other war service; what country they came from to America; first settled — county and State: always giving full names (if possible), and never referring to an ancestor simply as such without giving the name. It is desirable to include every fact possible, and to that end the full and exact record from old Bibles should be appended on separate sheets of this size, thus preserving the facts from loss.

10. If you owned land or other property at the opening of the war, state what kind of property you owned, and state the value of your property as near as you can:

11. Did you or your parents own slaves? If so, how many?

12. If your parents owned land, state about how many acres:

13. State as near as you can the value of all the property owned by your parents, including land, when the war opened:

14. What kind of house did your parents occupy? State whether it was a log house or frame house or built of other material, and state the number of rooms it had:

15. As a boy and young man, state what kind of work you did. If you worked on a farm, state to what extent you plowed, worked with a hoe and did other kinds of similar work. (Certain historians claim that white men would not do work of this sort before the war.)

16. State clearly what kind of work your father did, and what the duties of your mother were. State all the kinds of work done in the house as well as you can remember — that is, cooking, spinning, weaving, etc.:

17. Did your parents keep any servants? If so, how many?

18. How was honest toil — as plowing, hauling and other sorts of honest work of this class — regarded in your community? Was such work considered respectable and honorable?

19. Did the white men in your community generally engage in such work?

20. To what extent were there white men in your community leading lives of idleness and having others do their work for them?

21. Did the men who owned slaves mingle freely with those who did not own slaves, or did slaveholders in any way show by their actions that they felt themselves better than respectable, honorable men who did not own slaves?

22. At the churches, at the schools, at public gatherings in general, did slaveholders and non-slaveholders mingle on a footing of equality?

23. Was there a friendly feeling between slaveholders and non-slaveholders in your community, or were they antagonistic to each other?

24. In a political contest, in which one candidate owned slaves and the other did not, did the fact that one candidate owned slaves help him any in winning the contest?

25. Were the opportunities good in your community for a poor young man, honest and industrious, to save up enough to buy a small farm or go in business for himself?

26. Were poor, honest, industrious young men, who were ambitious to make something of themselves, encouraged or discouraged by slaveholders?

27. What kind of school or schools did you attend?

28. About how long did you go to school altogether?

29. How far was it to the nearest school?

30. What school or schools were in operation in your neighborhood?

31. Was the school in your community private or public?

32. About how many months in the year did it run?

33. Did the boys and girls in your community attend school pretty regularly?

34. Was the teacher of the school you attended a man or woman?

35. In what year and month and at what place did you enlist in the service of the Confederacy or of the Federal Government?

36. After enlistment, where was your Company sent first?

37. How long after enlistment before your Company engaged in battle?

38. What was the first battle you engaged in?

39. State in your own way your experience in the War from this time on to its close. State where you went after the first battle—what you did and what other battles you engaged in, how long they lasted, what the results were; state how you lived in camp, how you were clothed, how you slept, what you had to eat, how you were exposed to cold, hunger and disease. If you were in the hospital or prison, state your experience there:

40. When and where were you discharged?

41. Tell something of your trip home:

42. Give a sketch of your life since the close of the Civil War, stating what kind of business you have engaged in, where you have lived, your church relations, etc. If you have held any office or offices, state what it was. You may state here any other facts connected with your life and experience which has not been brought out by the questions:

43. What kind of work did you take up when you came back home?

44. On a separate sheet, give the names of some of the great men you have known or met in your time, and tell some of the circumstances of the meeting or incidents in their lives. Also add any further personal reminiscences. (Use all the space you want.)

45. Give the names of all the members of your Company you can remember. (If you know where the Roster is to be had, please make special note of this.)

46. Give the NAME and POST OFFICE ADDRESS of any living Veterans of the Civil War, whether members of your Company or not; whether Tennesseans or from other States.

VOLUME ONE

Federal Soldiers (Acuff–Wood)
Confederate Soldiers (Abbott–Byrne)

NAMES OF VETERANS FOUND IN THIS VOLUME

UNION
Joel A. Acuff
George W. Adair
James David Adair
Uriah S. Allison
John Fain Anderson
William Landon Babb
Harry Bales
John Wilson Barnett
Josiah B. Bewley
Benjamin F. Bennett
Albert Birdwell
William C. Blair
Samuel S. M. Blankenship
Creed Fulton Boyer
Joseph Bozarth
John Bray (Gray?)
William Brewer
John Brimer
Samuel Arthur Brown
Charles Lafayette Broyles
Marvin Bullington
Moses S. Carlisle
John Wesley Carter
Oliver P. Chambers
Isaac Chatman
Wiley M. Christian
Joseph Cogdell
Peter Collman
Leroy Pate Cox
Tom Davis
George DeLaVergne
Robert E. Depeer
William Dickson
John W. Dinsmore
Wiley Dotson
William A. Douglas
William Franklin Duncan
Marion Finger
Gilbert Fox
George W. Frank
S. George
William H. George
Surbetus Gerard
Cyrus G. Giles
Overton Gore
Isaac Grandstaff
Irvin Hampton
Isaac Addison Hannah
William Harrad
Garry N. Hawkins
John W. Headrick
Joab Helton
William J. Hickerson

John Hoback
Alfred Meigs Hocker
A. T. Holmes
W. J. Johnston
Frederick J. Jones
Henry H. Jones
James Keaton
William Pressly King
John Fletcher Knowles
Mike Krantz
Moses E. Lane
Asa Layman
Charles Layne
George W. Loutham
William W. Lowry
Thomas Mason
Joseph McCloud
William Smith McCollum
Samuel D. Miles
Moses Miller
Benjamin Mills
Cyrus Miranda
William T. Mitchell
John Mooney
John L. Moore
Courtland Latimore Morris
David Moss
Jackson L. Naugher
George W. Norwood
William M. Parker
D. T. Patton
James W. Pierce
Richard K. Pinkley
John Pitts
Martin V. Prince
Anderson J. Roach
William Roberts
William Robinson
George W. Shelton
Mark Shelton
Isaac R. Sherwood
Samuel Shrader
Charles Henry Smart
Newton Smelcer
James M. Smith
Jacob Spickard
Edwin A. Sprague
Joseph A. Stamps
William Starbuck
James Taylor
John Wesley Tucker
Eli T. Walters
Lot Warren
David U. Weagley

George Washington Westgate
Timothy Whitaker
William Whitaker
James Lawson White
Stephen Logan White
Marcus Wiks
William Alexander Wilkins
Ezekiel Harrison Williams
James Wilson
Jefferson Wilson
Francis Marion Wofford
James T. Wolverton
William T. Wood
CONFEDERATE
Napoleon Bonaparte Abbott
Alfred E. Abernathy
J. Press Abernathy
Milton Thomas Abernathy
Ritchard Tucker Abernathy
Stokley Acuff
Robert President Adair
Charles Wesley Adams
Ford Norfleet Adams
J. M. Adams
John R. Adams
Samuel James Adams
William Thomas Adams
George Lafayette Adkisson
Samuel Adkisson
James K. Polk Agnew
James Aiken
Thomas Joyce Aldrich
Andrew Jackson Alexander
E. C. Alexander
E. F. Alexander
George L. Alexander
George Washington Alexander
Jackson Allen Alexander
James Knox Polk Alexander
McKager Cooper Alexander
T. B. Alexander
William Thomas Alexander
John Benton Allen
John Simpson Allen
Myrick Roberson Allen
William Gibbs Allen
W. J. Allen
Frank Oglesby Anderson
Henry Anderson
James A. Anderson
James Berey Anderson
John B. Anderson
John Moultrie Anderson
Mark LaFayette Anderson

J. W. Andes
William Leonades Andes
J. K. P. Andrews
Mark L. Andrews
James Frederick Anthony
Rody S. Anthony
William Lee Anthony
Cincinnatus Apperson
A. W. Applewhich
William Wryley Archer
William Richard Arnett
Francis Marion Arnold
Thomas C. Arnold
Thomas W. Arnold
Henry Clay Arrington
William Ary
J. W. Ashcroft
J. F. Askew
W. T. Askew
Archibald Atkins
Augustine Taylor Atkins
James Merdth Atkins
Lucullus Can Atkins
S. W. Atkinson
George W. Austin
James Austin
J. T. Austin
Robert Austin
William Clanent Aydelott
John M. Aymett
Charles Boyles Bagley
Leander K. Baker
William P. Baker
William T. Baldridge
James Wood Baldwin
Josiah Turner Ballanfant
James Howard Bandy
David Monroe Banister
Romulus Barbee
M. T. Barfield
James Madison Barker
Elijah C. Barnes
J. W. Barnes
William Thomas Barnes
Thomas Alexander Barnett
John M. Barron
George Washington Barron
Samuel Lee Barron
W. H. Barron
Thomas Van Buren Barry
Issac Anderson Bartlett
James Lemuel Bary
Joseph Peter Bashaw
George Booth Baskerville

Gideon Hicks Baskett
James O. Bass
J. B. Bass
William Jones Bass
Robert Baxter Bates
William Brimage Bates
Benjamin Blanks Batey
Robert R. Bayless
Willis Baugh
W. S. Baxter
Andrew Jackson Beaner
Richard Beard
Charles Davis (David?) Beard
William David Beard
William Edward Beard
Ed. Maney (Haney) Beasley
Richard Thomas Beech
Lemuel Jackson Beene
John Walter Bell
W. T. Bell
Ambrose Bennett
Samuel Bennett
William James Bennett
George W. Benson
Zack Briggs, Jr.
Felix Grundy Bilbrey
Lee T. Billingsley
Lewis Green Bing
John Calvin Bishop
John Holland Bittick
W. W. Black
James Knox Polk Blackburn
William Henry Blackburn
Charlie Fleming Blackwell
  (spelled Flemming on form)
Thomas J. Blackwell
Samuel Tate Blair
Henry Pink Blakely
Louis Jefferson Bledsoe
T. N. Bledsoe
W. F. Blevins
David Shires Myers Bodenhamer
G. R. Boles
J. H. Bond
Benjamin T. Bondurant
Thomas Booker
Peter Boring
Berry Rice Bostick
Edw. Bourne
Jefferson Bowden
Robert Lucius Bowden
Adam Alfred Boy
Charles Washington Boya
William Townes Boyd

William Carroll Boze
John Bradford
Andrew Jackson Bradley
J. W. Bradley
Thomas Edward Bradley
Stephen Garrett Bradsher
A. T. Bransford
Soloman Norman Brantley
John N. Brawner
J. F. Bray
J. A. Brewer
Mathew N. Bridgman
William Herschel Briggs
William Jackson Briggs
Edw. S. Bringhurst
Thomas C. Brittain
Jesse E. Broadaway
Joe C. Brooks
B. R. Brown
George Washington Brown
Hiram Riemes Brown
Isaac Brown
James Amos Brown
James P. Brown
Jesse C. Brown
John William Brown
Ridley Shadrick Brown
Russell Lasetor Brown
Stephen J. Brown
Thomas Brown
Isacc N. Broyles
A. M. Bruce
John Hardiman Bruce
John I. Bruce
John Henry Brummitt
Robert Jackson Brunson
Thomas Ledbetter Bryan
John David Bryant
R. A. Bryant
Wylie Richard Bryant
Claudius Buchanan
Daniel L. Luckner
Augustus Gus Buffat
Sam D. Bullen
Francis Marion Bunch
Robert Lee Burks
W. D. Burnley
Jack Busly (Busby?)
Thomas Jefferson Butler
Melmon Marion Butts
E. J. Bynum
James Jordan Byrd
George Dallas Byrne
James Polk Byrne

VOLUME ONE
Federal Soldiers (Acuff–Wood)

ACUFF, JOEL A.

(FORM NO. 1)

1. Joel A. Acuff, Washburn, Tenn.
2. I am 76 years old the 15th of March
3. Tennessee, Grainger county
4. In Tenn., Grainger county. I enlisted in the Federal
5. Farming
6. Farming and preaching
7. I was not 21 years of age and lived with my father on his farm.
8. We did not own any slaves.
9. My parents owned about 150 acres.
10. I suppose my parents were about 5 or 6 thousand dollars.
11. In a two story log house three rooms
12. I worked on the farm. Plowed and hoed the corn and cut the wheat with a craidel and also the oats. I also cleared the land and maid railes and fenced it.
13. My father worked on the farm doing all the kinds of work that I did, described above, and my mother spun thread out of wool and cotton & flax and wove it into cloth and cut and maid garments out of it to cloth the family. They alsoe cooked and scrubed and washed.
14. None
15. It was at that time thought to be the most honorable way this was to make a living.
16. Yes, Sir.
17. A very small persent.
18. Yes what fiew owned slaves in our county was just like the rest of us. They seamed to treed all respectable men alike.
19. Yes, you could tell no difference.
20. They all seamed to be frindly.
21. No but we did not have but fiew slave owners in our county.
22. No. Farm products wear cheap and wages very low. So that the opportunities was bad and it was a hard task for a young man to buy a farm or start into business.
23. They wear not encouraged very much I don't think the slaveholders wanted to elevate the poor boy very high.
24. Common country schools. The Civil War came up when I was about 16 years of age and I served 3 years in it and was deprived of gitting much school.
25. I went from the time I was 6 years old till I was 16, 2 months out of the year.
26. About a mile but we had very poor school when we got there.
27. None but county free schools.
28. Public
29. 2 or 8
30. Yes when they did not have to pull fodder or dry fruit.
31. Man
32. In August 1862 at Cumberland Gap Tenn. I enlisted in the Federal Army.
33. 2nd Tenn. Cav'y. Capt. Irick Sts Oaks and Butcher S. R. Meritt(?) Isaac Kitts Gran Hodges Rial Jennings John Casady, John Gery? Thomas Clapp, William and Joe and Andrue Guy, Wm. Smith, Will and Sam Ramsey, Sam Collins, Elbert Witt, J. M. Wilson, Isaac Ruth?, George Cloud, Jeracy and Riley Romines, Jerry Trambel?, S. Ruth. My last com(manding?) officers was J. H. Bird and St. Sackitt.
34. We went from Cumberland Gap Oak Hill Ohio then to Louisville Ky... then to Nashville, Tenn.
35. About 3 months. We went into the Battle of Stone River in Jan. '63.
36. Stone River or Murfreeboro
37. Any experience from then to the close of the war was hard times with plenty of hard fighting to do. We went from the Stone River fight over to Chicamogga (Chickamauga) and there helped fight one of the hardest Battles of the war. From there we went from place to place and lived out in the weather like dogs exposed to cold and heat wet and .....
38. At Nashville Tenn. about May the 13th 1865.
39. I was given transportation to Straw Bery Plaines Tenn. and came to that point on the train and walked from there across the Clinch Mtn. to my home and caried my suit case and all of my belongings on my back.

1

ACUFF (cont'd.):
40. I went to work on the farm again just as I had dun before the war.
41. In Nov. '65 I maried and settled down to farming and after a hard
     strugle I finaly suceeded in buying a farm and raised my family on
     it.
42. John D. Acuff; Read Hill; Grainger co.; Tenn.; Red Hill (now
     Washburn).; Father did no war service but was Captaine of a co. of
     militia.
43. Winney Kitts; Peter Kitts; Amey Kitts; near Rutledge, Tenn.
44. I am unabel to give you eney thing acurate on this question.
45. & 46. (Nothing shown for these questions)

(Following is on **separate** paper):
     In question 41 I did not heave room to state my Church relations...
which I regard as importent. I am a member of the Missionary Baptist
Church and a ordained minister of that Church I heave bin preaching over
30 years I am and heave bin all my life making the best fight I could
for the right aginst the wrong.

(Q #45):
William Wilkins   Parsons, Tenn.
J. D. Adair   Parson, Tenn.
     These are all I know who are alive to day.

ADAIR, GEORGE W.

(FORM NO. 2)

1.   George W. Adair, Decaturville, Tenn.
2.   77
3.   Giles county, Tenn.
4.   Federal
5.   C. Second Mounted Infantry
6.   Farmer
7.   Isac Adair; dont know; ---; ---; Giles co. Tenn. later in Decatur
     co. Tenn.
8.   Susan Goats; George Goats; _____ Goats; near Decaturville, Tenn.
9.   not known
10. owned none
11. no
12. 130 acres
13. $1500
14. 3 room log house
15. Farm work, plowing and hoeing.
16. My father did general farm work such as clearing and fencing land...
     plowing hoeing gathering etc. My mother did the usual work of a
     house wife of her day such as cooking, spinning, weaving and sewing.
17. no
18. yes
19. yes
20. very little
21. yes
22. yes
23. friendly
24. I think not
25. reasonably
26. I think they were encouraged
27. rural school
28. 36 months or 3 month per yr.
29. about 2 miles
30. rural schools
31. public and private
32. about 3 mo.
33. not much
34. men and women
35. 1864, Jan. 6 at Clifton, Tenn.
36. Nashville, Tenn.
37. we were never engaged in battle
38. ....

2

ADAIR (cont'd):

39. we staid at Nashville about 1 mo. came back to Clifton and from there Johnsonville Tenn. and from there to 54. lived well in camp, had good clothes and plenty to eat.
40. Jan. 6, 1865 at Galitan, Tenn.
41. Came on train to Johnsonville and then on boat up Tennessee River home
42. farming
43. I have spent my life since the Civil War on the farm in Decatur county, Tenn. have been active in the work up to about 3 yrs. ago when I became blind.
44. --

ADAIR, JAMES DAVID

(FORM NO. 2)

1. James David Adair
2. 76
3. Tenn. Giles co.
4. Federal
5. Company c; 2 Tenn. Mt. Inf.
6. Farmer
7. Isaac Adair; Giles co.; none
8. Susan Ghoats; George Ghoats; Elizabeth Ghoats; Giles co., Tenn.
9. no
10. no; $700
11. no
12. 128 acres
13. $700
14. Log 4 rooms
15. Plowing, hoeing, farm work in general as in pertaining a crop
16. Cooking, spinning, weaving
17. no
18. yes
19. yes
20. 20% did not work; 80% worked
21. some did and some were social
22. very few
23. some were and some were not
24. yes
25. no-opportunities very poor
26. they were discouraged by slave owners
27. rural country schools
28. 2 mo. in year to 17 yrs. old
29. 4 mi
30. Houston
31. Public
32. 2-4 mo in yr.
33. yes
34. both
35. Federal; 1-6-'64 near Decaturville, Tenn.
36. Clifton
37. 60 days
38. Battle of Clifton
39. Johnsonville, Tenn. was in no hospital in camps. small huts. a lot being good. sleeping quarters on bunks we made . rice beans bacon crackers coffee sugar
40. 1-20-'65; Gallitan Tenn
41. was discharged at Gallitan Tenn from there to Nashville for a wk or morein the zollise copper houses and ...... rooms ...to Paducah on the....River....and had to walk home which was about 200 miles
42. farming
43. when I was discharged and came home and engaged in farming and in general work pertaining to fa ming and have done nothing since then but farm as long as I have been able to do anything.
44. ----
45. ----

3

ADAIR (cont'd):
46. W. A. Welkins   Parsons, Tenn
     J. B. Hays   Parsons, Tenn
     G. W. Adair   Decaturville, Tenn

ALLISON, URIAH S.

(FORM NO. 2)

1.   Uriah S. Allison; Guntersvill, Alabama; Marshal county
2.   83 years 10 months 14 days
3.   Tennessee; Rabun county
4.   Federal soldier
5.   H and B.; 1 Tennessee
6.   farmer
7.   Robert M. Allison ; North Carolina; Register of Deeds Deputy Serif
     and Jailer
8.   Nancy Bird; Jesse Bird and Clark(?) dont know; Paint Rock, Rone
     county, Tenn
9.   Thomas Allison my grandfatherwas in the Revolution War my father
     told me
10. --
11. --
12. --
13. --
14. --
15. cleared ground, hoed and plowed, all kinds of work on farm
16 through 30: not answered
30 through 44: not answered
45. Col. Robert K. Bird; Capt. Langley; Lt. Pharron Evaritt(?), James
     Clark, 1st Sgt. All the above named have passover(?) since the last
     roll call.Lt. Wylie M. Christian was still alive last heard from.
     He lives at Johnson City East Tenn. if he is still alive and could
     give you more history of the First Tenn Regiment
46. Wylie M. Christian Johnson City Tenn.
     C. f and B Luit. 1 Tenn signed Uriah S. Allison

ANDERSON, JOHN FAIN

(FORM NO. 1)

1.   John Fain Anderson; Washington College
2.   Born November 17, 1844 now in 78 year
3.   Tennessee; Sullivan County; Town Blountville
4.   Tennessee; Roan County; Loudon Town
5.   Schoolboy farm hand
6.   farmer and merchant died in 1849
7.   did not own any my mother was interest in property and managed it
     for her parents. they old
8.   one negro boy
9.   none
10. do not no value this home burned up Sept 22, 1863
11. part logs part frame 16 rooms 194 feetlong 80 feet wide one half
     other half 40 feet wide. This home burned up Sept. 22, 1863 fight
     over town I was absent not there on 22 ofSeptember and did not wit-
     ness it-Batle
12. I howed droped corn ploughcorn carried sheves water helped clare 25
     acres of ground moved rails choped piled brush plouged with big
     plough harrowed picked weed out of hay hauled hay all work on farm
13. My father died in 1849. My mother was best housekeeper I have ever
     seen best cook She sent dinner daily to 8 hands in basket to farm
     supper and breakfast at table conciderable company W. K. McCalister
     and his daughter Fan have eat at this home
14. Yes. 15 negroes slaves servants each one performed its part. I and
     my sist ours
15. Yes and was preformed by all able to do it if they did not work they
     ware concidered trifing worse than a mean negro.
16. They did

4

ANDERSON (cont'd):
17. Thare ware none
18. Slave holders and non slave holders mingled freely.
19. They did.
20. They ware frendly
21. no it did not
22. yesir and a man who could not reed or writ comenced making spining toffs(?) shuttles and like marrid a poor women had 12 child...each form from 40 to 150 acres Oldest son died in confederate army
23. They ware encouraged by slave holders
24. 3 month school and Miss Marget McMurry (1850) 3 months school under Miss Mary Smith and Miss Fannie Smith (1851) 3 months school Rev George Snopp (1853) 5 months school George Anderson 10 months Rev. W. H. W. H. Hunphris-1855 10 Brown and Dily 3 months W. D. Haynes.. monts to W. C. Sept to April 3 months to Col. I. A.(?) Rhea 1865
25. about 41 months
26. about ½ mile Jefferson Acadamy of Act of 1806-built before 1815 ½ mile to female acadamy built about 1844
27. Male Acadamy and Female Acadamy in Blountville and a school house in all voting districts.
28. Publick
29. Schools in Blountville run 10 monts from 1855 to 1860
30. Regularly
31. Boath
32. I wa in U.S. Goverment Employ Feb. 1865 or about
33. Ct. S. F. Tru Acting Quartermaster Releved Captain Chamberlain and Capt Titus his Regment was 14 Illanoys Volenteer Cavelry Regment was never a soldier in ether Confederate or US Army only employ in QM Department as a mesenger carying O.B. Envelops gathering up reports of shops Generalls(?) daily work etc etc nothing to do with railroad transportation only taking such envelops and recept as was nessary
34. to Knoxwell releving Capt. Chamberlain and Tytus (Only chief acting QM)
35. Never
36. None
37. My experiance was pleasent agreeable well fed well clothed well horzed(?) only in office with Lt. S. F. True his clerks Ed Field T. S. Masoner T. C. Gains. O. F. Rench. Thomas Jones. Frank Stowell. (Written on next line: NY-KY-Tenn-Ma.-Tenn. unknown forgotten)
38. Knoxville, Tenn. May or June 1865 by request
39. First day took dinner with Mrs. J. M. Thornburg wife of Colonel J.M. Thornburg. Stayed all nigh(t) with Mrs. Colonel Tolbert grandmother of Rev. Geo. Rutledge Stewart nee Barshaby Col 1 marriage Mr. Stewarts second Co. Tolbert nex(t) nigh(t) Joseph Earnest first cousin of my mother next nigh(t) Samuel Doak Mitchells a brother in law of my mothers
40. commenced work on farm plowing corn any and all work up to 1866 went to stay in Dossers & Fens Store remained untill 1867 went to Brownsborough with goods Failed in 1874
41. Have live here since 1851. Go to Salum Church Oldest Presbyterian church in Tenn. I and wife have 15 children 14 were baptized in Salum Church
42. Samuel Anderson; 6 Civell District; Sullivan; Tenn.; Blountville - Born 7 May 1805 Died 9 February 1849; nothing
43. Hannah Crawford Fain Born May 17-1811 Died Jan. 27-1891; John R. Fain Ellen (Crawford) Fain; Blountville, Sullivan co., Tenn.
44. Nicholas Fain and Elizabeth Taylor born about 1730 married 1752 came from Ireland 1752 to Chester County Pensylvania 1852 to Washington county Tenn in early seventeys two sons John & Samuel Fain to Point Pleasant batle October 10-1774 five sons ware in batle of Kings mountain S. C. Oct. 4-1780 one son in law Andrew Evans who wonded sons John Samuel William Thomas and Ebenezer Fain This John Nicholas Fain was my great grandfather

(Next on film is a page beginning with question no. 34:)
34. As a girl and young woman, state what household or other work you did; whether or not you made your own dresses; and how young women generally lived around you.
A. My sister assisted my mother in all work in garden milking cows

5

ANDERSON (cont'd):

seowing cleaning up and all ladies around us
35. Was it considered dishonorable for women to work?
   A. it was not
36. Did you or any of your friends teach school or do clerical work of
    any king?
   A. My sister tought some 15 months
37. Describe the social customs and entertainments of the times of your
    girlhood and young womanhood.
   A. 1855 cornerstone of Masonick Institute was laid by Masons..Loan-
      don Curter Haynes made adress..Diner was served in courthouse..
      Tickets sold 100 each by R. E. Anderson..Mace Rhea..Anace Rut-
      ledge..R. E. Anderson sold over 1800 worth..100 each on ____..
      2000 for one..1000
38. What part did women take in religious, political and educational
    affairs?
   A. Women helped repaer churches..organize Sabath School..build chur-
      ch, etc. Netherland a fiew..J. T. Harris many
39. Tell your recollections of the war and conditions following it.
   A. Early in 1861 May 7 I seen many boys older than I in 37 Virginia
      Regment two Company ware forming for 19 Tenn., etc., etc. by time
      I reach my 18 birthday Nov. 17-1862 all ware gone.
40. Give all your reminiscences of anti-bellum and post-bellum times.
   A. Comenced making niter by a detail Nov. 17-1862 continued to Jan
      1st 1862 when I was furnished with substitute papers papers..come
      home town was lonesom not enough men to carry remains to graves..
      left home August 1863 to school at Laurel Hill (A. E. written in
      about Hill)..Burnside came..I remained at school never going to
      main road..hard batle of Limestone Tennessee Sept. 8-1863..Hard
      batle of Blue Spring all day and sundy..a sesaw up and down main
      road..Nov 17-1863 comences Seige of Knoxville..Nov. 29 it ends..
      I was sent annother detail and ordered to go to work at making
      salt peter which I did.. Soon they sent me 55.00 greenback and
      told me to go north and under no circumstances join no army as a
      volenteer..This I did.. I never was a Volenteer soldier.. simply
      an employee..my substitute paper ware from 60 North Carolina Reg-
      ment..I never seen it or name of man on it..paid 1000.00 for it
      to John Henry Barkley QM of 60 Volenteer Regment..Barkley, E. D.
      Blake and others ware selling substitute papers..it was a bogas
      afair..many ware sold so ended my stay in Southern Confederacy..
      went to Loudon Roan county Tenn...sold goods for Joseph Anderson
      & son 12 month..Bridge across river was built mutch of Shermans
      army was ree equiped at Loudon..Sheridans, etc..I learned 23 cars
      4 cars and seen Thomas army onloaded and ree loaded, etc., etc...
      and I have amused myself in reeding history cuting from nuse
      papers and preserving them..William Anderson an uncle..his wife
      a daughter of General George Rutledge..he was Sircuit court clerk
      1820 to 1832 of Sullivan co. in 1853 had a son George Rutledge
      Anderson living at Athens, Alabama..he desired visiting him..They
      lived in houses____ had 12 or 15 negros _____ erected for them.
      ..one had a melon patch broom corn patch..one a tobaco patch and
      so on..What they raised was theirs..he was a good horseman and
      had a fine sadle horse..he aranged with them living dining room
      and kitchen open to them..front part of house open..closed..he
      rode to Athens Alabama when he got there he wrote these negroes a
      letter..mention names of each one to them..this letter is written
      on blue paper sealed with a wafer and to colect postage as was
      custom..think postage stamps come into use in later part of 1853.
      ..John Isaac Smith was uncle of _____ Cox, one time Governor of
      Tennessee. He weighed 350 to 400 lbs..looked as large around
      wast as a coal oil barrell..squeaked when he laughed. John Isaac
      Smith had a negro Henry Smith and he, J. I. S., had bought Henry's
      wife. An unusual rain come up..he handed Henry a ruber coat um-
      brella..Rain began..Mr. Smith folowed wagon back in rain..he had
      on low shoes and road was a sheet of watter soon...I was returning
      from mill..pild my load of feed up covered over..droped chain..
      got under wagon..soon water drove me out..Henry Smith colrd and
      some team wagon come to Blountville..hauled a load of Volenteers
      leaving Blountville for organization of 60 Volenteer Infantrey

ANDERSON (cont'd):

Regiment Colord...John Hammer Crawfords Redgment among them was
Henry A. Cox who deposeted his belongings in wagon and laid his
arm on hid tire and took a noble manley crye and got into wagon.
This Henry A. Cox was father of Governor John Isaac Cox..he died
at Vixburg, Mississippi.

John Fain Anderson

Single page-numbered 40:

Three of J. R. Fains negroes run off..volenteered in First Tennessee
Heavy Artilery US..one was kill day they ware discharged..they had
stock armes and ware wating..this soldier and another took guns and
went to fencing..trying to knock Bayonets..others gun was loded..
discharged..it killing him..I went to their Regment in early 1864
and to their tents..seen them. All three have been dead a no of
years..older one buried at Jonesborough by Mr. S. H. Anderson, a
grand sone of J. R. Fain. Mr. Anderson hauled him in his hurse..
paid expences..he was a deserter..come home..was arested by confederate soldiers and many of them knowing him..he was permited to stay
with a confederate Redgement..Mr. Anderson new this and new he never
would be paid for it.

Single page-numbered 40:

I visited Chatanooga Cemetry going to office..given names..got sections..they ware burried in..a negro hand was sent with me as he
was not in section I hunted for his grave till I found going to
office..I reported it..book ware corrected..you are first man or
person who ever looked aft these graves..your correction of section
shows this..the soldiers mother drew a considerable pention but never
visited his grave (I did) and have nobers (numbers?) of graves and
sections on my book..older Negro soldier who came home deserted wife
(underscored with 3 lines; written along side is women) never returned. Colonel J. A. Rhea and Rev. John Waverly Bouchman kept him from
being punished by C. S. Soldiers as they new him, etc., etc. This
Rev. John Waverly Bouchman is Chaplain General of Confederate Veterans Organization. Seen him join Blountville Presbyterian Church
October 5-1855..herd him preach 100 Aniversity surmon of Blountville
Presbyterian Church Sept. 1920...Gov. John J. Cox had a child baptized by J. W. B...I showed him wher wagon stood when his father
deposeted his belongings and got in it.

Single page-numbered 44:

William Anderson came to Cecil county Maryland from Ireland about
1736. Married Ione Brian an Irish woman who died in Sullivan county
August 19-1819. These were my great-grandparents and come to Sull-
ivan county in 1773. Lived and died there. John Anderson born in
Ciscel county Maryland 1765. Removed to New Jersey thence to Augusta
co. Va with his parents then to Sullivan co. Tenn. in 1773. John
Anderson to Rachel Roberts 29 of Dec. 1792. Tennessee Historical
Magazine Page 10 sais Anderson, John to Rachel Roberts 28 Dec. 1792.
Miss White's is isuiing of licens mine marriage next day. John
Anderson was Register of Sullivan county 47 years. His son William,
Clerk of Sircuit court 1820 to 32. Henry Anderson his sone mad(e)
plot to Bristol 1853 surveyor of Sullivan county. I and his son,
J. R. Anderson, cut wood, made fires..his son John R. Anderson was
surveyor at 21 soon resigned.

Single page-numbered 44:

John Fain sone of Nichlas, my great great grandfather..made him my
great grandfather. His wife was Nancy Augnus McMahan daughter of
John McMahan, first Register of Washington county Tenn. John Fain
my great grandfather after his engagement at Point Pleasant Oct. 10-
1774 and at Kings Mountain Oct. 7-1780, was killed at Citico 1788.
I have a certified copy of his will July 15-1788. My grandfather
John R. Fain born Jan. 4-1788, died Apr. 18-1869. Another brother
of 5 Fain Brothers of Kings Mountain Battle... David Fain was killed
by Indians at Crab Orched Ky so two were killed by Indians..John see
Ramsey 421 page for John Fain. Correctly or incorrectly spelled
Fayne..he was my great grandfather.

Single page-numbered 44:

Samuel Anderson my father was the son of John Anderson, grandson of
William Anderson and great grandson of James Anderson.

John Fain Anderson

ANDERSON (cont'd.):
45. ---
46. Moses Lane   Sevierville, Tenn.
     Ruben C. Sims   ----   Tenn.

ATCHLY, WILLIAM D.

(FORM NO. 2)

1.   William D. Atchly; Sevierville; Sevier co.
2.   81
3.   Tennessee
4.   Federal
5.   B; 6th E.T.V.In. / I was 2nd Lt. Co. B 6 ET Vol Infty
6.   Minister of the Gospel
7.   Wm. Atchly/Sevier co./Tenn./He was a musical teacher
8.   Anna Bowers/ Augusteen Bowers/name not known
9.   My great grandfather was born in Mercer(?) co N. J. He served in
     Maj. Duns Regt in the Revolution war for independence.
10. --
11. they did not
12. 140
13. $750
14. 2 story log house
15. I taugt school and worked on the farm
16-31: no answers
32-46: no answers

BABB, WILLIAM LANDON

(FORM NO. 2)

(Answers typed, not hand-written.)
1.   William Landon Babb; Grceneville
2.   I am seventy six years eight months old
3.   born in the state of Tennessee
4.   I was a Federal Soldier
5.   Batery E. First Tenn.
6.   Farmer
7.   Isaac Eweuan Babb/Green County, Tenn./near Greenville/he was a powder
     maker for a good many years
8.   Katherine Goodin/James Goodin/Kathrin - I dont remember her maiden
     name/on Gray Creek, Green county
9.   --
10. I oned no property at the opening of the civel war
11. I nor my parents owned slaves
12. My father owned 300 akers of land
13. 1000 dollars
14. it had seven rooms two story log house weatherborderd and seald
15. I plowed choped wood made rales built fence and done all kinds of
     farm work that was requird to do at that time
16. My father was a powder maker a number of years and a farmer in his
     later years my mother all kinds of hous work such as cooking warsh-
     ing weaving making quilts cuting and making clos for the family
17. they oned no servant nor kept none
18. by the laboring clas of people, but not by the welthy slave holders
     they thought themselvs elevated above the laboring clas of people
19. as farm work
20. it was the slave holders that led the idal life
21. the slave holders was always elevated above the comen laboring man
22. no, they always moved in circle to themselves thinking themselvs on
     a hiar plane than the laboring man
23. the laboring was looked by the slave holder as being down on a level
     with the slave or not as quit as good as the slave
24. no, evry thing had to be in favor of the slave holder
25. not by the slave holder, but he was encoraged and helped by the
     laboring man.
26. they was discouraged by the slave holder

8

BABB (cont'd.):
27. I dident have the oppertunity of attending any mutch I got to go to
    the free scool a few months was all that i gotto go
28. about eight months all to gather
29. --
30. free scools, the slave holders sent there children off to colage was
    educated at colage
31. the most of the schools was privat scools
32. from three to four months
33. no they had to work
34. I went to a woman about three months and to a man a bout five months
    was all the scooling that I got
35. I volenterd in november 1863 in knox county Kentucky in the Federal
    Government
36. Camp Nelson, Kentucky
37. about six months
38. Moristown and Bulls Gap Tenn.
39. ours went from Camp Nelson Kentucy to Nashville Tenn, and went in to
    what was called the Zolicoffer barix and stade there about two weeks
    then we was moved out to what was called Camp Gillam
40. I was discharged at Nashville Tenn. In August 1865
41. I was given free transportation home to Greenville, Tenn.
42. Farming
43. Two years I farmed then I went to the wagon shop and my apprentisship
    then I worked at the wagon business for about ten years, then I left
    the shop and got out and worked at the carpenters trade for about
    ten years, then I droped the carpenters trade and took up a still
    liter trade as a orchard business and still work a little at the
    business yet when I am able to work
44. ---

BALES, HARRY

(FORM NO. 2)

1. Harry Bales/White Pine/Tenn./Jefferson co.
2. 98 years old
3. Greene county, Tenn.
4. Federal Soldier
5. M co./First Tenn. Cav. Vol.
6. Farmer
7. Jonathan Bales/Blutown/Green county/Tenn./or near Bluetown Green
    county
8. Eliza Jane Humbard/Henry Humbard/(no mothers name)/Rheatown
9. --
10. None
11. No
12. 100 acres
13. 1500.
14. log house 4 rooms
15. all kinds of farm work
16. Father all kinds of farm work Mother done all kinds house work inclu-
    ding cooking spinning sewing washing & mending
17. None
18. yes sir
19. they shure did
20. a very small persent
21. in my community the slave holders whitch lived there was vurry sosi-
    able
22. they did
23. frindly
24. no for there was more non slave holders than slave holders
25. yes
26. --
27. free schools
28. I cannot say
29. one half mile
30. free schools

BALES (cont'd.):
31. publick
32. --
33. yes
34. both
35. (Federal Government)/ I voluntered in Co M first Tenn. cav. vols. on the first day of April 1863 at Nashville Tenn in the Federal army
36. Trynne Tenn.
37. Just a few days
38. a little brush near Trynne
39. them that followed J. P. Brownlaw that kept no diary cannot under-take to tell how many engagementshe was in but a plenty..I assure you my _____ was like other soldiers that was almost constantly on the go
40. at Nashville Tenn on the 19 day June 1865
41. took train at Nashville Tenn to Stuville stade all night and came to Greenville...my home town the next day pennd my father without coming on home.
42. farm work
43. I have engaged in farm work. When I was younger I served Jefferson county as Depty Sheriff & Sheriff 8 years..4 years as Depty and 4 years Sheriff..so I am old and forgetful and you must not expect me to give all my past history
44. ---
45. Capt. J. A. Collins; 1 Lt. Samuel Love (Lane?), 2 Lt. George Harris; Jim Huggins; Hamilton Huggins; David Morrison?; Jos. (Jas.) Morrison; Mash.? Ambrose: Abner ____; Jameson ____; ____; ____; William Huffman; L. R. Bales; Andres Huggins; John ____; Frank B____; Calvin Sutter (Sutton?); Alford Northum?; Benjam Wade_
46. James White   White Pine
    John Gartlin   White Pine
    Andrew Huggins   White Pine

BARNETT, JOHN WILSON

(FORM NO. 2)

1. John Wilson Barnett/Achille, Bryan co., Oklahoma
2. seventy four
3. Bradley co., Tenn.
4. Federal
5. Co H/12th Tenn. Cal.
6. Farmer
7. William Hazelett Barnett/Knox co., Tenn./Cleveland, Bradley co., Tenn. no war service, no books
8. Elizabeth Odonelly/Isaac Odonelly/Mary Odonelly/Virginia (co. not known)
9. My fathers ancestors came from England and settled in North Carolina. I dont (know) their names. My Mothers grandfather and grandmother came from Ireland. They settled in Virginia.
10. I owned no property
11. Didn't own any
12. 160 acres
13. The value was $5000.00 as near as I can remember
14. Log house..it had 3 rooms
15. I done all kinds of farm work. I plowed..hoed out ditches and done anything that is to be done on the farm.
16. My father farmed for a good many years and took up the coopers trade. /My mother did her own house work..had no servants..she spun and wove her cloth and made all of our clothes.
17. No.
18. It was
19. yes
20. About 10% had other men to do their work.
21. No./they did
22. No
23. They were antagonistic to each other.
24. It helped the one that owned slaves to win his contest.
25. no

10

BARNETT (cont'd.):
26. Discouraged
27. Not much of any kind.. oney a short subscription school.
28. About 2 miles
30. Nothing..only short subscription schools.
31. ---
32. about 3 months
33. yes
34. men
35. I enlisted in the U. S. Army Feb. 20th 1864 at Cleveland Tenn.
36. Nashville, Tenn.
37. About 6 months
38. Tryune, Tenn.
39. I went to Pulaski Tenn. we went to scouting over the country fighting
    guerillas..Tullahoma 2 hrs. Tryune about 4 hours. Columbus Tenn. 12
    hrs. Nashville Tenn. about 4 days. Lynville 6 hrs. Surphia Testle 6
    hrs. Franklin Tenn. 24 hrs. Pulaski 1 day Cliften Tenn 2 hrs.
40. June 26th 1865 Washington, D. C.
41. I was sick all the way home and for a year after so cant tell any-
    thing.
42. Farming
43. I lived in Tenn. until 1868 and moved to Georgia and stayed there
    untill 1885 and moved to Bonham, Fannin co.Texas and from there near
    McKinney, Collin co. Texas and from there near Ravenna, Fannin co.
    in 1893. In 1897 I moved to the Indian Territory near Durant and
    have lived in this vicinity untill the present day. This is Bryan
    co., Oklahoma since state hood. Have been farming all the time up
    untill the last few years. My church relations are Missionary
    Baptist.
44. --
45. Abner, Burk, Burnett, Barnett, Burns, Crowe, Cordell, Davidson,
    Dennis, Farrell, Goodson, Golden, Hips, Honeyman, Johnson, Langley,
    Nettles, Swasgood, Sinyard, Parker
46. W. P. Rice   Calera, Okla.
    Paddy Cox   Calera, Okla.
    R. R. Halsell   Calera, Okla.
    John Porter   Calera, Okla.
    J. H. Mashburn   Mannsville, Okla.
    J. B. Coleman   Colbert, Okla.
    Allan Goolsby   Colbert, Okla.
    George Marsh   Platter, Okla.

Separate sheets to question 39.
      The results at Trune were 500 or 600 killed. At Tullahoma about 150
were killed. At Columbus about 3000 were killed..several hundred
wounded. At Nashville about 7000 were killed and hundreds wounded.
Probably 10,000 at Lynville-very few killed probably 40 or 50. A
great many wounded. Surphia Trestle-about 300 men killed and 500 or
more wounded. At Franklin 6000 men killed and probably 7000 wounded.
At Pulaski-400 or 500 killed at lots of men wounded. At Clifton
only 10 men killed lots of them wounded. it was only a guerilla
fight. The Federals were victorious in all the fights that I was in.
We were driven back twice..once at Franklin and once at Pulaski, but
succeeded after all. I lived fine in camp. I were well clothed all
the time. I slept sometimes on dry land..sometimes in mud and water.
We scraped the snow off of the ground in winter and layed down and
slept on the bare ground. We had bacon and beans, coffee, beef, hard
tack, dried fruit, onions, sugar and had a little whiskey when we
caught the quarter master gone and could steal it. We were exposed
to cold often and I have went as long as 5 days with out food. I
was never in the hospital or prison.

                    BENNETT, BENJAMIN F.

(FORM NO. 1)

1. Benigian F. Bennett/Watertown, Tennessee
2. seventy four yrs. 12 days old of March 14, 1922.
3. DeCab county State of Tennessee

BENNETT (cont'd.):
4. I live in Tennessee and enlisted in Smith co, in the Federal Army.
5. Farming
6. Farmer
7. did not own any
8. did not
9. fifty five acres
10. two thousand dollars
11. a double log house with a entry between them
12. I never plowed very much before the war..I thinned corn, hoed corn and pulled weeds.
13. done all kinds of farm work. my mother cook, carted and spun, wove, made all her clothes at home, washed and ironed, done all the house work in general.
14. not any
15. Honest toil was look at as respectable and hones liveing.
16. yes sir
17. The majority of them tended their own lands..made their own living at home.
18. the most of them slowed respect to them that had no slaves. they would swapt work with each other in harvesting their fields.
19. yes
20. They were friendly and sociable and more reliougious than they are now.
21. I was to young to remember much about that.
22. It was good to them that exceppeted it but most of them prefered to stay at home till they were twenty one years old.
23. dont know
24. just common free schools.
25. not very much
26. something like three quarters or a mile from where I was raised.
27. free schools
28. free school but if a man was 21 years old and wanted to go to school he paied for his tuition
29. about four months genearaly
30. yes
31. men most of the time.
32. I enlisted at Carthage Tenn. the county seat of Smith co. in the year of 1863. I was 15 years old 14 March and enlisted 8 day of April Stokes Cavelry.
33. 5th Tennessee Calervery. I enlisted in Capt. Bass co. Co K..their names as I remember of my comrades are: Leutient Roberson, Billie McDowell, Mat Dickens, Brade Dickens, Sid Suemake, Tim Bush, Creed Jones, Jim Jones, John Clubs, Henry Nothing, Prudaman Cleamans, Joe Cleaman.
34. Bridge Port, Ala.
35. dont remember
36. I wasnt in no battle at all
37. I had good clothes, slept in dog tents..plenty to eat most of the time eat around..a scaffold stood up and eat exposed some time.. pretty tuff some time..faired pretty well.. wake us us some time at 2 o'clock in the .... ride the rest of the night..false alarm..we would think the bush whaxers were after us.
38. at Pulaski, Tenn. Giles co. Aug. 14-1865
39. I went from Plulaskia, to Nashville..got my discharge and pay..went on the train then from Nashville home in a 2 horse peddling wagon with Uncle Wilse Jackson and Mart Foutchs..I paid 3 dollars for 50 miles ride and walked half way.
40. Pretty soon after I come home I began cutting cord wood with a chopping ax...cut down large beech trees with my ax and chop it up limbs and all..use no saw.
41. I kept family grocery for a long time ___ it peddling..done most all kind of honest work..I dont belong to know church now..the church busted up and I have never gone know where else.
42. Benjaiam Bennett/North Cla./dont know/North Cla/Alexandria, Tenn.
43. Miss Liza An Bennett/dont know/dont know/they died in time of the war. my grandparents on my mother side. I was young and dont know much about them.
44. I am old and absent minded cant remember way back there. my grandparents.. I have answered the questions the best I could remember.

12

BENNETT (cont'd.):
I dont belong to any church but am trying to live right.
B. F. Bennett

BEWLEY, JOSIAH B.

(FORM NO. 2)

1. Josiah B. Bewley/Greeneville
2. Seventy Six Jan. 10-1922
3. Tenn./Greene County
4. Fedral
5. Co A/2nd Tenn. Calv.
6. Farmer & stock dealer
7. Philip Meroney Bewley/Warrensburg/Greene/Tenn./Warrensburg also
    Cocke county, Tenn. at Newport/local minister in M. E. Church
8. Manerva Jennings/Anderson Jennings/Zilpha _____/Tazewell, Claibourne
    county, Tenn.
9. My father Philip Meroney Bewley..local minister in M. E. Church..my
    grandfather Jacob Murphy Bewley, soldier in Mexican War..Great Grand-
    father, Anthony Bewley, came to Greene co. from Va. his parents from
    England..I think Holland.
10. no was only a boy
11. my father owned 2 slaves
12. about 500 acres
13. about four thousand dollars..fifty thousand now.
14. old fashion framed house..six rooms
15. Did all kinds of work done on the farm and worked every day..worked
    with the slaves & employed white men.
16. My father works on the farm..what time he was not out buying & trad-
    ing in stock....my mother assisted in house keeping..cooking..
    weaving etc.
17. Yes, two slaves..hired men & women..all worked together.
18. Respectable and honorable
19. yes
20. Very few. All communities had a few idlers but were not respected
    as those who worked.
21. ---
22. yes
23. yes, all were on friendly & social terms
24. no
25. yes
26. encouraged
27. Subscription schools
28. About 16 years from 3 to 5 months per annum.
29. 2½ to 3 miles
30. No colledges or high schools..people erected school houses and the
    vicinity employed the most compitent teacher they could get. School
    term depended on the people who employed them.
31. Private and public. . at that date very short terms of public schools
    ..two to three months.
32. 2 to 3 months
33. only moderately..parents at that did realize the importance of an
    education.
34. Both..sometimes a woman..more often men.
35. I enlisted in the Federal Army Sept. 1st 1863 at Nashville, Tenn.
36. Decater, Ala.
37. About two months. While at Decater Ala. we fought General Forest
    men most every week.
38. ---
39. As above stated stationed at Decater Ala. had small fights with
    Forest men. When General Hood(?) attempted to go to Nashville we
    engaged in battle with him at Decater while his army was crossing
    Tenn. river at Mustle Shoals..evacuated Decater and engaged in
    battle at Sulpher Trustle and other points Duck River Franklin
    followed him on retreat.
40. At Nashville Tenn. July 6th 1865.
41. Took train at Nashville Tenn in co with the regiment. Some got off
    at Chattanooga. All along to Bristol, Tenn. I got off at Russell-

BEWLEY (cont'd.):
ville, Tenn. 12 miles from home..made rest of trip on horseback.
42. Farming and stock growing
43. Farming. South east of Warrensburg, Green co, Tenn. 16 miles west
   of Greeneville Tenn. A member of M. E. Church..Was P. M. at Pates
   Hill Tenn. 11 years. Magistrate 15 years. Chairman of County Court
   3 years. My home is on the banks of Chucky river. Reared 5 boys
   and one boy (girl?). After becoming too old to farm much. The
   Government established a national cemetery around the grave of
   Expa___ Andrew Johnson. I was appointed Supt. of that cemetery and
   took charge 13th of Nov. 1908. Am here now and hope to remain here
   while I am able to attend to the business of the office.
   I knew W. G. Brownlow. Horace Maynard. N. G. Taylor..his sons.
   Robert L. (our Bob). A. A. Taylor. Andrew Johnson. W. P. Brownlow.
   Hons. Wm. & Robert McFarland. Judge Clark. Dewitt Senters. Senators
   Shields & McKellar. Senator Bates & others.
44. ----
45. I have no roster. Most of our old company have answered the last
   call. My first Capt. was Capt. Aric of Union county, 1st Lieut
   Leafate Oaks of Union county. Second Lieut. Robert Locket of Louden
   county. Later Capt. John H. Bard of Morgan county. Lst Sergt. M.
   Wilson of Union county, Tenn. John Casady, Ryle Jennings, Granvill
   Hodges, Isaac Kitts, Joel Acuff, Elbert Witt. Wm. Philips, George
   Cloud, Jerry Tramble, Andrew Sneed, Tom & Wm. Smith, Thos. North,
   Wm. Greer, William Ausbin, George Clowlinger, Jos. English, William
   & Ike Guy..this is about all I can remember at this time. Most of
   my regiment were made up from Greene, Cocke, Sevier, Claibourn,
   Union, Morgan & Louden counties.
46. W. T. Mitchell   Greenville, Tenn.
    John Gray   R. F. D. Greenville, Tenn.
    Silas Fornay   R. F. D. Greeneville, Tenn.
    Charlie Broyles R. F. D. Greeneville, Tenn.
    ---- Moss   Cedar Creek, Tenn.
    ---- Jones   Greeneville, Tenn.
    Jacob Hybarger   R. D. #22 Greeneville, Tenn.
    W. E. F. Millburn   Greeneville, Tenn.
    W. H. Harrison   Greeneville, Tenn.
    Jas. Maloney   Greeneville, Tenn.
    John E. Wisecarver R. D.#2 Midway, Tenn.
    Joseph Alexander   Greeneville, Tenn.
    Dr. Dobson   Greeneville, Tenn.

                    BIRDWELL, ALBERT

(FORM NO. 1)

1. Albert Birdwell/Buena Vista/Carroll co./Tennessee
1. 81 years
3. Tennessee/Carroll co.
4. Tennessee/Carroll co.
5. Farming
6. Farming
7. I owned no property
8. not enny
9. 150
10. my parents was dead when the war opened.
11. log house/3 rooms
12. I plowed when needed and used the hoe the same..did all other farm
    work.
13. my father farmed for a living..my mother did all kinds of house
    work
14. not enny servants
15. yes
16. yes
17. cant answer
18. naw
19. yes
20. yes
21. do not know

BIRDWELL (cont'd.):
22. fairly good
23. cant answer
24. Privet
25. about 6 months
26. 3 miles
27. Walnut Grove and Holly Springs
28. Privet
29. from 2 to 3 months
30. yes
31. both
32. 14 of Aug. 1862/at Maple Creek
33. 7th West Tennessee Caverly/Furman Sanders/Arsra Gooch/James Burton/
    Thomas Essary/Green Batman/Cole Harris/Brad Harris/Thomas Dodd/Stan-
    ley Dodd/Silas Johnson/Silas Brinkley.
34. Trenton, Tennessee
35. 5 month
36. the Lexington Battle
37. Went to Browns Station, Tennessee. Was not in enny other Battles.
    Clothed good. Slept and ate very good. We took the weather as it
    came.
38. October the 25-1863 at Sails Bury, Tennessee
39. Boarded a boat at Memphis, Tenn. and come to Carroll then took
    another boat up Tennessee River to Bomans landing then walked 25
    miles home.
40. Farming
41. Farming has bin my ocupation
42. Isac Birdwell/dont know/ -0-
43. ----
44. ----

BLAIR, WILLIAM C.

(FORM NO. 1)

1. William C. Blair/Huntingdon, Tennessee
2. 89
3. North Carolina/Macklinburg co.
4. (Federal Government)/Tenn./Carroll co.
5. Farming and school teaching
6. Farming and teaching
7. 317 acres/$1200, and other farming inpliments & stock of all kind
    which goes to make up a farmer.
8. my parents owned 3
9. 200
10. Land and negores $3000
11. Log & frame 4 rooms
12. Farming, all kind of work done one the farm
13. My father farmed and my mother done all kind of house work including
    spinning, weaving, etc.
14. nothing, but 3 slaves
15. yes with all good people
16. yes
17. They did not
18. Yes they mingled freely and seemed to all be in one class.
19. They certainly did.
20. Good feeling
21. I think not
22. Yes by close work
23. Encouraged by all
24. Public schools
25. 15 years off and on
26. 2 miles
27. Common public schools
28. Public
29. 3 months
30. yes
31. man
32. (Federal Government)/Paducah, Ky.

15

BLAIR (cont'd.):
33. 2nd Tennessee Mounted Infantry Co G/my Captain was Capt. Chambers
34. Johnsonville, Tennessee
35. only a short time
36. Battle at Hico Tenn. where our Major was killed
37. From this time on we had a hard time..many battles, and exposed to
    hungry and cold but had good clothes. I was in hospital with accute
    broncal trouble.
38. At Galatin Tenn. in 1865
39. I came down the river to Paducah and taught school for a while and
    then returned to my home at Huntingdon, Tenn.
40. Farming and school teaching
41 I still farmed and taught until I was to old. I served my district
    as magsistrate for a no of years.
42. Wm. Blair/Raligah/Montgomery/North Carolina/just a common farmer
43. Margaret McAuley/Old Man McAuley/Mandy McAuley/----
44. Grandmother came from Scotland and grandfather came from Ireland.
    This is about all I remember now.
                                    William C. Blair
                                    Huntingdon, Tenn.

                    BLANKENSHIP, SAMUEL S. M.

(FORM NO. 2)

1. Samuel S. M. Blankenship/LaFayette, Tennessee
2. age 80   3rd March 1921
3. Tennessee, County Macon
4. Federal
5. I/9th Kentucky Infantry
6. Farmer
7. David Blankenship/Franklin, Virginia/Franklin/Virginia/Moved to
    Smith county, Tennessee 1820/no ware service/books none
8. Judie Holland/John Holland/Polly Holland/LaFayette, Tennessee
9. Virginia. No office held. Great uncle served in Revolutionary War.
    Came from Holland. Virginia. Bedford county.
10. No land or other property.
11. No slaves
12. About 300 acres
13. Value of land about $150.00 (other property about $75(00.
14. Log house. only three rooms
15. Worked on farm practically every day..plowed and used hoe to great
    extent.
16. Father worked on farm all of life. Mothers work house chores..wove
    and spun all the cloth to make clothing for the children, husband
    and herself.
17. None
18. Among most classes it was considered respectable and honorable for
    anyone to do.
19. Yes
20. Practically all did their own work. Very few had slaves
21. Cant remember
22. Cant remember
23. So far as can remember they were allright to each other.
24. Cant remember
25. Opportunities were poor unless one had a good capital of which he
    had heired.
26. Those that depended on daily labor for their support were discour-
    aged because of less work to do and also got smaller wages.
27. Country school
28. Lasted about three months each year. In all about 30 months.
29. about one mile. road leading to the school was rough.
30. only one school could have handily been reached while boarding at
    home.
31. most public
32. about three months
33. yes
34. all men teacher

BLANKENSHIP (cont'd.):
35. December 1, 1861 at Columbia, Kentucky
36. Glasgow Kentucky and and shortly to Nashville
37. 4 months
38. Battle of Shiloh engaged in this battle only one day
39. Had experience which proved to be beneficial after leaving army.
    After battle went to Corinth Mississippi made preparation for battle
    but enemy left before any battle, Murfreesboro & Love Joy Station
    about two days results good Well taken care of in hospital
40. Huntsville, Alabama January 8, 1865
41. From Huntsville we came to Nashville to Bowling Green Kentucky thence
    to Scottsville Kentucky and then home
42. working on farm with father
43. Working on farm as long as physical ability allowed me. Lived in
    Macon county Tennessee since I came from army. Was married to
    Katherine Jane White March 8, 1865. 7 children were born six boys
    and one girl all of whom are living except one. Four of them have
    taught school in Macon county one after made a medical doctor and
    also he served in the Worlds war as first Lieutenant but did not go
    over seas. Another gr M. Blankenship studied lay and afterwards
    went to Los Angeles California. Other four are farmers. Belong to
    Missionary Babtist Church.
44. .....
45. L. Pate Cox   Lafayette, Tenn.
    Tom Dixon   Trousdale co, Tenn.
    Albert Meador   Lafayette, Tenn
    (all of these are living)
    Same regement
    Capt. Reed   Scottsville, Kentucky
    M. Reed   Scottsville, Kentucky
    Lou Whitney   Red Boiling Springs, Tennessee
46. Pate Jenkins   Scottsville, Kentucky
    M. Durham   "
    Pate Cox   Lafayette Tenn.
    Robert Deckerd   Lafayette, Tenn.
    Wilson Bray   "   "
    Wesley Bandy   "
    Jake Butram   "
    Will Dillard   "
    Jim Meador   Westmorland Tenn
    Logan White   Lafayette Tenn
    Gilbert Wakefield   "
    Will West   "
    Jim Bill   "
    Jim Pedigo   "
    Mike Krantz   "
    Neut Marsh   Red Boiling Spgs. Tenn.

BOYER, CREED FULTON

(FORM NO. 2)

1. Creed Fulton Boyer, Newport Tenn. Box 224
2. 75
3. Cocke County Tennessee
4. Federal
5. A; 3rd Tenn. Mounted Infantry
6. Farmer and tanner
7. Isaac Boyer; Shenandoah Valley; Rockingham; Va.
8. Elizabeth Sims; Elliott Sims; Joanna Galen; Wilsonville, Cocke
    County, Tenn.
9. Grandfather Jacob Boyer came from Germany settled 1st in Mass. was
    a private in the revolution war; moved to Penn. and from there to
    Va. and from there to Tenn. Grandfather Sims came from Scotland to
    S.C. and from there to Tenn.
10. I was a miner during the Civil war mustered out of service at 18th
    birthday.
11. father owned 7 negroes

BOYER (cont'd.):
12. about 1000
13. Father died in 1854. Mother owned about 240 acres value then about 3000.00 that is at the beginning of the war
14. log house, two storries two porches and kitchen two rooms to main house.
15. I plowed, hoed, cut wheat, hay and oats, gathered corn. In the early young manhood we cut wheat with a cradle and sych. Husked with flail and tread mill.
16. Father worked on the farm and tannery. Made some apple and peach brandy and corn whiskey. Mother and girls 6 sisters wove spun on big and little wheels the(y) sewed washed cleaned house. Spun and wove cotton and flax cloth and made that into wearing apparel for the 9 boys and father.
17. no
18. yes
19. yes
20. none that I know of
21. they seem as one
22. yes
23. There seemed to be no difference
24. no
25. yes
26. encouraged
27. common country
28. about 3 months @ annum
29. about 2 miles
30. Parrotsville, Goodhope and teach (?) colledge 'this colledge was built of bunch logs no chinking nor daubing)
31. Public mostly by private subscription
32. amed to run 3 mos but stoped through fodder pulling and molasses making this would...the time to something like two months
33. not very
34. both
35. I enlisted in the Federal army on the 11th June 1864
36. Strausburg + Plains (+ Strawberry?)
37. about 2 mos
38. Bulls gap
39. From bulls gap we went to Straw Plains had a battle there then to Greenvile (?). There when Morgan was killed. Then back to Horsey(?) Creek belonged to Gillams brigade. horse shot while carrying message to Catauga(?) bridge. We had no camp outs during the civil war plenty of crackers, coffee and sow belly.
40. Mustered out at Knoxville Tenn on the 12th Dec. 1864
41. nothing of interest only 65 miles from Knoxville to my home
42. farming
43. Since the war I have farmed sold goods taught school worked the public roads been J. P. for 4 years Sheriff 10 years. Circuit Court Clerk 8 years Mayor 2 years. Cashier of bank 2 years. Worked for the Rejean River lumber & Iron Co. 12 years. been member of the Legislature 3 times. I have lived all my life in Cocke County. I affiliate with the M. E. Church. I am a royal arch mason. I hung two men while sherif the only local hangings that ever occurred in the county. I also _____ two men to Shock(?) whle in the line of duty as sheriff.
44. ....
45. Iranius Cisenburn?
    Thos Heritage
    Thos Safley
    Thos Swaktell
    John Davis
    John Shumaker
    John Pitman
    John Smith
    Wm. Burnett
    James Jones
    Hartwell Balch
    Wm Creesman
    Hickory Johnson Sr.
    Hickory Johnson Jr.

18

BOYER (cont'd.):
    John Archer
    Pleas. Williams
46. C. F. Boyer   Newport Tenn
     John Dowell   Bly....   "
     John Heritage   "   "
     John Smith   Parrotsville Tenn
     Foreman Fancher   "
     Joseph L Green   Hartford Tenn
     Henderson McMillan   Denton Tenn
     Da.... I Davis   Hartford Tenn
     J. S. Redwine   Byl.......
     Wm. Stringer   Rankin Tenn

                    BOZARTH, JOSEPH

(FORM NO. 1)

1.   Joseph Bozarth; Silver Point, Tenn.
2.   77 yrs old
3.   Tennessee, Dekalb county
4.   Tennessee
5.   a farmer
6.   farmer
7.   none
8.   none
9.   300? acres
10. Valued at 2500 dollers
11. a log bilding made of hued logses 4 rumes
12. I plowed with a how as round as and egg with a bull long plow
13. mi father was a farm by trad. mi mother was a cook spun all of the
     thread that she used wove her on cloth
14. none
15. very mutch in this community
16. the whit man was the Depenace in this communities
17. som men was very idle as the are in ther communities
18. I cold not tell any diferace between the men that owned slaves and
     them that did not own them
19. awll the same as I can recelect if thar was any diferac between them
     I dont recelack.
20. all right so far as can remember
21. if thar was any ill feling be tween them I dont now it
22. som men used ingenuity when others lirked aroun and don nothing
23. som of them tried to mak something of them other did not
24. free schools
25. about three months
26. one mile
27. shart free schools and not very well taut
28. public
29. ... 2 months
30. not very mutch
31. a man all of the time
32. was at Carthage Tennessee in the month of October as well as I can
     rember 1863
33. first Tennesse monted infantry
     I dont know of but one living out ___ of myself and that is Asbery
     Thames
34. from Nashvill back to Carthag
35. in a continuel giriler fit all of the time in the comberland mount-
     ain contry
36. at Calf Killer Whit and Putnam county Tenn
37. was very critical very well fed and cloth
38. at Nashvill Tennese
39. a traveled on steem boat the most of the time
40. farming
41. I have bin in the lines of farmin most of the time. I hav bin a
     member of the county cort most of the time. a Baptis in belief
42. William Bozarth; I dont ....; Birth dont no his county; as I under-
     stand it was in Tenn.

                         19

BOZARTH (cont'd.):
        he was not a soldier at all.
43.   Nancy Burton; Henry Burton; as it has bin so long i don no her ....
        nation
44.   I dont no any of ther arridganations.

                        BRAY (GRAY?), JOHN

(FORM NO. 2)

1.   John Bray; RFD #10 Greeneville Tennessee
2.   seventy four (74)
3.   State of Tennesse county of Greene
4.   I was a Federal Soldier
5.   H; 13th Tennessee Vol Cav
6.   Mill rite and miller
7.   Adin Gray(Bray); S'anah; S'anah; North Carolina; Greenville South
        Carolina
8.   Malinda Nelson; John Nelson; Tabitha Nelson; Horse Creek Greene
        County 1s Sivel Dist.
9.   grate grad Father Jeremiah Gray came over from Grat Britton in 1768.
        He went in the war at the out back with George Washington. Served
        all through the Revolution War. his son Joshua Gray my gran father
        was an old Virginia miller. he went through the war of 1812 under
        Capt Sharp of Va at Norfok, V.A. My gran Father John Nelson served
        in War of 1812 at Charlston South Carolina
10.   I was two yount t own land. I lived hom with my father Adin Gray.
        who owned a farm on Horse Creek Greene County
11.   none
12.   150 acres
13.   I can not say but about $2500 Twenty Five hundred Dollars
14.   First a good log house. Second a Fraim House 3 Rooms and a citchen
        and .. one room and Proch
15.   I worked on the farm every day suitable to work only school. I
        plowed joad choped drove a team. Atended to the stock splitt rails.
        Built fence
16.   My father worked on mills as a mill rite. seen after his farming.
        My mother looked after the cows the sheep chickens carded spun knite
        ware make cloth for us children. Don all most all of her house work.
        untill her Daughter got big enough to help her.
17.   had no negroes but hired help when most needed
18.   Hones labor was considered honerabel a man that did not work was
        loocked down on a lasey man........negros white man worked in they
        neighborhood.
19.   They did. all worked a like. Negros did ther work and white men
20.   all worked to make a living in my neighborhood.
21.   I worked with slave and the owner of slaves. all good old genial
        men treated all a like
22.   as far as I could see they did
23.   There was a general good feeling All assoiated to gether at Balls
        and hunting Fishing
24.   to som extent the nonslave holder sitisans seamed to vote the ____
        man to help him out some
25.   yes it shure was. when he was inclined to be saving the richer men
        helped him if hones.
26.   incouredg
27.   I atended a Free school som tim and sum time a subscription school
28.   six month to good school
29.   a half mile
30.   Plesant hill school. Plenty of schools in the Destrict
31.   Public schools
32.   a bout 3 month
33.   pretty regular
34.   men
35.   In the month of Oct. 9 1864 at Bulls Gap Tennessee
36.   after I enlisted I went in to a battel at Bulls Gap known as Bulls
        Gap Stampeed
37.   one day
38.   Bulls Gap

BRAY (cont'd.)
39. I was on the go all the time after the Bulls Gap Stampeed went to Knoxville drew new equipents horses & co went on by rail to Virginia. Destroyed the salt works burnt the bridge to cross new river had several scurmeshes. then back to Knoxvill then joined the Stonman Raid south
40. At Knoxville Sept 5,1865/Tenn.
41. I left Knoxville Sept 8, 1865 on an old freight train to go to Greenville Tennessee it taken us all day to go the 74 miles. I stoped in Greenville over nite then made my way home 15 miles a foot. Happy to get home.
42. Went at once to farming on my fathers farm went to school for some time.
43. Just after a quitt school I went to carpenters work. worked as contractor and builder untill 1890 I . I get one apointment as....store keeper and.....I helt that....for eleven years. then came home got a comision as seneter state Pension at witch I still hold but I am at this tim disabel to do any kind of business what ever.
44. ......
45.

Capt. Landon C. carter	Laken T. Dempsey	Dennis Noland
1 Liet. James M. Freels	M. B. English	John Oliver
2 Lt Ralph M. Ernest?	W. C. Emmert	Dimond Rockhold
Sgt G. N. Littenal	With French	Calvin Rae
Sgt Loranz D. Scott	W. C. Fain	Isaac Rales
Sgt James E. Piesgor	James Foust	Mose Robinson
Sgt M K Williss	Calvin G....	James L Scalf
Cap W. F. Stansky	John Gibson	William Scalf
Cap Charles R. Monday	James Garroway	Elcane Shell
Cap Peter Hart	George W. Greenway	Alford Shell
Pr... James Shell	John Geay	Isaac Stover
Cap J M Heatherly	John Holman	Marion Sams
Cap Green E Wadly	James L Hays	James Scarborough
Cap John L Baker	W C Howell	Rufus Treadway
Cap Robert P Shell	Arvil Harnett	William Treadway
Cap Samuel Thomson	Roland Hammert	W. B. Taylor
Cap W H H Demsey	Christey C Kost	Alfrod D Taylor
Cap Laird Lynn	Daniel Helford	John Triggs?
Cap W A Cambell	Wilson N Hegan	William Taylor
.... William Turner	James H Kellis	Jeremiah Taylor
Sally ? Benn Lane	James Lousar	Charles M Vantassel
Privat Felder Asker	James Loudermild	William Lewis
Jess Boles	F W Malone	Andrew Had.....
Anthony Ballard	Andrew Mathus	Jesse A....man
Hence Britt	Patric Maloney	Deserted
David C Boing	Robert R Milland	Isaac Archer
John Borin	Z T Allister	Benjamin Talent
Andrew C Cara	T J M Moore	Jessie Talent
Alfred Car	Andrew J Malone	Thomas Woods
H T Clemons	Patrick A/O Baine	

46.

Andrew J Alexander	Greenville Tenn.
Thomas Bowman	RFD 9 Greenville Tenn
Thomas Broyles	RFD 10 "
Landen F Babb	Greenville
Abner Babb	"
William A Dunber	RFD 11 "
Silas Flanney	RFD 9 "
Dick Humphry	RFD 15 "
John Geay	RFD 10 "
John Whison	RFD 15 "
John D Marshall	RFD 10 "
William Kelly	RFD 15 "
Joseph Willson	RFD 10 "
Alexander W. Kelly	Greenville
West? Gerge	RFD 10 "
Robert McGee	RFD 15 "
Charly L Baxter	RFD 10 "
William T Mitchell	Greenville

Confedret soldiers only on in this sivel distrt
R B Oliphent Co H 64 North Carlina Inft Frasher Brigad
Buckners Disvision. Borned in Greene conty Tennessee near Greenville

BRAY (cont'd.):
in the year 1841. On the 16 day of Oct. Ben a farmer all his ....
Did own two farms.

BREWER, WILLIAM

FORM NO. 2

1. William Brewer; Jasper, Marion county, Tennessee
2. 75
3. Marion county, Tennessee
4. federal soldier
5. D; 7 Tenn cav.
6. a farmer
7. Eliga Brewer; North Carlina; hea was no soldier in any war
8. fannie Mason; Walker Mason
9. i cant rember ever seeing gran pa Brewer. i can remmber gran pa
    Mason a little. they awl died when i was litle and bee fore.
10. nothing
11. no
12. non
13. nothing
14. a litle 1 room log cabbin rented
15. i plowd and hoed corn and some cotton. this valey was full of pore
    men. Had to wourk hard on farming to raise there famly at a bout 12
    dollards per month
16. father worked on farm. mother did her one (own) house wourk carden
    and sping to make us children close. she was the mother of 12
    children.
17. neaver one
18. yes
19. awl pore men had two to live and they was plenty of them
20. i cant give a good ida
21. o very well most of them some was two stuck up.
22. knot awl together but very well
23. yes as a rule
24. i cant tell at this date
25. no no chance for a pore white boy was slim
26. discuragd had no chance
27. free
28. from 2 to 3 months a year; 1 to 4
29. 1 2 3 4 miles
30. free
31. public
32. 2 to 3
33. when they could live with out working some had to wourk.
34. men altogether
35. federl army at Tracey City 1863 October stayed at tracey a long time
    then went to Tulahoma staid ther a good while kep that post
36. Tracey city
37. wee did knot fite much onley skirmshe with Bush whcers it was tough
    thoe
38. lincol county hills
39. wee did knot do much fiting wee was generl Milrays scouts wee did
    knot camp much our main company place was tracey city and Tulahoma
    wee never was sent off South wee wanted to go but ginerl Millroy kep
    my company a round him
40. at Steavenson Ala June the 16th 1864.
41. i cant tell mutch about my trip home wee went to Nashville from
    Steveson i...to get dischard and our pay i tuck sick there it was
    12 month i did knot no much
42. farming
43. i rented land far 15 or 16 year then my brother went in a little
    grocery store far 3 or 4 years wee broke hea was a penciner hea got
    a litle holt and tried it gav? hor died Jan 20 1921 i tuck up shoe
    coblin kep it up a long while till i got disable to do it so i am
    living on my pencion me and my wife wee have no children
44. .....
45. G W Brewer   Bob Lochart

22

BREWER (cont'd.):

L P Brewer   Jack Laine
H C Russell   Oliver Kilgore
James larimore   Bemr? Killgore
John Doogan   Sam Eakin
Bill Awls   James Colwell
Miller Hick   Gabe Disaroon
James Conatser   Wesley Owdem
John Lame   Jasper Revles
Andrew Coggins   Wiley Revles
James Laine   John Laine
Billey Gaught   Rafe Gaught
Hiram Killgore   Jim Killgore

46. wee have a gar pots?
    W. J. Jonson   Jasper Marion co Tenn
    Lot Warren   "
    Calvin Lewis   "
    J G Lancster   "
    Ezeakil Haines   Sequachie Tenn
    James Laine   "
    J J Johnson   Dunlap Tenn
    John Doogan   "
    Louis Carlton   "
    Sam McWilliams   "
    Albert Cross   Victoria Tenn
    Dan Pitman   "
    Dallas Dickson   Sequachie Tenn
    Sam Bennet, Bot Price, John Myers & many confederats
                             Jasper tenn.

BRIMER JOHN

FORM NO. 2

1. John Brimer; Dandridge Tenn. RD #7
2. 76
3. Tenn. Jefferson county
4. Federal
5. F; 9 Tenn. Cavelry
6. Farmer
7. Vinyard Brimer; near Dandridge Tenn; Jefferson county; Tennessee;
   same place all life
8. Roda Miller; Jack Miller; Lizzie Miller; Muddy Creek
9. ....
10. none
11. no
12. none
13. $600
14. log cabin 1
15. Farming Plowing though sumer months clearing and cleaning up lans in
    winter months
16. Farming hoeing in summer months cleaning in winter months. cooking
    spinning niting and careing for childern
17. none
18. regarded as right it was considered honorable
19. yes
20. none
21. no slaves in my comunity
22. none
23. none
24. no
25. yes
26. none
27. subscription only
28. 12 months
29. 1½ miles
30. Plesant Hill Hickery Ridge Hill Chapel
31. Privet
32. 2½ months

23

BRIMER (cont'd.):
33. not much
34. mostly men
35. I inlisted July 24-1863 in Federal
36. Knoxville
37. 2½ months
38. Siege at Knoxville
39. I went from Knoxville to Camp Nelson Kentucky as a gard next Straw-
    berry Plains 26 hours small amount killed Bull Gap a scatered battle
    from Knoxville to Welhful Virginia cloth good slept on ground cover-
    ed with wool blancket plenty of rought food not in prison not in
    hospital
40. Knoxville Sept. 15-1865
41. at home 3 time about thirty miles trip
42. farming
43. Farming lived in Jefferson county all my life I belong to Methodist
    Episcopal Church no ofice in state
44. ....
45. Mode Miller, Sam Swaderm/Bill Edmonds, Joe Rutheford, Bill Aslinger,
    John Rainwater, Jules Justis, Gib Fox, Jim Bird. These are the
    living ones.
46. Mode Miller   Dandridge, RD Tenn
    Sam Swader   "
    Bill Edmonds   "
    Joe Rutheford   "
    Bill Aslinger   "
    John Rainwater   "
    Julis Justis   Sevierville Tenn
    Gib Fox   "
    John Bird   "
    Andy Lingey   Sandridge

                    BROWN, SAMUEL ARTHUR (2 files)

FORM NO. 1

1. Samuel Arthur Brown; McLemoresville Carroll co Tenn.
2. 80 years old (b. Feb 20, 1842)
3. State of Tennessee Carroll Co
4. State of Tennessee Carroll co.
5. Farmer
6. Farmer & Miller (saw & grist mill)
7. I owned no property as I was only 20 years old when I enlisted con-
    sequently I owned nothing.
8. none
9. about 600 acres
10. Fathers land was valued at about $10 dollars per acre which would
    make it worth about $6000 dollars
11. Log House at first later on a frame house with about 3 rooms
12. I plowed with all kinds of plows we had at that time one horse plows
    made at the blacksmith shops also our hoes was made at the shops
    made of iron but few still hoes then and the most of the hoe handles
    was of a Papaw bush peel the bark off and put it on the hoe and go
    to work.
13. My father stayed mostly at his mill some times worked on the farm.
    My mother did all kinds of cooking done her own washing & ironing
    She spun and wove clowth of all kinds even coverlets counterpaines
    made bedquilts made clowthing of all kinds for the family she spun
    shoe thread for the shoe makers during the war and Father tanned the
    leather in a troft at first then afterwards put up a tanyard & run
    a shoe shop in connection with the tanyard.
14. None he would hire a negro some times to help work but his hiring
    was mostly white labors.
15. It was and those who did not work was considered lazy and no good.
16. yes
17. None all most every body worked but few led idle lives as they was
    not considerd of mutch importance.
18. You could not tell any difference in those who owned slaves or who
    did not. as far as sociability concerned in this locality all about

                              24

BROWN (cont'd.):
on a level
19. could tell no difference in my neighborhood
20. yes
21. no
22. no
23. no not discouraged
24. both public & private
25. we had no long terms of school only between work times
26. 2 to 2½ mile
27. no high schools near than 3½ or four miles McLemoresville the near-
    est. our common schools in loghouses and wooden chimnys & very open
28. both about 3 months of each
29. 6 months & sometimes not that long
30. Most of them did but many had to work on the farm to make a living
    & could not go regular
31. I never saw but one woman teacher and that was when I was too young
    to go to school
32. Federal/ on the 24th day of March 1862 at Fort Henry Tenn which was
    located on the Tennessee River about 75 miles above the mouth of the
    River
33. I enlisted in Co F 52nd Indiana Inf. said Co was commanded by Capt.
    A. J. Ross. This co. was detached from the Regement and was left at
    Ft. Henry to garrison the place while the regement was sent to Pits-
    burg landing and was in the battle of Pitsburg landing. Comrades
    from Tenn. was as follows. Feliz W. Moore now at Union City Tenn.
    James D. Thompson Miland, Tenn. Cyrus G. Giles McLemoresville all
    living. James H. Ledsinger, James Moore, R. K. Rhoads, John R.
    Simpson all dead. John R. Simpson died a few years after the war
    the other 3 died during the war all 8 was from Carroll Co. Tenn.
34. after staying at Ft. Henry until about the midle of July we then
    joined our regement at Memphis Tenn then our regement with the 178
    NY and the 32 Iowa was sent to Fort Pillow where we stayed fir 16
    months then about the 20 of Jan. 1864 we was ordered to join Sherman
    army at Vicksburg Miss. then the whole comand
35. 16 & 17 army core was ordered out on a rade went to Jackson Mississ-
    ippi our first battle or the first one I was in.
36. no name only a small engagement but few casualities the color bearer
    of the 52 Ind. was kiled dont remember of any more.
37. We marched from Jackson Miss. to Maredian drove the enemy out and
    took possession. The Band of the 178 NY went to playing Dixie &
    went out playing Yankee Doodle we marched to Canton Mississippi and
    at this place my regement found the Veteran Core which gave them 30
    days furlow & $300 dollars bounty but there was a few of us who did
    not enlist for 3 years more so we was put in the 8_ Ind. & sent up
    Red River to reinforce Gen Nathaniel P Banks so Gen. Gen Shumary?
    Loared? Banks 10,000 men under to make this hard under Gen A J Smith
    who had command of the 16 Army Core (see extra sheet for balance of
    this question)
38. ....
39. When we landed at Paducah Ky it was dangarous for us to go home so
    we had to stay there untill about the 27 of May I received a letter
    from Home stating the thought it would be safe to come home we
    started and arrived at home June 1st the happiest boy you ever I
    saw when I met my loved ones.
40. Went in to the tanning business & sewing machine business later got
    married. Farmed it some a few years I then offered myself as a
    candidate for Regester of Carroll co. was elected and held office
    12 years.
41. I was elected Co. Register in 1886 served 12 years was magistrate
    3 times 6 years each was President of the Farms & Fents? Groves
    Association about 12 years and Commander of Isaac R Hawkes Post 58?
    FAR for 25 years.
42. Isaac Brown; North Carolina; in the year 1805; North Carolina; dont
    know where he lived in North Carolina but died hear in June 1875.;
    held no office
43. Mayan McConnell; John McConnell; dont know; near near Columbia Tenn
    on Duck River afterwards moved to Carroll co Tenn.
44. My grandfather Arthur Brown was born in North Carolina in the year
    1761. Was in the Revolutionary war in Cap. Anthony Shark Co. Blounts

BROWN (cont'd.):

    Batalion 25 North Carolina Malitia was wounded by having a bayonet run clear through him by a British solideir and left for dead but survived and live to the age of 88 years. Moved to Carroll co Tenn in the year 1821 and died in 1845 was buried at McLemoresville the writer erected a soldiers mound to his grave a few years ago.

45. ....
46. ....

(Seperate sheets - Question No. 37 continued)

    Our first battle up Red River was the capture of Fort Dernsa? March 14, 1864 which was located on Red River. We captured the fort with but little loss. We got 200 prisoners and a lot of arms and amunition. We then after this battle marched to Alexander, VA then we met Gen. Banks army then we started to Shrevesport, La the 10,000 under A. J. Smith was in the rear. But the Confederated objected to Banks going to Shrevesport with all that army so they met him at Mansfield and gave him and his command a terrible bad licking - this was April 8, 1864. Captured at least half of his wagan train-supplies- amunition and lost of prisners. It was badly demoralized. Now Gen. Smith was not in this fight- he being 2 days march behind Banks-so Banks men fell back one day and we marched up one day which brought us together at Pleasant Hill (April 9) 40 miles from Shrevesport. There the Confederates met Gen. Smiths men and thinking it was going to be another easy going things came onto us with there usual Rebel yell. But this little squad of 10,000 of the 16 Army Core was stubborn and failed to move back as we was not used to being whiped. So we faught them until dark. Commencing about or a little after sunup we drove the enemy off the field and stayed there untill about 4 o'clock next morning then we fell back with Banks army badly demoralized every day skirmishing back to the mouth of Red River and while we was waiting to get across the River and Bayous the Rebels attacked us again (May the 18th) giving us a fairwell salute. Now this was the hottest little battle I was ever in. Commencing about 2 PM and lasted untill about 5 PM. Many casulities but we drove them back with many killed on both sides. Next day we crossed the bay on Pontoon bridges to the mouth of the River. After being up the river on the march from about the 10 of March until the 19 of May we now started for Memphis and here we met our 52 Ind. which had left us on a furlow and we was then back with our regement. We landed at Memphis Tenn. and after a short rest we then as we thought had orders to march through the county to Mobile Ala dont remember the date. We started and we marched to Pontotock Miss. and hear again the Confederates abjected us to going any further that way-so Gen Smith thought it advisable not to try to force his way and decided probably it might please them better for him to go back to Memphis or some where else so we filed East and let them have there way-so the Confederates was inclined to want us to hurry up consequently and they started to hurry us up and on the evening of the 13th day of July attacked our rear and give us quite a warm reception. Gen Foust being in command got his little toe shot off in that little fight and so the next day July 14 they attacked us again at old Harrisburg or better known as Tupelo. This battle lasted nearly half the day. The Confederated had to fall back with considerable loss of dead and wounded. Not being satisfied with this they attacked us again about 9 o'clock that night-The writer of this was on the skirmish line about 150 or 200 yards in front of my regement when the attack was made. I lay as flat on the ground as I possibly could so I would not stop any bulletts as they passed me by and if I could have found a hole in the ground big enough I would have crawled in but this was soon over. The Confederates was driven back with not mutch loss. Next day we resumed our march with but little happening on our way back to Memphis. We made several short raids while we stayed at Memphis of not mutch importance. Along about the 10 of Sept we left Memphis for Jefferson Barracks Mo to Watch Gen. Pike who was making his way towards St Louis on the 1st day of October we got abord freight cars went through St Louis as ___ men road in 28 miles of that place. We met them at a station on the RRhoad 25 miles and turned back after a light skirmish. We followed them to Kansas & Mo line-followed the line 2 days then

26

BROWN (cont'd.):

turned East and went to a place called Lone Jack. They had been a little town there but then was nothing left but brick chimneys all been burned up. Thence back to Lexington thence down the Mo. River to St Louis thence to Nashville and was in the fight at Nashville when Gen Hood made his rounds-was in the 2 days battle then we follow-ed Hood to Tenn River-camped at East Port Miss for about 2 or 3 weeks. Thence down the Tenn river to New Orleans..arrived there on the 22nd day of Feb-Geo. Washingtons birthday-there a few days-got abord the steam ship Guiding Star for Mobile Bay on Dauphine Island there for a few days. We 4 Tennesseans got our discharge from the army thence back to New Orleans thence back up the old Missippi River for Paducah Ky our nearest port home which was in Carroll co Tenn.
While in the service I will say I had good clowths and plenty to eat such as it was. Except at times when on a march and away from our supplies. We sometimes suffered for provisions but as a rule we had plenty-the writer never was a prisner and only ½ day in hospital among my 3 yrs service.

BROYLES, CHARLES LAFAYETTE

FORM NO. 2

1. Charles Lafayette Broyles; RFD #10, Greeneville, Tennessee
2. 78 yr 3 mo 11 days
3. Tennessee, Greene County
4. Federal
5. M; First Tennessee, Calvary
6. Farmer
7. James A. Broyles; Horse Creek; Greene; Tennessee; Horse Creek, Greene co, Tenn. and Birds Bridge, Greene, co, Tenn.; Post Master at Birds Bridge, Tenn. Tax Collector, no war service, wrote no book
8. Nancy C. Waddell; Benjamin Waddell; Rachel Bowman; Camp Creek, Greene co, Tenn.
9. My Grandfather, Jacob Broyles, settled on Horse Creek, Tennessee, dont know just what state he was from. He was a soldier in the Revolutionary war and drew a pension of $5.00 per month. He had two brothers that went on into Georgia, James Broyles and Lewis Broyles. My grandmother on the Broyles side was Salley Jones. My father lived to be 70 yrs old, my grandfather Broyles was 80 yrs old.
10. owned none
11. no
12. my father owned 150 or 160 acres
13. $2000.00
14. Log house with five rooms
15. Worked from sunup until sundown from 9 years on till war opened, plowing, hoeing, making rails, cutting wheat and all general farm work.
16. My father did all kinds of farm work, clearing land, splitting rails to make fence and through the winter made shoes for the family. Also he raised flax and prepared it for the whell. My mother did the cooking, made the clothing by weaving, spinning, and sewing, often working untill 9 to 10 o'clock at night, working by tallow candle light.
17. no
18. yes, both
19. yes
20. The slave owners I know of worked as well as their slaves.
21. The slave owners associated with the ones that owned no slaves free-ly and seemed to fell on equality with them.
22. yes
23. yes
24. I think not, the slaves did not vote and there fore that would not help or hinder.
25. Good, considering the times.
26. Encouraged
27. Mostly, subscription, consisting of from 3 to 4 months per yr.
28. about 23 months
29. 2½ to 3 miles

27

BROYLES (cont'd.):
30. Subscription schools
31. private
32. 2½ to 3
33. no
34. Sometime man, sometime woman
35. I enlisted in Federal army November 15, 1861 at Chimney Top Mountain in Northern part of Greene co, Tenn.
36. Louisville, Kentucky
37. about eleven or twelve no.
38. Murfreesboro
39. Went to Triune, had skirmish with Wheelers calvery and also fought with Forrests "bush whackers" at Sparta, Tenn. Killing and capturing the majority. From there on to Chattanooga. Had a hard battle with Hoods army winning a great battle. Then to Knoxville, routed the enemy there. Then to Cleveland, Tennessee, and rested there one day and night.
40. 13 day of April 1864 at Nashville, Tenn.
41. I came on an old freight, cattle car riding part of the time on top of it. Arrived at Greeneville my home station about 8 or 9 o'clock at night. My self and another comrade walked toward home about 4 miles and stayed all night.
42. Farming, general farm work
43. I married pretty soon after the war, settled down to farming principally, and raised a large family. My wife died leaving me to raise the younger children I have lived in the 2nd Civil District of Greene County, Tennessee since the war. I was deputy sheriff, school director, and enumerated the cencus in 1890, for my district and one more. I have voted in every election, county, state and national. I joined the United Brethren Church. The county in which I now live has made wonderful improvements since the war. I now live with one of my sons. I have retired from farming and am taking life easy.
44. ....
45. I have a History of my Regiment written by W. R. Carter Co. C and he gives the Roster of each company. If you so desire I can send you a copy later. I do not know of a single one of my co. now living.
46.

Name	R/RFD	Location
John S. Toney	R #12,	Greeneville, Tenn
William Dickson	"	"
John Devis Marshall	R #10	"
Henry M. Harrison		"
William M. Kelly	R #12	"
Thomas Johnson	R #10	"
James Rhea	RFD Afton, Tenn	
W T Mitchell	Greenville	
Landon Babb	"	
James Maloney	"	
John Gray	R #10	"
Silay Flournoy	"	"
C W George	"	"
Joe Wilson	"	"
Newton Smelser	RFD	"
Gideon Sentelle	"	"

(on seperate sheet-question 39:)
    From Cleveland we were ordered South into Georgia, the motive of this was to capture Atlanta and try to release the Federal prisoners at Macon and Andersonville. We were almost captured several times. All that kept us from being captured was the brave and daring captain we had, and fiting qualities of our boys. This campaign lasted 100 days, it was known as the Atlanta Campaign. The rail roads were torn up in several places. My regiment was ordered back to Nashville before Atlanta was captured, but we claim that we aided a great deal in the capture of that great city. My co. had some hard time in this march. We did not get to sleep any hardly and had to swim the Chattahoochee River. We went by rail from Marietta Ga. to Nashville Tenn., by way of Chattanooga, we went into Camp for a while 3 mi East of Nashville and faired fine for a while, but soon General Wheeler, headed for Nashville, and our fun job ended. We were remounted and ordered to fight him. He was turned back with out much loss to our company. The First Tenn. sustained the follow-

28

BROYLES (cont'd.):

> ing loss. 8 killed, 8 wounded. We were next at Franklin, we had fought General Forrest and Wheeler, and now we were against Hood's army at Franklin. This was a great and decisive battle for the Union soldiers. We were next fighting Hood at Nashville. Here Hoods army was routed and he retreated South. This was the last raid by the Confederate army attempted in Tennessee. After this we went on down to Waterloo Alabama, remained there one month; then went from there to Nashville by water and were mustered out. The First Tennessee was called the "fighting" Regiment with a colonel at its head that would not surrender. I went through all this fighting without getting wounded or having to go to the hospital, I had the measles but staid with a private family. I walked through to Kentucky most of the way after night. I suffered from thirst and hunger quite a bit. I am thankful that I am still alive and had the experience of helping to save the Union.
>
> C. L. Broyles Sergeant Co. M

BULLINGTON, MARVIN

FORM NO. 1

1. Marvin Bullington, Gainsboro R #3 Tennessee
2. 74 yrs & 10 mos
3. Tennessee; Jackson county
4. Putnam County; Federal Government
5. Farmer
6. Farmer
7. no property
8. no
9. 300 acres
10. 1500 ? worth of land and property
11. Log house 2 rooms
12. Boath-plowed and hoed
13. Father worked on the farm and Mother cooking, spining and weaving and so on
14. no
15. yes
16. yes
17. All worked them selves
18. They mixed with each other. All held them selves the same
19. Yes they did
20. Their feelings was good
21. yes
22. no
23. ....
24. Free schools
25. one year
26. one mile
27. Only one schol in the comunty name Shipley
28. Public
29. thre months
30. yes
31. man
32. I enlisted in 1864 Oct. at Livingston Tenn
33. First Tennessee Mont Inf Capt. G. W. Masey A. M. Jone frst Lutenant Geo. Gilbert first Sargent
    D. D. Laycock, Thomas Carr, Al Hataway, Joe McCline
34. Carthage Tenn
35. Never no battles
36. ....
37. In camps about 9 months good cloths Slept on the ground Eats was poor
38. at Nashville Tenn
39. Walked home
40. Farming
41. Lived in Jackson county all or most all my life
42. Henry Bullington; Va.; Cookville
43. Elyza? Howard; James Howard; Sparta Tenn.
44. ....

BULLINGTON (cont'd.):
45. ....
46. ....

CARLISLE, MOSES S.

FORM NO. 2

1. Moses S. Carlisle; Boston, Tenn.
2. 76 years Born March 16th 1846 A.D.
3. Wiscasset, Lincoln co., Maine
4. a Federal
5. G; 28 N Y ; 2 years Navy one year Co A 14th Maine 13 months
6. Naval Service
7. John A. Carlisle; Clifford; Lawrence; Kentucky; Washington, D.C.; dont
8. Leatate C. Lous Der Florsses; De Louis La Florsses; Abigail Spencer; lynn, Mass. with LaFayette
9. the Bible was lost. Fathers Mother was Mary Pinkham the daughter of Captain James S. Pinkham of 1812 A.D. War of James River Va. We had slaves but do not know how many. My sister told one of my parents Father had property do not know how much. I did not have any in 1861 A.D. Enlisted 1861 in New York city in Comp J 28th N. Y. My father was dead.
10. none. my guardian sent me to school under Prof. Eastman at Pough- keepsie N. Y.
11. parents did on Fathers side
12. they own land but do not know how mutch
13. dont know
14. lived in a city but do not know what kind of house it was. I travel- ed after the navy. I moved down in this state in Dec. 1877.
15. Gathers grandfather was John A. Carlisle of James River Va. he owned slaves but can not tell how many. His wife was E. A. Lee first settler of Va. Mothers grandfather was Captain W. R.? Spencer and his wife was Mary Adams first settlers of Mass.
16. My father was in the navy and my mother did the house work
17. dont know
18. honorable
19. yes
20. good many
21. sometimes they did
22. Some time did and other times they did not
23. not always
24. yes
25. sometimes
26. sometimes encouraged
27. mostly city schools
28. about 9 years
29. in Kentucky 2 miles but in the city lest
30. I cannot tell
31. mostley private
32. I cannot tell it was too long ago
33. Just medium
34. I went to both
35. July 1861
36. to Va. then went to Pittsburg Landing. I was in Grants Army
37. the first fight was at Pittsburg Landing. we was in a few fights before.
38. in the Spring of 1862
39. we lived very rough. some time did not have enough to eat nor was our clothes good. I never was in the hospital nor in prison. I only stayed two years in the New York Regiment. I was discharged as Corporal July 1863. I joined the Navy in Washington D.C. for 1 year
40. July 1863
41. I did not come home. I joined the navy July 1863 discharged in 1864 Joined Comp A 14th Maine at Washington D. C. I went to Shenandoah Valley Va L Bre 2 division 19th Corps our division
42. was sent to Gen Bill Sherman march to the sea made me Sergant instruc- tion we took.

CARLISLE (cont'd.):
43. Augustia Ga we releave 4th Michigan Cavlery 3 miles west Augusta and Com A. 14th Me. guarded Pres. Jef Davis, Steven, Gen. Wheeler, P.M. Ragen and Senitor Clay of Ga. Mrs. Davis and her sister and Mrs. Clay to Fort Monroe Va in steam ship Fheneston? at the close of the war we we had two Lieut. three sargents four Corp 22 Privates all of Comp A 14 Me. I am the only one living that I can find now in the Comp. I am sorry what I have done more for my country.
44. ....
45. I am now member of the red cross. I dont know were the roster is to be had.
46. ....

CARTER, JOHN WESLEY

FORM NO. 1

1. John Wesley Carter; McLemoresville, Carroll county, Tennessee
2. I was born June 22, 1848 age 78 past
3. Tennessee, Carroll county
4. I was living in Carroll county, Tennessee when I enlisted in the federal army
5. I worked on the farm with my father. I was only 18 years old
6. Farmer
7. I did not own any property at the opening of the war as I was just a boy working under my father.
8. nether of us owned slaves. my grandfather owned one cole man only
9. he owned 200 acres
10. two thousand dollars worth in all
11. a log house for the seting and sleeping room. and a kitchen made of logs to cook and eate in.
12. when I was a boy & hoed I mostly howed as my older brother could do better plowing then I could do. when I got old a nuff to plow I plowed and hoed too.
13. My father worked on the farm the most of his time. Ther was seven boys in my fathers family. My mother did the cooking and spinning and weaving and made all of our waring clothes. I was her girl. I have spun many a web of cath.
14. we did our work our selves.
15. yes it shurly was I can call to mind now quiet a lot of men that owned slaves to the amount of 30 and 40 slaves that ther white boy worked in the field with the slaves
16. yes, the slave holders boys worked on the farm with slaves
17. no one as I can think at presant of course there was som hoboes you know that got along com way with out work.
18. as a rule they were a little hauty. I dont think they thought them selfs better men then the no slave holder but a little richer.
19. I think so as I have been in such gathering my self and I saw no difference shown in such gatherings.
20. There shurley was a friendly feeling for they stood for what was wright when the test came.
21. I dont recalect any contest coming as of that kind. a slave holder and non slave holder running for office before the war
22. I think not as the products of the farm was very cheap at that time.
23. They were encouraged by slave holders
24. a veary poore one I should say
25. I dont know about two months in the summer to a teacher that could not purse Johns hand trimbles.
26. two miles
27. one school house made of loges with chimney down to the mantel peace with dirt floor with banches split out of a log with holes board in and leges put in them about 3 feet long.
28. public
29. two in august and July
30. yes
31. a man about six feet and 5 in tall
32. I enlisted in the Federal Government on 20 day of September 1862 in Carroll county Tenn.
33. it was the 7th Ten Cav. Col J. R Hawkins reigament. Cap. A. W. Haw-

31

    kins, S. W. Hawkins, Leut. John T. Robinson 1 Leut. Lafatte Robinson Magor, B. F. Morgan pri. Joe McCracken Allen Johnson S. J. Montgomery George Fry, J H McKinney James Evens George Little Charley Wilson George Morgan John Tucker Tom Tuvkers? Walker Kee Walter Pugh

34. to Trenton Tennessee
35. about 7 months
36. it was Lexington Ten
37. after the battle of Lexington our reigment nearley all captured and them that was not captured was sent to the gand Jouncan Ten after that I was onley ____ skirmishes. We had plenty of warm clothing and plenty to eate never was in prison or in hospital. I was captured by som out laws they told they were going to kill but I talked them out of that and they turned me loos.
38. At Saulsbuary Tennessee
39. I went to Memphis Tennessee and taken a boat to Hickman Ky and went on the train to Union City and me and comrad Joe Branch footed it home through the woods and home
40. farming
41. I farmed up till 1894 I rum for trustee of my county and elected in 1894 and served two turms which was 4 years
42. Reubin Ellis Carter; Born in Chester; county C. S. 1816; moved to Tenn.; when but a boy.; He was Class leader in the Methodist Church all of his life.
43. Sara Herron; John Herron; Sara Herron; John Herron and his wife Sara Herron was schoch irish.
44. My father from S C when but a boy. They were anglo sexion they were english. My grand came from old Ky to Tennessee I dont know what year it was he was scoch irish and a noble man. I have filled this out as best I could what I lack you will have look over.

                J. W. Carter

CHAMBERS, OLIVER P.

FORM NO. 2

1. Oliver P. Chambers; Dandridg RFD 7 Box 104
2. 74 years April 16, 1822
3. New Jersey; Warren county
4. Federal
5. Co A; 11 Regt Tennessee Cavlery
6. Tanner by trade
7. Moses Dewitt Chambers; see at coming scraft?; North Hamton; Penselvany; North North Hamtt county
8. Rebiceg Trigg; Aren Trigg; Amanda Trigg; Pittsburg, Penselvany
9. My father came from New Jersey to Chattanoga Ten aboutt the year 1858 and went in the taning busnes with John J Bynum and Thomas Richerson
10. non
11. no
12. House and lot in town Parottsvill
13. House and lott about 800 eight hundred dollars Taning stock about two thousand dollars
14. Log with a frame addition five romes
15. My work was in the tanyard till I enlisted in the armey
16. he was a tanner by trade and awlways worked at that ocupation my did her house work and was a weaver of fine cover lides and counter pains and all kind of the old day weeving
17. non
18. there was more of our people that owned slaves that worked in the field with them and considered and it honorable and some of them the leading citizen of Cock county Ten.
19. yes
20. there was verry few idel people in cook county up to the commencin of the civel war
21. Slave holders and no slave holders met at church Sundy equal term and associated together as all friends
22. there wasent any diferent between slave holders and slave holders children at school they seemed to be all one

CHAMBERS (cont'd.):
23. in Publick gethering you could not tell the difents between slave
hold and the non slave holder all firends
24. in a political contest it was geneeraly the caracter of the asperi-
ents whether a slave holder or a non slave holder
25. yes if the nerv and push was in him
26. yes I hear of some slave holders who had taken up som poor boys and
pushing them right square to the front
27. subscriptions schools
28. about two or three months
29. across our block in Parrottsville
30. no school only a short subscription school
31. just subscription school
32. two or three months
33. generally pretty regular
34. first was a man and the second a woman
35. I first enlisted in the firs Batalion of East Tennessee Scouts enlisted near Morris Town and went through the mountains to Camp Nelton
Kentucky there our organized our Batalion
36. to Cumberlan Gap
37. about 75 days
38. after the surender of Cumberlan Gap we moved toward Verginia
39. our comand first brigade of the thurd division of the army of the
Cumberlan we was mustered to the 11th Tenn Cavly I was of Co A an
served as the 11 Cavely till 22 February 1864 then one batalion was
all killed and captin I at wheman Mill Va then we ree consolidated
with the Bloody 9th Zen Cog during our virginia camp and we fight
and kirmish nearly ever day
41. Discharged Knoxville 13 day Sept 1865
Left Knoxville Sept 15-1865 with Trasparttion to Genatr? Ten - hiked
home on fot met one of my frends of befor the war who was a confedrate
soldier and had bin in prison at Camp Chase and we were friends till
his death
42. I went west after I was discharged
43. I went west after the war and cared the Star rout male from Larence
Kansas to vilage called Abton but later the name changed. when I
left that I taken the ocupation of cow puncher or herder. I finley
left the west and returned to Jeferson county Ten my ocupation saw
milling thrashing and farming I have bin elected five times for
constable in my district and have served as deputy sherif my member
ship is in M. E. Church a Hascues / Chappell I have seene Aberham
Lincoln Andrew Johnson General Grant General Joe Wheeler one of the
best cavlery generals america ever produced
44. ....
45. Field Officers   Privates
Joe Parson Colonel   Acra, John   Johnson, Plesent
Patan Gutherford lt Colenel Anderson, George R.   Kesterson, James R
James Hornsby 1st Mag.   Bookhart, James L   Kelley, William T
John G Wright 2ns Mag   Barnard, Joseph A.   Lane, James W.
David L Dossitt 3rd Mag   Byrd, William
            (see loose sheet for continued list)

John G Wright 2nd Mag   Bellers, Andres J   Leadbetter, Hamilton
David L Dossett 3d mag   Byrd, William   Lanhennch, James
Samuel Greer Regt Chaplain Boyd, David C   McAnelly Thomas
   Camping Officers   Barger, Johan   "   William T
John W Herrington Capt   Choat Gabe   "   Walter A
Benjamin J Holland 1st Lt Chambers Oliver P   Overstreet William A
James L Lacy 2d Lt   Coffman William P   Odom William H
   Non Commisioned officers Cox George W   Prevost Samuel
John Wright 1 sergt   Dyche William H   Posey William F
John N Massengill 2d Lt?   Goodman John H   "   Benjamin M
John M Little __ seger.   "   William N   "   Jubilee
William Reegan 1st duty S. Gibson John R   Pitts John
Francis Winchester 2d DS   Gadis William   Parson William
Joseph D Thach 3d DS   Gilbreeth James A   Reggon Jessy F
John F Goforth 4th DS   Greer John   Rice Asher
James Hall 5th DS   Garner George W   Read John A
   Corprells   Henry Samuel   Shipley Milem G
Daniel Huddleston   Harrison William   Strand Jacob

33

CHAMBERS (cont'd.):

James M Holder
George W Reagon
Samuel R Chambers
Sawleberry Kerby
William P Collins
Cevin S Mullens
Martin Crawford
46. James Bird
Tilman Hank
John Brimer
Will Edmons
Asa Laymon
Bud Whitehead
Sam Shroder
Gilbert Fox
James Johnson
George Blazor
Crockett Newcombe

Helton Daniel
" James
Hodge William
Hurst Alexander
Johnson Noah M
Jenkins George W
Johnson Plesant
Seveirvill Tenn
"
Dandridg
"
New Port
"
Dandridg
Seviervill
Dandridg
Seviervill
"

Snider George
Stockley Edward
Sims Thomas J
Templeton James M
Trent Wriley
Underwood George
" James

(Seperate sheet)

Deceased:
Miller Wesley
Reagan Robert D
White William M
White Flaid G

Deserters:
Dyre James
Duncan Peter
Franklin Hedley
McClellan David R

Miller William
Morgan John R
Smith Burten
Smith Emanuel
Wilson Andrew M

I cant give the names of the killed in action for I havent any record of killed.

Oliver P Chambers

(Seperate sheet)

West Joseph A
" George W
" John H
Webb Iredell

Wilkins Noah
Williams Frances M

Discharged:
John H McNeutt 2d Lt
Billberry Chamberlan
Justin John M

Lallard Joseph B
Overton Isaac
Perdew Granville C
Rich Georde W
Reagan James D
White James E
Walker Edmond

CHATMAN, ISAAC

FORM NO. 1

1. Isaac Chatman; Sparta Tennessee Route 5
2. 82 yr
3. Tennessee; Smith County
4. Tennessee; Smith County
5. Farming
6. dont know
7. no property
8. no
9. none
10. none
11. log house, two rooms
12. I plowed and also hoed
13. Father died when small. Mother spun, wove, cooked, and knit.
14. none
15. It was counted respectable and honest
16. They did
17. About ¼ of them
18. They mingled freely. The majority of them did.
19. They did not
20. There was frindley feeling between them.
21. It did not help in a contest for the man to hold slaves.
22. The chances were not good.
23. They were discouraged by slave holders.
24. Free schools
25. Three months and three days

34

CHATMAN (cont'd.):
26. one half mile
27. Just a free school
28. Public
29. three months
30. They did
31. Man
32. In 1861. December. Hickman Tennessee Smith County. In the Federal.
33. 44 Tennessee. Capt. James, Bill Lerry, Lt. Deckens, Lt. Noner, Dos Garnet, Sim Jones, Jess Aged, Lewis Duby, Jim McCall, Jerry Butler, West Wentry, Joe Beard, Efrom Rageille.
34. Camp Trousville, Tennessee
35. one year
36. Perriville Kentucky
37. After first battle went to Murfesborrough. Went into battle, murfes-borrow battle, Shilo Miss. Chickamauga, Chatt. Knoxville, Bean Station from Bean Station to Richmond Va. Bruys Bluff. each battle from five hourse to all day and some 3 day and nights, 4 battle for Edereral but retreated in two.
38. When war closed in was in prison at Camp Lookout Maryland. they made me take an oath and sent me home.
39. I come from Washington City home on the train part of the way at part of the way foot.
40. farming
41. Farming in Tennesse & Texas. no office. Christion Church
42. He died before I can remember
43. Lucindy Chatman; Peggy Chatman; dont know; Smith county, Tennessee
44. Dont know any thing of that.

CHRISTIAN, WILEY M.

FORM NO. 2

1. Wiley M. Christian, 215 Boone St., Johnson City, Tennessee
2. eighty five years old; April 5, 1922. (date he filled in questionaire -year.)
3. Tennessee; Roan Coutny
4. Federal soldier
5. Cos F & B; 1st Regt. Tenn. Vol. Infantry from enlistment to May 1863 was mounted and did service raiding, scouting etc.
6. Farmer Miller & Wool carding machine man
7. Gilbert Christian; Boatgan now Kingsport; Sullivan co; Tennessee; he lived at Boatyard until he was 18 years old then moved to Kingston Tenn.; was Capt. of Malisha and Justice of the Peace and sorely afflicted for years with dispespy.
8. Mary Terry; Jessee Terry; Hanah Terry nee McNair; in Cherochee Nation and removed to Roan county, Tenn.
9. My fathers ancestor Israel Christian came from Denmark and settled in Virginia Just before Revolution had two sons Gilbert and Robert who participated in that strugle after the war one located in Old Virginia the other moved to Territory of Tenn. whether Robert or Gilbert I do not know. I think it was my father uncle Gilbert who was speaker of the first house of representatives of Tenn. My gran Father Robert Christian married Mary Adair in Knox County.
10. I had none. not over one or two hundred dollars personal property and a third interest in town house a lot value at $300.00
11. owned none
12. none
13. Small amount personal property not over three hundred dollars
14. My first recollection an log house but as a ____ octer we lived in different kinds of house at the beginning of Civil war a small frame house in Kingston, Tenn.
15. Worked on farm untill 18 years old did any and all kinds of farm work then learned the shoemakers trade.
16. My father did all kinds of farm work when well enough. ____ grist mill and wool carding machine. Mother was woman of general house work cooking washing spinning weaving. Serving, making the clothes for a family of 10. She was a busy Christian woman not only in name but in fact. She has been dead for nearly forty years and yet she

35

CHRISTIAN (cont'd.):
lives.
17. no
18. Cant say as to public, but I have always _____ all honest labor as honorable
19. Yes for very few of them was regarded as rich and a rich man then would be a poor man now.
20. Hardly any extent. None but the drones. We all had to work in order to make ends meet. not one in ten were slave owners.
21. ....
22. Very few of them owned slaves what their feelings were I do not know. but they had to associate with non slave holders or be quite lonesome and _____ alone
23. generally friendly and sociable
24. dont remember of a contest of that kind.
25. not very good as very few did
26. no special encouragement or discouragement I know of at present
27. comon school
28. altogether not over 3 years
29. general about two miles
30. The public schools suported by public funds ocasionally a private subscription school.
31. Both Public and private but very little of both.
32. about 3 month
33. Only moderately. There was no cumpulsory school law.
34. Most generally men, but ladies ocasionly specialy the private schools.
35. August 9, 1891. Marching through the mountains wading rivers for about 200 miles to Camp Dick Robinson Ky to place of rendivous. Started between suns marching in night and day in sunshine and rain with a promise of reward or compensahon, only to uphold and preserve the union of states and we did it.
36. We remained at Camp Dick Robinson until November and were sent to Wild Cat, Ky. where the first battle was fought.
37. About four months Jany 17, 1862 Fishing Creek or Mill Springs.
38. Fishing Creek Gen Zollicofer was killed there and the confederates were completely routed.
39. We went East from there to Cumberlandford Ky and assisted in the capture of Cumberland Gap a generally suposed strong hold in June 1862. Remaining there building forts and fortifying generally till Sept 1862.
    Gen. Braxton Bragg cut our supplies by getting in Ky and we had to march through the mountains through Eastern Ky to Greenupsburg Ky on _____ river then we went to Charleston Maulding in Kanaw Vally West Virginia.
40. Nashville Tenn Aug 4-1864
41. My trip home uneventful except we got to ride in passenger coaches instead of on top of frieght cars. We had RR to Loudon at Loudon bought a cannoe and for 30 miles we paddle our own canoo.
42. Merchant for eight years. Then book keeper and manager for Knoxville Car Whell Cos. Furnace and property Carter county Tenn.
43. Was merchant for 8 years Roan County Bookkeeper and manager for Knoxville Car Whell Co for 10 years then moved to Johnson City After I had accumulate over $10 dollars and engage in merchandizing again and because my credit was too good and my leniency in trusting others. I lost it all and left Johnson City and Bankrupt. I have been a local preacher since 1880. as so I preached as a supply for a few years then moved to Morristown doing what ever I could for a year or so then continued to preach as a supply for while longer the conference being full of regular members. I dropped out and employd my time as agent for Universal book and Bible house and agent Hosiery Mills. Six years came to Johnson City and engaged as retail agent for White Ribbon Manufacturing of Perfumed toilet goods and flavoring extracts which I still continue.
44. I have met a good many. Great men but greatest of them Billy Sunday an ambassador for God.
45. (As near my Cos. roster I can remember)

Capt. E. Langley decsd	Alex Dunington	Martin Redman
Lieut Moore "	Thomas Green	Granan Duncan
Lieut. Neuman "	Greenbury Green	Rufus Jones
" M. Stephens	Amos Green	Dudley Jones

36

CHRISTIAN (cont'd.):

Lieut Mose Everett	Jessie Mitchell	James Langley Senr
" W M Christian	Lewis Jones	Robert K Robinson
" Walter Dalton decsd	Reubin Smitee	Ransom Viles
Sgt James C Clark	John Smitte (Smith)	William Taylor
" Martin Lyons	....	James Roberts
" James Langley	John Pendergras	John Hawkins
" Joseph Davidson	John Burton	George Lee
" Abraham R Cox	Mason Hinds	John Lee
" Lewis F Natzachke	Israel Wright	John Cox
A. B. Delozeer kill in action	Samuel Ladd	Charles Cox
Nanton Delosur "	William Wright	Thomas Lyons Sr.
Jesse McKeehers "	Thomas Childress	Thomas Lyons Jr.
Orville R. Everett	John Y Christian	John Lyons
William Magill	Uriah S Allison	Nicholas Lyons
William Langley	William Allison	John Moore
James House	David Depue	Jackson Honeycut
Absolom Potter	William McNeas	Pheling Newport
Solomon Potter	Henry McCall	William Hodgden
Martin Bardetl	Herman Thurmer	John Bardell
Charles Mueller		

46.
Joseph McCorkle   Johnson city, Tenn.
Thomas Harrison   Morristown Tenn
James Rodgers   Morristown
Porter G Witt   Morristown
William Rightsell   Morristown
Cant recal full name of but few living vetrons and they are all federal

(Seperate sheet)
39. and from thence we went to Stone River and was in that battle and then back to Lexington Ky and was mounted at Camp Dick Robinson and in June we made the Sander raid into Tennessee burned the depot of supplies at Lenoir Station on E.T Vir & Ga RR. tore up the RR to Knoxville, atack the forts at that place and after a demonstration withdrew, tearing up RR tracks to Flat Creek, burned the Flat Creek bridge, then marched for Strawbery Planes, fording the Tennessee river two or three miles below Straw Planes, captured that place, spiked their guns, parolled the prisners, burned the RR bridge across Turn? River, camped there over night, fed and rested our horses and next day marched to mossy creek burned the RR bridge at that place then retired for Ky; this done by a force of about fourteen hundred men. After a skirmish or two we crossed the Cumberland mountain into Ky arriving there in time to assist in the capture of John Morgan and a part of his force making his big Indiana & Ohio raid, in the mean time fighting Scotts forces from Winchester Ky to Cumberland river 10 miles south of Sumerset Ky capturing about half of his command. After this was done went to blue grass region of Ky fed and rested our horses until latter part of August or first of September. Then led the advance of Burnsides army into Tennessee Went as far South to Cleveland skirmishing daily with Confederate forces. at Charston Tenn we met forces of Forest & Hodges and in skirmish with them Lewis F. Nitzschke my former 1st sergt but hospital steward lost his right arm by canon ball shot which also cut off the head of a colored boy servant of Dr. E. M. Norwood. Our comand was driven back to Louden Tenn; the next day my company scouted down to Cottonport road south west of Sweetwater Tenn. the next day went scout down Tenn river to Kingston returning monday we remained in Louden till return of the regiment from southern expedition for two days. Then joined the comand and marched to Kingston where I releived the Provost Martial and filled that place for over one month my company provost guard. During the time we were getting our supplies for horses from south of the river, skirmishing for it with confederate forces who occupied the country south of Tenn river. My Regt went down Tenn river picketing all the fords and ferries. A Mr. Thomas Sevier captain by my command came from Longstreets command give about the number his command and what were his intentions which telegraph to Gen. White at Louden and he Genl Burnside at Knoxville. Long crossed the river in spite of Burnsides forces and fought several battles between the crossing and Knoxville. My company at

CHRISTIAN (cont'd.):

Kingston forty miles west of Knoxville constituted the force at Kingston but my regt 1st Tenn up in day or two then the 16 Ky Regt, 25
Michigan Infy, 2nd Tenn Cav and some other regt of Col Motts command
arrived making a force of 3 to 5 thousand and on Nov 17 Gen Wheeler
with a large force of Cavelry attacked the post my company was on
picket duty and fought the attacking force of Wheeler for more than
an hour. My co at time prisent was 18 men (other part of co on
detush.....senic) at day light we were back to Infantry picket the
battle line for the day. We learn afterward that the 18 men with me
did great execution but one of my men was hurt till after day light
(Joel Griffy was severely wounded, and we learn afterward from pretty
reliable authority that 18 men were brought back to the improvised
hospital in my aunts backyard) before daylight one man was killed
with one my mens blanket around him, and there was no guns fired by
federal troops till after day light. When we got back to Infrty
picket we had on the Capt Davis Co of 16 Ky ½ Co 28 men of 25 Michigan 2 pieces of Old Elgian Batter in command of 2nd Lieut asked me
where are the enemy. I showed them to him in the underbrush less
than half mile away he said what I do my reply was gime them a few
shot he replied I will do it and he did. And the confeds reply with
a gun less than mile from us. At day light two sechons of 5 pound
steel Parrat Gun to position on the highest elevation and the first
Tenn Infry came up from the town and moved to the left 25 to the
right my Co in the center 2nd Tenn Cavelry still further to the right.
Wheeler was no.... with considerable loss. Our loss was small seven
were wounded none killed. We remained at Kingston for winter. Turned back our horses to the Government in Dec. or Jany and remained in
Kingston untill June when we joined Sherman army and participated
in the battles from Burnt? Hickory to the investment of Atlanta in
Sept 1863. When regt was ordered to Nashville for discharge; but the
regt. having .... largly 4 to 500 recruits were held to make good
their time, and every officer held to command the recruits-2 field
and 6 line officers were retained. I was one of the retained. (My
rank during the war Private to July 30, 1862. 2nd Lieut. to Aug.
1863. Then 1st Lieut. to Aug. 5, 1864 when discharged and I remained with the men until the last man of the organization was discharged.
When the regt. was mustered out in Sept. the recruits and retained
officers were given 30 days furlough and at its expiration was
ordered to Knoxville for reorganization and formed into Cos. A & B
and a detachment. My asignment was to Co B. The field officers
all discharged, then all the line officers except Lieut. Wm. Hartly
and myself and I being the senior it fell to my lot to command Co.
A B & A detachment to time of discharge Aug. 1864. My soldier experience was similar to experiences of other soldiers; climg mountains; ..... through the mud; slept on the ground and many time in
the mud, endured the rain and snow, the heat & cold. had thre derious
spells of sickness, measels, jaundice, rhumatism. Generally were
clothed and well fed, except at times but I know what it is to be
on half rations and what it is to be entirely out. We were fed on
hard tack, bakin bread, side bacon, coffee and sugar dry beans some
times rice and mixed vegetables not always she most palatable but
nutritious.

COGDELL, JOSEPH

FORM NO. 2

1.   Joseph Cogdell; Greeneville Tennessee RFD 11 Box 40(46?)
2.   80 years old
3.   in Cock County Tennessee
4.   I was a federal soldier
5.   Co. J.; 10 Tenn. Calvery
6.   ___maker by trade
7.   Fredrick Cogdell; Maston county N C; lived at Cock co Tenn
8.   Mairy Davis; J M Davis; not none; North Carolina
9.   ....
10. none

COGDELL (cont'd.):
11. no
12. none
13. ....
14. it was a log house had three rooms
15. worked on a farm. worked with a hoe and a plow.
16. my father was a shot maker by trade. mother wove and spun as well as the cooking
17. no
18. it was
19. yes
20. every body worked in those days
21. you couldnt tell any difference
22. they did sir
23. their was a friendly feeling between slave holders and non slave holders
24. no
25. very good
26. they was encouraged
27. free schools
28. about 4 years
29. it was two miles
30. they was all free schools
31. public
32. about 4 months in the year
33. yes
34. most of them were men
35. I inlisted in Cock county Tenn. in July 1862
36. Nashville Tenn
37. it was about six months
38. Florence Alibama
39. My calvery just chased in and out. We was in the saddles most all the time after we first battle we fell back to Lexton Alibama our clothing was good
40. I was discharged at Nashville Tenn in August the first 1865
41. I took the train at Nashville and came to Greeneville Tenn and walked from that point home
42. farming
43. I have worked on the farm ever since I got out of the army & I have lived in Greene county Tennessee since 1866.
44. ....
45. (most of the names unreadable)
46. ....

COLLMAN, PETER

FORM NO. 1

1. Peter Collman; Whiteville, Tenn.
2. age 79
3. Paris, Tenn
4. in St. Louis Mo
5. farming
6. ca____
7. nun at all
8. no we was slave our self
9. did not own no land at all
10. nun at all
11. log house one room stick and durt cimbey
12. plow and hoe to
13. carper (carpenter?); she cook and spining and weaving
14. no whe was a serven(t)
15. no we done all the work
16. no thay was the boss
17. yes (rest of sentence unreadable)
18. yes
19. no
20. thay was difen between them
21. yes

COLLMAN (cont'd.);
22. no
23. they discurge
24. nun at all
25. nun at all
26. near by
27. nun
28. private
29. to and three month
30. when they coud
31. dont no
32. year 61 August Spring Ill
33. 29 Ill first
34. ....

(letter on seperate sheet; first reply from a colored soldier)
page 1   Whiteville Tenn Feb the 16, 1922
    Dear sir in the regards of you well i have been working all of my
    days and hardly can get a living the times is hard work all the time
    and dont get a living work aints worth nothing you mite say and we
    aint aloud to say what we are worth we just work and the white people
    pay just what they want to pay and a man cant get a living out of
    what they are giving now it aint enought to get you some to eat mus
    less close to wear so we just can make enought to get something to
    eat and by the white people old clothes some times cant do that
(no second page)

34. sent to chilow
35. fore mount
36. Shilou
37. Vickburge the re___ in camp was good and bad we eat hard tick and
    we was exposed in col and hungry and disease we was not in hospilat
    an was no prison
38. Springfeld ill
39. after i went in camp i had no trip home
40. on steam boat
41. sometime a nair rise for my life i engage in a farming union hill
    church i have not helt no office
42. i hav not had no; Prible to S Rice?; rite off Peter Akns; (father)
    in space for state of; He lived at Paris Tenn
43. Gilie Chester; she was the daughter of Mary Chester
44. ....

COX, LEROY PATE

FORM NO. 2

1. Leroy Pate Cox; Lafayett
2. 79
3. Smith County
4. Federal
5. J; Ninth Ky
6. Farmer
7. Dunkin Mackfarlie Cox; North Carolina; lived at Tenn.
8. Elizabeth Cox; Warn Coker; Polly Coker; Ky.
9. ....
10. one mule
11. no
12. 100
13. $3000.00
14. log house three rooms
15. plowed-hoed
16. Father a farmer Plowed hoed. Mother cooking spinning weaving washing.
17. no
18. honorable
19. yes
20. no
21. yes
22. ....

40

COX (cont'd.):
23. yes
24. no
25. yes
26. encouraged
27. 3 months free school
28. 8 months
29. 1 mile
30. yes
31. public
32. 3 months
33. no
34. man
35. Columbia Ky 16 Oct
36. Shilo
37. 1 year
38. Stone River
39. clothed very well. diden suffer with cold. beans Porked beef, vel-
    egable. in the hospital 3 weeks
40. Louisville Ky
41. Came to Bolden Green Ky on the train. Them walked home.
42. Farming
43. very good health Member of the Church 40 year
44. ----
45. Sam Blankenship   Ace Blankenship   Co. I (J?)
    Tom Dixon   Mitch Gannon   "
    Ike Ellis   Dee Gammons   "
    Ples Shrum   Walker Hinton   "
    Pellie Hinton   Ben Hanes   "
    Em Napier   Pate Hooper   "
    Warn Cox   Marina   "
46. -------; LaFayette, Tennessee

DAVIS, TOM

FORM NO. 1

1. Tom Davis; Liberty Tenn. R. 5
2. 76
3. Tennessee and DeKalb Co.
4. Tennessee
5. Farming
6. farmer
7. none
8. none
9. none
10. none
11. Log House one room
12. I worked on a farm. I used a forked Dogwood for my Plow. and hoe
    shop made ----- hoe
13. my father died when I was 4 years old. my mother carded spon made
    her owned cloth. colared with walnut hulls and moss that grew on
    logs
14. none
15. I used stears for Plowing and hauling. Was respectable and honor-
    able.
16. yes
17. Seveal had slaves to do there work.
18. some fiew felt them selves better and some did not.
19. mijorty were equal some thought them selves better
20. kind feelings to one another
21. wasent aloud to help
22. quite a task
23. lots were encouraged by slaveholders
24. free schools. they would run a bout 3 months
25. 6 or 8 month
26. 3/4 of a mile
27. onely free schools
28. Public

41

DAVIS (cont'd.):
29. 3 months
31. man
32. I enlisted 1862. Alexandria Tennessee
33. 4th Tennessee regiment Mt. Inf. J. H. Blackburn was my Kernel. Mart-
    ain Quin my captain. My General Gerdon Stokes Henry Blackburn 1st
    Lutenent Tom B--lten 2nd Luetenent Pruit(?) soldiers Henry Jenkins,
    Henry Tugles, Wesley Morgain, Felt Culwell, Alex Culwell, John hehdon
    Bud Herman, Bill Phipips, Bill Botts, Bill Vares
34. White County
35. 5 days
36. Calf Killer
37. I was in the Murfreesboro fite. Nashville fite. Lebon fite. My
    last fite was with the Bush wackers. Our camp life was just out on
    the ground. we cooked in a big kittle out on the ground.
38. Aug. 1865 Nashville Tenn.
39. come home on a wagon and enjoyed it fine
40. farming
41. farming. genealy
42. John Davis; Alabama; do not no; Alabama; he was in the Mexican War.
43. Polly Snow; Billy Snow; Mahaley Braswell; Dry Creek, Tenn.
44. un none

DeLaVERGNE, GEORGE

FORM NO. 2

1. George DeLaVergne, 239 W. 41"St. Los Angeles, Calafoiner
2. in my 82d year
3. Ohio, Washington County
4. Federal
5. Lt. Col.; Eighth Tenn. Vol. Inf.
6. Farmer and had a flower mill
7. George W. DeLaVergne; Butches; New York; lived in N.Y. Ohio, Tenn.-,
   Mos. & Colorado; He was a member of the guard of Honor that escorted
   Lafaette into NY in his second visit.
8. Mary ......; Wm. Yates;......; at New Hackansack Dutches Co. N.Y.
9. Have not now access to one old family Bible. He was born in NY in
   1800 Died 1898(3?) Was a devout Christian. Elder in the Prsbyerian
   Church. My father, grandfather & great grandfather were born in NY
   and of Hugernot French stock Great grandfather was a celebrated
   physian.
10. Was barely of age; had no real property
11. no
12. about 300 acres
13. about 3500 dollars
14. part(1)y frame & partly log, 7 rooms
15. Did all kinds of farm work & helped in mill
16. fathers work was all kinds of work pertaining to a farm & grist mill.
    Mother did all kinds of house work, spinning, knitting cooking etc &
    the care of nine children. Extra help at times
17. No regular sirvants, empoyed.
18. it was, wher properly executed
19. they did
20. a few hunters(?) did a little, but their wives & children did the
    major part
21. Not many owned slaves in our section & those were good friendly
    neighbors, until they war came on, then some estrangement
22. yes, in our section
23. yes (words "or were they antagonistic to each other?" have lines
    drawn over them.)
24. Do not think it did
25. should say not; being too poor & too isolated
26. incouraged rather than otherwise, but rather indiferent
27. Public & neghborhood schools. was tootered by my sisters who were
    educated & refined
28. a part of sixtien years; each year
29. one mile
30. as above stated

42

DeLaVERGNE (cont'd.):
31. both
32. about six
33. yes
34. men mostly
35. I inlisted first in the 47 New Y-N-J- in Brooklyn N.Y. were sent to Fort McHenry, near Baltamore Md.
36. as bove stated
37. No battle while in the 47. At Person Bownbows solictation came to Ky... drilled & organized refugees
38. Siege of Knoxville, & other battles in uper East Tenn.
39. My first act was to cast my first ballor for the State to remain in the Union; after this I was treated as an outlaw & was obliged to go north; Was in 2d Brgade 3d Div of the 23 Army C--s; took my part in near all of the battles that took plase, between Chatanooga & Kennasaw Mt near which plase I received severe injurey in battle; then a hospital campaign
40. At Detroit Mich. 1865
    Was ordered by the War Dep to report to Gen Hooker in Cincenatti Ohio
41. was so broken up, did not go directly home but to Chattanooga Tenn. where I engaged in manufacturing business, in a small way, with a partner
42. stated above
43. On reporting to Gen Hooker he gave me a Dep Court over which I pre-sided while under his command; while under Gen. Ord, had the same duty, til was mustere(d) out. Married Emily D. Rice, neise of Chan-celor Abwood Hyde of Jasper Tenn. Moved to Mo.; Engaged in Merchan-tile business. from there to Colorado Springs Colo.; Engaged in merchandise ranching & banking & some mining; Got too high for health sold out; spent 5 yrs in (Harwell?) then came here to reside. where I am living a retired life having lost my wife & one of my two sons & now have one left Judge G. H. DeLaVergne.
    Have met quite a few noted men; one Sec. Chase of the US Treasury, once offered to me his kind services, but I wanted to "paddle my own canoe" and through the Love & mercy of God & our Lord Jesus Christ I have no complaint to make.
44. (written on seperate sheet of paper-see bottom of this sheet)
45. ----
46. Felix A. Reeve, Col & Tenn Vol Inf 1626 13st NW Washington DC
    (at the bottom of space for #46;)
    Respectfully submitted for what it is worth Co The Tennessee Histo-rical Committee Nashville Tenn.
44. above
    Los Angeles, Calif. - Apr. 29" 1922
                239 - W 41 St
    Mr. John Trotwood More
    Nashville, Tenn.
    Dear Sir: Enclosed herewith you will find the statement requested to be filled out. I doubt very much if you will find anything of public interest for your State. While I have not much to give, there is nothing to conseal. When we have grown old, those things that looked large & important when young, now look small! Wishing you the utmost success in your Department, I am very truly yours.
                Geo DeLaVergne

                DEPEER, ROBERT E.

FORM NO. 2

1. Robert E. Depeer; Fordlawn Rout 2 Tenn
2. 80 May 8 1922
3. Sulivan co Tenn
4. Fedrel
5. Batry E; First Ky Light Artillry
6. Farmer and brick mason
7. Isaac Depeer; Idont no; dont no; dont no; I dont no; he had nun
8. Sarah Campell; John Campebel; she was a Ward; I dont no
9. ----
10. didnt one (own) eny

43

DEPEER (cont'd.):
11. nun
12. Idont no
13. nun
14. Log one room
15. I worked on farm. Did all kinds of work
16. My father was brick laer; cooking spinning
17. nun
18. Respectibel and honerbel in my comunity
19. most of them did
20. such as that did not exsest only among the slave holders
21. they did not in my noing
22. much so as for as I no
23. so far as I no thare was no ill feeling
24. not as I no
25. it was kindley hard
26. to some exstint they descouraged
27. buy subscripsion
28. about 12 monts
29. 1½ miles
30. nune onley buy subscripsion
31. private
32. deffernce with schools
33. prity much so
34. both
35. I inlisted in the fedrel governent at Luyville Ky in Sept 20 - 1863
36. Camp Nelson Ky
37. I cant tell
38. Lexiton
39. ----
40. Lexiton Ky Oct. 8, 1864
41. I left Luyvulle came to Knoxville Tenn then home
42. farming
43. I have all way worked on a farm   I belong to the Church of the Brothern
44. ----
45. I havent enything of intrust to give you as I havent eny thing historical I will remian as ever yours
                                   Robert E. Depeer

                          DICKSON, WILLIAM

FORM NO. 2

1.   William Dickson; Greenville, Tenn. R 12 Box 5
2.   100 hundred yrs and 8 months
3.   Sery county North Carolina near Salem
4.   I was federal soldier
5.   first Ten Calvery; east Tenn.
6.   shoe maker
7.   David Dickson; Sery county, North Calonia; North Carlonia; Chapel Hill North Calonia
8.   Eliezeph Stillmen; George Stilman; Bekie --ilman
9.   ----
10. I was a renter I own 2 cow and 8 hog 2 mules and 2 heifers worth 600 dollars worth of property
11. didnt own no slaves
12. he was a renter
13. 800 dollars
14. a big hued log house
15. I worked on farm while I was a boy I plowed
16. My father run a shoe shop; my mother spun weaving and carding and cooking and other work also
17. Nary one
18. plowing hauling and other hone-y(?) work was honorable
19. did they delighted in plowing and other work
20. good many white men had negroes to work for them
21. they felt biggety and above poor folk who did not have slaves
22. ----

                                44

DICKSON (cont'd.):
23. they would not mingle togather at all
24. no sir
25. no the times was not good
26. they was discouraged by slave holders
27. free school 3 month in a year
28. 6 month
29. 2 mile and ½
30. free school
31. private
32. 3 month
33. very regular when ther was school
34. man teacher
35. 1862 August 8
36. Western Virginia
37. Just 3 days exactly till we were fighting
38. big creek gap
39. starved most of time slept just like bruts big battle stone River
    gia gap houia(?) gap Bridge port last 3 hours and some 23 hours
    hard fighting Alpine georgia lasted half day Chicamogia 3 day fight
    look out mountain knoxville
40. Nashville Ten
41. I came home on train to Knoxville
42. farming
43. farming on paint creek Tenn
44. ----
45. Westly George; Charley Broyles; Nute Smeler; Cornel Brounlow; Luet-
    enet dyer; R--s onburg; William didwell; James Elkin; Major Trent
46. William Rule   Greenville Ten

                    DINSMORE, JOHN W.

FORM NO. 2

1.   John W. Dinsmore; mine is Rogersville tennessee
2.   mi age is 75 years
3.   hawkins co tennessee
4.   I was a federal solgar
5.   a & f; first tennessee light artilary
6.   mi father was a farmer
7.   felldan f. dinsmore; Washington Co.; ----; Va.; aftar he got grow
     he cam to hawkins co tenn; he never was int eney official he nevr
     riten eney Book
8.   Juda Presley; (the name Nancy Presley is in the space for fathers
     name and the phrase "and his wife" has been crossed over) Nancy
     Presley she was bornd in north carlner; north carliner untill she
     was girl then cam to tenn
9.   my gran father on mi mothers side was revluchanary solgar an mi gran
     father on my fathers side was in the war of 1812 mi father nevr ond
     eney land aftar tha cam out of the wars tha was farmers
10. I one a hous an lot in Rogersville hav bin for 2 years I ond a
     litel farm befaur I cam to Rogersville
11. We nevr ond eney slaves
12. tha nevr ond eney land
13. the gest ond a mild cow tha was vary pore men tha gest liv in a log
     caban
14. onla 1 rume
15. I worked on a farm befour I went in the arme an aftar I cam home
     out of the arma I was a farmear an un tell I got too old to farm
16. mi father was a farmer an mi mother kep house she spun flacksan to
17. tha nevr kep eney servants
18. such work was respected an onest but the price for such was offel
     low in price 40 an 50 cence per day at that time.
19. yes tha in gaged in such work
20. ----
21. tha dident with them that dident one eney slaves tha thought them
     a litle betr than the no slave holars
22. the slave holdars thought them selves a litel betr
23. when the sivel war began to com up the non slave holders wasent a

                            45

DINSMORE (cont'd.):
laud to say eneything
24. the slav holdar was genrealey democrats a poshan of the non slav holdars was democrats an part waw whigs
25. the pore men wasent given eney incurgment to mak eney thing tha was kep down as much as pasleb.
26. tha was discuredg an keep down all tha cold
27. not eney onley subchripshan choals
28. In all the cholling I went was about 2 years I ges in all I went
29. about a mile
30. subshripshams chools
31. privet
32. three month
33. yes tarleb well
34. tha was all men
35. I inlisted in the federal arma her at Rogersville tennessee hawkins county
36. we remand her at Rogersville un tell we had a litel fight at Big Creek 3 mil east Rogrsvill
37. a bout a month or the rise
38. Big creek 3 mile east of Rogersville hawkins county tennessee
39. the first place we went aftar was Kantucky camp Nelson we went from Camp Nelson Kantucky to nashville tennessee to the Zalea Coffer (Zollicoffer) house an from thar out in the west part of tenn to camp gilam then I was sent from thar to the hospitel nashville then from the hospitel to fort martan.
40. I was discharged at nashville tennessee on the third day of August 1865
41. then I got a free transpertashan to Bools gap tennessee then I had to walk home a bout 28 miles
42. I went on the farm
43. I hav bin a farmer evr cence the sivel war I hav liv sevarl places cense the sivel war but not over 16 miles from Rogersville tennessee mi church relashan is what uther pepel call dunkerd but we call our selvs Brethren I went in that church when I was onley 26 years old and I hav remand thar evr cence we bleve in gest takin the new testment an falring evry precept we read in it we dont beleve in eney organashan but the church of crist an we dont want eney book onley the bibel an good equel chashan book we blev in egachashan.
44. ----
45.

James Adams	Berks	Bixler
Briten	Brown	Bentlea
Be Brams	John Brown	Boon
Cashan first	Cashin second	Castillaw
Carnind	Copick	Caraway
Chrech	Colbart	Carsan
doolea	dant	Duning
davis	ed ing	gastar
glass	Haw Ltan	Hagrman
herlea	Pactr sinilea	J. E. Sinila
salan	sha	shen
stanfield	stuBelfeld	richman smith
william smith	trent	turner
tomas harner	danal harner	houseright
henley	ismer Burg	Jackeba
lench	law	makery
magarener	magraw	sustrd
mefard	mathas	noa ?
nix	osBarn	fagan
Pain	Portor Robert	Portor Pall

this is the names I will giv you of mi compney
46. JoPes right of the 13 Cal Tennessee Rogersville Tennessee
lues J. Davis of mi co 1 lit Tennessee Rogersville Tennessee
John Minan of mi Co 1 lit Tennessee Rogersville Tennessee

DOTSON, WILEY

FORM NO. 2

46

DOTSON (cont'd.):
1. Wiley Dotson; R.D. #2 Bx 84 LaFayette, Tennessee
2. 75 years June 13, 1922
3. Macon County, Tennessee
4. Federal
5. D; ith Tennessee mounted Infantry
6. Farmer and showmaker
7. Thomas Jefferson Dotson; don't know; ---; Tennessee; Macon County, Tennessee; He brought the mail from Fountain Run, Ky. to the people in his settlement.
8. Melinda Scott; John Scott; ---- Woods; Salt Lick, Tennessee Macon County.
9. There were seven brothers, Dotsons that came over in the Mayflower from England. My fathers people came from North Carolina and my granmothers from South Carolina. I do not have any record of the name of the settlement.
10. Did not own any kind of property.
11. My mother heired some slaves but she took land for her part.
12. I don't know don't have any record.
13. ----
14. Log house - one room - cooked in the smoke house
15. I lived with a widow Mrs. Sarah Turner; plowed and worked with hoe, did all kinds of work that was to do on a farm.
16. My mother died when I was about 5 years old. My father then broke up housekeeping and went from house to house and made shoes. The women raised cotton an flax and spun and weaved made everything wove also bedclothes.
17. no
18. With all respect - There were no aristocrats in our community.
19. yes
20. No- the white men worked as well as the slaves
21. no, I dont know as they did. as I was nothing but a small boy.
22. yes
23. yes
24. Don't know as I was to young to remember
25. Nothing was worth anything much you could buy a real good horse for $25.00-slaves were high
26. ----
27. 3 month free school
28. About 6 month, just long enough to read and write a little
29. 1½ mile
30. 3 month free school beginning first Monday in Aughts.
31. Public
32. 3
33. some did and others only a few weeks at beginning
34. man
35. Mar. 1, 1865, Gap of Ridge, Tennessee
36. Carthage, Tenn
37. was not engaged in battle at all. I was sick with measles long time.
38. we were sent to Carthage for a guard as the gorillas were so bad.
39. My camp was alright, plenty to eat such as it was Beans, fat meat and hard tack was the fare had good coffie and sugar - Had extra good clothes, slept on a bunk in the tent, Had the measles while in Nashville would not go to a hospital as there were so many in it.
40. Aug. 31, 1865 at Nashville
41. We come up to Gallatin on the train and there 5 or 6 of us hired a wagon to bring us to LaFayette
42. Everything that was done on a farm
43. Have always lived on a farm. oun a hill farm of about 60 acres in Macon County, never had held any kind of office. Been a member of the Missionary Baptist at Liberty since 1867 or '68.
44. ----
45. W. S. Dotson   Booker Freeman, First Lieutenant
    Bishop Hudson   Wiley Barton Hudson
    Corporal Woods   Hiram Dotson
    Tom Dotson   Logan White
    sec. Lieutenant Bandy
46. William Smith   LaFayette R.D.#2 Tennessee
    Shephard Green   Akersville Ky
    Henry Andrews   LaFayette Tenn

DOTSON (cont'd.):
    Bishop Scott   Akersville Ky
    Hiram Dotson   Westmoreland Tenn
    Haley Kirby   LaFayette R.D. #2 Tenn

                        DOUGLAS, WILLIAM A.

FORM NO. 1

1. William A. Douglas; Wildersville Tennessee
2. 78
3. Henderson County Tennessee
4. Henderson County of Tennessee, Federal
5. farming
6. farming
7. didin own any
8. father owned 15 slaves
9. 400 acres
10. $2,500.
11. two log rooms
12. plowed and hoed and any thing that came to hand
13. Father plowed made shoes bottom chair was a blacksmith, rum a griss-
    mill done this with horsepower Mother cooking spinning weaving
    milking churning
14. no
15. yes
16. yes
17. They didin do any odleness white men worked every day.
18. They mixed and mingle with each other they did not think them selves
    better and they respected honorable ___ who did not own slaves.
19. at churches & school they mingle and all went to gather me and slaves
    all went pare footed to gather to church
20. They were all friendly and good feelings toward each other
21. no they didin do that
22. yes
23. they encourged him tryed to help him
24. didin have any free schools had a very few subscriptions
25. guess I went about 10 months altogether
26. It was two miles to the nearest school
27. subscriptions white people didin have any negros schools
28. private
29. 2 months
30. yes
31. man teacher didin have any women teacher
32. Aug 1862 Jackson Tennessee
33. Co A 7th Tenn Calvary Kernal Hawkens regiment Capt Moore Leut Royal
    Sargent Dennison Sam Coffman Whig Adams Frank Berket Bill Berket
    Jasper Teague R. Teague Dock Teague Ben Camp Bill Mullins, Milt
    Bartholomew Daniel Meals, Harper Meals, Drew Massey John Wipe,
    George Morgan Frank Morgan, Hareson Thomas John Christphor Clark
    Pritcherd
34. Henderson station Tennessee
35. 1 month
36. Korrent Miss. lasted too days
37. Cross roads 1 day. Trenton one day Hallow springs half day Union
    City 1 day captured and cared to Anderson prison and stayed 9 month
    eat 1 spoonful Bow peas a day lost 1400 thousand slept on ground
    nothing under us or over clothed pretty well until got in prison and
    we didin have any cloth. exposed to cold hunger and disease
38. Aug 1865 Nashville Tenn
39. Left Nashville and had a hundred miles home had a right nice trip
    home
40. farming
41. magstrate farming grocery business Henderson Co. Tennessee
42. William A. Douglas; N. Carolina; ----; -----; Henderson County Tenn-
    essee; ----:
43. Nancy Jane Douglas; Billie Milan; Pollie Milan; Henderson County
44. Came from N. Carolina to Tennessee settled in Henderson County Tenn
                            William A. Douglas   Wildersville, Tenn

                                48

DUNCAN, WILLIAM FRANKLIN

FORM NO. 2

1. William Franklin Duncan; Tasso Tennessee
2. I am eighty years and four months old
3. In Ashe now Alleghaney County North Carolina
4. Federal soldier Civil War
5. M4th Tenn Cav; 4th Regiment Tennessee Calvary Volunteers; I was credited to Washington County Tennessee
6. Farmer
7. George Washington Duncan; Sparty; Ashe now Alleghany; North Carolina; in Ashe County NC and Washington Co. Tennessee; He was a farmer and Ex Mexican Volunteer Soldier
8. Jane Elizabeth Edwards; William Edwards; Nancey Edwards, Near Gap Civil Ashe County North Carolina
9. John Duncan great grand father a soldier of the Revolutionary Wa 1776 John Duncan grand father soldier of 1812 George W. Duncan father Volunteer Mexican War. William Edwards great grandfather an Englishman first settled in New York William Edwards grandfather first settled in Penn and then in NC Nancey Edwards and Duncan was from Ireland. Scotch Irish Descent
10. Father owned a farm
11. No did not own slaves
12. About one hundred acres
13. About one hundred acres worth $500.00
14. Common country log house
15. As a boy I worked on the farm and attended public and private schools three to five months each year
16. Father George W. Duncan was a farmer owned land and mill worked the farm and run the mill at times. Mother done house work cooking spinning and weaving making our wearing appeas
17. No slaves only domestic white girls
18. yes Respecable by every body
19. yes
20. No idleness was not tolerated
21. In Verriable did associate together as friend and citizens
22. In Vernables so without Fricsun up to 1860
23. Naborly and friends up 1860
24. I think not
25. It was and evry Industrus person taken advantage of the opportunity
26. Evry body was encoraged to work and be honest.
27. Public schools 3 to 5 months and Private schools after public schools expired
28. More or less each year up to 1860.
29. Four to five miles
30. Public and private subscription schools
31. Public and private
32. Three to five or six months
33. They did
34. Men
35. I William F. Duncan was enlisted for Company M. 4th Regt Tenn Cavalry United States Army May 6th 1864 and credited to Washington County Tenn. I was offered $750.00 to be credited to New York City as substitue for New York
36. To Nashville Tennessee to Camp Catlelto
37. Stoneman Raid into Georgia in June or July 1864 Sherman campaign.
38. I was on detached service at a Block house gaurding a RR Bridge near Decatur ala until Battle of the Sulphur Trusler and capture of the 3rd Tenn Cav
39. While on detached service seargt in charge of 100 one hundred men having to occupy to Block house contracted fever and bowel trouble and was in Railroad and injured treated in hospital at Nashville Tennessee and at Jeffersonville Ind.
40. July 12th 1865 at Nashville Tennessee
41. I landed at home in Jonesboro Washington County Tennessee in July 1865
42. Work on the farm Hoeing corn for a Nabor for one pick of corn per day.
43. I began work on the farm farming next clerking in a country store in

DUNCAN (cont'd.):
    Washington County Tennessee. I have lived in Bradley County Tenn-
essee Forty years was Census Newmerator in 1891 & 1900 and 1910
Justice of the Peace member of the County Court Notary Public for
years Depot and Express Agent seven years Pension agent or attorney
Clerk in store and Assist Post master at Tasso Bradley County Tennessee for last ten years up to the present time. A Master Mason
Chatata Lodge F & AM Member of the Christian Church

44. (On 2 separate sheets of paper)
    Honerable John Trotswood Moore
    Director Nashville Tenn
    1-1-1923 Dear Sir
    In reply to yours of recent date I give you further history of my-
self after the Civil War I was 1st Lieut. of Co E 2nd Regt NC State
trooper and Adgt of the Regt and was elected Lieut Colonel of the
same. I married Martha Jane Hensley Sept 28th 1865 She was mother
of one son David Washington Duncan Borned March 24th 1867. He was
a Legislator He was killed by RailRoad train near Cleveland Tennessee March 24th 1922. On his birthday on a crossing. He was stock
inspector for Tennessee appointed by Cap Peck and Govenor A. A.
Taylor. I am yours truly,
                        William F. Duncan
                        Tasso Tennessee

    Honerable John Trotwood Moore
    Nashville Tenn
    1-1-1923 Dear Sir
    On March the 12th 1871 I was married to Malissa Christena Briggs
she was the mother of Martha E. Duncan Borned 8-13-1873 now living
John Thomas Duncan Born January 21, 1877 living William L Duncan
1-17-1879 living Marion D. Duncan 11-22-1881 Decd 7-6-1903 Isham
F. Duncan 1-1-1884 living Oscar L. Duncan 2-16-1886 Died at Donelson
Tenn 3-31-1921 Fredrec R. Duncan April 8, 1889 Decd 6-8-1890 Evan P.
Duncan 2-12-1892 Now living My wife Malissa Christena Duncan Decd
Nov 5, 1921 members of the Christian Church I am yours
                        William F. Duncan
                        Tasso Tennessee

45. Company M 4th Tenn Cav

Capt. A. D. Stone	Lieut. Robert Kettrell
Sarg. Joseph Hicks	William F. Duncan
James D. Rice	John Munely
Abraham Owen	Anthony Weaver
Henry H. Hood	Thomas J. Marshall
John Anderson	William Anderson
Wesley A. Bryant	John D. Carter
Thomas Cox	John Duncan
William P. Dunble	Ezekiel Davidson
Tarver Hempfield	Jasper Guinn
Parker Hoover	William H. Higgins
George W. Hale	Andrew C. Kelley
James W. Miller	Samuel Muller Maddix
John Edward Moser	John Penix
William F. Rodgers	Jasper Rodgers
Hiram H. Roy	Ross B. Smith
August Silwell	William H. Sims
Andrew J. Thomas	David Watkins
Fredrick White	Andrew Young
James McKechan	Hamilton Bunton
James R. Evans	Loyal Henson
William M. Bivins	James Allen
George Bittle	Michael Bowler
John Chriswill	John Galliger
Dolphus Kerby	Wiley Mayfield
George W. Mallicoat	Price John
Bivens (?) C. (?) Phillips	Henry H. Thomas
Andrew Thomas	James Cl_ck
William Wit	

    Hoovan Gamiel (?) He killed in Battle at Franklin Tennessee. He
                 told boy I will be killed today.
    James W. Holland Deid March 30, 1865

DUNCAN (cont'd.):
```
      Powel Lansay          Deid June 26 1864
      Maddex Thomas         Deid Augst 2 1864
      Maddin James          Deid Dec 28 1864
      William E. Welkins    Deid on Board Sultann
```
I Wm. F. Duncan Have a Roster Repot of soldiers of Tennessee Adgt Genl Report

46. I William F. Duncan Co. M 4th Regt Tennessee Cavalry that is L____ky that I know any thing of at present time.
When I left hospital I was sent to Vicksbury Miss and to New Nleans La then to Fort Barrancus Florida then to Mobelle Ala then marched by land to Batton Rogue La then to Nashville Tennessee by boat Excuse me for takin up so much time I am yours truly

Wm F Duncan

Tasso Tenn

My own hand
Writing age 80 years old

FINGER, MARION

FORM NO. 2

1. Marion Finger; Grunback, Tennessee
2. 78 yrs.
3. Tennessee
4. Federal
5. Company H; 5th Tenn.
6. Farmer
7. Jonas Finger; 8th district; Blount; Tennessee; in Blount & Knox counties all his life;
8. Delilah Sliger; Adam Aliger; ____; in Washington County
9. My parents died when I was five years old, no records had been kept. I do not remember any thing about them. and have never been able to trace their ancestry.
10. I owned one mare & some farm tools the value would have been about $100. (one hundred dollars)
11. no
12. did not own any
13. ----
14. log house 3 rooms
15. Did all kinds of farm work. I went to work before the sun was up and quit at sun down worked every day except Sundays.
16. My father worked on a farm. My mother cooked, wove and spun and did the house work
17. no
18. yes
19. yes
20. Several owned slaves and kept then at work but they also worked
21. The majority of the slave owners did not feel them selves better but a few did.
22. yes
23. yes
24. no
25. no
26. discouraged to some extent
27. Subscription schools
28. six months
29. two mile
30. Peppermint branch school
31. private
32. 3 months
33. no. the people were poor & had to stay out to work
34. man
35. 1862, February, Barbersville Ky
36. Cumberland Ford Knetucky
37. about two months
38. Cumberland Gap
39. We were surrounded at Cumberland Gaby? by Gen Bragg & men we went to Ohio we were then ordered to Murfreesboro Ten, but the battle had

51

FINGER (cont'd.):
ended just as we arrived. I was in a battle at Chattanooga, Ten. on Lookout Mt. I fought one day, we went back to city as they were about to surround us. Kennasaw Mt in Georgia lasted one day, we won it. Resacca battle lasted all day, we won

40. 11th of May, 1865 at Nashville, Ten.
41. The goverment gave me a free pass I got a train at Nashville and got off at Concord. walked from there home it was about three mile from there to where my sisters lived
42. farming
43. I have always lived on a farm and been engaged in farming. I lived in Blount County until twenty three years ago I moved to Loudon County where I now Live.

39. Question 39 con't on separate page:
Battle of New Hope Church in Ga lasted one hour, I was wounded in left arm at elbow. taken to hospital at Jeffersonville Ind. I stayed from 2nd of June to 9th of Aug. My regemint was Marietta Ga. I joined them there. the next battle was at Franklin Tenn. lasted two hours, we won. we had a blanket to sleep on in camp, we had good clothes. sometimes we had food and some times it would be two and one half days we would not have food. we were expoused to cold and hunger while we were at Murfreesboro Tenn. exposed to small pox.

44. ----
45.

Capt J L Dungan	Private	Jim Vallalee
1st Lieut. R L Cudgeonton	"	Fleur Reed
2nd Lieut. John Carpenter	"	Bill Phillpot
Sargeant Jim Hammontree	"	Davy Carrol
Sargent Andy Boyd	"	Jim Summit
3rd Sargent Joe Allen	"	Hugh Campbell
1st Corp. Alex Hammontree	"	Adam Finger
2nd " Harris Anderson	"	Jim Finger
3rd " Gran Kittrell	"	Henry Finger
Private Marsh Tipton	"	John Finger
" Asbery Robertson	"	Frank Finger
" Sam Blackwell	"	Doc Tallent
" Sam Keer	"	Jack Tallent
" Dave Rosin	"	Jim Scrimpture
" Harve Rosin	"	Jake Carter
" Sam Marney	"	Hankins Daniel
" Vance Marney	"	Marion Willis
" Bill Hammontree	"	Tom Cannon
" Samuel Marney	"	Jim Jones
" Tom Hammontree	"	Marion Jones
" Harve Hammontree	"	Lee Thompson
" Hiarm Hammontree	"	Sanders Orr
" John Hammontree	"	Jim Simpson
" James Hammontree	"	Gib Martin
" Harvey Hammontree	"	John Martin
" Bill Ball	"	Marion Finger
" Bob Hacker	"	Jack Snider
" Bill Smith	"	John McGlothen

46.

Isaac Hannah	Maryville Tennessee
John Carpenter	Maryville Tennessee
Bill Tulloch	Maryville Tennessee
D. V. Weagley	Maryville Tennessee
John Allen	Maryville Tennessee
Bill Hannah	Binfield Tennessee
Cam Walker	Greenback Tennessee
Joe Lamon	Maryville Tennessee
Andy Goddard	Maryville Tennessee
Russah Cabe	Greenback Tennessee
Cam Carver	Greenback Tennessee
XCass Tipton	Knoxville Tennessee
XHouse Allen	Knoxville Tennessee
Bill Edmondson	Maryville Tennessee
Jack Snow	Loudon Tennessee
Pink Dockery	Greenback Tennessee
Bill Rule Capt.	Knoxville Tennessee

FOX, GILBERT

FORM NO. 2

1. Gilbery Fox, Sevierville Tennessee
2. Seventy Seven
3. Sevier County Tennessee
4. Federal
5. Co A; 9th Tenn Cav Vols.
6. farmer
7. George Fox; Sevier County Tenn; Sevier; Tennessee; Fair Garden Tennessee; He was a farmer wrote no books, but was an excelent stiller in his day.
8. Ruthie Derrick; Jonas Derrick; _____; Fair Garden Tennessee
9. Cant give any of the above information
10. Dident own any property at the commencement of Civil War.
11. No
12. 222 Acres
13. $1500.00
14. Log house with stick and clay chimney with three rooms.
15. Plowed hoed cleared lands worked all the time on farm worded at different kinds of work as was needed on farm.
16. General farm work and was a stiller. My mother done all kinds of house work and weaveing of all kinds of cloth made all the cloth that went to make up our clothing such as cotton wool flax.
17. did not own any
18. honorable and honest and it had to be done to make a liveing (LIVEING) and a man that did not work was considered no good.
19. yes
20. there was none such in my community.
21. mingled with each other at times you would find some fellow who thought him self better than his neighbors due to the fact he owned slaves.
22. All atended church one one footing.
23. To some extent they were antagonistic but not generly speaking.
24. Not in this community.
25. No
26. No.
27. Free school
28. some thing like six months all togather.
29. One half a mile
30. Just free schools some thing like two months in fall of the year.
31. Public
32. some thing like two months.
33. No
34. Man
35. 1863 in the month of Sept 13, sowrn in Army at Knoxville Tennessee
36. went to Camp Nelson Ky.
37. About three months.
38. At Knoxville Tenn.
39. After leaveing Knoxville we went to Ky and from Camp Nelson to Nashville, Tennessee and from there to louisville Tenn from there to Knoxville Tenn, was in battles with Gen. John Morgan in different places and finely captured and killed Gen Morgan at Greenville Tenn in 1864. and in the battle of Bulls Gap Tenn, In the rade at Marion Va. and was finely discharged at Knoxville, Tenn.
40. In Sept 1865, at Knoxville Tenn.
41. Left Knoxville on foot and spent the night at the old Sunn farm 7 miles from Knoxville Tenn. the second day we arrived at the Home of John McMahan a (confederate) and spent the night there and then on through Sevierville Tenn to my fathers home 12 miles east of Sevierville.
42. Farming. till a few years ago when I sold my farm and moved to Sevierville Tenn.
43. At the close of the War I returned and rented a farm for four or five years then bought a farm of 220 Acres. later I bought more land makeing a total of 300 acres. I have been a member of the primitive Baptist Church for the past twelve years was a methodist before joining the Primitive Church.
44. _____
45. Capt. Lafayett Jones   Lieut. Peter E. Walker

53

FOX (cont'd.):

Caswell Fox	Bill Williams
Perry Webb	Milos Webb
John Thomas	Abner Gentry
Bill Blake	John Weeden
Joe Banch	Allen Hendrics
Marion Davis	Jim Davis
Jake Walleford	Jim ....
Leander Ray	Tom Willson
Louis Spoon	

46.
Jim Bird	Sevierville R F D #11 Tennessee
Perry Chambers	Dandridge Tennessee
Geo Blazor	Sevierville R F D #11 ....
Tillman Houk	..................8 ....
Edward Loveday	....
Julious Justice	
Moses E. Lane	Sevierville R F D #13 ....
W. D. Atchley	..................2 ....
Jack Norhor	Sevierville Tenn
Jessie Atchley	Sevierville Tenn
George DeLozier	Boyds Creek Tenn R F D #1
Sam M. Hammar	....
Alex Gann	Sevierville Tenn R F D #13
Sam Shrader	Dandridge Tenn
Mode Miller	....
Bill Edmons	....
Asa Layman	New Port Tenn
Creed Boyer	....
Sam Maples	Pigeon Forge Tenn
Geo McFalls	....
Rance Sims	....

FRANK, GEORGE W.

FORM NO. 2.

1. George W. Frank; P. O. Sweetwater Tenn. R.#7.
2. 77 yrs. old in April 1922
3. In loudon county, Tenn.
4. Federal soldier
5. Company C; 11th Tenn Cavelry
6. Farmer
7. James Frank; unknown,Jefferson; Tennessee, in McMinn, Roane & Loudon
    counties; _____;
8. Betsy Woods; unknown; unknown; _____;
9. ____
10. nothing owned by myself at the beging of the war.
11. No.
12. No.
13. at the opening of the war my father was a renter and owned 4 horses
    & 3 cows valued at something near $500.00
14. Log cabin with 2 rooms.
15. I plowed and hoed on the Farm. we considered hoeing more important
    than anything else back then. I also made rails and builded fence.
16. My father plowed and hoed made rails and fenced and cleared up land,
    etc, my mother did all the house work such a cooking spinning card-
    ing the cotten & wool and made clothes for the family also done the
    weaving and made garden etc.
17. No
18. yes sir this kind of was considere very respected and honorable.
19. yes almost everybody
20. Just a few that practiced the above life
21. the slave holder mingled freely with respectable, honorable men who
    didnt own slaves. they were nice comidating men.
22. yes they ween equal at all such gatherings.
23. yes ther was in a friendly feeling between them
24. no that I remember, I seen no Difference.
25. Yes
26. I think they would encourage them to go ahead and make something out

54

FRANK (cont'd.):
   of themselves.
27. Free school it was about two months long and it came in fodder puling
    time and wheat sowing time
28. I only got to go about 2 weeks
29. about 2 miles
30. The wilson school house
31. public. free school.
32. about 2 months
33. yes. them that was close.
34. a man. his name was "Dolphos Low"
35. I enlisted in August 1863. at the edge of Pond Creek.
36. Camp Nelson in Kentuckey. We came to Cumberland Gap, engaged in
    scrirmishes there.
37. about 3 week we begin to engage in scrumishes.
38. we were in no real battles
39. we were in no real battles but scrumishes. We all escape unhurt and
    always gained all scrumishes. we had very good clothes, but we didn't
    have sufficient clothing to keep us warm in winter at nights, we
    slept on the ground with rock under heads. plenty to eat, never was
    in the Hospital, but was exempt from 12 day on account of deseases.
40. at Knoxville. in 1865
41. We came home on the train, free fare got home same night we started.
42. I went back to farming the same kind of work we did as before we
    went to the army.
43. I have engaged in farming every since the civil war on up till became
    to feeble. I have lived in Loudon, McMinn and Roane counties since
    the war. In 1862 I joined the Baptist Church and been a minber
    every since. Held no offices.
44. On two separate pages - handwritten
    (pg 1) Certificate No. 526360
    I was drove away from home by the soldiers. I was only about 18 yrs
    of age and didn't want to join the army never was away from home a
    single night.
    I didn't want to join the army when I did but in leaving home with
    my Brothers and associates the enlisting officer over persuaded me
    and I joined with the balance of then. being just a mere boy.
    I will state I went through a great deal of exposure and hard ships
    while I was in the army. we had plenty to eat except when we were
    away from the wagon train for days at a time when we suffered with
    hunger and cold.
    I want to state further that I havent seen a well day. or felt well
    since. since the war like I did before I joined the army. and it
    seems like I am getting worse and worse every day of my life. I
    have live now untill I am entirely a past work. I can barely see
    enough to feed my self. My eyes are so weak.
    (pg 2) I have some body with me to take care of me and do my cooking
    and work. I have them hired.
    I have six in family encluding the one that is doing my work. and
    have to buy everything to live on, am not making anything.
    I have to hire all my outside work done such as getting wood and
    plowing my truck patches and garden.
    I buy my medicine that I use I have no Doctors waiting on me now I
    can thing of nothing else at present.
                          Yours Very truly.
                          George W. Frank
45. Captain Dossett   Order Sargent Henry Farmer
    Major Black   Tom Whitlock
    King Bowman   James Cannon
    Joe Bivins   two Brothers
    James Arnel   Jessie Hufacre
    John Weese
46. Geo W. Payne   Erie   Tenn
    Baily finley (Col)   Loudon   Tenn
    A. P. Hutcheson (Con)   Erie R #1   Tenn
    A. W. Guffie (Con)   Kingston R #1   Tenn
    Hardie Guffie   "   Sweetwater R #7   "

55

GEORGE, S.

FORM NO. 1

1. Gassaway, Cannon county Tenn.
2. Eighty-six year old
3. Wilson county Tenn.
4. Wilson county Tenn. I enlisted in the Federal Army Co. B. 5th. Tenn. Ca. Vol.
5. Farmer
6. Farmer
7. No land at the time I enlisted. I have no property now.
8. No
9. None
10. just a smal amount
11. Log house
12. General farm work
13. Rather did general farm work. My mother manufactured our clothing by carding, spinning, weaving and sewing our garmens.
14. No
15. Yes it was considered Honorable and respectable and all the people followed farming and did general farm work.
16. Yes
17. There was no idleness among our people.
18. I dont remember that there was any diffence among us white people.
19. yes
20. Friendly feeling
21. I never noticed it then.
22. Yes, but not all did it.
23. No
24. Common or free schools, last only a few months during the year
25. a short time only could barely write.
26. One fourth mile of the school hose for sever years
27. Common or free schools, only.
28. public
29. three or four
30. fairly well only
31. Man
32. Enlisted at Nashville Tenn. at the fair grounds, Aug. 2nd. 1862
33. Co. B. 5th Tenn. Cav. Vol. Col. W. B. Stokes, Capt. Tom Waters, J.K.P. Lance, Joshua Bryant, Wathertown Tenn, Gernal Bryant, Eli Hear, John Davis, Zack Davies, Arch Davis, Leui Rodgers, Dock Rodgers, James Compton, Dick Compton, James Grindstaff, Bump Grindstaff, James Kitchesn, Jerome Goodner
34. Drilling, then sent to Smith Court Tenn. to bring out some recruits that wanted to come.
35. Only a short time.
36. Near Nashville Tenn
37. One battle at Sparta Tenn. lasted for two or three hours, and other places in White county, Murfreesboro or Stne River, Charleston battle Knoxville Battle I was prisoner at Chattanooga Tenn. I was captured at Carthage Tenn. my horse was killed from under me, I was well treated generally. We were well clothed and fed as a rule but I did not eat a bite for three days and nights at Murfreesboro Tenn. We had considerable exposure in the three years, but I judge not more than other soldiers had. Slept in the open largly, and on the ground with a little straw or leaves under a blanket and one over us.
38. June 25th of June 1865 at Fayettville Tenn.
39. we went to Nashville and was parolled there, and on home with no unusual incident.
40. Farming
41. Farmed since the war, I had nine boys and reared eight to be men, I reared one girl, all live in Tenn. But one
42. Charles George; Wilson Co. Tenn.; ____; ____; Alexandria Tenn.; nothing more than an ordinary citizen Without much education.
43. Vasti Hughes; came from Virginia to Tenn.; ___; ___; ____;
44. _____

GEORGE, WILLIAM H.

FORM NO. 1

1. William H. George; Smithville Tenn R #6
2. About 82 yrs
3. Wilson County Ten. 13 Dist
4. DeKalb County
5. Farming
6. Farming
7. I did not own any
8. no
9. 800 acres
10. as the Land He owned then was valued at $100 per acre the full amount would be about $1000.00
11. Log House two rooms
12. I plowed with a bull tongue plow and Hoed Lots
13. Father plowed Hoed cleared Land Mother knit spun rasid chickens cooked for the Family and made the garments.
14. no
15. yes sir
16. yes mostly
17. mostly all of them did this work them selves
18. I did not think they did I think they felt themselves a little above the other who did not
19. I think there was a slight difference the slav holding people mixed together and the non slaving people together
20. yes they were Friendly
21. I think it did
22. If they had been saving and industion (?) they could but what they co__ do now
23. I dont know anything about it if they did
24. Just a very simple rural school
25. not over 6 or 8 months
26. about 2 miles
27. Free school of the poorest _____
28. public
29. two or three months
30. no
31. man
32. 1863 May 1st at Cathrage Tenn
33. 5" Tenn Regment C E Adamson, John Ashford, Jim McGee, John Estos, Fate Hale (HALE) Joe Blackburn, M__n Tilery (?) & Bill Trent
34. I think it was Granville Tn
35. two months in scrurmish
36. at Cathrage
37. Afte my First Battle I was sent to and Fro all over the state living what was called Dog Tents are "Eats" some tim were full rations some tim scanty "Calf Killer" about 2½ hours It was the hottest tim I ever seen and only about 19 were killed the fight resulted betun a bunch of our scouts and the __o called Bush Whacker
38. at Nashville Tenn 14 Day Aug 1865
39. I came home in a wagon. The man name was Snow, Jim.
40. Farming
41. Farm laborer most of the time in DeKalb Co a conststent member the Free Will Baptist Church nevr held an office in Life
42. James George; Wilson Co Tn; _____; Tennessee; Stateville, Youngblood, Smithville
43. Mary Dunn; William Dun; Elizabeth Dunn; Some where in Wilson County Tenn
44. If any of them evr held an office I dont remeber it. My grandfather William Dunn was in the war of 1812 Butler Co and I think he was in some of the Indians Engagements.
Signed, William H. George

GERARD, SURBETUS

FORM NO. 2
Continued

57

GERARD (cont'd.):
1. Surbetus Gerard; Manchester tennessee
2. 74 last October 28
3. Ohio Ross Co.
4. I am a fedrel soldier
5. Co C; 10 Ohio Cavlry
6. grocrie helper
7. james madison; chilocoth; Ross; Ohio; midway the last time we saw him; ___
8. Susanna Recob; daniel Recob; cant tell; _____
9. ----
10. Dident one evey thing a tall
11. dident one nothing
12. dident one nothing
13. dident one evey thing bu children
14. the house was a big 2 Room house 2 miles out of town midway ohio madison Co
15. when a boy I lived with my uncle I worked in the kitchen and wash house and milked cows twice a day that was my ocupation.
16. my mother did spin and all so was a weaver and in fact would work at eney thing for bread and diner for us poar hungry children 6 of us and nothing too go on for a living
17. none a tall
18. the best peopel we had then choped cord wood and falawed the plow all day and work part of the night yet.
19. they certenly did all of then we dient have no nigers a tall.
20. there was no idel men in our cuntry they all worked hard for bread and diner
21. we dident no hardly what a slave was in ohio
22. dont no eney thing a bout sutch stuff
23. dont no eney thing a bout stuch stuff
24. dont no dident try it
25. it was if he would save it and work all the time but no time for fooling a Round
26. had none of that class of men in my state ohio
27. white school of corce
28. generly 3 months in a year when we dident work
29. from one mile too too miles generly
30. just comen schools a b c crack a louse and kill a flee (?)
31. publich of corce
32. generly a 3 months school was all we had them dayes
33. they did it if wasent too cold too go
34. we generly had men teachers then wimen dident no how
35. in 1862 nobenber 6 at Camp Chase ohio I was a privet in the 10 ohio cavlery and of corce a federl soldier
36. sent too nashville tennessee
37. I cant just tell
38. the only one I was in was the battle of Resacca.
39. After the battel of Resacca I was detailed as an ordlie for generel hill patrick and after a while I was capturd and put in prisen at andersonvill staid and starved 3 months on 3 tabel spoons full of corce meal 2 of flour
40. dischaged at Camp Chase onio a bout the 25 of June 65
41. I lived and was raised close too wess Jefferson ohio close too camp chase ohio
42. a working for the other felow what over he put me at
43. I came home and mother and I lived too gather till I was 48 years old then I took a notion too get maried and wife and I ar a living too gather yet have lived in tennesee 25 tears and I expect too live heer what little time I have to live yet well there is a fiew federl soldiers heer mr sweatland mr law mr gilbert and my self is I no of I falawed plastering for seven years since then I have bin a farming the most of my time I have bin a memer of same branch of church since I was 25 years old but I cant work mutch eney more just a staying heer live in town have for 16 years manchester tennessee
45. ----
46. mr. sweatland   Manchester   Tennessee
    mr. law   manchester   tennessee
    mr. gilbert   manchester   tennessee

58

GERARD (cont'd.):

I was capturd one night by 13 buxhwackers the took me off in the woods and put me in an old corn crib till next morning then they got an old man or too and took me too a little Railroad station and the had severl others there they sent us too old andersonvill prisen and from there too charleston from there too clarence prisen and there I was paroled and sent home there they had a whipen post they would srip them off naked and give them so meney lashes but they never did get a holt of me they treated them every way hang them up by the thumbs and I saw it all my self.

s gerard   manchester tennesee

GILES, CYRUS G.

FORM NO. 1

1. Cyrus G. Giles; McLemoresville Tenn.
2. 81 years
3. Tennessee Carroll Co.
4. Same as above
5. Farmer
6. Mechanic
7. none
8. no
9. 120 acres of land
10. about $1200.00
11. Frame
12. ordinary farm work plowed & hoed made a full hand
13. Father a mechanic Mother did all kinds of house work including cooking spinning & weaving
14. no
15. It was
16. yes
17. none of them did this
18. they were all on an equality
19. (ink spilled on this page obliterates answers
20. to questions 19 and 20)
21. I think not
22. very good for the times
23. They were usually encouraged
24. Public & Subscription
25. 3 months each year for 9 years
26. 3/4 mile
27. Public & Subscription
28. Both
29. 3 months
30. yes
31. men altogether
32. in March 24 1862 in the Federal Army
33. 52nd Ind. Infantry. I didnt know any thing about the Co only the ones who volunteered with me. R.K. Rhodes - James Moore - James H. Letsinger - John R. Simpson - Felix W. Moore - James D. Thompson - S.A. Brown
34. Fort Henry
35. about 21 months
36. Harrisburg Miss
37. I fared just as the common run of soldiers so far as eating & sleepint and was continually on the march in La. Miss. Ark. & Western Tenn. Was in Overton Hospital in Memphis in 1862 for 3 mos never in prison and was for 15 months exposed to cold hunger & desease.
38. at Dorphene Island at mouth of Mobile Bay March 23 1865
39. Came by water from New Orleans to Paducah Ky and came from there at close of war with a crowd.
40. Farm work
41. Have engaged in farm work principally
42. Jessie Giles; ----; Chester District; South Carolina; Carroll Co Tenn since 18 yrs of age; no connection with war
43. Chloer Bogle; "Dont know"; ----; ----
44. Dont know much of my ancestry   Signed C.G.Giles

GORE, OVERTON

FORM NO. 1

1. Overton Gore, Livingston, Tennessee
2. 75 years
3. Overton County, Tennessee
4. I was Living in Overton County Tenn., and enlisted with Federal Government at Carthage, Smith County, Tenn.
5. Farmer
6. Farmer
7. I did not own property at the opening of the war.
8. None, neither me nor my parents.
9. Parents owned about 300 acres, or more.
10. The land was the Principal estate and it was very cheap at that time they owned some stock, and few farming tools.
11. It was a frame house. 4 room house.
12. I worked on a farm. I plowed and hoed corn; we raised a crop every year, until the war come up.
13. My father was named Mounce Gore, he did farm work. I dont recollect a great deal about that. My mother did all kinds of house work, gardening, spinning, weaving, cooking, and all other tasks that came to hadn.
14. No, they kept no servants; all the work was done by my mother and the children
15. Yes, generally it was. But there was a class of people who thought they was too good to work and regarded labor as a low calling, it least to be done by some one else. This class however, was much in the minority.
16. Yes, generally they did. But the people lived easy as a rule and did not get up and work the way people do now. All they wanted was an easy living.
17. Not much in that respect. They worked some as a rule, but just enough in order to have a living, and took no interest whatever in trying to accumulate property.
18. Well, there was a division here on this point. Some of the people who owned slaves equalized themselves with the poor class who did not and was one of them in every respect, while it is true, some of the richer slave holders held themselves above the poor class who did not own slaves, and refused to associate with them.
19. They did in my immediate community.
20. Friendly so far as I know. They associated togather in friendly good spirit.
21. They seemed to try to use that some, but I do not know just how much it helped or whether any or not.
22. Yes, the opportunities were good, and there were few who tried to take any advantage of them.
23. I don't know that they were either encouraged or disencouraged.
24. Very little school in our community. I went to school a little but not as much as 1 year all togather. Opportunities were very meager in this respect.
25. about 1 year
26. about 2 to 3 miles
27. A 1 teacher school was in session a short period in the Fall.
28. We had some of both, the public school however was very short.
29. About six weeks for the public school.
30. No
31. Some times one and some times the other.
32. Federal Army, December, 1864, at Carthage, Smith County, Tenn.
33. 8th Tennessee, Mounted Infantry
34. To Nashville, Tenn.
35. Not at all
36. None
37. We was very well taken care of, at Carthage, Tenn. and Nashville, Tenn., I was never in Hospital or Prison.
38. Nashville, in August, 1865.
39. I came to Gallatin on train, and from there to Carthage on a hack, and from Carthage home on horseback.
40. Farming
41. I have been in Farming business ever since the war. Held no offices,

GORE (cont'd.):
nor have not ask for any. Belong to Methodist Church.
42. Mounce Gore;----; Overton; Tennessee; Windle, Overton County, Tennessee; ----
43. Becky Simcoe; ----; ----; ----
44. The family came from Virginia to Tennessee and settled here in Overton County.
This Sept. 8th, 1922.
Overton Gore
Livingston, Tenn.

GRINDSTAFF, ISAAC

FORM NO. 2

1. Isaac Grindstaff; Hampton Tennessee Carter County RFD #2
2. 80 years
3. Carter County Tennessee
4. Federal soldier
5. "G"; 13th Tenn Calvary
6. Farmer
7. Mike Grindstaff; near Hampton; Carter; Tennessee; Hampton & vicinity
all his life; Held a commission as Major under Gen. Scott but did
not participate in any War.
8. Sarah Chambers; ----; ----; in Carter County Tennessee
9. Ancesters came to Carter Co with the first settlers from N. Carolina.
Originally came from Germany & Ireland
10. none
11. none
12. 30 acres
13. approximately $1000.00
14. Two Room frame house
15. General farm work - plowing hoeing & other misc. farm work.
16. Father farmed all of his life - mother did own house work such as
cooking, weaving, spinning - & making clothes.
17. none
18. yes
19. yes
20. none
21. Every body mingled -- very few slaves holders in this immediate community -- slave holders as a rule working with their slaves.
22. They did
23. There was
24. none
25. A young man had a hard time -- very little work to do --- & given
small wages for what there was.
26. Encouraged --- & given employment wherever possible
27. Attended Free School - 3 months after the war closed - none before.
28. 3 months
29. 4 miles
30. one free school - known as Fisher's Field School
31. Public
32. about 3 months
33. yes
34. men
35. Aug 1862 - Captured at Powell Sta Lee Co Va in 10 days after enlistment --- & before being assigned to company -- was sent home in
about 15 days. Re-enlisted Sept. 1863
36. Strawberry Plains Tenn
37. eleven months
38. Bulls Gap
39. Battles Greenville - Bulls Gap Md Morristown - Rogersville - Limestone Carters Depot (now South Watauga) - Va Raid under Gen Stone -
Wilberville Va to Knoxville - staid in Knoxville until spring of '65
then south Carolina raid - home sick when war closed - only wound
received was by being thrown from horse.
40. Discharged at Knoxville - Sept 5, 1865
41. Train Knoxville to Johnson Depot (now Johnson City) walked home -
15 miles

GRINDSTAFF (cont'd.):
42. farming
43. have followed farming all my life - was Sheriff of Carter Co - 3
    terms - Constable 6 years and Deputy Sheriff 2 years.
    Am now living within two miles of where I was borned and have never
    lived any farther away.
44. ----
45. The roster can be obtained from Charlie Wilcox son of Lieu. Wilcox -
    of 13th Tenn Address Elizabethton Tenn
46. Joe McCloud   Hampton   Tenn
    Ancil Carden   "   "
    W B Wolford   "   "
    J M Wilson   Cardens Bluff   Tenn
    John Hedrick   Elizabethton   "   R F D
    Jim Jackson   Johnson City   Tenn
    Wes B. Smith   Elizabethton   "
    John Stolly   "   "

HAMPTON, IRVIN

FORM NO. 1

1. IRVIN Hampton; R #3 Huntingdon Carroll Co. Tenn.
2. 77 yrs last Nov. 6
3. Gibson Co Tenn
4. In Carroll Co Tenn
5. Farmer
6. Farmer
7. I owned none
8. None
9. My father owned 100 acres of land
10. $1000.00 or $1200.00
11. Double log house with side room, in all 4 rooms
12. I both plowed & hoed as the needs of the crops demanded.
13. Clearing land making rails & fencing it as well as leading in the
    planting & cultivation of the crops grown. Also he made shoes for
    the family. My mother made our clothes from cloth she had woven,
    from thread she had spun and many times carded the wool to make the
    rools from.
14. No
15. yes
16. yes, only a very few exceptions
17. None of them were worthless by idle I only knew two who had others
    do their work. Although many of them owned slaves they worked with
    and among them.
18. yes there was no difference in their treatment of their neighbors
    on this account.
19. yes; there was no difference
20. they were friendly
21. Not one bit
22. yes
23. Generally encouraged by both slave & non-slave holding neighbors
24. Pay schools mostly known a loud school because the students studied
    as well as recited out or aloud we had about 1 month Public school
    each year.
25. about 1 month in the year, some times 6 or 8 weeks
26. Subscription schools at Mud Creek Primitive Baptist Church house at
    Concord Missionary Baptist Church house. Mostly 10 months alternate
    years.
28. 4 to 6 weeks public schools and the rest private
29. Private schools were run from 2 to 10 months
30. yes, at the short terms
31. Man, a few women taught short term privite schools
32. I enlisted in Aug 1862, at home in the U.S. Army.
33. 7th Tenn Cav Co G US Army Thomas Bellew Captain, Alton Hardy 1st
    Lieutenant,Joel W. Chambers 2nd Lieutenant, Thos. Hampton, Thomas
    Scott, Jim Scott, Henry C. Scott, Scott Pinckley, Sell Pinckley,
    Allen Pinckley, John Brandon, Allen Brandon, Frank Phillips, Frank
    Hood, John Grogan, Ode Parker, Billy Bridges, John Laycook, Clark

HAMPTON (cont.d.):
>Pinckley, John Scott, Ren Springer, Hosea Springer, John Halbrook, Nath Wilson, Jim Hendricks, Matt Wilson, Henry Wilson, Harry Brandon, P. W. Gordon

34. Trenton Tennessee
35. three or four months after I was mustered in which was in Oct 1862.
36. Lexington Tenn
37. I was captured at Lexington Tenn by Gen N. B. Forrests Command. I was parolled on the 3rd day after capture then ordered to Camp Chase Ohio to wait exchange. We had plenty provision most of the time. I was in hospital about 1 month and was well treated here. We were exposed to cold rain & snow many times with no shelter of any kind
38. Oct 25 - 1863 at Saulsbury Tenn we were mustered out here & received our pay & discharge at Memphis Tenn
39. We walked from Columbus Ky & had an exciting & wearisome time suffering from both hunger & exposure.
40. Farming lying out every night & plowing in day time. I lay out to keep from being mistreated, perhaps killed by Guerrillers.
41. Farming all my life, I am a Primitive Baptist. I have lived to see my children & grandchildren married to the sons & daughter & neices of the boys who wore the Gray.
42. Thomas Hampton; in about 1819; Williamson or Gibson; Tennessee; Carroll County near Clarksburg Tenn; He volunteered into US Army in Aug 1862 was captured & sent to Andersonville & died in Richmond Va. (Note in margin: "N.B. family records being burned I give from memory")
43. Katherine Parsons; Henry Parsons; I do not remember; S.C. as children before moving to Carroll Co. Tenn. ("children written over "a girl")
44. My great Grandfather _____ Hampton was a soldier in the Revolution in the Va. army and entered a claim as a soldier of the Rev. on land near Franklin in Williamson Co. Tenn. My great uncle James Hampton of Carroll Co Tenn was with Gen Jackson when he marched to Natshly Miss & at New Orleans. My uncle Kit Parsons was in both the Mexican & Civil Wars.
>This is correct to the best of my recollection.
>>Sincerely yours,
>>Irvin Hampton per T.M.H.son

HANNAH, ISAAC ADDISON

FORM NO. 2

1. Isaac Addison Hannah; Maryville Tennessee Route#7 Box 101
2. 78
3. Tennessee Blount
4. Federal
5. H; 2nd
6. Farming
7. John A. Hannah; Maryville; Blount; Tennessee; Maryville Tennessee; ------
8. Margaret Scott; William Scott; Jane Scott; Blount County Tenn.
9. ----
10. land $2000.
11. no
12. 150
13. $2000.
14. log house
15. worked on a farm
16. worked on farm cooking spinning weaving
17. no
18. yes
19. yes
20. not many
21. no
22. yes
23. yes
24. no
25. no very good

HANNAH (cont'd.):
26. ----
27. subscripion school
28. not very I was the only boy in the family and had to work
29. 1 mile
30. subscription schools were the only ones
31. private
32. 3
33. no
34. man
35. Oct 11 1862 Blount County
36. lovington kentucky
37. 2 mo
38. Murfreesburg Ky
39. We stayed at Murfressburg until spring of 1863 I drive a team we did not have any _battles_ while there I stayed in the wagon most of the time we were in camp. We wore government uniforms bread an meat beans etc
40. Nashville Tenn July 17 1865
41. We came on train to Knoxville Tenn and walked the rest of the way
42. on Farm
43. worked on Farm. Then worked on railroad lived in Maryville Tenn
44. ----
45.
John Carpenter	Anderson McCulloch
T. F. Wallace	L. L. Wallace
Lamar Wallace	Joe Bradley
Aron Everett	Robert Everett
Jim Simerly	Henry Simerly
Adam Simerly	Jim 2nd Simerly
Henry 2nd Simerly	William Simerly
Abraham Simerly	John Urier
William Wallace	Robert Bell
Lefs Kagley	Absasloon Kagley

46.
John Carpenter	Maryville, Tennessee
William Hannah	Bingfield, Tennessee
Fletcher Wallace	Maryville, Tennessee

47.
William Waters	Maryville, Tennessee
Silas McMillan	Maryville, Tennessee

HARRAD, WILLIAM

FORM NO. 2

1. William M. Harrad; P. O. Athens McMinn Co. Tenn
2. 78
3. state of tenn co. of McMinn
4. federal soldier
5. B. Co; 7 tennessee mtd inftry
6. farmer
7. William M. Harrad; Decature; Megs; tenn; Athens McMinn Co tenn in 46 or 47 was in the war of mexico; there lost his life
8. amaindia butler, allen butler, Rachel butler; athens tenn
9. great grand parence from Guilford Co NC my great great grand parence was from scotland my parence was borned in tenn
10. I owned 80 achors valued at 3 hundred Dolars
11. ----
12. ----
13. ----
14. 2 rooms log cabin
15. farm work plowd hoed Don all kinds of farm labor naly Don on a farm
16. as I was bornd 8 of sept 1844 and as I am infirmed that pa left in 46 war of mexico and neve returned mother died when I only was 3 moths old then I was left in the hands of aslave holder and as all alphens sured Did see one hard time
17. ----
18. sure it was
19. that was common with all white me
20. about 1/3 was living an idallife
21. about ½ was selfish would not mingel with the common whit man

HARRAD (cont'd.):
22. varry little most of the time vary cool at the common white man
23. not mutch friendly
24. no they was for self
25. the poor man was alwayes respectable but could not save mutch money he could make an honest living
26. poor man never received any encouragement from any slave holder always saul one of their one first
27. free school in a log house
28. 18 months
29. one and ½ miles
30. free schools
31. public free schools only
32. 6 months
33. as mutch as possbell
34. a man
35. firs inlisted in Co. B. 8 michaghn intd inftry in Oct 1862 US Army then in Oct 1864 I inlisted in B. Co. 7 tenn Mtd inftry of the federal government
36. all parts of southern Ky
37. about 4 months
38. (?) paryvill K.y.
39. good close good quarters most of the time to sleep except on long marches. as I was member (?) of army of the Cumberland 14 army core on the march from Chattanooga to Knoxville under General Sherman
40. 27 Day of July 1865 at nashville tenn
41. my tripe home after the many long and Dangers seens ____ ____ was handed my transfe and pass free to return home once moor as a citizen of this our America country
42. farming railroading worked most of time on farm
43. as to my past life I have bin a true republican true to my country have lived an honest life was a member of county court 6 years my firs wife ____ ____ was Sarah Sansia lamar of Guilford County No.C. as I ame now alone some times at the soldiers home and then with my grand children I have many good firends in the county of McMinn.

45. first sergent Ewin Attlee   James Crow
    Donald Sails   W. L.Rice
        wattenbarger   Allen ellis
    H. H. Nutsell   B underwood
    W. W. Lowery   M. M. Carpenter
    fletcher carpenter   W. allen
    Joseph Hampton   J.R. Yetters
    W. S. McGaughy   B. B. McGaughy
    D. L. Moore   John McChristan
    Elijah Dyer 3 tennessee inftry army of the Cumberland
    Edmand Tucker   J. W. Shariets 3 tenn Cav
    John D. Long 4 tenn Cav   ____ fite 4
    James Small 4 Cav   Scott foyea
    J. K. foyea   C. C. Clayito 2 ____ Cav
    George G. Guffy K.Y. Cav   James Nix
    James Cochran   R. Cochran 4 tenn Cav
    W. f. McCra_n   James Norusley
    W. M. Hart   John Key

46. James Crow   athens tenn   tenn
    C. C. Clayton   athens   tenn
        ____ fite   ----   ---
                        Cleveland   ---

    Elijah Dyer
    George Johnson   Cleveland
    M. M. Carpenter   athens   tenn
    fletcher carpenter ---   ____
    H. H. Hutsell   athens   ____
    George W. Guffy   athens   tenn
    W. W. Lowery   Ricevill   tenn
    William M. Harrah   athens   ____

65

HAWKINS, CARRY N.

FORM NO. 2

1. Carry N. Hawkins; Gainesboro Tenn R. 1
2. 75 years
3. Jackson Tenn
4. federal soldier
5. B; 8 Tenn
6. Farmer
7. John C. Hawkins; ---; Jackson; Tenn; ---;---
8. Hally Lee; Curry Lee; Polley Hawkins; Jackson
9. ----
10. had no property
11. did not one any
12. 75 acres
13. 1000
14. Log house to rooms
15. work one farm plowed and hoe other kind of farm works
16. he was a farmer she don the cooking washing spinning weaving
17. non
18. yes
19. yes
20. wasant but few but what work
21. no
22. yes
23. yes
24. no
25. no
26. no
27. free schools
28. six month
29. 3 miles
30. free schools
31. public
32. from to and three month
33. no
34. man
35. 1865 feb carthage Tenn federal government
36. Nashville
37. ----
38. ----
39. ----
40. Nashville Tenn Ag 1865
41. whee came par of the way of the trane walked the uther part was all
    glad to get home whee had a good time coming in home
42. farming
43. farmering in dry goods store some of the time raisen stock and corn
    hay wheet otes.
44. ----
45. Jef Wilson   Pink Gipson
    John A. Draper
    this all that know of my company
46. Chammbles(?) Allen   Cooksville   Tenn
    John Smith   Cooksville   Tenn
    pink Gipson   Gainesboro   Tenn
    Jeff Willson   Gainesboro   Tenn
    John A. Draper   Hadenborg   Tenn
    John H. Stfferd   Fainesboro   Tenn
    Jim Tarnilent   Gainesboro   Tenn
    Bill Whitker   Gainesboro   Tenn
    Curry N. Hawkins   Gainesboro   Tenn

HEADRICK, JOHN W.

FORM NO. 2

continued next page

66

HEADRICK (cont'd.):
1. John W. Headrick; Elizabethtin RFD No. 4 Carter County Tenn
2. bore Sept 29, 1844 age 77 year 8 mintes
3. Tenesee Elizabethin Carter County
4. was a federal solder US Army
5. belong to A Co; 13 Tenn Vil Cav I enlisted under Capt Lawson W.
   Fletcher at Carters Depot. Carte County was mustered in the servis
   at Straw Planes
6. was a Brick masen by trad
7. Charles Headrick; in the state of Va; an now on Bige Sandy ro;
   Virgine; came to Tenesee when a small boy ____ Carter; un till his
   deth he was a pore man never hel any ofice
8. Jane R. Chambers was borne South Car; John Chambers; Jane Turner
   bef__?; moove frome South Carulin to Elizabethtin Carter
9. grandfather was a soldier in the war of 1812 statind Charlstin SC
   my father Charles Headrick was a soldier in the federal army in Cop
   A 13 Tenn Cavely was in all the batels and marchs of the regment and
   was dischage at Knoxvill Tenn Sept 5 1865 and live an honer ctizen
   till his deth in 1881 at Valy Forge
10. we had no land was renters durg the war when bougt lot and bilt a
    home at Valy Forg
11. no we nevr oned a slave
12. a too acor lot at Vally Forge
13. none the price of land in this mountan conty was ver low then to
    wat it it now
14. a loge hous with too rooms and chicken the common peopel lve moslely
    in looge houses in thos the best farmer had fram develg
15. I worke one the farm from the time I doo any thige plow and hoed
    corn and done all cindes of work that was to be done and worke ver
    hard and receivd from five delas a minth to fifty cents per day th
    young men dine a gooded mer work Dune than th lyes of this time
16. father worke at most all cindes of work was a molder in the _en
    founder of the time dune teans lay brick mad looms for to weave
    cloth to make our clothing Mother dune all cinds of house work
    carding and spining yarn weaving cloth cutting and making garments
    for the famly
17. No we had no servans done all our work
18. yes work was honerbill and the peopell was jonerely happy in havin
    plenty of work to doo and their was plenty to doo Sutch as cuttin
    timber bilding houses and larens and fenein(?)
19. Shure they did a man tha woodent work was not though mutch of
20. thear very few men idell in thos days
21. Most jeneraly so some of our bes citiens war slave oners.
22. as far as I can realet(?) the was jeneraly good feling be twine all
    the people of our county
23. jenealy So
24. in polical mate the pore man vate counted as mutch as the man with
    slaves
25. I dont think thar was for miny was scare and hart yet and the young
    man did not have the chance to get an edatin that they doo at this
    time
26. i dint think the was
27. I got vere litill schoolin my first scholing was in a primar schoole
    taut
28. Mrs. Timey (Tinney?) Badget in a litill schoole House in Elizabethton
29. a bout one and a half mile thear was a bit schole all so in our tow
    but parents had to pay for them
30. and pore men cold not tent to them
31. mostely prvat schools
32. about 4 minths in the fall and winter and parents had so mutch work
    to doo that nine but the small one got the good of it
33. jeneraly in the winter minths
34. Mo jenearly Wimen tacher
35. in September 1863 I enlisted ine the Servis of the United States arm
    at Carter Depo in Carter County
36. to Strawberry Planes near Knoxvill Tenn wher we war musterd in fed-
    eral army
37. we was sent from thear to Camp Nelson Ky from there to Nashvill Tenn
38. we war fist in batill at Rogersvill

HEADRICK (cont'd.):
39. we war next ingage at Moristoun Bull Gap Greenvill Carter Depo ---
     Spot lick creek Bristo Marin Va Salt vill was ine the batill of
     Greenvill when the noted general John H. Morgan was cild my exper-
     inge was a bout like all solders of the war
40. Sept 5 at Knoxvill Tenn 1865 was paid all wages and balance of county
     which was dew me which amunty to 35400
41. one the mirne of the 6 of Sep we borded a trane for Johnson City then
     to our homes and dear ones that we had left 2 year be four
42. I went to work at any thing that I cold get to doo to get miney to
     pay yp detes that my mother had mad to live
43. as some as us nevr lived up I went to work at my trad laying Brick
     whilep I folered up to 1910 when I broke dow with deseas have been
     abill to do any work sine I maid Mis Cordela Fletcher March the 25
     1866 we live hapy to gather till 1910 when the lord take her a way
     I joined the Christan Church in 1887 and have lived a fathfull
     member to the presant time I have raised a family of 6 children one
     sone five girles I have got a nie litell home at Valy Forge one the
     ETWN railrod 3 miles south of Elizabethton county sete of Carter
     County I ame now car by the government I spent 2 years of my young
     manhood to save and wating for the master to call me to a biter
     home beyend whear I cane by doneth toiles of this life
44. ----
45. Danel Ellis   Eliza D. Harden   James R. Swaner
     Danel S. Nave   John W. Harden   Gerge Simerly
     Bus B. Stone   William Hodge   Jackson Sims
     Isag (?) Lewis   Wiliam Hamptin   Alexander Williams
     Robt L. Smith   Elbert Hamptin   W. W. Williams
     Abham Nave   William Hyder   Hunt Weste
     Charles Headrick   William Jenkens   William West
     Benjamin H. Peaters   Hugh Jenkens   James Woods
     Thomas A. Dugger   A. N. Kite   Aren Woodford
     James A. Pane   Gideen Lewis   Plesant Williams
     Thomas A. Mills   John Loveless   Henry Pearce
     John B. Williams   Alexander Martin   A. N. Carver
     John W. Headrick   Willia R. Morell   Bene Ashly
     James A. Genlery   Benjmen Moody   T. N. Bowers
     Samuel E. Smith   Frane Moody   David Bowers
     Jas A. Dugger   Rubin Mosley   Wiliam Coppely
     Mashal Morell   Josep P. Mekiney   John C. Crow
     Mark Nave   Henry Miller   David Lewis
     Wilson McKiney   Jas Matherly   Isac Moody
     Samuel M. Estep   Frank Martin   David Farr
     D. S. N. Alen   Plesant Nave   Ely Pilips
     Gerge Blevins   Isac N. Nave   Andrw Sells
     Andew Bowman   Peter Nave   James Stufilstreet
     David T. Chambers   Gerge Oliver   A. C. Carden
     Dave Oliver   Bengaman Clemmens   James Oliver
     Wiliam H. Dugger   Thomas Peaters   James Delouch
     Lewis M. Pearce   Richard Glover   John H. Fair
     Ely Harden   Andew Rilley
46. David T. Chambers   Elizabethton   Tenn
                            Elizabethton   Tenn
     George Simerly   Elizabethton   Tenn
     J. W. Headrick   Elizabethton   Tenn
     A. C. Carden   Hamptin   Tenn
     John Loveless   Elizabethton   Tenn
     W. H. Morell   Elizabethton   Tenn
     Jas Oliver   Elizabethton   Tenn
     David Fair   Elizabethton   Tenn
     W. M. McKiney   Elizabethton   Tenn
     all living of Company A
     Isaac Grindstaff   C G Hamptine   Tenn
     Joseph McCloud   C G Hamptin   Tenn
     John Holeg   C G Elizabethton   Tenn

FORM NO. 1

1. Joab Helton; Rutledge Tennessee
2. 75 years
3. Grainger County, Tennessee
4. Grainger County, Tennessee, enlisted in Federal Army
5. Farmer
6. Farmer
7. Nothing
8. Father owned two
9. 200 acres
10. $3600.00
11. Log house. 6 rooms
12. I plowed and hoed corn
13. Father plowed, hoed corn and did farm work. Mother cooked, spun and wove
14. 2 negroes
15. yes
16. yes, generally
17. Several
18. At the beginning of the war they did after the war opened faction of differences became so great they they did not until the war was over
19. Yes
20. Not very friendly. Some were friendly and some were not
21. No
22. Yes
23. Encouraged
24. Free schools lasting about three months.
25. about six months
26. Mile and a half
27. Old time free school and old time subscription school
28. Public
29. About three months. Most of us stopped to pull fodder etc.
30. Not much. Not much interest in schools at that date.
31. Both
32. New Market, Tennessee, in 1864
33. 9th Tennessee Volunteer Calvary Company "M" L. Jones Captain. Lieutenant Gross.
34. We were sent to Morristown, Tennessee, and had engagement with Confederate General Baughn. Fought him up to Bulls Gap Tennessee, and was then driven back to Knoxville, Tennessee.
35. About ten days
36. Battle at Morristown, Tennessee
37. We went from Knoxville after having been driven back from Bulls Gap to Virginia on what was called the stoneman Ridge, then returned to Sweetwater Tennessee. Then back to Knoxville, and was mustered out at Knoxville, Tennessee, in August 1865. We were roughly clad, sometimes plenty to eat and sometimes nothing. We slept on the ground most of the time.
38. Knoxville, Tennessee, August 1865.
39. After being discharged I received my transportation to Morristown, Tennessee. At Morristown I hired a horse and returned to my father's home in Grainger County, Tennessee. The different events that occured on the trip home were so tame as compared with camp life, and I was so anxious to get home, I did not pay much attention to anything I did see.
40. Farming
41. Farming ever since at Rutledge, Grainger County, Tennessee. Belong to Baptist Church at New Prospect, Grainger County, Tennessee.
42. Alexander Helton; ----; ----; North Carolina; ----; ----
43. Nancy Boatman; Henry Boatman; Kazih Boatman; near Morristown, Tenn
44. ----

Joab Helton

HICKERSON, WILLIAM J.

FORM NO. 2

1. William J. Hickerson; Linden Tenn Route #2
2. 82 in July
3. Wayne Co Tenn
4. Federal soldier
5. E; 2nd Tenn
6. Farmer
7. Jefferson Hickerson; ----; ----; Kentucky; New Era, Perry Co Tenn.; ----
8. Nancy Ann Bishop; --- Bishop; Sallie Bishop; --- Ky
9. ----
10. ----
11. ----
12. 100
13. $500.00
14. Log 1 Room
15. General farm work and chopped wood.
16. General farm for father. Mother general housekeeping spinning and weaving.
17. no
18. very honorable
19. yes
20. none
21. yes
22. yes
23. yes
24. no
25. yes
26. no
27. country school
28. about 3 months each year
29. about 3 miles
30. 1 room one teacher schools
31. private
32. about 3 month
33. yes
34. man
35. 1861
36. Clifton, Wayne Co, Tenn.
37. about 3 months
38. Centreville Tenn
39. In hospital 4 months
40. Nashville, at the close of the war
41. Came from Nashville to Johnsinville on a train. Came from there to New Era in a steamer on Tenn river.
42. Farming
43. Been engaged in farming since. Lived on Ceda Creek in Perry Co. Tenn. Held no office. Member of M. E. Church south
44. ----
45. Alec Guthrie Cap   Linden   Tenn (dead)
    Col. Murphy
    Col. Haynes   Ky
    P. A. Hickerson   Texarkana   Texas (living
46. Geo. Shelton   Linden   Tenn
    Wm. Starbuck   Linden   Tenn
    John Kedring   Trenton   Tenn
    Wm. Ary   Flatwoods   Tenn
    E. Inman   Peters Landing Tenn
    Geo. Bridges   Flatwoods   Tenn
    Dr. I. M. Black   Linden   Tenn
    D. W. Treadwell   Linden   Tenn
    Doc Byrd   Linden   Tenn
    E. Steele   Peters Landing Tenn

HOBACK, JOHN

FORM NO. 2

1. John Hoback; Athens Tenn R# 1
2. 77
3. Tennessee McMinn Co.
4. Federal
5. I; 3rd Tennessee Calvery
6. Carpenter and joiner
7. William Hoback; Withville; With; Virginia; Virginia and later in Tennessee; he served in 7th Tennessee mounted Infrantry
8. Elizabeth Hutsell; John; Christina Hutsell; Withville Va.
9. My uncle Alford Hoback (brother of my father) served in the regular army in the Mexican war he served 5 year. Another brother of my Father served in the Cival War. George Hoback, he was captured and served in Kahaba prison in Ala. he lost his life on the Sultana that was blown up near Memphis.
10. No
11. No
12. 320 acres
13. $2500
14. Frame, 4 rooms
15. I did all kinds of work on the farm. hoe, plow, sprout, and evry kind of work required in farming
16. My Father worked at carpentery. My mother spun, wove, carded, knit, cooked, washed and all kinds of house work. and bore and raised 12 children.
17. no
18. yes
19. yes
20. very few
21. yes
22. yes
23. very friendly
24. no, I think not.
25. no. not as good as at the present day.
26. I do not think thay were discouraged
27. country free school
28. not more than 2 year
29. one mile
30. Public school
31. Public
32. 2 to 3 months
33. no
34. man
35. Oct 7th 1863 at Louden Tenn. I enlisted in the Federal army and served until the close of the war
36. Nashville
37. I was in Calvery skirmishes
38. Knoxville
39. I was in several skirmishes. The hardest fought battle I was in was at Decatur, Ala. We were well fed and plenty to eat. good clothes and good quarters when we were in camp.
40. Nashville. 1865
41. ----
42. Farming and then I worked at carpenter trade for several year.
43. I went to school at Athens, one ters, spent 2 year in Chattanooga building houses. went to Arkansas. spent 2 yr. married then bought a farm in Meigs Co. and lived on it 40 year. left the farm and mooved to Athens 4 year ago. I am a member of the G.A.R. I have been a member of the M. E. Church 40 odd year.
44. ----
45. I cannot give names of members of my company as I was put on detach service soon after I enlisted.

HOCKER, ALFRED MEIGS

FORM NO. 2

1. Alfred Meigs Hocker; Athens Tennessee
2. 76
3. McMinn County Tennessee
4. Federal
5. H; 5th Regiment 5th Tenn - Volunteers
6. Farmer
7. Alferd Hocker; Morgan County; at Wartbury; Tenn; Morgan County near
    -----; He was a Confederate Soldier In McKenzie Co.
8. Margaret Hocker; Pete Freeman; Sallie Moorehead; Rutherford County
    North Carolina on Big Pee Dee River
9. great grandparents came from Germany and he was in Revolutionary
    War under General Washington 1777 and grandfather was in the war of
    1812 and great uncle --- Hocker and Peter Freeman my grandfather on
    my mothers side came from England and my uncle on my mothers side
    Morehead came from Ireland.
10. none
11. none
12. ----
13. $165
14. log house one room
15. plowed and hoed
16. farming and mother done house
17. no
18. honorable
19. no
20. them that had slaves was idle and did no work
21. no
22. no
23. the slave holder would no migle with men how had no slaves
24. the man that on slave give all of his hep to the candidate that on
    slaves
25. no
26. Discouraged
27. Free School
28. 6 month
29. Five miles
30. Free School
31. public School
32. 3 month
33. yes
34. man
35. Baboreville Ky on the 25 Feb 1862. Enlisted in the Federal army.
36. Cumberland Ford on Cumberland River
37. 6 month
38. Tasville on powel River
39. we sleeps on ground and blnkets and are grond was had Tack and Bocan
    coffee when we could get it
40. Nashville Tenn May th 18, 1865
41. I went from Nashville to Loudon Tenn on Train and from Loudon to
    home on wagon
42. farming
43. farming. Rone County 6 month and in Magis County 1 year and McMinn
    Co 40 years
44. ----
45. ----
46. ----

HOLMES, A. T.

FORM NO. 2

1. A. T. Holmes; Bithpage Tenn
2. 90 past
3. Tenn Summer
4. Federal

72

HOLMES (cont'd.):
5.   Co A; 43rd
6.   Farmer
7.   Albert Garner Holmes; ---; Sumner; Tenn; on Trammel Creek Tenn; ---
8.   Millie Turner; Yancy Turner; Polly Turner; on Trammell Creek Tenn
9.   ----
10. none
11. none
12. 100 acres
13. about $4000
14. Log house
15. Farming - all kinds
16. Farming - Mother did general house work
17. none
18. honorable
19. yes
20. all worked
21. yes they mingled freely with slave owners. for very few had slaves
22. yes
23. yes
24. ----
25. yes very good
26. ----
27. Pay school
28. about 5 years
29. about 1 mile
30. Trammel school
31. Public
32. about 6 months
33. yes
34. man
35. Missouri - can't recall year and month
36. stayed in Missouri during war
37. about 5 or 6 months
38. Wilson Creek
39. plenty to eat, wear, sleep, good warm place no disease. fairly good
     time
40. Jefferson City Mo
41. Lived close by
42. Photographing
43. Lived in Mo. until about 20 year ago I came back to Tenn. I belong
     to the Presbyterian Church. For the past 10 years have not done any
     work.
44. ----
45. My memory is not very good and can't recall very many
     Capt Yarnel
     Lieut
     Col - Haycocks
46. Brick Stone   Bichpage   Tenn
     Jerry Rippy

                        JOHNSTON, W. J.

FORM NO. 2

1.   W. J. Johnston; Jasper Marion Conty Tenn
2.   I will be 80 the 24 of July 1922
3.   Marion County Tn
4.   I was a federal _____
5.   E 6th Tenn; 6 Tenn Mounted Infantry
6.   Black Smith
7.   Charles Johnston; I don't know; dont know; Tenn
8.   Nance Griffin; don't; ---; ---
9.   ----
10. Havent got in Jasper Tn
11   no
12. Havent got
13. over one thousand dollar
14. Loge house

                        73

JOHNSTON (cont'd.):
15. farmed until the war then after the war worken at the Black Smith
     Trade
16. Black smithery
17. no
18. yes
19. yes
20. farming
21. yes
22. yes
23. yes
24. no
25. yes
26. no .
27. Publick Schools
28. 5 months a year
29. abot 3 Hudred yars
30. Publick Shools
31. Publick
32. 5 month
33. yes
34. man
35. year 63 fedrel soldger
36. camp Hunser (?)
37. 6 month
38. at Layfayet Googar?
39. ----
40. Nashvill Tn
41. on the Train
42. Blacksmithing
43. I ____ after the war & then follow Blacksmithry & was Elected Regis-
     trar of deeds & then I was Elected justice of the Peace 2 year the
     I was Elected Sherff of M Court 2 year the I was Elected Justice
     of the Peace ____ 12 year I Blacksmith for ____ can I was Elctr
     Justice of the ___ I and I am slaving the san officer now
44. ----
45. ----
46. ----

                        JONES, FEDERICK J.

FORM NO. 2

1.   Frederick J. Jones; P. O. Dunlop Tenn
2.   78 years old
3.   I was born in Catoosa Co Ga
4.   Federal
5.   Co E 6th; 6 Tenn
6.   Farmer
7.   James Jones; in Virg. 1804; Dont know county; Virginia; ---; ---
8.   Hariet M. Pitner; John Pitner; ---; ---
9.   ----
10. ----
11. They did not
12. 150 acres $1,000.00
13. one thousand dollars this includ all
14. a log house 3 rooms
15. we plowed hoed cut whet mowed grass all kinds of work done on the
     farm.
16. My Father wagon Hauled wheat. to Chattanoog Grasville Ga. Hauled
     goods from Nashville Hauld Salt from Saltwords in K.Y. my mother
     was a taylor by trad. spun. made cloth &
17. Not any Done their own work
18. This kind fo work was respectable & honorable
19. They did
20. about one out a Thousand
21. They did mingle as though both owned slaves
22. They did They mingled the same. No diference

                              74

JONES (cont'd.):
23. There were a friendly feeling between them
24. Did not make any difference as I culd see slaves some times eat at
    the same table with their masters
25. yes
26. They ever encouraged
27. Free & Subesition
28. Abut 3 years in all
29. averaged from ½ mi to Three miles
30. publick & private
31. Both
32. from 3 to 4 months
33. They did
34. Both male & Fe
35. 1861 & 1864 federal
36. To McMiville
37. 9 months
38. Shilough
39. I had a discharge from Confederate Army after the Battle of Shilough
    sometimes we had plenty to eat & others very scant. any one knows
    that we did not sleep on flower beds ease
40. from the federal army at Nashville the other at Columbus Miss.
41. I went through Mobile on cruches Landed at Mongomery A.L.A. Thence
    to Atlanta. Eat some melons & Thence to Chicmoga & then to my Half
    Bro. & then from there to Home in Sequachie Co. Tenn from the fed-
    eral army. from Nashville from Strait home & went to work.
42. ----
43. I worked on the farm & went to school after whick I taught school
    till I was disabled for the business. I am now just able to sit up
    and write
    P.S.--I-would-like-to-write-but-Dont-feel-like-doing-questions-on
    my-self
44. (at the bottom of the page:)
    "P.S. read the above if you can. & Then Excuse me pleas."
45. ----
46. John J. Johnson   P.O. Dunlop   Tenn
    Robert Eckhart   P.O. Dunlop   Tenn
    Selich Green   P.O. Dunlop   Tenn
    Thomas Grant   P.O. Dunlop   Tenn

                          JONES, HENRY H.

FORM NO. 1

1. Henry H. Jones; Alexandria
2. Seventy Six (76)
3. Smith County, Tenn.
4. Smith Co. Tenn (Federal Army)
5. Farmer
6. Farmer
7. none
8. yes two (2)
9. about 200 acres
10. $6000.00
-1. Frame house Six rooms at beginning of war
12. Plowed about all the time while making a crop.
13. Father did general farm work Such as plowing hoeing and etc Mother
    did general housekeeping Such as doing the cooking, washing, ironing
    Sewing and spining.
14. Yes, one part of time to help do Some of household duties
15. yes
16. yes
17. very little idleness at this time, most every one worked
18. yes all classes mingled freely and one class didnt think themselves
    better than the other
19. yes. freely
20. They were very friendly toward each other
21. I think owning slave, helped no one in winning a political contest.
22. They were reasonably good.

JONES (cont'd.):
23. They were encouraged to save money and buy property.
24. common country schools
25. about four month each year for about eight years
26. Two Miles
27. common grammar schools
28. Publice
29. about Six months
30. no
31. men always
32. Federal army Oct about 15th 1864
33. Fourth Tennessee Mounted Infentry US Vol James P. Paty Col., S. B. Whitlock 1st Lt., J.H. Kitchings 2nd Lt., Geo E. Courtney N.C.O., D.B. Gwaltney , Arch Gwaltney, Tom Cowen, Moses Preston, Bartley Jones, Kerry Agee, Wm Agee, Jas Nowlen, Tom Nowlen, Jno. Watt, Jno. Enoch, Simon Hires, Jno Hunt, Joe Hunt, Fredrick Buckner, Burr Manning, Jno Barbee
34. Stationed at Carthage Tenn first.
35. Never was in a regular battle, but in Several Small Skirmises
36. Skirmish in east Tenn. on Obdes (?) River
37. Were stationed at Carthage for a while after 1st battle and later at New Middleton. I did general camp duties. Smal brush at Lebanon Tenn, Slightly wounded, about 10 minutes, the Con were routed out of Lebanon and persued toward Nashville and part of them were captured at Stones River. I lived well and had of good clothing and plenty to eat. we slept in tents on bunks while in camp.
38. Nashvill Tenn Aug 25, 1865
39. Just at time when discharged I was taking Thypoid Feaver and was broth home sick
40. Farming
41. Farming until the year 1911 Since 1911 have been engaged in insurance business. lived since war mostly in DeKalb Co near Alexandria Member Baptist Church
42. Isaac Jones; don't know; don't no; North Carolina; dont no what county or town; he had no war service Served as J.P. for 18 years in Smith Co was Chairman Smith Conty Corty several times
43. Elizabeth Malone; James Malone; dont no; Alexandria Tenn
44. Grandfather Jones lived to be 96 years old Settled in what is now DeKalb Co
This is about all I can tell about my ancesters.

KEATON, JAMES

FORM NO. 2

1. James Keaton; Mcinville Tennessee R# 4 Box 91
2. 76
3. Tennessee Wilson Co.
4. Federal
5. E; 4 Tennessee; Mounted Enfentry
6. Farmer and stone mason
7. John Keaton; Tennessee; Wilson; Tennessee; his fathers farm; ----
8. Annie Fuston; James Fuston; Betsy Fuston; Liberty in DeKalb Co.
9. ----
10. I did not own land. but owned one horse worth $125.00
11. did not own no slaves
12. did not own any
13. $500.00
14. log house and had 2 rooms
15. I plowed and hoed both. the white men that owned slaves worked that lived near me
16. Cooked wove and spun
17. no
18. it was
19. yes
20. none in my neghbor of that kind
21. some were on an equl and some were not
22. most of them were. a few were not
23. yes they were friendly

KEATON (cont'd.):
24. no it did not
25. no
26. I dont know where they were or not
27. Literary
28. Not more than one year
29. half mile
30. Literary Primary
31. Public
32. about 3 month
33. no
34. a man some time and some time a woman
35. in the year 64 month sept place at Liberty DeKalb Co. Federal
36. to Nashville Tennessee
37. about 3 months
38. it was at Nashville
39. After the first battle we returned back to Liberty DeKalb Co and stayed there a while then went through White Co Vanburn and Overton Co then in battle at Lebanon lasted one hour. one in White Co. lasted ½ day.
40. in August 64 place at Nashville
41. come home sick. and as soon as I got well I went to work as I did before the war
42. Farming
43. I have worked on the farm some. have worked at stone mason some have lived in Wilson Co. Cannon Raulford and Warren Co. I hope in building a church house in Cannon Co also in Warren Co. I belong to the church at Providence in Warren Co. Baptist Church. have held no office
44. ----
45.

Captain	Private Soldier
McVanattie	James Okley
1 Lieutenant	Joe Okley
Columbus Vick	Leman Hale
2 Lieutenant	J.M. Johnson
James Williams	

46.

Hiram Robson	McMimmville	Tennessee
Obie Rich	Woodbury	Tennessee
A.D. Denton	Smithville	Tennessee
Gene Cripps	Liberty	Tennessee

KING, WILLIAM PRESSLY

FORM NO. 1

1. William Pressly King; Westport Tennessee
2. Seventy three   73
3. Tennessee Carroll Co
4. Tennessee and Carroll Co
5. Farming
6. Farming
7. I owned nothing
8. I dident But my parents owned four.
9. One hundred and sixty acre
10. about 25 hundred Dollars
11. Log house two rooms
12. I plowed the most of the time and the rest I worked with a hoe.
13. My father was a farmer and raised cotton as his pleasure and my mother spent her Time in cooking carding spinning and weaving cind she would spin until late at night
14. X
15. I say it was
16. yes
17. Just a few But not many
18. I say they did and dident seem to feel thier selves above the none slave holders
19. yes I say they all seem to be on a level.
20. yes there were. no quarling be twen the two party. the slave holders and non slave holders.

KING (cont'd.):
21. yes in some cases they did and in some they dident
22. yes I say that the chance were very good
23. yes they were encourage
24. a subscription school. we had no free school
25. not over 8 months all togather in my life did I go to school.
26. about 3 miles
27. None except at the Hall School House and it was a subscription school
28. it was a private school
29. it run from one to two months
30. yes the one that made the school up attended it regular.
31. a man. here are their names Mr. Jim Barger, Mr. Lem Beckidite and
    William King
    (Elas Parish in margin)
32. enlisted March 1, 1864 at Paducky Kentucky
33. my regiment 7th Tennessee Calvery Siam Parish, Rylie S. Edd Hall,
    Jim and George Burton, Wess and Bill Pendergrass, Jim Guinn, Jim
    Lamblic, John and Ryle Boteman, Albert Bridwell, Turner Boyd, Jofus
    Boyd, _ermon Sondey(?), Call Mcauley, John and Earvin Perdue, John
    and Jim Porter, Charlie Cumore, Jas and Green Jones, John and Wight
    Singleton, Jim and Clay Scot, Siah and Edd Tosh, William and John
    Wall, Sid hatch, Lem Anderson, William Baberson, Henry Robinson
34. Scot Ky
35. The guns were firing when I enlisted
36. it was near murey kentucky
37. one day with another it was if they wasent after us we was after
    them. I went back to camp at Paducky. still on duty. our battles
    was just in scrmshing over Ky and Tenn short pieod of Time. we
    goined every Time we faired rough - my clothes good we slept on the
    ground Just where night over taken - meat Beef. Crackers. flour Bread
    Beans pease onion coffee. sugar. We just took the weather as it
    come. we dident go hungry when we could get to it. I had none -
    in hospital once to see a friend. no imprison ment
38. I was discharged at Nash. Tenn Aug. 6, 1865
39. I got transportation to Johnsonville walked the rest of the way home
    in Carroll County Tenn.
40. farming
41. farming. Carroll County missionary Baptist and a decon. none.
42. Cheslie King; N. Carolina; ---; N. Carolina; ---; ---
43. Katie Kelen; Jim Keler; Pollie Spencer; lived in carroll county
44. my parents were Weltha and made thier living at home and toiled hard
    on the Tenn hill sides. My great grandparents on Father. Thomas
    King come here from N.C.he run away when a young boy being an orphan
    child his parents died when my Father was young my parent great
    grand parents none of them never fought in any war.
                              William P. King

                        KNOWLES, JOHN FLETCHER

FORM NO. 2

1. John Fletcher Knowles; Sparta Tenn R 6
2. 80 yrs and 3 mo
3. White Co Tenn
4. Federal
5. Company F; 3rd United States Infantry
6. farming
7. James A. Knowles; Pisgah; White; Tenn; Pisgah White Co Tenn; Justice
    of Peace for many years
8. Matilda Webb, Jere Webb; Sarah Webb; Pisgah White Tenn
9. ----
10. none
11. none
12. 150 acres
13. $2500
14. a five room frame house
15. I worked on a farm all the yr. and worked hard
16. my father worked on his farm and my mother worked in the house spin-
    ing weaving and cooking.

                               78

KNOWLES (cont'd.):
17. none
18. yes
19. yes
20. yes
21. society seemed to be on an equal
22. yes
23. were friendly
24. no
25. I think so
26. I do not think they discouraged them
27. public
28. 20 months
29. one mile
30. Shady Grove
31. both
32. an average of 4 months
33. some did
34. man
35. at Rock Island Ill in 1864
36. To the frontiers
37. we were guards against the Indians
38. I was not in a battle.
39. I stayed on the frontiers till it closed. I was fed and clothed
    very well while in camp.
40. 1865 in the state of Kansas
41. came home on the train
42. Farming
43. I have been a farmer in White Co Tenn ever since the war. I am a
    southern methodist I have never asked for an office
44. ----
45. Jasper Knowles   Polk Fincher
    It has been so long I can not remember many of them
46. Andy Beaver   Sparta White Co.   Tenn
    John Tery   Sparta White Co.   Tenn
    James Fuson   Sparta White Co.   Tenn
    Nate Quarles   Sparta White Co.   Tenn
    Gamon Dibrell   Sparta White Co.   Tenn
    Will Montgomery   Sparta White Co.   Tenn
    James Mormon   Sparta White Co.   Tenn
    John Kirby   Sparta White Co.   Tenn
    Billy Hayes   Silver Point   Tenn
    Carroll Jones   Dibrell Warran Co   Tenn

                         KRANTZ, MIKE

FORM NO. 2

1. Mike Krantz; R 4 Box 4 LaFayette Tenn Macon Co
2. 77
3. Tenn Smith Co
4. Federal
5. D; 8th Mounted Inft Tennessee
6. Farmer
7. Joe Krantz; ---; ---; Virginia; LaFayette, Tenn; ----
8. Litha Krantz; Billie Donoho; Polly Donoho; Carthage Tenn
9. ----
10. none
11. no
12. ----
13. ----
14. Log house one room
15. worked on the farm
16. spinning and weaving making clothes that we used also cooking
17. none
18. yes
19. yes
20. every one done his own work
21. all about equal

                              79

KRANTZ (cont'd.):
22. yes
23. yes
24. yes when they were called on
25. yes
26. dont know
27. none
28. 3 or four weeks
29. one mile
30. free school
31. Public
32. Three monts
33. some did and some did not
34. man
35. Carthage 1865 March
36. Nashville
37. not any
38. none
39. clothed very well provision short slept on the ground part of the time in snow and rain
40. Nashville
41. Had to walk home
42. Farming
43. Lived in Tenn
44. None
45. Wes Bandy   Dock White
    Sigh Jones   Alse Kenifr
46. Neute Marsh   LaFayette   Tenn
    Wiley Dotson   LaFayette   Tenn
    J.K. Perrigo   LaFayette   Tenn
    Tom Dixon   LaFayette   Tenn
    Bill Smith   LaFayette   Tenn
    Gore Whitley   Red Boiling Springs   Tenn

LANE, MOSES E.

FORM NO. 2

1. Moses E. Lane; Sevierville Tenn   R.F.D. #13
2. 84 years
3. Cocke County, Tenn
4. Federal soldier
5. Co. "B"; 3rd Tenn Vol Inf
6. Farmer
7. Sanders Sims; Cocke County, Tenn; ---; ---; ---
8. Mary Lane; Azaria Lane, Nancy Furgeson Lane, Cocke County, Tenn.
9. ----
10. Did not own any at begining of war
11. none
12. about 500 acres
13. about $500.00
14. Log house, one room
15. Worked on the farm
16. worked on the farm and my mother done general house work
17. none
18. Yes, such work was considered respectable and honorable.
19. yes
20. very few men of that kind in this community
21. yes
22. yes
23. yes
24. did not
25. yes
26. encouraged
27. common free school
28. about 3 months in the year for 2 yrs
29. 2 miles
30. County free schools
31. public

LANE (cont'd.):
32. 3 months
33. no
34. man teacher
35. Feb 10th 1862, Flat Lick, Ky.
36. Camp Pint Not, Ky. or Tenn
37. about 60 days
38. Gaylor Tenn
39. After the first battle, we went to Cumberland Gap Tenn., and I engag-
    ed in the following battles during the war: Knoxville, Tenn and
    trough the Georgia Campaigne, Nashville, Tenn. We were very well
    clothed.
40. Feb 28th 1865 at Nashville, Tenn.
41. ----
42. Farming
43. farming
44. ----
45. Sam. Borun Sergent   Joe Borun Sergent
    Moses O. Cox Sergent   William James
    Lewis James   Andrew Cassady
    Alex Cassady   James Renfro
    Simon Bird
46. George Blazer   Sevierville Rt 8   Tenn
    D.C. Newcomb   Sevierville Rt 8   Tenn
    W.D. Atchley   Sevierville Rt 2   Tenn
    Alex Gann   Sevierville Rt 13   Tenn
    Jack Naugher   Sevierville Rt   Tenn

                          LAYMAN, ASA

FORM NO. 2

1. Asa Layman; Newport Tenn
2. 82
3. Sevier County State of Tenn
4. Federal
5. M; Second Tenn
6. Farmer
7. James Layman; Fair Garden; Sevier; Tennsee; ---;---
8. Vina Fox; George Fox; ---; ---
9. ----
10. ----
11. Two slaves
12. 175
13. 10,000
14. frame house five rooms
15. work on the farm Plowed and hoe
16. father work on the farm done all kind of work Mother done all kind
    of house work spining weaving
17. no
18. yes
19. yes
20. ----
21. yes
22. yes
23. friendly
24. yes
25. yes
26. encouraged
27. Subscription schools
28. 2 years
29. 2 mile
30. Fox school
31. Private
32. 2 month
33. yes
34. man
35. in the year 1862 month November Place Kentucky Federal
36. sent to Mussburrow

                              81

LAYMAN (cont'd.):
37. one month
38. engaged Wagon train
39. ----
40. 1865 Nashville
41. ----
42. Farming
43. ----
44. ----
45. Tilbert   Hank
     Ed long
     Cracked   Newkor

LAYNE, CHARLES

FORM NO. 2

1.   Chas Layne; Whitwell, Marion Co, Tenn.
2.   72 years
3.   Marion County State of Tennessee
4.   Northern Soldier
5.   ----; ----
6.   Farming
7.   Abrem Layne; Penne; ---; ---; ---; ---
8.   Becky Killgore; Bill Killgore; ---; ---; ---
9.   ----
10. own 50 achres value $100
11. no
12. 200 acres
13. $200
14. Log house 2 rooms
15. Plow on farm
16. cooking and spinning
17. no
18. honorable
19. yes
20. work for them selfs
21. no
22. ----
23. ----
24. ----
25. no
26. ----
27. free school
28. 6 month
29. 2 miles
30. free school
31. Public school
32. 3 month in a year
33. yes
34. man
35. about 66   Buress Cove
36. Pellham
37. 2 month
38. ----
39. ----
40. Discharge 67 Stevison Ala
41. enjoyed it fine
42. farming
43. ----
44. ----
45. ----
46. ----

LOUTHAM, GEORGE W.

FORM NO. 1

1.   George W. Loutham; Westmoreland Tenn

82

LOUTHAM (cont'd.):
2.   78 years
3.   Richland Co Ohio
4.   Harden Co Ohio
5.   farmer
6.   farmer
7.   did not own any
8.   did not
9.   80
10.   4000
11.   log house two rooms
12.   general farm work thrashing grain teaching school
13.   genealy farm work such clearing land cultivation of crops thrashing grain
14.   did not
15.   it was
16.   all wite people in neighborhood no colered.
17.   no idles all worked
18.   cant answer as I was not in this state in the days of slavery
19.   ----
20.   ----
21.   ----
22.   fairly good
23.   ----
24.   country schools and high school
25.   5 or 6 year
26.   about half mile
27.   comon and graded
28.   public
29.   from thre to nine
30.   they did
31.   we had both
32.   in federal service nor 64 in Dunkirk Ohio
33.   in spt 64 in Kenton Ohio
34.   Camp Chace Ohio
35.   about a month
36.   ----
37.   in campagn from bul run to Gettesburg campagn from nashville to Atlanta back to nashville
38.   June 17 Nashville Tenn
39.   took the train at Nashville to Lousville then by boat to Cincinnati then by horse to Kenton then home
40.   agriculture and teaching school
41.   farming and   ment and farm   has been my principle occupation have been Tennessee
42.   Henry; ---; Beaver; Pennsylvania; ---; ---
43.   Jane White; William White; dont know; in Beaver Co Penn
44.   my grandfater on my father   came from scotland and stled near Wheeling Va in 1746 served in Indian war   My mother parents came from Ireland cant give date

      you will see I have omited some questions that I cant not ansar as I was in the south all the war

                         LOWRY, WILLIAM W.

FORM NO. 2

1.   William W. Lowry; Riceville McMinn County Tennessee
2.   79 years 15th January 1922
3.   Virginia Washing county
4.   Federal
5.   D; 5th Tennessee Mountry Inftry
6.   Farmer and school teacher
7.   Jas H. Lowry; Lebanon; Russell; Virginia; also in Washington County Va; he was local preacher M.E. Church
8.   Abigal McNew; Elisha McNew; Jane McNew; in Washing County Va
9.   My great grand Parents were scoth Irish desent lived in East Virginia and served in the Revolution. My grand father hauled goods in wagons

                              83

LOWRY (cont'd.):
    from the East to the south country.   This was long before Railroads.
10. was not a land owner before the war
11. none
12. 160
13. about $3000.00
14. Log house 5 rooms
15. I worked on farm as a regular hand in all crops thru all the year
16. all kinds farm work raising stock some mechanical work such as tan-
    ning leather shoe making coperage work carpinter work anything
    essential to the up build and accumilation of a living and support.
17. none
18. was no disgrace to labor for a living
19. yes except those owining slaves
20. about 10%
21. slave holders and non slave holders had the same respect for each
    other
22. Practicaly so
23. generally friendly
24. often this occured
25. yes this was an ambition when the man was Industrious
26. encouraged
27. Rural county schools
28. from 7 to 18 years old
29. ½ mile
30. subscription schools until advanced to about 12th grade after this
    accadamy
31. Public
32. 9 months
33. yes
34. both sex
35. In the federal army August 31, 1864
36. to Cleaveland Tenn nearest Army Post
37. 4 months
38. It was a battle with Confederate deserters and out laws
39. After the first battle transfered to North Georgia for front duty
    as scouts wher we were in many samll engagements of short duration
    gaining the Victory. We lived in army tents well clothed slept on
    the ground I at Hard tack Meat. fresh & drid ones
40. Chattanooga Tenn 26 June 1865
41. After being discharged and paid off we furnished free transportation
    home feeling gay and happy for our service and victory. Though some
    of our men dide a few Kild in engagements did not ____ _____
42. Rail road service as baggage man then to freight and passenger con-
    ductor for 25 years
43. Engaged in Railroad business my home was Riceville Tenn   am
    a Methodist. was Post master in town Riceville for 16 years have
    been in Politics for last 30 years as delegate most all Political
    Campaigns am now retired from any active employment.
44. ----
45. ----
46. John P. Underwood   Athens Tenn   Tenn
    L.G. Hoouck   Athens Tenn   Tenn
    Geo Gilbert   Athens Tenn   Tenn
    Nute Barnet   Englewood   Tenn
    Geo. Horster   Athens Tenn   Tn
    Nuton Hacker   Athens Tenn   Tn
    J.J. Jackson   Athens Tenn   Tn
    Geo. Henderson   Athens Tenn   Tn
    Burt Fite   Athens Tenn   Tn
    H. Dugan   Athens Tenn   Tn
    F.M. Underwood   Athens Tenn   Tn
    I.R. Bolton   Athens Tenn   Tn

                            McCLOUD, JOSEPH

FORM NO. 2

1. Joesph McCloud; Hampton, Tenn Box 86 Carter Co.

                                84

McCLOUD (cont'd.):
2. 82 years old
3. Tennessee
4. Federal
5. Co G; 13 Tenn VC
6. was a farmer
7. Isam McCloud; Johns River; Lanora Co; N.C.; Tailorvill; known as
    Mountain City now; none;
8. Mary Fain; Joseph Fain; Mirea Fain; Culval County on the waters of
    Mulberry
9. Don't know aney thing about great grand parents. The only thing I
    do know about my great grand parents; They were from England
10. Dident own aney property
11. "No"
12. my father owned about 50 acres
13. $100
14. Log house, one room
15. I plowed, hoed corn, cut wheat etc
    (questions 16 - 44 missing but 6 separate handwritten sheets answering
    #39)

Battle at Morris Town

(39) The day before the battle at Morris Town, we scrape all day with them,
     then the next morning we had the battle, was cool nastey morning.
     We captured about one hundred prisoners. our commanding officer was:
     General Gilam They was fighting pretty bad on the left of the Rail-
     road coming East; the Rebels was just east of the town in line of
     battle clear across the valley as far as I could see

2

They was fighting on the left; the first and third pertalian of my
Rigement arnal patten of eight Tennessee was coming up from the
center in coloms of companies. Just before patten made his charge
General Gillan said draw that "Damned old Rustey saber of his and
go and   of his pertalian" General told magor underwood that
an old straw cat would fight this morning.

3

about that time the confederates broke their center lines come about
half way through Morris Town yellowing arnal paten was coming up in
coloms of companies; Thats twelve companies togather. The Jonnies
whealed at run when they saw patten Regiment. Dident fire a gun.
General Gillam hollored to curnel patten to move his Regiment forward. He was onley about fifty yard from the Johnies.

4

followed seven miles and they dident get time to form any more
            we capture general wan in the time off it. He got away -
But we skined his head before he left us with the saber. we onley
followed them to Russelvill, but they diden't stop running for two
or three days, they was scared so - They threw away nearly all of
their baggage away when they go to Alington V.A. Thats where they
stop -

5

running. We were clothed pretty well, had plenty to eat we slept on
the ground nothing over us onley a blanket. we were expose to all
kinds of desease wasent in hospital, or prison. we dident have
much of camps. just had little shantes built out poles, bark and
whatever we could find   we were in several battles
besides this one, this is the first

6

we went to Va. about Christman and tore up the sault works. we went
from Marion VA. up to Withwal and tore up some of the Railroads and
burned some bridges Then come back to Knoxville. we were in many
battles after that to numerous to mention.
From Joseph McCloud

45. Isice Grindstaff   Hampton Tenn

85

McCloud (cont'd.):

Joe Green		Butler Tenn
James Jackson		Johnson City Tennessee
Daul Sailor		Johnson City Tennessee
Gim Wilson		Hampton Tennessee
46.	----	

McCOLLUM, WILLIAM SMITH

FORM NO. 2

1. William Smith McCollum; Chuckey R. 2 Greene Co Tennessee
2. 93 yr April 6 1924
3. Tennessee Greene Co
4. Federal
5. F; Third Tennessee mounted infantry
6. Farmer
7. James McCollum; House where I now live; Greene; Tennessee; at this same place all his life; was magestrate for 8 year
8. Rachel Jones; ---; ---; ---
9. The McCollums came from scotland Three McCollum brothers came from Philadelphia Penn. Tom McCollum (my grandfather) settled in Tennessee and built the house where I now live 10 miles north of Greenville Tennessee
10. I owned 100 acres. value $1000
11. none
12. 300 acres
13. about 3000 dollars
14. a log house built double with two large stone chimneys 5 large rooms
15. Worked on a farm with hoe & plow did any and all kinds of work.
16. Father was a farmer and did all kinds of work. Mother took care of the children and done the cooking also weaving and spinning
17. none
18. This work was considered honorable.
19. yes
20. very few kept servants
21. no distinction between the slave holder & others
22. yes
23. a friendly feeling existed
24. no
25. fairly good
26. They were encouraged. as there were very few slave holders in my neighborhood.
27. District schools generally.
28. I do not know, but I got an english education
29. ----
30. Clear Spring Accadamy and Dodds Seminary
31. Public
32. about 3 months
33. yes
34. men
35. conscriped about May 1862 in Confederate and was in that for five months. I left and scouted a while and then enlisted in the federal army.
36. To Knoxville
37. never in a regular battle
38. Just a skermish
39. never in a regular battle. at Strawberry Plains we had a little skermish. I was once captured and was put under one man and I took the gun from him and got away. In camp we were well fed & well clothed and I was not exposed to cold.
40. I was discharged at Knoxville 1864
41. I was only about 80 mile from home & walked all the way.
42. Farm work
43. I have been a retail merchant I sold good at then (Laurel Gap) now Baileyton and at Newmansville my old home place. never held an office of any kind except Postmaster at Newmansville from 1886 to 1891
     I am living on the farm and in the same house I was born in and also the house my father was born in. This house was built in 1791. My

McCOLLUM (cont'd.):

      wife and I have been married 70 years. my wife is 90 years old. We
      had 13 children - 3 died in infancy 10 living the youngest one 46 the
      oldest 63.

44. ----
45. Joe Bowers   Captain
      My mind is frail I can't recall the names
46. Ephriam McAmis   Afton   Tennessee
    William Lane   Afton   Tennessee

MASON, THOMAS

FORM NO. 1

1. Thomas Mason; Alexandria Tennessee DeKalb County
2. years 75
3. Tennessee Smith County
4. Tennessee DeKalb County Federal Army
5. Farmer
6. Farmer & carpenter
7. none
8. yes 3 mother & 2 children
9. 342 acres
10. about $3000.00 slaves, not included neither Personalty
11. Log 3 rooms Also 2 rooms seperate cook & dining four f_ ases (?)
12. general farm work plowing hoeing fencing & so on
13. Fathers work at opening of Rebellion Carpentering Cooperage & Wheel-
    wright. Mothers work when able cooking spinning & general house
    work
14. only as above mentioned
15. yes
16. yes Except those that were too lazy.
17. about one tenth I suppose
18. Those that owned many slaves did not associate freely with non slave-
    holders expecially the children of the slaveholders
19. somewhat few exceptions
20. generally Friendly so far as I remember.
21. I cant say
22. Not altogether good wages & labor for hirelings were scant
23. encouraged by the older slave owners
24. mixed
25. up until the Rebellion about 12 months schools terms about 3 months
26. from ½ to two miles
27. Free & subscription
28. common
29. 3 months
30. not all
31. Both
32. 1865 February at Alexandria Tenn
33. 4 Tennessee mounted Inft Co K Captain Rufus Dowdy, G. Plumlee, Jim
    Moore, George Roberts, Jim Jones, Dan Hall, Jim Bohanan, James
    Wilhoitr, Bill Wilhoitr, Frank Courtney, Houston Clark, Crockett
    Clark, Bill Hider, Roderick Poe, Jim Hardaman, John Herington, Will
    Capshaw, Champ Furgeson, Coleman Grier, Porter Hill, Confederate
    soldiers names J.F. Mason, Philip Mason, William Mason, Benton
    Cantrell, Bethel Cantrell, Perry G. Potter, Bill Richman
34. Divided Carthage Tenn & Alexandria
35. Scouting all the time after guerrillas & others
36. my horse was stolen the same day at night after reaching Alexandria
    was not remounted again
37. not being mounted any more I was not in any battles. Just remained
    in Camps & obeyed orders as given towards first of may those that
    were not were discharged by fulough & sent home with orders to go to
    work to make some thing to live on would say it is not so since
    world was they dont want to work & seem to keep them up. Our sleep-
    ing in tents on Blankets eating Hardtack Pickled Pork & Coffie. Not
    much exposed to cold disease mumps & mesealles
38. Nashville Tennessee August 25, 1865
39. I bought a   grey mare & rode all night leaving Nashville about

MASON (cont'd.):
      sundown second day reaching my mothers home six miles southeast of
      Smithville 70 miles trip
40. Farming while at home. in 1867 march I left home & hired out for
      5 months & lived 4 years instead of 5 months at same place get in
      cash for all of my work. Besides captured the old Ladys grand
      daughter & still remained on the farm.
41. Farming for 16 years then went in to goods business for 17 years &
      busted (?) under Freetrade Admineration & then went back to farm-
      ing again
42. Thomas Mason; in 1800 Dec 13 (illegible); Hanover I think the; Vir-
      ginia left there; at Lebanon Tenn or about far along time never
      written book; never held office no war service
43. Nancy Johnson Born May 1805; Philip Johnson; I don't know died before
      I was born; Tuckers Xroads Wilson County Tenn
44. I don't know a great deal of ancestry of my parents. My Fathers
      mother I heard him say before he died was of Irish descent. My
      mother of French & English & cant give a full History of my grand-
      parents (?) N.B. I was away from home when this came & never received
      it until April 6, 1922.

MILES, SAMUEL D.

FORM NO. 2

1. Samuel D. Miles; RFD No. 4 Chamberlain, Kingston, Tenn
2. 84 years and 3 months
3. Tennessee Roane Co
4. Federal
5. Co #; 2nd Tenn Cavalry
6. Farmer
7. Samuel Miles; White Out Mt; ---; ---; on Tennessee   Roane Co
8. Jane Rollin; ---; ---; on Dixon Highway Kingston Knoxville Road
9. ----
10. Plenty of stock and other property no land.
11. ----
12. none
13. ----
14. Log house - one big room
15. Farmer boy _____ and hoed corn
16. a farmer in the field. mother wove and spun and made cloth to ____
      eight children all gone except me
17. none
18. It was considered honorable and respectable
19. They did
20. worked hard
21. They mixed & mingled but held themselves a little aloof as they were
      as a class better educated
22. all went to the same church
23. Fairly friendly
24. The Slave holder stood a better chance
25. not much chance
26. encouraged
27. Log school house on Co Joseph Byrds place father of Col. Bob Byrd.
28. Several terms
29. 3 miles
30. Joseph Byrds farm the only school within 9 or 10 miles - Kingston
      Rittenhouse Landing was its nearest school to us
31. Private Had to pay tuition
32. 3 or 4 months
33. yes
34. man - always one of the Byrds
35. 61 May
36. Fishing Creek
37. about 3 months
38. Battle of Fishing Creek
39. After first battle went to Cumberland Gap "and it was a long ____
      way" Several battles & skirmishes. Our worst fight was at Murfrees-
      boro. Many killed there and fearful fighting. good clothes full of

MILES (cont'd.):
    lice (?)
40. August 65
41. Taken from Andersonville to Vicksburg. walked, no shoes, and weak
    from poor food. about 3 weeks. Federal Army at Vicksbury clothed &
    fed. It was HEAVEN. (in the right margin) up & down the river In
    prison Richmond Bells Island May - March (upside down at top of
    page) no food to be gotten. Most of them died - disease. then
    taken to Andersonville - the awfullest place was built for men to
    live in - Torment on earth
42. Farming - Farmed 50 a. on John Wilson Island - John Wilson bought
    this Island from Samuel Morton who ____ for the land.
43. ----
44. ----
45. Capt. Centre (?) from the upper end of East Tennessee. Finc looking
    and a good man can't remember his first name Jone 1st Lieut 2nd
    George Needham a round thousand men and he remembers the names of
    all the offices. Doesn't know where the Roster is __ Remembers
    Morgan and Joe Wheeler. Col. G Regiment Sam Carter
46. Last member of his regiment as far as he knows ---- Mr. Miles is
    what we call here a Mohegeon - you are familiar with the history of
    these people. He has a marvellous memory and talks clearly and
    lucidly. I believe if you could interview him it would be well worth
    while - His tale of the war is a romance
    Came to Kingston this spring as my guest and I'll have him in Kings-
    ton itself is full of history. Oliver Martin Kingston Tenn.

MILLER, MOSES

1. Moses Miller; Dandridge Tenn R#4 Box 4
2. 78 yrs
3. Tennessee Jeff County
4. Federal;
5. F; 9th Tennessee
6. Farmer
7. Christopher C. Miller; Virginia; X; ----; ----; ----
8. Lucy Hall; Benjiman Hall; Eda Hall; Jefferson County
9. Grand father came from Germany Kentucky State
10. X
11. 0
12. 80
13. $1500
14. log house three rooms
15. on a farm plowed
16. Father was a farmer. My mother spun, weaved, cooked & made clothes
17. 0
18. yes
19. yes
20. not very many about 3
21. some did and some did not
22. no they did not very much
23. yes they were very good
24. no did not
25. no
26. not any way
27. Free school
28. about 6 months
29. 1 mile
30. Free school
31. public
32. 2 or 3
33. some did and some did not
34. man
35. Jefferson County Fedral army.
36. To Knoxville Tenn
37. 2 months
38. Long Street
39. good experience. Camp Nelson Kentucky Winter quarters 8 - 4 Octock(?)
    Yankees drove them back had plenty, good clothing slept on ground

MILLER (cont'd.):
crackers meat Irish potatoes bread exposed to Cold a lot good many
diseases no.
40. at Knoxville 11 Sept 65
41. had to walk very long walk
42. Farming
43. Very good helath Jefferson County Medothist.
44. ----
45.

Perry Hall	Frank Brown
Ples Poe	Tommie Brimer
Hogue Poe	Rote Brimer
Henry Ketner	John Patterson
Bill Hill	John Allen
J.P. Hill	Bill Ivy
Andie Moore	Huston Ailey
William McGallra	Joe Holbert
Bill Millir	Dock Burchfill
John Moore	Jake Baker
Bill Moore	Christopher C. Miller
Louis Reneau	Tip Granklin
John Reneau	Ellik Gan (?)
Joe Hill	Henry Gan (?)
George Hill	

46.

John Brimer	Dandridge	Tenn
Sam Shrader	Dandridge	Tenn
Tip Franklin	New Market	
Jim Byrd	Sevierville	Tenn
Ellik Gan	Sevierville	
Julis Justice	Sevierville	

MILLS, BENJAMIN

FORM NO. 2

1. Benjamin Mills; Beacon Decatur Co Tenn
2. 83 year
3. Tenn Henderson Co
4. Federal
5. A; 48 Illinois in Volunteers
6. Farmer
7. James Mills; Some Where, I dont no; North Carolina; ----
8. Fanny Johnson; Benjamin Johnson, Salley Johnson; ----
9. ----
10. non
11. non
12. non
13. ----
14. log
15. I plowed hoed and dun all most all kind of farm work
16. cook sin weaved maid ____ did her familey clothes Fathe Plowed hoed
    cleared land
17. non
18. yes
19. yes
20. non tha I no of
21. No
22. yes
23. Thair was a friendly feeling
24. no
25. ----
26. thy had a chance
27. short terme subscriptions
28. 12 months
29. som times one mile others three
30. short term subscription
31. privet
32. ----
33. no
34. man

MILLS (cont'd.):
35. 1862 march 24 at Savana Tenn
36. Shilo
37. two weaks
38. Shilo
39. Coreth missippi from there to Vixburge mis then after gen Johnson to Jacson mis thence back to vixburg then up the river to mempis on Boats then on a fors march to Chatanoga ten to Noxvill then to Atlanta gorga then savan gor
40. littl Rock Ark 15 of august 1865
41. then they we tuck boatts down White Rive and up the missipy to caro ill to springfield Ill Where we wer Discharged and paid and all stared home
42. farming
43. Run a sta_ mill Blacksmith sold grocerys Chuch relation non Served one term as Justc of the Pease I hav Bin a mason for forty year
44. ----
45. ----
46. ----

MIRANDA, CYRUS

FORM NO. 2

1. Cyrus Miranda; Pulaski Tenn R #6
2. 78
3. Knox Co Ilinois
4. Federel soldier
5. M; 16th Illinois
6. I don't know
7. don't know; don't know; don't know; Indiana; ----; don't know
8. don't know; don't know; don't know; ----
9. ----
10. none
11. none
12. don't know
13. don't know
14. don't know
15. farm work milked cows and fed stock
16. don't know
17. No
18. yes
19. yes
20. don't know
21. there werent any slaves
22. ----
23. ----
24. ----
25. yes
26. there weren't any slave holder
27. public school
28. about 3 years
29. 1 mile
30. don't remember
31. public
32. don't remember
33. yes
34. man
35. 1861 in march
36. Covington Kentucky
37. about 18 months
38. scurmish
39. I had a very good time. After first battle went to Cumberland Gap Tenn. battle atlanta Georgia next Nashville Tenn next Franklin Tenn next spring hill Tenn next Pulaski Tenn
40. Nashville Tenn
41. I went from Nashville to Decatur Ala
42. farming
43. farm always lived in _____ tenn belonged to Christian Church

91

MIRANDA (cont'd.):
   my father and mother died when I was an infant and I know very little
   of their life I was raised an orphun and cun neither read nor write
44. ----
45. ----
46. William James Hammonds   Aspen Hill   Tenn R 1
    Abe Varner   Puluski   Tenn R 6
    C.N. Harris   Puluski   Tenn R 6
    Press Abernathy   Puluski   Tenn R 6

MITCHELL, WILLIAM T.

FORM NO. 1

1. William T. Mitchell; Greeneville Tennessee
2. Seventy seven
3. Greene County Tenn
4. Greene County Tenn in Federal Army
5. cabinet maker
6. same
7. none
8. none
9. House & lot
10. about $2000.00
11. Frame house
12. I worked all the time when not in school
13. my Father made furniture and my mother keep the House
14. none
15. Boath
16. they did
17. they ware very few idlers
18. they associated together as Equals
19. they did
20. they ware Friendly
21. I think not
22. I think so
23. They ware equal no difference shown
24. Pay school
25. Six month
26. In the Town whare I lived
27. Pay school all went to gether Boys & Girls
28. Private
29. about six months
30. Fairly well
31. man
32. Oct 12, 1863
33. 4 Tenn Infantry Co E they are nearly all dead
34. Knoxville Tenn
35. about a year
36. I was not in any as I was _____ Sargent
37. We was well taken care of
38. Nashville Tenn Aug 2, 1865
39. In a Freight car nothing to eat
40. cabinet maker
41. I have live in Greenville Tenn all my life Furniture maker the last
    30 years I have been a Justice of the Peace
42. John J. Mitchell; Knoxville; Knox; Tenn; Knoxville Tenn; He was just
    a Plain man 65 years old
43. Manamma (?) Britton; Major James Britton; Jesamine Britton; Greene-
    ville Tenn
44. I have no Record of my former? Grand Pareant
                                    William T. Mitchell

MOONEY, JOHN

FORM NO. 2

1. John Mooney; Scott Hill Tenn Henderson Co

92

MOONEY (cont'd.):
2. 80 years in March
3. in Tennessee Henderson County
4. a federal soldier
5. C 6th Ten Calvy; 6 Tenn
6. potter and farmer
7. Mark Mooney; NC; I dont know; North Carlinia; ----; none
8. Sally   ; George   ; I don't know; North Carlinia
9. I did not have any land or property.
10. none
11. we did not
12. one hundred ackers 60
13. 16 steers I don't know
14. Log house 3 rooms
15. worked on the farm and in the potter shop
16. ----
17. none
18. it was
19. they did
20. very few
21. they did
22. they did
23. they were
24. it did not
25. they was
26. neither as I can remember
27. None
28. None
29. ----
30. None
31. we did not have any
32. ----
33. ----
34. ----
35. I enlisted at Grand Junction Tenn in April 1862 in the federal
36. Helena Ark
37. ----
38. at Bolivar Tenn
39. general service
40. near nashvill tenn
41. My eyes were Bad I came on a boat
42. farming mostly
43. ----
44. ----
45. Henry Johnson   surelis   Ten
    Calvin Hannah   surelis   Ten
    James Dickson   surelis   Ten
    Rily stanfield   surelis   Ten
    Luke Rogers   scotts hill   Ten
    J.N. Davenport   scotts hill   Ten
46. ----

MOORE, JOHN L.

FORM NO. 2

1. John L. Moore; Greenville Greene Co Tennessee
2. 78 will be 79 Apr. 20, 1922
3. Tennessee Greene County
4. Federal
5. E; 4th Tenn Inft Vols
6. Farmer and school teacher
7. Jeremiah Moore; 5 miles from Greenville; Greenville; Tennessee; 5
    East of Greeneville on old Stage Road; no war service He taught
    Private or Subscription schools
8. Mary Rice Holt; David Holt; Betsy Paxton; 3½ miles North East of
    Greeneville
9. My Great Grand father Anthony Moore came from North hampton county
    Pa in 1778 he was a soldier of the American Revolution Belonged to

93

MOORE (cont'd.):

Penn State Guards or Milistia My Grand Father David Moore was my Great Grand Fathers only son 9 years old and Inherited the 500 acres of land Intered by

10. By Inheritance from my Father and Mother
11. no. none
12. Fathers 77. Mothers 107
13. 15,000. no building on either tract. My Father died when I was 2½ yrs old. My Fathers Brothers built a log house for my Mother.
14. The log house had 2 stories. Two rooms down and up stairs (See in question 13) It was built on land Inherited from her Father David Holt.
15. All kinds that was needed. Plowing hoing mowing with scythes. Clover and Grass. cuting wheat and oats with grain cradle. I could and did swing a cradle or bind wheat from morning till evening for 6 days in the wk; one day bound days and helped shock 75 dozzen of wheat 60 dozzen good work
16. Dying yams in blue pot Sowing kniting and all kinds general house work. and was known as a special good cook besides much work with a hoe in garden as my mother was left with two children my sister yonger than I.
17. No
18. Honest toil was highly honered and and practicede by both Precept and example by Both my grandparents Families
19. yes
20. a few exceptions I heard of men owners of land allowing their lands to grow up in sprouts and _____
21. I think they did generally; some felt self important and puffed up with pride
22. As to this question I cannot say as in my _____
23. ----
24. as not being a voter then and my Father dying in my child hood my thoughts were not called in that line.
25. ----
26. I cannot say definitely yes or no
27. Subscription
28. very little before Civil War
29. one mile
30. Tusculine College
31. subscription old time county school
32. Four or Five
33. yes
34. a man
35. 1863 mch 15 in Greene County Tennessee
36. Louisville Ky
37. Oct 3rd 1863
38. Picket fighting at McMinnville Tennessee
39. After our Regt. surendered to Gen Jo. Wheeler under flag of truce we were turned loose or Parole not to take up arms till legally exchange and in event Burnside held E. Tenn to re organize at Greeneville Tenn
40. Aug 3rd 1865 at Nashville Tenn
41. Was returned home on train
42. work on Farm with my mother My sister had died in May 1864 when I was at Loudon Tenn
43. In Oct 1865 I entered Tusculern College with 23 enrolled that year with one Teacher Prof Samuel S. Dark. I spent one full and two half terms begining Sept at 1st and stoping off in Feb of years 1867 & 1868 to work on farm. My church relations have been in th Bethel Pres. Church since I was 13 yrs a member served as a deacon 7 yrs and as an elder 49 yrs since 1873. Served as a _____ of Pres. _____ Pub. of 1322 Chestnut Street Philadelphia Pa. for 15 or 16 yrs 1871 to 1887. Riding horse back mostly in winter months being on Farm in summer. This for Walston Presbytery U.S.A.
44. (On a separate sheet of paper)

MOORE (cont'd.):

Greeneville Tenn
R.D. 8
Mrch 20th 1922

John Trotwood Moor
Dear Sir
I have answered some of the questions I hope you can put them to
proper place. If you should like some incidents of how we East
Tenn Sta__feeders got to Ky I will try to give some of my experience
Hand(?) ever nead(?) the Book of Capt Dan Ellis of Elizabethton
Carter County Tenn. He was a Union _____ and guide to get the union
men thro the lines

With best wishes
Sincerely yours
John L Moore
Co E 4th Tenn Vols

45. Wm. T. Mitchell Esq.   Greeneville Tenn
     A.F. Babb   RFD
     Joseph G. Fellers   Afton Greene Co Tennessee
     All the commission officers have died. A few years ago a comrade
     who lived and died in Greenville told me he kept a roll and only 13
     comrads of our Co E were living then some of them have since died.
46. Capt W.E.F. Milburn Greeneville Tenn. A Tenn soldier as a lawyer.
     and of some educational and literary attainment might give you some
     facts if you have not allready a letter from him - Capt Newton
     Hacher of Jonesboro Tenn was Capt of Co C 4th Tenn Inft Vols he is
     84 now and very feeble he may not be able to write.

(Question No. 9 continued)
     My great grandfather Anthony Moore My grand father David Moore had
     9 children at his death the land was divided into 9 tracts of which
     my father Jeremiah Moore got 77 acres (see question 12) My great
     grandfather Anthony Moore's parents were Scotch Irish from North
     Ireland. He was an Original Elder of Mt Bethel Presbyterian Church
     Bringing the Name with him from Mt Bethel Pa. Organized on lands
     where the town of Greeneville now stands. The first preaching in
             of Greene County was by the Pioneer Samuel Doak(?) in
     the house of my Great Grand father so reported in Centenial discusses
     for 1876

MORRIS, COURTLAND LATIMORE

FORM NO. 2

1.   Courtland Latimore Morris; Plymouth Indiana
2.   79 years
3.   Huron Co Ohio
4.   Federal
5.   Co C; 83rd Illinois Vol
6.   Farmer
7.   William Morris; Danbury; Fairfield; Conn; Norwalk Ohio; ----
8.   Angeline Swetland; Daniel Swetland; Lucy Gates; ----
9.   Amos Morris Conn War of 1812. Samuel Morris, Agur Hoyt, Capt Comfort
     Hoyt, Serg. Miles Boughton of Danbury, Ct, Nathaniel Gates, Luke
     Swetland and William Gallup of Wilkes Barre Pa served in Revolution.
     Colonial Wars; Col. Benedam Gallup, Capt. John Gallup, Lieut Joseph
     Morris, John Winston, Capt Nicholas Olmstead, Capt John Gorham and
     Dr. Thomas Starr
(on two separate sheets of paper)
     Question No. 9
     Grandparents
     Amos Morris & Polly Hoyt, Danbury, Ct.;Daniel Swetland & Lucy Gates,
     Beaver Meadows Pa
     Great-grandparents
     Samuel Morris & Jerusha Hinman, Danbury, Ct.; Agur Hoyt & Lois
     Boughton, Danbury Ct.; Joseph Swetland & Salome Hall, Wilkes Barre,
     Pa; Nathaniel Gates & Lucy Gallup, Kingston, Pa.
     Great, great-grandparents
     Ephraim Morris Jr. & Eunice Hoyt, Danbury Ct.; Hon. Noah Hinman &

MORRIS (cont'd.):

Lydia _____ (Widow Wildman) Woodbury Ct.; Capt Comfort Hoyt & Anna Beach Danbury Ct.; Miles Boughton & Mary Benedict Danbury, Ct.; Luke Swetland & Hannah Tiffany, Wilkes Barre, Pa.: Thomas Gates & Sarah Rowley East Haddam, Conn.; William Gallup & Judity Reed, Kingston Pa.

Thomas Morris signed the Platation Covenant of New Haven, Conn 1639. Mayflower Ancestors; John Tilley, wife Bridget Tilley, daughter Elizabeth Tilley, John Howland and Edward Fuller.

(page 2)

Members of the General Court, a position of great honor in those days. Capt John Starr, Capt Josiah Starr, George Gates, Hon. Nicholas Olmstead, Hon. Noah Hinman, Benjamin Hinman.
10. none
11. none
12. 100 acres
13. Parents both dead.
14. Log house
15. Worked at farm work. Plowed and worked in fields as necessary to farm.
16. Farming. Household duties such as cooking, spinning and etc.
17. no
18. Considered respectable and honorable
19. yes
20. very little
21. None owned
22. No slaveholders lived here.
23. ----
24. ----
25. yes
26. ----
27. Public school
28. 10 years
29. ½ mile
30. Public school
31. Public
32. Six months
33. yes
34. Both
35. July 19, 1862 at Monmouth Illinois
36. at Harriman Tenn
37. 8 months
39. Remained at Ft Donaldson until late summer 1862 when moved to Clarksville Tenn was detached from Company with about 30 others & formed an independent company and mounted for Scouts hunting Outlaws Gurrillas & Roaving Bands with num erous fights & skirmishes for 2 years
40. Nashville Tenn June 26th 1865
41. Moved to Chicago, Ills and rec'd final pay July 5th 1865.
42. Started to school at Monmouth Academy from there to Oberlin Business College and telegraph school.
43. After going to school for 1½ years entered the services of the Pittsburgh Ft Wayne & Chicago RR as Telegraph Operator & later as station agent. Served about eight years then resigned and engaged in the lumber business and later added Manufacturing was Post Master and Notary Public.
44. ----
45.

L.B. Cutler	H.J. Baily	J.H. Jones
J.C. Gamble	C.H. Brown	L.M. Lusk
S.L. Stephenson	J.N. Caldwell	A.L. McReynolds
Jas S. Campbell	G.D. Chapman	C.L. Morris
A.B. Chaffee	M. Crosier	J.A. Beard
E.H. Crandall	L. Real	J. Carrick
J. H. Montgomery	Wm. Crosby	J.A. Gordon
Jacob Dively	J.B. McKown	J.E. Stewart
E.H. Brittan	W.L. Edwards	G.L. Mitchell
A. Caskey	V.W. Earp	J.F. Mitchell
A.B. Hawkins	A.R. Foster	Jonas Murdock

MORRIS (cont'd.):

J.W. Green	A.C. Foster	A. Matterson
C.S. Patton	J.C. Ford	S.T. McWilliams
G.W. Robinson	J.L. Ford	T.T. McWilliams
W.T. Livermore	J.I. Francis	A.E. McCombs
A. West	L.B. Frazier	W. McIntyre
J.W. Strong	G.W. Folsom	J.R. Nichols
Allen B.B.	T. Gowdy	J. Pherman
Allen D.B.	J.W. Grubbs	S.M. Pike
Augst Jonas	J. Godfrey	G.L. Real
G.W. Anderson	H.M. Griffin	B.F. Robinson
J. Anderson	W. Griffin	H. Rice
H. Amey	D.W. Graham	N.B. Rouse
C.H. Butler	B.F. Hill	Elias Smith
Ira Butler	M. Holoners?	J. Smith
A.W. Bunker	F.M. Higgisen	A. Sellman
E.G. Benkert	G.T. Henry	S.J. Shirley
G.L. Barrett	J. Jones	L.T. Stewart

46. ----

MOSS, DAVID

FORM NO. 2

1. Cedar Creek Tenn
2. David Moss 85 years
3. Cherokee Co NC
4. Federal Soldier
5. Co K; 13th Tenn Cav
6. Farmer
7. Jeff Moss; Buncomb Co NC; Buncomb; North Carolina; ----; my father
    was in War 1812 under Jackson
8. Margret Henderson; Arch Henderson; Jinnie Henderson; neare Ashville
    North Carolina
9. My grand father william moss my Grand mother Moss was Hooper from
    Jermny my grate grand father Hardy Henderson was in the Revolution
    under Marian my grate grand father Hooper was under Washington my
    great grandfather on my mother side was Kild at Bunavista Mexico.
10. oned 150 acres in Charokee Co NC other Property 77 Head Horses 25
    Head cattle
11. 13
12. 300 acres in 61 worth 2000.
13. 6000 Land value of slaves 5,000
14. Doble log House 4 rooms Roch chimny
15. when I was a Boy I Prowed Hode about 15 acres every summer the white
    men in my country all worked the citizens of my co nearly all lived
    in log houses
16. my father farmed and my mother spun and wove nearly all our clothing
    She carded and spun the wool for clothing & Blankets and fancy
    Coverlid olls flax and to
17. two some times more
18. yes By some it was Bute the Big slave holders it was not. They
    would not let a Pore white man eat at their table.
19. as farming generally
20. the slave holders Boys generly lived in idleness
21. yes the most slave holders thought they better than men that did
    not own slaves just so with the Boys and Girls.
22. no the was a ____ Differance the slave holders would not mix with
    the non slaveholders.
23. the slave holders the did not mix the slaveholders thought them
    selves Better.
24. yes the slave holder allway had the advantidg He had a little money
    & always taken the the advantidge
25. no the oportunity for a Pore young man was Hard
26. Discouraged. some ambitious young men made the slaveholder Had the
    advantidg and used it.
27. Subscription school about 3 months to year and some had to go about
    4 miles
28. 3 months to year

MOSS (cont'd.):
29. 3 to 5 miles
30. spelling Reading & Rithmetic
31. Subscription the Parrents paid according to how many children
32. 3
33. yes
34. man
35. I enlisted in the Aug 63 federal gov
36. from Ky to Knoxville Tenn come in to Tenn in Burnside army.
37. about 3 months
38. Bigcreek Gap Tenn
39. we was egaged in the Big Creek Gap the at Knoxvill then at Morris-
    town·Tenn then at Bulls Gap then at Greenville Tenn when the galen
    John Morgan was Kild on the 4 morning in Sept 64. I dont no just
    how many one at <u>Bristol</u> Va Seag of Knoxville one at Bun Station
40. Washington DC
41. my trip home was very disheartening I some times could get something
    to eat sometimes nothing 2 days at one time just one small Piece
    corn bread finding all Burnd Houses Deserted & Burned.
42. farming
43. I was a farmer in Cherokee Co NC ____ Tenn now in Green Co Tenn I
    am a Baptis and a Republican. I met Theodore Roosevelt and US Grant
    & McKinly and <u>House</u> Presidents <u>General</u> Thomas McCelan & Mead & Wood
    Burnside ____ at Murphy burrough I've Mit Both the govners ____
    I was wounded at Battle of Morristown Tenn in 3 spaces of the galant
    Gen Vaughn this is my hand Rit at 85 years old I served a while in
    the ware with Spain in the Battle Santiango I cuba a little ____ of
    the Battle of Greenevill Tenn Left Bulls Gap about 8 oclock at night
    marched all night just at daylight we encountered the Confederate
    Pickets We all ____ in town to gather morgan was Kild Between
    Daylight and sun up we Tick charge of his Boddy till it was I
    Inteffed.
44. ----
45. Jake Kiker   13th Tenn Cav   John K. Miller was Col
    Mart Kiker   13th Tenn Cav
    John Bissell   W.H. Ingerton St Col
    Luther Hilton   the Bravest of the BRave
    John Bageal   Stacy was St Col
    James Rollins   when the Regt ment
    Henry M. Walker Lieut CoK   was Discharged
    Jno G. Dervan Capt Co K   I fought for my govmnt
    William Spivy   and I vote the way I shot
    Canady foster   David Hardigree
    Gard Wyrick   William Dorsett
    Lee Wyrick   Martin Anderson
    James H. Cox   Osker Payne
    Will Payne   Will Spivy
    Richard Pilsher (Pilther?) Anteney Pilsher (Pilther?)
    Logan Densley
46. John Gray 13th Tenn Cav Greenville Tenn James Marshall
    nearly all dead

NAUGHER, JACKSON L.

FORM NO. 2

1. Jackson L. Naugher; Sevierville Tenn
2. 81 yr
3. York County SC
4. Federal
5. 1st Tenn; Battery E Light Artillery
6. Farmer
7. William F. Naugher; Ireland; ----; ----; York Co SC; War of 1812
8. Celia Pendergrass; ---- Pendergrass; ----; ----;
9. ----
10. none
11. no
12. yes
13. ----

NAUGHER (cont'd.):
14. Two story log house
15. Plow and hoe corn chop wood split rails
16. General farm work. Mother general house work
17. no
18. yes
19. yes
20. small per cent
21. yes
22. no
23. Friendly
24. no
25. no
26. ----
27. common country school
28. 12 months
29. 2 miles
30. common country schools
31. Public
32. 3 mo.
33. yes
34. men
35. Knoxville Tenn Oct 1863 Federal army
36. Ky
37. 10 months
38. M y Creek Tenn
39. Regular ____. 8 or 10 battles camped in tents. In battle at
    Greeneville Tenn when Gen John Morgan was killed
40. Nashville Tenn Aug 1, 1865
41. Made the trip in as short a time as possible without accidents or
    unusual occurrense
42. Farming
43. Farming. Lived in Sevier and Knox Cos Tenn
44. ----
45. ----
46. ----

NORWOOD, GEORGE W.

FORM NO. 2

1. George W. Norwood; Good Spring Tennessee Route 2
2. Eighty six years
3. Tennessee Lincoln Co.
4. I was a Federal soldier
5. Company 'H'; 13 Ind Cav
6. House carpenter in the days of his manhood
7. William Norwood; in SC July 1, 1804; ----; South Carolina; ----; ----
8. Lucinda Larwood she was the daughter of; Edmund and Tabitha; Larwood;
    they lived in Marshall Co Tenn.
9. my fathers (William Norwoods) ancesters came from England. my
    mothers (Lucinda Larwoods) ancesters came from France. my great
    grandfather Edmund Larwood was a Revolutionary soldier.
10. I owned no land then.
11. owned no slaves
12. about 200 acres
13. about one thousand dollars
14. a log house with a framed room at one side two rooms
15. my work wa on the farm and commonly with the plow.
16. House carpentering. House keeping and governing the children. card-
    ing spinning weaving sewing knitting and cooking
17. none
18. It was certainly considered respectable and honorable.
19. They did except a few that owned many slaves such were very few
20. Such was very limited
21. There were very little aristocrasy in this part of Giles County.
22. There was no difference made.
23. Altogether friendly.
24. it certainly did not.

99

NORWOOD (cont'd.):
25. it would have required a long time
26. They were encouraged
27. just our little district's free school and not much of that
28. not more than one year in all
29. about two miles
30. none but the district school a short term each year
31. generally public
32. about three months
33. They did
34. commonly taught by men
35. on the 19 day of feb 1864 I enlisted in the federal army at Mitchell Indiana.
36. To New Albany Indiana
37. I don't remember the length of time, but it was when Hood tried to take Nashville.
38. ----
39. When Hood approached Nashville I was on detail duty. and was not in the battle I never disobeyed an order and as to how I lived in camp it was the strictest time of my life. during all the time of my service I never swore a profane oath nor drank a dram.
40. Nov 18, 1865 at Vicksburg Mississippi
41. had no trouble in getting home - got of the train at Mitchel Indiana and walked a few miles to my little home I had paid for with my wages. There I met my dear wife and my little boy.
42. farm work - for about a year. I then moved back to Giles County Tenn right in the neighborhood where I was raised and have worked in a wood shop ever since.
43. I have done some farm work but my work has generally been in my wood shop. my home has been all this time right here in Giles County Tenn. I have been a member of the Methodist Church since before the war. I have been a district tax assessor for four years and a Notary Public four years.
44. ----
45. Now I could give the names of the men of my company in full but as they were not Tennesseans I think it will not be required. I will use a part of this space to give you the whereabouts of a few old Tennessee soldiers.
    E.G. Prince   Good Spring Tenn   Route 2
    he was a confederate soldier and is a nice old gentleman
    J.S. Coffman   Minor Hill Tenn
    a confederate soldier and a good citizen
    Abe Garner   Prospect Tenn RFD
    a gederal soldier a good citizen

    Now Mr Moore if you would like to hear anything else from just let me know
              your friend   G.W. Norwood
    I should have written this in the space below
46. ----

PARKER, WILLIAM M.

FORM NO. 1

1. William M. Parker; Bradford tenn
2. 77 yr the 2nd dec 1921 Past
3. state of tennessee Gibson County
4. state of tennessee Gibson County
5. farmer
6. farmer
7. owned farm
8. none
9. 150 acres
10. ----
11. log house 3 rooms
12. farm when a Boy done all kinds of farm work
13. ----
14. no

100

PARKER (cont'd.):
15. yes
16. yes
17. none all work
18. wasnt eny slave holders in the neighbor hood
19. ----
20. ----
21. ----
22. yes
23. no
24. Public and subscription school
25. about 10 mo
26. 1 mi
27. do not know
28. Both kind
29. 6 mo
30. reasonibly
31. mna
32. I enlisted in the federal army the first da of August 1862 at North
Gibson tenn
33. Regiment 6th tennessee cavalry
34. Dresden Tenn
35. forgot
36. Salen Tenn
37. ----
38. Palaski tenn the twenty sixth da of July 1865
39. I walk from Nashville home Had all the good whiskey I wanted.
40. farming
41. ----
42. Henry Parker; ----; ----; ----; ----; ----
43. Mytilda Parker; ----; ----; ----;
44. ----

PATTON, D. T.

FORM NO. 2

1. D.T. Patton; Lewis Co.
2. 76
3. one mile ½ mury co
4. federal soldier
5. Company E; 9th Tenn _____ command by C.F. Akins
6. Farmer
7. Subaison (Sebastian?) Patton; ----; north kitter; dont no; dead; no
8. Liss Beath (Elizabeth?); Joseph Patten; dont no; one mile ½ hamper
9. I dont no nothing about them
10. no
11. no
12. no
13. no
14. Hued log house one side room and one Pig room and one up stares
15. I farmed when the war come plowing a mule making corn
16. She done her cooking with a skillet and lid before the fire. She
had a pole on the rack hung before the fire cooking Hog jaw cooking
it with Turnept salet. she had a loom Kind a little (reel) to
Hucket the thread on a had a cord and spinning wheal and working
hard ---- winter
17. none
18. old bar shun old time cradels and reek took th old big how with the
big eye in it
19. how in such work
20. some of them had niggers there was ----
21. no it did not make eny Difference with they show not
22. yes sir
23. they war all friendly and tredt them with except.
24. no
25. they was good to him
26. no he was not
27. I tried one school on drie fork By Jack biggan but he wanted to whip

101

PATTON (cont'd.):

me some <u>Fork</u> with with ricketts and I quit being by the wood not go one school on driy

28. about 4 months to a free school <u>Perkins</u> it was not my mother will but I wood not go besase they wanted to whip me
29. one mile
30. there was not but one it was and their to dry forks that I all that I no about
31. I had to pay for and one I did not
32. 4 month the free school the other from 4 to 6
33. yes
34. man
35. Left morey Co 62 and alline <u>brach</u> <u>Currie</u> _____ and went to Cpo biffel Co E march the last day on the <u>first</u> of april I dont Rember first whe now.
36. it stay their in <u>nirskin</u> and Had Currie orders I dont no how _____.
37. I dont no the <u>first</u> one the first reed wook brige.
38. _____ Jackson _____ _____ with the niggers and white ____ and ____ them.
39. I was not in hospital nor in prison I had plent to eat and slept all right. I had good cloth and good Blankett and rain coat I keep the hu___ _____ full Before I got hungry I _____ my _____ _____ and got It full agan.
40. Salt bury north killery as well as I can rember.
41. we come home all right untill we come throw till general grant _____ __ ____. He let us ____ and horse saddes and bridle and side army when we come to starw bury ____ __.
42. farming
43. I spent it the most in ___ I have hell no office or nothing.
44. ----
45. the roster is ____ _____ _____ of Co E

Gorge _____ 1 Luet   Joe Patton 2 Luet
_____ Curry 3 Luet   Sgt
_____ 2   _____delk Pvt
                       Nute Cury

Joe Love   Bill _____more
Jakey love   purley
John   Billey tready
Jake "   willes lies
      cury   dude lies
Gorge cury   ~~Jaek~~
      "   ~~Jaek~~
George Pay   john fuller
      "   Sam   "
Sam   "   walker
Bill "   Bell
Jim   spencer
Joe
John fuller
Sam   "   John Page

Bill
Jake
Hardy

46. John   taspy   tenn
Andy   Hanper   tenn
                       Mury   tenn
Jake   Mury   tenn
Bill turner   taspy   tenn
that all I no of now.

PIERCE, JAMES W.

FORM NO. 1

1. James W. Pierce   Post Office Add _ _, Tate, Tenn
2. 75 years
3. Carter County Tennessee

102

PIERCE (cont'd.):
4.   Green County Tenn.
5.   attending school and assisting my Fathers sadlers shop
6.   saddle and harness maker
7.   none
8.   no
9.   none
10. none
11. a two story framed house of 6 rooms
12. was a helper in fathers saddler shop
13. My father devoted about all his time to saddle and harness making
     until the autumn of 1862 when he rented and moved to a farm in Green
     Co Tenn
     Mother did the ordinary housework
14. no
15. yes
16. yes
17. very few such
18. many of them mingled freely but some of them felt themselves above
     the non slave holder
19. In majority of instances they did
20. a friendly feeling
21. I do not remember
22. They were limited
23. am not prepared to say
24. some small subscription schools, and later attended school at Suffield
     Academy at Elizabethton Tenn
25. about three years
26. a half mile
27. The Suffield Academy and a small private school
28. Private "subscription schools"
29. eight months
30. yes
31. man
32. Sept 23 1863 federal service
33. 13th Tenn Vol Cavalry Names in my company J.G. Burchfield, John M.
     Wilcox, Jo. Badgett, Solomon Turner, John Bishop, S.W. Scott, S.F.
     Angel, Geo. Angel, Landom Folsom, James P. Angel, C.P. Pierce, John
     Hilton, Andrew Campbell, John Campbell, G.D. Roberts, Robt Wilcox,
     Frank Perkins, Wm Folsom, Landon Carden
34. To Camp Nelson, Kentucky
35. about 6 months
36. a short engagement at Morristown Tenn.
37. The battles were all small that is no great battles All my service
     was in Tenn mostly in Tenn was in ____ fight at Moristown Blue
     Spring Bulls Gap Greenville Johnson City Carters Dept. We usually
     had hard tack bacon coffee sugar dried vegetables except where we
     had to forge off the country - Some times we subsisted on _____
     corn for a day or two
38. At Knoxville Tenn in Sept 1865
39. was not far from where my father then lived ____ Creek Green Co
     Tenn a few hours travel by rail to Bulls Gap thence three miles to
     destination - nothing of interest enroute.
40. was at leisure till november then took a job of salesman in a store
     genl. merchandise in Elizabethton till spring of 1867 then took the
     study of medicine at Morristown Tenn.
41. Practiced medicine from Apr 1869 to the present located in Union Co
     Tenn later Claiborn County two years in first place 7 yrs in second
     & 42 years here
42. James Pierce; in Misouri; don't know Co; Mo. came to Ky when a child,
     to Jefferson Co Tenn. when young man; later to Elizabethton; held no
     office & never in war service
43. Caroline Wilcox; know nothing of; ----; her history
44. ----

PINKLEY, RICHARD K.

FORM NO. 1

1. _____ Richard K. Pinkley; Hallaw Rock Tennessee
2. 80 years and 7 months
3. Tennessee - Carroll Co
4. Carroll Co - Tennessee - In the service of Federal --
5. Farm hand
6. farmer and shoe maker
7. ----
8. mo
9. ----
10. ----
11. Log house 2 rooms and wide hall
12. I did all kinds of farm work
13. In crop times he did farm work and other times made shoe. did all kinds of house work. Cooking spining and weaving and various other things that women did at that time.
14. no
15. yes
16. yes
17. very few
18. In our part of the country I never could tell any differance.
19. They did here.
20. All friendly so far as I remember
21. To some extent it did
22. very poor opportunities
23. ----
24. Public school
25. about 3 months
26. 3 miles
27. Just a primary school
28. Public
29. 4 months - 2 in summer & 2 in winter
30. yes
31. man
32. 1862 Aug 15 Beuna Vista Tenn
33. 7th Tenn Calv E.R. Kyle, Young Cooper, Geo Cooper, Gray Butler, Henry Butler, Dock Butler, Jess Pickler, Levy Ozier, Jim Taylor, Arch Allen, Colombus Williams, Geo Williams, Jas McCracken, Randolph Rust, Tinker Williams, Danial Meal_, Ben Greer, Will Greer, Bill Rushing, Dock Mizzell, Bob Priutt, Bobe Pruett
34. Humbolt Tenn
35. about 3 months
36. Battle of Trenton Tenn
37. After the first battle my regment was captured & sent to a parole camp 'Camp Chase Ohio'. We stayed there 6 or 8 months. We were then exchanged and sent to Union City Tenn. We were kept there as scouts through Tenn & Ky. 4 month Battle of Union City Tenn all were captured but 100 men. I was one that was not captured. it lasted about ½ day the men that were captured were sent to Andersonville prison. I lived all right. well clothed. some times in tents sometimes out in open
(continued on a separate sheet of paper)
We had plenty to eat some times rough but didnt go hungry - I was in hospital one time had pneumonia.
38. Aug 9 1865
39. I came on train from Nashville to Johnsonville Tenn and then rode my horse home.
40. Farming
41. I married and began my farm work and later dealt in cotton for 14 yrs. lived most of my life near Buena Vista member of Christian Church
42. Michael Pinkley; ----; ----; ----; ----; ----
43. Ann Tosh; ----; ----; ----
44. ----

FORM NO. 1

1. John Pitts; Henderson, Tenn
2. 80
3. Tennessee McNairy County
4. Tennessee Hardin County Federal Government
5. Farmer
6. Farmer
7. Farm land 200 acres $1000.00
8. Father owned three
9. Father owned 600 acres
10. Land $3000.00, slaves and other property $4000.00
11. Log weather boarded & _____ two rooms 2 story
12. Farm work gerally full time
13. Father did not work he had boys who did his work Mother worked all the time cooking spinning weaving and general house work & ____ work.
14. no special servants
15. Considered very honorable - the white man who did not work had very low standing in my community.
16. yes Hardin County was loyal to Federal Government 800 majority approved secession
17. Practically none
18. Slave owners respected those who owned no slaves but at the opening of the war there was apparant differences.
19. yes
20. Friendly until war opened.
21. This fact made no difference
22. Fairly good
23. encouraged
24. common public schools
25. about 12 months
26. one & one half miles
27. Public school
28. Public
29. Three months
30. yes
31. men generally
32. In   1862 Jan conscripted by confederates March 6 at home on furlough on March 11 1862 joined U.S. Army. 46 Ohio continued until disable 1864 Nov 28.
33. 46 Ohio
    Tom McQueen, John McQuees, Tom Travillian, George Shipman, John ____, Bud Hunt?, Tom Wood (Tennesseans) George Adams, Wilse(?) Barba__, Bill Obideer.
34. Shilo
35. From March 11 to April 6
36. Shilo
37. After Shilo battle went to Corinth Miss (?) Vicksburg Chatanonga, Tenn atlanta Ga Savannah Ga. I was wounded by accident by a comrade near Macon Ga Nov 27 1864 and was not in actual anymore until close of war, was never in prison was clothed well had plenty of ____ and hard tack to eat camp life reasonably comfortable had fever in 1863 and suffered ____ ____ during this winter Battle of Shilo won by Federals Vicksburg same Atlanta same Savanah same
38. was sent from Savannah to Hilton Head SC from to Davids Island NY from there to Camp Denison Ohio where I was discharged May 1865.
39. Came to Cincinnacti to Lewisville Ky there to Nashville Tenn from there to my home in Hardin County Tenn May 7, 1865.
40. Farming
41. Farming merchandising ____ mill & cotton gin to about 1900 since which time have done no work and had no business, held no offices.
42. Barbee Pitts; √ ; Davidson; Tennessee; √ ; Held no office except Colonel of Malitia was in Fla. war
43. Felisia Wilson; William Wilson; Sallie Wilson; Hardin County Tenn & McNairy County Tennessee
44. Grandfather Burrell Pitts resided in Davidson County Tenn.

John Pitts

Chester County   Henderson Tennessee

PRINCE, MARTIN V.

FORM NO. 2

1. Martin V. Prince; Turtletown, Tenn
2. Eighty-Five
3. Union Co Ga
4. Federal
5. Co K 12 Tenn Cav; 12 Tenn Cav
6. Farming
7. Cooper C. Prince; South Carolina; ----; South Carolina; Cherokee Co NC; ----
8. Malinda Givens; James Givens; ----; Monroe Co Tenn
9. My great - grandparents came from across the ocean.
10. just´mountain land Value 200
11. No
12. something over 100 Acres
13. about a $1000
14. Log house Two rooms
15. Made rails Plowed & hoed corn
16. Farmed Cooked served and knit Weaved
17. No
18. Yes
19. Yes
20. very few but what done their work
21. Yes
22. Yes
23. Yes
24. No
25. No
26. No
27. Grammer school
28. Three months
29. ever three mild
30. Grammer school
31. Public
32. three
33. No
34. Man
35. Twenty th day of March 1864 enlis Loudon Tenn Federal Government
36. Nashville Tenn
37. about five or six months
38. Franklin Tenn
39. Nashville Tenn. Two days and part of one night clothed very good Very good in camp some of the time on the ground and some of the time on bunks Hard tack bun bread meat coffee sugar mix vegetables.
40. 7th day of Oct 1865 Fort 1ith worth Kansas
41. Come to Nashville Tenn. From Fort 1ith Worth Kan from there on to Charlistin Tenn
42. Farming
43. Church Relations Baptist I have been a member of the Baptist over 45 years.
44. ----

ROACH, ANDERSON J.

FORM NO. 1

1. Anderson J. Roach Rutledge Tennessee
2. 75 years old
3. state of Tenessee Granger Co
4. I inlisted in the Fedral State of Tennessee, Grainger Co
5. Farmer
6. Farmer
7. none
8. none
9. about thirty-five acres
10. about five hundred dollars
11. one room log house

ROACH (cont'd.):
12. I put in full time plowing hoeing and other farm labor
13. Father did farming and blacksmith work. Mother's occupation was cardind spinning, weaving, cooking, and all other jeneral house work.
14. none
15. Such work was considered respectable
16. yes
17. But verry few.
18. slave holders did not mingle freely with those who did not own slaves they seem to feel them selves better than those that did not have slaves
19. They did not. The slave holders did not mingles with the non-slave holders but verry little at any place.
20. They seemed to be on friendly terms but there was no perticular association between them and when a slave holder hired a non slave holder he was principally looked on as being no better than a slave and was treated as one.
21. I have no rememberance of it, if it did
22. no
23. They were no incouraged by the slave holders. The slave holders kept the poor class of people down as much as possible.
24. a public primary school
25. about 10 months
26. about 1½ miles
27. Primary schools
28. Public
29. 3 months. The teachers salary was $8.00 per month
30. was not regualry as every body was poor and the children had to work
31. man
32. July 16 '63 Camp Nelson Ky
33. Cl F, 8th Tenn Calvry. Cap. Cal Massengill, (Lieut) Geo R. Cambel, Robert Loyod, Geo Burleson, Mike Uankey, Wess Bull, Jeff Bull, R.D. Taylor, Will Goens?, Rafel Akins, Sam Phelps, James Wood, James Evans, Cal Runions(?), Tom Overbay, Jeff Fryor, Dock McVey, Sam Collier, Champ Collier, Geo. Collier, James Grant, Will Sulphridge, Dan Sulphridge, Banister Sulphridge, Clint Sulphridge (con't on a separate page) Eliga Sulphridge, A.J. Calahan, Samuel Hodge, Jake Hyder, Ernie(?) Musgrove, Geo. Lyons, John Right, Samuel Hunter, John Cole, Samuel Hodge, John Baker, Murry Lafyerd, Nathaniel Gorley, Lafeatt Kinder, Green Boatman, Geo. Maston, John Boseman, Mark Hudgison, McCaniel Collins, Clint Carter, James Burkett, James Feuget, James Dovison, Will Mooney, Ben Mooney, Lenord Bea Marytt, Thomas Marytt
34. into Ky to raid Scott. We drive Scott out of Ky back into Tenn. Then we returned to camp.
35. A short time. The Scott raid.
26. The Scott raid.
37. After the Scott raid our next place was Cumberland Gap. We went up on the north side of the gap under Jeneral De Coursey. De Coursey had no orders to make that move so he was arrested for disobeying orders and put under guard. There was other regiments of Union soldiers on the South side of the gap which the rebels surrendered to without battle. The next was Kings Port under Jeneral Alvin C. Gillen. We captured the principal port of the rebel army. The next ingagements was at Bluntvill. (con't on 3 separate pages) Tenn. We captured the principal port of the army and burned the town. We burned the town in order to drive the rebels out from Bluntville to Bristol Va. picket fighting at Saltworks Va captured it, spiked two of the wells and burned the buildings. from Saltworks to Abbington picket fighting. From Abbington to Maryon. Ingaged in an all day fight. Drove the enemy through Withville Va captured a great many prisoners and several pieces of artilery. The rebels ingaged us on the west of Withful. We captured their two largest guns "Lady Buckner and Lady Breckenridge" then we returned to Knoxville. and went into winter quarters in the month of Dec '63. While in regular camps we had plenty to eat plenty to wear and good treatment, but when we were on raids, as we were most of the time, we suffered untold agony from cold and exposure. There were several hundred of the soldiers feet froze and had to be amputated. In the spring we left Knoxville to make a raid in Va. NC SC and Ga. We had a regualr

107

ROACH (cont'd.):

battle at Saulsbury which lasted about 8 hours. We captured about
eight hundred and distroyed the most of the town by fire. The
remainder of our fighting in Va NC SC and Ga was of a short duration
We went back to Tenn Lon St. beseiged us at Knox. which lasted
eighteen days. Our sufferings were great but we saved the town. Our
next pitch battle was at Morristown Tenn. which lasted about four
hours. We defeated the enemy captured about four hundred prisoners
and killed eighty-seven. We lost six dead and twenty two wounded.
We went from there to Bulls Gap and there we ingaged in an all day
battle in which we were defeated and retreated to Morristown. there
we made a stand. we met with defeat. The loss in life was small
but we lost most of our artilery and our provision wagon. we
retreated on to Knoxville. in forty eight hours after reaching Knox.
we were called to battle at Straw-berry Planes, which lasted a short
while with defeat for the enemy.
A sketch of our marches during the war = Starting from Strawberry
Planes and ending at Knoxville where I was mustered our of service.
The Regiment in its various marches and counter marches traveled
three thousands three hundred and twenty three miles, less than
fifty miles of this distance by rail, the balance except from Strawberry Planes to Camp Nelson, a distance of 170 miles, which was
traveled on foot, was on horseback. We crossed seventeen large size
rivers and streams including the Holston or Tennessee, the Cumberland,
Watauga, New River, Yadkin, Savannah, Calawba Clinch and Kentucky
besides innumerable small rivers and streams We passed through the
following states or some parts of them Tenn Ky Va NC SC and Ga. We
passed through more than fifty towns cities and villages, among these
were the following; Lexington, Danville, Lebanon, Lancaster, Barbours-
ville, Loudon, Crab Orchard Nicholasville and other towns in Kentucky.
Nashville, Gallatin, Lebanon, Sparta, Kingston, Knoxville, New Market,
Mossy Creek (Jefferson City) Morristown, Russellville, Rogersville,
Rutledge, Tazewill Kingsport Blountsville, Bristol, Greenville,
Rheatown, Jonesboro, Zolli Coffer (Bluff City), Elizabethton, and
Taylorsville (Mountain City) Tennessee; Estelville, Abington, Marion,
Witheville, Hillsvill, and Taylorsville in Virginia; Ashville,
Hendersonville, Marion, Rutherford, Morgantown, Willksboro, Mount
Airy, Saulsbury, Statesville and other smaller town in North Carolina
Greenville Anderson in South Carolina and Washington Milledgevill,
Grensboro, Athens and other towns in Georgia
We crossed and recrossed the various ranges of the Alleghene Mountains
the Cumberland, ___aka and Smokey Yellow, Iron, Clinch, Stone and
Blue Ridge and a great many more to numerous to mention.

I might mention that in the beseige at Knoxville that Sherman came
by the way of Chattanoog to our aid.

38. Knoxville Tenn Nov 11 '65
39. I walked from Noxville to my home which was about 33 mile
40. farming
41. Farming Grainger Co Tenn I have been a member of the Baptist Church
    ever since Dec '65. D. shierfand Con. (?)
42. Alferd Roach; Tampaco Tenn; Grainger; Tennessee; Tampico; ----
43. Mary Ann Cullifer; Benn Cullifer; Elizabeth Cullifer; Tampico,
    Grainger Co. Tenn.
44. my ancestors are from Hallon (Holland?)

ROBERTS, WILLIAM

FORM NO. 1

1. William Roberts   Rl Greeneville Tenn
2. 85 year old April the 10 1922
3. Madison County NC
4. Greene County Tenn
5. farming and Black smith
6. farmer
7. I did not own property before I enlisted in the federal army
8. none
9. 150

ROBERTS (cont'd.):
10. their land was worth about five dollars per acre
11. a log house with 2 rooms
12. I plowed hoed done all kind of farm work
13. my father worked on the farm my mother cooked and did general house work.
14. no
15. yes
16. yes
17. the white men that owned slaves did not do much work them that had no slaves did honest work.
18. yes the men that owned slaves felt themselves better than the non slave holder never had no dealings with them only on business.
19. no
20. the slave holders seemed to be above the non slave holder
21. ----
22. not much
23. discouraged
24. private school
25. about 3 weeks I was a bound boy had no chance for school
26. one half mile
27. subscription schools
28. private
29. 3 months
30. yes very well
31. a man
32. I enlisted 11 day of June 1863 at Indianapolis Ind. Co D 6 Ind
33. John Green it has been so long and I am so forgetful I caint remember anymore
34. to Kentucky then to Tenn then to Ga
35. I caint remember
36. at Dalton Ga we had a fight ever day from Dalton to Atlanta
37. I had _____ to eat but I was exposed to the cold and wet day and night
38. at Indianapolis Ind Aug the 31 1865
39. ----
40. Black Smithing
41. lived in Greene Co Tenn most ever since the war was a blacksmith until I got to feeble to work.
42. Jessie Roberts; ----; Maidison; NC; near Marshall NC; ----
43. Anna Finny; caint remember; ----; ----
44. I was bound out when young caint remember so much about my people only I know my parents come from England and settle in North Carlina.

(on a separate page)
37. cont. Battle southe of Nashville the 16 of December, was take to nashville kept there two weeks. sente to Camp Chace at Columbus Ohio was in priso ther two months the carryed too Baltimore then down Chespeek bay to Point lookout from ther up James River to Richman Va was kept ther utell 10 of march 1865 as to how I faired duerg the war it was tough the most of the time never had a regular unifor of cloths; after the battle of Shilo had to ware any thing I could get in war wether could make out with any kind of clothes, but winter it was tough; the last two years we had to sleep on the ground and take the wether as it come, as to what we had for rashing it was Corn Bread and pore Beff but wee live thrue the war. have lived very well since.
41. cont. I have bin associattions bin withe Baptis

ROBINSON, WILLIAM

FORM NO. 1

1. William Robinson; Buenavista Carroll Co Tenn
2. 83 year the 7th of last March
3. Tenn Carroll Co
4. Tenn Carroll Co
5. Farmer
6. Farmer

109

ROBINSON (cont'd.):
7. I ond 2 hed of mules an 1 Cow an Hogg in all in all a bout 7 seven hundredd Dollars
8. No
9. 240 Acres
10. About 4000 thousen Dollars
11. Log 2 Room
12. I worked at all sort of Farm work.
13. Farmed Mi Mothe Dide when I was small boy But mi fathe Married the 2 Time she Dun the work of the Clening up of the Hous and maid cloth for the use of the Family.
14. No
15. yes
16. yes
17. They _____ Dun ther one Laber
18. ther was but very few men ond slavies in our Neighberhood they was sociable with good citisons.
19. I suppose so.
20. I think so
21. I think not
22. the oportunitys was bad.
23. they was in curreged by all good citizens
24. I atinded Free schools
25. O i guess 24 month
26. 1 Mile
27. Free schools
28. Public
29. a bout 2½ months a year
30. Risionabl well
31. Man
32. I inlisted in the Fedrel army Jan the 1st 1865 at Padch Ky
33. 7 Tenn Cav under Col Hawkins Comorid James Smdhus
   T.J. Norwood
   I Can not call to memery all the Boys
34. we was stationed at Paducky Ky
35. we was not in ay Regular gagement was in sevral scurmishes
36. all redy answered
37. we was on scout the most of the time We lived in ____ good warm close had plenty to was subject to Diseas I was in hospitle a bout two weeks well caird for.
38. Nashville Tenn on Aug the 14th 1865
39. I went home on Frait Car
40. Farming
41. I have Farmed livd in Carroll Co Tenn I am a Locle Preacher in ME Church south
42. Thomas F. Robinson; Dont no; ----; ----; ----; ----
43. Susaner Smothers; Jacob Smothers; Nancy Smothers; in Carroll Co Tenn
44. yours
                    William M. Robinson
                    Beaunavistu Tenn
                    Rl

                SHELTON, GEORGE W.

FORM NO. 2

1. George W. Shelton; Linden Tenn Box 14
2. 78 years
3. Williamson Co Tenn
4. Federal soldier
5. Co G; 2 Tenn Mounted Infantry
6. Farmer & stone and Brick Mason
7. Washington Shelton; I Don't know; ----; ----; ----; ----
8. Mary M. Fields; ----; ----; ----
9. ----
10. I Didint own any Property at the Begining of the War
11. My Parents owned 18 slaves
12. about 250 acres
13. abot thirty thousand dollars

110

SHELTON (cont'd.):
14. huld log house 4 Rooms
15. I Plowed hoed and other simerlar work on the farm
16. My Father worked at his trad such as making Brick Buildin Building houses and Chimneys My Mother done the house work.
17. yes 2 one to do the cooking one to tak care of the children
18. Hauling was done with oxens.
19. yes
20. they done their own work
21. yes if they Respectable men
22. I suppose so
23. not that I knew of
24. No some of our officers dident own slaves
25. yes
26. no
27. Jus common subscription schools
28. I dont remember
29. one Mile
30. Just common subscription schools
31. Private any Body Could that Paid to go
32. 3 or 4
33. yes
34. Man
35. I enlisted the Federal army at Linden Tenn
36. Clifton Tenn
37. I dont remember
38. Clifton Tenn
39. ----
40. Nashville tenn
41. i went from tenn to Johnsonville tenn on the NC RR from there to Perryville by Boat from there to Linden tenn to my home
42. farming
43. ----
44. ----
45. ----
46. ----

SHELTON, MARK

FORM NO. 1

1. Mark Shelton; Tate Tenn
2. 81 years
3. Tenssee Claborne Country
4. State Tenessee Claborne Country
5. Farming
6. Farming
7. none
8. none
9. 20 or 25
10. $500
11. Log caben 2 room
12. I plowed. Hoe corn and done any kind of work had to be done on farm
13. Farm. Mother cook spin wove
14. none
15. any kind of work was honrable in my day
16. yes
17. Ever Body in olden days done ther own work. no hiring done
18. no they was as any other People.
19. yes we all mix as one
20. we was all as good to each other. no high brown we all was common people.
21. no
22. yes fairley good in some part of country.
23. no slave holder try to keep them
24. Chabone country school
25. about 3 years
26. 2 miles
27. civil school

111

SHELTON (cont'd.):
28. Public school
29. about one month in year and some 3 week
30. yes as long as it lasted
31. man
32. I enlist month July 16 1862 federal first tenessee calvary Co H
33. ----
34. Nashville Tenessee
35. about one hoer
36. Cumberland Gap Tenessee
37. Pine Mountain Ky next Battle Midden Tenesse. one charge right after anthe ever day. live in camp 3 years.   chothe and good chothe We sleep out door all time hardy ever in house expose to cold night day. Pretty good eating we need sontig (something?) eat Could get it
38. Nashville Tenessee
39. I walk all way from Nashville 3 hundred miles part time ? parts hungry. and sleep out side all time
40. farm
41. no offices no Business I have not been able to hold big job my Educate was good enought.
42. Ralph Shelton; Clabone County; Claben contry; Tenessee; Clabone Count; ----
43. Anna (?) Taylor; Tom Taylor; Mollie Johnson; ----
44. ----
45. ----

SHERWOOD, ISAAC R.

FORM NO. 1

(Microfilm was a very poor job. One complete page missing; all others cut off.)
1. Isaac R. Sherwood; Washington DC
2. was 86 Aug 13, 1921
3. Dutchess Co New York
4. Williams Co Ohio
5. Journalist
6. Farmer
7. owned house and lot and printing press at Bryan Ohio
8. ----
9. 200 acres
10. $6000.
11. ----
12. Worked on farm until 17 years old
13. (page cut or town. Questions 13-33 missing)
34. West Virginia
35. 60 days
36. Philippi W Va
37. After 1st 3 month service reinlisted for 3 years on during the war in another Regiment. Was made 1st Lt then adjutant; then Major, then Lt Col. then Colonel, then Brevet Brig General - was in 42 battles.
38. ----
39. ----
40. Editorial work and politics
41. Since the war have been 28 years in public life, as Major Secretary of State 7 years as Judge 16 years in Congress.
42. (part of question 41 answered in spaces provided for name of father. No information on father)
43. Maria Geomans (Flowers?); ----; ----
    (the rest of this page is cutt off)
(on a separate sheet of paper)
      Letterhead: Cable Address "Conghall"
                               Congress Hall
                               American and European
                               S.A. Manuel, Pres & Gen'l Mgr.
                               Washington, D.C.
                               Feb 7 - 1922

SHERWOOD (cont'd.):
Dear Friend Moore,
  Glad to get your letter and to know that you and your wife are
still alert and worth while.
  The beautiful poen my wife wrote on Albert   Johnson I will
try and find when I go home to Toledo Ohio early in March. I remember my visit to your home and the pleasure it gave me. Among my
best and most frequent memories. That was a great day at Franklin?
No 30th 1914. Best regards to your wife.
                          Truly your friends,
                          Isaac R. Sherwood

                    SUPPLEMENTARY STATEMENT
                 by First Lieutenant John M. Woodruff

First Lieutenant John M. Woodruff, of Co. D, 111th O.V.I., who was
so severly wounded in the charge made by the regiment at Peach Tree
Creek, Ga. July 20th, 1864 makes an interesting addition to the
heroics of the 111th O.V.I., in the following;

                          Fostoria, O., Nov. 12, 1907
To the Surviving Comrades of the 111th O.V.I.:
  In the intersting Sovenir pamphlet issued to the "old boys" at
our last reunion, October first, two important engagements are
omitted which we participated. I refer to Lost Mountain, at the
right of Kenesaw, and Jonesboro, Georgia. This makes the battle
list of our regiment 42, instead of 40, as printed in the Historic
Sovenir.
  It is now over 42 years since the war closed, and before we are
all gathered to Abraham's bosom, let us ask what Ohio soldier holds
the record of that great conflict for long and arduous service.
  April 16, 1861, Isaac R. Sherwood, then Probate Judge of Williams
County, and Mayor of Bryan, enlisted as a private soldier in Company
C, 14th O.V.I., at $11 a month; started with a gun in the ranks,
participating in three of the first battles of the war- Philippi,
Cheat River and Carricks Ford- serving four months for $44.00. Then
he jumped through ten grades to Brigadier General. Private Sherwood
had no friends in court at Washington, and the movement that caused
President Lincoln to endow him with the Stars came from his comrades
in arms.
  The reason why President Lincoln made our Colonel a Brigadier is
found in the following lucid papers, prepared by the officers and
soldiers of the 111th O.V.I. at Nashville, Tenn., December 4th, 1864,
four days after the battle of Franklin;

                    "Nashville, Tenn., Dec 4, 1864.

To President Lincoln:
  Lieutenant Colonel Sherwood has proved himself one of the most
gallant, daring and efficient officers of the army. It has been the
good fortune of the regiment to be led by him in every engagement in
which we have participated since we entered the field, and the cool,
determined bravery displayed by him on every occasion, particularly
that on the bloody field of Rasaca and the terrible struggle at
Franklin, is an example worthy the emulation of all true soldiers."
  The above testimonial was signed by every officer of the 111th
Ohio then alive and present, also by the line officers of the Brigade;
was endorsed by every regimental officer of the Second Brigade,
Second Division, Twenty-Third Corps; recommended by Major General
Schofield commanding the army, and forwarded to Washington. On
February 26th, 1865, President Lincoln made our Colonel a Brigadier
General by BRevet.
  What I would like to know is this, what soldier of the war has a
record more remarkable?
  What other Ohio soldier went out as a private, served four months
as a private, carring a gun, and ended up four years' career at the
front including forty-five battles and one hundred and forty-four
days under fire, coming home with the stars of a Brigadier?
  Would like to hear from the admirers and historians of all the

                              113

SHERWOOD (cont'd.):
    colonels and brigadiers and majors, captains and corporals of Ohio
    on this proposition.
                                    John M. Woodruff

From the Toledo Blade, Toledo, OH Monday, August 13, 1923:

                        (Picture of IRS)

                        General Sherwood
                        In Fighting Trim
                        On 88th Birthday

    Brigadier General Isaac R. Sherwood is 88 years young today!
    This fine old gentleman, present representative of the Ninth Ohio
District in congress, unchanged health, appearance and activity in
several years, chose Toledo and the Grand Circuit races, his favorite
sport, as the places of celebration.
    Mr. Sherwood reported Monday that he is feeling like a "fighting
cock" and all set to honor Toledo with his presence for many years
to come.
    Seated in his favorite chair in his home in the Scottwood apart-
ments Monday morning, Mr. Sherwood enjoyed the early hours of his
88th birthday receiving the telephone and personal calls of his
friends and opening the scores of letters and telegrams of "best
wishes" from friends throughout the United States.
                    Receives Many Messages
    Many telegrams and other messages of congratulations, bearing the
official stamps of the United States government continued to arrive
at the Sherwood apartment throughout the morning. They were from
his congressional friends at the capitol where Toledo's represent-
ative has spent so many years of his life. No one forgot him.
    One of the most pleasing birthday presents Mr. Sherwood received
in the mail Monday, he announced, was a letter froma publishing
company that it was about to publish the letters, written by
General Sherwood and printed in the Blade, in book form.
    A day of entertainment has been planned for the genral. Monday
afternoon he was the honored guest at a box party at the Grand
Circuit races. He occupied the honored seat in a box beautifully
decorated with American flags and red, white and blue bunting.
                    To Be Banquet Guest
    Mr. Sherwood will be the guest of honor at a banquet in the Elks'
Club Monday evening. The table, set for 25, will be decorated with
the colors of Old Glory and alarge birthday cake will grace the
center of the table.
    The cake around which 88 small American flags will be decorated
will have an icing of red, white and blue flowers. The place cards
will be small American flags.
    Oliver S. Bond, of the Merchants and Clerks' bank, will be one of
the guests at the dinner. Mr. Bond has attended a birthday dinner
for Mr. Sherwood every year for several years. Mr. Bond and Mr.
Sherwood have been life-long friends. The general, while secretary
of state of Ohio, issued the charter for Mr. Bond's bank.
    Isaac R. Sherwood was born Aug. 13, 1835. He was educated at
Antioch college and at the Ohio Law school in Cleveland. His career,
both in military and civil life, has been a most distinguished one.
                    Joins Army in 1861
    He entered the army April 18, 1861 and served in West Virginia
as a private for four months.
    He was commissioned First Lieutenant in the Eleventh Ohio Volun-
teer Infantry and then was appointed adjutant which postion he filled
during the Beull campaign in Kentucky. He received the appointment
of major early in 1863 and participated in Morgans' campaign as well
as that of East Tennessee.
    A year later he was appointed Lieutenant Colonel. He fought in
a number of famous battles of the Civil War including those of Resaca,
Burnt Hickory, Pine Mountain, Lost Mountain, Kenesaw Mountain, Peach
Tree Creek, Atlanta and Duck River.
                            114

SHERWOOD (cont'd.):
"For gallant and meritorious services" in the battle of Resaca he
was promoted to the rank of brigadier-general of volunteers to date
from Feb. 27, 1865. At the close of the war, he resigned his commission and left the service.
Service as Civilian
Since that time Mr. Sherwood has held a number of responsible
positions in civil life. He was secretary of state of Ohio from
1869 to 1873, and was a member of the forty-third congress, from the
Sixth Ohio District. He was elected to the Sixtieth congress and up
to the presnt time has held office almost continually. His most
recent election to this position was in 1922 when he defeated
Congressman Chalmers for re-election.

Speech of Honorable Isaac R. Sherwood on "The Horse in all Civilization"
from 4 Mar 1915 pages 1-5 (incl) and pg 8.

SHRADER, SAMUEL

FORM NO. 1

1. Samuel Shrader; Dandridge Tenn. R.4
2. 77 yrs 9 mo 17 days
3. Cold County Missouri
4. Sevier County, State of Tennessee
5. Farming
6. Carpenter, Shoe-maker, and farmer
7. I did not own any property at the opening of the war.
8. my parents did not own any slaves
9. 75 acres
10. Three horses about $300; cattle 5 about $100; land about $400; total
    about $800.
11. Log house and had two rooms
12. I plowed, hoed, chopped and grubbed on my father farm.
13. My father made shoes during the winter months. During the summer
    he farmed and worked at the carpenter trade some. My mother and
    sisters did the cooking, spinning, weaving and sewing.
14. No
15. It was regarded as respectable and honorable
16. Everybody worked in our community.
17. There were no such men in my community that I knew of.
18. I did not know very many but what few I did know were just the same
    in actions as those who did not own any slaves.
19. Those that I knew mingle freely with the non-slaveholders.
20. There was a friendly feeling both. Those that I knew were kind and
    clever.
21. I never knew a slaveholder to run for any office.
22. The opportunities were medium; a boy might get a start by raising
    stock and selling the.
23. There were only three slaveholders in our neighborhood and we could
    not tell any difference in them and the non-slaveholders. They were
    encouraged.
24. I attended subscription schools, my parents paid $1 per months for
    each schoolar. During my last school days I attended public school
    run by the co. about 2 mo.
25. I went to school about six months in all.
26. about one and a half miles
27. Subscription schools
28. For the public
29. about three months
30. They did
31. man
32. I enlisted for the Federal Gov. Sept. 13, 1863 at Knoxville, Tenn.
33. My regiment was the 9th Tenn Cavalry, Company F.
    The following soldiers are dead;
    Capt J B Sharp, Lieutenant Cyrene Mott, 2nd Lieu. John Layman,
    R.M. Henderson, Sim Layman, S.A. Byrd, Jake Byrd, Mike Byrd, Wm.
    A. Byrd, Harry Hicks, Tip Gillen, Peter V. Folden, Tip Franklin, Wm.
    Rickard, Press Hill, Bill Hill, Wm. Newman, Tom Walker, Tom Brinner

SHRADER (cont'd.):

Rote Brinner, James Hartley, Wash Shrader, Cris Shrader, Arnold Ailey, Harrison Ailey, Wm Miller, John Allen, John Patterson, Lewis Reneau, (on a separate page)
2nd page Q. 33 James Gadys, Col. John Moore, Ben Langston, Ransom Mooneyham, Ransom Cross, Granville Kite, Henry Thomas;
The following are living;
John Sartin, Dave Sartin, Chas. Lisenbee, Moses Miller, Jim Byrd, Julius A. Justus
The following are dear or alive I do not know;
Jake Milliford, Geo Johnston, Jake Reneau, Bill Weeks, Albert (?) Yarberry, John Weeks

34. after enlistment at Knoxville we were then sent to Nashville Tenn.
35. In about a month after we enlisted there was a battle at Knoxville Tenn where we were but we were not in the thickest of the battle.
36. after the seige of Knoxville the first was at Sparty Tenn.
37. From Sparty we went to Knoxville then on to Strawberry Plains and spent the night there went on up the R.R. track to Morristown where we had a battle which lasted about about 2 hours. We captured most everything the enemy had. We then went to Bulls Gap where we fought for three days and nights. There I stood on picket for three days and nights without anything to eat or any sleep or rest.
(on a separate page)
3d page Ques 37. Next we went to Greenville where a part of us had a little skirmish. Then to the Watauga River where we had another skirmish. We prowled around there awhile and heard of John Morgan coming and we started to meet him and met him at Greenville where we had a pretty severe battle in which John Morgan was killed. Then we came on to Knoxville but was ordered immediately back. We then had another at Bulls Gap where the rebels got the best of us. Got two of our cannons. From here we again went to Knoxville. Just at the time we were ready to leave here I took sick and was sent to the hospital. I had fever at first I didn't get very much care. I then got so sick they began to wait on me pretty well. The hospital was a tent, we lay on a cottonseed bunk, after I began to eat our food was good. I was there two months. I then went to the camp just outside Knoxville. I fared pretty well while at camp. Then we began to march up and down the R.R. track, stayed around Rogersville about a week or two. Then we went down to Sweetwater, Lenoir Station Loudon and around there then back to Knoxville and stayed around there until we were mustered out. I was in several battles and skirmishes and only one time were we whipped and had to retreat. My clothes were good all during the war. So long as we were along the R.R. track we had plenty to eat but when we were back it was rough. We slept on the ground where ever night came over us.
38. I was discharged Sept. 11, 1865 at Knoxville Tenn.
39. I was mustered out only about 50 mi from home. we started early in the morning walking. on our way we met a boy and he took us in his buggy about 8 mi toward home. We then walked in home by sundown of the same day.
40. I took up farming when I got home.
41. Have followed farming since the war lived in Sevier Co. then moved to Jefferson Co. where have lived ever since.
(on separate page)
Ques 41. I have been a member of the Methodist Episcopal Church for fifty years. When I first bought my farm here there was no church or school close so I, with the help of a few of the neighbors built a school house on my farm, and it served as a church and school house both. a few years later we built a nice Methodist Church. I was class leader and held class meeting regular as long as I was able. I had one son who served in the "World War" in the navy, for nearly two years. He came out safe and sound as I did.
42. Henry Shrader; Sevier Co Tenn; Sevier; Tenn; Fairgarden in Sevier Co.;
----
43. Elizabeth Barnhart, Conard Barnhart; Evasoul Barnhart; Fairgarden in Sevier Co.
44. Christopher Shrader, my grandfather was born in Germany, came to Va while young lived in Withe Co Va then came to Sevier Co Tenn and took up land. Christopher Shrader joined the war of 1812 and went as far as Lookout Mts. and camped, but the war ended and he

SHRADER (cont'd.):
```
     never had to fight.
     Moses Miller              Dandridge  Tenn R4
     Harrison Williams         Dandridge  Tenn R4
     Jake Williford            Jefferson City  Tenn R3
     Jim Byrd                  Sevierville  Tenn R11
     Ace Layman                Newport  Tenn
     Nip Reneau                Dandridge  Tenn
     John Brimmer              Dandridge  Tenn R7
     Cam Fox                   Dandridge  Tenn
```

SMART, CHARLES HENRY

FORM NO. 2

1. Charles Henry Smart, 319 7th Ave N., Nashville Tenn
2. 77 years
3. Walpole, Cheshire Co., N.H.
4. Federal
5. C 1st Battalion; 13th US Infantry
6. Bricklayer and Plasterer
7. Harrison Gray Smart; Skipton; ----; Lower Canada while my parents
    were sojourning there; Walepole, N.H.; Garnavills(?) Iowa, New
    Albin Iowa
8. Emily Agusta Guild; Samuel Guild; Sarah-Smith-Guild (S.H. Guild
    marked over; written above it:) Annie Hoadley Guild; Bellows Falls,
    Vt.
9. Can give nothing
10. ----
11. No
12. ----
13. House & town lots -- about $1500.00
14. Frame house. Five rooms.
15. up to 12 years of age did light work on farm & afterwards worked in
    printing office
16. See answer to No 6. My mother simply did housework.
17. One servant - off and on
18. yes
19. yes
20. No per cent that I knew of - everybody worked
21. Slaves not owned in our state.
22. See No 21
23. See No 21
24. See No 21
25. yes
26. See No 21
27. Country school & High school
28. about five years
29. quarter of a mile
30. See no. 27
31. Public
32. about 8 months
33. yes
34. Sometimes man - at others woman
35. Nov. 1. 1861. at Dubugore(?) Iowa
36. Newport Ky (Reco____ at Jefferson Berricke(?); went to Alton. Ill, &
    guarded Confederate Prisoners & then went to Newport.
37. A little over a year.
38. Chickasaw Bayou Miss
39. Arkansas Post, Ark.; Champion Hills, Miss.; Black River, Miss.:
    Charge of May 19 1863 at Vicksburg, and during the siege; Missionary
    Ridge, Tenn; Nashville Tenn.
    Clothed well, fed well, slept well. Never in hospital
40. St. Louis, Mo., Feb. 13. 1867
41. Was at Nashville where I have since resided, discharge sent to me
    from St Louis Mo.
42. Printing business
43. Sketch alread sent to you.
44. ----

SMART (cont'd.):
45. Not deeming that the department needs a roster of this regiment, as
    it is not a Tennessee organization. I omit names, though I have a
    list of the members of my company as of July 31. 1863.
46. ----

SMELCER, NEWTON

FORM NO. 1

1. Newton Smelcer; Greenville Tennessee
2. (80)
3. Greene Co. Tennessee
4. Greene Co. Tennessee
5. Farming
6. Farmer & House carpenter
7. owned one mule. value $125.
8. no
9. 3
10. $300
11. Log house   five rooms
12. all kinds of gernal frarm work plowing corn. cradling wheat diging
    potatoes.
13. Father followed his trade as house carpenter. Mother a invalid as
    far as can remember. sister older than me did the house work.
14. none
15. alway has been respectable in east Tennessee.
16. about all the kind of men there were
17. a veary few of that kind always more or less dead beat than any
    country.
18. all the same
19. They always appeared to be all the same.
20. No all frindly
21. All went together worked to gogether
22. I was about as poor as any of them and saved up enough to buy three
    hundred acres of land.
23. This question is answerd   above
24. Private school
25. 2 years
26. 2 mi
27. Private school. Taught by any man that could get as many as twenty
    one scholars subscribe a little money left in Co. treasure after
    expenses were paid a little left divided out among the _____.
28. Private
29. gereal about five
30. some times did and dident
31. man
32. I inlisted Louisville Ky. year 1862. month Dec.
33. First Tennessee Calvery   Col. Johnson, Henry G. Flga, Cap. Co. E.
34. went to Nashville
35. 3 months after at poplar grove Tennessee
36. Poplar Grove
37. Amont the first was sent to hospital no first June then returned to
    my reigment wenchester from there our campain went through the
    mountains to the battle Chickimogge on the whelard raid through
    Tennessee and Alabama back to winchester Tennessee with a little
    _____ then to sparty Tennessee among camp. person and his grillars.
38. at Nashville Tennessee
39. my trip home was in a stock car
40. farming   as best I could being wounden and broke down in health.
41. Joined the protison Methodist Church have tried to live a constince
    member of the same married me a nice little wife raised 5 boy and
    2 girls.
42. James Smelcer; Greene Co Tennessee; Greene; Tennessee; Caney Branch
    Tennessee; None;
43. Annie Freeman; John Freeman; Polly Lauderdale; Greene Co. Tennessee
44. Great Grand Father Lauderdale John a soldier Inn the Indian war I
    being the first soldier of any wars we hav any record of many serve
    in the civil war under the old flag.

SMITH, JAMES M.

FORM NO. 1

1. James M. Smith; P.O. Yuma Tenn Route #1
2. 78 years
3. State of Mississippi County of Tippa
4. I lived in the state of Tennessee County of Carroll
5. Farming
6. Farming
7. I did not own any property. I was young I was about 19 years of age.
8. none
9. about 400 acres
10. The land was worth about $4500. He owned horses, cows & Hogs aplenty worth $500 anyway.
11. Log house weatherboarded and criled two log rooms this way & two rooms framed. Five rooms in all.
12. I did both in the general run of making a crop.
13. He did general farm work - plowing & hoeing. My mother cooked, spun, weaved & did other general house work.
14. My Father kept one hired hand.
15. Yes it was considered honorable.
16. Yes
17. To no extent in my settlement.
18. I could not see any difference.
19. Yes. They did.
20. I did not observe any ill feeling.
21. I dont think it did.
22. They were
23. I dont know that they were incouraged or disincouraged.
24. I attended free schools which ran about three month in a year.
25. During about 12 years of my life.
26. 1½ miles
27. Just the country free school.
28. Public
29. 3 months
30. The best I remember I think they did.
31. The Teacher was a man.
32. 1862 August 5, Clarksburg, Carroll Co. Tenn.
33. 7th Tenn Regiment. H.S. Brandon; J.D. Brandon, Scott Pinkley, George Johnson are all I remember now, but I know them all then.
34. Trenton, Tenn.
35. About three month
36. Battle at Lexington, Tenn.
37. I went back to Trenton, Tenn. we had a scrumish next day and were captured and paroled. We went to Camp Chase Ohio we fared all right there and had plenty of good clothes. we slept on bunks in houses. we were warm and comfortable. Plenty to eat of ordinary food. We were exposed to small pox some took it but some did not. I was in hospital at Camp Chase
    (cont'd. on separate page)
    Ques. 37. When I left Camp Chase I went to Louisville, Ky, to a hospital. I was suffering with Typhoid Fever. When I got up I came home.
38. Oct. 25, 1863. At La Grange, Tenn.
39. As I stated in answer no. 37. I was sick at Louisville, Ky. when the officers at La Grange discharged me on account of sickness. and when I got able I got on a steamboat at Louisville, Ky. and boated to Paducah where I got a horse and rode home.
40. I went back to the old home to my mother and brothers & sisters and went to farming again.
41. I farmed some and then worked in the merchantile business I have been Justice of the Peace & County Judge. I am member of the M.C. Church (South)
    (on a separate page)
    Ques. 41.   I have lived in Henderson & Carroll counties.
42. Charles Bird Smith; ----; ----; North Carolina; He lived in North Carolina, Mississippi & Tenn.
43. Sarah A. Bridges; Francis Bridges; ----; Somewhere in Tenn.,

SMITH (cont'd.):
44. I have given all information that I knew in the above answers.

Answers written by A.C. Bridges
(signed) James M. Smith

SPICKARD, JACOB

FORM NO. 2
1. Jacob Spickard; White Pine Tenn.
2. 91 yrs.
3. Jefferson Co. Tenn
4. Federal
5. A; 9th Tenn Cal
6. Harness maker & Tanner
7. Jacob Spickard; ----; ----; Penn.; ----; ----
8. Mary Jenkins; ----; ----; ----
9. ----
10. ----
11. No
12. ----
13. My Father & Mother were both deed before the war broke out.
14. Loghouse
15. Farmed till about 21 done all kinds of work on the farm.
16. Harness maker My mother died when is was about 1 month old
17. none
18. Yes
19. not a great deal
20. about one half
21. They did not. they seemed to think them selves better.
22. not a great deal.
23. They were friendly But the slave holders Thought they were a little better.
24. some times not often.
25. Not good.
26. The slave holders rather encouraged then They helped to build school houses and helped support the school.
27. Free school not much of that
28. about 6 months
29. about 1 mile
30. None but a little country public school.
31. Public
32. 3 months
33. some did some did not go any
34. man
35. Aug 23 - 1863 in Comberland Mountains on the line between Ky & Tenn.
36. Knoxville Tenn
37. about 3 months
38. at Knoxville just before the siege
39. we was in the siege in Knoxville. I was a black smith and was not in any battles of importance. When we was where they could get it to us we had plenty good clothing slept on the ground.
40. Nov. 11 - 1865
41. I was discharged in Knoxville about 45 miles from home and the sent us home on the train.
42. Blacksmith
43. I went to Knoxville and worked in the quarries around there at the blacksmiths trade worked in the quarry where the rock was obtained that built the Knox County jail and from there I moved to Morristown Tenn and from there to Jeff. Co near White Pine Tenn where I now live.
44. ----
45. Cop(?) Bunch(?)
    2nd Cop Haynes
    Tom York

I am so old I dont remember any names. I was Blacksmith and stayed in the waggon yards and done all the shoeing and did not have much

SPICKARD (cont'd.):
time to learn there names.
46. P.J. __itt   Morristown Tenn
    Will R̄itsell   Morristown Tenn
    Jno Sartain   White Pine Tenn
    Dave Sartain   White Pine Tenn
    Harvey Boles   White Pine Tenn
    J.L. White   White Pine Tenn
    Col. J.W. Gladding   White Pine Tenn
    A.J. Huggins   White Pine Tenn

                    SPRAGUE, EDWIN A.

FORM NO. 2

1.   Edwin A. Sprague; Gainesboro Tenn
2.   91 yr.
3.   State of New York Alegany County
4.   A Federal soldier
5.   Company. I. third West Con Calvery; 3
6.   Farmer
7.   David W. Sprague; Alegany County; ----; New York; Alfred Alegany
     County New York; ----
8.   Zadia Maraih Haliton; Josep Haliton; Mary Laura; Alegany County
9.   Grand mother Haliton was borned in New York. My Fathers Grand ma
     Boddie was borned Kindred Hook. near New York.
10. ----
11. ----
12. about 160
13. ----
14. Log house and two Rooms
15. I work by month before I went to war. for _____ on the _____in
     winter I choped.
16. my father Farmed. my Mother done Genral house work.
17. ----
18. of course respectable and Honorable
19. yes
20. ----
21. No slaves in the country
22. ----
23. ----
24. ----
25. ----
26. ----
27. just comon school
28. about 7 yr
29   ½ mile
30. ----
31. Public
32. about 6 month's
33. yes
34. Both kind's at different times
35. in May 62. Edgerton West Consion Rockey County.
36. Levenworth Cansis
37. next day
38. ----
39. Our Busness was fiting Bush Rappers and guarding trains. Big Battle
     was in 6 Oct 84 Boys Burried in one hole. Besides some they carried
     to Fort Cotl.(?). slept on the ground. in hospital 3 times.
40. duvall Bluff on White River (DuValls Bluff is in Prairie Co Ark on
     the White River)
41. went on Boat's duvall bluff down White river up Mississippi to the
     Karo Ill. from there to Chicago. to Edgerton West Consin.
42. went to Nebraska in one month and 4 days and went to Farming
43. dident have any office onery post master on the road. Just mostly
     Farmed.
44. ----
45. Captian Name   Joe Hood
     Conley   William Shook

                              121

SPRAGUE (cont'd.):

first Lutenten	Jessie Smith
Caert	John Smith
Second " " (Lieut.)	Marian record
Banster	John Ganon
first Sargant	John Janor
Jones	Ab Woodall
Another " " (Sgt.)	Marion Woodall
Sam Heart	Bolgalvy (?)
Another " " (Sgt.)	Milford Coon
John Splinn	Joe Preston
Corpial	Abe McCoon
Giorg Beirns (?)	You may find a Roster
Privates	Lekion Nebraska
pond	
David House	
Donalson	
Calvan Voman	
Lige Voman	
Saller	
Narrice (?) Brown	
Charlise Brown	
John Litny	
Joe Litny	
Jessie Green	
Dirf Springer	
Burtan Ganse	
Joe Lilley(?)	

46. ---

STAMPS, JOSEPH A.

FORM NO. 1

1. Joseph A. Stamps   Westmoreland Tenn
2. seventy seven years and 6 mo
3. Allen Co. Ky
4. Warren Co. Ky
5. Farmer and work on and help grade the Main L&N R.R. that runs from
    (on separate sheet)
    Louisville Ky. to Nashville Tenn. in the year of 1856. Also made
    trip to Nashville Tenn on the first Through train that went over the
    road. in 1856.
6. Farmer
7. did not own any farm
8. Father owned 2 slaves names Harriett & Lucy Stamps
9. 100 acres
10. Land slave $3000.00
11. Log House 2 story open Hall - 4 rooms
12. Plowed and Hoed about the same. and did all other kinds of work
    pertaining to farm work - worked just as same as the slaves
13. Father did all kinds of farm work. and in winter made shoes for all
    of the family and for a lot of the slaves. Mother carded and spun
    and made cloth for the family. and did all of the other House work.
14. 2 - Wommen slaves
15. yes we could not tell that there was any division made.
16. yes most all of them worked
17. no body idle except the real old men
18. all men seemed to be on equal basis - slave holder and non-slave
    holder. all mixed and mingled togather.
19. They did
20. All on good friendly terms
21. No They were no such
22. opportunities was not very good in my boy hood days
23. they were encouraged to make and effort for themselves.
24. a little log school house out in the woods about 16X18 ft one log
    cut out a cross one end. which served us as a window - no glass was
    in some
    (on separate page) We had a fireplace which extended about 2/3 a

122

STAMPS (cont'd.):
cross one end of the House. we had logs bursted open - with holes
bored in them. and legs put in which made our seats. We had for
a desk a plank running a long with the window. on which we done our
writing.
25. 5 or 6 mos
26. 3 miles through the woods and we had for a leader one John Read.
and, on one particular
(on separate page) time - We were going home through the woods.
and our leader stopped almost as sudden as death. and threw up his
hand which we all knew was a signal for us to stop. We all came to
a Halt. and stood there for a few minutes and our leader advanced
a little further and behold. he saw two wild Turkey gobblers fighting
in a Thicket of briers and bushes. and our leader slipped up to them
and held them until - all of the children - arrived and assisted him
in capturing his game.
27. the one that I attended was all the school that was very close.
28. Private school
29. 3 months
30. yes
31. man teacher and never known him to sit down when on duty.
32. Aug. 1863 Scottsville Ky --
33. 52nd Ky. Mt. Inf.

Jon Mitchell	Wickliff Taylor
Willis Mitchell	Alford Taylor
Harry Mitchell	Baley Wade
Tom Lee	Tom Boyd
Jno Satterfield	Joe Claypool
Rafe Lomb (?)	John Richman
Wesley Stamps	sid Williams

34. Was drilled at Scottsville Ky - about 4 mos - and was sent from there
to Franklin Ky
35. about 8 months
36. salt work of Virginia
37. We had good clothes and plenty to eat. We had very poor sleeping
quarters. Never was in prison. stayed in Jail one night for disobeying orders. _____ (?) in hospital about 6 weeks very distressing.
38. at Bowling Green Ky. Jan 17th 1865.
39. only had 5 miles to go. but was very glad to get them.
40. Farming
41. Farming is all lived in Warren Co Ky until 1872. I moved to Sumner
Co Tenn April 5th 1873 and have resided here ever since.
42. James Stamps; ----; dont know; Virginia; Allen & Warren Co Ky.;
none;
43. Rebecca Waite; Jno Waite; Anna Benedict; Allen Co Ky
44. ---
45. ---

STARBUCK, WILLIAM

FORM NO. 2

1.   William Starbuck; Linden Tenn RFD 1
2.   I will be 74 years old the 4th of Sep nex 1922.
3.   Perry County Tenn
4.   Federal
5.   E; Second Tenn Mtd. Infantry
6.   Farmer
7.   Erastus Starbuck; Linden; Perry; Tenn; Cypress Creek Farm until
Civill War in Perry Co Tenn.; he served in the 6th Tenn Cavalry.
Died at Boliver Tenn Jan 8th 1863.
8.   Marry Ann Burcham; William Burcham; Marry Garrett Burcham; Lick
Creek Perry Co. Tenn. came here from North Carlirna.
9.   my grand Father Daniel Starbuck came to Perry Co Tenn. from the New
England state & was Colonell of Malittia here before I was born:
& owen & Matthew Starbuck Belonged to the Navy under John Paul Jones
& served on the Bon home Richard was in the Battle with the Serepis.
Owen Starbuck was captian of the Battery during the Battle Jones
called out Cap Owen . . (meaning Owen Starbuck) to raise his guns

123

STARBUCK (cont'd.):

he Didnot want to sink the Brittish Ship as they had to ride on it.
Matthew Starbuck in that battle arm was shot off
(on separate pages) the kindship of Cap Owen & Matthew Starbuck to
my grand father Daniel Starbuck I can not produce the family history
as my Fathers family records was Destroyed in the civill war. Father
Erastus Starbuck & 3 Brothers was in the civill war & of the 4
Brothers only one lived through the war. they were equely Divided.
2 in the federal and 2 in the confederate army under general Price
in Jacksons war with Indians & Britch I had 2 great ucles Harris &
Allfred. Whitson. was in the Battle of horse shoe Bend & others
allso Battle of New Orleans with the Brittish
On my Mothers side my great grand Father John Burcham was a Solder
of the Revolution under Washington. 2 uncles was in civill war one
Jessie Burcham was on the federal side & Pleasant Burcham confederate
Both was in the Battle of Shiloh. I had 2 grandsons in the world
war James Starbuck went over seas allso Floid Dickson served garding
lake Canal Reenlisted on Battle Ship Tenn. P.S. This questionare
answered mostley from memory as I am the oldest of the connexion(?)
living & no Records Do Not Know what county my family came from to
America.
10. None except interest in fathers Estate was a minor.
11. None
12. About 1200 acres
13. Land about $3000. Horses & mules $1000 Cattle Notes && $1500 total
    $5500.00
14. they lived in a 2 Room log House with open Hall way.
15. i Did all kinds of farm work that I was able to do Plowing hoeing
    gruling & fensing. Did Plowing at 8 years old. & ever since except
    part of the war time.
16. My Father Did Plowing hoeing chopping cleering Fencing Makind Rails
    && My Mother Did cooking for the Family Spining weaving & Making
    Clothing & washing &&
17. Father generaly hired one white man or a Plow Boy to help in the crop
    Mother sometimes hired spining.
18. allways respectable and honorable
19. yes. was considered Disgraced if they would Not work.
20. there was But few slaves in this section seldom owend But 1 or 2
    slaves to the man. Practicaly all worked.
21. Did Not Notice any Difference in my community.
22. allways Did Except a few youngsters
23. there was a friendly feeling. So far as my observation goes. I was
    young. was born Sep 4 1848.
24. can Not answer
25. was Not good. wages was low and & few manufactures allthough land
    was cheap a man could Bye a little farm for $500 to 1500 Dollars.
26. it seames to me that worthy young men was encouraged by all.
    without regard to slaves or slaveholders.
27. verry common country schools 1 month free & 2 month Subscription
    3 months in all Beginning in July.
28. about 11 months
29. about 2 miles
30. all was Primary taught by common country teachers. whoes education
    was very limited.
31. Public & Subscription
32. in my section 3 months all Told.
33. No. the Boys had to stop school about half the time to work on the
    farm.
34. men with one exception.
35. March 25 - 1864 Federal at Linden Tenn
36. to the fort at Clifton Wayne Co Tenn
37. was Not in Big Battles we fought gueriles Mostly.
38. we was attacked at our post By Clo. Bipple & his command in fall of
    1864. My Captian Ham (Horn) was Kiled.
39. Soon after our fight our 6 Companys was ordered to #54 on the L&N
    R.R. to gard same. So I was taken down with measles about the last
    of Nov 1864 and conveyed home by frinds the Effects of whitch I
    Never Recovered. Camp life was bad we slept on Bords Leaves or hay
    whitch we could get. our grub was most of time hard Bread side
    bacon & coffee some time

124

STARBUCK (cont'd.)
40. at Washington
41. See No 39
42. Farm work
43. I've Ben a farmer all my life Bought a farm on Cypress Creek Perry
    Co Tenn 2 miles from Fathers Farm. and I and my wife are still
    living on this farm I bought in 1870. I married Nancy Jane Simmons
    in July 1865 just after the civille war closed. Never held office
    except Road sverver & Never was a candate for office in my life.
    I and wife had Boath Belong to the Christian church we have raised
    7 children live to Be grown we Now have 33 grand children and 12
    great grand children.
44. ---
45. I do not know of But one of my company living Now his Name is Jack
    hickerson address Linden Tenn
    I Doe Not Know where the Roster is my second Captian R.A. Guthrie
    has Ben Dead about 10 years he left 3 sons living in Linden Tenn they
    mite give the information of company Roster.
46. Galathiel Trull   Linden   Tenn
    Add Baston   "   "
    Jack Hickerson   "   "
    J.N. Black   "   "
    Nathan Horner   "   "

                        TAYLOR, JAMES

1. James Taylor, Buena Vista Tennessee
2. 77 this Dec 6 day 1921
3. Carroll County Tennessee
4. Obyon County Tennessee, I enlisted in Federal Army
5. assistant Black-smith and farmed some of the time.
6. carpenter by trade.
7. none
8. no
9. some town property
10. $1000.00
11. Framed House, three rooms one being up stairs.
12. what time I worked on the farm I done the actual work my self using
    plows and hoes.
13. my father was a carpenter. My Mother cooked, spun, hand wove. She
    made the clothing for the family.
14. none
15. yes with the poor class of people But not with the rich.
16. the poor class did But the welthy did not
17. The rich whites had the poor whites to do the work.
18. Slave owners did not mix with the poor very much. They proved by
    their actions that they felt their selves above the honorable men
    who did not own slaves.
19. no
20. they were rather distant, not verry friendly.
21. yes
22. slim chance
23. Discouraged
24. Subscription school, about 30 days is my full attendance. my parents
    were not able to school me.
25. 30 day
26. 5 or 6 miles
27. Subscription schools
28. Private
29. about 3 months
30. Attendance was small among the poor class
31. Man
32. I enlisted Jan 10th 1864 in the Federal army.
33. 7th Tennessee Calvary Voluntary   Private Joe McCrackin, Private
    Bill Smith, Private G.D. Taylor, Pvt. Jim Huffman, Pvt Hugh Colwell,
    Marion Hodge, J.H. Green, Rich Green, Bill Grooms, Ike Grooms, John
    Edwards, Ruth Bloodworth, James Taylor, Josh Green, Shoat Moore,
    Jim Doighty, Nelse Moore, Will Right, Jessie Neighbors, Jake Barn-
    heart, Dude Mizell, Goat Butler, Cant thank of the rest

TAYLOR (cont'd.):
34. 7th Tennessee Regiment Union City, Tenn.
35. Christmasville Tennessee Just my company out on Scout Duty. The
    Fight was in February 1864.
36. Scrumish fight, near Christmasville, Tennessee
37. I went to Union City Tenn with my regament next fight was in March
    24 - 1864. about _day(?) and surrendered about 11 a.m. all of our
    regiment being captured accept one company that was out on scout
    duty. lived in tents on the ground with blankets. food and clothing
    was good in camp. Good Treatment in Hospital, Federal. I was
    prisoner of war about 13 months and treatment was verry bad. one
    man food supply for 24 hours was about ½ what a man ordinarly has
    for one meal.
38. Nashville Tennessee Aug 9th 1865.
39. From Nashville Tenn to Johnsonville Tenn by train from Johnsonville
    Tenn to Buena Vista Tenn on a mule. From Buena Vista Tenn to old
    Molbrough Carroll County. Tenn. Still on the mule. This was my
    home.
40. Farming
41. I have farmed every year up untill two years past. Primative Baptist.
42. Jarrett Taylor; North Carolina; ----; North Carolina; ----; He
    volunteered in the Mexican war and Civil War also.
43. Emily Elizabeth Smith; Levy Smith; X; North Carolina
44. My Father was born in 1814. My Mother was born in 1810. I have
    had a hard time all of my life.

TUCKER, JOHN WESLEY

FORM NO. 1

1. Mr. John Wesley Tucker; Leach Tennessee
2. 78
3. Carroll Co. Tennessee
4. Carroll Co. Tennessee
5. Farming
6. Farming
7. I was a boy and dident own any.
8. no
9. about four hundred dollars
11. Log house one room
12. I plowed worked and hoed
13. My Father farmed My mother cooked, spun, wove and knitted.
14. No sir
15. It certainly was.
16. Yes sir
17. None were Idle as far as I know.
18. They thot them selves better to a certain extent.
19. They mixed and mingled.
20. There was a difference shown before the war, and friendly afterwards.
21. No sir
22. yes sir
23. They were encouraged.
24. Litterary rural schools.
25. about one year
26. one half mile
27. common schools
28. public
29. about three mo.
30. yes sir
31. a man
32. I enlisted in the federal army in Nov 1862 in the State of Kentucky.
33. my first Regt. was the 7th Tenn Cavalry. Hugh Mathes, Demps McMullen,
    Gim Burns, Irvin Pedue.
34. I re enlisted in Co B Illinois Cav and was sent to St. Pillar Tenn.
35. about a month
36. The Okolna in Miss.
37. I had hard service. I went to Baton Rouge Louisana after the first
    battle. The Battle of Clinton Louisana. It lasted all day. The
    Oklona lasted three days and nights. We fell back at Oklona and

126

TUCKER (cont'd.):

won at Clinton. Ft. Blakely and from Fort Blakley. was clothed
pretty well, slept very well when I did sleep in Tents. ate Potatoes
Beans, Bacon & Beef Salt Pork. In marching was exposed a great deal.
Had the Small Pox. was exposed to cold as a guard. Was in Hospital
& was well treated.

38. I was discharged at Sanantonia Texas, on the 27 of Nov. 1865.
39. I came by railroad, steam boat and hack.
40. I Farmed.
41. I farmed since the Civil War lived at Leach Tenn.
42. Robert Emerson Tucker; dont know; Lincoln; North Carolina; Huntingdon, Carroll Co. Tenn.; He was a Farmer.
43. Mary Jones Gullett; Mr. George Gullett; Dont know her full name;
near Huntingdon Tenn.
44. My Grand father name was George Washington Gullett dont know my
Grand mothers full name. He came from Delaware. Grand mother came
from England. My Grand father was in the War 1812 also my Grand
father on my mothers side.
(P.S. I was mustered out on the 27 of Nov 1865.)
In Co. C. by 2nd Ill. Cavalry. By consolidation of cos. my former
Co. was Co. B. 2nd Ill. Cav.

WALTERS, ELI T.

FORM NO. 2

1. Eli T. Walters; Jonesboro Tennessee Washington Co.
2. Seventy Four
3. Cob County. Georgia
4. Federal
5. Co. G; 1st Alabama Cav.
6. Brick Mason
7. William B. Walters; ----; ----; ----; Marshal Co. Ala; ----
8. Francis Ragsdale; ----; ----; Georgia
9. ----
10. None
11. None
12. Three Hundred & Twenty acres
13. Nine Hundred Dollars
14. Log House. Three Roms
15. I was a Farmer. and done much plowing
16. My Father was a Brick Mason my Mother Run a Loom and made clouth
and done the rest of the House work such as cooking on cts.
17. none
18. yes
19. yes
20. none
21. none
22. So Far as I know
23. They were Friendly
24. ---
25. yes
26. ---
27. public schools
28. Two years
29. Two Miles
30. Literary school
31. public
32. Six months
33. yes
34. man
35. at Decatur, Ala March 1863.
36. Moseville Ala
37. about three months
38. The Battle of Resaker, Ga
39. Next Battle of Kenasa Mountain next at White Point S. Carliona next
was in Piny Woods in N. Carliona lasted three hours and half. We
drove off the confederats. Had a tough time was clothed in uniform.
Food was scarce at Times.

127

WALTERS (cont'd.):
40. Huntsville. Ala. Nov. 1865.
41. ---
42. Farming.
43. Farming most all the time Arkansas most of the time. Belong to
    Southern Methodis Church.
44. ---
45. ---
46. ---

WARREN, LOT

FORM NO.2

1. Lot Warren; Jasper Marion County Tennessee
2. 75 year old May the 16
3. in Georgia Gilmore Co.
4. Fedrel
5. C; first Alabama and Tenn Cavrley mixt was the Ala videt
6. a famer
7. John Warren; I dont no; ----; Georgia; Bridgport Ala; he was a
    Privet solger in the Fedrl armey.
8. Frances Halaway; _____ Halaway; Saley Halaway; Lafaite Walk Co. Ga.
9. my Gand fathe Haloway was Farme When I new him he was a solger in
    the 1812 war. I nevr seen my Grandfathe one my fathe side my Grate
    Grandfathe got killed in the Old Revlushen war as I have Ben told
    at a Place that call Bunker Hill.
10. my Fathe ond land I was a Boye and hade nevr tried to have iney.
11. he ond som But not meney.
12. 180
13. 4 or 5 thousan
14. Loge house 6 Roomes But he ond a saw mill at the time the war
    Broke out it was a water mill and a sash saw.
15. I have Plow and it as what we call a Cultoonce(?) Plow and old
    ____. Have weed Bee Worth nothen now. We wood not look at it now
    the Plow wood be worthless now.
16. My Fathe worke some But thaded some my mothe and the Girl Maid cloth
    spun the thread and wove the ____ that we wove in 1858 my mothe got
    a cookin stove that was the firste stove she ____ and she cooked
    in the Fre place up until then.
17. I think 5 is about the numbr.
18. it was work seemed to onorable.
19. they did.
20. Huntin Sea and Fox hunten was Good sport item dys some Bose hutd.
21. in our countrey they seemed as there was no difernce.
22. they dide
23. Frindley
24. they wood
25. he cold Home stide 160 achers
27. incurdeg
27. Primar in a Loge House with splite out slabs for the seets.
28. one year 3 months at a time
29. 3 miles
30. we wood not call them iney now.
31. Publeck.
32. 3 to 4
33. they did
34. some men and some
35. time a woman
36. to Stevenson Ala
37. 6 weeks
38. Lookeoute Mountan
39. we was sent back to Stevenson Ala then from there Back to Chattanooga
    Tenn with confedrete Prisner to exchange and then one with Sherman
    to dalton Ga. from Dalton Ga. Back to Bridgport and from there to
    Huntsville Ala. had severe scrumsh one that live I cant tell you
    all of the Place I was.
40. at Nashville Tenn

128

WARREN (cont'd.);
41. did not hav far to come. came home ane a frait train
42. Farmer
43. i hav lived in Marian County ever since the war closed and have
    worke most of the time ane a form hav Ben in the Merchendise Bessne
    som and have Raised 6 children 4 boys and 2 Girl. I have held
    service Privtes of such as JP - sheriff I am a JP now wont say
    iney more now.
                                   Lot Warren
44. ----
45. William Blalock   John Blevens
    Ganes Bleven   Lewis Blevens
    Jack Smith   Henry Smith
    Johnson James   Will Canaley (?)
    William More   William Hawkins
    Lewis Hawkin(?)   _____ Hawkins
    George Slatan   John Slatan
    Jime Loull   nathan Baldan
    William Cogan   Graves Cogan
    Lewis Morgen   Gails(?) Adknson
    shell yenge   sam yenge
    John yenge   ham warren
    henry warren   Jim Lee

    there was 108 in the company when we were in the services But I cant
    with call all the names now I dont no of But I liven Bee side my
    self.
46. J.G. Lankster   Jasper   Tenn
    W.J. Johnson
    _____ Lewis   Jasper   Ten
    _____ Hanes (?)   sequche   Ten
    John Myars   Jasper   Ten
    J.C. Hense
    J.D. Deakins (?)   Jaspe
    A.? Weolfe   Jaspe
    I dont think of iney more to tel now I am so fogetfully I dont
    Remembr so fil Beck

                        WEAGLEY, DAVID U.

FORM NO. 2

1. David U. Weagly; Maryville
2. 79
3. Indiana County, Pennsylvania
4. Federal
5. Company E; Tenth Ohio Cavalry
6. Minister,United Brethren, and a Miller
7. Jacob Weagly; Don't Know; ----' Pennsylvania; Pennsylvania; Maryland
    and Ohio; None of these
8. Elizabeth J. Unger; George Unger; Sarah J; Pennslyvania.
9. The Ungers and Grandfather were of German descent. Grand mother was
    Irish descent.
10. No land in Tennessee. Was in Ohio at that time.
11. No
12. None here
13. Can't inform on that.
14. Log for a time; then framed. The first I remember was round logs,
    with chinks and daub.
15. common laborer
16. General work, and father a miller and preacher. Mother - general
    house work, cooking, spinning, &c.
17. none
18. Honorable as any other vocation
19. yes
20. very few
21. Did not own them
22. No - no slaves there
23. ---

                               129

WEAGLEY (cont'd.):
24. ---
25. yes
26. No slave holders
27. Public country school
28. a year about.
29. One mile
30. Public
31. Public
32. At first 3 months - afterwards to 9 months
33. yes
34. Both - sometimes one, again another
35. I enlisted in the Federal army Oct 20 1862, in Van Wert Co. Ohio -
    10 Ohio Cavalry.
36. First Cleveland, Ohio
37. 3 or 4 months
38. Don't remember which
39. I was not in prison - Was once captured but exchanged on the battle
    field. Was in quite a number of engagements, and part of the service
    was in raids.
40. July 24, 1865, near Lexington, N.C.
41. Railway
42. Carpenter
43. Went back to home at Van Wert County, Ohio, came to Tennessee 30
    years ago, first settling in McMinn County, lived there six years,
    then moved to Maryville, where I have lived ever since.
44. Met General Kilpatrick, Grant, Thomas, and other Generals of the
    Civil War.
45. ---
46. ---

WESTGATE, GEORGE WASHINGTON

FORM NO.1

1. George Washington Westgate; Linneus Mo.
2. 80 years old
3. Illinois Le Salle Co.
4. In the state of Ills - LaSalle Co.
5. Farming
6. a mason by trade until the age of 37 he then emigrated from Marietta
   Ohio to La Salle Co. Ills.
7. I owned forty acres of land valued at $400. (four hundred dollars)
   and about $300 worth of live stock.
8. none
9. 240 acres
10. about five thousand dollars
11. an eight-room brick house which was built by my father Abner D.
    Westgate.
12. I did all kinds of farm work - plowing hoeing &c.
13. All kinds of farm work including plowing hoeing fencing rail splitt-
    ing and every thing usually done on a farm. My mother did cooking,
    washing and general housework.
14. No servants but hired help for my mother.
15. All legitimate work was considered honorable.
16. most certainly
17. There were very few men belonging to the idle class. in the community
    in which I lived.
18. There were no slave holders in my community as Illinois was a free
    state.
19. yes if they chanced to meet.
20. ---
21. no slave owners in Illinois
22. very good
23. no discouragements for such young men as far as I know
24. country school
25. about 4 months each year
26. about one mile.
27. a common District school

WESTGATE (cont'd.):
28. Public
29. about four months as a rule
30. Fairly so.
31. Sometimes one and sometimes the other.
32. I enlisted in Mendota, in 61 in the month of August. (In the Federal Army)
33. 7th Illinois Cavalry. Henry Eby, Wm Orris, Jno Hill, Chas Hodge, Cap. Bartlett, Jno Shaw, Wm Christopher, Wash Eddy, Jos. Eddy, Levi Eddy, J. McKean, Geo McKean, Dan Townes, Jos. Driver, H. Dewey, Chas. Dewey, K.D. McCord, Sam McCord, David Porter, Sigh Arnes, Reed Munger, Gus Hehnstine, Chas Everette, Wm Buchan, Albert Scudder, Rube Lewis, Geo. Glenn, all these men have passed over except the three first named.
34. To Camp Butler, near Springfield I-1s.
35. We moved from Camp Butler to Birds Point, Mo. the following winter and were engaged in several skirmishes in that vacinity.
36. the Murfreesboro Battle
37. I was wounded in the battle at Murfreesboro was shot through the right arm. I was taken to a hospital in Nashville and stayed one night where it was so unpleasant that I preferred to return to the battlefield after the battle was over, Gen. Palmer under whom was an Orderly got me a Furlough and I went back to Nashville and took a boat, left Nashville in the morning and went down the river about 80 miles I think.
(on a separate page)   At this point our boat was bolted by Jos. Wheeler's forces which were making a raid inside of our lines. where he had a small Battery where he captured 9 of our boats which were loaded with wounded men who were on the way to the Louisville hospital in Kentucky. After holding us there an hour, he got all the boats together except one and   as the one boat on which he loaded all the wounded, set fire to the other boats. I then went home where I remained all winter. In the spring I returned to our command. I well remember the day after Christmas our company was an Escort for General Palmer. we left camp on the 26th of Dec. and started to take a strong hold of Murfreesboro. Gen. Palmer surrounded a Division on the extreme left of Crittenden's Corps When we got to Stone River it was about sun-down. The officers held a consultation and decided they would sleep on their arms and attack Murfreesboro in the morning. Gen Bragg with a full force attacked our right wing and drove our forces back. The noise from the fighting reached our ears and Gen. Palmer ordered his Staff officers - Simmons, and myself to change our front from the East to the South which we did and we planted 36 pieces of artillery on the Nashville and Murfreesboro Pike, which was supported by our Division. When we returned and reported to Gen. Palmer - Sharp Shooters were firing on us from the front. I was hit in my right arm but being so heavily clothed no bones were broken
(on a separate page)   Oposite a cotton field - (probably about 80 acres of land) South of this there lay a rocky, bushy stretch of land where our right wing was being driven in confusion back to where we were. The Confederates came out and reformed and charged on our Forces which were repulsed - I think - three times. The ground was litterally harrowed with grape and cannister shells and I think they were completely demorelized. The next day I was sent back to Nashville.
38. At Springfield, Ill's
39. nothing special
40. Farming and trading
41. I married in Illinois conducted a farm 1 year. sold out and came to Mo. in the year 68 - bought 280 acres of land and as there was plenty of range &
(continued on another page)   I handled a great deal of stock of all kinds. I followed buying and shipping live stock the better part of my life. I am a member of the Methodist E. Church South. My home has been in Linneus for 42 years. I was Deputy Sheriff for Lime Co. for a number of years - was also President of our Local Telephone business for about 6 years. During the time of my office as Dept. Sheriff - I captured four bank robbers who had robbed a bank at Brookfield of $5-00. I followed them with a "Possee" until

WESTGATE (cont'd.):

we captured them the 3rd day on Sheridan river near Kirksville, Mo. I brought them back to Linneus and lodged them in Jail. Court was in session and they plead guilty and were sentenced to a 25 year term in the penitnetiary. The money was all recovered except a small amount. This was done under Gov. Crittenden's administration.

42. Abner D. Westgate; ----; ----; Vermont; Marietta Ohio since boyhood; ----
43. Caroline Waterman; ----; ----; ----;
44. My father was born in the year 1799. He was a farmer and lived an uneventful life. His ideas were fine on the subject of Litigation. My parents were both American born.
(on a separate page)

Feb. 15-1922

Hon. John Trotwood Moore
Dear Sir:

Hoping that my answers to your questions will be satisfactory I submit the same to you today. I hope you will fell perfectly free to eliminate any thing I have written that you would not consider helpful in compiling your history mentioned. My wife and I were delighted to hear from you again and would be more than pleased to have you and your lovely family visit us in the near future. With kind regards to all I am Sincerely your friend.

Geo. W. Westgate

WHITAKER, TIMOTHY

FORM NO. 1

1. Timothy Whitaker; New Tazewell Tenn.
2. 82
3. Tennessee Claiborne Co.
4. Tennessee Claiborne Co
5. Farmer
6. Farmer
7. Did not own any land.
8. No
9. about 200 acres
10. $300
11. Log House 2 rooms
12. Plowed hoed cleared land & general farm work.
13. Father done general farm work. and Mother done general house work and spinning and weaving
14. None
15. yes
16. yes
17. Most people done their own work
18. Men who owned slaves always seemed to think them selves some better than People that did not own slaves.
19. Not much
20. generally friendly feeling towards each other.
21. In some cases they did
22. Verry poor chance
23. In some cases they would help them
24. Free school
25. about one year & 6 mo
26. 2 miles
27. only one Free school
28. Public
29. 2 months
30. yes
31. man
32. Flat Lick Kentucky March 1861
33. Co I 3rd Tennessee Infantry.   John Roark, Henry Poore, Bartes (?) Poore, Ike Poore, Marion Wyatt, Andy Duncan, Paroce(?) Dobbs, Bill Romsey, Mack Romsey, Jim Roark, Wiley Cox, Newt Cox
34. to Williams Burg Ky
35. about 3 months
36. Nashville Tenn.

WHITAKER (cont'd.):
37. awful Rough and verry tough Mufresborough Tenn Chattonooga Tenn.
    Resocka Ga from that Point to Atlanta Ga then back to Nashvill Ten.
    Lots of men killed and wounded. 3 years Verry good clothing on the
    ground Beef & verry Poare(?) got verry hungry went to hospital but
    did not stay went to Private home.
38. Nashville Tenn 1864
39. come from Nashville Ten to Knoxville Tn on train and walked
    Tazewell Tenn
40. Farming
41. Farming. Tazewell Tenn. Babtist Church. none.
42. Andrew Whitaker; near Tazewell Tenn; Claiborne; Tenn; Tazewell Tenn;
    ----
43. Anna Williams; ----; ----; ----
44. ---

WHITAKER, WILLIAM

FORM NO.2

1. William Whitaker; Gainesboro Tenn R2
2. 85
3. White Co Tenn
4. Federal
5. 9 cansis (?); 8
6. Farmer
7. William Whitak; ----; ----; ----; Gainesboro; ----
8. Rhodia Kinnard; ----; ----; ----
9. ---
10. ---
11. no
12. $100
13. $200.00
14. Log house on room
15. worked general farm work Plowing howing Raised corn _____
16. Father farm work Mother spining weaveing cloth for family Youse that
    being all the means by which the Family clothing.
17. no
18. yes
19. yes
20. no
21. yes
22. yes
23. yes
24. yes
25. no
26. Discouraged
27. short subscription school each fall.
28. about 12 month in all
29. 3 mile
30. subscription schools no Free school in my Boy hood days
31. Private
32. 2 to 3
33. no
34. man
35. I inlisted in 1862 in the confederat army. I inlisted at King hill
    Ark.
36. Springfield Mo.
37. Aug 10 1862
38. willson creek Geo.
39. we lived on the March on the Road in day at night we camped under
    Tents had good clothes and Plenty to Eat was exposed to cold and to
    Disease was in hospital at Kansis City Mo. staid 2 months.
40. Levonworth City(?) Cansis
41. I came to Glasco Ky on train came foot to Gainesboro Ten
42. Farming
43. I came home and one yeare after was married to Cansadie(?) Halkum(?)
    My occupation has bin farming. Got no children I am and have bin a
    Pensioner for several years and Drawing now 72 pr month. and am in

133

WHITAKER (cont'd.):
        Reasonble good Health can go any wher without youse of stick for
        which I am verry thank ful.
                            April 1 1922
                            William X (his mark) Whitaker
44. ---
45. ---
46. ---

                            WHITE, JAMES LAWSON

FORM NO.2

1. James Lawson White; White Pine Tennessee
2. 81 years
3. Carter Co Tennessee
4. Federal
5. Co g, Thirteenth Tennessee Cavalry
6. Farming
7. Richard C. White; near Elizabethtown; Carter; Tennessee; This place
    for more than 50 years; He was Circuit - Court Clerk and a Justice
    of the Peace.
8. Elizabeth Moore; Rufus Moore; Catherine Moore; in Johnson Co.
    Tennessee
9. came to this state from Virginia. aside from this know very little
    as Grandfather died before I was born and Grandmother died when I
    was very young.
10. Owned nothing.
11. Grandparents owned several but parents owned none.
12. about - 200 acres
13. Land was very cheap at that time in the Mountains and I should say
    it was worth 1000.00
14. Log house with rock chimney.
15. Farm work with plow and hoe.
16. Father worked some on farm and some at carpenter work. Mother cooked
    spun wove served washed and ironed and all other work belonging to
    the home.
17. none
18. yes
19. yes
20. none of these
21. knew no difference, all associated as equals.
22. yes
23. Friendly
24. no
25. yes - wages low but land could be bought cheaply.
26. not much attention given them in any way.
27. a very primitive school in a log cabin - with puncheon floors and
    slab seats
28. about one year
29. about 3/4 mile
30. The public school and an occasional subscription school.
31. Public
32. about Three
33. No
34. Man
35. 1863 in September at home
36. to Strawberry Plains Tenn
37. about one year
38. Lick Creek Tenn
39. Stayed in E. Tenn. one battle at Morristown one at Kingsport.
    Greenville near Johnsonvile Marion Va. Bulls Gap Tenn and other
    skirmishes. lived rough, good clothes slept on bunks, ate pork,
    bread hard tack etc. exposed to all contagious diseases in Hospital
    at Nashville for two weeks (in the right hand margin) We ate in
    addition to this beans pickles vinegar coffee and sugar when they
    could reach us.
40. September 1865 Knoxville Tenn
41. Went on freight cars to Johnson City occupying two days and walked

WHITE (cont'd.):
the remaining 25 miles.
42. Farm work.
43. Have farmed ever since war closed. lived in Carter Co. four years
after close of war. then came to Jefferson Co. to my present home.
Presbyterian Church. no office. Have raised a large family. have
7 children, 21 grandchildren 14 great grandchildren living and five
children dead.
44. ---
45.

Joseph Green	Butler	Tenn	Johnson
Isaac Grindstaff	Hampton	"	Carter
Joe McCloud	"	"	"
James Jackson	"	"	"
Wm. Smith	Elizabethton	"	"
Jas. Sheffield	Whitmore	Colo	
Daniel Baker	Butler	Tenn	

These all the living ones I know. These all I have any knowledge
of now.
There were one of my brothers and four cousins enlisted, but I am
the only living one. None killed in war but one died with measles
and one with small pox at Nashville during war. Others have died
since. My health is fairly good for one of my age.
46.

Jno. Sartain	White Pine	Jefferson Co.	Tennessee
David Sartain	"	"	"
Harvey Bales	"	"	"
Andrew Huggins	"	"	"
Jno. Backsley	"	"	"
Ad. Lane	"	"	"
Jacob Spickard	"	"	"
Capt. J.W. Gladding	"	"	"
W.B. Caldwell	New Market	Jefferson	"

WHITE, STEPHEN LOGAN

FORM NO. 2

1. Stephen Logan White; La Fayett Tenn Macon Co
2. born 1845 76-5 mo
3. Macon Co. Tenn
4. Federal
5. B, 37 Ky Reelisted in Co. D. 8 Tenn.
6. Farmer
7. Joseph White; ----; ----; Va; Macon Co Tenn; ----
8. Malinda Mays White; Billy Mays; Katy Mays; Scottsville Ky
9. ---
10. No
11. No
12. No
13. ---
14. Log
15. hoed
16. plowed & hoed   Mother cooked spun and wove
17. no
18. yes
19. yes
20. yes
21. yes
22. yes
23. yes
24. I dont know
25. no
26. no
27. Free school
28. 3 mo.
29. 2½ mi
30. Free schools
31. public
32. 3 mo.
33. no

WHITE (cont'd.):
34. man
35. 1863 - June 1st
36. Lousiville Ky
37. about 1 yr.
38. Salt works or Saltville Va.
39. came back My Sterling Ky then to Louisville Ky nothing of importance lived out in the open clothed and fed well part of time   I was exposed to cold and sometimes to hunger and disease. in prison at Glasgo Ky
40. 29th Dec 1865 at Louisville Ky
41. I traveled on train much of way home.
42. Farming
43. Farming   Macon Co Tenn   Never joined any church but Baptist in belief.
44. ---
45. Jim Bean Carr
    Bill Smith
    Geo. Glover
    Jim Driver
    John McDonald
    Zack Brooks
    Haid(?) Witt
    Jas. King
    Wess White
    Dock White

46.	Jas B. Carr	Westmoreland	R2	Tenn
	Will Smith	Lafayette		"
	L.P. Cox	"		"
	S.S.M. Blakenship	"		"
	Dock White	"		"
	Will Dillard	"		"

WIKS, MARCUS

FORM NO.1

1. Mart Wiks; Westmoreland Tenn   RR 2
2. 81 the 27 of next may
3. Sumner Co. Tenn
4. In Sumner Co near Hartsville
5. Wool carding in summer season and tobaco prising in the winter season
6. Had none   he was a crasey man
7. I didnot own any land nor any property I was a hireland.
8. None
9. None
10. House hold and kitchen furniture
11. Log cabin
12. I didnot Work on the farm I worked in the summer season in the carding factory in the winter season in the tobaco factory prising tobacco.
13. The duty of my mother was Cooking Spinning and weaving had to work hard For her living.
14. None
15. The Slave done the farm work mostly There was 80 per cts idelness in the white people.
16. They did when they Had to get them a bu(?) of corn from a slave holder.
17. The slave holders idled and there slaves done the work.   The moset of the poor class idled around untill they Had to jump out and work a bu of corn or a fiew Lbs. meat.
18. They did in most Respects they wanted a man to have one thousand Dollars or own a slave before they would have mutch To do with him.
19. In some respects they did.
20. I wouldent consider it was if he was not worth One thousand dollars they did not want him to stop on the high way and talk to his slaves slaveholers Kept out gards to keep there slave at home.
21. The slave holder helt a cold shoulder to him unless he as mutch as

a thousand dollars.
22. he could not unless it was handed to him by His ancester land at
    that time had to be entered and The poor young men could not get the
    money.
23. Discouraged the slave holders wanted to hire him at a low rate and
    trafick out his labor reason whip. I no this by self-experience I
    was hired out in 1854 and at the same place become a servent till
    I was Twenty one and took the fair as the slaves except sleeping.
24. None
25. One day
26. was about three hundred yds.
27. white school
28. Public
29. Three
30. Pretty regular where There parence was able to send them
31. Man
32. In Oct 1862 at a place known as the rock house on the gallatin and
    scotsvill pike in the US armey.
33. Enlisted in dumonts(?) devision when first enlisted Then went south
    to fort donelson I was exchanged to diferent Plases and did not get
    acquanter verry mutch. They was mostly northern men and not under-
    stand Ther language as I had no education the first full Suit of
    close I ever out and out uncle sam gave me befre this my clothing
    come one at a tim At this time recolection is not as god as it has
    bin.
34. Fort donelson and stayed on this side of the river till the fight
    was nearly ove The reason why we did not cross I was undrilled
    man.
35. It was a bout five weeks Before we engaged in a curmish near union
    citty Obion Co.
36. The curmish near union citty.
37. 1) mighty rough 2)muffelbourk 3) garded railroads and stock cades
    to keep the railroads from being tore up 4) the next time we fought
    at the court hous at mcminvel warn co tenn lasted about one hour
    we Reinforsed with blackburn Brigade 5) pretty rough partly Lay on
    they ground 6) hard tack and sow belly and not Hardly enough of
    that 7) exposed pretty bad to cold in winter Had hardly half enough
    to eat 8) in hospittel in carthage tenn
38. Nashville tenn
39. sent me home by the way of gallatin I come home with my enemies
    my enemies were all around me but one darkey and he was afraid to
    own he Was in the armie and I was not I went to Brownville Ky and
    spent the first winter.
40. Rail making
41. Hard labor timber cutting mostly Lived in macon co Tenn Jeneral
    baptist church, no office, my health is verry bad disable to work
    at any thing
42. Sam Wiks; dont no; Sumner; Tenn lived two thirds; In Tenn Sumner
    Co and died in grave co Ky; None
43. Mary Prock; Jimmie Prock; Winnie Prock; They in macom co tenn
44. My grandfathe on my fthers sid his Name Johney Wikes my grandmaw
    on fathe sid Gelila Wiks my fore parents come from oldforgina

WILKINS, WILLIAM ALEXANDER

FORM NO. 1

1. William Alaxander Wilkins; Darden R.F.D. #2 Box 23
2. I was 79 years old the 9th day of last December Dec of 1921.
3. Deatur county Tennessee
4. Decatur county Tennessee near Deaturville
5. farming and stave making and general farm work
6. taner and farmer
7. I owned no land only and undivided interst in 240 acres one third
   int I owned one horse wort $100
8. my mother owned one a boy her father gave her
9. they owned 309 acres
10. my father was dead the value of all property owned by my mother was

WILKINS (cont'd.):
about $2,000 dollars at begining of the war.
11. a three room frame building ceiled and weathe borded a kitchen 20X24 feet made of hewed loggs crcks lined with bevel eyed plank.
12. I plowed hoed cut wheet and oats mde rails and stves boards and done all other kinds of work that is done on a farm.
13. he taned leather and done all kinds of farm work = my mother cooked spun and wove abundance of clth to clothe the family which was a large one - being maried twice She also was a tayloris made clothig for many people.
14. Occasionally the had servants one and two but not always
15. it was respected as a greteal more honerable than loafing which was desised by all honerable people.
16. Almost all engaged in farming and other honerable work with fiew exceptions.
17. Just a fiew of the largest slave owners did not work and several no account people that had nothing and dident appear to want any thing.
18. as genera thing they mingled freely with all honerable people there were a fiew exceptions with the largest slave owners and a fiew whose heads were turned that dident own may Just a fiew were the excetions.
19. most them did on a perfect eqalety but some did not would send children off to city schools while young.
20. very friendly feeling between them geneally speaking a fiew of them dident want a poor boy to go to see his girls but these cases were verry fiew.
21. my observation is that help him any there were verry fiew save owners that sought office.
22. yes were verry good for any industrius young man to make and save up enough to buy a small farm or go into business for him self.
23. Jenerally speaking they were encouraged by good advice and sometimes financial help if they worthy and industrius.
24. country school made up by subscription for 3 months.
25. about 20 months is best recolection
26. 3/4 of a mile but I went as far as 2½ miles part of the time.
27. common schools with verry poor teachers taught the old blue back speller and smileys arithmatic as far as the rule of three
28. we had no public shools all made up by subscribers.
29. 3 months
30. yes most of them did sometimes the teacher was sorry they stop sending.
31. 2 of them woman this rest were men
32. feb 4 1864 in the federal army at Clifton tenn.
33. secon Tenn mounted ifantry camel barnett, Jefferson barnett, James Jenings, Isra Jennings, K.M. Ivy, M.H. Fowler, John Keen, thomas frizell, John Turnbos, John Grimes, Larkin Grimes, Davy Green inef(?) Surratt, tacket tim reves, Jack Puley (?), Hammonds, Charly tubs, hutch mcgee, 2 named clark, Jerry Halbrooks
34. we stayed at Clifton till about sep then sent Johnsonville in the winter to 54 on the N Western RR to nashville in December in January to galatin in february back to Clfton.
35. nevr was in regular battle about 3 months we had a small fight near Clifton had another near crumps landing on tennessee river
36. we were surrounded at Clifton in summer 64 for 3 days & nights had several hot skirmishes was relieved by _____ gun
37. while we was 54 apart of our regiment in a hard fight on beaver dam in hickman county lasting about 3 hours we got the worst of it we lived verry well in cam had good clothes had plenty to eat but badly prepared slep in bunks made of boards under tent on 2 blankets under 2 we were badly exposed in cold weather while on 3 to 5 days without any thing to eat one time for 3 days and nights slept in rain in feb 65 was hospital about 5 days in the army is worst place for exposure I ever experienced.
38. we were discharged at nashvill Tennessee on the 5 day of may 1865
39. came home from nashville to Johnsonville on cars from there on aboat to the narrows 9 miles and very tired.
40. went to plowing mad a crop cut wheat threshed it and gathered my crop and kept on farming.
41. farming lived right her in Decatur county Joined baptist church 54

138

WILKINS (cont'd.);
    years ago was Justice of peace for 12 years I own 207 acres of land
    worth $4000. 81700 in bank.
42. George Washington Wilkins; near Knowville; Knx; Tennessee; lived
    ther till quite grow and moved to Decatur county; none
43. Marry Ann Rebcca Graves; George Washington Graves; Charlotte Rains
    Graves; near Decturrvile Tenn
44. Gerge Washington Graves & Charlotte rains graves was born raised
    maried near Charlott NC moved to giles co them to Decatur county
    Thomas Wilkins my grandfather came from Englan when twelve years old
    to Knox County Tenn grew up maried raised a family then moved to
    Decatur County Tenn his wifes name was Sally but know her maiden
    name.

WILLIAMS, EZEKIEL HARRISON

FORM NO. 1

1. Ezkiel Harreson Williams; Dandridge Tenn R.F.D. 4
2. age 81
3. Tenn Jefferson Co
4. Tenn. Jefferson Co. Federal Government
5. Farming
6. carpenter
7. no
8. no
9. 50
10. $250.00
11. Framed house 3 Rooms
12. all kinds of Farm Plow and Howed
13. Feather carpenter mother Died when I were a child
14. no
15. yess
16. yess
17. non
18. yess
19. no
20. antagonistic against each other
21. no
22. no
23. Discurage
24. 3 month country chool
25. about 5 months
26. 1½ mile
27. country chool
28. Public
29. 3 months
30. Jest _____
31. man
32. Kentucky March 1862   Federal Government
33. 8 Tenn Enfantry Lutinent Lun Bibb, Jack Robison, Carter taity(?),
    Bill Ker, Charley Smith, _____ Bibb, Tom Bibb, Bill Prater, other
    Praters Bill Engling, Gabe Ruth
34. Watoga Bridge Tenn
35. about 5 months
36. Wautage Bridge
37. after first Badle went to siege at Knoxville tenn when the siege
    was over at Knoxville I went thru Georgia with Genl shearmen I was
    in at Battle in George went by the name of Burnt Hicory last 7 days
    we _____ lived in camp 2 years 4 months we had good close and
    slept on the ground
    (on a separate sheet)   What we Had to Eat
    meat crackers Brans coffee Rice mixt(?) vegables suit(?)
    _____ Had to take _____ Just like it come not exstosed to diase
    except By cold I had the measles I was at Privet House wasent at
    any Hospitle neaver was in Prison
38. June 31 1865 compay shops north cali(smeared)
39. I came from the shops sity Point crossed the Bay to Batman from
    thir to Rittens Burg Via Rikers Burg Via from thir to Louisville

WILLIAMS (cont'd.):
     Ky from ther to nashville tenn
40. Farming
41. Farming lived in Jefferson Co. church Mount Zaon Methodist Church
42. James Williams; near Morristown; Jefferson Co; tenn; ----; none
43. _____ Williams; Joe Williams; ----; ----; ----
44. ---

                         WILSON, JAMES

FORM NO. 2

1.   James Wilson; Hampton Tennessee Route #2
2.   93
3.   Wilkes County N.C.
4.   Federal
5.   Co G, 13th
6.   Farmer
7.   Cornelius Wilson; N.C.; not known; ----; Wilkesboro N.C. was in
     French & Indian war
8.   Betsey Roberts; ----; ----; ----
9.   ---
10. I did not own any land until after the Civil War
11. none
12. none, rented land
13. owned no land
14. part time in a log house.
15. worked on a farm Plowed hoed did our own work on the farm with out
     slaves
16. my father worked at the different jobs on the place my mother
     cooked, spinning & weaving for the family clothes.
17. none
18. People worked hard and regarded loafers as the worst citizens in
     the community.
19. yes
20. not much Idleness in our community.
21. They mingled together They did not.
22. yes
23. Friendly
24. not as I know of
25. not very good
26. I do not remember
27. none. about 5 weeks altogether
28. ---
29. about 2 miles
30. ---
31. do not remember
32. short time
33. no
34. man
35. 1863 about nov near Greenville Tenn
36. sent to Strawberry Plains from there to Ky & from there to nashville
37. some time
38. do not remember but I think it was Bulls Gap
39. ---
40. at Knoxville Tenn
41. came home on train
42. Farming
43. Have lived near Hampton since I ____ back. I farmed until a few
     years ago. Since then I have not been able to do any thing at all.
     I have been a member of the Baptist Church for Thirty seven years.
44. ---
45. Captn Columbus Wilcox
     Lieu Clabe White
     Lieu John White
     Sargnt John Humphreys
     Sn. S. W ___ly McCa____
     Ser. Ham Kennick
     Dav_ Baker

                              140

WILSON (cont'd.):
      Joe Green
      David White
46.   ---

                        WILSON, JEFFERSON

FORM NO. 2

1.   Jefferson Wilson
2.   76
3.   Jackson Co. Tenn
4.   Federal
5.   B, 8th Tenn. Mtd. Inf.
6.   farmer
7.   Thomas Wilson; Robertson Co; ----; Tenn; Rough Poinet, Jackson Co.
     after moving from above Co.; none
8.   Basha B. Braswell; John Braswell; Tabtha Price; Jackson Co Tenn.,
     near North Springs
9.   John Braswell and wife also Basha B. Braswell came from North Carol-
     ina
10. I did not own land.
11. No
12. owned some, tho do not recall amount
13. only a small amount.
14. Log dwelling
15. I did general farm work, as plowing, hoeing, wood cutting and in
     other work necessary.
16. Father did general farm work. Mother did the house work. and
     also worked at spining weaving and any other work incidental to
     housekeeping.
17. No
18. yes
19. yes
20. all white men worked, and none spent idle lives.
21. all stood on a level
22. yes
23. yes
24. I was not old enough to recall all facts pertaining to political
     contests.
25. Some did
26. Encouraged.
27. Short subscription schools
28. Only a short time. Was forsed to work for a widowed mother.
29. one mile
30. New Bethel and Rockie Mount
31. private or open only to those paying tuition.
32. about 2½ or 3
33. yes
34. man
35. Dec. 1864, Carthage Tenn.
36. Nashville, Tenn.
37. Served on guard duty
38. ---
39. slept in tents. age pickled pork and Beef. Crackers and Biscuits.
     Was on guard on Battery Hill, Carthage about ½ times. remainder in
     town. Clothed in regular Blue uniforms.
40. Nashville Aug. 17 1865
41. Walked from Gallatin Tenn
42. farming
43. Lived in Jackson Co Tenn since the close of Civil War. Engaged in
     farming only. Am a member of the Church of Christ. Have served
     as United States Deputy Marshall for a number of years.
44. ---
45. Capt. Bill S. Long
     1st Lieut Johns Hopkins
     2nd   "   Geo. McDuffy
     Cds Jack Clorland
     John Draper (?)

                          141

WILSON (cont'd.):
    Shafer (?) Richardson
    Doob Huffines
    Uriah Lee
    Murph Craighead
    Thos Gentry
    Bill Gentry
    Curry Hawkins
    Wesley Carter
    Henry Quick
46. John Hicks   Haydenburg   Tenn
     Lee Sadler   Gainesboro R4 Tenn
     John Howell   "   "   "4 Tenn

                    WOFFORD, FRANCIS MARION

FORM NO. 2

1.   Francis Marion Wofford; R7 Athens Tennessee
2.   72
3.   Hall County, Georgia
4.   Federal Soldier
5.   Co g; 10th Tenn Cav
6.   Farmer
7.   James Whitney Wofford; Polksville; Hall; Georgia; in Hall County
     until the close of the Civil War, when he moved to McMinn Co. Tenn.
     where he died.
8.   Mary Miller; Henry Miller; Betsey Miller; Polksville Ga;
9.   They came to Ga from S.C. The Wofford name came from Scotland but
     Just when I do not know. Neither do I know what country's the
     Millers were orginally from.
10. No
11. No
12. 250
13. $500
14. Frame House, 2 Rooms
15. worked on the farm. Plowed with a bulb Lounge plow and hoed with an
     eye hoe.
16. My father farmed raising corn mostly. My Mother spun carded wove
     and made clothes for the family.
17. No
18. Not much by the high class.
19. yes, those that did not own slaves
20. about one fourth
21. most of them did not
22. no
23. They were against each other
24. I think not
25. no
26. Discouraged
27. Subscriptions
28. 15 months
29. 3 miles
30. subscriptions schools
31. Everybody could go that paid their subscription.
32. 6 to 10 months
33. not much
34. a man
35. 1864. Feb. 15th Lumpin County Ga went from their to Nashville Tenn
36. From Nashville to Shelbyville Tenn
37. ---
38. Franklin Tenn
39. Hood Battle at Nashville Tenn we mostly done Guerilla hunting around
     Murfresborough, Shelbyville, Tullahoma, Fayettsville, Pulaski,
     Franklin and Gravel Springs Ala. from here to New Orleans from here
     to Natches Miss to Lumpkinville from here to Nashville Tenn.
40. at Nashville Tenn Aug 1st 1865
41. went from Nashville to Atlanta in Freight box cars, from Atlanta home
     in a wagon a distance of 70 miles from Atlanta Ga.

WOFFORD (cont'd.):
42. Farming
43. I moved from Hall County Ga to McMinn County in 1875 where I have
    been living since that time engaged in Farming. Holiness Church.
44. ---
45. Capt Baker   Ind.
    1st Lieut Magill   "
    2nd Lieut Fitgerald   Bradley County   Tenn
    Bob Munroe   Va
    Alford Hyden   Bradley County   Tenn
    Privt Gaber
    Privt Weavers   Bradley County   Tenn
    Privt Stinnett   Polk County   "
    Privt Gerron (?)   Bradley County   "
    Privt Elrod   Fannin County   Ga
    Privt Lingenfielt   "   "   "
    Privt McGlocklin
    Col. Geo. Bridges   Athens, McMinn Co   Tenn
    MaJ. Storey   Polk Co   "
    Col Abernathy   Rhea Co   "
    Polk Forrester   Polk County   "
46. J.J. Jackson   Athens   Tenn
    Robt. Underwood   "   "
            Hacker   "   "
            Gilbert   "   "
            Hicks   "   "
    John Hoback   "   "
    M.M. Carpenter   R3 Athens   "
    W.F. Carpenter   Athens   "
    Henry Carroll   R3 Athens   "
            Barnett   Etowah   "
    G.W. Guffy   R7 Athens   "
    F.M. Underwood   Riceville   "

                        WOLVERTON, JAMES T.

FORM NO. 2

(35 additional pages with this-part of this typed part handwritten)
1. Adamsville Tennessee; James T. Wolverton
2. 77 year
3. Tippi County Mississippi
4. Federal
5. Company G; 6th Regt Tenn Cav.
6. Machanict (Carpenter and Mechanic)
7. Robt. Huston Wolverton; Maury county, Tennessee; Maury; Tennessee;
    He moved with his father (James Wolverton) from Maury county to
    Hardeman Tennessee about 1831, then to Tippah county, Mississippi,
    where he married; none
8. Elvira Hughes(Eliza Hughes); Thomas Hughes; dont know; ----
9. Grandfather was James Wolverton The Wolverton First Family came From
    England to Amerca and Settled in New Jersey. Grand Father Hughes
    Served in the Indian war
10. none
11. none. They were opposed to slavery, and would not invest in what
    they were opposing.
12. 4 acre Town Lot
13. None. Owned household furnishings, tools and so on, but not of
    very much value.
14. Log 3 rooms. which in that day were very common for living shelter,
    since in his section, only the wealthiest lived in framed or brick
    homes.
15. General farm work a garate maney whit people had it to do and it
    was considerd honerable.
16. macanical work was done by my Father. mother cooked spun and
    weved cloth.
17. none
18. yes it was considerd honerable & Respectable.
19. yes

                                143

WOLVERTON (cont'd.):
20. very few - only those who owned slaves
21. a small majorty of young women only did so
22. verry much so
23. ordernarly so
24. It was considered slave holders was allowed a vote for each slave owned.
(Questions 25-37 typed)
25. Rather poor, since wages were cheap, and money making was very slow, young men saving only by sheer economy, and sticking closely to work. Wages then were about eight dollars per month for farm hands.
26. Yes, they were by the best element of slave owners, however slaves were owned in small numbers where I grew up, there being no large owners. Honest young men then as now were always encouraged, if he showed thrift, with honest principles.
27. A short term of a country school, of which was poorly equipped and short termed.
28. About ten to fifteen months all told.
29. From one ½ of one mile to two miles distance, I living at different places, in my boyhood.
30. Very poor country schools, with short time terms. The Webster old blue backed speller being the principal text book, and very few ever had anything else, from which to study.
31. Private, as we then had no public school as provided of later years. The young man who attained to the single rule of three, as the term then expressed, was considered a scholar.
32. About two months.
33. No many never attended since only those who expected sell goods, or do professional work, thought it necessary to educate.
34. Men teachers mainly, but attended one taught by a woman teacher.
35. At Bethel Springs, Tennessee on the 15th day of September 1862, in the Federal army, where I served until July the first day, 1865, at Pulaski, Tenn.
36. to Boliver, then to Grand Junction, Tenn.
37. about 1863, at Ripley Miss. Holly Springs.
38. Holly Springs Miss
39. I am not able to do Justice by my war experience as I saw to _____ (either much or work.)
40. at Pulaski Tenn 1st day July 1865.
41. I went via Nashville to draw my pay of about $500.00 which amount had accumulated during my confinemnt in Prison. Then I went by Rail to Johnsonville Tenn then by River to Crumps Ldg near my Home.
42. Farm work for sevral years then later pension attorney. which I have served in this capacity for 40 years or more. and Notary Public about 22 years.
43. merchantile(?) Pension Atty NP to lived at Adamsville Tenn since the close of the Civil War. with the exception of 2 years - 1 yre in Ala. & one yeare in _____. I was captured by the Rebels in the Springs of 1864 neare Adamsville Tenn. was parolled sevral months in the fall of 1864. I was sent to prison 1st at Meridian Miss. from thence to Cahawba Ala where in remained untill the Spring of 1865. then footed it most of the way to Vixburg Miss and was exchanged at a Pontoon Bridge at Black River neare Vixburg about the first days of April 1865. we remained here sevral days & Just after the assasination of President Lincol 2608 (2603?) of us placed on board of the Ill fated steamer Sultana which blew up up 9 miles above Memphis Tenn on the 27 day of April 1865. I was rescude at Memphis about 5 oclock in the morning. have floated 9 miles in the cold ice water it has been stated by one person that the explosion ocured about 4 oclock at Night this person lived at Hen Island or Paddys Hens & Chickens at the time of explosions.
44. Gen Buell & others Gov. Hooper & Taylor & others Sevetos(?) Sims & others
45. All that are X are dead

Hezekiar Wilson	Co G 6th Tenn	Adamsville Tenn
W.G. Tegrum	Co G 6th Tenn	Finger Tenn
Riley Holmes	Co G 6th Tenn	Adamsville R.R.No.2 Tenn
Capt Wm Chandler X		
Elisha Chandler X		
Lt. W.L.T. Boolman X		

144

WOLVERTON (cont'd.):
    Lt. John R. Ray   X
    Thomas Guthrie   X
    Benjamin Baker   X
    Henry Wolfe   X
    Mark Wolfe   dead
    William Smallwood dead
    Jackson Wilson   dead
    George Smallwood dead
    Robert Barns   dead
    Elexander Barns dead
    Willis Sweat
    Willis Gray
    the muster roll of the 5 Tenn is at Finger(?) Tenn Dr. Hodges can
    give you information concerning it Capt Hodges had pesission of it
    hes is dead I might fing it

46. Randolph Wesson   Adamsville   Tennessee
    Co 6th Regt Tenn Cav
    Waran Kemp Co C-6th   Adamsville   Tenn RR
    Calvin Plunk
    Co Regt Tenn Infty   Adamsville   Tenn
    William J. Phillips
    US Navy   Crump   Tenn
    John C. Doss   Bethel Sprs   Tenn
    Co M 7 Tenn Cav   Bethel Springs Tenn
    George D. Manars   Adam.

First of many separate sheets.

                             Adamsville Ten. Sept 29 1922
Gentleman
I have some more importent war History in conection with this - if
needed. I saw a good deale of service - the capture of our Col.
Fielding Hurst - his cescue and many outher thrirling incidents If
can only find the time to write it sure would make a good sized
volumm parden me for my delay
                    Yours truly Jas. T. Wolverton

(Typewritten letter signed James T. Wolverton Sergt Co G 6 Tenn
Cav dated 29 Jan 1920 2 pages)

                    Adamsville, Tenn   Jan. 29, 1920
Editor Commerical Appeal (out beside this is written I did not sent
        Memphis Tenn this)
Gentlemen:
    Having read in your paper of Jan 25 1920 a detailed history of
the Sultanna desaster 9 miles above Memphis April 27, 1865. It
brought back to mind that awfull night of suffering and death Capt.
Woolrige has added some detailed accounts to the story I have not
known. I was on board of the illfated steamer at the time of the
explosion. I was stationed on harrican deck on the east side of
the steamer near the center. Just behind me was a saloon and an ice
chest, the water was leaking from the chest and had wet my blanket.
So I had decided I would rather remain up than attempt to sleep on
a wet blanket, and as I had no other Place I could occupy. As
every other place was crowded with human sleepers. The saloon
keeper and one other man had just Passed out of the saloon just
before the explosion. I did not thirst after any of the liquor, I
gave no thought to that, at that time, and did not know that I would
have to swallow some before daylight. Which I did, when they
pulled me out of the river as stiff as a Poker. They put me aboard
of a steamer some one was standing there with a bottle of whiskey
and gave me about half of glass and in a few minuted after I revived
and could walk alone. As I said every avaleble space I could see
was occupied by sleeping soldiers Perhaps dreaming of the loved ones
they would soon meet. But alas what a terrible fate awaited them.
While drearly slumbering there all at once I felt a terrible shock
followed by a deafning explosion, and before I could think my head
struck water and I went down, down struggling for breath. Finaly

WOLVERTON (cont'd.)

I come to the surface exausted for breath. I began swiming the best
I could with my clothes and shoes on. I grabbed at anything I might
get a holt on, as I knew it was my only chance. At last I grasped
my Peices of the boat with my left arm, whitch was hardly sufficient
to support me. A little later some Pieces came up between my legs
which helped me to keep my head above water. I went whirling down
the river and soon landed in a drift with some others and went
whirling in a circle. We could see the burning wreck of the steamer
then as the next view would be the lights at Memphis, which looked
like hundreds of stars beckoning to us. I have allready told what
time we landed at Memphis. As the Capt. has told what time the
explosion occured about 4 oclock if so it took us to near daylight
to float 9 miles to Memphis. The Place of the explosion was called
Hen Island and (words written over unintelligible) Hens and Chickens.

#2

There are many other incedents I would like to relate but I fear it
would tax the good editors Patience. I wrote a short story of this
some years ago, it was Published in the Nat. Tribune and I have a
large batch of interesting letters from different ones, some who
were on board and some who were not. I have thought of having them
Published by some Paper but, have not asked them to. Now I cannot
think of that terable night of the disaster without deep sorrow.
The terrible screams of the victims, which haunt me when I hear it
mentioned. It was like an old camp meeting before the war when the
Preacher worked every soul up to shouting. I have two Pictures of
the Sultanna taken at Helena showing her crowded condition. I with
many others went aboard her at Vicksburg. We had been confined
(words written over and smeared but may have been "in Cahawba"
Prison and exchanged at Vicksburg. The story of this disaster given
by Capt. Woolridge is about correct. I never knew before what
became of the hulk and that the Island had disappeared. After
remaining in the hospital for severel days I was sent to Camp Chase
Ohio and from there to Pulaska Tenn where my Rigemnt was stationed
and was discharged. I am now 77 yr. old and have lived at Adamsville
Tenn. nearly all my life. The river was at it highest stage, thawing
ice & snow in the north. Two or three years ago the survivors held
a meeting and reported that only about twelve of the survivors of the
Sultana was living but perhaps there were some other outside billie
goats like myself that they did not know about. It is remarkable
that any of us could be alive after such great exposier in the ice
cold water.

                    James T. Wolverton
                    Sergt. Co G 6 Tenn Cav

(handwritten note)
P.S. I have Just Read an interesting story of this by _____
(no name; just the line)

(Small newspaper article - Newspaper unknown article dated 27 Apr
54 yrs would be 1919)

                "Sultana Survivors Meet"

"Gather for Fifty-Fourth Reunion in Mount Olive, Near Knoxville"

Knoxville, Tenn, April 27 --- The fifty-fourth annual reunion of the
survivors of the ill-fated steamer Sultana, which were held at Mount
Olive Baptist Church near here today, was attended by hundreds of
citizens from Knox and adjoining counties. Also hundreds of world-
war veterans enjoyed the all-day programme. Short addresses were
delivered by the young soldiers also by the veterans of the Civil
War and the few survivors of the Sultana, which sank in the Missis-
ippi River near Memphis April 27, 1865.

This disaster resulted in the loss of 1,700 killed or drowned.
The Sultana was carrying 1,966 federal soldiers released from
Confederate prisons at Cahaba, Ala. and Macon and Andersonville, Ga.,
the soldiers being in route to their homes in Tennessee, Ohio,
Indiana, Kentucky, West Virginia and Michigan.

WOLVERTON (cont'd.):

The war between the states had been concluded and the men were
returning to their homes after a long campaign in the south. A large
number of the members of the Third Tennessee Cavalry Regiment,
organized at Knoxville and composed of men from Knox and adjoining
counties, were killed. There are only 12 survivors of the disaster
living in East Tennessee. J.H. Sympson is the only survivor in this
city.

A few of the veterans have passed away every year and the attendance of Sultana survivors grows smaller every reunion day.

Rev. Thos. J. Espy, pastor of Mount Olive Church, delivered the
annual sermon this morning at 10:30 o'clock.

An imposing monument erected a few years ago to the memory of
Sultana survivors is one of the attractive markers in Mount Olive
Cemetery.

Business card of Elias Shull:
"Attorney at Law and Abstracter of Titles"
111 West 6th st. Ground Floor Topeka Kansas
"He That Reapeth Receiveth Wages"

(Letter from Winfield S. Colvin to J.T. Wolverton - 4 pages)

Mackville, Ky Sept 21st, 1912

Mr. J. T. Wolverton,
Adamsville, Tenn.

Dear Sir & Comrade: I have just read an article in the National
Tribune of the 12th, inst, written by you in regard to the Sultana.
I was glad to see it because it agrees very nearly with what I saw
in that fearful disaster.

I was a member of Co. F. 5th Ky Cav. at the time of the explosion
I was sleeping with a member of my company on the upper deck right
by the side of the pilot house. My comrade was a good swimmer and
in the grand rush that was made shortly after the explosion he went
with the rest and was lost. I had never learned to swim and so I
waited until the rush was over and until the fire compelled me to
move. I then pulled a shutter from the pilot house window and
started to climbed down, but when I came opposit the cabin windows
the flames were coming out with such force that I let go and fell
into the water. On coming to the surface I got hold of a man or he
holt of me (I hardly know which) and after a considerable struggle
we somehow separated and I cought holt of a large trunk over another
mans (page 2) shoulder and held to it until it floated into the
wheelhouse. Then we let go of the trunk and took holt of the wheel.
In a short time the wheelhouse burnt loose and fell over on its
side. There were about a dozen men in the wheelhouse when it fell
and if any of them got out except myself I do not know it. I was
almost gone when I came up with the wheelhouse and it was sometime
before I was able to get on top of it. After I had been on the
wheelhouse sometime two other men - one of the 9th Ind. Cav. and one
of the 3d Tenn. Cav. got on the wreck of the wheelhouse with me (I
wonder if it was you) We floated along by the side of the hull till
it sunk. Then we floated on down the river. A little after sunrise
we passed a soldier who had floated down beofre us and struck a
small willow tree and climbed up it out of the water. He was
perfectly naked and the mosquitos were about to eat him up. He was
fighting them first one hand then the other. He was making a most
gallant fight and I am glad to say that he got out. He belonged
to a Michigan Regiment. We had long since quit trying to get our
wreck to the shore and just let it float, as we knew that it would
not be long until we would meet a boat coming up the river, and
sure enough sometime between 8 and 9 o'clock the boat came in sight,
ran up to us, and put out a yawl and took us in. You may be sure
that we felt good then.

I do not remember that name of the boat that resuced us. But I
do remember that if had the pilot and second engineer of the Sultana
on board. The pilot was not hurt but the engineer was the most
pitiable object I every beheld. Every particle of the skin was
burnt from his face and breast yet I could see that the heart was
beating faintly. I am quite sure he did not live long after I saw

147

WOLVERTON (cont'd.):
   him.
      I saw an article in the Louisville Herald the other day saying
   that Clem D. Strahan who died at Huntsville, Ind. the other day was
   believed to be the last survivor of the Sultana. You say there are
   about 30 survivors. I do not know the number but am inclined to
   believe that you make the number too small. Of the three members of
   my company who escaped I am the only one living, and also the sole
   survivor in my (Washington) county.
      I attended a reunion near Willisburg, Ky. on the 20th Inst and
   there met Charles Higdon Co. C. 4th Ky. Infty. and he is the last
   survivor of the disaster from Marion County, Ky.
      Well I guess I have writen (sic) enough but I will give you a
   short history of my life. I was born in Washington Co., Ky. March
   10th 1847. I enlisted Co. F. 6th Ky Cav and served until the 14th
   of July 1865 but fortunately was exchanged in about 10 days one
   week of which time I spent in the prison pen at Meridian, Miss.
      I married when I was about a month over 20 years of age and we
   raised ten children - eight of whom are still living. I have been
   afflicted with a lung trouble ever since I was in the army the result
   of taking cold while I had measles. I farm on a small scale and
   have spent about half the time for the last forty years in teaching.
   I am a pensioner at the rate of $16.00 per month.
      Now I hope you will answer this and if you are not the man or
   rather you were a boy then who rode on the wreck with me that sad
   morng and can give me the his name of him who did ride with me I
   will be more than gratified for it is what I have wanting to know
   for years.
                              Very sincerely yours,
                                Winfield S. Colvin
   Address Mackville, Ky. R.F.D. No (1)

   (Letter from J. Sam Johnson to J.T. Wolverton dated 12 Apr 1912)

                         Department of Justice
                               office of
                         United States Marshal
                      Western District of Tennessee
                               Memphis

                            April 12, 1912

   Hon. J.T. Wolverton
   Adj't & Q.M., G.A.R.,
   Adamsville, Tenn.

   My dear sir:
      Replying to your favor of 10th instant, inviting me to address the
   Grand Army of the Republic on the occasion of your memorial services
   May 30th, beg to say that it affords me much pleasure to accept your
   invitation, and I desire to express my thanks to you, and to the
   Post you represent, through you, for the honor you do me in inviting
   me to participate in these patriotic exercises on this great battle
   field of our country. If nothing interferes I will be on hand with
   a short address. The United States Court convenes here on May 27th,
   and it is possible that I might not be able to leave, but I will
   try and arrange to get off afternoon of 29th to Jackson via way of
   Selmer to Pittsburg Ldg. I want no expenses. I would appreciate
   it if some conveyance would be furnished me from Selmer. You can
   arrange for that, if you will. I will want to get back to Selmer
   for night train. Kindly advise me as to time of trains, if you can
   furnish me conveyance out etc.
                              Very truly,
                              J. Sam Johnson

   Article "The Burning of the Steamboat Sultana" by John Leisk Tait
   date? paper? *
   Article from Nashville Banner "Rivaled Loss of the Titanic dated
   27 Apr *
   Letter from Lincoln Post No. 1 Department of Kansas G.A.R. Elias

WOLVERTON (cont'd.):
    Shull to J.T. Wolverton *
    (* Did not copy)

    Names on the letterhead:
    J.M. Miller   Adjutant
    J.E. Stewart   Sergeant Major
    H.H. Louthan   Post Commander
    A.M. Fuller   Istalling Officer
    Elias Shull   Quartermaster
    J.F. Carter   Quartermaster Sergeant

    Geo. Hanley   Chairman, Relief Committee
    C.N. Bacon   Chairman of Trustees
    J.F. Carter   Secretary of Trustees
    C.N. Bacon   Chairman Memorial Committee
    A.W. Knowles   Chairman Finance Committee
    R. Reed   Chairman Employment Committee
    F.M. Kimball   Chairman Entertainment Committee

    Geo. Hanley   Senior Vice Commander
    W.R. Reed   Junion Vice Commander
    H.C. Suess   Surgeon
    J.W. Sidwell   Chaplain
    J.E. Pennick   Officer of the Day
    Geo. McCaslin   Officer of the Guard
    Elias Shull   Historian

    All members of Lincoln Post No 1 of Dept of Kansas G.A.R. who met
    1st & 3rd Sat. every month in Post Hall No 118 East Sixth St.
    between Quincy Street & Kansas Avenur. Topeka Kansas

                              Sept 19 1912

    To J.T. Wolverton
        Greeting:
        I have read with much interest your recently printed article in
    The National Tribune under the title of "A Sultana Survivor"
        There now lives, about a half mile outside of the City Boundary
    here, one of the Survivors, named John Sanderson, who was a Soldier
    in the Co. "K" 58th O.V.I. and escaped by the use of means much
    like those you set forth as resorted to by you; only differing in
    that he did not float down to Memphis, but got into a tree-top near
    the fatal disaster and clung fast there till rescuing craft went
    up from Memphis.
        He was not one of the releast prisoners, but one of a guard of
    20 put on the boat to preserve order whilst the trip was expected
    to be made. The prisoners had not all been collected from Cahawba
    the many of them did - but a considerable number had come from
    Tyler, Texas, and other places west of the Mississippi River.
        At the time of the loading of the boat I was not in the ranks of
    the army - tho I had been and honorably discharged. I was then a
    Quartermasters Clerk in the office of the Q.M. in charge of River
    transportation there; and had instructions about sunset the evening
    the boat was loaded, from the Q.M. to the effect that whenever the
    memorandum came to me from Captain Williams giving the name of the
    ranking officer aboard, and the number of Soldiers entire, I should
    issue the order to the Sultana to carry them up to Cairo. That
    memorandum came to me, as I remember, about 9 or a little later and
    I then wrote out the order. (which had been signed in blank by the
    Q.M.) Afterwards, I testified before a Court of Inquiry there in
    regard to the matter of the order being based on the memorandum.
        Then I did not personally know John Sanderson, nor for more than
    30 years thereafter: I settled here before his coming. But now we
    are well acquainted and belong to the same G.A.R. Post. I would like
    if you would write for me the names of as many of the survivors now,
    as you know, their P.O. addresses as far as you know them, and the
    companies or Batteries in which they served. It will be edifying to
    John Sanderson and to me.   Ever
                              Elias Shull

                              149

WOLVERTON (cont'd.):
    (Next letter from Wolverton   3 Nov 1922)

    Adamsville   Nov 3/22
    Gents
    I am sending you one dozen letters from difernt ones who know about
    the disaster of the Sultana 9 miles above Memphis on the day April
    1865. I have another good history of it in a magazien will look it
    up - Capt Woolrige P.O. I do not address the Com. Appeal whil was
    gone to Jackson. Our house keeper missplaced my papers - & could
    not find your stamped envelope & c. Hence my delay. will soon have
    my Photo taken and send it in.
                                        yours Truly
    see the other side   Jas. T. Wolverton

    (Letter from Wm Crisp to Maud W. Bell   Notation across the top of
    letter "this to my daughter __ell")

                            December 18th 1910
                            Osceola Nebraska
    Writen to Maud W. Bell Tenn
    From William Crisp Survivor of Sultanna
    Dear Friend I saw your name in National Tribune that your father
    was in the Ill fated Steamboat was your father name F.M. Bell who
    belonged to third East Tenn Cavelry Company A. if he did he was on
    the Sultana with me for I was on the Boat that Terable night. I was
    acquanted with him I don't know if he got out alive or not I don't
    think he did their was nearly two thousand perished that awful night.
    Write me dear friend when you get this. My address is Osceola
    Nebraska Polk Co. now tell me more about your father when you write.
    I reman your friend in F.C.L.
                                        William Crisp

    (Letter from Wm B. Floyd to J T Wolverton 23 Jan. 1913)

                            Great Northern Express Co.
                            Auditors Office

                            St Paul, Minn. Jany 23, 1913

    J.T. Wolverton
    Adamsville Tenn
        Dear Sir
        I read an article in the Washington Tribune in regard to the
    burning of the Steamer "Sultana" during the Civil War. I was in the
    US Navy at that time & the vessil I was on was lying at Memphi & I
    went out & picked up twelve of the survivors as they floated past
    the city. I hav always been interested in anything relating to this
    terrible disaster & have kept clippings & have added your acct to
    those already collected. Would be glad to hear from you
                            Respectfully
                            William B. Floyd
    937 Ottawa Ave

    (Letter from Wm B Floyd to J T Wolverton dated 14 Aug 191<u>5</u> (may be
    1913) 2 pages)

                            Great Northern Express Co.
                            Auditors Office

                            St Paul, Minn. Aut 14 191<u>5</u>

    Jas T. Wolverton
        Dear Sir & Shipmate
        I duly recd your letter of Jan 27th in answer to mine of Jan 23d.
    You may think it strange that I shld delay so long in answering.
    There are several causes one was I wanted to have made an acct of
    my experience at the time of wreck to send you & another & most
    important is that altho 73 years old I am still employed as a clerk

                            150

WOLVERTON (cont'd.):

in this office & each day am expected to perform as much work as the
ordinary clerk which I do & more. Then when my office work is done
I have a Horse Cow & Chickens & about an acre of lawn to look after.
& I will hav to own up when I get thru I am not in fit condition to
do much writing. I enclose the type written copy of what I know
about the accident. You can see I was not the one that rescued you.
shld you publish your book let me know & I will purchase a copy. I
know you will be interested in my narrative & can place it among your
files.

I will close with well wishes for your health & prosperity.

                                    William B. Floyd
937 Ottawa Ave.

(Letter from Wm Crisp 31 Dec 1910 from Osceola Nb - 3 pages)

                          December 31th 1910
                          Osceloa, Nebraska
Comrad yours in F.C.L. William Crisp
Dear Comrad your letter received to night and I was glad to get the
letter from one that was on that Ill fated Sultana that night of
darkness and Death in fire and water and men crushed beneath the
Burning Timbers I never shall forget the work awful dont express it.
I enlisted in the 18th Michigan Vol Infantry at Hillsdale Mich in
August 1862 for three years or during the war under Colonel Dolitle
we started in our Campaign at Covington Kentucky and we drove the
Rebels Back from there and we follered on to Atlanta and then we
was sent back wit General (illegilbe - Torenas?) to Nashville Tenn
that was 1864. while going back I was taken prisoner the 24th of
Semptember 1864 and was sent to Cahawba Prison for seven months and
was taken to Vickburg and then we was loaded on the Sultana for St
Louis we had got to Memphis Tenn and started from their about 12
oclock and we got about nine or ten miles up the River when the
Boiller exploded and deckes fell in and then the fire began to do
its work
                              2
I was asleep on the Boiller deck about sixteen feet from the Boiler
and the great side of the Boiler was Blown out and shut down over
me breaking my left shoulder and the heat was so intense I seemed
to be nailed to the floor I could not stir hand or foot I thought I
should be roasted alive then and there I was scalded and Burned to
death almost when the heat got out some I fould I could move and I
cralled out of that Hell to the the front of the Boat and then it
was I saw what happened I could look into the fire and see hundreds
of men burning up among the Timbers that Boiler saved me from being
crushed to death by the falling timbers finely the fire drove me of
into the water and I swam three miles and a half and landed in the
trees on the Arkansaw sid and I was there until nine oclock in the
morning this took place about two oclock of the morning of the 28th
of April 1865. We started from Memphis the 27th we made slow work
getting up that River we did not go very fast so you see it was 27th
and 28th of April 1865 you will remember when the water came into
our Prison dont you how the men died in the water about five hundred
men died then in that Hell Hole after 12 days they took us out
                              3
and then we started for Vicksburg I never shall forget that awful
night tongue(?) cannot tell. it was the greatest Mareine disaster
on record the greates loss of life. I think nearly two thousand
men perished that night out of all the men that was on the Sultana
there is about 27 of them living now & near as we can tell of what
a sla___ter (slauter for slaughter?) of human life after suffering
what we did in that pen of starveation and death you and me was in
Cahaba Pen we are out of the filthy place we are out of the rageing
water to tell the horred story of degration and death that we endured
that this nation might live all Hail to the Boys in Blue they have
a name that will live as long as time does last they was Brave and
true to there flag and there Country write me again soon will you
you can do what you like with this letter you can give it to the
national Tribune if you want it printed I belong to Post No 26

WOLVERTON (cont'd.):
    Department of Nebraska am it Chaplin I remain your Comrad in F.C.L.
        William Crisp

(Letter from C M Kendall to J T Wolverton   30 Oct 1912 - 1 page)

C.M. Kendall
Real Estate Headquarters
Loan and Trust Building
Milwaukee, Wis.

Oct 30, 1912
J.T. Wolverton
Adamsville Tenn.
Dear Sir:
    A few days since one of my Comrades of the Wolcott Post, knowing
that I saw much of the Sultana disaster, handed me a cliping from
the National Tribune which prooved to be a letter from you.
    The evening you landed at Memphis, I with the manager of the
Sanitary Commission, went to the landing and distributed Tobacco
and other necessary things that would convey some comfort to our
boys in blue.
    I was acting as commissary steward of the Adams Hospital having
been severely wounded at Champion Hills on the 16th day of May - 63.
    That night at some hour (I never did know what hour it was) I was
awakened in great haste by our sergent of the gard, and asked to get
out all Surgeons, nurses and stretchers and report at the landing
at once, the Sultana had been wrecked.
    I hastened to comply and soon reached the landing where I was
ordered by the Gen'l Sup of Hospitals to see that every boat landing
with survivors or dead bodies was properly taken care of the living
sent to the different Hospitals &c.
    Well you know what I saw, and you may be sure I never will forget
it.
    You are the only survivor I have ever heard of since the close
of the war.
    If you were in the Adams Hospital, I am sure you got plenty to
eat.
    I hope you may live many years yet and enjoy good health.
                    Yours most sincerely
                        C M Kendall
                        Co K   29th Wis.

(Letter to J T Wolverton from Joel C. Hume dated sep 1912 - very
    poor handwriting)

Grantsville Utah   sep __ 1912
Mr. J.T. Wolverton
    Dear sir   I notice in the _____(National?) Tribune of your sketch
of the Sultana survivors: and will say that I at the time was a
member of I Co 113th Ill vol Inft was camped on the bluffs next to
the river or on front row as it was called in Memphis and was that
morning detailed as guard at the military Prison but before reaching out post of duty was switched off to guard _____ or anything
to convey the Rescued to the Hospitals of the city being camped on
the Banks of the River the circumstances of the affair come back to
my memory very distict on the night before the disaster a soldier
whom had been with our Regt for some previous stoped off of the boat
over night with our company and who had been prisoner of war and
was paroled missed the boat after coming of the river and was saved
another one who was a member of our own Company K Bradley of Kentucky
was
                            2
on the Boat   He Had Deseret our Regit but had went _____ to Ky and
enlisted again was on the boat returning as Parolee Prisoner that
was an awful calamity I remember how I was placed as guard on a
carriage and went to the river all day for wounded one women floated
down the River to Memphis with her babe in her arms and Both were
rescued one boy about four years old lost father mother and all I

WOLVERTON (cont'd.):
    seen Bad is of union soldiers laid out on the warf. it was Horrible.
                                    your Truly
                                    Joel C. Hume
                                    Col I 113th Illinois Inft
    P.S. Hurrah for Teddy

(Letter to Wolverton from L.A. Deerman - Boaz Marshall Co Ala dated
 19 Sept 1912 - 6 hand written pages)

Marshall County
Boza Ala Sept 19 1912
    Rout 5 Box 3
        Dear Old Comrad
I see in the National Tribune a letter that you written Stating that
you was a Servivor of the Sultana that was Blowed on the Miss River
April the 27 - 1865. Now as I am one of them old Sultana Servivers
I thought that I would write you a few lines to let you know that I
havent for gotin
                                    2
that aufful Night of disstress I am proud to here of any that is
still living that was on that Boat they isent but one besids my self
in this part of the country his name is W.F. Battles they is a few
of our com living in this part of the country I belonged to 3th
Tenn Regt Comany R + my Regt was captured at Athens &c Sulphertrusel
Ala. The 25 of Sept 1864 &c was sent to Cahaba Ala
                                    3
and we staid down there tell March 6 1865 & then to Vicksburge &
staid there over a month to _____ recrut up we had lay in that
old prison all the winter & was a bout half ded when we come out
We had bin water over a week befor we come out, the River got up &
the Back water from a bove Cahaba rune in to the prison & overflod
it they give us cord wood to make pens so we could scafel on them
so we set on them over a week
                                    4
before we come out you dident state what Regt you belong two our
Camp was J.H. Mortan Mayor Mines Col Thornburg they was a good many
of our men come from Sevire (Sevier) Co. & Blunt (Blount) Co. I am a
Ala. I was bornd & rased in Ala they was 25 or 30 Alas belonged to
Co K 3 Tenn Cav I am geting to be a tolerable old man on barred
time I was borned in 1837 Augt 11 I am drawing a pension of 15
dollars a month
                                    5
I recon that I will get a Rase under the new law I sent in my
application & they notified me it was on file Just me & my wife & son
at home I Rased 11 children to be grone all marred but one & he is
36 years of age I want to here from you a gain by letter if posable
I love to here from the old Comrads all the time I have bin taking
the National Tribune 30 y or more
                                    6
So I will close tell I here from you after I red your letter in the
paper I couldent help but study a bout it So I thought I would
write you a few lines in my simple way I am a bad composer   So
yours respectfully in F.C.&L.
                                    L.A. Deerman
Marshall Co. Boaz Ala
RFD 5 Box 3

(Letter from James Demeritt to J T Wolverton from Monterey Mexico
 5 Oct 1912)

Monterey Mexico Oct 5th 12
J.T. Wolverton
Dear Comrad
I saw a comunication of yours to the Editor of the National Tribune.
I was a prisoner of war at the Cahaba Cotton press from Sept 64
untill we wer brought to Bicksburg in April 65 So we wer in the
same prison together. Do you remember the time we disarmed the
guard and they suronded the prison with artillery. When the Alabama
overflowed and we had to drive stakes but skilled covers on top to

                                    153

WOLVERTON (cont'd.)"
        cook our corn pon! Thy wer pretty tough tines still we wer reasonaly
        happy.
        I would like to hear from you most all the old boys answered last
        roll call before this. I am now nearly 70.
                                Very respt
                                James Demeritt
                                  66 Zuazua St.
                                    Monterey Mexico
                                2
        P.S. While you went on the unfortunate Sultana We went on the Ruth
        to St. Louis. I ran away from St. Louis rejoined my regiment and
        went through Texas musterd out Dec 18th 65 at New Orleans.

        (Notation made on this letter by Wolverton:)
        yes I was in the same Prison at Cahawba the prison became overflowed
        it stood on the Bank of the Tom Bigba & Ala. River after the water
        receeded we were exchanged & I _____ how _____ wheel Barrow dead
        Rats were removed
                                Jas T. Wolverton
                                Comrades Post #7 GAR

        (Letter from Esther Patmor to Wolverton from Sheldon Ill 20 Oct 1912)

                                Sheldon Ill
                                Oct 20th 1912
        Mr. J.T. Wolverton sir: saw your ad in the national tribune where
        you went down in the illfated Sultana now i had a brother by the name
        of James Martin who made his escape out of andersonville prison and
        we never kew what his fort was he belong to K ovi rigement he might
        have gone down on that boat now would you please infome me if you
        knew any thing of that brother or not and oblige me
                                2
        i am a soldiers widow and have 3 good homes in sheldon Ill and a
        pension of 10 (?) a month you see im in a good shape i am a true
        friend to the boys in blue. blease answer soon and oblige me.
                                very respectfully
                                Esther Patmor
                                sheldon Ill

        (Letter from John E. Clark to Wolverton from Meridian Idaho 25 Sept
          1912)

        Meridian Idaho Sept the 25 1912
        Mr. J.T. Wolverton
        Adamsville Tenn

        Dear Comrad -
        I see in the National Tribune Sept 12th your account of the Reck of
        the Sultana on Apr the 27th 1865. I enlisted in the first Ala Videt
        Cavalry Sept the 16th 1863 at Valey Head Ala we crossed the mountain
        with McCook to Chickamauga after that fight we were sent back to
        Bridgeport Ala to gard the Railroad
        When Gen Hooker crossed the river at Shellmound Tenn. 50 of my Co
        C was sent there to Pilot him across the
                                2
        mountains we had a small fight at Lookout Bridg and then at wahatcha
        we were with Hooker untill after the mission Ridge fight then we
        were sent back to Bridgeport
        we seen hard service scouting against the Rebel Raiders
        on the 17th of Sept 1864 I was taken Prisner with others we were
        sent to Cahaba arrived there some time in Oct staid there untill the
        _____ water in march I left there on the Boat Riendeere was landed
        at Sellma we were taken from there to Demopilous on the tom Bigby
        River Down the River on a boat to McDowells landing
                                3
        then to Meridian Miss then to Jackson Miss then to Camp Fisk neare
        Vicksburg as I Remember we arrived at Camp fisk March 19th I left
        Camp fisk with the Bunch that left there on the 22nd of April on the
        Boat Olive Branch to the Benton Baracks at St. Louis Mo

                                154

WOLVERTON (cont'd.):

I staid there untill the 15th of May then went to Johnson Co Ill
In Aug I went to my old home in Ala found everything Burnt houses
and Barnes and all the fence it was a Desolate looking Place my
folks had Been Driven away from home I found them in

4

Marion County Tenn
we heard of the great Disaster of the Sultana a Day or so after we
arrived at St Louis
I hav Been Reading the tribune carfuly to see if I could ever heare
of a Cahaba Comrad that went thru the Starvation with me I was not
one of the leaders of the mutiny when we made an attempt to Break
out But I was one of the helpers I was at that time 19 years old. I
was not caled by my name in the prison by my Comrads I was called
Alabama By them all that called me at all

5

I will Be 67 years old the 8 of next Dec. I get a Pention of $12.00
per month. I hav Ben farming untill 5 years ago.
I hav Been connected with a feed store the last 5 years.
I would be pleased to here from you and here some of your expereance
of the war and Prisen life. I am as ever your Comrad and friend.

John E. Clark
Meridian
Box 151   Idaho

WOOD, WILLIAM T.

FORM NO. 1

1. William T. Wood Darden, Tenn, Route 1
2. I am 76 years of age
3. Tennessee, Henderson County
4. Henderson County, enlisted in Federal army
5. Farming
6. Farming
7. I owned no land before the war.
8. no
9. they owned none
10. $500
11. Log house, with two rooms
12. Plowed and worked with hoe about equally.
13. My father farmed enterely for a living. my mother did the house work
    in general, and spun and wove practically all the cloths for the
    family.
14. no
15. yes
16. yes
17. To no extent in general, however, a few white men had slaves and
    they didn't work much, but generally looked after the business.
18. They mingled freely with those who did not own slaves and didnt seem
    to think themselves better than those who didn't own slaves
19. yes, about the same
20. yes, in general. Just as the war was coming up there seemed to be
    a little coolness between them.
21. I do not know that it did.
22. yes, about like it has always been
23. I do not consider they were antagonistic. they seemed to be on an
    equal footing with other men. There were few who owned slaves in
    the community where I was born and raised.
24. Subscription schools in very poor houses with poll benches.
25. I do not know, not much I never got futher than baker in the old
    "blue back speller
26. about two miles
27. I have forgotten the name
28. private, or subscription
29. two or three months
30. not much
31. man
32. I enlisted in the Federal army the 8th day of January 1864 in

155

WOOD (cont'd.):
Henderson County, was mustered in at Huntingdon   Carroll Co Tenn
33. 7th Tennessee Cavalry.
John B. Hays, Houston Wood, Elijah Bradfield, Shade Owens, Joe Robins,
Nath Overman, Tab Rogers, Judge Reid,Clark Prichett
I can't think of the given names of any others
34. Union City
35. about two months
36. at Union City
37. my company was captured at Union City, and taken to Andersonville
prison. We suffered greatly from exposure and hunger.
38. Nashville Tennessee
39. came on a train from Nashville to Johnsonville thence on a boat to
Perryville, and walked from the latter place home, a distance of
20 miles.
40. Didnt do anything for some time, because I was not able, owing to
exposure and starvation in Andersonville prison. When I did go to
work, I took up farming.
41. I have made part of my living since the war by farming and working
in timber. I haven't done anything in particular for several years,
owing to disability. Baptist. Never held public office.
42. Jasper Wood; Don't know; Don't know; Don't know; the time of his
death in Madison County, near Milan; He was a plain common citizen.
43. Hanna J. Essary; Don't know given names; ---; ---
44. I can't give you anything upon the above questions. I know practically nothing of my ancestry, of which I am sorry.

156

Confederate Soldiers (Abbott–Byrne)

ABBOTT, NAPOLEON BONAPARTE

FORM NO. 1

1. Napoleon Bonaparte Abbott, Frankewing R 2, Tenn.
2. Will be 84 yr old Apr. 17, 1922
3. Tenn., Lincoln county
4. Tenn., Lincoln county - in service of the Confederacy
5. farmer
6. farmer
7. did not own anything
8. did not own slave
9. did not own land
10. $100.00
11. log cabin two rooms
12. worked on farm every work day with plow or hoe or other implements used on the farm or chopping wood or at making rails, ect.
13. father worked at all the kinds of work on the farm continually. Mother did all the duties of the home - cooking, washing and ironing, spinning, having corded the cotton, knitting and sewing, ect.
14. they did not
15. it was considered respectable and honorable
16. yes
17. approximately 10% were large slave holder, having from 15 to 30 slaves. These men did not work, except occasionally at some profession - doctor, lawyer, etc.
18. Some of the slave-holders seemed to feel themselves better than the non-slaveholders and hold themselves aloof. Many mingled freely with non-slaveholders making no distinctions.
19. In the main they did. A few slave holders held aloof.
20. There was a friendly feeling.
21. It did. They could buy votes, with liquor and cigars
22. They were not good. Very few poor men ever became more than laborers
23. They were discouraged
24. Rural free one-teacher schools of three or four months duration per year
25. Ten or twelve years
26. about one mile
27. Rural free one-teacher school
28. Public
29. 3 or 4 months in the late summer and fall
30. Very regularly between work times
31. man
32. April 22, 1861 at Boons Hill, Lincoln co., Tenn. in the service of the Confederacy
33. 1st Tenn. Confederates - went out before State seceded
34. to Lynchburg, Va.
35. Supported line at Manassas - no fighting - July 21, 1861. Fired first time at Seven Pines on Chickahoiny (Chickahominy) river May 31, 1862(?) (N.B.: Seven Pines or Fair Oaks, Va.- Manassas Junction, Va.)
36. ----
37. Engaged in many skirmishes and in following battles; Mechanicsville (Va.) June 26, 1862, Gaines Mill, (Va.) June 27, 1862 Gettysburg (Pa.) 1st day. Captured in morning of 1st day. Exchanged in Mar. 1864. Battle Fredericksburg (Va.) Dec. 13, 1865(?). Feb. 5, 1865 fought at Mine Run, right of Petersburg. Captured at Petersburg (Va.) Apr. 2, 1865. Fraziers (Frayser's Farm) June 28, 1862
38. At Port Delaware, May 9, 1865 from Federal Prison
39. Federal Govt. furnished transportation from Philadelphia to Wartrace (Bedford co.) Tenn. Yankees were friendly
40. Raising cotton
41. ----
42. Flemming Abbott; b. in Halifax co., Va.; lived in Lincoln co., Tenn. after he was 20 yr. of age; always worked on farm - raised large family
43. Lamiza J. Owen; David Owen and Manerva Owen (nee Irving); Boons Hill, Lincoln co., Tenn.
44. Maternal grandmother's people were pure Irish. Maternal grandfather's

159

ABBOTT (cont'd.):
    people were Virginians. My father's people were Virginians.
45. ----
46. ----

                    ABERNATHY, ALFRED E.

FORM NO. 2

1.   Alfred E. Abernathy
2.   79
3.   Giles county, Tenn.
4.   Confederate
5.   Co. E, 32
6.   farmer
7.   Jas. Abernathy; Brunswick (co.). Va.
8.   Eliza Abernathy; Elisha (?) Abernathy and Martha Reed
9.   ----
10. none
11. Parents 2
12. 150
13. about 6000$
14. frame 4 rooms
15. farmed
16. farming - cooking, spining, carding and weaving
17. 2
18. it was
19. they did
20. very few
21. they did - they did not
22. they did
23. they was - they was not
24. they did
25. it was
26. encouraged
27. private and sub(scription)
28. 11 years
29. 1½ miles
30. ----
31. booth(both)
32. 10
33. they did
34. man and woman
35. 61, Oct.-Elkton
36. Camp Trousdal(e)
37. 5 monts (months)
38. Fort donnelson (Fort Donelson, Tenn.)
39. ----
40. I was on detail and was not discharged at all
41. I footed it home
42. farming
43. farming - same place that I went from - Methodist
44. ----
45. I am the only one of my Co. in the State. One in Ala. that is of
     the Company left. W.S. Brigforth (Bridgeforth?) and my self.
46. ----

                    ABERNATHY, J. PRESS

FORM NO. 2

1.   J. Press Abernathy, Aspen Hill, R.F.D. No 2, Giles co., Tenn.
2.   If i live until November nineteenth (19) next will be 82.
3.   Giles co., Tenn.
4.   Confederate
5.   Co. A, 3rd Tenn. Reg.
6.   farmer
7.   Hartwell P. Abernathy; Brunswick co., Virginia; lived at Giles co.,

160

ABERNATHY (cont'd.):

    Tenn. from childhood; he was to(o) old fer the Civil War.

8. Loucinda Meadows; Lileston Meadows and (unknown); Giles co., Tenn.

9. My father had an uncle Elisha Abernathy who served in the Mexican War and his father, James Abernathy was one of the founder's of a Methodist Church Bethesda in Giles Co.-in 1818 my ancestors came from England, five brothers and settled in the state of Virginia date unknown, first Abernathys in America.

10. I was 20 years old when I entered the Civil war and served, no property - lived with my father. Joined army 16th day of May 1861.

11. My father owned 3 slaves

12. My father owned 200 acres

13. $10,000.00

14. My father lived in a log house 1½ stories 5 rooms built of yellow poplar and white ash logs and black walnut sills put up in 1842.

15. I did any kind of work that belonged to farming - plowed, howed, split rails or any thing that came up.

16. My father did all kinds of farm work. My Mother cooked served spun thread wove cloth and clothed her family of 11 children with the fruits of her labor.

17. ----

18. It most certainly was

19. They did

20. Very little idleness done at all in those days

21. They were very social and frindly and most all had a kind respect fer all their neighbors.

22. they did

23. in any community a family of non slave holders was considered in every way equal to the ones that had slaves.

24. it did not

25. they were

26. as a usual thing they were encouraged by most people

27. common country schools

28. I went a part of 10 years not full time

29. about 2 miles

30. private schools, that was before the days of public schools

31. private

32. about 10 months

33. they did - some had to work part of their time

34. both

35. I enlisted May 16th 1861 at Elkton, Giles co., Tennesse(e) in the Confederate Army

36. To Lynnville Tenn. where the famous 3rd Tennessee Regiment was organized electing Capt. John C. Brown(?) Col.

37. In February at Fort Do(nelson?) where I was captured and sent to prison at Camp Douglas Chicago with the command I was with

38. Fort Donelson 15th Feb. 1862

39. After first battle I went to prison and staid 7 mo. and went down the Mississippi River to Vixburg, Miss. and was exchanged and soldiered about their about a year and was in the fight at Raymond, Miss. May 12 1863. Wounded in right arm, rations were short sometimes but we were very well fed had plenty clothes I was wounded again at Chickamage 19th Sept. 1865 in arm and on head. (Chickamauga)...

40. Wounded in head again skull fractured at Jonesboro, Ga. Aug. 31st 1864(?) part skull removed and have suffering 12 years from it.

41. I had a furlough from the Medical board at Macon, Ga. and was at home when the army surendered never fit for service any more. I walked home from Mississippi - no cars through here then about 100 miles. We walked it in about a week two other soldiers and myself.

42. farm work

43. I was raised on a farm and after coming home went to work and bought a small farm and have engaged in farming fer 56 years - was Justice of the Peace of my district fer 20 years - have been a member of the Methodist church for over 50 years. Joined the Mason Lodge in June 1867 at Elkton, Tenn. and have lived in Giles county all my life only the 4 years that I was in the civil war. I am over most 82 years old and 12 years ago my head wound began to give me trouble and I suffer at times with falling sickness or apoplexy. I was born

ABERNATHY (cont'd.):

in the year 1840, November 19th - am now in my 82 year. Hoping this will be of benefit I am,

Respectfully,

J. Press Abernathy

44. ----
45. M.T. Abernathy, J.L. Abernathy, Sam Abernathy, W.H. Arthur, W.J. Adkins, T.(?) C. Barber, (Cap.?), ___Budmew, T.E. Devenport, O.(?) P. Bruce, J.P. Barr (or Bass), H.M. Beatty-Sargent, W.D. Carden, W.W. Wren, W.J. Hargrove, F.G. Wilson, J.A. Hollin, W.H. Hodge, W.F. Tucker, Tom Reed, W.C.(?) Garrison, Larkin Gorden, H.W. Watson, Tom Beatty, S.J. Bates, D.B. Boswell, J.G. Bra line, James Bracline(?), D.J. Bridgeforth, G.B. Brice(?), J.W. King,A._. Culps(?), T.J. Bruce, W.G. Buchanan, John W. Bull, W.A. Campbell, John Carter, W.H. Cheat-ham, J.W. Childers, G.W. Chiles, W.R.(?) Davis, M.A. Daugherty, T.A. Degraffenried, Abder Dunger, F.M. Dunger, J._. Dyer, George Elder, E.(?)_. Estes, J.P. Ewell, W.I. Franklin, J.B. Fuller, J.M. George, W.H. Gibbs, H.C.(?) Gilbert, George H. Grant, P.H. Hardeman, W.B. Hargroves, H.B. Hazelwood(?), T.B. Henderson, A.B. Hollis (Hollin?), John W. Hollin, Cal Ewing, J.L. Nelson, Jim Nelson, Charley Nelson, J._. Reilly, Tom Henderson, Polk Henderson, Cuck (Dock?) Whitfield, Dub Whitfield, Bill Scruggs, W.H. Jones, Andrew Reed, Logan Steffe(?), W.H. Jackson, Tom Hues(?), Jim Hues(?), Ed Bowers, J.A. Bowers, Tip Stone, John Osborn, Jim Osbourn, John Simpson, Tom Silvester, Fletcher Stevenson, Bill Kenedy, Reps(?) Petty, Dell Bass, J.M. Bass, Billie Gilbert, Oscar Campbell
46. M.T. Abernathy   Pulaski, No. 5, Tennessee

M.T. Abernathy	Pulaski, No. 5, Tennessee
J.T. Dyer	Pulaski, No. 5, Tennessee
F.M. Bunch	Pulaski, Tennessee
J.F. Nelson	Aspen Hill, No. 2, Tenn.
E.P. Park	Elkton, Tenn
John Curtis	Frankewing, Tenn.
A.E. Abernathy	Pualski, No. 5, Tenn
L.B. Oderneal(?)	Pulaski, Tenn.

ABERNATHY, MILTON THOMAS

FORM NO. 2

1. M.T. Abernathy (Milton Thomas), Pulaski, Tenn. R. #5
2. 76 yrs. 10 mos.
3. Giles co., Tenn.
4. Confederate
5. Co. A, 3rd Tenn.
6. Farmer
7. Hartwell Passon (Abernathy*); Virginia, Dinwiddie co., Va.; Pulaski, and Elkton (N.B. *see J. Press Abernathy questionnaire and 1850 census)
8. Lucinda Green Meadows; ----; Elkton
9. ----
10. none
11. yes, two
12. 200 acres
13. $2000
14. log house four rooms
15. plowed, hoed and every sort of farm work
16. farm work. Mother did spinning weaving sewing making candles
17. none only slaves (2)
18. by most people it was considered honorable - small percent consider-ed disgraceful to work.
19. yes
20. about 5%
21. to some extent they felt themselves better
22. not altogether
23. generally there was
24. ----
25. I was too young to remember
26. encouraged
27. common country school

162

ABERNATHY (cont'd.):
28. 4 or 5 years
29. 1½ miles
30. Center point
31. private
32. 10 mos.
33. I went to school 1 yr. and others worked (time about) - yes
34. man
35. Elkton, Giles co., Tenn., June 1861
36. Camp Cheatham
37. 7 mos.
38. Fort Donaldson (Donelson), Tenn.
39. Taken prisoner at Donaldson (Donelson) exchanged after being in prison
    7 months. Was in battle at Springdale Chckasaw Bayou, discharged
    at Port Hudson (La.) by being under age, rejoined my command after
    4 mos. - wounded at Jonesborough - had gangrene.
40. Payroled at Augusta, Ga. April 1865
41. Walked on crutches from Atlanta to Dalton (Ga.). Yankees then gave
    transportation home.
42. farming
43. Engaged in farming. Methodist Church South
44. ----
45. Roster of our Company will be sent to you
46. J.P. Abernathy   Pulaski, Tenn
    A.E. Abernathy   "
    R.J. Brunson   "
    J.T. Dyer   "
    Fate Nelson   "
    J.R.D. Williams   "
    D.C. Neal   "

ABERNATHY, RITCHARD TUCKER

FORM NO. 2

1. Ritchard Tucker Abernathy, Bells, Tenn. R.F.D. No. 4
2. 78 the 29(th) of last April
3. Giles co., Tenn.
4. Confederate
5. C - 53rd Tenn.
6. farmer
7. Elisha Abernathy; Virginia; lived near Petersburg, (Tenn.?)
8. Mary Ann Rebecca Evans; dau. of Henry Evans and a Miss Pool; Dinwoody
   (Dinwiddie) co., Virginia
9. ----
10. ----
11. 2 negroes - 1 woman and 1 child
12. 90
13. $1500
14. log house 2 rooms open hall
15. i done general farm work anything that was need to be done
16. General farming my Mother woked(?) washed spun weave cloth
17. no
18. yes
19. yes
20. not many
21. they mingled right freely
22. to some extent
23. friendly
24. i do not know
25. yes
26. i do not know
27. Subscription
28. something like ten months
29. about one fourth mile
30. Brown / Paynes / Bethesda
31. Private
32. from 4 to 6 months
33. yes

ABERNATHY (cont'd.):
34. man
35. 1861 - Dec. Mount Pisgah Church, Giles co., Tenn.
36. Nashville
37. something near two months
38. Fort Donaldson (Donelson) was wounded 5 times
39. i went to the Hospital after i was wounded i stayed in the hospital
    3 months then was carried out to Gilbert Abernathys and stayed 4
    months. Camp was good had plenty to eat and wear i was not in Camp
    long before i was wounded.
40. i did not get a discharge
41. i was carried home in a buggy and made the trip very well - my
    Mother was going to have my funeral preached sunday and i got home
    saturday afternoon - she heard i was dead
42. farming
43. i have never done any thing but farm and i have not been able to
    do that for the pas(t) 20 years i have lived in west Tenn. for 58
    years i belong to the M E Church So.
44. ----
45. Alf Abernathy, Col,; H.H. Ammett, Capt.; Pone(?) Macklin, 1st Lt.;
    Cred Ammett, 3rd Lt.; Henry Ammett, Orderly Sgt.; John Sisk, private;
    John Wilson, private; Alfred Wilson, private
46. William Acuff   Bells, Tenn
    J.L. Shelton   Bells, Tenn
    J.L. Betts   Jones, Tenn
    Doc Harris   Bells, Tenn.

ACUFF, STOKLEY

FORM NO. 1

1. Stokley Acuff, Powder Springs, Tennessee
2. 77 yrs.
3. Granger (Grainger) Co., Tenn.
4. Granger co., Tenn
5. Farming
6. Farming
7. none
8. no
9. 300
10. $2000.00
11. Log house 4 rooms
12. all kinds of work nesersary on a farm
13. my Father did all kinds of work pertainning to the farm. my Mother
    worked in the house cooking spinning weaving also patch work
14. no
15. yes
16. yes
17. none
18. all mingled togather
19. yes
20. yes frendly feeling
21. ----
22. I could not tell any difference
23. encouraged
24. Publick
25. 3 months
26. 1½ miles
27. Primary Publick schools
28. Publick
29. 2 mo.
30. no
31. man
32. Sept. 1862
33. 26th Regiment. Albert Acuff is the only surviving members I know of
34. Mossey Creek now Jefferson City then sent to henderson Station then
    my co. transfered to Redgiment 26 at murfresborough
35. near 4 months
36. Murfhriesborough or Stone's river (Murfreesboro), Tenn.

164

ACUFF (cont'd.):
37. I was wounded in the first battle I maid my way to Knoxville was
    signed to the hospittle and then was sent home on 30 days furlow
    never able for service any more and no call was maid for me I never
    was in service any more.
38. never was discharge
39. left Murphisborough to go to georgia but prevailed with conductor
    and paid ½ fair and he took me to Knoxville was sent to hospittle,
    then my father came and I was carreyed home in an ox cart
40. none for 15 or 16 years for I was not able to do any thing sence
    then what work I have done have been farming
41. ocipation (occupation) farming. Lived in Tenn most of my time - was
    in the west 17 yrs. Belong to Baptist Church ever since I was 16
    yr of age
42. Thomas D. Acuff; Granger co., Tenn.; ----; none
43. Clara Vittitoe; Thomas Vittitoe and Susan Vittitoe; Locust Grove,
    Granger co., Tenn.
44. ----
    (On Separate page)
41. My life sence the war has been filled with untiled pains and aches.
    I received an _____ ball in my shoulder in this battle at murphis-
    borough. I carried that ball for 42 years in my body. it went in
    at my shoulder worked down through my body and back part of my
    thigh. the coruption that run from me has bee(n) awful. it was
    almost a constant drip for 30(?) yrs.

                        ADAIR, ROBERT PRESIDENT

FORM NO. 2

1. Robert President Adair, #44 North Adair Street, Clinton, S.C.
2. I will be 81 years of age December 19, 1922
3. South Carolina, Laurens county
4. Confederate soldier
5. A-13th Regiment S.C.; Veterans, McCowans Brigade. Fought under Lee
   and Jackson, and A.P. Hill.
6. Farmer
7. Robert James Adair; b. in Jacks Township, Laurens co., S.C.; lived
   same as above; Private citizen
8. Sallie R. Jacks; Isaac Jacks and Annie Whitten; Jacks twp., co. of
   Laurens, S.C.
9. I do not know my great grandfathers name, but he lived in the state
   of Maryland, and served in the Revolutionary War. My grandfather
   James Adair (I think that my great grandfather was named James Adair
   also), came to South Carolina from Maryland, and settled in Laurens
   county.
10. No
11. My father owned twenty odd slaves
12. 480 acres
13. Approximately $18,500.00
14. We lived in a house that was partly log and partly frame. It con-
    tained five rooms.
15. The work that I done on the farm was mostly plowing, of course I
    went to school, but often I stayed away from school to plow, and I
    plowed and worked on the farm in general during the summer months.
16. My father was an extensive farmer and he was kept busy looking after
    the whole farm. My mother had a house servant, but she superintended
    the house work, the cooking and the spinning, and she did her part
    in the actual work. Quite a bit more than the average woman of
    today does. She did the entire sewing for the family, and there
    were seven in the family, besides making the clothing for the slaves.
17. One House servant (Cook)
18. All farm work was considered respectable and honorable
19. Yes, fully
20. There were very few men in my community that led lived of idleness
    not as many as there are today by a long way.
21. There was no such feeling at all between the slaveholders and those
    men who did not own slaves they were the same toward each other as
    they were toward one another

                              165

ADAIR (cont'd.):
22. As stated above there was no feeling of animosity. The slaveowners had no more importance than a respectable man who did not own any slaves.
23. Very friendly and not the slightest antagonism existed.
24. The people did not consider whether a man owned slaves or not. He was elected on his merits and not on his wealth.
25. Everything possible was done for such young men, and was often aided in buying his land or going into any other kind of business.
26. They were encouraged by slaveholders, equally as much as by the none-slaveholders.
27. An old Field school
28. About nine or ten years
29. Three miles
30. Clinton School and Hurrican School
31. Private
32. Nine to ten months
33. Fairly regular
34. Both
35. I inlisted in the Confederate Army August 6th 1861 in Laurens co. S.C.
36. Near Columbia, S.C. for a camp of instruction
37. about 8 months, before I was in a battle; my comapny was in battle earlier
38. The Battle of Chancellorsville (Va.)
39. I fought in the following battles, though this is not the order as they came - Cahncellorsville (Va.); Wilderness (va.); Pottsylvania (this may be Spottsylvania, Va.) - I was under the Big 188' tree* that was shot down by minnie balls; Sharpsburg (Maryland); Falling Waters (Maryland); Cedar Run; Riddle's (Riddell's) Shop (Va.); Deep Bottom (Va.) on James River. Two battles - one of these battles against negroes, I killed some of the negroes and we rum them back, Gettysburg, Harper's Ferry (we captured 11,000 prisoners), Petersburg (in this battle I was wounded). (N.B.: See additional page) I was never discharged - I was not with my company at the time of the surrender. I had been wounded (this answer goes on into the space for Q. 40)
(*This was probaly the oak tree at the fight of the "Bloody Angle")
40. See above
41. After I was wounded at Petersburg, I was sent to a hospital at Appomatox, and from there to Danville (Va.) and was fourloughed at Danville. (I walked from Appomatox to Danville. From Danville I rode Jeff Davis Train to Greensboro (N.C.). We walked from here to Charlotte (N.C.) and rode train from here to Chester, S.C. and walked from there hom. (see additional page)
42. Farming, as soon as my wound got well.
43. I lived on the farm until 1897, which was about three miles north of Clinton, and then I moved to Laurens, S.C. to serve as Supervisor of Laurens County, which office I held for five years. Then I moved to Clinton, S.C. and since then I have served two years as City Alderman. During this time I continued to look after my farm and up to a few years ago. I have served as Stewart of the Methodist Church for about fifty years.
44. ----
45. The Roster is in the County Clerks Office at Laurens, S.C. (see addisional sheet). Members of Company A, 13th Regiment South Carolina Volunteers, McGowns Brigade, Jackson's Corp., A.P. Hill's Division; (Our entire fighting was done in Maryland, Virginia and Pennsylvania under General Robert E. Lee.)
Capt. Romulus L. Bowden; 1st Lt. J.D. Copeland; 2nd Lt. S. _. Wier; 3rd Lt. J.W. Rook; 1st Sgt. W.A. Stone; 2nd Sgt. J.L. Cunningham; 3rd Sgt. W.R. Jones; 4th Sgt. J.S. McCrary; 1st Corpl. J.C. Raiford; 2nd Cpl. W.L. Cunningham; 3rd Cpl. W.W. Walker; 4th Cpl. B.E. Hunter; 5th Cpl. Henry Suber; 6th Cpl. D.A. Watson; 7th Cpl. R.W. Bobo; Privates; W.J. Anderson, R.A. Atchinson, Q.Q. Adair; R.P. Adair, I.J. Adair, Frank Abrams, J.W. Bailey, W.P. Buchanan, W.J. Brock, T.S. Boyd, Henry Boyd, A.M. Butler, Thomas Burnett, J.F. Bell, I.C. Bell, J.T. Braddock, J.N. Boshell, William Brown, B.M. Copeland, Harry Coleman, Boyd Clopton, J.H. Cunningham, Watt Cunningham, J.C. Calhoun, Patrick Calhoun, Charlie Denson, T.J. Dillard, Joseph

ADAIR (cont'd.):

Duncan, David Dalrumple, G.H. Davidson, Marcus Foot, I.W. Finney,
Berry Graves, Frank Graves, G.W. Horton, C. S. Horton, R.A Hudgens,
.T. Henderson, Elisha Hellams, Alex Henry, Robt. Hatton, William
Husky, Marcus Harris, R.G. Hitt, H.A. Hitt, W.Y. Jacks, J.M. Johnson,
C.H. Johnson, B.N. Johnson, Hiram Johnson, Gary Johnson, T.R. Jones,
J.A. Jones, R.J.Y. Little, Thaddeus McCrady, C.M. McCrady, W.H. Mc-
Crary, S.R. McCrary, Cally McCrary, Isaac Morris, Mattison Milan,
W.R. Nabors, A.E. Nelson, J.W. Neil, S.A. Oliver, J.H. Odell,
E.C. Odell, John Odell, E.T. Oxner, W.S. Pearson, W.S.Palmer,
E.A. Pitts, R.G. Pitts, T.Y. Prather, H.W. Prather, H.W. Prather,
G.R. Ray, J.T. Ray, R.C. Ray, J.A. Ray, W.W. Ray, J.H. Ramage,
I.W. Ramage, L.B. Ramage, P.P. Rock, J.T. Richmond, Elam Richey,
Albert Smith, William Simms, James Simms, Geo. Simpson, T.J. Tigert,
W.A. Tarrent, T.F. Tarrant, W.D. Watts, W.P. Watson, Drayton Watson,
W.G. Watson, Johnson Wesson, W.W. Walker, Simon Wolfe, ___ White,
A.C. Young, H.B. Young.

46.
J.W. Copeland	Clinton, S.C.
H.P. Blakley	Clinton, S.C.
H.Z. Wright	Clinton, S.C.
George M. Hannah	Cross Hill, S.C.
R.P. Adair, Sr.	Clinton, S.C.
R.J. Copeland, Sr.	Clinton, S.C.
T.F. Milam	Clinton, S.C.
John W. Young, M.D.	Clinton, S.C.
A.M. Copeland	Clinton, S.C.
J.W.C. Bell	Clinton, S.C.
J.L. Simpson	Clinton, S.C.
W.H. McCrary	Clinton, S.C.
B.M. Copeland	Nashville, Ark.
M.M. Buford	Newberry, S.C.
J.D. Mock	Laurens, S.C.
O.G. Thompson	Laurens, S.C.
M. Fleming	Lanford Station, S.C.
J.C. Davis	Clinton, S.C.
Irby Chandler	Clinton, S.C.

(on additional pages)

39. These are the only battles that I cam remember. There was one more
that I remember, but do not recall the name, however, we boys called
it where we Made the Fur Fly. I got the majority of my clothing from
home during the war, but during the last two years I was often half
clothed and many times with out shoes. There was a shortage of
rations during the entire four years, but during the last two years
there was a serious shortage and we often had to go hungry. We
slept under a little tent, my partner and I. There were many times
we ate raw green mutton corn, and stewed apples without any season-
ing whatever. During the cold weather our soldiers suffered
immensely from the cold as we did not have one-half enough clothing
and blankets to keep us warm in the day time much less at night.

41. During my entire trip home I walked two hundred miles, having a
wound in the abdomen. I was wounded on the second of April and
did not get home until the 18th of April, and Lee had surrendered
on April 9th. Afther I got home I came near dying from my wound,
it having contracted gangreen.

45. Out of my company at the beginning of the war of 124 men, there are
only three living today, and they are: R.P. Adair, Sr., B.M. Copeland and W.H. McCrary.

ADAMS, CHARLES WESLEY

FORM NO. 2

1. Charles WEsley Adams, Manchester, Tennessee
2. Seventy-eight years old August 18, 1922
3. Warren county, Tennessee
4. Prisoner one night - paroled next day
5. Company A, 48th Tenn. Cavalry, Col. Hayes
6. Farmer

ADAMS (cont'd.):

7. James Bazel Adams; Monroe county, I think, Tennessee; he afterwards lived in Bradley county, Tenn. and moved to Missouri in the year 1858, and then moved back to Tennessee and died about 16 years ago in Coffee county.
8. Sallie (Crosslin) Adams; Charles Crosslin and Annie Crosslin; in Coffee co., Tenn. where they died
9. ----
10. Was just a boy when the war began and young when I came back
11. no
12. ----
13. ----
14. ----
15. Been a farmer all my life
16. ----
17. ----
18. It was
19. ----
20. ----
21. ----
22. ----
23. ----
24. ----
25. It depended then, as it does now, on the young man himself
26. ----
27. Common school
28. ----
29. ----
30. ----
31. Public
32. Do not recall
33. Yes
34. Man and a good one
35. Enlisted in October 1st, 1863 in Coffee co., Tenn.
36. South
37. About two months
38. At Haynes Tanyard, Alabama
39. ----
40. May 8, 1865 at Blue Mountain, Alabama
41. I walked home, crossing Sand Mountain in the night and it was a slow and lonesome trip.
42. Farming
43. Have lived in this county (Coffee) since the war, engaged in farming
44. ----
45. Jim Kidd, Dan McMahan, Ford Jetton, Lee Hulatt, Tom Jones, Rob Crow, Elias Braxton, Lock Hitts, Perry Phillips, Jim Anthony
46. ----

ADAMS, FORD NORFLEET

FORM NO. 1

1. Ford Norfleet Adams, Adams, Tenn.
2. 80
3. Tenn., Robertson county
4. Tenn., Robertson
5. Farmer
6. Farmer
7. Did not own property before the war
8. Parents did, 10 or 12
9. about 350 acres
10. about $21,100.00
11. Frame house 4 rooms
12. I did all kinds of farm work, including hoeing and plowing
13. Father was in bad health and did very little work but supervised the farm work. In addition to household duties Mother cooked, spun and wove.
14. Yes - 1 woman
15. All honest toil was regarded respectable and honorable

ADAMS (cont'd.):
16. They did
17. Very few white men, led lives of idleness all working
18. Yes, all mingled freely
19. They did
20. Always a friendly feeling
21. It did not, always voted for the most capable man, regardless of slaves.
22. All honest young men always had help
23. They were encouraged by slave holders
24. 1 room log school
25. about 10 years
26. 2 miles
27. Subscription schools
28. Private
29. 6 to 7 mo.
30. Fairly so
31. Man
32. Nov. 17, 1861, near Guthrie, Ky.
33. 50th Tenn., Officers Capt. Cyms Sugg, J.B. Dorth, 1st Lt. Joel Ruffinf, 2 Lt. O.W. Tyler, 3d Lt. T.J. Adams, R.T. Adams, G.W. Adams, R.S. Adams, Geo. W. Adair, Wm. Trice, Emmett Fields, Robt. McReynolds, J.A. Moore, Robt. S_ry, Robt. Ogg(?), J.L. Qualls, G.J. Qualls, Tip Goodman, Buck Harris, G.S. Hinberger, J.O. Lawrence, J.S. Dunn
34. Ft. Donelson, Tenn. Steward Co.
35. 3 mo. before battle of Ft. Donelson
36. Ft. Donelson
37. on 10th Jan. 1863 was sent to Ft. Hudson - after exchange in Calvary was in bombardment in Ft. Hudson, La. eveing came up river in gun boats - bombs were heavy all night long - we drove them back with guns from land. Went into hospital Mch. 1, 1863, remained about 4 weeks, had very bad treatment. After being released from hospital was sent to Clinton, La. for a week, went to Jackson, Miss. and joined our command at Enterprise, Miss. - we left Enterprise, Miss. went on to Mount Bluff Church, Miss. and went into camp.
38. Left prison, Columbus, Ohio on account of ill health
39. Came home on train via Cincinatti, Louisville to Allensville, Ky. and walked from Allensville to Adams.
40. After recovering from sickness took up farming
41. Have lived in Robertson co., except 4 yrs. in Montgomery co. about 4 yrs. in mercantile business at Adams, balance time a farmer, member of Baptist church.
42. Rubin Adams; near Danville, ----, Caswell co. N.C.; lived at Adams, Tenn. 55 years
43. Precilla Robertson; Jno. Robertson and Miss _____ Thompson; Robertson county
44. Lemuel Chilton, an uncle by marriage, served in War of 1812.

(N.B.: on separate sheet of paper headed "Town of Adams, Adams, Tenn.")
37. From Mount Bluff Church we went to Vicksburg, Miss., when we were about 1 days march the Ft. at Vicksburg surrendered. We went to Jackson, Miss. where another engagement was in force on our right. but we did not engage in this, but were in sight, from there went to Enterprise, Miss. left Enterprise for Meridian, Miss. in ___ about 1 day and night from there to Mobile, Ala. camped there 1 night, crossed Mobile Bay fer Atlanta, from Atlanta to Chicamauga battle field and entered the battle, Sept. 25, 1863 - after this battle driving the enemy back to Chattanooga we went into camp at the fort of Lookout Mt. 2 mo. in camp we had the battle of Missionary Ridge. They drove us back to Ringgold, from there we went to Tilden, Ga. where we went into winter quarters for winter 1863-1864 (following on 2nd sheet) ---- Apr. 1864 we went to Selma, Ala. camped there for some time, from there to July 22, 1864 we were engaged in flanking, for 3 mo. we were forced to Atlanta, Ga. where we had a big battle July 22, 1864. Aug. 3, 1864 I was captured from pickett line sent to prison, remained 8 mo. to 29 Mch. 1865. My health giving completely away was sent directly home from Columbus Ohio arrived home Apr. 1, 1865 about 10 days before the surrender. In prison we

ADAMS (cont'd.):
    had very little to eat, but managed to keep from freesing by piling
    up together.

                        ADAMS, J. M.

FORM NO. 1

1.   J.M. Adams, Kinton, Tennessee Rout 6
2.   77 year old
3.   Dyar co., state Tennessee
4.   Dyear county stat of Tennessee
5.   farming
6.   farming
7.   not iny thing
8.   Parents own 1
9.   197 acres
10.   about five thousend dollers
11.   log house wether boarded and seald containg 6 rooms
12.   howing plowin eny kind of work cam to hand
13.   father a farmer mother cooking sweeping spining weving all kind of
      house work
14.   not
15.   yes it was
16.   yes
17.   not eny
18.   the men migle(mingle) freely, the slave holders they did not
19.   yes they did
20.   all naberd and worked to ge ther
21.   thire was not eny candidate of slave holders in my country
22.   yes very good
23.   there were encouraged
24.   a subscription school
25.   about 6 mounts in a year
26.   1½ miles
27.   Miler Chapel
28.   Burit (?) school
29.   10 monts in the year
30.   whin not bisie they was regularly
31.   men and women
32.   year 1863 in dyer county
33.   15th Tennessee Regiment Co. F - Don Wells, George Wells, Andu Whitson,
      Pvt. More, Lt. Gr_fey, Bill Mosby, _iat Willson, Jsh. Whitson, John
      Bealhouse, Wilce Fra__, Jeff More, Da__ More, Henry Hodg, Francls
      Hodg, Will King, Herb King, Bill Fillaups, Will Turpin, Bill Bruce,
      Bob Johnson, Jake (John?) Brooks, Van Bibbs, John Redeck, Amas Reed,
      Dick Doud.
34.   all ovr the cuntry getharing up solgers
35.   about 5 monts at esternalie(?)
36.   at esternalie
37.   on the road to missippi had a fight at Whitewell(?) and at wolf
      station not long results furty rough for a month rugh a gin sum was
      closed (clothed?) very good and som was very bad and ____ purty bad
      it was vary cold wuther my eting was vary good at this time
38.   wasint discharged
39.   rugh and cold wether got hongry at times
40.   help my dadie farm
41.   farmin evur since the war in dyer county and Gibson
42.   George Washing(ton?) Adams; Franklin, Willims co., Tenn.; lived
      at franklin
43.   Jane Arms
44.   no record of my grand parents
      (N.B.: the following is written on separate pages)
      after the Battle of Esternolia (see Q. 35 and 36 for spellings) and
      we went to Whitevill the second day and had a battle - the battle of
      ours captured 36 presners and left 5 ded on the feilld - lost 5 men -
      1 kill and 4 wounded - captured 4 lods crackers and bacon then one
      march on to Woolf Station - theay farde on us once from the Brest
      works and then theay run and went on to Miss. - camp in Miss. one

                            170

ADAMS (cont'd.):

month and ½ and we went from ther to West point had a battle that
lasted 12 hours - general Jef foerst (Jeff Forrest) then we left
thir and went to yassou sity (Yazoo City) and left thir and went to
Tenn and some of us went fort Pilar (Pillow?), Ky. memphis then we
went to Boliver (Bolivar, Tenn.) and had a battle then we went back
to Tupelo Miss and had a battle thir at Byce (Bryce? Bice?) Crossing
captured 2,000 negros and four or five white men and then we had a
battle Tupelo it lasted 12 hour and we lost abut 100 men and theay
lost nearly that meny and we went to harican creek (Hurricane) and
we fought 15 days and nights - theay run us back to oxford then we
stayed thir one night then we stayed one day thir and that night we
started to memphis and we traveled 2 days and 3 nights and we got to
memphis about daylight we went in town and to fall back we brought
760 prisners and 700 head of horses and then we went back acrost a
lyk___al(?) river - then we went to West point Miss and come to Tenn
into Jackson and went from Jackson to Jonsonville on Tenn River and
then we come back to musels soles (Mussels Shoals) and met Hoods
army thir and detailed 'J.P. Thurmond as lieutenant to com back west
Tenn to pick up all lost soilders and had 15 men when we started
back together thin up and had a ruff trip comin home whin we got
home we stayed in Tenn and Kentucky 1865 untill the war ended could
not git back to the army on the coun of being cut off from thim and
we rambled untill we met the soilders comin home and that is the
reason that i didint git eny discharge.

J. M. Adams, Kenton, Tenn.

ADAMS, JOHN R.

FORM NO. 2

1. John R. Adams, P.O. Selmer, Tenn.
2. 80 yrs old 4th Jany. 1922
3. McNairy co., Tenn.
4. Confederate
5. E-19th Tenn.
6. County Court Clerk and Merchant
7. John R. Adams (Sr.); Bedford co.,; lived at Purdy, Tenn.; co. of
    McNairy; my father died in last part of the year 1842.
8. Sarah H. Young; dau. of Memitrus Young and Delila Young, Henry co.,
    Tenn.
9. ----
10. ----
11. Yes my mother owned 5 or 6 slavis
12. ----
13. the negroes ware worth about four thousand dollars. we owned a small
    town lot in Purdy, Tenn.
14. we occupied and owned small lot and small framed house and 3 rooms
    in same
15. I was clerk in dry goods houses upon small boy up to the war
16. My father as before stated was county court clk. and run the office
    and sold goods. My mother after his death, made most of our living
    with her needle.
17. Yes some 5 or six. after my father died - during his life I thinkk
    we kept one.
18. yes - of course any honest work was considered respectable.
19. yes
20. the community generally worked
21. all hones labor was respectable
22. yes
23. The feeling was quite friendly
24. No, every man ran on his own merrits - regardless of slaves
25. yes
26. The holding of slaves had nothing to do with it.
27. Attended small town shcool
28. 5 or six years
29. From one hundred to 500 yards
30. don't remember
31. both

171

ADAMS (cont'd.):
32. about 10 months
33. yes
34. both, but mostly man
35. I enlisted in Confederate army about summer of 1862
36. I went to Col. Forrests command in Alabama.
37. dont remember I think though about 3 months
38. Around a grave yard in the Vally of Ala. I believe am not certain.
39. ----
40. In few days after Genl. R.E. Lee surrendered. Went to Paducah Ky.
    where I was disc'ged by taking oath.
41. In few days I came up Tenn. River with some Purdy friends. to one
    of whom I hired to sell goods and sold goods in Purdy for R.B.?
    Turner.
42. as above stated
43. I was borned in Purdy Tenn. in 1842 reared might hard by Widow lady.
    My first clerking in store was at price of two and 5/100 dollars
    per month and barefooted. walked 10 miles to borrow yoke oxens to
    haul up one winter wood - when war came up between the states I was
    18 years old - after about 2 years I taveled (traveled) one hundred
    miles and joined Col. Jessie Forrest - Report as a private. very
    soon was elected Lieut. in the co. when the war closed I was in
    command of the Co. as Capt. After war closed I gathered around
    Purdy my old home. Was 3 terms of 4 years each elected County
    Court Clerk of McNairy county. after serving 4 years as deputy in
    said office and quit the office of my own accord a thing that is
    seldom done. Generally have to beat a man out before he quite. I
    am now in the McNairy Cnty. ___? as cashr same at Selmer Tenn.
44. ----
45. "Haven't the time to spare for this side. 22 March 1922- J.R.A"
46. ----

ADAMS, SAMUEL JAMES

FORM NO. 2

1. Samuel James Adams, Lewisburg, Tenn.   RR #5
2. 81 years old
3. Bedford county, Tennessee
4. Confederate
5. Company B, 4th Tennessee Cavalry
6. Farmer
7. Archibald Adams; ----; ----; North Carolina; He died before the war.
8. Jane Ramsey; dau. of Samuel Ramsey and Elizabeth Ramsey; near Lewis-
    burg, Tenn., Marshall county.
9. ----
10. 174 acres farm land valued at $4,350.00
11. Yes eleven (11)
12. ----
13. They died before the war (this answer for question on value of prop-
    erty of parents.)
14. Part log and part frame with 6 rooms
15. General farm work. Plowing and hoeing along with the slaves
16. His father was a farmer. He raised corn, oats and wheat. His
    mother did most all the house work and cooking. The slaves did the
    weaving and spinning for the family and slaves.(This form must have
    been filled in by someone other than the veteran...cme)
17. ----
18. Yes
19. Yes they worked just as much as the slaves.
20. ----
21. Yes some mingled with men who did not own slaves and some would not.
22. ----
23. There was a fiendly feeling between slave-holders and non-slave-
    holders.
24. ----
25. ----
26. ----
27. A one room log school house with long benches extending across the

172

ADAMS (cont'd.):
room for seats.
28 Just received a grammar school education
29. A mile
30. Just ordinary country schools. Free and subscription schools.
31. The free school was public.
32. 3 months
33. No
34. A man most of the time
35. In 1862 and in Bedford county in the service of the Confederacy
36. ----
37. ----
38. ----
39. He was scantily clothed, slept between two blankers on the ground,
     had scarcely nothing to eat at times, was exposed to cold and hunger,
     but not to disease and was not wounded.
40. Discharged in Virginia after the war closed.
41. ----
42. Farming and seeling goods.
43. Married Oct. 16, 1866 to Cleopatra Low. The father of three child-
     ren, two grand sons and two great grand-daughters. A Southern
     Presbyterian - his active life has been spent in Marshall and Bedford
     co., Tenn. except three years in Texas. A merchant and farmer noted
     for his honesty. Sometimes needy but too independent to ask for a
     pension.
44. ----
45. ----
46. Dock Chapman   Belfast, Tenn.
     Frank Dillard   Belfast, Tenn.
     Edd. Woodard   Farmington, Tenn.

ADAMS, WILLIAM THOMAS

FORM NO. 1

1. William Thomas Adams,   Tenn.
2. 78 years
3. State of Tennessee, county of Dickson
4. State of Tenn County of Dickson
5. Farming
6. Farmer
7. Did not own any property.
8. My parents did, owned five, Three men and two women.
9. Two hundred and eighty acres.
10. $6,400.00
11. Log house having three rooms.
12. Plowed and hoed as the occasion demanded.
13. Father worked the farm, mother cooked, weaved and did the spinning
     and general house work.
14. None except the slaves mentioned above.
15. It was considered respectable and honorable.
16. Yessir.
17. All worked in my community.
18. There was no difference shown as between men who owned slaves and
     those that did not own them, so long as a man was honorable he
     looked upon in the same manner as though he owned slaves.
19. They did.
20. Friendly feeling existed all around.
21. The owning of slaves did not help any, every thing was based on
     honesty in them days.
22. It was.
23. They were encouraged.
24. About three months of public school per year.
25. Not over twelve months.
26. Union and Wesleys Chappell.
28. Public
29. Three months
30. The attendance was fair.
31. Man

ADAMS (cont'd):
32. May 10th, 1861. I was sworn in to support Tenn. Sworn in at Nash-
    ville, Tenn.
33. 11th Tenn. Regiment Company Co. There was 110 of the company ages
    from 17 years to 25 years. Names J.I.J. Adams, W.T. Adams. Paul
    Averet, A.B. Olison, Jno. and Clabe Chester, J.L.V. Schmmittou and
    Tom Martin, Don McNeely, Poney Dodson, Matt. Owens, Jess Owens,
    Sam Cathie, Sam Green, Capt. W.H. McCauley, Dr. J.D. Slayden, Monroe
    Rogers, J.M. Skelton, W.H. Mathis, Bill Hayes and Jno. McCauley,
    Newt and Jno. Dickson.
34. Camp Cheatham, located in Cheatham county, state of Tenn.
35. Five months
36. Wild cat or Rockcastle, Ky.
37. From the first battle we went back to Cumberland Gap, Tenn. Guarded
    Cumberland Gap, for the next ten months. During this period of time
    Buels army tried to take the place at three diferent times, we held
    them off until the 4th, of August, 1862. Then Buels army give way
    and we followed them into Kentucky. We fought them on to Louisville
    there they were reinforced by Grant, then we retreated back over the
    same ground back to log mountain 13 Mile from Cumberland Gap on the
    Kentucky side, from here we went to fight the battle of Murfreesboro
    this was in the last days of 1862, in this battle I was shot in the
    head and lost the use of my right arm.
38. Was discharged at Ft. Doanldson (Donelson), Tenn. in June 1864.
39. I left place of discharge a few days after I was discharged, went to
    work for Geo. Stacker, at Cumberland City Tenn. my duties was to
    haul saw dust from a saw mill using two horse wagon. left this job
    and went to Lion (Lyon) county Ky. and taken a job on the farm etc.
40. stated in question 39.
41. My occupation has been farming, have lived the county of Dickson,
    State of Tenn. for many years. Church relations, none except my
    belief is in the old primitive Baptist. Have been a mason for 54
    years.
42. Bej. Adams; Dickson co., Tenn.; Just simply lived in Dickson county,
    there was no towns at that time near him; None
43. Nancy Reynolds, dau. of Jno. Reynolds and Susan Reynolds; Dickson
    county, Tenn.
44. I have no facts that I can state, hence I will have to answer - I
    dont know.
45 & 46. Page not included.

ADKISSON, GEORGE LAFAYETTE

FORM NO. 1

1. George Lafayette Adkisson, Columbia, Tenn.
2. 76 yrs.
3. Tennessee, Maury co.
4. Maury co., Tenn.
5. Farming
6. Farmer
7. 1 horse and saddle
8. No
9. 125 acres
10. About $3000.00
11. Six room, two story frame house
12. Farming - plowing, hoeing, grubbing bushes - Everything
13. My father did farm work in general and my mother did all of the
    house work - cooking, spinnin, & weaving, sewing.
14. No
15. Yes
16. Yes
17. There were none.
18. They mingled freely
19. They did
20. They were friendly
21. No
22. They were not. Times were strenuous, owning to the war.
23. Encouraged.

ADKISSON (cont'd.):
24. Private school. There were no public schools then.
25. Until I was 16 yrs. of age
26. From 1 to 2 miles
27. A private school
28. Private
29. 6 months
30. Yes
31. Sometimes a man and sometimes a woman
32. 1863, Campbell Sta., Maury co., Tenn.
33. 1st Tenn., Co. H - William Adkisson, John Hobbs, Lafayette Hobbs, Wiley Smith, John Smith, Owen Smith, Bob McLaurence.
34. We scouted in Maury co. and then met Hood's army at Florence, Ala. Re_opled (Reported?) there to Forrest. He put us under Armstrong.
35. Every day from Florence, Ala. to Franklin (Tenn.)
36. Franklin and from there all the way to North Carolina.
37. We were constantly fighting the enemy and skirmishing. Riding miles and miles through rain, snow and sleet. Hungry and without food often. At one time I foraged and found corn for my horse to eat after several days hungar. Then I gathered up the grains it lost in the much and parched them for my supper.
38. Washington, Ga.
39. I came horse back to Chattanooga, Tenn. and from there on the train to Campbell Sta., Tenn.
40. Farming
41. Farming. Transfer business.
42. Yearba Adkisson; near Columbia, Maury co., Tenn.; on Little Bigby Creek-Sunnyside; Veterinarian.
43. Permelia Harris; dau. of George Harris and Sarah Harris; near county line of Maury and Giles.
44. ----
45 and 46. Page not included

ADKISSON, SAMUEL

FORM NO. 1

1. Isac Samuel Adkisson, Decaturville, Tennessee
2. 76 yr 2 mo 9 days
3. State of Tennessee Decatur county
4. State of Tenn., Decatur county (in confederacy)
5. Farming
6. Farmer and blacksmith
7. I own no property. I lived with my father.
8. No slaves
9. about 200 acres
10. about $2500.
11. Double log house with 3 rooms with a kitchen extra
12. I plowed, hoad, and cut wheat, and drove a team. all kinds of work on the farm.
13. Father worked on the farm and in the balcksmith shop. Mother cooked, washed, spoon (spun), wove and all kind of house work.
14. no servants
15. yes it respectable and honest
16. yes
17. there were no idleness
18. They mixed and mingled with one an other and did not show thir action that they thirselves were better.
19. yes couldn't tell any differace
20. yes there was a friendly feeling
21. they would not
22. yes I thank so
23. yes they were encouraged by slaveholders. that there were no big slaveholders here.
24. primary subscription school
25. about 10 months
26. about 1 mile
27. Private school or subscription school
28. Private

ADKISSON (cont'd.):
29. about 2 months
30. yes what time it lasted
31. man
32. last of Oct or first of November 1861 Decaturville Tennessee county of Decatur. Conferacy.
33. 51st Regiment 51st Tennessee rigment. Thos. Aarons, Wiley T. Brasher, Samuel J. Brasher, Sam Brasher, Jr., C.C. Bussell, John H. Fisher, Alex Fisher, Jonethan Fisher, Will Fisher, Trask? Fisher, Mile Fisher, Charles Fisher, Nick Yarbro, Will Crowley, John T. Walker, Brad Walker, Clay Walker, George Thortnon (Thornton?)
34. Henson Station now named (Henderson)
35. Nov. 1862 till April 1862
36. Shilo
37. I went to Grand Junction to the hospital then to Jackson, Tenn. hospital, then forowed home. Sick about one year. I went to my rigment at Tullahoma, Tennessee and on to Murphysboro, and on detail to Farst (Forrest's) Calvery (Cavalry), came back into West Tennesse, what was called the Cross-Road fight. Then retreated back into Middle Tennessee, We were on the Scouts most all the time, part of the time had tents, very poorly clothed, slep under tent and out on the ground. had scarcely anything to eat, we were exposed to cold for the want of shelter and clothing as were out on the Scout most all the time. I was captured at Cathrin? ferry and taken to Camp Morton Indiana put in prison and stayed till the close of the war and payrolled (paroled) June 12, 1865.
38. at Camp Morton Indiana, June 12, 1865.
39. We had a train reck (wreck) killed several I jumped out at the window and never recived a wound. We were loyaly treated and recived by the ladis on our way home.
40. Farming
41. Local preacher in the M. E. Church South. Lived in the Town of Decaturville, Tennessee and have served as Marshall of my Town.
42. Abslom Adkisson; Perryville, Perry co., Tenn.; lived at Perryville; Farmer and blacksmith is all.
43. Kizie Brasher; dau. of Samul (Samuel) Brasher and (dont know); Perryville, Tenn.
44. as to referace to the above question the Bible and Records were destroyed during the civil war and I cant trace my ancestors back.
                              Yours truly
                              Isac Samuel Adkisson

                    AGNEW, JAMES K. POLK

FORM NO. 1

1. James K. Polk Agnew, Camden, Tenn.
2. 76 yrs
3. Marshall co., Tenn.
4. Giles co, Tenn. in the Confederate army
5. Farming
6. Farmer
7. I owned no property
8. none
9. none
10. Just the household goods
11. log house, stick and dirt chimney, 2 rooms
12. I plowed with bull tongue shovel, but no turning plows, hoed and cut wheat with an old fasion cradle
13. Father worked in the field with aboved described tools. Mother cooked on the fire place, spun and wove cloth that went to all the clothed we wore
14. no
15. Honest and honerable and so considered
16. yes
17. none of that kind all worked
18. All seemed to be on ewual, not may (many) slaves owned in my community
19. yes

AGNEW (cont't):
20. Friendly feeling among all
21. I do not know
22. Yes good
23. Encouraged
24. Public free school
25. 3 months each year for about nine years
26. about one-half mile
27. Mostley free schools, some subscription schools but I did not attend.
28. Public
29. About 3 months
30. yes
31. man
32. Sept. 1864 at Pulaski in the Confederate Army
33. Reg. 11th Tenn. Cavalry. Wm. Pickens, Miner Wilks, Clay Stroud,
    Columbus Pickens, George Cavender, Was McConnell, Jack McConnell,
    George Davener, Sam Davener, Dutch Rothrock; Rothrock, all dead
    except Minor Wilks as far as I know.
34. In Alabama, along the line of Mississippi, we had no regular stopping
    place.
35. Only a very short time before we had what we called a skirmish battle
36. Our regment was all the time on guard, no regular battles
37. We were shifting from place to place guarding ammunition, provisions,
    etc. Slept on the ground no tents, eat cornbred and bacon, very
    plentiful (plentiful), clothed with the same clothes we wore from
    home, no clothes drawn from the army, wore the same clothes all the
    time, exposed to all kinds of weather, never captured.
38. Gainsville, Ala. May 9th 1865.
39. We were allowed our horses and we rode hoseback to our homes in
    Tenn. Eat one time from the time we were discharged until we
    reached home. Horses fed once, two days and nights on the trip.
40. farming
41. Farming, resided in Marshall co., Tenn., moved to Benton co., Tenn.
    have resided here every since. Belong to the Cumberland Presbyterian
    Church
42. William Robert Agnew; Marshall co., Tenn; lived at Mooresville; (no
    other particulars)
43. Narcissus Leonard Wilks; dau. of Mi-or Wilks and (not known to me);
    Giles co., Tenn.
44. None of importance
45 and 46. Page not included

AIKEN, JAMES

FORM NO. 1

1. Mr. James Aiken. Telford, Tenn. Route 2
2. eighty seven years
3. Va. Scotch Co.
4. State of Tennessee Washington Co.
5. Farming and black smith
6. Farming
7. Did not own any land. Owned one horse, two cows and sixty hogs,
   The value of property about $200
8. No slaves
9. Did not own land
10. ----
11. log house
12. plowed and hoed to a certain extent
13. my father did farm work. my mother did cooking, sewing, spinning
    and weaving and all kind of house work.
14. Did not keep servants
15. This kind of work was considered respectable and honorable at this
    time.
16. The white men engaged in this work where they did not own slaves
17. Thire were not many idle people at that time.
18. The men who owned slaves mingled very freely with the other people.
19. They all went to geather at all public gatherings

177

AIKEN (cont'd.):
20. Thire was a friendly feeling between the slave holders and none slave holders
21. yes
22. They were not very good time for a young man. He had to work hard and save every thing and not indulge in the good time to spend what he made.
23. mostly encouraged
24. district school payed one dollar a month what schooling we got
25. about one year
26. about mile and half
27. prescription (probably means "subscription"...cme) schools
28. private
29. from 4 to 5 months
30. they attend all they could for the chance they had.
31. a man. Thire was no women teacher in that day
32. In the year of 1863 Aug. Washing.(ton) Co. 17th Civil district of Tenn.
33. Artillery Co. - Billy Brown Presell Newman, George Cashady, Sprowls Jackson, Roe, Sam _ouse, McNab, John Moore
34. Knoxville, stay a few month and went to Mobile Ala.
35. was not in battle
36. ----
37. Lived in very well in camp. Clothed very good and warm. slept on a bunk and on the ground on any way to get to sleep. Slept in water. Had buf., (probably beef), bacon, stock pease and hard tack bread. Was not exposed to cold very much. was hungry did not get much to eat was exposed to some disease. In hospital ___ day treated very well.
38. Jackson, Miss. 1865 in April
39. we got transportation home.
40. Farm work. plowed corn my first work when I came back
41. Farming lived in east Tenn. 17th district in the same house sence the close of the war. United Brethren. Have been blind twelve yrs. caused by shop work (pertains to blacksmithing...cme)
42. Abraham Aiken; Scotch co., Va.; born Scotch co. Va. (repeat on this answer. This is Scott county, Va....cme)
43. Peggy Puvler; dau. of Henry Puvler (this name not clear); (no name on wife); Sullivan co. (no state).
44. ----
45 and 46. Page not included

ALDRICH, THOMAS JOYCE

FORM NO. 2

1. Thomas Joyce Aldrich, Smyrna, Rutherford county, Middle Tennessee.
2. 78 years old July 13th, 1921.
3. State of Tenn. Davidson county
4. I was a confederate soldier
5. Co C Buchanans 1st Tenn. Cavelry. I first joined Luit. Col. M.M. Gordons? Battalion Cavelry then in year or origin in the army at Corinth, Miss. Biffles and Gordons were thrown together and we elected Col. James Wheeler?
6. he was a merchant farmer and land trader
7. Joseph Arnold Aldrich, P_____ (this may be Providence); lived 9 nine miles out on Murfreesboro Pike Road
8. Miss Sulan (Susan?) Caroline Joyce , Lincon (Lincol-Cos_); dau. of Thomas Joyce and Mrs. Thomas Joyce, Nashville, Tenn.
9. ----
10. I was 17 yrs old when I volunteered in the army I had no (p)roperty
11. Parents owned about 20 twenty
12. about 200 acres $35,000.
13. $35,000
14. It was a log house weatherboarded 2 times above and 2 times above (this may also be "tier") 2 tier? wide halls. front and back porches and ell. cedar log meat? house
15. I did all kinds work on farm ploughed at 8 eight since then I have farmed and traded in live stock my occupation now and I have done

ALDRICH (cont'd.):
  well (or I have some bull one a good ones?) I have silver on my
  tables taken on my colts in 1859? on the old b____ Creek fair
  grounds State Fair. Old Vermont Boy my old friend stalion the lat
  Tolbert Fa___ President of Franklin? Coolidge
16. My father looked after all farm work. Kept all hands busy had all
  we could do. My mother looked after all house keeping had servants
17. had 15 fifteen servants
18. It was considered respectable and honerable
19. they did
20. not buy very few did that
21. they mixed and mingled all went forwards? to help each other
22. they did
23. There was a frindly feeling between all
24. It did not in the least
25. They were fine
26. Encouraged; even wanted them to have something
27. The common pay school of the district. did not go to school any
  after the war.
28. about 6 months in twelve
29. about 1 one mile
30. Syruebkd? (Syruinld) hill, Ecadeny - Smith Springs - Wallces School
  house
31. both, we paid our teachers all men poor (could not pay, free)
32. about 9 nine months
33. They did free? schools
34. man two at time
35. At Nashville, Tenn. Confederacy in spring 1861 and went to Nashville
  Tenn. offered my service to Gov.? Sam G. Harris he would not receive
  me said buddy you one to young and little for a soldier now. you go
  home we will want you later. I said I am going now. and I went on
  soldier ____?
36. Camp Weakly East Nashville
37. After our army left Ky.
38. At Murfreesboro Tenn. on Sunday morning July 13th with Gen. N.B.
  Forrest we took them all
39. I was with Gen. N.B. Forrest 13 months on staff duty he was my best
  friend in all the war. he took care of me. I was with Maj. Gen.
  Contes?. L. Stevenson staff from Dalton to at Atlanta had two horses
  shot down under me in battle.
40. wounded twice. prisoner twice. I was discharged at Greensboro
41. (cont'd from above) North Carolina Apl. 1865 ____ Tenn. in Tenn.
  sent home under Gen. J.B. Palmer of Murfreesboro Tenn. we were
  R____ at Greenville Tenn.
  of____ we had good trip down the French ____
42. trading and farming and going to see the girls and having good time
  all around and over? ____ and hope to for many ____ to come only
  79 years in July '22
43. I stayed at my fathers and traded two years. then I went to Smyrna,
  Tenn. Ritherford co. I rented 120 acres land teams impliments every
  thing to make a crop. with I put 120 acres in cotton I paid Mr.
  Licurgus Nelson $1.440. dolors rent for some ____plain note of ____
  I paid to up on materials I made 50 B.C.
  sold for 13 cts to 15 cts per lb. I ate my meals with Mr Nelson
  and family. Slept up in my little g__cy house for protection of my
  stores. this was in 1867 the next year in 1868 Mr Nelson employed
  me on saleing to run his farm of 300 (330?) acres. In 1869 I worked
  for Maj. Houston Dudley? and Mr. Jim Rofs? in Mercantol (mercantile)
  business in Smyrna, Tenn. Mr. Robert Espry(Espey?) Grand old farmer
  and gentleman. We have 4 daughters and 1 son. Educated-son and 2
  daughters married?
44. (N.B.- on separate paper; Smyrna, Tenn. Sept. 20th 1922)
  I know Governor Sam. G. Harris met him at Capital Nashville, Tenn.
  and at my father he was out there often before the war between the
  states. I knew Judge Jo. Gild? of Summer co. I knew Maj. General
  William Bates Met him in our war a great man, afterwards Governor
  William Bates of Tenn. after Senator William G. Bate of Tenn. who
  died in the harnace (harness). United States Senator. I knew Gov.
  Robert L. Taylor afterwards Senator ....my great and true friend.
  I knew Andrew J. Caldwell: Nashville, Tenn. Attorney Gen. I knew

ALDRICH (cont'd.):

      Governor Benton McMullin? and voted for him in the last primary for
      nominee for Gov. 1922. I knew Gov. Malcom R. Patterson and suported
      him in every race he ever made for anything. my frind. briliant
      man on the Stump as briliant as man as I ever listened to.

45. all gone a way cant give name and post office
46. I cant give names of my comrades in arms and friends which one (are)
      all gone they are all gone passed away.

ALEXANDER, ANDREW JACKSON

FORM NO. 1

1. Andrew Jackson Alexander, Columbia, Tenn.
2. Seventy eight
3. Maury co., Tenn.
4. Maury co., Tenn.
5. farming
6. Farmer and stock dealer
7. none
8. yes two men
9. five hundred
10. valed about fifteen thousand dollars
11. Frame house. Eight rooms. Log house lathed and plastered
12. All kinds of work, usually done on a farm, such as plowing, hoeing,
    splitting rails, and etc.
13. My father was a hard working man and stock dealer. My mother was a
    complete domestic woman, did all of her own work.
14. ----
15. Yes by a certain class of people.
16. All that did not have slaves to do it.
17. Majority did
18. ----
19. Somewhat
20. Not so much so
21. Yes
22. Had a hard time to gain much
23. ----
24. ----
25. about three years
26. Three miles
27. ----
28. Private
29. From four to six months
30 Yes
31. Both
32. November 1, 1862. Columbia, Tennessee
33. Maury Artillry - Captain Sparkman, I Leiut. Lige Thompson, II Leiut.
    Cook, III Lieut. Watson Cook, E.C. Alexander and L.B. Alexander.
34. I joined the company at Port Hudson, Louisiana
35. They had already been engaged in battle at Fort Donelson and were
    taken prisoners and when exchanged went to Port Hudson
36. Battle with gunboats at Port Hudson, La.
37. Came back to Tennessee after first battle and joined cavalary.
    Furnished my own clothes, on a blanket, anything that we could get.
38. at Charlotte North Carolina about the 19th of May 1865.
39. Started home on our horses as I was then a member of the 9th Battalion
    of Cavalry. Horses were taken away from us at Strawberry Plain in
    East Tennessee were then put on a train and brought to Columbia on
    May 18, 1865.
40. Farming
41. Last twenty-one years have worked for L&N Railroad, before that was
    a farmer
42. Ebenezer C. Alexander; ----; ----; North Carolina; ----; ----
43. Lucy Sellars; Isacc Sellars; Martha Sellars; Maury county, Columbia
    Tennessee
44. ----

ALEXANDER (cont'd.):
Article from Covington Leader Ap 28 1927

Reunion of Four Brothers, All Confederate Veterans
Held in Columbia - Oldest 90, the Youngest 83 Years

One of the most unique celebrations ever held in the South was
that of the recent reunion in Columbia, Tenn. of four brothers, the
only children of their parents, each of whom has a distinguished
record of service in the Civil War, says the Maury County Democrat
of April 21. The four Confederate veterans, all bent with years,
but still full of vigor and interest in the events of ancient and
modern history, met at the home of the youngest, Andrew Jackson
Alexander, aged 83 years.
Ebenezer C., aged 90 years, lives at Godwin, T.B., aged 88, near
Thompson Station; G.W., aged 86 near Trenton, and Andrew Jackson of
Columbia, aged 83. The combined ages of the four brothers is 347
and the average age 87. The two oldest, E.C. and T.B., served
throughout the entire bitter conflict of the sixties, spending the
latter part in prison at Fort Donelson, and were exchanged at the
close of the war. G.W. enlisted in Bragg's army in 1862 and served
gallantly in Gen. John Morgan's cavalry until the close of the
conflict. A.J., the youngest, enlisted in November, 1862, and was
taken prisoner at Fort Hudson and was later paroled and sent home
and after exchange joined Gen. Grant's cavalry and served until the
close of the war.
Many messages of congratulations were received by the illustrious
brothers Sunday, as well as gifts and flowers, conveying the admire-
ation of many friends and relatives.
The birthday celebration has been made the occasion for the
reunion for several years and will continue to be as long as two of
the gallant old soldiers are left. They have all been blessed with
good health and vigor and the eldest is considerably more active than
many men that are several years his junior. Their record is probably
unequalled in the annals of southern history, and much public interest
has been aroused in the annual gatherings at the home of the junior
brother.

ALEXANDER, E. C.

(He filled out two different questionnaires)
FORM NO. 2

1.   E. C. Alexander, R.R. 3, Columbia, Tenn.
2.   Eighty seven
3.   Henry Co Ky
4.   Confederate
5.   Maury artillery
6.   Farmer
7.   E. C. Alexander; ----; ----; North Carolina; moved to midle Tennessee;
     ----
8.   Lucy Sellers; Isaac Sellers, Julia Sellers; Maury Co. Tennessee
9.   My brother G.W. Alexander of Trenton Tenn can give this correctly
     than I
10. two hundred acres worth thirty dollars per acre
11. Two negro men
12. Seven hundred acres
13. about Fifteen thousand dollars
14. part log and frame eight rooms
15. all kinds of work usual done on farm
16 thru 44. Not answered
45. E.C. Alexander
     T.B. Alexander
     A.J. Alexander
     Pat Adkins
     M.M. Butt
     James Shaw
     Anderson Walters
     Pink Fitzgerald

ALEXANDER (cont'd.):
        J.M. Dockery
        Clay Bridgeforth
        Brooks Barnes
        James Goad
46.   E.C. Alexander   R.R. 3 Columbia   Tenn
        T.B. Alexander   Thompson Sta   Tenn
        A.J. Alexander   Columbia   Tenn
        G.W. Alexander   Trenton   Tenn
        M.M. Butts   Columbia   Tenn
        Pat Adkins   Water Valve   Tenn
        James Shaw
        Williams Willis   Columbia R.R. No. 3   Tenn
        Anderson Walters   Santa Fee   Tenn
        Pinkney Fitzgerald   Theata   Tenn
        J.M. Dockery   ville   Mo.
        Clay Bridgeforth
        Brooks Barnes
        James Goad   Union City   Tenn

FORM NO. 1

1.   E.C. Alexander; Columbia Tenn
2.   Be 85 years old 19th day next April
3.   Graves County Knetucky
4.   Maury County Tenn
5.   Farmer
6.   Farmer
7.   I did not anything but one horse
8.   my parents owned 3
9.   850 acres
10.   About 15000 Dollars
11.   Log house wether Boarded and sealed inside
12.   well I plowed hoed and other kind done on Farm
13.   worked on Farm & Traded.
      my mother cook and done all kinds house work
14.   we had 3 servants
15.   it was
16.   well if he had property he did not work mutch
17.   half of them worked and half did not
18.   well they seemed to think themselves better
19.   not mutch
20.   Jest tolerable
21.   well not mutch
22.   well yes
23.   well I think not
24.   country school
25.   well I recon 3 years would get it
26.   2 miles
27.   Chapples
28.   private
29.   3 months
30.   well yes
31.   man & sometimes woman
32.   Maury County Tenn
33.   Maury Artillery
34.   Nashville Tenn
35.   5 months
36.   Fort Donelson
37.   ----
38.   Georgia
39.   walking from Atlanta Ga to Chattanooga cars? to Nashville   walked
      to Columbia
40.   Farming
41.   Farming
      no church
42.   E.C. Alexander; North Carolina; I dont know; ----; he lived here
      since year 1843; ----
43.   Sellers; Isaac Sellers; I don't know her given name; ----
44.   I don't know

                              182

ALEXANDER, E. F.

FORM NO. 1

1. E.F. Alexander; Jackson Tenn 541 East Collige St.
2. Age 83 & six months the 18 of this month Feb 1922
3. Madison County State of Tennessee
4. Tennessee Madison Co Jackson
5. Carriage Painter
6. My Father Died when I was about 2 and one half years old I supose he was a carpenter by trad.
7. I owned no property at all
8. No slaves
9. My Parents owned the House and lot they lived in
10. I do not Remember No Land when the war opened.
11. A Samll 2 or 3 rooms House A one story building frame house
12. (N.B.: The words of the question "As a boy and young man" and "certain historians: are underlined. He answers what he did as a boy in one sentence & then answers the "certain historians...." question with the rest of the paragraph)
    I went to learn my trad at 14 years old Have spent all my life at Painting Business and no other work that statement is a mistak men who owened slaves Did not have to work but they hired whit men to over see the farme and have the negro to do the work but whit men who did not own servents don their own work with hired help a way Back younder before the Family fuss they all got along all right
13. my Father worked at his traid my mother kept the House and sewed for and suported six children untill they were able to help her she was a Seamestres but they have all passed over the river but my self and I am nearing the crosing.
14. No servents only as they needed them then they hired them.
15. it was
16. when ever they needed work they did it themselves if they needed help they hiered it.
17. To a very little extent Lazy triflen white man they generaly let his own whip whip his own back. he was not respected by any one.
18. Some did some did not
19. Some did some did not in some cases money makes the mare go when the negro is not in the question all.
20. as A a general thing there was a freindly feeling between both if the Poore man needed help from the slave owerner he could get the negro help or the money which ever he needed worst there was by fare a beter feeling then between the colard race and the white raice than ther is to day.
21. no I think not the qualification of the man was more in queston than it is day.
22. if the man was all right he could all wais get help it was better for him then thar now what we neede to day is confidence in our fellow man
23. I think a man Like that had abetter showing than he has to day.
24. we had individual Pay chools the chool system to day is by far better than it was then
25. about 5 years
26. About ¼ of A mile
27. All chools were Privete Pay chools there was no Colord chools in my raising up only what their oweners taught them we had white Preachers to Preach the gospel to them
28. Private chools.
29. 10 month from 9 to 12 from 1 to 4 each day
30. they did
31. one was a woman the other was a man
32. in January 1862 at Jackson Tennessee in the service of the Confederacy.
33. in the 51 tennessee regment Comp E there is only 2 of my comp. living Mr. John Price & Jim Day Both in Jackson Tenn
34. to Henderson Station 18 miles from Jackson Tenn
35. 9 months at Peraville Ky
36. Pereville Ky
37. in the spring of 1862 we took up our line of march from Corinth missippi by the of chatnooga to Louisvill Ky 8 day of October 62 we

183

ALEXANDER (cont'd.):

   fought the the Perevill fight drove the eamy off the Battle field
   held the field untill 12 o clock that night the enima renforce their
   army and we had to back by the way of of Cumberlin gap our next
   fight was muferbor 3 days fight we drove the enimay back we had a
   bout 3 to our one to fight then we fell back to through east tennessee to Missionry Ridg whre we fought again then we fell back to
   Dalton Georgia then Los Angle Ga then AtLanta

38. Brownsville Tenn in 1865. then my last fight was Franklin Tenn
    where I was shot off the Brest works the 30 day of November 1864
    I was sent back to Corinth Mixx.

39. then from there home the last night of December 1864 then when I got
    able to travell I had to go to Brownsvill Tennessee to be Parroled
    and tak the Perrod oath in 1865.

40. went to my traid Painting Buisniss But two old now to do much work.

41. ----

42. Granderson Alexander; I do not know where; ----; North Carolina;
    ----; I dont know any thing particular about his life he died in
    1841 I was 1838.

43. Martha Wilson Alexander Cabarris County N. Carolina; ----; ----;
    ----

44. I am of Irish desent about 4 generation my greate greate Grand Father
    was was a a full Blodded Irishman from canocchy my g great Grand
    mother was Scotch laddy so that make me the 4 generation this is
    about all I can say about on Ancestry.
                              yours very truly
                              E.F. Alexander
                              541 East College St.
                              Jackson Tenn

                         ALEXANDER, GEORGE L.

FORM NO. 1

1. George L. Alexander; Brownsville Tennessee Route #4
2. 80 years
3. Haywood Co. Tennessee
4. Haywood Co. Tenn
5. Farming
6. Farmer and surveyor
7. Didn't own any thing
8. 20
9. 1000 acre
10. $50,000
11. Frame 6 rooms
12. I did all kind of work that was done on the farm
13. My father farmed and surveyed. My mother kept house helped with the
    cooking spinning and weaving.
14. Yes, they owned 20 slaves and they helped with the work.
15. It was, those that worked were thought just as much of as those that
    didn't have to
16. They did
17. Very few
18. They did mingle freely with those who did not own slaves and did not
    think they were better than those that were not able to own slaves.
19. They did
20. There was a friendly feeling
21. It did not
22. It was
23. Encouraged
24. No public schools all subscription
25. 5 years
26. about 2 miles
27. Subscription School
28. Private
29. about 4 months
30. yes
31. sometime men and sometime wemen
32. Enlisted in April 1862 Dancyville Haywood Co. Tenn

                              184

ALEXANDER (cont'd.):
33. 9th Tenn   Captain W.J. Lyle, Charly Ballard, Fred Ragland, Bob Montgumry, Joe Thomas, Jake Elrod, Billie Carnes, _____ Perry, Asberry Harrison, Fayett Hall, Joe Neble-1
34. To Corinth Miss
35. t months
36. Perryville Ky.
37. I was wounded in the battle of Perryville Oct 8, 1862 and was taken prisoner and held by the Federals untill Feb 18, 1863 was exchanged at City Point Va. from there went back to my regiment at Shelbyville Tenn and was given indefinite furlough and was never able to serve any more. I lived in camp like a dog, I had as few clothes as a man could wear. I slept on the ground. very little to eat was exposed to cold hunger and disease on all side. My life in prison was as hard as a man could stand.
38. I was never discharged I came home from Shelbyville on an indefinite furlough and was never able to serve any more, lost the use of my arms.
39. ----
40. I was not able to do any kind of work for about four years, since then have done what I could at farming.
41. My life has been spent on the farm. I married Mary Josephine Wilkerson Jan 28, 1869 to that union was born four children 2 girls & 2 boys all are living. I belong to the M.E. Church South
42. Oliver Alexander; Knoxville May 26, 1812; Blount Co.; Tennessee; he moved from there with his parent to Hardaman Co. 1825 on to Haywood 1826; he represent Haywood Co. 1876 also magritate for two terms. He died Aug. 31 1888.
43. Elizabeth Lucas Gee; George L. Gee; Sara Schler Gee; Mecklenburg Co. Va.
44. Oliver Alexander married Elizabeth Gee March 1836 lived the rest of his life in Haywood Co Tenn near where I live now. he did a lot of good by helping the poor and church work and died with very little means. The family record was distroyed in a fire

ALEXANDER, GEORGE WASHINGTON

(2 questionnaires for Alexander - no file folder preceding them. See T.B. Alexander for notes written by G.W. Alexander and also newspaper article of death of G.W. Alexander)

FORM NO. 2

1. George Washington Alexander; Trenton Tenn
2. Eigty three years old
3. ----
4. Confederate Soldier
5. Co E; 9th Tenn Cav Col Bifles Regt Dibbrells Brigade
6. Farmer
7. Ebenezer Crawford; Maryville; Sevier; Tennessee; Columbia Tenn 50 years; he was an uncompermising Democrat a true Southern man (N.B.: See E.Crawford census)
8. Lucy Sellars; Isaac Sellars; Judah Johnson; ----
9. my Great Grand Parents on Fathers side come from Scotland. my my Maternal Grand Parents came from England and settled in North Carolina Chatham County. my Paternal Grand Father settled in Westmoreland County Va. my Great Grand Father and Grand Fathers were in the revolutionary war from Beginning to end
10. I owned none. My Father owned 832 acres four miles from Columbia
11. yes. only three one man two women
12. 832 acres
13. land $26,600; mules and horses $2000.00 slaves $2500.00
14. a hewed Poplar log house ceiled weather boarded and painted white four rooms below and as many above.
15. I began Plowing when Seven years old. I did every kind of work required on farm used hoe and ax. cut wheat with a scythe used mowing blade built fence and other work.
16. he was a Farmer and did all kinds of work required Plowed hoed split rails repaired fences and kind of labor necessary. he also was a

ALEXANDER (cont'd.):

    trader and stock raiser. Generally had from thirty to forty head of mules and horses for market every year.

17. from three to four
18. every man engaged in any kind of work was respected on an Equality with all honest citizens.
19. they did most of the work but few slaves in my community.
20. I think there were none I remmember no one.
21. they certainly did no difference shown all on Equality provided the Poor man was honest.
22. no difference shown like one Family
23. ----
24. It did not the man and not property decided the contest.
25. yes if a young man would work and save his earnings he could soon have a home of his own. the People would help him. Credit him and endorse note.
26. they were always encouraged assisted every way would lend them money on long time
27. country schools
28. I attended school at Six about 4 months a year two in Summer
29. three miles through the woods and canes
30. Jackson College in Columbia four miles was the nearest and only one.
31. mostly Private Public school two month in year
32. Generally four months sometimes in winter we had no school.
33. the attendance was good
34. a man
35. I was sworn in June 27th 1863. I enlisted at the commence of hostilities but was discharged on account of Typhoid Fever re-enlisted June 27th 1863.
36. Moulton Alabama
37. three months
38. Chickamauga Sept 18th 19th 20th 1863
39. Athens Tenn. engaged in Battle there Nov 16th I Believe captured 276 Head of fine Beeves was detaild to drive them to Bragg army the Battle of Missionary ridge occured Nov 26th confederated defeated retreated to Dalton Ga. I drove the cattle there
40. I was discharged at Abingdon Va. April 28th 1865.
41. I walked home following Rail Road to Knoxville stopped two days at Strawberry Plains was kept 6 days in Knoxville went from there to Chattanooga kept one week walked from there to Nashville and home.
42. I went to farming my former business. though we had no stock scarcely to work Federals had taken all worth anything.
43. After the war I resumed farming stock raising and all things connected with it. I clerked in a store several years for Wisener Sto_e & Co. then I began the same Business for myself seven years. Bought a farm four miles from Columbia on Santa fe Pike lived there till 1892. I have never held an office. I am a member of the Primitive Baptist sometimes called Hard Shells but few in number. I lived to be fifty years old before I married. My parents were old and feeble I took care of them. there are two things a pleasure to me one is I was a Confederate Soldier the other is I looked after the welfare of my old Father and mother made their lives as pleasant as my ability would allow.
44. -----
45.

Gideon Adkisson	Capt
John Leftwich	1st Lieut
Pop Nichols	Sec Lieut
Joh. A. Pigg	3 Lieut
Blue Fitzgerald	Sarg.
E.P. Alexander	Private
Jim McMahon	"
John Ragdale	"
Frank Ragdale	
Tom Douglas	
Alf McManue	
Jim Dowell	
Bill Dowell	
Jim Weaver	
John Weaver	

ALEXANDER (cont'd.):
      Josh Weaver
      Newt S _ awn
      Rube White
      Dan White
      Ab Reeves
      _ill Duncan
      J_ Duncan
      Len Fitzgerald
      Jo Vestal
      Jake Dupree
      John Church
      Jerome Church
      William Church
      Buck Alderson
      Tom Oneal
      Sam Armstrong
      Dick Stockard
      Frank Robinson
      Sparks Skelly
      Lum Fain
      Van Fain
      Ike Connor
      Pleas Whitehead
      Jo Vestal
      G.W. Alexander

No.	Name	Place	State
46.	Jesse Jackson	Trenton	Tenn
	Squire McRee	"	"
	Doctor Osborne	"	"
	Dave Mills	Milan	"

I was in the Battle of Chickanauga Sept 18th 19th 20th Athens Tenn
Nov 16th 1863
Dublin Va May 9th 1864
Mt Sterling June 9th 1864
Cynthiana two Battles June Saturday 11th Sunday 12th Greenville Tenn
Sept 4th 1864 Sunday Gen Morgan was killed
Saltville Oct 2nd Sunday 1864
Saltville Decr 14th & 15th 1864 the _ook the works and Distroyed
that ended my fighting in civil war

FORM NO 1

1.   George Washington Alexander; Trenton Gibson County Tennessee
2.   81 years old April 17th
3.   Tennessee Henry County
4.   Maury County Tenn Confederate Army.
5.   I was a Farmer
6.   he was a Farmer
7.   I owned no property.
8.   My Parents owned three slaves one man and two women
9.   My Father owned 832 acres
10.   My Judgment is they owned about thirty thousand Dollars worth of
      Property including land slaves and live stock.
11.   it was a Log house made of Poplar trees weather boarded and ceiled
      in side. there were four rooms below same number above. two
      porches
12.   as a boy and man I did every kind of work on the Farm. I Plowed
      and used the hoe from Planting crop till it was laid by.
13.   My Father was a Farmer mule and Horse trader he did very little work
      after I could remember. My Mother did the cooking in younger days
      spinning cloth and and making same in to clothes for the Family.
      hired the weaving
14.   they kept none
15.   yes it was considered Honorable and respectable.
16.   nearly all work was done by white men and white boys
17.   there were very few living in idleness at least 90 percent or more
      worked.
18.   they did. men who owned no slaves were treated as well and was on
      equality Socially Provided he was Honest and industrious slave

ALEXANDER (cont'd.):

Holders were ever ready to help that class of Poor men

19. at all those Places they freely together you could not have told the rich man from the Poor man.

20. there was always a friendly feeling between them. I never heard a man say ought against his neighbor because he owned slave or did not own them

21. No sir it did not the man that was most competent was generally elected.

22. yes sir it was some did other did not. any Poor young man could have saved enough in a few years to buy a home.

23. they were always encouraged if they were worthy Poor men. they would help them any way they could lend them money endorse for them in Bank or _____ their Security to Individules.

24. Subscription school one dollar per month twenty days a month

25. about three years

26. three Miles

27. there were no schools in operation only in Summer of crops were finished and in the winter month after crop were gathered.

28. Public

29. Generally Five July August December January February Sometimes March.

30. All Boys and Girls of School Age Attended

31. a man

32. I enlisted in July Confederate army 1861.

33. 9th Tenn
Blueford Fitzgerald, E.P. Alexander, Buck Alderson, Dan Pigg, Joh Pigg, Francis Ragsdale, John Ragsdale, Jo & Bill Dunca, John Jay and Jerome Church, Ab Reeves, Dan White, Jim & Bill Dowell

34. we remained in Middle Tenn

35. Bragg retreated to Georgia we went out with with his army

36. Chickamauga was the first Battle of any consequence then Missionary Ridge.

37. (on first line: "corn bread & Bacon" under the words "what you had to eat"; "yea" under the word "hunger" ; "----" under the word Disease"; "7 days" under the word "hospital"; "no" under the word "prison".)
Provisions clothing and every thing else become scarcer. Athens, Tenn Nov 1863. 3 hours. captured 276 fine Beeves Dublin Va. May 9th 1864 2¼ hours we had to retreat. Mount Sterling Ky 2 hours defeated Cynthiana all day Saturday and Sunday Greenville Tenn Saltville Va. in Oct and in Dec 1864 Second Battle At Saltville. Defeated.

38. Abingdon Virginia

39. Walked to Knoxville Tenn rode in Freight train to Chattanooga stopped there a few days rode on Freight to Nashville walked from there Home.

40. I went to farming raising cotton corn cattle and Hogs.

41. After the war till 1893 I was engaged in farming and raising stock. Since then I have sold good. I am now retired.

42. Ebenezer Crawford Alexander; Maryville; of Blount Tennessee; in Maury County three miles of Columbia; he was Capt of the Minute Men in 1861 till the Yankess come.

43. Lucy Sellars; Isaac Sellars; Juda Sellars; in Maury County 3½ miles North of Columbia;

44. My Paternal Great Grand Father come from Scotland. My Maternal Great Grand Father come from England. Both of my Great Grand Fathers were soldiers in the Revolutionary War. Great Grand Father Johnson was a Capt under Gen. Marion.

ALEXANDER, JAMES KNOX POLK

FORM NO. 2

1. James Knox Polk Alexander; Gleason Tennessee

2. 79 years old

3. Sate of Tenn. Henry County.

4. Confederate Soldier

5. Company I; Fifth Tennessee Strawls brigade Hallum was our captain.

ALEXANDER (cont'd.):
6. a Farmer
7. Joseph Alexander; ----; ----; South Carolina; He was of Dutch
    descent; ----
8. Flora Shaw; X; X; X
9. My father was an immigrant to Tenn from South Carolina in 1828 and
    died on his farm in Henry County in 1858. They had six children.
10. X
11. Yes but dont know how many but several I know.
12. Yes but dont know how much.
13. X
14. Small frame house
15. My parents died when I was quite small and I was reared by my uncle
    Simpson Alexander in Henry Co. with whom I remained untill 18 years
    of age. At the out-breaking of the Rebellion I enlisted and saw
    service for four years and returned home May 20th 1865. Yes I
    worked plowed and hoed both before the war.
16. My father was a farmer. Yes cooking and spinning was done in my
    home.
17. NO
18. yes indeed very respectable
19. yes
20. There were not very many men to work but they all worked and did not
    lead an idle life.
21. no they did not.
22. To some extent
23. They were friendly.
24. X
25. X
26. X
27. Very poor
28. a very few years I attended Bluff Springs school in Gibson County
    and was there when the war broke out.
29. ----
30. ----
31. Public what few we had.
32. X
33. X
34. ----
35. ----
36. ----
37. ----
38. Battle of Shiloh
39. I was in the battles of Shiloh, Perryville, Murfreesboro, Chick-
    amauga and Missionary Ridge being severly wounded at the latter place.
    I was sent to the hospital at Marrietta Ga. I was wounded twice.
40. ----
41. ----
42. Farming
43. After my discharge I returned to Gleason Tenn and begun farming and
    in 1866 entered the mercantile business was also freight and express
    agent. When the Dresden Bank of Dresden our County seat was
    organized I was elected Vice Pres which office I still hold have
    had that about 25 years. Jan. 19th 1861 I was married to Sue F.
    Burnett daughter of Dr. G.H. and N.M. Burnett. We have had six
    children three of whom are living now. Mrs. Hugh McClain Greenville
    Texas Mrs. Elbert S. Craig Memphis Tenn and Homer Alexander Gleason
    Tenn. I am a member of the Methodist Church.
44. ---
45. You will find my war record in the History of Tenn 1887 on page
    985 under Weakly Co. Do you care for a photograph? If so do you
    return same?
46. ----

FORM NO. 1

1. McKager Cooper Alexander; Shelbyville, Tennessee
2. 77 years
3. Tennessee, Bedford County
4. Bedford County Tennessee
5. Farming
6. Farming
7. None
8. No
9. About two hundred acres
10. About $5000.00 to $6000.00
11. Double log house with four rooms.
12. Done all kinds of farm work.
13. My father did all kinds of farm work, my mother did all the house work of every kind.
14. No, the children and parents did all the work.
15. yes
16. yes
17. Very rare case of a man that did not work.
18. they did mingle freely with people that did not own slave, and I never remember of any slave holder who consider himself above those who did not own slaves
19. yes
20. they were always on the most freindly terms.
21. No
22. I do not think so.
23. encouraged.
24. Public free school.
25. about two months each year
26. about one mile
27. none but the free schools.
28. public
29. 4 to 5 months
30. No
31. Both, generally a man
32. November 1861, at Camp Trousdale.
33. 45th, Tennessee, regiment commanded by Col. Searcy, Capt Moore, Leut Parsley, Leut Miller, Leut Grimes, Sam Mitchel, Dock Barkclay, Rufe Haynes, John Puckett, George Lane, A.J. Carver.
34. To Murfreesboro, Tenn.
35. about one year.
36. Murfreesboro, Tenn.
37. Went south from Murfreesboro, ingaged in the battle of Chicamauga, Missionary ridge, Resaca Geo., Atlanta Ga, Jonesboro Geo, was wounded at Jonesboro Geo., 31st Aug 1864, sent to hospital at Augusta Ga. staid there two months, and then come to Tennessee, with Gen Hood, was never in prison.
38. at Augusta Ga, May 19th 1865 and returned home on May 13th 1865.
39. rode the train part of the way and walked the rest was glad of the chance to get to even walk home.
40. Farming
41. Have living in Bedford County Tennessee, ever the war and engaged in farming ever since, have been associated with the Cumberland presbyterian church, have never held any office.
42. Was known as Capt. Jim Alexander; North Carolina; Do not know; ----; Near Shelbyville, in Bedford County Tennessee; Was early settlers served in the Indian wars and after the indian wars was captain of the malitia.
43. Elizibeth Cooper; dont know; ----; ----
44. ----

ALEXANDER, T. B.

1. T. B. Alexander; Thompson's Station Tenn
2. 83 yr. Feb. 22 1922 Williamson Co.
3. Henry Co. Tenn
4. Maury Co. Tenn
5. Farmer
6. Farmer and raiser
7. none
8. yes two men
9. Four hundred acres
10. $12000.00
11. log house two story 5 rooms
12. all kinds of work usual done on farm.
13. My Father worked on farm & my mother being a very domestic woman done the house work.
14. two men
15. before the war some in community looked down on working people as rather low class but later on had a better opinion of the laboring class.
16. where no way to get without work.
17. But bery few majority had to work more or less.
18. I think majority did.
19. with some exceptions they did.
20. I never knew of any bad feeling between slave holders & non slave holder in my section co.
21. I never heard of anything was not a voter and did not take any stock in elections.
22. opertunities was very slim.
23. Poor men was not looked after ___ them days very much.
24. poor country school.
25. In broken doses 3 or 4 mo in yr
26. Three miles
27. Private
28. Private
29. about 5 months
30. not as they should have done
31. man
32. In October 1861
33. E.C. Alexander of Columbia & Marion Dockery & James Shaw of Culaoka (Culleoka?) Tenn. I cannot call to mine another one whom went in my company To Fort Donalson. I enlisted at Santa Fee Maury Co. Oct 1861 by Captain Griffith in Maury Artillery.
34. To Fort Donalson Tenn and there we were surrendered and sent to prison at Camp Douglas Ill. This was in Feb 1862.
35. Feb 1862 and was surrendered on 16th day of Feb and sent to Camp Dougla prison.
36. Fort Donalson
37. In September 1862 we were exchanged and sent to Port Hudson La. In March we were attacked by the Gun boats and our company had a pot shot batery & destroyed the Gun boat Missippi it burned some 30 or 40 minutes in front of our batery & then floated down the river & blew up before reaching.
38. Baton Rouge after surrend at Port Hudson all of the Maury Artillery men not paroled and the sick & wounded
39. were sent to New Orleans. the sick and wounded after being exchanged were sent to Mobile and later to ft morgan Ala. and was surrendered there and sent to prison at Elmira N Y this was in fall of 1864. and remained
40. there until March 1865 was sent to Richmond Va paroled and reached home May 18 1865.
41. I resumed farming on my return home and claim to be law abiding citizen never held any office
42. E. C. Alexander; Dec 13 1804; Blount Cty; East Tennessee; ----; ----
43. Lucy Sellers; ----; ----; ----;
44. ----

ALEXANDER (cont'd.):
Newspaper article from The Maury Democrat Thursday March 3, 1932.
Includes a picture of the four Alexander brothers.

Last of Four Brothers Dies

Left to right and age when picture was made in 1926-- E.C. Alexander
89; T.B. Alexander 87; G.W. Alexander 85; A.J. Alexander 82.

The death of George Washington Alexander, 90, at his home in
Trenton, Tenn., Tuesday, removes the last of four brothers who
served valiantly in the confederate army and whose annual reunions
at the home of the youngest, A.J. Alexander in Columbia, were
interesting events for several years, or until the group was broken
by the death of A.J., the youngest, who died in September 1927 at
the age of 82.
The four brothers volunteered for services at the outbreak of the
Civil War and served throughout. Their annual reunions were unique
in the fact that no other family is known to have had four of its
members in the war. The annual meetings were held at the home of
the youngest, A.J. Alexander in Columbia; E.C. made his home at
Godwin; T.B. near Thompson and G.W. at Trenton.
Deceased was married a few years ago to Miss Lizzie Pennington of
Trenton, who preceded him to the grave. He is survived by several
nieces and nephews and despite his mature years was active and alert
until his fatal illness. Mrs. J.R. Ogilvie of Columbia, daughter
of the late A.J. Alexander, is one of the nieces. Funeral services
will be conducted today at Trenton.

(In printed hand: "Younger pictures T.B. Alexander Grandfather of
Dr. Allen A. Foster")
1
Our Grand Father Ebenezer was born in Washington County Va in
1765 married Elizabeth Rogers in Fauquier Co Va moved to Blount
County Tenn. From there he moved to Williamson County in 1807
Seven miles east of Franklin near Harpeth River. From there to
Graves County Ky. and died August 1835 both Great Grand Fathers are
buried in Maury County Oliver Alexander 4 miles South of Columbia
Cap Johnson 5 miles North up the River from Roberts Bend.
G.W. Alexander
2
Our Great Grand Father Oliver Alexander was born in Westmoreland
County Va in 1732 was in Washington Company at Braddock defeat by
the Indians July 9th 1755. was wounded in his knee went through
the American Revolutionary War under Gen Washington he married
Mary Craig an Irish girl he moved to Washington County Va. where our
Grand Father was born. 15 miles North of Abingdon Va near the Salt
works now called Saltville
3
Our Great Grand Father on Mothers Side was Captain Johnson who
was under General Marion during the war of 1776. he was a North
Carolinan lived in Chatham County. Moved to Maury County Tenn and
died in 1823. Our Grand Father Isaac Sellers and Juda Johnson were
born in Chatham NC and married there. come to Maury Co. in 1802
and died where Dick Hughes lived he also was a soldier in the
American Army under Gen Green in North Carolina

ALEXANDER, WILLIAM THOMAS

FORM NO. 1

1. Wm. Thomas Alexander; 525 Battery Place   Chattanooga Tennessee
2. 75, at next birth day June 23rd 1922.
3. Alabama Calhoun Co town of Jacksonville
4. Calhoun Co Ala my birth place
5. School boy
6. Planter & trader
7. I owned no property at opening of the Civil War between the states.
8. Yes, my recollection is near 77 young & old slaves.

ALEXANDER (cont'd.):
9. about one section
10. I should think the value to be ninty to one Hundred thousand dollars.
11. I was born in double log house, but when I was 8 or 9 years old my
    father built a large frame house with 8 or 10 rooms & 6 or 8 frame
    cabins for the negro family.
12. When not at school, I worked on farm, plowed some and hoed & drop
    cotton seed (we had no cultivators then) & help to attend to the
    stock & attend the cotton gin in fall season.
13. My father was very industrious man; looked after his plantation &
    was also a trader in buying & selling stock & real estate. My
    mother devoted her time to caring for her 7 daughters & 5 sons,
    cooking washing spinning & weaving & other household work was done
    by the servants & my sisters when not at school, done the sewing.
    No sewing machines then.
14. yes about 77
15. yes. very honorable. a man that did not work at some kind of
    employment was looked up as a no body.
16. yes.
17. I do not know of any that come under my knowledge.
18. So far as I know there was no social differences as to men who
    were slave holders & the non slave holders
19. yes
20. I never heard of anything of this kind.
21. No I have known non slave holders being elected in Co. offices over
    the slave holder.
22. Yes if he had the honor & integracy could get help from his neigh-
    bors both of slave holders & non slave holders.
23. As a rule they were always encouraged. May of been a _____ _____
    in some communities where they were not helped.
24. old fashion country school
25. about 3 years
26. two Miles & then later 3 Miles when I went one year in town Male
    Accademy in the town of Jacksonville Ala.
27. Each township was supposed to have a school, teacher selected & paid
    by the patrons.
28. Private so far as I know no public money went to schools
29. Don't know some run longer than others
30. only fairly so.
31. a man
32. Feby 1861 Jacksonville Ala called out by Gov. Moore of Ala & was
    then State Ala. Troops.
33. 2nd Ala D.F. Forney Captain, W.M. Hawes 1st Lieut, H.T. Snow 2nd
    Lieut. the Co. had about 100 men & was ordered to Fort Morgan Ala
    and when the Confederate was organized the Co. disbanded & in the
    reorganization I enlisted in Co B 30 Ala & served there when not on
    detach services until the surrender.
34. Talladega Ala & then to Montgomery Ala & Knoxville Ten.
35. in the spring of 1862 & on the 11th Augst 1862 engaged in the battle
    of Tazewell Ten & on into Ky, with Genl Bragg army of which I was
    made Military Post Master
36. Several skirmishes but the first battle of any note was Tazewell,
    Tenn.
37. After Bragg retreat from Ky in winter of 1862 engaged in the battle
    of Murfreesboro Ten on Stone River & then went to Vicksburg Mis &
    in battle Warrenton, Port Gibson & Bakers Creek & Big Black & then
    into Vicksburg where we were beseiged for 47 days lived 47 days on
    10 days rations. Ate Mule Meat & went half naked and on July 3,
    1863, surrendered to Genl Grand & was paroled after being fed by
    the federals ten days to enable the men to walk & go home as best
    they could, were exchanged Oct 4 1863 and mobilized at Demopolis
    Ala & reorganized & put in Genl E.W. Petters Brigade Stevenson Div.
    Harders Corps took part in Battle Missionary Ridge Nov 25 1863
    after being in the battle above the _____ on Nov 24. after the
    battle of Missionary Ridge went into winter Quarters at Dalton Ga. &
    was with Gen J.E. Johnston through Ga to Atlanta when Hood took
    command. After the fall of Atlanta was in Battle of Jonesboro Ga
    where I was slightly wounded & sent to the Ala Hospital at Montgomery
    Ala & when convalescent was put in command of 2 Co. of convalescent
    men & sent to F_____ Ala & head off a Yankee Cavalry raid.

ALEXANDER (cont'd.):
   After which I _____ to Montgomery Ala.

38. Paroled some time in April 1865 near Talladega Ala
39. I had good luck in getting home, the Post surgen at Montgomery wife
   was there & he furnished Cap White & myself with pair mules &
   ambulance to take his (the surgen Dr C.J. Clark) wife home, were
   some days enroute & had to flank several Yankee raiding parties.
40. Done what I could to help my old father & mother to keep together
   what the Yankees had left some of the Negro servants on the plantation for years & worked the land on shares.
41. After leaving the farm was Express Agt & Post Master of Jacksonville
   Ala engaged some in Merchandising, was member of the City Council &
   last 25 years have lived in Chattanooga Ten & a traveling salesman
   I have been a member of the Protestant Episcopal Church for 50 years
   or more, have at times been vestryman & _____.
   Tennessee Divis of T.P.A. of American & have been a traveling salesman for 26-27 years, I am also a Master Mason Temple Lodge No. 430
   & R.A.M. Chapter No. 40. I also affiliate with some of the Chandler
   Associate of our city. Please let me know if I have given you the
   desired information. Yours truly W.T. Alexander 525 Battery Place
   Chattanooga
42. Robt. Alexander; Charlotte; Mecklenburg; North Carolina; Jacksonville
   Ala at the time of his death; Member of home guards & at one time was
   Shff of Co.
43. Mary Smith; Peter Smith; Hanah B__t Smith; near Lincolnton N.C.
44. My grandfather was Robt. Alexander & he served as a Capt. in
   Grahams NC Regiment in the Revolutionary War with Genl Greene. My
   paternal ancestors was Scoch Irish decent & my mother German.

   (on a separate page)
   Mr. Moore
      Dear Sir
         I have given you some of my life & war experience & could
   write much more but expect you have all you want. I am now & have
   been for 26 years a Citizen Chattanooga Ten, and as far as I know
   the youngest Confederate soldier that served 4 years in C.S.A. I
   am member of NB Forrest Camp No. 4 U.C.V. at Chattanooga Ten &
   member of Genl. Hickmans staff. I am
                              Yours Truly
                              Wm. T. Alexander
                              525 Battery Place
                              Chattanooga Ten

                  ALLEN, ANDREW JACKSON

FORM NO. 1

1. Andrew Jackson Allen, Gibson Co. Bradford Tenn.
2. 83 years
3. Gibson Co. Tenn.
4. Gibson Co. Tenn.
5. Farming
6. Farmer
7. One horse bridle & saddle
8. No
9. 400 acres
10. Land worth a bout $8.00 an Acer. stock about $200.00
11. two store log House a bout 3 or 4 rooms to Each a partment.
12. plowed hoed or split Rails or any thing was to do on the farm.
13. Father did any thing that come to hand plowed or used a hoe at any
   thing there was to do. cooked all her meals on the Fire place and
   spoon & weving cloth made the Most of our Wearing close.
14. No
15. Respectable
16. yes
17. a bout 10 percent
18. Not classed
19. they did
20. yes

                        194

ALLEN (cont'd.):
21. wasent Discussed at all
22. yes
23. X
24. Subscribions School
25. 6 or 8 mo.
26. 2 miles
27. Subscribion was all no High Schools
28. private
29. 2 two 3 mo.
30. yes
31. Man
32. Jun 5th 1861 Musterd in at Jackson Tennessee
33. 12th Tenn Reg. Co G Tom William's, John Gibbs, Frank Young, L.D.
    Walker, Harry Breakhouse, Young Allen, John Hartsfield, Bob Bradford,
    Buck Mullins, John Gallard, John Warren, Pryer Warren, John Dowed,
    _____ Dowed, Harve Smith, All Smith, Wash Biship, Jim William's,
    George William's, F.M. _____, Dick Wade, Chas. Wade, John Wall's,
    Billie King
34. Union City
35. 4 mo.
36. Bellmont Mo.
37. wounded in Bellmont and sent to Memphis Tenn _____ in Ky. Raid at
    Lexonton 1 Day. We won the Fight and captured Lots of Suply's &
    Big Lot of prisnors. Big hard Fight at Perryville & the Feaderals
    won there. retreated from there in to Tenn and had a battle _____
    we won the Fight there next we had 7 Day's Fight at Murphisbur.
    wounded there in the brest & sent Atlanta Hosp. Stayed there 2 mo.
    next Battle was Missionary Ridge. captured several of our soldiers
    I got captured there and stayed in prison 17 mo. got home 1st of
    June in 1865. (there they tryed to get me to vote for Harper & I
    would not do it.)
38. Discharged at Rock Island sometime the last of May 1865.
39. Come down by water to Hickman Ky. From there I walked home a
    Distant of 40 miles.
40. Macanic
41. Farmed all my life. Magristrate for 12 years Decon in the Missionary
    Baptist Church about 55 year's.
42. Young Washington Allen; ----; ----; N.C., In Gibson Co., was Col.
    Dureing Mexican War after was Magristrat & served for year's.
43. Nancie Shy; Franklin Shy; Dont Remember; Smith Co. Middle Tennessee
44. Have no Record of them and could not truthfully say of any thing of
    them.

ALLEN, JOHN BENTON

(two questionaires - first rec'd. 1922)
FORM NO. 1

1. John Benton Allen; Cleveland Bradley County Tennessee
2. Born June 11th 1844 78 years 2 months 20 days
3. Jefferson County Tennessee
4. Hamilton County State of Tennessee
5. Farmer
6. (Farmer) My Father died when I was only 4 years old.
7. I did not own any land but my Foster Father owned about 400 acres
    situated at what is now known as King Point near Chattanooga Tenn-
    essee worth I would say about $6000.00 or $8000.00 dollars as it
    mostly River and Creek bottom. My Foster Fathers name was Absolem
    Sivly.
8. My Foster Father owned only Three one male and two females.
9. 400
10. Personal $1000.00 Land 8000.00 3 slaves @ 800.00=2400.00 worth I
    supose about 11000.00 or $12000.00 dollars
11. It was a Two Story log house with ceiled and weather boarded and
    contained 6 large rooms.
12. when not in school I did all kinds of work that is done on a farm.
    Everybody both white and black worked. Pepole did not think that
    work was a disgrace (Some few exceptions among the young)

195

ALLEN (cont'd.):
13. I supose a farmer. Mother did general domestic work including card-
    ing spining weaving to as Pepole made most everything in the way of
    clothing before the war.
14. My Foster Father owned three slaves but I never did hear them called
    servants.
15. Pepole considered honest labor of all worts to be honorable and
    nessasary. there were less loffers before the war than there is at
    this time.
16. Yes. However there is always a class of pepole that will not work
    if they can get out of it.
17. To my knowledge there was very few Probably a few young dudes as
    I class them as I stated above labor was not considered disgraceful
    before the Civil War.
18. Yes I did not see any distincion between them realaly not as much
    difference between the rich and the poor as there is at this day.
19. yes
20. yes
21. In that case money always has its influance in such cases.
22. In that case money was scarce and wages was low and the laboring
    class did not strive very much to accumilate money.
23. In some cases there might have been but in general way there were
    no discouragement presented to the pepole.
24. In the cuntry schools there was no high schools only what we call in
    this day Grammar School.
25. I supose about 5 years.
26. From my home it was about one mile.
27. One was called Chickamauga School the other one was called Boyce
    School.
28. Always Public
29. abot three months sometime as long as Four moths.
30. yes from the ages of 6 to 21 years
31. Generally speaking they were men. sometimes a woman
32. at Ooltewah Tenn on October 31st 1861 I Joined Co. E 37 Tenn Inft
    (Col Mosses White) Capt Isaac Nichols
33. I served 12 months in Company E 37 Tenn Inft after that I Joined
    Company H 2nd Tenn Cav. Co H was mostly made up in Hamilton County
    by William Ragsdale and the Regt when first made up was in command
    of Col. Gillespie but in the consolidation was commanded by Col.
    Henry M. Ashby who afterwards was made a Brig. General.
34. To Germantown near Memphis Tenn Thence to Knoxville Tenn
35. Something over Two months
36. Fishing Creek or Mill Springs
37. Fishing Creek we Joined Gen A.S. Johnston at Shiloah Thence to
    Corinth Miss Thence back to Chattanooga Tenn Thence on Gen. Braxton
    Bragg raid into Kentucky Battle of Perryville and other engagements
    Thence back to Knoxville after this I was with the 2nd Tenn Cav. at
    this time we was the imediate Com of Col. Scott and about the 1st
    of July 1863 we was ordered into Ky to intercede for John H. Morgan
    who was then in Ohio. On July 31st 1863 at Lancaster Ky I was
    captured and taken to Camp Chace Thence to Ft. Deleware Released
    June 20 1865.
38. Released from Fort Deleware Prison June 20th 1865 I was kept a
    prisoner of war from the 31st of July 1863 to June 20th 1865.
39. Boarded the cars at Philadelphia went to Pittsburg Pa. remained all
    night next morning got on the cars went Louisville Ky Thence to
    Nashville Tenn from Nashville I came to Chattanooga my home.
40. I went clerking in a Mercantile line of business for about 6 years
    then up the carpenters trade and followed that business as long as
    I was able to work which has been about 10 years.
41. I have belonged to the Baptist Church for about 55 years.
42. John Allen; dont know; don't know; ----; When last seen we lived in
    Bradley County Tenn; In regard this I know nothing.
43. Mary Ann White; Thomas White; ---- Chattanooga Hamilton County Tenn.
44. my Grandfather name was Benton Allen who lived at New Market
    Jefferson County Tenn this all that can tell you about my ancestry.
    P.S. Excuse bad writing as I am very feeble.

ALLEN (cont'd.):
   second questionnaire - rec'd. 1915
FORM NO. 1

1. John B. Allen,Cleveland Bradley County Tennessee
2. 71 the 11th of June 1915
3. Jefferson County Tennessee
4. Hamilton Co. Tenn.
5. a farmer
6. a farmer (only a God Father)
7. none
8. yes my adopted parents owned 3 slaves (I was adopted when quite young)
9. about 500 or 600 acres
10. about Ten Thousand dollars
11. a Two story log house ceiled and weatherboarded containing 6 rooms.
12. I did all kinds of aarm work when not in school. as a general rule
    pepole were much more industrious before the war than now especaly
    the woman folk. a spining wheel and loom made about all the music
    they had.
13. my adopted father did all sorts of farm work untill he become too
    old. my adopted mother did General house work such as it takes to
    keep house besides carding wool & cottons spining weaving & making
    all kinds of cloth.
14. not in the oridnary way that we class servants at this time.
15. There was no other occupation that was considered more honorable
    than to be a good farmer at that time it was not a disgrace to work.
16. I do not remember any one that did not take any active part on the
    farm.
17. I can not remember of a single man only in rare cases where they
    could live without work however in that day there was but very few
    drones among the pepole.
18. yes all classes of pepole mixed and mingled to gether in a social
    way more so than pepole do to day however there were some bigots
    then Just like there is now but not near so many of them.
    However farthur south there were more distinction shown.
19. If there was any distinction between the Two classes of pepole I
    was not able to find it out there might have been on some special
    gethering to some extent but nothing that could be called offencieve
20. I do not remember any antagonistics in my boy hood days any more
    than in a regular course of events. The slaves attended the meetings
    the same as white pepole but always sit in the back seats.
21. not near so much then as pepole do at present to help a man that
    has plenty of money there were not so much log rolling in that day.
22. They opportunities offored to young men was Just as good or better
    then than now all things considered however that of course depends
    largely on the man his chances were slow but very good.
23. If there ever was discouragment or obstructions placed in the way
    of any young man because he did not own slaves or because he was
    poor. I do not know anything about it (I did not own any slaves)
    the negro race is much more against the poor white man than now.
24. I always attended a common country school but generally speaking we
    had good teachers for that day sometimes tuition was charged there
    was not so many books then but the pupils learned them.
25. I supose altogether I went to school about five years three & four
    moths at a school term.
26. about one mile from where I lived
27. the one that I attended there were other common schools farther
    away from me. We did not have as many school then as now and but
    very big schools in the state.
28. nearly always they were public schools some time the Cittizens paid
    the teacher.
29. From three to four months beginning about the first of August.
30. Yes more so than now considering the size of the population. I was
    glad when school time come.
31. Sometimes they were men at other times they were woman (My bes
    teacher was a woman)
32. At Oolewah Tenn on October 31st 1861 and served out my twelve months
    then reinlisted at Lenoirs Station near Knoxville in March 1863.

ALLEN (cont'd.):
33. Co E 37th Tenn Inft Moses White Col, Bob Frazier Lieut Col, Capt.
    Isaac Nichols some of my Comrades in Co E were Thos Sively,Dug Ball,
    John Ervin, H.T. Spivey, J.P. Moon, T.T. Cobb In the month of March
    1863 I reenlisted again in Co H 2nd Tenn Cav. Col. Gillespie Alas
    Col H.M. Ashby, Generaly known as Ashby's regiment Capt. William
    Ragsdale raised the Co. but Capt. Thodes commanded the Co. when I
    enlisted W.T. Newman 1st Lieut John D. Traynon 2nd Lieut Comrades
    of Co. H 2nd Tenn Cav Mart Bell, Sam Burnett, John C. Doyle,
    O.S. Green, J.P. Tymes, J.W. Webster
34. To Germantown near Memphis Tenn then to Knoxwille Tenn then to
    Fishing Creek then to Murfreesboro Tenn then to Corinth Miss then
    Mobile Ala then to Montgomery then to Atlanta Ga then to Chattanooga
    Tenn then Gen Braggs raid through Ky to Knoxville
35. About three months at Fishing Creek however on regiment did not
    participate in the main battle when Gen. Zollicoffer was killed.
36. At Fishing Creek around Corinth Miss at Perryville Ky. and many
    other small engagements.
37. Hard times does not expres fully what the old Confederate soldiers
    went through with. I have marched three days & nights with out
    food waided creeks waist deep in the middle of winter been in the
    sadle day & night three & four weeks at a time had to forage & beg
    food for ourselves & horses had to go thinly clothed had to get our
    clothing the best way we could after the first year after the
    beginning of the war. After all this I am not sorrow that I suffered
    for my dear old Southland.
38. I was Payroled or discharge at Fort Deleware military prison on June
    the 20th 1865. I was captured on Col. Scotts raid at Lancaster Ky
    July 31st 1863 was a prisoner of war 22 months 20 days.
39. We was taken from Fort Delaware up to Philadephia where we received
    good treatment by the old soldiers & citizens of that place we were
    well treated all the way through Ohio Indiana and Kentckey to
    Chattanooga my old home town.
40. I went to clerking in a dry goods store and followed that business
    untill 1876 but on account of my health had to get out in the open
    air and worked what I could at the carpenters trade since I think I
    have done my part.
41. I was raised a Baptist and belonged to that order about 40 years
    but at present I am antisectarian and believe in only one church
    which is the Church of God. I am not a holy roller but try to be a
    Christain. I have never held a state or county office I never did
    want any office. I only have a few more days to live on old earth
    then I shall pass over the river of death to meet the most of my
    old comrades at the Judgment with the few that is left behind to som
    follow on then there will be no more old Confederate soldier I think
    it a great honor to be called a Confederate Soldier don't you
    P.S. I would like to write a more detailed accont but my physical
    condition will not admit of my doing so at present. my memory is
    getting bad.

ALLEN, JOHN SIMPSON

FORM NO. 1

1.   John Simpson Allen, McKenzie, Carroll Co, Tenn.
2.   76 yrs. since Nov. 10, 1921
3.   Rutherford co., Tenn.
4.   Rutherford co., Tenn.
5.   Farming
6.   Farmer
7.   I had no property at that time
8.   No
9.   160 acres
10. $10,000
11. Log house, weather boarded and ceiled and had 5 rooms
12. I did all kinds of general farm work and certain historians were
     mistaken
13. General farm work and mother did the house work, such as cooking,
     spinning, weaving and washing for a family of 10

ALLEN (cont'd.):
14. 1 hired hand a negro
15. Yes, for everyone did their work
16. Yes
17. To no extent
18. Social equality was the ruling spirit, only with questionable characters
19. yes
20. They were friendly
21. no
22. Yes
23. They were encouraged
24. Public school
25. About 5 months in each year for 2 or 3 years
26. 2½ miles
27. Public school
28. Public
29. About 5 months
30. Yes
31. Men
32. In autumn of 1862.
33. 4th Tenn. Cavalry. Bill Allen, Al Mathews, Tom Mou___?, Ras Jennings, Bob Hyght, John Arnold, Julius Williams & many others I fail to call to mind now.
34. To Chattanooga
35. on the next day we had a schmirsh (skirmish)
36. Sand Mountain, Alabama
37. From San Mountain we went to Chatanooga & had many small fightings around there but we were scouting all the time and were fighting most every day but were in no big battles. We had scarcely any clothes and slept on the ground and ate anything and everything we could find available. We were exposed to cold, hunger and disease in every possible way. ___? a case of pneumonia was at a house in Alabama
38. I was discharged in April 1865 at Charlotte, N.C.
39. When we surrendered we were to keep our side-arms and horses but on animals at Sweetwater Tenn. we were ordered stopped & dismounted, but 16 of us banded & came home on our horses as agreed.
40. Farming
41. I have fathered 13 children and made my living farming & logging. I lived in Rutherford co., Gibson co., & Carroll co., of Tenn. and am a member of Christian Church.
42. Robert John Allen; Murfreesboro. Rutherford co., Tenn.; near Murfreesboro. Rutherford co., Tenn.; He was a staunch supporter of the Confederate Army but no office
43. Elizabeth Jane Lassater; Jacob Lassater and Laracey(?) McMinn (McMimm?) near Murfreesboro, Tenn.
44. My Grandfather Eli Allen came from Ireland and settled in Rutherford co., Tenn. together with one brother & sister where he lived until the time of his death.

    I am just recovering from a six weeks siege of sickness & my mind isn't as clear as it has been but I have answered as near as possible under existing circumstances & as soon as it was possible for me to. Hoping you will obtain all desired information.

Very Truly,
J. S. Allen

ALLEN, MYRICK ROBERSON

FORM NO. 2

1. Myrick Roberson Allen, Belfast, Marshall co., Tenn.
2. Born the Elenth (11th) day of April 1834
3. South Carolina
4. Confederate
5. Company G; 32 Tenn.
6. Farmer
7. Myrick Allen; Virginia; M.E. Preacher
8. Sarah Porter; Dr. James Porter and Mary Porter; in S.C.

199

ALLEN (cont'd.):

9.   ----
10. Did not own any
11. yes five or six
12. owned land about 150 (180?) acres
13. My father was dead when the war opened and the land had been devided among the Heirs.
14. log house two Rooms
15. Farmed, worked with plows and hoes and with a cradle.
16. Cooking, spining, weaving
17. Did when lived in S.C. But had none when they came to Tennessee
18. Yes
19. Yes
20. they worked on farms and at their other occupations
21. yes they all associated together
22. yes you could not tell any difference
23. they were all on good friendly terms
24. they made no difference
25. yes they were good
26. they were not
27. common country school
28. about 12 months in all
29. about 2½ miles
30. none
31. Private
32. 3 or 4 months
33. yes
34. Man
35. in the year 61 in a little village called Belfast Tenn in Oct. 1861
36. Camp Trousdale
37. four or five months
38. Fort Donalson
39. Captured at Fort Donalson was taken to Camp Morton indiana stayed in camp Morton 7 or 8 months, exchanged at Vicks Burg Miss. very well treated in camp Morton. I in all the Battles in Joe Johnston Retrest. I was with Hood in the campane in Tenn.
40. in Florence Ala 1864
41. to Nashville Tenn on Boat and from Nashville home on foot
42. farming
43. I have been engaged in farming and other general labor since my return home. I have never held any public office. I have lived in Marshall county tenn ever since the war
44.   ----
45.

James Wood	Thomas Barons(?)
Bill Barrons	Bill Neil
Jess Leonard	haree Neil
Dock Cahpman	Mike Cannon
Bill McAdams	Sam McAdams
Arch McCool	Col. Coffee
Jasper Smiley	Alex Crawford
George yarbrough	Roof yarbrough
R.L. Bowden	zan Bradshaw
Tom twity	Andy Calahan
A.D. Armstrong	Bill jones
Dock Doddy	Wiley O'Neil
granville Goltrath(?)	james Beckham
Bill Sharp	Green Bowden
Newt Finley	

46.   ----

(on separate sheet - handwritten)
the Public men I have met are -
I was present when Gen. Grand and Gen. Buckner met and shak hands at Ft. Donalson. I was personaly acquainted with Gen. Brawn, Gen. N.B. Forest, Jefferson Davis. I marched by the boddie of Gen. Leonidious Polk as he lay dead at or on the Battle field at Pine Mountain. Gen. Hatch give my Discharge at Florence Ala.

ALLEN, W. J.

FORM NO. 2

1. W. J. Allen, Martin (?) Tenn.
2. 78
3. Tenn. - Weakly county
4. confederate soldier
5. A - 31st Tenn Infantry
6. Farmer & Merchant
7. James G. Allen; North Carolina; Granville co., N.C.; ----; ----;
    ----
8. Agnes A. _____; Herndon ____; can't answer; Lauderdale co., Tenn.
9. cant give this information
10. did not own any property
11. Parents did. I did not
12. about 250 acres
13. about 10.00 per acre
14. a framed house
15. an Farmer - Regular farm work
16. Father worked on farm and Mother was house keeper
17. yes
18. yes
19. yes
20. none
21. yes
22. yes
23. yes
24. did not
25. yes
26. encouraged
27. common county school
28. 1 year all told
29. 1½ miles
30. county school
31. Private
32. 3 months
33. yes
34. man
35. 1861 June(?) 20th Tenn.
36. Trenton Tenn.
37. about year
38. Island No 10
39. Fort Pillow - Corinth Miss. - was wounded & sent to hospital 6 weeks
    Next Battle was Perryville(?) Ky fight lasting 24 hours & went to
    Camp Dick Robinson(?) fighting at several places - Drew 5 days
    rations went to Knoxville had rough time - Enough eatables & cloth-
    ing fairly good -
40. had a furlough from army and at time of surrender was at home on
    furlough
41. walked from Corinth Miss. home
42. Farming
43. I have tried to live an honorable life since the war & I believe I
    have succeeded in this as I believe those who have known me would
    testify - have been a farmer most of my life
44. I knew a number of great men - Gen. Cheatham was an great man.
                    signed   W. J. Allen

ALLEN, WILLIAM GIBBS

FORM NO. 1

1. William Gibbs Allen, 651 South Market St., Dayton, Tenn.
2. I have passed my 86th birthday (follows: I am as __ __ __ __ -
    not readable)
3. at Larkinsville, Jackson county, Alabama
4. confederate - I was living at Washington, Rhea county, Tenn. when I
    enlisted.
5. I was a merchant and farmer

ALLEN (cont'd.):
6. Farmer
7. I owned a small farm value of property about Two Thousand Dollars. I was Trustee of Thea County and Deputy Register. hold a small stock of goods. I resigned both and went into Captain John George Morgan, Montgomery, Bradley co., Cavalry, company.
8. None
9. 211
10. Land $2500 - house hold goods Horses and cattle about $1500
11. one large log house later a two story frame with porch in front 2 rooms down and 2 up stairs
12. I was ten years old when war came between American and Mexico. Father and Uncle Abner Frazier had a 4 horse crop rented on Tenn. River bottoms Uncle Abner and A. Richardson volunteered and left Father the 4 horse crop to tend. I had made a hand with hoe now I made a plogh hand.
13. Father did all kinds of work on the leased land. we boys for their was 7 boys and one girl, grubed, burt (burnt?) bush. Mother cooked, washed, patched, made tow cloth when a web of cloth was wove. She made us long tow shirt. I helped her was shed(?) would card a pile of reals(?) and I would spin till bed time. I helped to glear(?) the Loom and fill the real and weave the cloth at night.
14. no. sometimes Father would hire help to work on the farm.
15. our neighborhood considered a lazy man who would not work as worthless as mean _____ Day Labor was respetable, in Rich and poor families.
16. yes, Rich and poor worked
17. Thier was but few men that would not work. and the few thier was was not respected and hated by rich and poor. Mothers, the girls of that day would not keep company with such dudes.
18. I married into a slave owner family. My wife Miss Mary E. Thomison, associated with Daughters of slave owners. My wife had one beau who owned 40 slaves and _____ 10 slaves. My best man had no slaves. My wife best young(?) Lady had 30. At our wedding their was 80 invided gest. Rich and poor were invited.
19. At church gatherings of all kinds you could not tell by dress or groups for all classes were respected save the lazy worthless fellow at our social parties the poor boy would have as his pardner the rich girl.
20. _____ so much as then, in Politics my father wanted me to marry into a Democrat family but I chose the daughter of a whig family and we was raised into _____ of _____ and went to a three months school to gather once.
21. It did not as you can see from appended sheet neither in marage relations it was character and work that made the man
22. It was honesty and willingness to work was all that was required character made the man not negroes or money.
23. A slave holder & a Whig once hired me to work in his store. I had just made & hauled and built into a fence 5000 fence rails. Hauled them with a yoke of oxen. Hired me at $12.50 per month to work in his store at the end of 6 months I was half owner on a credit extended me.
24. a Subscription school 2 months in Miss.(?) a subscription school in Washington in 1845 father boarded me and paid $3.00 for my tuition. 3 months at Kerr (?) Springs. 3 months at Black Jack School. log houses, penchen floors, 4 leg benches
25. Some fifteen and half months
26. two miles
27. None but subscription schools
28. Public all white childer went Rich and poor that could pay $1.00 per month.
29. from 1½ to 3 months
30. all was glad to go
31. All were Men
32. In Confederate March 1st 1861. would of in sooner if it had been for my family and my officer.
33. Fifth Tenn. Cavalry. Col. George W. McKenzie. Co. D. First Captain John George Morgan, Montgomery, Bradley, county. Company. I had made an Infantry(?) _____ for Col. J. M. Gillesford(?) 43 Regiment but owing to my family and my Trustee office I could not leave till

202

ALLEN (cont'd.):

after sell____ and the company of my wife when I went to Knoxville. I found Col. Gill (empines?) Regiment full and he took me to Col. James T.(?) H____. I found him drunk and I would not serve under him.

34. To Brimstone(?) KY. then to London(?) Ky to Camp Dick Roberson to Danville Ky - at Dick Roberson we bumed (burned?) a large supply of bacom and several wagons under Gen. John Peg____.

35. two week at Bornston(?) Kentucky and Barberville Ky at Goose Creek. I had a horse shot by bushwackers.

36. at Williamsburg Ky we fought the fifth Ohio. Lost a Lt. of Co. G. Horner and 11 detailed(?) men

37. we furnished our own horses and arms our armes was a shot gun or Colts Piston (Pistol). Some times an old flint locke rifle. our saddels poor. we soon captured better guns and saddels - the western horse was no good to a Tenn or Kentucky cavalry man they wanted mediam size horses. Keen and active. we had no tents. the Rich and Goverment furnished a Blanket a pick(?) for each man the Heavens was our covers Rain or Shine by Day or Night in Cold or heat.

38. At Charlott, North Carolina on twenty day of April 1865

39. May 4th 1865 we mustered(?) passed thrugh Ashville N.C. at Gap of Mountain. we found one Col. Hick and some 3 or 4 hundred bush-whackers. Robert Hick (Kirk?) demanded our horses and side arms of the Officers. After a long Parley between Col. McKenzie and Kirk, Col. McKenzie ordered me to bring forward.

40. I made a little crop in fall of the year. Judge Locks nephew Hunihal Paine was a merchant in Washington. he died and Judge F. Locke sold me his stock of merchandise on a credit and I made good. was able to bye a good farm. Trusted a friend and lost all

41. I farmed traded in Grain Horses Cattle and sold goods. Lived at Washington on a farm and have been a member of Southern Methodist Church since August 20th 1850

42. Vallentine Allen; or near Fatewill? Bedford county in 1809, Tenn.; lived at Larkinville, Ala. two 6 yrs in Miss. came to Rhea County 1843; he had little education. he served as peace officer was in Scotts(?) war with the In.

43. Ann Frazier; Beriah Frazier and Barbara Gibbs; their home in Fraziers Bend on Tenn River.

44. My grand father Vallentine Allen came to South Carolina in 1774 married and settled in South Carolina. he was Scotch Irish. my grand Mother was Scotch and French came to South Carolina. her maden name was Barbra Collin(?) Grand Father fought for independence of America and was at the Battle of Neworleans under Genl. Carroll. Grand Father Frazier was under Genl. Green in wars for Americas indep____.

Dayton, Tenn. Jany. 1922
W. G. Allen

(N.B.: For additional material see - Confederate Collection - Memoirs - Allen, William Gibbs)

ANDERSON, FRANK OGLESBY

FORM NO. 2

1. Frank Oglesby Anderson, Clarksville, Tenn.
2. 84 years & 6 months
3. Green county - State of Kentucky
4. Confederate
5. Company A; 14th Tennessee one of the regiments composing the justly famous Tenn. Brigade which served in the Va army throughout the war, surrendered with Lee at Appomattox.
6. Planter
7. Peter Anderson; in Louisa County, Va.; moved when a young man to Green co. Ky. he was still an extensive Planter, was very highly respected; esteemed, loved by every one in his community, was a very fine business man.
8. Lucilla Jane Montgomery; Gen. John Montgomery & Ann Casey(?) Montgomery; Stanford? Ky. later moved to Columbia Ky.

203

ANDERSON (cont'd.):

9. Frank Oglesby Anderson is the son of Peter Anderson, sone of Garland Anderson, 2nd son of Garland Anderson 1st who was a member of the House of Burgesses of Va.. Chairman of the Committee of Safety Hanover Co., Va. 1775 a delegate from Hanover in the Va. convention at Richmond. July 17, 1775 a member Provincial Congress at Richmond 1774 & 1775, elected delegate to the Continental Congress.
10. I was a minor and owned no property. My father was living.
11. My father owned about 40 slaves.
12. My parents owned 1000 acres in Green co., Ky.
13. I would say about $50,000.00 slaves and land
14. Two story frame house with seven rooms
15. When I was a young man I did general work plowing, hoeing, etc.
16. My father did general farm work & overseed his slaves. My Mother had the slaves to do the house work such as cooking, spinning, weaving and all other house work.
17. about 40 slaves.
18. Yes
19. Some did and some didn't. generally at that time the negroes did work of that sort
20. Very few
21. To the first question, yes - to the second question, no.
22. There was a very friendly feeling between them - slave holders and non slave holders mingled together.
23. ----
24. Not independent of his personal character
25. Very fine
26. They were encouraged
27. First I went to Preparatory schools and later graduated at Centre College, Danville, Ky.
28. about 10 or 12 years
29. Very near
30. Schools all over the country in every neighborhood.
31. Private
32. Ten
33. Very regularly
34. Both
35. I enlisted in the Confederate Army in April 1861 in Clarksville, Tenn. 14th Tenn. Regiment. William A. Forbes was Col.
36. My company went on the Cheat Mountain Campaign in wester Va. under Gen. Robt. E. Lee.
37. about 5 months
38. Cheat Mountain
39. After 1st battle went to Karracha(?) Valley. My Brigade was the only one that was in every battle & skirmish fought by Gen. Robert E. Lee. I had the experience of the average Southern soldier. I was in prison 3 weeks.
40. after the battle of Appomattox
41. ----
42. Went to Law School at Lebanon, Tenn.
43. Practiced law at Clarksville, Tenn. was a member of the First Presbyterian Church there. Was Attorney General of the Criminal Court of Montgomery Co., Tenn. at Clarksville for one term. (F. O. Anderson of Clarksville, Tenn. was appointed Judge Advocate with the rank of Capt. on the staff of Gen. John L. Jones, commanding the second brigade of the Tenn. Division U.C.V. F. O. Anderson is a member of Forbes Bivouac U.C.V. at Clarksville, Tenn.
44. ----
45. The Roster of the 14th Tennessee Regiment I believe can be found at Clarksville, Tenn. at the First National Bank
46. ----

(on separate pages - handwritten)

1

39. Extended answer to the war record of Frank Oglesby Anderson, Confederate Soldier Member 14th Tenn. Reg. Clarksville, Tenn. Frank O. Anderson was severely wounded at the battle of Chancellorsville shot in the knee was taken to the field hospital, the surgeon in command (who was a personal friend) and the other Dr's. thought it best to amputate the leg, stating he had little chance of recovery unless that was done, he told them he would rather die than lose his

ANDERSON (cont'd.):

    leg, that he would take the chance, so they did not amputate and he recovered sufficiently to be removed to the home of a relative, Dr. Ben Anderson's, near Richmond, Va., he remained there about 4 months. On account of his wounded leg he was not able to again go into the Infantry so he joined Morgans Calvary and was captured at Cinthiana Ky, on his way to Camp Douglas, to be imprisoned, as the train slowed up at Chicago, he was on the rear end of a coach with a guard, he pushed the guard off on one side, spent 1 night with acquaintances in Chicago, went from there to St. Louis, spent a short time at the home of his uncle, Col. Barrett. Gen. John B. Castleman & he went from St. Louis to Cincinnati working their way back to the Confederate lines, at Cincinnati they were informed they were wanted to join an expedition to release prisoners at-

2

    Frank Oglesby Anderson's war record - Camp Douglas, Col. C.C. Clay, Jas. P. Halcomb & Jacob P.(D?) Thompson were commissioners from the Confederate States. to enprovise the expedition to Chicago, they organized the expedition at Toronto Canada under command of Gen. John B. Castleman and Gen. Henry T. Hines. They selected the date of the Democratic National Convention at Chi cago in 1864 as the time to make the effort failing to receive the assistance that had been promised, they had to abandon the attmep. Each man was released on his own resources to get back to the Confederate lines. Frank O. Anderson was selected to carry the report to the Confederate Government at Richmond, Va. he went over the northern route through the great lakes the Gulf of St. Lawrence to Halifax Nova Scocia from there went on a blockage runner (Sir William Armstrong) to the Bahama Islands, then to Wilmingont N.C. then on to Richmond, Va. delivered the report to the Government, Jefferson Davis being President of the Confederate States.

    (These are some of the incidents told by Frank Oglesby Anderson, of his experiences in the Civil War of 1861-1864, to his daughters, Mrs. J.W. Hayes at Clarksville, Tenn. and Mrs. Jas. L. Glenn at (9)322 Harding Road Nashville, Tenn.

ANDERSON, HENRY

FORM NO. 2

1.   Henry Anderson, (Troy?), Tenn. Box 55
2.   75 years
3.   Cumberland Co., North Carolina
4.   Confederate
5.   Co. d, 40th N.C.
6.   Farmer
7.   James Anderson; Cumberland Co, N.C.
8.   Mary Bostic -----
9.   James Anderson Grandfather came from England before the Revolutionary war and fought with the colonys for Liberty
10. ----
11. No
12. 75
13. _____ as the _____ of war owned 75 acres of land. His land was in Cumberland co, N.C. and valued about $23.00 per acre.
14. Log house with 2 tooms and stick and dirt chimny.
15. We yoused home mad(e) plows and crude hoes and did our own farm work.
16. My father tended his farm & stock, my Mother did her cooking before the open fire. her spinning and weaving of all house hold goods also made all clothing by hand.
17. No
18. Yes, in our community it was
19. Yes
20. in our comunity most every man did his own work.
21. Slave holders did not mix to any extent with non slave holders
22. They did not
23. Antagonistic
24. It did
25. No

ANDERSON (cont'd.):
26. Discaraged by slave holders
27. a little log school house
28. about 2 months to the year
29. Four miles
30. only one little school
31. Public
32. Three months
33. No
34. Man
35. I inlisted in the confederate army Dec. 12 - '61 at Goldsborough, N.C.
36. Wilmington, N.C.
37. about four years - this Reg. was heavy Artillery and moved a gruad__!
38. Fort Fisher
39. ----
40. Almira New York
41. we were discharged with no money and made our way home sometimes on foot sometimes on flat cars took about 8 days to make the trip.
42. Farmed
43. My Mother died the first year after the war and in 70(?) I went to Granada, Miss. married there and lived until 78 when mooved to Memphis Tenn. lived there until 94 and mooved to Troy(?) Obion(?) co. Have lived here since that time and all ways farmed.
44. ----
45. Everet Dixon, Turkey, Samson co., N.C.,Charley Grady, Kennonsville?, N.C., Jessee Jones, Rocky Mount, N.C.
46. ----

ANDERSON, JAMES A.

FORM NO. 1

1. James A. Anderson, Hendersonville, Tenn. R.R. 2
2. 82 the first day of March
3. Jackson county, Tenn.
4. Overton county State of Tenn.
5. farmer
6. farmer
7. None
8. Owned one-old Uncle Abe
9. 108 acres
10. about $3000   in land
11. a four room double log house
12. farm worked at anything on farm that come to hand
13. He was a farmer and my mother did her house duties & also spun & wove & made all our clothes & even tanned leather & had our shoes made.
14. one slave
15. extremely so
16. yes all did
17. mighty few that was idle
18. not in the least they felt they were no better
19. yes
20. they were friendly
21. did not
22. good
23. they were encouraged
24. country schools
25. 6 or 8 sessions
26. ½ mile
27. free schools
28. public
29. 3 months
30. tolerable regular they were kept home to work
31. man
32. April 1, 1861. Livingston, Overton County
33. 8th Tenn. Infantry A.S. Fulton Col., Will Windle, Fate Wendell, Lafayett Gore, Jim Cullem?, Milt Oakley, Treb? Bledsoe, Jack Harrison,

ANDERSON (cont'd.):
  Jack Tompkins
34. Celina, Tenn. to Nashville & then to Camp Trousdale, Sumner co.
35. about 4 months
36. Perryville, Ky
37. From P., Ky to Stanton, W. Virginia then to Cheek Mountains then
    back to Stanton & So. Carolina Donelsons brigade
    Battles 1 Perryville - 1 day held the battle field
    Battles 2 Parkers Cross Road W. Tenn. 3 hours gained
    Plenty to eat first 1½ years reasonably well. Slept in tents.
    Twice in hospital & was never in prison
38. Washington, Georgia year 1865
39. Went to Kingston(?) East Tennessee & were allowed our horses & side
    arms then to Chattanooga there our horses were taken and walked
    Sparta disbanded there & then walked home. On the last days of the
    Dec. I was transfered by exchange to the 8th Tenn Calvery.
40. farming
41. farming, lived in three counties, Jackson, Sumner and Davidson.
    Never held any offices.
42. Mathew M. Anderson; b. Virginia; lived Jackson co.; War of 1812
43. Elida Cummins; ----; ----; lived Kentucky - Baron county
44. Parents ----; Grandparents: Robert Anderson lived in Jackson county.
    (7 or 8 small lined sheets handwritten; war experiences - difficult
    to read)

                    ANDERSON, JAMES BEREY

FORM NO. 2

1. James Bery Anderson, Dickerd, R #1 Tenn
2. 76 years 2 months & 3 days old
3. in Franklin co., Tenn.
4. i was a confederate soldier
5. Company D - 28 Regiment general Morgan Calbry
6. farmer
7. Lewis Anderson; b. Virginia; Justis of the peace for sometime -
    inroling officer later part of war
8. Charlotte Moore; (don't remember); Mary A. Moore; begining of civil
    war in franklin co Tenn.
9. my grand fathers and grand mothers on both sides com heare from
    vriginia before father and mother wer married. Father was tax
    collector of this county 1 term also he rode on horse back 2 trips
    to virginia to wind up grand father Moore estate.
10. none
11. not eny
12. six hundred acres
13. a bout two thousand dollars
14. log house two rooms one used for kitchen with a dirt floore grand
    Pa Anderson first name is Garlant
15. farm work plowed howed cleard land maid rails built fences dug
    ditches out and hauled wood and rails with a yok of oxens. I cut
    wheat oats and rye with __zen blade or cradle.
16. father wasant able to work he bossed us boys showed us how to work
    Mother carded cotton spun theat on a spining sheal wove cloth of all
    kinds on a loom made home spun dresses died indigo blue and c____
    made us boys c___ pants cooked on the fier place had a pot rack
    hanging in chimmy to hang pots on
17. non
18. all honest toil was considered respectable and honorable
19. they did
20. ther was non of that class of men in my community that I knew of
21. yea they migled freely with non slave holders I dont thing they
    felt themselves beter than other honorable men
22. thay did
23. there was a friendly feeling between them
24. it did not if they wer honorable men bouth of them
25. it was
26. they wer encouraged
27. the cuntry free schools is all the kind I attended about 2 or 3 month

                            207

ANDERSON (cont'd.):
in the year
28. may be about 12 months or more the civle war cut my schooling off
29. about one mile
30. cuntry or districk free schools
31. it was public except some subscription schools
32. from 3 to 4 months
33. tolerbly regular from laying big time to gethering fodder time on
34. I have went to bouth man and woman
35. in september 1864 I enlisted in Franklin county Tenn. the federal
    army was in possesion of this country - a a recruiting officer from
    General Morgan command name Coln. Hays who elisted all the boys who
    wanted to be taken out of heare to the reble army
36. wee scouted hear in Tenn. and alaba and never got out thrugh fedrals
    lines
37. wee wer engaged in scirmishes a month after joining with yanky
    cavalry.
38. wee wasant ever in a regularly battle as colon had a good scouter.
    didnt fite much
39. our captian and a few of us was sent out on scout as wee wer crosing
    the nashvill and chatanoogy R R in the night wer fierd on by sevral
    yankys killed 2 of our men and 2 horses mine from under mee - wee
    went to north alabam and tore up the Rail Rood a(nd) burnt the ties.
40. severl of us was cut of(f) from our commd. in january 1865 so we
    just stayed hom.
41. well just dodging about in the woods to keep from runing in to a
    squad of Federal soldiers
42. farming
43. I came home and took charge of my fathers farm work and other kinds
    of work - hav lived here in Franklin Co. Tenn. on the place my father
    mooved to when I was only 9 years old except 3 years in lincolin co.
    Tenn. and 5 years in south Ala where I worked in the cotton fields
    3 years. I run a saw and gris mill 1 year tended to wair house at
    Boat landing on Ala River stoerd freight in wair house and keep
    book of storage and billed and shiped cotton and other stuff. I
    joined the seperate Baptis Church in year of 1866 served as church
    clerk about 35 years is all office I hav held.
44. ----
45. Dave Anderson   John Reagin
    William Anderson   Jim Partan
    Edward Burks   hop Sarton
    low Burks   Jim Moore
    tol Gest   George Sanders
    sol Wagner   sam Riley
    Ammus Aristell   Bob Abbernather
    tom getton   John Williams
    Joe Starnes   tom Modeny
    William Starnes   linzy Jones
    Pery Philips   John Purtrim
    tomst phillips   Nox? Champion
    Jo. Beryhill   John Bass
    George lanahan
    ike camp
    abe Greenlee
    frank Staferd
    John Hinton
    Pe Nevill
    Gris little
    Captain
       Rufe Roseborro
46. Ben Cambell   Estells Springs Tenn
    Dave Coble?   Dicherd Tenn
    Henry Hold   "   "
    Alex Ursery   "   "

208

ANDERSON, JOHN B.

(File folder contains a single page from questionnaire and 2 lined
pages handwritten - cme)

33. (First part missing)
Peter Howard Shell, Fst. Sargent, Noah Hubbard, Sec. Sargent, Ray
Bollen, Corp. John Anderson, Corp'l, P.V.'s - John Debust, John
Cloud, Elic Cloud, George Cloud, Own Cheek, Billy Hartgrove, John
Hoose, Sol Hoose (this may be House), Felt Hoose, Bill Hoose, Nute
Breeding, Bill Ayers, John Ayers, John Wilson, & James Laremore,
Capt.
34. Red Bud, Ky.
35. 7(?) weeks
36. Red Bud, K.y. Cavalry
37. from Red Bud, Ky. to Washington co, Virginia salt works. Next battle
at the plaise(?). Negro soldiers in Yankee army. We the Confederates
repulsed whiped the Negroes and held the salt works. From there to
Withville Va. Dismounted us thare than one to Richmond Va. but on
guard duty awhile from Richmond to Cumberland Gap in Va. K.Y. &
Tenn. thare I was taken prisoner to Camp Chase C.H. From to Fort
Deleware
38. In Prison when Surrender. I left Fort Deleware the 20th day of June
1865 for home.
39. From Ft. Deleware to Baltimore, M.D. to Richmond, Va. to Roanoak, Va.
walked one hundred miles home
40. Farming
41. Farming to Griss Miller
42. Joseph Anderson; Washington co, Va.
43. ----
44. ----

(seperate pages rec'd; Sept 15, 1922)
My name is John B. Anderson i was married(?) at at Greenville Green
co tennsee 1847 i inlisted in the war 1862 in lee co Va i joined
James larmore compa the 27 Battalion the calva our Battalion was
chang into the 25 Battalion Will give you some the captans name i
Be longed to James Larmore compa(ny) H Captans Gipson Capton Bishop
Be longe to the 27 _____ our magers name was macdoel(McDowel?) and
_____ name was edison jineral Marrchell was our jinerl for A while
we ware put under him we went to _____. we went in Al(Ala.?)
Gap and down on red Bud we had a 2 hous(hours?) figt thar and jinerl
Marchel(Marshall?) retreted and we com Back went to Salt works Va
and had a fight thare we _____ _____ _____ _____ _____. I
served in the war yer in the west and east I was under jinerl Jones
we had a fight her at Jonesville i was under jinerl Marchel for a
while _____ (rest is difficult to understand. It appears he was put
on a train & sent to Richmond, Va. where he was in a battle near
Norick?, Va. He was "all over the bush.")

ANDERSON, JOHN MOULTRIE

FORM NO. 1

1. John Moultrie Anderson, Fayetteville, Tenn. or Flat Creek, Bedford
co, Tenn.
2. 85 next Oct.
3. Georgia, Screven county
4. South Carolina Barnwell District
5. M.D. Practiced medicine
6. Farmer
7. Land & slaves about $10,000.00
8. yes 8 or 10
9. about a 1000 acres
10. $10,000.00
11. Frame house 6 Rooms
12. worked on farm some plowed or any kind of work required
13. He did all kinds of work on farm as required Mother did such work
as helping about house etc.

ANDERSON (cont'd.):
14. yes - _____?
15. yes
16. yes
17. Not much of such idleness as every one ___ head of family had to look after their ___.
18. Yes they mingled & thought as much of those did not own slaves as those who did provided they were honorable & upright
19. yes
20. Frindly
21. no
22. yes
23. encouraged
24. Mostly private
25. about 7 years
26. about 2 miles
27. Private mixed schools
28. Private
29. 10 months
30. yes
31. man
32. Nov. 1861 Confederate
33. I was not long in the co. Capt. Smart was in Command of my Co. while at war in the Co. as I was put on detached service and was not with the Co. any more.
34. coast of South Carolina
35. I do not know
36. ----
37. I have no personal knowledge of the action of the Company after I left it as I was sent back to my neighborhood(?) to look after my mother in and _____ farm & to my medical practice in the neighbor-hood.
38. I never was officially discharged as we were scattered over the country
39. None
40. Practice of Medicene
41. Practiced medicine ever since principally in Tenn. Member of the Christian Church.
42. William Anderson; Screven co, Georgia; lived at Black Creek, Ga.; He was in the battle around Atlanta with Georgia_____.
43. Sarah Dowdie; James & Mary Dowdie; Middle Ground, Screven co, Ga.
44. My grandfather Jezekiah Anderson was a soldier in war 1812 and my foreparents came from Scotland.

ANDERSON, MARK LaFAYETTE

FORM NO. 1

1. Mark LaFayette Anderson, Orlinda, Tenn. R.F.D. #1
2. 77 years, last Oct. 14
3. Tenn., Putnam co.
4. Putnam co., Tenn.
5. Farmer
6. Farmer
7. None
8. None
9. 100 acres
10. $500.00
11. one-room log house, "stick & clay chimney"
12. I did a man's part with plow after I was eleven years old.
13. Father made full time hand at regular work on farm. Mother cooked, did her own spinning & weaving. (No servants)
14. No
15. Such work was certainly considered respectable and honorable.
16. Yes
17. None
18. No
19. Yes
20. A friendly feeling

210

ANDERSON (cont'd.):
21. No
22. Yes
23. Encouraged
24. Free school
25. I attended a three months term school each year from age 7 years to age 18 years
26. One mile
27. I was raised in one mile of Cookeville, Tennessee, where there were higher grade schools that I never attended. I only received education from the free school at that place.
28. Public
29. Three months
30. Yes
31. Man
32. October, 1862, at Cookeville Tenn.
33. 8th Tenn Cavalry, under Colonel Geo. Dibrell and Lieut. Tenant Daugherty. Other members of my Company were; Captain, Isaac Wooley, 1st Lt.Wood, 2nd Lt. John Smith, 3rd Lt. Andrew Lacy; John Speck, 1st. O. Sgt.; Jackson Davis, Henry C. Davis, H.M. Davis, Stephen Davis, John Davis, Ben Smith, John Smith, George Grimsley, Peter An-erson, L. Thompson, H.H. Beasley, Isaac Romins.
34. Maury co., Tenn.
35. about 3 months
36. Parkers Cross Roads, in West Tenn.
37. First battle lasted about 3 hours. After this was sent back to Maury county and in July 1863, was sent to Chattanooga before any engagements there. Was later sent to Sparta, White county, where I was captured August 1863. I remained a prisoner until the close of the war, being held at Camp Chase, Ohio, about 6 months, and at Fort Deleware about 12 months
38. I was exchanged out of prizon about 4 days before the Confederacy surrendered, went to Richmond, Va., where I received a 40 days furlo, and was never called to report again.
39. No special events in this trip, except I walked a good part of the way from Richmond, to my home.
40. Farming
41. Continued farming to this date. Never held office. Spent a part of my life in the West, but the greater part has been spent in Tennessee. Have been a member of the M. E. Church, South about 38 years.
42. James Anderson; Raleigh, N.C.; lived Putnam co., Tenn. at about 18 year, and later went to Maury county, just a farmer
43. Elizabeth Mathews; ---- & Harty Mathews; Raleigh, N.C.
44. ----

ANDES, J.W.

FORM NO. 1

1. (Not filled in)
2. 77
3. Marion co, Tenn.
4. Marion co, Tenn.
5. Farming and stock raising own a small scale.
6. Farming
7. No Land
8. No Slaves
9. 60 acres of cleared 90 timber
10. Land was cheap then cant ans. that
11. 2 Too(?) rumes Living Rume 20x20 head(?) Logs 5 inx12 and 14 in Siles and Plates 12x12 in Kitchen 2414 (24x14?) No Loft Chimny stick and mud 8 ft wid
12. Ploud barefooted. how ____ it was to wet to plow. We ploud 5 times in every row or in outher words 5 times to the row
13. Father farmed. Mother did all kinds of house work. We used coton. Mother carde and spun wove coten cloth allsoe spun woole roles and wove it in Jeans. hom made Shirts and pants. Finger pick the cotton of nights.

ANDRES (cont'd.):
14. No servants
15. Every body did all this work and was proud to do soe.
16. all jus plane honest farmers dident know iney other way to live.
17. Sir we dident have any of thous
18. Just as plane people as we had comodating
19. You cudent tell any difant. Role loges togather. S(h)uch corn
    togather - Rais houses togather
20. No difant
21. Not atall
22. Opportes (opportunity) was not good we was all poor alke (alike)
23. Dident seame to Bee
24. Free schooles
25. about 2 or 3 months a year cant saey jist how much
26. 1 Mile
27. Red Hill
28. Public
29. 2 or 3 months
30. not regular
31. man with beard
32. July I beleave
33. Fourth 4th Tenn Calvey Company H Our captain was James Kanather,
    Lt. J.M. Rogers, Lt. Kenisy(?) Harness(?), Lt. J.E. Teague, J.N.
    Smith, R.J. Moore, John Lewis, W.D. Richards, Frank Kanatche, Billey
    Rogers, Arch Bracher(?), M.A. Lewis, Newt Lewis, Ned Lewis, Dock
    Maeimore(?), Tom Turner, Johny Turner, J.F. Richard, Mige(?) Turner,
    S.H. Benett, Wes Waren, H.C. Grayson.
34. After I joined in a little while Gen. Hood made a rad (raid) to
    Nashville.
35. Then our Calvar(y) Regeament was sent west of the Tenness River to
    tare up R.Roads. Then we had ____ on Calvry Regement had to forde
36. (this is still continuation from Questions 34 & 35) Brod River.
    Looked(?) Ca____? after night to ford or? swim we soone hit the
    R.Road and the _____ somme had friz. (doesn't appear clear)
37. Calvary soldiers was allways on the goe. Some times a few coud get
    shelter in Barns and hous(?) if clost to camp if it was bad night
    outhers wood duble up put there blankets togeather and kind of
    shelter. in that railroad company we dident eat much if we was
    pushed we wood mack (make) up a calvera. Shoat get was kitchen cook
    Sweat (sweet) potatoes and pork all togather
38. We surrendered at Rome(?) Trent(?) Georga. sent from ther to Chatta-
    nooga Tenn. from Chatt. to youre _____ (beautiful?) city Nashville
    than we was Paroled. May 25th 1865. We was sent back to Shelmont
    then every one did the ____(best?) he could.
39. (Question 38 continued into 39.)
40. We plantted a littel corn and hired out to work for others
41. Ben farming ever sinse. No Offices
42. Ale____(scrawled - can't read, may be Alick --- cme) Andes; raised
    Screven(?) co, Tenn. or Sevier co.
43. Sarh (Sarah) Lewis; Archabel Lewis & _____
44. (No remarks on ancestry; More discussion of how his home was built)

ANDES, WILLIAM LEONADES

FORM NO. 1

1. Wm. Leonades Andes; Whitwell, Tenn Marion Co. R.1
2. 83 yrs old
3. Tenn. Marion co.
4. Tenn. Marion co. Confederacy
5. Farming
6. Farming
7. 2 Horses cow some hogs value $250.00
8. None
9. 260 acres
10. $400.00
11. Log house 2 rooms
12. plowed oxens halled on sled

212

ANDES (cont'd.):
13. Plowed cleared land maid rails built fence cooking spinning weaving
    making cloth
14. No
15. yes
16. yes
17. to no extent
18. they wer all the same. thare wer no difference in them
19. they did
20. yes absolute friendship
21. no
22. not much
23. they wer incouraged
24. free school
25. about 1 year
26. 1 mile
27. county school
28. Public
29. 3 months
30. yes
31. man
32. Enlisted in Confedracy 1862 - Sep.
33. 3 Confederate changed to 4th Tenn. swaped places with John Owen
34. Kentucky
35. about 6 months
36. Fort Donelson
37. Badly clothed not much to eat exposed to weather most of the time
    after first went to Murphesburrow then to Chicamogia then to Knoxville
    then to Dalton, Ga. then to Atlanta then to Decab co., Ga. Staye
    thar till the surrender never was a prisoner was in a hospital was
    shot through the sholder.
38. in May 1865 at Nashville
39. I was sent to Shellmound in a box car
40. Farming
41. Farming held no office
42. Alexander Andes; Sevearvill, Sevear co., Tenn.
43. Sarah Lewis; Archie Lewis and _____ Mitchell
44. ----

ANDREWS, J. K. P.

FORM NO. 1

1. J. K. P. Andrews, Columbi Mury co, Tenn RFD-5
2. 82
3. Tenn Maury co
4. State of Tenn. Maury co.
5. Hous carpenter
6. both farming and house (horse?) _____.
7. no land at time no propty of valy
8. no slave at all
9. my father ond about ____ _____
10. about $2000 - dolars work
11. a fram hous six ____
12. at ten yers old ploud had an did all canes of work on the farm tha
    boy cold do
13. My father was a mity find macanic he did macanic work and farm my
    mother ____ she spun an wove mad all our clothing at hom and mad
    cloth(?) sold and bough goods from the store for the famly sonday
    wair. She worked in the som of the time (word left out)
14. Non at all
15. (this answer so poor in grammar, etc we have not attempted to copy
    but will edit---cme)
    (cont'd. with regard to honest toil) It was with most of the people.
    Those who thought something of themselves thought good labor was
    all right. They were looked on as being good honest citizens.
16. the most of them did
17. at that time I would say about _____ per cent (this number blurred)
    was engaged at some kind of a occupation

213

ANDREWS (cont'd.):
18. They did to some extent. They seem to want to stay _____ to them self.
19. At some times very little difernce
20. As a rule they were friendly or (an) would take a part in service
21. At times the slavehold thought he ought to have some preference as he was a slave holder
22. ----
23. I cant say there was very little differance in that
24. Near home in the country
25. In my school days about three months in the fall
26. ----
27. mostly free schools
28. they was publick schools mostly
29. as _____ three months
30. For a short school they did
31. At that time was men old most envabely(?) men (invalid?)
32. In April 1861 at Estel Springs
33. 17th Tenn. My first Col. was T_____ Dinman(?) second. Connel was A.G. Marks (next part not clear)
34. To Estel Spring then we were organized? in a regiment there we were sent to Camp Trousdel near the line of Ky. after being there some time was sent to Nasville then to the battle of Mannasas
35. Some 3 or 4 months at Mannassas or Donlson(?)
36. Manases
37. After the 1st battle at Manasses we came back to Bostel? Tenn. then to Louden co Tenn. then to Cumberland Gap then to combng (Cumberland) ford then to Rockcasel 60 miles north of cumbng gap we then com back to combing ford then we moved to Mills Springs then we went in winter quarters just north of ____ place on fishing Creek we had a nother battle got defeted fel back to camp we then retreted by the way of muffrber (Murfreesboro?) then to decator Alabamy
38. (another difficult answer to read) I was a prisoner but had made my escape from the Federals and was on my way back to _____. to join my old command which had been sent to General Lees
39. My self and others on our way to our old command? when the _____ of Lees army? we were stop then (doesn't make much sense)
40. Farming - as I have some space I will give a few more lines(?) we fought the battle Shila(Shiloh?) in the spring of 1862 our next battle Tenvill(?) Ky then back to Murfreesboro was taken prisoner 19 Sept. on _____
41. ----
42. M.S. Andrews; b. 1805; Maury co. Tenn
43. Martha Patrick; Samuel Patrick and _____.
44. My grand father John Andrews was in the war under General Jackson at New Orleans. My father came from Virginia my mother from North Carolina

ANDREWS, MARK L.

FORM NO. 1

1. Mark L. Andrews, 1011 16th Ave. S. Nashville, Tenn.
2. 80 years and 6 months
3. Williamson co., Tenn.
4. Williamson county
5. attending school
6. Circuit Court Clerk of Williamson co., Farmer and Minister
7. One horse, bridle and saddle, and shotgun. Value about $250.00 which I carried with me into the war.
8. My father owned about 40 or 50 slaves
9. About 300 acres
10. $75,000.00
11. Brick house, containing 10 rooms
12. I began work on farm at ten years of age, hoeing and plowing in season and attending school in winter
13. My father was a county official and spent his spare time in preaching. My mother looked after the house work - spinning, weaving, cooking, etc.

214

ANDREWS (cont'd):
14. Forty or fifty
15. It was
16. They did
17. The men of my community were mostly men of means, owning and conduct-
    ing their own farms.
18. The slave owners were very considerate and showed no disposition to
    look down on those who owned no slaves.
19. Yes
20. They were on friendly terms
21. No
22. Yes. I know of a number of instances where deserving young men were
    materially aided in there efforts along this line
23. They were encouraged. Many young men being aided in a finacial way
    by slave holders.
24. Attended the district school until I enrolled at the Harpett Academy,
    taught by Profs. Andrew and Patrick Campell, at Franklin.
25. About ten years
26. one mile and a half
27. The district school about 3 miles west of Franklin and Harpett
    (Harpeth?) Academy at Franklin also a school for girls at Franklin.
28. Private
29. District school about 6 months. The Academy about 10 months.
30. They did
31. District school was taught by Mrs. Sue Brown. Academy by Prof. Camp-
    ell
32. In 1861, in July, at Franklin.
33. Fourth Tennessee Cavalry. Col. J.W. Starnes was Captain; H.L. McLemon
    1st Lt., T.F.P. Allison 2nd Lt., Green Harrison 3rd Lt., Oscar Boyd
    Orderly Sgt.; We started with 62 men but before the war closed we
    had about 300 in the company. As near as I can arrive at it, about
    15 are now living.
34. To Camp Cheatham for training
35. About 5 months.
36. Raccoon Range, in Kentucky
37. We went from Russellville, Ky. to Fort Donelson under Gen. Forrest.
    When we retreated from Donelson, we went to Nashville. When Bragg
    went into Kentucky we went through Cumberland Gap to Richmond, Ky.
    From there we went to Louisville and then to Perryville. We came
    back to Nashville and to Spring Hill. Next fight we had was at
    Thompson Sta.
38. I was taken sick in Oct. 1864 with typhoid fever; was captured and
    was sick at the time the war closed.
39. I was sick in Hickman county and on my recovery returned to my fathers
    house in Williamson co.
40. Farm
41. Farmer; was Trustee of Williamson county; was in grocery business in
    Franklin; published the Re___(run?) & Journal; came to Nashville and
    engaged in Coal business.
42. Mark L. Andrews; b. Virginia; lived at Lexington, Ky.; moved to
    Williamson co., Tenn.; Circuit Court Clerk of Williamson county 36
    years.
43. Eliza Dean; Alexander Dean and _____; lived in East Tenn.
44. My grandfather George Andrews came from England, lived in Virginia
    where my father was born, moved to Lexington, Ky. and then to
    Williamson co. I am not familiar with the early history of the family
    at my age my memory being very faulty.

ANTHONY, JAMES FREDERICK

FORM NO. 2

1. James Frederick Anthony, Bell Buckle, Tenn.
2. 76½ yrs.
3. I was born in Franklin co., Tenn.
4. Confederate
5. Company B - 28 Tennesse Cavalry
6. He was an old style Methodist Circuit rider.

215

ANTHONY (cont'd.):

7. William Horace Anthony; Thompson's Creek, Bedford co., Tenn.; lived on Turkey Creek and Big Hurricane practically all his life in Moore co. He and his two older sons joined Peter Turney's 1st Tenn. regiment in 1861 and he served as chaplin in 1865 (The following was on a separate page) After serving as chaplin during the year 1861 he resigned in the spring of 1862, came home, and continued his ministerial duties to his death.

8. Elizabeth Pollock; I can not recall her mother's and father's names; my mother had three brothers John Pollock, Benjamin Pollock & Robert Pollock.

9. My father was a full blooded German - his grandmother & grandfather on both sides came from Germany. His grandmother on his father's side was a Shofner but farther than that I do not know.

10. I owned no land or other property.

11. Neither I nor my parents ever owned slaves.

12. My parents owned about 100 acres

13. All the property my parents owned when the war began would not have sold for exceeding one thousand dollars ($1000).

14. My parents lived in a one room log house to within two years of the war and in a frame house of five rooms the remainder of their lives.

15. As a boy I did all kinds of farm work that a boy can do. The land was practically all in woods and had to be cleared the land was necessarily full of roots and stumps and could be plowed only with a ball tongue plow - many times have my shins been beaten blue by roots breaking and flying back. There was no such things as turning plows or double shovels in those days.

16. My father being a minister had often as many as 15 churches under his charge and preached every day in the week and so of course was at home less than 1/3 of his time. While Father was gone, Mother had charge of her six boys, did all the house work, carded and spun and wove and would cut and make the clothes for her family, including her own, doing the sewing with her fingers. She never used a sewing machine in her life.

17. They had no servants

18. The man who worked the hardest stood the highest in our community.

19. There was but few negroes in that part of the country; white men did practically all of the work of every kind.

20. We had practically none of that sort.

21. So far as my limited knowledge goes they were all on an absolute equality.

22. If there was ever any antagonism between slave holders and non-slave holders my attention was never called to it.

23. The above answer will cover this

24. I remember no such contest in my neighborhood

25. I would not say they were exceptionally good but with industry and economy he could accumulate.

26. They were never discouraged - if they had sand in their gizzard they could succeed.

27. The school I attended was called a free school and run about three months in the fall of the year.

28. I went to school two or three months every fall - advanced rapidly - had completed the Bluebacked Speller at 14.

29. About three miles

30. Only one and it was a nondescript Public

31. Answered above

32. It seldom run over three months

33. Just as regularly as their parents would allow them or make them.

34. Most always a man-women were supposed not to be able to control big boys.

35. I enlisted in the Confederate army in November 1864 and was sworn in in the woods in Lincoln county in compnay B 28th Tenn. Cavalry, Capt. Reed Holmer, Major Jordan Hayes Battalion; Brig. Gen. B.J. Hill.

36. We started to Follow Hood's army out of Tennessee but got cut off. We turned back and went out through East Tenn.

37. Our company was in only one regular battle and I was 30 miles away with a scouting party at the time.

38. I was always with a scouting party - Our battles were "shoot and run" but we did not always work in the lead.

216

ANTHONY (cont'd.):
39. I was cook for my mess and I will tell how the best bread I ever ate
was made. The boys got the meal and of course it was not sifted but
I spread an oil cloth on the ground, put the meal on it, took a can-
teen of good branch water, poured it on the meal and worked it to
the right consistency. Took a flat rail, rolled out my dodgers and
filled my rail full. Sat it up before the fire until it toasted
brown on one side - then turned the bread over & toasted the other
side - of course there was some in the middle not quite done.
(The following was on a separate page) But we had appetites and I
want to say I never in all my life ate batter bread. And we ate
hundreds of meals of just such bread and nothing else and this is to
some extent how we lived in camp. Our uniforms were uniformly
ragged! There was no two suits alike. We had rags of all sizes,
rags of all shapes, rags of all colors, texture and makes; rags of
bright colors and gloomy ones too; rags of all shades the world ever
knew. "Rummage amongst them and twist them around; But a suit that
will please you can never be found!"
40. I was paroled in Chattanooga on the 16th day of May 1865. I have my
parole now.
41. We were discharged about sundown and given transportation to Tullahoma
on a freight car. We climbed on the top and laid down and were soon
asleep. The train either stopped or ran very very slow for we were
only about 30 miles from Chattanooga when daylight came. (The following was on a separate page) We landed at Tullahoma about two oclock
- walked six miles home, from there and found the whole family down
with smallpox - could not go in the yard - slept a whole week under
a shade tree - But oh! how thankful I could see and talk to my
mother.
42. Being under age I was subject to my father's demands for two years.
He sent me to school for ten months which is practically all the
education I ever got.
43. My life since the war has varied but slightly from the general run
of Confederate soldiers. The war taught me that a man could do
without everything he couldn's get so I took as my motto "Pay as you
go and when you can't pay don't go." I don't only preach this but
I practice it. My estate is not large but it is worth one hundred
cents in the dollar. I have had nine children born to me, six of
whom were raised to maturity - Five of them are now living and to my
credit - there is not one of them has ever served a term in the pen-
etentiary yet. I never held an office. I ran for a county office
once and I didn't think I had an enemy in the world. When the votes
were counted I concluded my friends were "darned nigh" as scarce as
my enemies. However "Alls well that ends well" and I have no fears
for the rest of my alloted time for I can say with the poet in all
sincerety, "What ever my lot, thou has taught me to say it is well,
it is well with my soul.
44. ----
45. Company B Haye's Battalion,
28th Tenn. Cavalry:
Capt. Reed Holmes
1st Lt. J.T. Roads
2d Lt. S.H. Roberts
3d Lt. Wm. M. Anderson
1st Corpl. Prank Stafford
2d   "   W.B. Helton
3d   "   James L. JOnes
1st Sgt. M.P. Jetton
2d   "   D.G. Taylor
3d   "   W.B. Brawley
            Privates
Adams, Charley
Anthony, James F.
Anderson, Naith   Lasitor, John
Braxton, Elias   McMahan, Wm.
Crow, Bob   McMahan, Dave
Eperson, W.   McMahan, John
Grens?, William   Matin, Jim
Holt, William   Muse, Tom
Hitson, R.L.   Newman, Geo. W.

217

ANTHONY (cont'd.):

Hulett, Lee	Owensby, Wat
Hendrix, Abe	Philips, J.P.
Hains, G.A.	Robinson, John
Hamilton, G.F.	Randall, Jim H.
Herron, G.	Sherrill, George
Hutchison, Brown	Scott, J.C.
Jones, Jesse	Smith, Jim
Johnson, John	Smith, Jim A.
Kidd, Jim	Speers, Hess
Lambert, Bill	Snipes, John
Lynn, Dallas	Strowd, W.B.
Harris, John	Strowd, G.S.
Harris, G.S.	Skastien, Jim
(Hains?)	Skastien, Jess
	Swafford, Al

46.
Adams, Charlie	Manchester, Tenn.
Strowd, Walter	Manchester, Tenn.
Newman, George	Hillsboro, Tenn.
Travis, John	Tullahoma, Tenn.
Jones, J.L.	Georgetown, Tenn.

The above are living members of my company
R.S. Anthony	Tullahoma Tenn.
Z.T. Crouch, Sr.	Bell Buckle, Tenn.
W.R. Webb, Sr.	Bell Buckle, Tenn.
J.C. Keysaer	Bell Buckle, Tenn.
Jim Cobb	Bell Buckle, Tenn.
Tom Hatchet	Bell Buckle, Tenn.
Bob Clemems	Bell Buckle, Tenn.
Bill Culley	Wartrace, Tenn.

(Letter - notation on top "I sent Jan. 26/22 never returned.)
Bell Buckle, Tenn.
Mar. 17, 1922
Mr. John Trotwood Moore - Having noticed your ad in the March Veteran
where you were asking for the old Confederates to hand in their war
experiences and records that they may be preserved. So I have in
the enclosed humble sketch tried to place the main points and cut
what ever is unworthy. I hope you may have great success in this
enterprise you have undertaken, and may it be completed soon, that
we may each one have a copy of the Confederate History for our book
shelf.   Respectfully,
                          James L. Anthony
Please pass the reminiscences on to the Confederate Veteran when you
are through. Perhaps they would publish it.

(more pages)
" My War Reminiscences"
    When the war of 1861 to 1865 began, I was barely fifteen years of
age but my father, W.H. Anthony and my two elder brothers, Robert H.
and Roddy S. Anthony volunteered in Colonel Peter Turney's 1st Tenn.
Regiment which was afterward designated "The 1st Confederate," it
having been mustered in and left the State in April '61, before the
state seceded. My father, W.H. Anthony served the regiment as
chaplin till May '62, when he resigned on account of being afflicted
with rheumatism, contracted in camp. My two brothers served throughout all the battles in Virginia, beginning with the first battle of
Manassas and continuing through to Gettysburg. They were in the
famous Pickett Charge where Robert H. lost his left leg, taken off
above the knee. On that fiercest day of the battle of Gettysburg -
the 31st day of July 1863, Roddy S. was captured and carried to Fort
Delaware prison where he remained till the close of the war.
    Robert H. Anthony died in Victoria, Texas at the age of 72.
    Roddy S. is now living near Tullahoma hale and hearty at the age
of 81.
    I had another older brother, Nicholas who volunteered in another
regiment in 1862 - the number I can't recall - he served only a few
months and was discharged on account of disability. Now comes the
humble part I played in the war. In the fall of '64, Maj. Jordan
Hayes had instructions to raise a battalion of cavalry, he raised

ANTHONY (cont'd.):

three companies of perhaps 50 men each. - or boys, I should say - for there were not sufficient whiskers in the entire bunch to line a birds nest. We attempted to go out with Hood's army but were cut off - we turned and went out through East Tenn. and into North Carolina across South Carolina and across Georgia below Atlanta into Alabama, to a point on Coosa River some miles below Gadsden, where we were when the war ended. We broke camp there May 15th 1865 and were paroled in Chattanooga on the 16th and come into Tullahoma in a box car - upright however - on the 17th. I make no claim to any heroic deeds, but am entitled perhaps to one distinction, I belong to a family whose father and four sons all served in the Confederate army and were all honorably discharged - the three oldest served or two of them at least, served in the first regiment made up in the state and I, the youngest - in the very last command made up in the Confederacy and perhaps the last whole command paroled.

I am also enclosing the muster roll of my company. You are at liberty to use this in any way you may see proper.

Very Respectfully
James F. Anthony
Bell Buckle Tenn.

of Co. B. 28 Tenn. Cavalry

ANTHONY, RODY S.

FORM NO. 1

1. R.S. Anthony, Tullahoma, Tenn. Route 1
2. 80 yr. 10 months
3. Tennessee, Bedford Co. on the waters of Thompson's Creek 1841
4. State of Tenn. Franklin Co. (now) part of Moore county
5. My occupation was a miller and farming
6. Traveling minister in the Tennessee Conference
7. None. Minor
8. None
9. 110 acres
10. $1500
11. Framed house 6 rooms
12. I plow, hoed, cradled, run a saw mill and griss mill
13. My father was farming when he wasn't on his circuit preaching. My mother done cooking, spinning, weaving cutting and making clothes
14. None
15. All work was honorable and highly respct. by our community.
16. They did - all of them
17. None of that character
18. Nothing of the sort. They were all as one.
19. They did
20. They were all symphetic to each other
21. Not at all slaves had no influence in the political
22. It was all he had to do was to show an(d) industrious will and he succeeded.
23. Not at all discouraged they encourage them very much
24. Public free school
25. 24 months for as my memory alow
26. Was at my door when I moved away then 2 miles away where my father died.
27. A free school was all.
28. Public school
29. About 2½ to 3 months
30. Not very regularly
31. Man they didnt think a woman could teach school them days.
32. In the year 1861. April. Winchester, Franklin county
33. Peter Tuney 1st Tennessee, Captain Nels. Sampson, Co. D (Lieut 1st) John H. Bevel, (2nd Lt.) W.M. Farris(?), (3rd Lt.) John Tribble, Drate Adams, James Allen, H.F. Anderson, Tom Anderson, Dobber Awalt, Bob Anthony, Rod Anthony, Joe Byrom, Jim Byrom, John Byrom, Giles Bowers, Arch Bowers, Lee Brown, W.M. Brazier, Lem Brazier, John Bevel, Tom Baggett, Joe Bolin, Bud Bolin, John Beaver, James Baily, Milt Byrom, Ben Childs

ANTHONY (cont'd.):
34. Richmond, Virginia
35. A little over a year
36. Seven Pine below Richmond, Va.
37. After the battle of Manna we went to Camp fisher on the Potomic
    river we were not in this battle (but) was on the battle field winter-
    ed and drilled. After Seven Pine the big battle below Richmond
    lasting several days. Cedar Run (in Virginia) Sharpburg, Maryland,
    Fredrickburg, Va., Chancelsville, Va. Getysberg, Penn. Captured
    there on the 3 of July 1863 placed in Fort Deleware prison till
    June 8, 1865 released on parol and sent home.
38. Paroled from Ft Deleware 8 day of June
39. Came on the train to Tullahoma transportation furnished free. W.A.
    Marshall and my self came on the same transportation from Fort
    Deleware home. I got home on the 10 of June.
40. Carpenter and cabinet work
41. Carpenters and cabinets work, lived in Wartrace 7 yr. at the death
    of my father bought this place now living here in Moore county.
    Methodist Church since my 3 (13?) yr. Justice of Peace 2 terms
42. William Harris Anthony; Thompson Creek, Bedford co, Tenn.; Bedford
    co., Thompson Creek; Chaplain of Turney 1st Tenn. regiment 1st year
    of the war.
43. Elizabeth Pollock; John Pollock and Alsey Pollock; Bedford co. near
    Roseville.
44. My great grand father and mother came from Germany & settled in
    German colony and thence moving to Tenn. lived and died in Tenn. On
    my mother's people came from Penn. they were from Ireland. as where
    my grand parents were in any war I do not no. These are the facts
    to the best of my knowlege and ability.
    (1 page #2 - p. 1 not on film)
    37(31?). p.3 - I lived in camp all right nothing to complain of.
    Very well clothed in camp. slept on our blanket some time cold some
    time warm had beef and flour bred had very little corn bread. Some
    of the boy complained of getting hungry but I never but one time
    when we were on our retread from Richmond to Yorktown. We had to
    take soldiers life in cold and disease. I was in hospital with
    attack of Rheumatism and Juandise something like a month with reason-
    able treatment at Lynchburg Virginia (1862). I was in hosipital
    while in prison at Fort Deleware with small pox about 40 days very
    roughly treated but got over it. This is my prison life in full.

                          ANTHONY, WILLIAM LEE

FORM NO. 1

1. William Lee Anthony, Brownsville, Haywood co., Tenn.
2. 82 years the 15th June 1921
3. Tenn. Haywood co.
4. Tenn. Haywood co.
5. I had commenced farming before the civil war, up to that time I had
    no special occupation
6. Farmer
7. I owned no land of my own but worked home of my fathers free of rent.
    I owned 7 slaves also several hundred dollars in money all I suppose
    about 8000 dollars
8. My father (spelled Farther throughout) owned about 200 slaves he gave
    me 7 slaves and some land free of rent to work.
9. He owned 2 farms about 3000 acres in all in Tenn. (con't. on separate
    pages)
10. I would estimate it at about 160000$
11. It was a two story frame house with 7 rooms 2 halls with back and
    front portico
12. As a boy and young man I attended school most of the time, but
    during vacation while not on a pleasure trip or visiting my father
    required me to hoe in the garden and truck patche near his house.
13. When a small boy I have known my father to plow in the fields with
    his slaves when the crop was badly in need of work. This he did
    untill he had accumulated enough from his own exersions & inheritance
    to employ an overseer on each farm, he being supereminent

                                220

ANTHONY (cont'd.):

(superintendent?) directing what should be done (see separate page)

14. There were several servants about the house to do the work that was necessary.
15. It was considered respectfull and honorable.
16. If they had no slaves or only a few they did.
17. As well as I remember there were very few.
18. As far as my observation slaveholders did not consider themselves better than respectable honorable men who did not own slaves.
19. That was owing to the parties of each. If they were respectable and honorable they did.
20. I do not think slavery antagonized the feeling between slave holders and non-slaveholders.
21. I think the question of slavery had nothing to do with the contest.
22. If he had the energy and management he had the opportunity.
23. They were encouraged.
24. When a boy I attended country schools untill I was nearly grown and then went to college one session.
25. I suppose about 10 years
26. When a boy, from 1½ to 3 miles; this was untill I went to college.
27. They were what we call country schools.
28. Private
29. About 9 months
30. They did except those that were poor who had to stop to work on the farm in the busy _____.
31. Generally a man but sometimes a woman.
32. Our company was oranised in Haywood co., Tenn. in April and sworned into servise May 23rd 1861 at Jackson, Tenn.
33. After being in for 12 months our Co. with several others and Logwo__ (see separate pages)
34. Fort Randolph on Miss. River tence (thence) to New Maddrid, Mo. tence to Columbus, Ky. Thence to Island 10 on Miss. River thence to West Tenn. Dowing scout and picket and having a few skirmishes in the mean time.
35. About 15 months though we were engaged in several skirmishes in the mean time.
36. Meaden in Madison county, was wounded in the battle.
37. From this time to close of the war we had no tents and had to sleep in the open suffering in bad & cold weather and frequently for something to eat and clothing. After being wounded I went to Miss. and staid with a relative untill I was well enough for duty. Reported for duty at Holly Spring after the battle of Corinthe. Helped to cover Van Dorm's retreat to Granada... Was with Van Dorn when he got in Grant's rear and
38. After hearing of Lee and Johnston surrender we marched to Ganesville Ala. and on the 11 May 1865 was parold by Maj. Gen. Canby.
39. As fast as each company was paroled we started for home under charge of our company officers camping at night, procuring feed for ourselves & horses from the citizens. Arriving in the county where the company was first organised we disbanded each going to his own home.
40. I hauled some cotton for my father & myself that was on hand after war. This cotton was hauled 50 miles to market as the railroads were not doing business. I did hauled for other people who had cotton they wished to sell.
41. About the latter part of Dec. 1865 at the solicitation of my father, I took charge of his farm of 1000 acres in the western part of Haywood county looking (see separate page)
42. William Austin Anthony; Richmon. (don't know the county) Va.; moved to Haywood, Tenn. 1835 died in same co. in 1884; he followed farming as a resort for support and attended his mothers business in Al (blurred is either Ala. or Ark - see separate page)
43. Malinda Dyson; Aquilla Dyson and Malinda before marriage (Miss Harris); in Madison co., Tenn. 7 miles north of old Denmak (Denmark)
44. I know but little of my mothers ancestors farther than her parents. Her father Aquilla Dyson was a farmer owning a farm in Tipton co. and one in Haywood co. had one in Madison co. on which he lived, owning many slaves. He married a Miss Harris. He died when I was very young. He leaving 5 children to inherit his property. My fathers occupation was a farmer all his life. My grand father J.C. Anthony was born in Va. (see separate page)

221

ANTHONY (cont'd.):
     Followed by several lined pages.
                              1
9.   He also owned land about 1500 acres wild lands in Ark.
13. He also look after his mothers interest in Ark. who had property
     there. My mother looked after household affairs such as cooking
     spinning weaving making garments for the negroes and many other
     things.
32. Captain Robert Haywood commanding. We were not faced (placed?) with
     a regiment for 12 months after being in service.
33. battalion was organised into a regiment in April in 1862
                              2
     as the 7th Tenn. Calvary. Col. Wm. Jackson commanding. I belonged
     to Co. D. After the organisation we supprised several companies
     of Federals at Lockridge Mill in West Tenn. capturing 67 prisners
     and stampeding the others. After this we retreated to Miss. Re-
     organised the regiment electing many new officers. Our Company
     D. electing Capt. W.L. Talliaferro, 1st Lt. H.J Livingston, 2nd Lt.
     J.H. Read, 3 Lt. T.B. Mann, 1st Sargent J. Eades, 2d Sarg. H.G.
     Winfield, 3 Sargt. M. McGrath, 4 Sargt. J.C.
                              3
     Holloway, 5th Sargt. R.M. Grizzard, 1st Corpul J.L. Elwood, 2 Corp.
     E.D. Dupree, 3 Corp, R.S. Ervine, 4 Corp. D. Dodge. Privates:
     W.L. Anthony, P.C. Archer, E. Austin, H.C. Anderson, J.A. Allison,
     J.F. Barbee, L. Bond, R.H. Browning, W.A. Blake, A. Boyd, W.P. Bond,
     M.H. Bradford, T.B. Claiborn, B.W. Chapman, W.D. Curry, F. Day,
     T.A. Davis, E.D. Dupree, A.M. Estes, T.(F.?)H. Estes, C.A. Estes,
     J. Elder, J.L. Elwood, J.H. Freeman, H. Freeman, E.S. Grove, R.
     Grove, J.B. Griffin, W.L. Grizzard, J.C. Holloway, E. Henderson,
     R.R. Hodges, Dr. A. Irvine, R.S. Irvine,
                              4
     H. Jarret, R. Jeffres, B. Jones, T.C. Livingston, N. Leget, J. Lilly,
     R. Mann, B.V. Mann, E.G. Mabane, J.W. Northcross, T. Northcross,
     E. Owen, R.F. Oldham, H.L. Penn, T.M. Perkins, R.S. Porter, H. Rains,
     R.P. Rains, G.J. Roads, R. Roberson, J.F. Roberson, J.W. Sanders,
     A. Shaw, W.H. Sallis, W.H. Schawb, A. Scerapa, J. Serape, W.W. Tucker,
     E. Taliferro, B.D. Taliaferro, J. Tharp, F.M.(?) Taylor, J. Wright,
     L.G. Walker, P. Wilson, M. Weaver, J. Wells and many others.
                              5
37. capturing his army stores & distroying them and paroling about 2000
     prisoners. Having the next day a fight at Davis's Bridge on Wolf
     river and losing some men. With drew and moved in the vicinity of
     Bolivar & Middleton where we did some fighting capturing about 70
     prisoners. Retreated to Miss. Arriving at Granada about the last
     of Dec. 1862. In March 1863 we were ordered to Fort Pemberton Yazon
     river doing out post duty & picketing. About the latter part of
     March we were ordered to report to Gen.
                              6
     Chalmers who command of the Cavalry of north Miss. In June we had a
     fight with the Yanks near Harmando, capturing near 90 prisoners
     Kill & wounding a good many. We were in a fight at Salem, Miss. in
     Oct. 1863 defeating the enemy and loseing some men. Shortly after
     this we attacked Colliersville, capturing over 100 prisoners &
     losing some men but had to retreat as they had reenforcements. We
     had an engagement after this at Moscow & in the vicinity of Colliers-
     ville.
                              7
     About Jan. 1864 we were placed under Gen. Forrest. Our first engage-
     ment after this with Gen. W.S. Smith. After 2 day hard fighting
     we drove him 50 miles capturing several cannon killing wounding
     many, and many killed wounded on our side leaving the enemy in a
     demoralised condition. Our next move was in Tenn. The 7 Tenn. was
     sent to Union City to drive Col. Hawkins out of Forrests way while
     on his way to Paducha. By a bluff game we captured
                              8
     Col. Hawkins with 500 men horses & arms. Our next move was on Fort
     Pillow. We we (7th Tenn.) sent in the vicinity of Fort Randolf to
     keep wach on the federal at Memphis while Forrest attacked Fort
     Pillow. The place was captured with many prisoners & many killed.

ANTHONY (cont'd.):
Our next fight was with Shurges (Sturges?) after 2 days hard fighting we roughted him, capturing his wagon train all his casons
ambulacks (ambulances?) and about 1500 prisoners. Our next battle
was Harris burg, Miss. after 2 days hard fighting.
9
The 7 Tenn. lost about 70 kill & wounded, besides many were exhausted
from excessive heat and carried from the battle field. The enemy
retreated to Hellys (Kellys?) Mills and New Albany, Miss. We
skirmished with them after they commensed retreat two days. Our
next move was to Middle Tenn. Crossing the Tenn. river at Mussle
Sholes by fording. Our first attack was Athens, capturing the
garrison with about 1500 prisoners besides one regiment coming to
there relief. We
10
then moved up the railroad attacked a fort at Sulphur Trussle.
After shelling the fort and killing about 200 the place surrendered
with about 850 prisoners 2 cannon 15 wagons 300 horses besides
small arms. Our next encounter was at Pulaska (Pulaski) after
driving the enemy into the fort we withdrew after night, flanking
Pulaska & going by Spring Hill and commenced our March south capturing several block houses & about 140 prisoners. We arrived at
Florence about
11
Oct. 5 & cross the Tenn. river at Newport. The next move of the
7 Tenn. was with Forrest on the Hood campain to Nashville; sharing
the hardships of that campain. I was not with my company on that
trip; being sick at the time. After the command recrossed the Tenn.
our next move was in Ala. to look after the Wilson raiders. We
encountered them at Tuskoloosa, driving them across the Cahawber
river. We then went to Marion, Ala. and hearing that Lee & Johnston
had surrendered.
12
41. after the cultivation of the crops & stocks on the place & repairs
for 3 years, he compensating me for same. He then divided the farm
between a son-in-law & myself. We paying for one half the farm, the
other half was a gift. I spent several years improving my part, in
building houses barns cabins and many other improvements, besides
looking after the products raised on the farm; continuing farming
until 1911. Then my wife and my health being bad, I rented
13
the farm & moved to Brownsville, Tenn. I married in 1880 a Miss
Taylor, & soon afterward join the Methodist Church. We have no
children of our own, but took 2 orphans to raise. The oldest a girl
married at 19 years of age. The boy 3 years old when we took him.
We adopted him when he was 20 years old & is about 24 years old now
& is now on my farm & attending to my business. It has been a great
pleasure to my wife & I to attend the confederate reunions; meeting
with old comrads & other friend of bygone days. Never held an
office.
14
44. but do not know the county. He married Mary Smith Lee, a daughter
of Col. Phillip Lee of Normini,(?), not far from the Statford place;
first settled by Richard Lee on the coast of Chesapeake bay. After
the death of my Great Grandfather Lee, his widow moved to Leeville
on Stanton river Va. From there she moved to West Tenn. settling
in the little village of Durhamsville near the east boundary line
of Lauderdale Co. about 1834; dying at the age 86 yr. I have a
Bible that belonged to her over a hundred ago giving
15
the records of her ancestors on her side (The Smiths). Also some of
her posterity. My Grandfather J.C. Anthony's father was Rev. John
Anthony who married Susan Austin. Rev John Anthony fought in the
revolutionary war enlisting in Bedford co., Va. Rev. John Anthony's
father, Mark Anthony, married Miss Banks. Mark Anthony's father
was also named John Anthony. He emigrated from England & settled in
Va. one of the early settlers. I do not know the date or place he
settled.
16
My Grandfather J.C. Anthony moved from Va. & settled in Little Rock,

ANTHONY(cont'd.):

Ark. about 1834 buying property in the city a farm near by. Grand
Mother was heir to this property after his death.

APPERSON, CINCINNATUS

FORM NO. 1

1.   Cincinnatus Apperson.   Cleveland, Tenn.   R.F.D. #9   Bradly co.
2.   75 years
3.   Verginia Sport Sylvania Co.
4.   Verginnia Orange Co.
5.   FArming
6.   FArmer
7.   Not any
8.   Not any
9.   about two hundred acres
10. I will say about ($1500.00) fifteen hundred dollars
11. Log house   house with three rooms
12. I plowed, howed, sprouted or general farm work
13. Father did ordinary farm work Mother knit spun carded made cloh and
     ordinary house work
14. None
15. It was considered honorably and respectably.
16. they did
17. very little if any
18. They mingled freely with each other.
19. They did you could not tell one from the other
20. Ther was they seemed all on an equal footing.
21. Not that I could tell
22. They were moderately good
23. They were encouraged by slave-houlders
24. In a log house with one for a fire place the desks were slabs with
     holes bored in them with stick for legs with no black board.
25. about two years
26. about one mile
27. All settlement school or subscription Schools
28. Private
29. From one to three
30. No not very
31. Man
32. first of April 1861 on the line between Orange co. and culpeper co.
     Verginia.
33. 7th Virginia Infantry. Will Aperson, N.J. Bartly, Billy Bisca,
     Charles Byum, James Byum, ____ Cruchfield, Jo. Coleman, Thommas
     Coleman, ____ Dempsy, Miller Davis, ____ Ingle, _____ Feely,
     ____ Finks, ____ Freeman, John Hall, Henry Hall, ____ Hawkins, ____
     Balden, Will Jenkins, E. Kilbe, Frank Fox, Jerry Pannel, George
     Liason, John Shotwell, _____ Sims.
34. Culpepper Court house stade two weeks to drill and get ready
35. Three or four weeks
36. Mannasa
37. After first battle went to Richmond. Fronted Mclellen. I was in
     the sevn (Seven) pines or fair oak. We drove the enemy back and
     then I was in cold Harbor. we were successful. we struck Mclellen
     at Williamsberg. we captured all his artillery we kill 62 horses to
     keep the enem(y) from getting them back. I was in the battle at
     Gainses Mill our company suported Major Wheat(?)
38. Never discharged but was with Lee till the 7 Aprile 1865. of the
     union army with three of our company and came home by way of orange
     courthouse Virginia with no mishaps.
40. General farm work
41. ----
     Followed by several pages.
1
37. we went to Tarburrow in North Carolina. and took the town captured
     a large amount of armes and amunittion and commisary. we destroyed
     seven baats. then we were ordered back to Richmon. we marched
     through Butlers army. we gave him our out side line and wated for

224

APPERSON (cont'd.):

Reinforcement the next day we struck him down at Drewis bluff on
James River. we tore him all to pieces I saw 13 flags surendered to
my colonel that day. and in their Brest works there were Bead stead
Rockers Dresser & other hous furniture and kitchen wares to numers
to mention I was detailed to scout the country for straglers and
the Ladyes of that settlement told me that after

2

they had taken those things from them they made them cook for them
that is Butlers army. Then we went to Fredricks Berg. and were
successful there army backed back a cross the river then we came
down to the second Battle of Manassa. we suffered a loss - but were
successful. we charged 8th R__deilands they would not surender they
limbered up and started of(f) we got orders to shoot their front
horses and there shure was a mess. then we went on to the Mairland
(Maryland?) campane & fought the Battle of Sharpsberg or Anteden
(Antietem?) we had a hard fight and had to retreat but they did not
follow we went back to Virginia then on to Pensylvana (Pennsylvania)
to Gettysberg we went in to that fight with a full crew of officers
commissioned and non commissioned we came out with any officers and
with but just men for a stack of armes. I took

3

charge of the company and commanded them the rest of the war. I saw
all the good times and bad times. I have slept on logs and rails to
keep the watter from getting to me. We had no tents. Some times we
had to live on parch corn some times half rations have moved our
camp fires to have a warm place to sleep and would have suffered for
something to eat if we had not got them from the union army.

4

41. after the war I came home and stad there for a while then went to
red clay G.A. stade to (2) years then went back to virginia and
married in the year 1869 then I came back to north G.A. I have
worked on the farm there for a number of years then I came to my
present place in 1884. I was an able Boddied man till a bout 7 yrs.
back. I was paratized and have just been able to get around over
my farm since then. I have always belonge to the Southern Methodist
Church. I have been an active member.

APPLEWHICH, A. W. (on file folder)

FORM NO. 1

1. A. M. Applewhite (Adolphus Monroe Applewhite) Collierville Tenn
2. 76 yrs old
3. Tenn. Shelby
4. Tenn. Shelby
5. School boy
6. Farmer
7. none a school boy 16 years
8. yes about 50
9. yes 2100 acres
10. about 35 dollars (perhaps his mistake - 2100 acres would be worth
more)
11. a 2 story log weather bourded plastered and painted
12. When I was not a(t) school I worked
13. Father attended to his own farm some times he had an overseer
14. Yes a cook a house girl
15. Yes every one worked
16. Yes
17. very few
18. Yes Sir evry honest man was respected
19. Yes sir
20. Yes sir
21. All treated a like
22. Yes sir
23. encouraged
24. log house we had a professor ____ who taught 10 months a year
25. 4 years
26. two miles

APPLEWHITE (cont'd.):
27. one
28. public
29. 10
30. yes sir
31. man
32. Confederate 1862 Mt. Pleasant. Miss. Marshall county
33. 34 Miss Col. Tom Burton Adolphus Monroe Applewhite
34. to Corinth, Miss.
35. a month
36. Forming Tenn - we moved to Tuplo (Tupelo)
37. we were at Corinth and after that at Tupelo I had the measles and soon had camp fever and nearly died - was discharged.
38. Tup(e)lo
39. came home for a month and then went to war again in the 18th Miss. Calvary.
40. None I was wounded at Brieset? Bend? under Gen. Forest. and lost my leg.
41. I came home after the close of the war and helped my (father) attend to his farms.
42. Jesse Applewhite; North Burrow?, Wayne co., N.C.; lived at Collier-ville; he was democrat and was opposed to
43. Piety? Killough?; Frema Killough?; moth. dont know. lived N.C.
44. I had two brothers killed in the war. one at Perryville?, Ky. the other at Chattanooga? Tenn. one sister her husband was killed at Gettysburg Va.

ARCHER, WILLIAM WRYLEY

FORM NO. 2

1. William Wryley Archer Petersburg, Tenn.
2. 83 yrs 4 months 19 days
3. Lawrence county, Alabama
4. Confederate soldier
5. Co. E - 41 Tennessee; 41 Tenn. was captured at Fort Donalson - I made my escape - went south & joined Fifth Confederate Comapny after 41 was exchanged I went back to my old command 41st
6. Shoe maker by trade and farmer
7. Isaac Curry Archer; Lynchburg _____, Moore co., Tenn.; when a boy he moved to Lawrence co., Alabama; he was Disipating(?) Handle Race Horses.
8. Margret Francis Williams; Doudley? Williams & Sallie Vandiver; Mount Hope, Alabama - Lawrence county
9. Don't know anything except my great grand mother Lizziebeth Vandiver. she told me when they came to Lawrence county and settled they had to pen their sheep and hogs to keep the wild animals from eating them up. She told me she spun and wove her weding dress. When spining she yoused chair backs to aly her thread on to keep it from breaking. soaked it in buttermile to whiten it.
10. Two brothers & one sister & myself owned forty acres of verry poor land
11. None
12. Not any
13. He owned very little probly two or three horses and a cow or two.
14. We lived at different places generly one room log house
15. Worked on a farm plowed are used a hoe one all the time. My My father died when I twelve years old. I was the oldest child. I worked and supported the family as best I could until my Mother died She died when I was 18 years of age. I have worked on a farm ever since.
16. My father was shoemaker and farmer. My mother generly spun and mad cloths for the family. Both being very industrious.
17. None
18. Yes - As a generel thing the county was very poor all the poor people had to work.
19. yes Sir
20. Very few of this kind of living in my county at this time

226

ARCHER (cont'd.):
21. they generly felt themselves better with some acceptions
22. As a general thing they felt themselves better than the non-slave-holders with some acceptions
23. Could not tell much difference
24. The slave holders would vote for him every time but as a general thing the poor man would not vote for him.
25. his chances was very hard for him hardly one out of every hundred that ever got any start.
26. As a general thing they were discouraged
27. little Prymary school
28. about two years altold
29. What schooling I got I walked from one to three miles
30. At that time most neighborhoods had little log school houses - went by the name of whose land it was on - very few high schools at that time - they were few and far between
31. Generly free schools
32. 4 or 5 months
33. ----
34. Male
35. 1861 - Oct. Petersburg, Tenn.
36. to Fort Trousedale to drill
37. about 3 months
38. Corrint (Corinth) Miss
39. My regement 41st T. was captured at Fort Donaldson. I was in hospital at dones(?) when regment was captured. I made my escape - went to Corinth, Miss. ½ m.(?) Joined Fith (5th) Confederate went to Vicburg (Vicksburg) - at the battle of Shilo from Vicksburg to Port Hudson.
40. from Port Hudson went west Knoxville into Kentucky retreat back to Knoxville 41 men exchanged
41. (continuation of Q. 40) and went back to 41st back to Mississippi near Holly Spring taken prison till 64 May took the oath and came home as to my trip home I had a very rough trip. my feet was blistered and sore
42. I culd hardly walk as to my work went wright on the farm to work
43. have been a farmer ever since have lived with in five miles from Petersburg every since have raised four boy and two girls and they are all farmers. I have never missed a crop untill 1911. My wife died and I havent been able to do much since. but I still like to work yet do what I can. as to my church relations have bin a member at the Christian church about 37 years. my seven children belongs to the same church - have thirty three grandchildren the majority of them belonging to the Christian church.
44. The best man I have ever known was Edward E. Carmack if he had lived would have been worth something to his country.
45. Captain ___, First Leu. Fondfield?: Sec. W.S. Beardin; Third Ed Beardin; John Andrews, Tom Harkins, Joe Yarnell, William Smith, Bill Williamson, John Craig, George Craig, Tom Bledsoe, Andrew Gilbert, Gid Hamby, George Hamby, Clay Oulls?, Clay Dyre, Jack Dyre, John Davis, Jiles Davis, Jack Smiley, Henry Smy___, John Gates, John D___, Ed D___, John Blackwell, ___ Hooper, Sam Woods, Pete Foster, Willis Foster, Bill Gillum, Tom ___, Bill Reader, Ja__ Welch, Henry Welch, Tandy Ford, J__ Clark, John Luna?, John Andrews, Tom McNorton, John Wakefield. All I can think of - only three of my company living to tell the tale that I know anything about out of 150 - Myself, Thomas Bledsoe, George Craig.
46. W.R. Lovin   Petersburg, Tenn.
    Jim Haynes   "   "
    Sam Leonard   "   "
    Newt Pylant   "   "
    Wash Coffey   "   "
    Dee Duckworth (Fed. Soldier) Petersburg, Tenn.
    Joe Dodd   Petersburg, Tenn
    John Blackwell   Belfast, Tenn
    Tom Bledsoe   Petersburg, Tenn
    Joe Fox   "   "
    George Foster   Fayetteville, Tenn.

ARNETT, WILLIAM RICHARD

FORM NO. 2

1. William Richard Arnett, Grand Junction, Tenn.
2. I was born May 29, 1848 (may be 1843-see answer to Q. 11)
3. Tipper (Tippah) county, Mississippi
4. I was a Confederate soldier
5. Company F First Tenn. Regiment. Peter Turner was the Colonel
6. Farmer
7. Richard Arnett; dont know; lived in Arkansas at the time of his death.
8. (no name given); dau. of James Woods and Elizabeth Embry; lived in Franklin county near Winchester, Tenn.
9. My grand mother Elisebeth Embry and great grand father Embry lived in Madison county-Richmond was the County Cite(site) Kentucky
10. I owed(owned?) some land but dont know how much
11. My parents died; mother died in 1843; Father died 1848 so I cant tell how much land
12. ----
13. ----
14. ----
15. I plowed hoed tied grain and helped to do all kinds of work on the farm.
16.

(N.B.: there are two forms filled for Mr. Arnett; the second differs from first and has added some extra material...cme)
1. Hardamen co., Tenn.
2. 78 years 8 months
3. May 19 1843, Tippah co., Miss
4. and 5. same as 1st form
7. where father lived - in Arkansas near Dardenell; he died before the war. I cant tel much about him
8. 9. and 10. the same
11. My father owned slaves. I dont know how many. He owned land. I dont know how much
15. As a boy I worked on the farm, etc. The historians are mistaken when they say that white men did not work on the farm. some of the best men with the cradit or tithe were white men.
(this next page is written in light pencil and very difficult to red)
16. He was a farmer as I was only 5 years old when he died I cant tell much about him and mother died when I was born so i cant tel much about her
17. yes I dont know how many not less than 20
18. It was considered respectful and honorable and the most honorable men in the county were self made and they were the best men we could put in office but not the man that was the money got the office
19. they did
20. ----
21. They did if they were honest
22. they did
23. They was
24. It did not but it is diffant now _____ (not able to read this)
25. They were
26. If he was industrious ____
27. county school
28. about 8 years
29. 1 mile
30. ----
31. Public
32. 10 months
33. they did
34. Both men and women
35. 1861. Now I think I went to Virginnie in the fall after the regiment went out in May. I think it was. I went too the 1st Tenn. Reg. and it was in Va. Peter Turney was the Colonel.
36. ----
37. ----
38. 2n battle Manasses Va

ARNETT (cont'd.):
39. I went back to Fredricksburg that was the 2 battle I was in Chancler-
    vill was the 3 battle I was in. There we lost Stone Wall Jackson.
    I was in his army. The last battle I was in was Gettisburg I was
    captured the 1st days fight got 75 of my reg. and ____ and ____
40. I was sent home from Fort Donelson
41. I had a hard time in getting home. I had to work my way home but
    that was my fault. their was 4 of that got tickets to Cinnati 1
    ticket with ____
42. Farming
43. Since the war I have followed farming. I lived 3 year in Mississippi.
    In 1869 I came to Hardman co., Tenn. and have lived here ever since.
    Church - I am a Missionary Baptist. Have held no office.
44. ----
45. Capt. Glen Arledge; 1 Lt. James Thompson (was living in Winchester
    last fall)
    2 Lt. Tom Foster (dead)
    3 Lt. W.E. Donelson (dead)
    Non commision Officer and Privates
    Jack Hall - dead killed at Gittis Burg
    John McClure dead killed at Gittis Burg
    James Donelson - dead killed at Gittis Burg
    Bill Nuckels - dead killed at Gettis Burg
    John Bell - dead killed at Gettis Burg
    W.E. Woods - died since the war
    John Mann - died since the war
    Mat Mann - died in Prison Fort Del(aware?)
    Art Martin - died since the war
    Tom Oliver dead
    Henry Wilson killed in the war
    Nute Brolin - killed in the war
    Thad Green - died in the hospital
    Ad Ra_L? dead
46. Capt. James Thompson - Winchester, Tenn. He is the only one that
    is living that I know of.
    (On extra lined sheet:)
11. and slaves they did own ____. My father owned a very large farm in
    Arkansas and number of slaves. He had 6 children. 3 boys and 3
    girls the slaves were divided among the children 3 to each child.
    the land was divided among the children both of my brothers were
    killed in the war.
24. it is Party now if the canidate is a Democrat most all democrats will
    vate the Democrat Ticket and the same with Republicans.

                    ARNOLD, FRANCIS MARION

FORM NO. 2

1. Francis Marion Arnold, Rutherford Co, Lascassas, Tenn. R. #2
2. 92 yrs. 1 month 11 days
3. Tennessee, Wilson county
4. Confederate
5. I-18th Tennessee
6. School Teacher and farmer
7. Davidson Arnold; Halifax, Virginia; Rutherford county; private in
    Civil War
8. Patsy Puckett; Isham Puckett and Sallie Puckett; Wilson county
9. ----
10. no
11. no
12. no
13. ----
14. he was a renter and moved a good deal
15. farmer, and plowed and worked cotton with a hoe
16. My father was a school teacher and a farmer when not teaching also
    a carpenter. My mother card, spin and weave cloth knitting and
    cooking.
17. no

ARNOLD (cont'd.):
18. this was regarded very respectable and showed the parents were raising their children right.
19. yes all of them
20. no every one worked
21. yes they were sociable and friendly
22. yes, every one mingled and had a good time
23. a good friendly feeling
24. dident see very much difference
25. no not like there is now. nothing only hard manual labor
26. encouraged
27. subscription and free school
28. three years
29. Three miles
30. ----
31. both
32. about four months
33. yes
34. man
35. I enlisted in November 1862 at Cainsville
36. Camp Trousdale near Bowling Green, Ky.
37. two month
38. Battle of Murfreesboro
39. went to Tullahoma in camp next battle of Chicamauga, several days lots killed, fairly good clothes, common foods, slept on ground sometimes had tents using guns for pillow, was in Mewan? Ga. hospital was in prison in Chi. 8 months very hard life
40. at Chi at end of war
41. me and a few of my neighbors came to Nash. on the train ran there I came horseback and no saddle but was very glad to get here any way.
42. farming
43. Has lived on the farm I am on now since 1861 and am a member of the Baptist church for 73 years have held no offices have always been well and am still very active for a man of my age have been married three times and might marry again
44. ----
45. F.M. Arnold, Bob Mathews, Garis Mathews, Sam Craddock, Bob Dillon, Will Thodes, Agie Batey, Jim Lemming, Arch Patterson, Bob Koonce, Al Rhodes, Buck Jennings, Dick Arnold, Jim Arnold, Lum? Arnold, Tinte? Jennings, Bill Harris, Sam Harris, Roof Patterson
You can get the Roster from Esq. Bob J. Mathew, Lascassas, R. #2 Tenn.
46. Al Matthews, Milton, Tenn.
Sam Craddock, Lascassas, Tenn.
Mr. Arch Heigth, Lascassas, Tenn.
Mr. Jim Williams, Norene, Tenn.

ARNOLD, THOMAS C.

FORM NO. 2

1. Thomac C. Arnold
2. 77 yrs
3. White County Tenn. (lived in Rutherford most all my life)
4. Confederate
5. Co. F, 23rd Tennessee
6. Farmer
7. America Arnold; unknown; Tennessee; he lived at Mally? in Rutherford co.; he was Capt. in 44 Tenn. Regiment
8. Mary Jane Tolbert; Jas. Tolbert and Vinie Tolbert; Cannon co.
9. ----
10. none
11. no
12. no
13. $500
14. Rented some logs house and sometimes frame
15. did any and all kinds of farm work
16. (16 thru 44 not answered)

230

ARNOLD (cont'd.):
45. Aaron Todd, Jno. Gum(Gunn?), Bill Ought?, Bill Knox, Geo. Benson,
Eli Benson, Tom Benson, Hugh? Benson, Dave Flemmins, Hiram Harrell,
Bill Hamilton, Crick Burks, Monroe Prater, Calvin Love?, Jim Kelton,
Abe Armstrong, Harrison Todd, Sam Brown, Levi Todd, Kalup Todd,
Russell Patrick, Jim Mathis, Jesse Jernagan, Jimmie Love(Lowe?),
William S. Prater, Asa Lee, Vick Lee, Jim Wiley Jernigan.

46. Geo. Benson   Murfreesboro R #8 Tenn
Jim Kelton   Christiana R #3 Tenn
Dave Flemmin   Readyville #1 Tenn
L.H. Hathcock   Beechgrove #2 Tenn
Jake McKnight   Readyville #1 Tenn
Frank McKnight   Readyville #1
Robt. McKnight   Sharpsville (Rutherford) Tenn
Geo. Hatchett   Murfasboro R #8 Tenn
Davis Murray   Readyville R #1 Tenn
Russell Patrick   Readyville R #1 Tenn
Jesse Jernigan   Bradyville Tenn
Capt. Jno. C. Knew   Christiana Tenn
W.J. Prater   Beechgrove R #2 Tenn
J._.J. Hoover (Hower?)   Murfreesboro R #4 Tenn
Wess Jacobi   Beechgrove R #2 Tenn
Jno Lee   Murfreesboro R #4 Tenn

ARNOLD, THOMAS W.

FORM NO. 2

1. Thomas W. Arnold, Postoffic now Creston(?), N.C.
2. going on 76 years old
3. Tennessee nox (Know?) county
4. a confederate soldir
5. A- 6 N.C. Cavelry Sixty fith regent
6. Farmer
7. John Arnold; jonson (Johnson) co. Tennessee; he lived in nox (Knox)
co. at the time of my birth; he was a jestes (Justice) of the Pease
8. Nancy King; Robert King and _____; a Methodist rev.
9. My grandfather name on my fathers side was William Arnold. my grate
grand father name was Jon (John?) Arnold. on my mothers side my
grandfathers name was Robert King a methodist preecher
10. I had no land in time of the war. I went in the war at seventeen
years old.
11. no
12. sumthing over 600
13. sumthing nere eight 100 or a thusen dollar land was cheap in these
mountains and humans lives two in that war
14. a log house one large room and fire plas at that time peeple warked
hard in this cuntry all about equal
15. I worked on the farme hoed corn and plowed with ox or horse, anything that was to do on the farm work is onerable in thes cuntry
and allways has bin with rich and poore so far as I can remember
16. My father pracktis medison a while and was jestes of the pease for
sumtime and worked on the farme part of his time. my mother dun the
cooking and spining and weiving all by hand and all the house worke
17. they had no servents
18. yes sir
19. yes sir
20. we had varry few idlers in this cuntry all men prety much thaut work
onerable
21. holdes did not act like they thaut them selves better than comon
peeple
22. yes sir you could tell no diferns
23. they did not seme to hav any hard feeling to ward each other in our
cuntry so far as I noe
24. noe sir ther seme to be no differens
25. in this cuntry land was cheap 50 year ago land sold at one dollar
a acar yung men could hav dun varry well at that time
26. poore yung men allway has had opertunity to make sumthing of them
selvs if they would and hav bin incureged tho lots wont try

231

27. subscription school
28. about 6 munths
29. 2 mile
30. subscription schoole all together in thoas days in these mountains and varry short schools in the year at that
31. privet we had noe public schools in this cuntry
32. 2 or three
33. yes sir what time they had school
34. a man we had noe women teechers in this cuntry at that time
35. I joined the army in bristol I dont remember whether it was in Va. or on the tennessee side as that plase is on the line. I joined company a 6 north carlina cavelry 65 redgment confederate army
36. to the lorend? of N.C. we stade ner kinston (Kingston?) a few weeks and went down on ronoke (Roanoke?) lines
37. nere plymath (Plymouth?) and stade thar tell lee serendred was not in gaged in
38. (continuation from above) varry series battles while I was in the army. they captured my horse the fray I go in
39. about the first truble I got in to a few days after I got to the rigiment I was on iron detale down nere newbern (New Bern?) I got my horse capturd and shot at hunderds of times them yanks was not good marksmen or they would hav hit me had sumthing to eate sum times pretty hungry too
40. ridgway, N.C. if I remember rite
41. come rite up throu N.C. cart road and by pathes and throu the woulds (woods?) we hav to look out plenty of bushwhacers at that time
42. when things setteld I worked on the farm
43. soon after the war I profest faith in Blessed sun of God I have joined the Methodist long ago the old me. church I have preecht a menny time. I have baptised and received in the church a good menny members in to the M.E. Church and marrieed a good menny cuple and hav done a good deal of church work and a lot of hard work on the farm I hav not hel any offic only in the cherch and I dont want any other offic I could giv you the names of sum good men if you can reed my riting. Bishop Joye? was one I was aqainted with Bishop Waleden a nother one and sum bad men up here in a_ country but that is noe use
44. ---- (N.B.: "you straiten all misstake")
45. Thomas Sutherlan   Creston, N.C.
    John Parker   Jefferson, N.C.
    Martan Warn   Mable, N.C.
    James Horton   Silverlake, N.C.
    William Greear   Bannerselk?, N.C.
    Calven Grable   West Jefferson, N.C.
    Roby. Brown, Capton off co. a 6 caverly, _____ Tennessee
    you must look over all mis stakes yorse fraternly, Thomas W. Arnold, Creston, N.C. R 1 Box 22
46. Jamson? Cornett   Creston N.C. Confederate
    Robert Arnold   Mountain city, Tennessee
    Thomas Barlow   fedral solair (soldier?) Trade, Tennessee
    Landon Netherly   Trade, Tennessee

ARRINGTON, HENRY CLAY

FORM NO. 2

1. Henry Clay Arrington, Cordova, Tennessee
2. 78 years and 6 months
3. Wilson county, State of Tenn.
4. Confederate soldier
5. Company _ 28th Tenn. Infrantry
6. a farmer
7. James Arrington; in North Carolina; Halifax, N.C.; he was magistrate 16 years in succession in Tenn.?
8. Martha Thomas; dont know; dont know; in Warren county, North Carolina
9. I do not know anything of my grand parents. I only lived with my parents one year after the war stoped I joined the army at 17.

ARRINGTON (cont'd.):
10. I owned none
11. No
12. 105 acres
13. $3000
14. Log house hewn cedar logs had four rooms and a seperate kitchen
15. I commenced working on a farm when but 6 years old and did all kinds of work usually done on a farm till I entered the army
16. My father did all kinds of work on the farm and my mother cooked, washed, spun, carded, wove, knit, milked the cows and made the clothing for all the family.
17. no
18. it was
19. They did only those who owned slaves did not work all the time
20. very few in number
21. As a general thing they did not visit the poorer classes much but were friendly when met with
22. They mingled together fairly well
23. They were friendly
24. I think not
25. Some did but they had to economize to the fullest extent
26. encouraged
27. subscription schools
28. about 30 months
29. one mile
30. pay or subscription schools
31. private
32. from three to five months
33. no. some had to work and could not attend regularly
34. Mostly men. I attended one school where a woman was teacher
35. In June 1861 near Gladesville Wilson county, Tenn.
36. to Camp Zollicoffer
37. about 8 months
38. Battle of Somerset or Fishing Creek in Ky.
39. We fell back after the Fishing Creek fight or run to Corinth, Miss. engaged in the battle at Shiloah on the 6 & 7 days of Apr. 1862. I was wounded on the first day. next battle was at Murfreesborough, Tenn.
40. Nashville Dec. 1864
41. I walked home; there was nothing amusing about this trip
42. Farm work
43. I have not held any office. worked on farms. went to school. taught school in Tenn. and Ark. Cleraked in the store. took a business course at Leittle Rock Ark. kept books in Ark. and Tenn.
44. ----
45. Wade Baker, Spencer Talley, John Colman, Robt. Talley, Wm. Colman, James Hill, Richard Mann, Wesley Mann, Solomon Shaw, Henry Cobson, Francis Underwood, James Coppage, Jasper Coppage, Jesse Clifton, Robert Clifton, Christopher Brown, Robt. Mabry, John Mabry, James Mabry, Roland Mabry, Robt. Chambers, Clay Palmer, Wm. Beard, John Taylor, Joseph Rogers, Wm. Smith, Solomon Smith, Houston Graves, Wm. Hal____, Wm. Tedford, John Barr, Thos. Barr, Nig Barr, J.W. McFarland, Thos. Bradshaw, Wilson Peak, Jonas CArver, John Carver, Riley Rogers, John Webber, Thomas Lane, George Eddins, John Eddins, William Garner, James Smith, John W. Taylor, Jonathan Eatherly, George Baker, John Smith, Pat Garrett, Frank Lindsley, B. Lofton, J. Lofton, Bluford Johns, Stephen Johns, Thomas Murphy, Robert Murphy, Thomas Fitter, Hampton Wade, Wade Hampton

46.
William Yates	Cordova, Tenn
James WEaks	Cordova, Tenn
Spencer Talley	Lebanon, Tenn
Thomas Barr	Lebanon, Tenn
William Hoolman	Lebanon, Tenn
Cam McNeely	Collierville, Tenn
Algie Seward	Eads, Tenn.
A.F. Yopp	Heazen (Hazen?), Ark.

These are all Tennesseans

ARY, WILLIAM

FORM NO. 2

1. William Ary, R. #1, Flatwoods, Tenn.
2, 82
3. State of Tenn. Perry county
4. Confederate
5. A-9th Mounted Cavelry
6. Farmer
7. Henry Ary; Salisbury, Roan co., North Carolina; Salisbury 30 years
    then came to Perry co., Tenn; none
8. Sophia Fraley; Jacob Fraley and (do not know her name); Salisbury,
    Roan county North Carolina
9. Ancestors came from Germany but I dont know their names
10. owned none
11. no
12. 360
13. $300.00
14. log house 2 rooms
15. worked on a farm plowed and hoed and other similar kinds of work
16. Father did farm work. Mother did house work cooking spinning weaving
    etc.
17. none
18. yes
19. yes
20. none
21. yes
22. yes
23. they were friendly
24. no
25. fairly good
26. encouraged
27. public schools
28. about 12 months
29. ½ mile
30. just common public schools
31. public
32. 2 to 3 months
33. not mutch
34. men
35. Nov. 1862 in Confederate Army
36. Jackson Tenn
37. the third day in battle at Lexington Tenn.
38. Jackson battle commenced at Lexington
39. Battles at Trenton Tenn. Union City Tenn. Sand Mountain, Ala. then
    to Straight Raid to Rome Georgia Chickamauga Knoxville Tenn Franklin
    Tenn Nashville Tenn Moss Creek Tenn in Camp we lived rough went
    hungry and half clothed was at the battle at Atlanta Georgia and
    Thompson Station Tenn.
40. Selmer Ala April 1865
41. found all on sufferance at home every thing spent and place all
    gon to rock
42. farming
43. have ben farming ever since the war live at the same place now that
    I did when I enlisted am a member of the M.E. Church and the Masonic
    Order
44. ----
45. P.D. Burns, John Walker, John Rasbury and myself are all that are
    liveing that belonged to my company
46. Dan Tredwell, R. #5, Linden, Tenn.
    The above answers are correct to the best of my knowledg. I was
    wounded in the head at Jackson Tenn. in the first battle I was in

ASHCROFT, J. W.

FORM NO. 2

1. J.W. Ashcroft, Newbern, Tenn.
2. 75 yrs
3. Decatur co., Tenn
4. Confederate
5. Co. I, 1st Tenn. Cal.
6. Mca.? and farmer (Mechanic?)
7. Joel Ashcroft; Raleigh, N.C.; lived at Decaturville, Tenn.
8. Malvinia Brown; Col. Harry Brown and Nancy Brown; born near Jamestown, Va.
9. Scotch Irish dec. and Mother French Hugnot
10. ----
11. about 18 or 20
12. 300 acres
13. about $15000
14. lof and frame com. of 8 rooms
15. I worked on farm as same as our negros untill I enlisted in con. army
16. My father master mechanic and negro foreman who managed farm. My mother died when I was 8 yrs. old negro women spin and made our cloths untill civil war
17. ----
18. all labor was resp. and very disresplbe. not to work
19. they did
20. none all worked or was not resp.
21. all on common level no distinctions made
22. all on common level
23. no distions (distinctions)
24. not in least
25. there was ample optuney and many taken advantage of it
26. encouragement was given all to make an hones endever
27. subscription school
28. 1 mile
29. ----
30. grammar school
31. private
32. about 3 mo. in year
33. yes
34. both
35. Feb. 23-'62
36. Linden, Tenn.
37. short time
38. Thompson Sta. Tenn.
39. ------- Gen Vandorcamp? in offise at Holly Springs from Miss to Tenn. VanDorn's army after Vandor was killed killed at Spring Hill served under Gen Forest till battle of Franklin and taken prisner
40. Went to Rock Glad remained at Rock Gland untill 27 Feb. "65
41. was carried from there to Richmond Va. and parroled 11 da March '65 left Richmond went to Johnson army? north and stayed untill surender
42. walked abot 1000 miles arrived about 1st of May worked on farm 65 and 66
43. worked in dry good store at diferenct places on Tenn. River from 66 till 1880. _____ with my brother in law H.W. Hooper and bot a farm on Tenn river and engaged in farming and mercantile business in 1880 Sol my business on Tenn River and moved to Dyer co. and bought 225 ac. farm and eng. in farming and mercantil business until 2 yrs ago and sold out and retired have never regreted part I taken in war and got no apologes to make
44. ----
45. Cap. H.R. Basham(Barham?); 1st Lt. Geo. Barham, 2nd Lt. John Salyton, 3rd Lt. Bob Kitrell; Ordly. Sgt. Frank King; 2 Ord. Sgt. Will Howard?, 3rd Ord. Sgt. Will Whitwell, H.A. Dean, Archar? Dean, Will Dean, Hiram Kelly, 4 Kelly boys, G.D. Price, Henry Blackburn, B___ Kitrall, _____ Shelton, W._. Shelton, Jes.? Wald, Dick Wald, J__Wald, _____ Wheat, Ben. Whitwell, Jo. Pouge? It is possible that som of Frank Ling descendants maight have the roster of Com. I. Rigret that I am unable to call to mind but few of my commrads.

235

ASHCROFT (cont'd.):
46. J.A. Hall   Newbern, Tenn.
     _____ Haskins   "   "
     _____ Wynn   "   "
     John Willis   "   "
     M. Cropton?
     B.R. Rhae
     Tom, Wilson
     C.L. Claborne   Dyersburg, Tenn
     J.W. Green   "   "
     _____ Dunn   "   "
     J.H. Tarant   "   "
     H.H. Brook   "   "
     Tom Sanders   "   "
     W.H. Pope   "   "
     F.A. Chitwood   "   "
     L.H. Firrill   "   "

dated: 4-1-'22

ASKEW, J. F.

FORM NO. 2

1.   J.F. Askew, Dee R__ (Del Rio?) Tennessee
2.   Born 1846 July 13
3.   Soorry conty north colininio (Surry co., N.C.?)
4.   confederate
5.   Co. E 53
6.   Machanic
7.   C.F. Askew; Randolph co., N.C.; Randolph co., N.C.; dont know; he
     went in the first year and me in the second
8.   Seno Doris; D. Doris; dont know; Flat shool creek surey co. n.c.
     (Flat Shaols Creek, Surry co., N.C.?)
9.   dont know
10. dident own none
11. no
12. they owned land dont know
13. none
14. framed house 5 rooms
15. carpenter work with my father
16. my father was a mechanic my mother was dead when the civil war began
17. no
18. yes
19. yes
20. dont know
21. dont know
22. dont know
23. dont know
24. dont know
25. dont know
26. dont know
27. free school
28. 5 years
29. one mile
30. feww school
31. public
32. 3 & 4 months
33. yes
34. some times a women and some times a man
35. my father went in the first year and I went second year i enlisted
     when i got to my regment Kingston North carolina
36. Richmond, W. Va.
37. not untill the Gettisberg fight
38. Gittisberg fight
39. Captured at Gettisberg took me to Fedrick city and from there
     Bottomoore went from there ft. Delaware put me in ft. Delaware prison
     kept 15 monts very bad clothed ___ slept cold hard tacks and meat
     esposed bad in prison

236

ASKEW (cont'd.):
40. Oct. 1864 at ft Delware
41. Got on steamer New York came from there to ft. Monroe and went up
    James river to Okren? Loudon got off confredetts bot and went to
    Richmond W. Va.
42. was sick couldnt do no work had chills and fever
43. i worked with my father he was a carpenter came to Brostoll Tenn
    (Bristol?) i am a member of the Babtist church no office i come to
    Morristown when the rail raod when it was just finished to Lead Vale,
    Tenn. and worked from there over untill it was finished from there
    to Neuport (Newport) Tenn. me and my father was in the same command
    the war. we both was captured togather at Gettisburg. we both was
    put in prison July 1863. we was parolled out Oct. 1864 and we both
    got back togeather. my father died hear in Green county. he was
    70 yrs. old when he died and has been dead 25 years.
44. ----
45. Cap. D. Hill of my Comapny E.; Ft. Lt. Jim Hill; Sa.(2) Lt. Winters;
    Col. Owens of my Rigment 53 North Carolina; Daniels Brigade was my
    brigade.
46. John Pock (Pack?) Del Rio, Tenn
    Bill Pock (Pack?)   "   "
    Dolph Askew   "   "
    i Filled this out myself an't much of a scooler i might to have made
    some mistakes if so hope you will rectfy them the best you can for
    iam a poor hand Trying to fill such thins out. Hoping you Will
    apresiate the same.

                          ASKEW, W. T.

FORM NO. 2

1. W.T. Askew, Goodlettsville, Tenn.
2. 78
3. Sumner county Tennessee
4. Confederate
5. H-44 Tennessee
6. Farmer
7. Whashington (Washington?) Askew; around Goodlettsville, Sumner co.,
    Tenn; most of the time around Goodlettsville.
8. Polly Pike; John Pike and Mrs. Pike; around Springfeild
9. As far back as I can remember my parents was born in Tennessee
10. Didn't own any land
11. none
12. 84
13. $84
14. log house 3 rooms
15. work on farm
16. Followed farming most of the time. she had a loom and made all of
    her own clothes.
17. ----
18. yes
19. most of them farmed
20. most done there own work
21. we mingle together
22. no
23. was friendly
24. It would help him to some extent
25. no show at all
26. yes
27. little
28. 2 years
29. 1 mile
30. just 1 school
31. free school
32. 3 months
33. yes
34. man
35, 2, 1861, do not remember month. place Shackle Island, Tenn.
36. Camp Trousdale and is now mitcherville? Tenn. Sumner co.

ASKEW (cont'd.):
37. about 3 months
38. at Ringo Georgia I was a sharpshooter
39. we went south after the first battle we drilled every day that we
    wasn't engaged in battle from south we went to mobile Ala. and we
    got on boat and went montgomery Ala. from there to serrville Ky.
    where we engaged in a 2 days battle
40. at Elmira N.Y.
41. was treated fine all along the road
42. worked in timber
43. worked in timber most of the time. never did belong to a church
44. General Hardee, General Boygard, General Bragg, Beneral Pat Claborne,
    General Bush Johnson, General Lee.
45. Dick Lizer, Jim Garret, Billy Frazier, Jim Pike, Lim La-siter
46. Jim Garrett, Hendersonville, Tenn.
    he was in our company
    Jim Frazier, Hendersonville, Tenn.
    Bryant Garrett, Goodlettsville, Tenn.
    D.F. Matherly, Hendersonville, Tenn.
    Dan McMurtry, Nashville, Tenn. address dont know
    Captain Bass, Goodlettsville, Tenn.
    Capt. Roscoe, Goodlettsville, Tenn.

ATKINS, ARCHIBALD

FORM NO. 1

1. Archabald Atkins, Idal,? Tenn.
2. 77
3. Grainger co., Tenn.
4. Grainger co., Tenn.
5. farming
6. farming
7. ----
8. no
9. no
10. ----
11. log house 1 room
12. used both plows and hoe
13. father farming mother cooking
14. no
15. yes
16. yes
17. not as I know of
18. all mingled together
19. yes
20. friendly
21. no
22. no
23. ----
24. none
25. ----
26. about 1 mile
27. ----
28. public
29. about 3 months
30. no
31. ----
32. about Aug. 1863 State of Ky.
33. 47th K.Y.
34. Camp Nelson, Ky.
35. 4 or 5 months
36. at Camp Nelson
37. ----
38. at Lexington, Ky. in 1864 I think
39. ----
40. farming
41. ----
42. Wyvright (Wright?) Atkins; Idol(Idal), Grainger co., Tenn.

238

ATKINS (cont'd.):
43. Sallie Bunch; dont remember
44. ----
45. ----
46. ----

ATKINS, AUGUSTINE TAYLOR

FORM NO. 2

1. Augustine Taylor Atkins, Covington, Tipton county, Tennessee
2. 76 1 20 (don't know what he means by this)
3. State of Tennessee Giles county
4. I was a Confederate Soldier
5. Company K, 11 Tennessee Cavalry, Hollman's regiment Bells Brigade
   N. B. Forrests Corps.
6. He was a farmer
7. John Atkins; North Carolina; lived near Pulaski Giles county he died
   in 1882. he was 84 years old.
8. Marth Croft; (rest not filled in)
9. I can not give you any information in this space
10. I owned no property at the opening of the war. I was only a school
    boy
11. They did they owned 21 slaves young and old
12. They owned land 408 acres
13. 21 slaves valued at $400 each $8400. 408 acres $13__ per acre
    $6000 = $14,400 horses at $800
14. A double log house weather boarded ceiled up stairs to each room
    stick chimney.
15. I worked on the farm, plowed, hoed when there was no school near by,
    and I and nother negro boy went to mill every Saturday with a sack
    of corn each horse back. These historians surely did not ever visit
    our community we had no slackers among us
16. My father did some work such as plowing hoeing and etc. but he
    looked after the slaves principally and kept tools ready for service
    when needed. My mothers duties were to keep the house in order,
    looking after cooking spinning weaving, etc.
17. One girl who did most of the house work another who did most of
    cooking
18. All honest toil such as your named above, was considered honorable
    in our community and approved of by our best citizens
19. They surely did and we had none idle they all labored daily
20. These were very few scarcely any which lived such lives in our
    community
21. Any one who was not personally acquainted could not tell any differ-
    ence with slave owners and non slaves owners
22. If there was any difference at either place it was not easily
    detected
23. There was a friendly feeling in our community of all people if he or
    she was worthy of such
24. I was not old enough to know much about these political contest but
    I never knew or heard of such, in our community
25. The opportunities were good if he would practice economy and take
    care of money
26. I am personally acquainted with several young men (school mates) who
    made useful men of themselves by being encouraged by slave holders
27. I attended a private school for our public school was hardly known
    then
28. I suppose it was 7 or 8 years a private school of our community
29. I suppose the distance was from 1½ to 2 miles
30. A private school which was generally operated from 5 months to 8
    months
31. Private lasted 5 months 2 weeks vacation and began again for 5
    months
32. Ten months ordinarily in each year
33. Our attendance was very good daily
34. I have attended schools of each as teachers, but the most of time
    men
35. In the year of 1864 in December near Pulaski, Tenn.

239

ATKINS (cont'd.):
36. to Franklin, Teen.
37. Only a few days when General Hood fought General Thomas there
38. Battle of Franklin
39. After the Battle of Franklin our CAvalry did no more fighting we
    brought up the rear of Hoods retreat until we crossed Tennessee
    River at the Mussells shoals. Our fair in camps were rough, badly
    clothed Slept under....
40. Forrests Cavalry were dischard at Gainesville, Ala. in April 1865.
41. Our trip home was made almost without any thing to eat for horses
    or men. We crossed Tennessee River at Eastport on our return home
42. I helped my father cultivate a part of the farm which he and the
    slaves had planted
43. After returning home I still remained upon the old home farm until
    it was sold for debts that was made before the war. I am a member
    of the Methodist Church. I have held no office. I have taught in
    our public schools. I an now not able to do work of any kind.
44. ----
45. Capt. James Rivers; Lt. Robert McNairy; George Cobbs, Robert Cobbs,
    Mack Conley, Wesley Ingram, Milton Woodard, Frank McNairy, John
    Watson, Billy Watson, Joe Lindsay, Frank Amiss, Davie Hannah, Billy
    Tidwell, Fred Kelley, I can not give you any information on this
    subject.
46. Dr. Gillispie   Covington, Tenn.
    Colonel Sanford   "   "
    Brock Sales   "   "
    M.A. Misenhaimes?   "   "
    Bill Grant   "   "
    John Beasley   "   "
    J.D. McFallin?   "   "
    John Shoaf   "   "
    George Eaverson?   Independence, Miss.
    W. . Miller   Coldwater, Miss.
    R.G. Wallace   "   "
    B.F. Richard   "   "
    Capt. W.A. Dougherty   "   "
    Morris Moore   Serratobia, Miss.
    Sam. J. House   "   "
    Davy Dean   "   "
    Billy Cathey   Thyatira?, Miss.
    George Puryear   "   "
    Willie Campbell   "   "
    Billie Harwell   Coldwater, Miss.

ATKINS, JAMES MERDTH

FORM NO. 1

1. James Merdth Atkins, Noeton(?), Grainger co., Tenn.
2. 88 years in May
3. Tenn. Granger co.
4. Tenn. Grainger co. Conferacy
5. Farmer and Backsmith
6. Farmer
7. 75 acres land, value $100.00
8. two
9. 120 acres
10. $120.00
11. log house one room
12. I worked with hoe on farm
13. He worked on farm. He made two hundred rails the day he died.
    Mother cooked and weaved and spooned (spinned)
14. No
15. yes
16. yes
17. noon (none)
18. thru 33. not answered
34. Murfresburough, Tenn.
35. Thirty days

ATKINS (cont'd.):
36. Murfresburough, Tenn.
37. ----
38. Cherackee Springs
39. I walked home about 100 miles
40. I went to work on farm
41. I have lived in Grainger co. and worked on farm. I served as Constable one term.
42. Merdth (Meredith?) Atkins; Thorn Hill, Grainger co., Tenn. lived at Thorn Hill.
43. Marah Fitchgearl (Fitzgerald); James Fichgeral (Fitzgerald); I do not no
44. ----
   (N.B.: small paper attached: This is to ceterfy that I have known Mr. Adkins for the past 35 years. I have found him to be a good law and cival citizen. As to his military service I know nothing. I have always regarded him of being one of our best citizins. I served in the confederate army from Va. Co. B 8th Va. Regiement.
                        C.H. Peron (Perrod?)

                     ATKINS, LUCULLUS CAN

FORM NO. 1

1. Lucullus Can Atkins, Adams, Tenn.
2. 76 yrs. old
3. Tennessee Montgomery co.
4. Tenn. Montgomery co.
5. Farmer
6. Farmer
7. Owned one 3 yr. old hose, value $100.00
8. Father owned 6 slaves
9. Father owned 350 acres land
10. Property valued at $14,500.00
11. Log house 7 rooms and hall
12. I farmed, and did all farm work, plowed, hoed, and similar work
13. Father did general farm work. Mother looked after house keeping but did not do any cooking, weaving, etc spinning.
14. Yes, 6 slaves
15. All honest work was respectable and honorable
16. White men did farming
17. Most white men worked in my community
18. Men mingled freely and there was no difference shown those who did not own slaves
19. I think all were on an equal footing of equality
20. Friendly feeling existed
21. I believe men were elected upon their own qualification rather than being a slave owner.
22. I think the opportunity was good for a young man to save money to buy a farm or go into business
23. Honest young men were encouraged by slave holders, when worthy
24. Short term subscription schools
25. about 6 years
26. about 1 mile
27. Private school taught by Esq. Johnson and wife - another school taught by Childs. Private school taught by Rev. Louis Lowe.
28. Private, subscription school
29. 6 mo. each year
30. they did
31. 1862 - May - Port Royal, Tenn.
33. 3rd Ky., Co. G
   Jno. B. Dortch, Capt.; Logan Williams, 1st Lt.; Fisher Merritt, 2nd Lt.; Henry Merritt, 3rd Lt.; H.A. Yates, T.L.? Woodson, Geo. T. Rosson, A.F. Rosson, Bill McLee, Hiram Grant, Bill Hogan, Horris Lurton, Frank Browder, Jim Jones, Hight Small, Monti Merritt, Bill Grizzard, Joel Grizzard, Monroe Mason, Henry Fort, Clark Johnson, J.W. Shaw, Alex Watts, Bill Adams, Dee Mason, Towps? Jones, Alex Roles, Milton Dam, Obb Greer, Jake Archer, Bob Weatherford, Henry Atkins, Dan Mason

ATKINS (cont'd.):
34. Sent to Riggins Hill. first battle 1862. then James Woodard Cavalry
    and sent to Russellville, Ky.
35. about 2 mo. after enlistment we had a battle at Riggins Hill
36. Riggins Hill, Montgomery co., Tenn.
37. From Russellville, Ky. joined Col. Morgan, went to Murfreesboro,
    then to Bowling Green, Ky. then Hortsville, Tenn. battle lasted
    about 1 hr. captured 22 "Yankees", carried them to Murfreesboro, in
    and around Murfreesboro we had several small battles. battle Snow's
    Hill, then to Smithville, Tenn., Readyville. we lived well in camp
    in the south, slept outdoors, 1 blanket, exposed to cold. Never
    slept outside during war except while in prison. July 1863 ordered
    to Indiana and Ohio, took two boats.
38. May 9, 1865 Washington, Ga.
39. (See supplement 37)
40. Did no work that year. My father gave me a horse and saddle and
    told me get go until next Jan. 1866 before I went to work
41. Jan. 1866 - I took charge of farm for my father at $500.00 each
    year. during this 5 yrs. I did a great deal of hauling. Rented a
    farm, bought a farm 1872. Port Royal Tenn. lived here 40 yrs.
    moved to Adams 1912. Member of Methodist Church 1908.
42. Jas. Thomas Atkins; Montogomery, Tenn.; Montgomery co.; was tax
    collecter Montgomery co., 2 yrs.
43. Virginia Carr; James Carr and Martha Ann ____; lived in Kentucky
44. Family came from Virginia - settled near Port Royal, Tenn.
45. & 46. not on film

(Supplement #37)
Town of Adams, Adams, Tenn.
#37-On Ohio River, and crossed and set fire after crossing. Then we
rode 11 days and nights on our horses, without sleep, one night we
rode 100 miles. The enemy fired on us several times each day. We
had two 6 pound cannon with us. We encountered? a stockade but our
guns were not sufficient to rum them out. At one time we were
ordered to burn this stockade but this was countermanded. We went
down below about 2 miles on Green River and crossed the river.
Timber was cut all along our way. All towns through which we passed
were deserted could not see a man. We were captured by Woolford
Cavalry near Penn. line, who (I lost my horse here) had followed us
through Ohio and Indiana. We were carried to Chicago, Ill. and put
in prison. We remained there 7(8?) months. Were fed on bread,
pickled meat and tin cup of rice (ten?). We were not allowed money
in prison. Slept on bunks with straw and 1 blanket. We were punished in prison if we disobeyed by being made to ride Morgan horse,
which was a rail. We were exchanged to Richmond, Va. there we were
given $130.00 30 days furlough. We went to Blacksburg, and spent
our 30 days among southern people. At expiration of our 30 day
furlough, Apr. 1865, we were ordered to mount and report to Washington, Ga. where we reported for duty. 9th of May we surrendered at
Washington, Ga. They gave us 33.00 gold. I sold my horse for $10.00
gold. We had free transportation home. We rode on train where
tracks were not torn up. Other times we walked. Atlanta to Dalton
we walked 100 mi. in 3 days, then entrained for Nashville, remained
there 3 days and could not buy food without gold or silver. People
would not take currency. Reached home at 9'oclock P.M. walked in
and my dog knew me after 4 years being away.

Members of Co. H.A. Yates, G.S. Woodson, G.T. Rossen. A.Y.? Rosson,
Bill McLee Hogan Hiram Grant (no seperation between these names)
Charly Linton, Horris Linton, Frank Browder, Jim Jhones, Hight Small,
Montgomery Mearritt, Bill Grisard, Joal Grisard, Monrow Mason, Henry
Fort, Clark Johnson, J.W. Shaw, Tomas phones, Elick Roles, Bill
Adams, Milton Dame, Demason Archer, Ob Greer, Bob Weatherford, Henry
Atkins, Dan Mason

ATKINSON, S. W.

FORM NO. 2

1. S.W. Atkinson, Redboiling Springs, Clay co. Tenn.
2. 75 years old
3. Fentress co., Tenn. (N.B.: this old gentlemen had very shaky hand)
4. Confederacy
5. 4 Batalion and 8 tenn. Calvary served 2 year
6. whickey tavern and tolegate
7. Will H. Atkinson, Near Jamestoen, Fentress co., tenn.; lived on
    Cumberln Mounton (Cumberland Mountain)
8. Nancey McFarlen; James Mc and ternay (James & Turney McFarlen?);
    on Sand Mounton
9. My gran ma and my father lost este they had on the Mouten. Wel my
    great gran Ma thair with them She lived 117 years old
10. land and stock other property
11. no
12. 3.h.d. (300 hundred acres?)
13. sed to be worth 25 thosend it is a soled bed of cole (coal?)
14. log 4 r and cook house
15. farmer all worked yes. white boys and white men worked sum got
    their living buy haird labor
16. My Ma made our close. spining weaving _iling and sewing. My father
    dun all sorts of work
17. few
18. yes
10. yes
20. very few
21. they was all sochebel with each other
22. yes sir
23. yes
24. yes sum times
25. yes
26. he was encureged
27. (can't make out answer)
28. dont rember
29. we lived close
30. generley 1
31. publick
32. 3 months
33. yes
34. man we had no woman techers
35. august 16th 1862 was Celiner (Celina?) tenn.
36. to the armey fares ____
37. very short time
38. Mupherdville Ky whiped 75 to 1
39. i got hurt and wente hom on ferlr (furlough) and staid on whil and
    then returned to the armey. served til discarged (discharged)
40. in Miltneck(?) 64 in ____ parte
41. footed they tuck my horse war was not over
42. farming
43. wel i ben farmer Book agent and veris other slaesman i Recken wil
    ring off yes you cante read it
44. ----
45. A.C. Masters, Celina, Tenn.; H.G. Tinsley, Hermitege Springs, Tenn.
    G.W. Daley?, Celina, Tenn. about all ded.
46. wel i had beter stop. What will i get out of this i dident eny
    pension. We hav a borde that wood ruther pension a man worth 20
    thousand then a pore men ____ ____ it Rite now, from S.W. Atkinson

AUSTIN, GEORGE W.

FORM NO. 1

1. George W. Austin, Sardis, Tenn.
2. 78
3. State Miss. disrember county
4. Texas - Red River County

AUSTIN (cont'd.):
5. farming
6. farming
7. not any
8. no
9. no
10. ----
11. log 2 rooms
12. plowed hoed sawed chopt
13. cooking spinning and weaving
14. no
15. yes
16. yes
17. every body worked
18. most of them did
19. they did not mingle much the slave holders feld a little better
20. thye were frendly
21. I dont know as it did
22. it was
23. Discourage
24. A Pay school
25. 18 month
26. ¼ mile
27. ----
28. Privat
29. 3 months
30. yes
31. man
32. Dec. 1861 Vanburn (Van Buren?), Ark.
33. Second Arksaw Co. G - Captin Cawhorn. 2 Hapins Boy 2 Story Boys
    Van Nash, Burtrum? Selavant, Billie Deton
34. Elk Horn. Ark.
35. 10 days
36. Battle of Elk Horn
37. Next battle was Richmond Ky. next Atlanty Ga. Camp Jackson Miss.
    Franklin Tenn. Nashvill Tenn. I was sorry fead. My clothing was
    mighty bad my far(e) was bad all through the war
38. neare Raligh North Carliner
39. When i started home I got sich in Miss. Was in care of a Dr. 7 week.
    I travel a foot i walked from Raligh N.C. to Montgomery, Ala.
40. farming
41. I have lived in Tenn. except 9 yr. in Texas. My ocupation has been
    farming. never held a office
42. Andrew Jackson Austin; Scoats (Scotts) Hill, Henderson co., Tenn.;
    lived at Scoats Hill
43. Elisbeth Smith (I dont remember)
44. I dont rember my grandparents and grate grand parents. They lived
    in .C.
45. & 46. not on film

AUSTIN, J. T.

FORM NO. 1

1. J. T. Austin, Portland, Sumner co., Tenn. R. #2
2. 84 yrs.
3. Tennessee Sumner Co.
4. Tennessee Sumner Co.
5. Farming
6. Farmer
7. no land two horses and 1 cow and a fiew hogs. Three hundred dollars
8. my Father owned 1
9. 200
10. Two Thousand Dol.
11. Logg House 5 rooms
12. Farmer Plowed and hoed
13. He was a farmer. My mother cooked spun and wove
14. No
15. Yes

244

AUSTIN (cont'd.):
16. Yes
17. The majority worked
18. Yes-No
19. Yes
20. They wer Friendly
21. No
22. The opertunity was not good
23. Incouraged
24. Country schools
25. not over two years
26. 1 mile
27. Austins and Nolins
28. Private
29. about three
30. No
31. Man
32. Year 1861 Oct. 19 at Gallatin - Confederate
33. 7 Batalion Tenn. Cav. Col. Jas. Bennett in twelve months we reorgan-
    ized and Col. C.R. Bartian was Col. Second Tenn. Cav. Names - J.M.
    Jink?, P.H. Corkran, Tom Wilkison, C.W. Wilkison Post Office Cotton
    Town, Tenn. R #2. Those or all that I know is living
34. To Gallatin Tenn
35. 6 months
36. Shilow
37. Hard. Times as we had no tents and but little to eat. Corrinth
    Miss. Brices Cross Road Harrisburg Ocolona Birmingham Paliglts?
    ___ These wer in Miss. Fort pillow Big Sandy Johnsonville Franklin
    Murphesborough Those or in Tenn
38. Gainsville Ala. May 10, 1865
39. Started from Gainsville the 11th and arrived home 23 of May we wer
    treated kindly by the people
40. Farming
41. I was Deputy Sheriff 6 years and ingaged in Farming again Sumner Co.
    near Portland Tenn. General Baptist
42. John Austin; Albermarl Co., Va.; Born 24 day of April 1807
43. Rhroda Groves (Graves?); Isic Groves (Graves?) and Mary ____; lived
    in Robertson co., Tenn.
44. ----
45. ----
46. ----

                              AUSTIN, JAMES

FORM NO. 2

1. Jas. Austin, Limestone, Tenn. R 2
2. 82 years
3. N.C. Yancy (Yancey) County
4. Confederate Soldier
5. B - 29 Regiment
6. Farmer
7. Sam Austin; North Carolina; Yancy county, N.C.
8. Carlina Banks; Andy Banks and Rachel Banks
9. ----
10. I own 150 acres land at the beginning worth about $500 at that time
11. ond (owned) no slaves
12. ----
13. ----
14. log house 4 room house
15. farmed hoed cradle plowed grubed choped wood cleared new ground
16. father farmed mother carded spun wove cloth cooked wash dishes made
    clothes washed clothes
17. none
18. as respectable as noe
19. yes
20. wasent as idle men then as there is now
21. sosated with one another just the same

AUSTIN (cont'd.):

22. yes
23. yes
24. yes just the same
25. yes
26. encourged
27. free school 3 month
28. about 9 month
29. 2 mile
30. free school no high school
31. public
32. 3 month
33. yes
34. man
35. in the year of 61. April best to my memery
36. Ashville, N.C.
37. 11 month
38. gun fight and canon
39. Azua? river a little fight from ther to Alabamy a fight there day and
    night won in fight fought one place 2 day and night one day fight at
    Walnetrige 3 days and night fight at comland gap 6 day fight pretty
    well clothed and fed
40. in 65 at fort della ware
41. ----
42. farming
43. havent bin in good health since the war had bad eyes and a bad cough
    since the war and cant hear none a tall hardly and I ant able to do
    any work a tall jest poke about with a cane
44. ----
45. John Robson, Young Robson, Robbert Roumple, Berry Creecemen, Press
    Blankinship, Cpt. Bert Creeceman, Ed Mack, John Mack, Ed Honeycut,
    Joe Honeycut, Cling Austin, Merian Forgson, Mack Will Young, Ed Austin,
    Sam Austin, Will Medcalf, Abson Medcalf, Elac Angle, Will Angle, Jim
    Angle, Sam Randol, Nis? Randol, Drue? Bradford, Tom Bradford, Sam
    Brackson, Tom Brackson, George Gardner, Tom Gardner, John Allen,
    Hyram Allen.
46. ----

AUSTIN, ROBERT

FORM NO. 1

1. Robert Austin, R.F.D. No. 1 Sparta, Tennessee
2. 89
3. White County, Tennessee
4. White County, Tenn.
5. Farming and working in Blk Smith Shop
6. Farming
7. I had one horse and two or three yearlings and a few hogs worth about
    $200.00
8. Yes Fifteen or Sixteen
9. Yes Six Hundred and forty acres
10. Twenty thousand or more
11. Log house three rooms
12. plowed and hoed in the field with slaves. we did all kinds of farm
    work together.
13. My father kept cattle on the Mountain - Ride out and looked after
    business in a general way. My mother cooked, washed for family and
    wove cloth made it into coats shirts briches wearing apparel of all
    kinds.
14. No
15. Yes they rooled up their sleeves and pitched into it. They cleared
    land and had big log rollings and a big jug of whiskey to boot and a
    big dance at night also the women had quilting during the day
16. Mixed up both whites and black at their work
17. Not many. Most all whitemen worked as well as the black
18. Yes they mingled with those that did not have slaves. They were
    sociable with each other and seemed to enjoy life better than they do
    now.

246

AUSTIN (cont'd.):
19. All upon a footing of equality. The young ladies would go to school
    and church barefooted. They did not dress then. They wore cotton
    and linsey dresses home made and spotted dresses of their own make.
    Young barefooted Briches rooled to their knese Jeans pants shoo fly
    and cotton.
20. yes they were friendly
21. I think not
22. Yes
23. Encouraged by those owning slaves
24. Free school white of course. Sometimes the teacher would come in
    drunk and the school boys would take him to the creek and duck him in
    the middle of the day
25. Two or three months
26. Half mile
27. The house had no name. A man by the name of King Kept it when he
    was sober enough.
28. Public
29. Three Did not have much school s then
30. Yes
31. Man
32. I dont recollect the yr. and month but enlisted at Sparta White
    County Tennessee
33. Eight Tenn. Cavalry D.L. Smith, Halliard Wilhite, Wm. Lowery,
    Lafayette Quarles, Henderson Clark, Wash Miller, Dave England, James
    Coakley, John Walker
34. Frankland near Nashville
35. Three or four months. It was at a place called Triene? in which the
    Yanks were victorious. Dibrell had to send about 60 of his men home
    till they got well
36. ----
37. After the battle of ____ (see answer to Q. 35), we went to Rome, Ga.
    and returned to Tullahoma and met the Yankees coming out from Nash-
    ville and we brought them clear over to Chattanooga. After this
    we made arrangements for battle at Chickamauga which was a heavy
    battle. It lasted four days and nights. We cleaned them up. Heavy
    loss on both sides. From there to Sweetwater Valley and we cleaned
    them up and went from there to Knoxville. We were engaged two days
    in battle. We whipped and starved them out. Thence to S.C. a fought
    a little. We laid out. Our clothing were very good. Exposed to
    cold, hunger and disease. We took a good many off of dead yankies.
    We would kill a hog or a calf on our way part of time. It was very
    muddy disagreeable. Sleep out on cold ground from which we suffered
    considerable. Discharged at Washington, Ga. I dont remember yr.
38. (see above)
39. We rode a part of the and walked part. the 1st day I walked 45 miles
    and the next day I was so sore I did not try walking. I hired an old
    poor horse from a negro and rode ten miles and walked bal. way home.
40. Working in corn field Stilled some and first one thing than another
41. Farming, Blk. Smith Shop, White., Tenn. None. None
    (End of his return)

AYDELOTT, WILLIAM CLANENT

FORM NO. 1

1. William Clanent Aydelott
2. 79 years
3. Maury Co., Tenn.
4. Maury Co., Tenn.
5. Printers "Devil"
6. Farmer and carpenter
7. owned no property
8. family owned no slaves
9. 40 acres
10. farm worth about $200.00
11. hued log house, 3 rooms
12. up to my 15th year worked on farm

AYDELOTT (cont'd.):
13. My father worked on farm and did carpentering at times for neighbors.
    My mother was a mid wife and sister. Spun thread and wove various
    kinds of cloth.
14. No servants
15. All honest toil was considered honorable
16. With few exceptions slave holders sons worked on the farm
17. There were very few idle men in our community in my early days
18. In my community slave holders were social with the upright noneslave
    holder.
19. They did with a few exceptions
20. Always a friendly feeling between the 2 classes
21. Too young to answer intelligently
22. It was a hard struggle to save up money in my early days
23. Generally encouraged
24. I attended school about 2 years all told sometimes public school
    and sometimes subscription school
25. about 2 years
26. From 2 to 4 miles and had to walk
27. Short term neighborhood schools say from 2 to 4 months
28. Sometimes public and sometimes private
29. Two to five months sometimes longer
30. No
31. Woman sometimes and then a man sometimes
32. May 2nd, 1861, at Columbia, Maury County, Tenn.
33. 2nd Tenn. Company; W.B. Bates Colonel commanding. My company was
    officered by: W.J. Anderson Capt., W._. Reed 1st Lt., Ed O'Neill
    2nd Lt., G.A. Jones? 3rd Lt., There is living to day of our old Co.
    Ed O'Neil, Charles Reynolds, Henry ____ , T.J. Steward, W.A. Smith
    and myself
34. Fredericksburg, Va.
35. Three months, July 2st 1861
36. First Battle of Manasas, July 21st, 1861
37. On Feb. 14, 1862 we re-enlisted in Va. and come back to Tenn. and
    about that time Fort Donaldson fell and we assembled at Corinth, Miss.
    and reorganized and on April 6th or 7th 1862 fought in the battle of
    Shiloh. It is impossible to answer the above question as fully as I
    would like to.
38. Charlotte, North Carolina
39. Was a hard one. I had captured a Yankee just 3 or 4 days before.
    He surrendered and had taken 3 or 4 from him (money?) that helped
    to buy something to eat for myself and 2 or 3 friends.
40. Printing business
41. Followed the printing trade most of my time, held no office.
42. Joseph Aydelott; cant answer; lived at McCain's Tenn.; two old for
    military duty.
43. Susanna Gilmer; Joseph Gilmer; dont know; near McCain's
44. My grandparents were Scotch Irish extraction and was amont the early
    settlers of Maury county and settled about 6 miles south of Columbia
    and cut the cane on their first homestead in the county. I was
    wounded at Shiloh Richmond Ky. Perryville Ky. and Chickamauga. Tenn.

AYMETT, JOHN M.

FORM NO. 2

    Notation at top of form: "When copied please reture to Mrs. J.A.
    Loyd, Pulaski, Tenn."

1. John M. Aymett, Pulaski, Tenn. R.D.D. 4
2. Eighty years Feb. 9, 1922
3. Giles co., Tenn.
4. Confederate
5. A-Entered army in 3rd Tenn. under Jno. C. Brown transferred to 53rd
   Tenn. Reg. when my brother Hance Hamilton Aymett was made Major of
   53rd Tenn. Reg. Was tranferred to 1st Tenn. Reg. just before close
   of war. Was made Sargt. Major.
6. Farmer
7. William (Jerre) Aymett; Newbern, N.C.; lived near Pulaski, Giles co.,

AMYETT (cont'd.):
Tenn.; served apprenticeship in shipyards at Philadelphia, Pa. was highly educated, decidedly literary.
8. Louisa Jane Hamilton Amyett; Hance Hamilton and Mary (McNairy) Hamilton dau. of Francis McNairy.
9. ----
10. ----
11. Yes twelve or more
12. Yes. 316 A.
13. ----
14. Frame house, three rooms
15. Worked hard on farm, ploughed and worked with hoe, in fact did all work necessary to making my crops
16. Father ran the farm. Mother did household duties, including cooking spinning and weaving. Directed.
17. Yes 8 or 10
18. Everybody worked and this was considered respectable and honorable
19. Yes
20. ----
21. ----
22. ----
23. ----
24. ----
25. Yes
26. ----
27. Mixed country school
28. 2 or 3 years
29. 2 or 3 miles
30. ----
31. Public
32. 3 or 4 months
33. Fairly
34. ----
35. May 16, 1861 at Pulaski, Tenn.
36. ----
37. ----
38. ----
39. Came home with J.W. Butler arrived about midnight went without waking mother and father.
40. at Charlotte, N.C. at the close of war
41. ----
42. farming
43. I have lived since the war where I was born in the 8th Civil District of Giles Co. on Leatherwood Creek 5 miles East of Pulaski. Have been a farmer all my life. I belong to the Methodist Church. I served a no. of years as Commissioner of the County Poor House and was a director in Peoples Bank at Pulaski until I resigned last year. I came home from the war without anything but a horse. I began farming and raising cotton, Corn, Hogs, and Cattle. Ginned for the public. Threshed wheat for the public. I own a good farm and owe no money. "People say I have made a success financially."
44. ----
45. L.E. Abernathy, R.L. Culps, G.W. Elder, F.M. Bunch, J.D. Flautt, E.F. Aymett, T.S. Pittard
46. L.E. Abernathy   Pulaski, Tenn.
    Lee Smith   "   "
    G.A. Pope   "   "
    W.N. McGrew   "   "
    Ed Adkins   "   "
    J.M. Hardiman   "   "
    Ed. Cox   "   "
    R.L. Culps   "   "
    J.M. Patterson   "   "
    Jim Tidwell   "   "
    S.F. Wilson   "   "
    A.E. Abernathy   "   "   R. 5
    F.M. Bunch   "   "
    J. Press Abernathy   "   "
    J.R.D. Willians   Aspen Hill R 2 Tenn. (R.F.D. No. 2)
    Dr. R.N. Herbert   Aspin Hill

AMYETT (cont'd.):
```
    T.J. Ray                Elkton, Tenn. R.F.D. (Bryson on 2nd copy)
    T.L. Ham                     "
    T.A. King               Aspin Hill
    G.M. Rothrock           Memphis
    J.S. Poag               Nashville
    J.K.P. Blackburn        Lynnville
    T.C. McMahon                 "
    Robt. Bugg                   "
    Mitchell Davidson            "
    Jack Waldrop                 "
    Owen Smith                   "
    Mack Edwards            Prospect
    J.M. Patterson          Pulaski
```

(N.B.: 2 forms returned for Mr. Amyett: one handwritten and one
typed. There follows another one basically same as above.)

BAGLEY, CHARLES BOYLES

FORM NO. 1

1. Charles Boyles Bagley
2. 78
3. Tennessee, Lincoln County
4. Tennessee, Lincoln County, Enlisted in the Confederate Service
5. Worked two years on the farm, then apprenticed to a watch maker and
   jeweler to learn the trade
6. merchant
7. did not own land. no property
8. two, old negros
9. only a small house and lot in Fayetteville
10. about $500.00, value of house. a small lot of merchandise, say
    about 4 or 500 $
11. frame house, 4 rooms
12. worked on farm two years, plowing, hoed etc. cut wood in winter
13. Merchant. Mother sewed for other people. My self and a two and
    half year younger brother did what we could to help support the family.
    (Father was very much given to the drink habit)
14. two old negro man and woman
15. My brother and my self worked, so did my mother and two sisters. We
    were as highly respected as any of our towns people. We had scant
    opportunity of schooling.
16. They did
17. Very few. There were very few of those able to live without that
    did so were those that owned land and negros worked and required their
    boys to work also. in fact boys in general were taught to work.
18. Yes honorable men of all classe and occupations fared alike with
    everybody.
19. They did.
20. No distinction made
21. It did not
22. Yes. Many of our poorest boys then are now many of them our wealth-
    iest men. Many of them died leaving good estates.
23. Always encouraged. I was often.
24. Very little of any, a few months free school and a short time pay
    or subscription school.
25. Only a few months (Mother taught us children as far as she could)
26. Only a few blocks
27. F.A. Kickerson kept a school of importance many years ____ during
    my early life and up to the civil war. He was from one of the New
    England States came here in his early young manhood married here,
    volunteered early in the civil war fought the war thru on the
    Confederate side, made a brave good soldier.
28. Both
29. Both Public and Private Schools ran the usual school year as I
    remember
30. A great many did
31. We had both men and women teachers

250

BAGLEY (cont'd.):
32. Fayetteville, Tenn. Summer of 62. June or July. Confederate Army
33. 41st Tenn. Infty. Company C. Capts J.D. Scott, J.R. Finney, B.J.
Chaffin from first to last. Lieuts. Milton B__d, Robt. Askins,
J.W. Davidson, J. Bonison?, Tomp Wilson, Joe English, John A. Formwalt,
James Webb, James Woods, James Woodard, Galon Woodward, Mc Beard,
Ben Beard, Duncan Beard, Sam Beard, J.B. Hill, W. Hill, W. Smith,
Dick Smith, Jack Smith, Bud Smith, Wm. Ellis, Hal McKinney, Jim
McKinney, Chas. McKinney, Wm. McKinney, Jack Delany, Jerry Frauley,
Tim Ward, Martin Cokely, Wm. Gracy, Berry Neece, Joel Neece, Jo
Askins, John Price, Jas. Conaway, Wm. Conaway, Doc Conaway, Arch
Conaway, Wm. Price, Others I cant recall just now. R. Farquarhson,
Col. J.D. Tillman, Lt. Col. Thos. Miller, Maj. (see accompanying
list marked X)
34. Camp Trousdale. I was a recruit joined the Regt. at Corinth, Miss.
after the battle of Shiloh. Most of the Regt. were taken prisoner at
Ft. Donaldson, I joined the Regt. Co. C, after the exchange of Ft.
Donaldson prisoners.
35. we did skirmishing on the _____ from Holly Springs Miss. did some
fighting around Vicksburg Miss late in 62. were then sent to Port
Hudson, La. 1st Jany. 63.
36. on Yazzoo River north of Vicksburg, Miss.
37. Remained at Port Hudson La. from Jan. to last of Aprl. saw the Miss.
Faragut's largest ship burned night of 14th Mar. 63, he was trying to
_____ our works to join Grant at Vicksburg. Adml. Geo. Dewey was a
Lieutenant on this ship at this time, it was burned by hot shot from
a two gun battery which I stood a short distance in the rear of at
the time and saw every shot fired all taking affect not a single shot
missed I was in plain view all the of the engagement. it occured
about midnight I also saw the soldiers and crew jump overboard all
that escaped many dead and wounded were burned with the ship. two
ships got by Hartford and Albetros, not returned? down the river
38. January after the Chicamauga battle, Marshall co., Ala. near
warrenton? the co. site originally.
39. I was severly wounded at Chicamauga taken to Marshall co., Ala. near
Warrington there remained with relatives the summer of 64 - my mother
having heard of my being wounded and taken to Ala. secured an old
condemned horse left Fayetteville at night came over to where I was
swimming Tenn. River dodging the Yankees they had at that time
possession from Tenn River noth. Mother then nursed me until I could
go home
40. For about 2 yrs. after the battle of Chicamauga, I was unable to do
any work of consequence suffering from a wound received at the foot
of Snodgrass ridge late sunday evening Sept. 20th Lt. Col. J.D. Tillman of my Regt. 41st Tenn. was also wounded at same time. he and I
went off the field together.
41. It was about 2 yrs. after the war closed before I was able to work.
I then with my brother engaged in the grocery business (he had gone
thro the war but escaped with out wounds) we did business together
about 40 years
42. R.H.C. Bagley; Guilford C.H., N.C. 1806; Guilford Co., N.C.; lived
at Fayetteville most of his life; his father came to this co in 1809.
43. Eliza Benton Boyles; (about the time of her birth Thos. H. Benton
and grandfather were friends): Charles Boyles, and Mary Old of
Amelia Co., Va. not far from Richmond; lived at Fayetteville at time
of his death.
44. In 1735 great grandfather came to America from North of Ireland was
of Scotch-Irish extraction, so tradition in our family has it. My
grandfather on father's side was Elisha Bagley, born in Guilford, N.C.
in 1764 named for his father Elisha Bagley a Capt. during the revolutionary war on the American side. My mothers grandfather Barnabus
Boyles was of Scotch Irish lineage also was in Ky. during the time
Daniel Boon was. Married in Ky. and moved to French Lick before Nashville was made name of the place-lived on the opposite side of the
river from the lick sometime after Nashville was named then moved
further out to where Franklin now stands game becoming scarce around
Nashville he was a hunter and when game began to get scarce around
Franklin he was living there.

BAGLEY (con't):
On letter head from The First National Bank, est. 1873; F.M. Bledsoe, Pres.; W.G. Cowan, Vice-Pres.; R. Ed. Feeney, Cahsier; J.J. Moyers, Asst. Cashier and C.F. Bagley, Asst. Cashier. Capital $60,000.00-Surplus $40,000.00 Fayetteville, Tenn.

37. after leaving Port Hudson latter part of Apl. our command went to Jackson Miss. thenice to Raymond 11th May and fought the battle of Raymond on 12th May 63. Our brigade (Greggs) held back a division of Grants forces all that day giving time for Joseph E. Johnson to get ____ Jackson we that night fell back to Jackson joing Johnson. Johnson moved immediately to canton causing Grants forces to go back towards Vicksburg. Our movement was then towards Yazzoo and big black rivers as we understood his (Johnson's) movements were to try to open a place in Grants forces to let Pemberton get out of Vicksburg, - the morning of the 4th July we moved rapidly towards Jackson arriving there just in time to take our positions in the works around the city before the federals arrived then we engaged them for 8 days and night. before we were forced to evacuate the place. our brigade was then sent to Enterprize Miss to recuperate there we remained until the latter part of Sept. being ordered ____ via Mobile Montgomery and Atlanta to Chicamauga. I am sorry I am not able to do better than this but know you will look over my imperfections.
very truly, C.B. Bagley Mr. G.W.D. Partin? Fayetteville Route - could give a lot of war history and I am sure he would be glad to assist you.

44. in that region when Franklin was organized, he moved further out on the frontier and located on Elk river 8 miles west of Fayetteville. before Fayetteville was located and died there. my grandfather on mother's side Charles Boyles occupied some official Co. position in Davidson and Williamson Cos. moving to Fayetteville after having married Mary Old at Franklin where 3 children William, Martha and Eliza BEnton Boyles (my mother's maden name) were born, after coming to Fayetteville he assisted in organizing Lincoln county with Thos. H. Benton and others.

41. I and all my family are members of the U.S.A. Presbyterian Church. Served 6 yrs. as one of our Poorhouse Commissioners - am now and have been one of our Co Judge? since 1906. have held no other office of honor and profit.

BAKER, LEANDER K.

FORM NO. 2

1. Leander K. Baker, Alamo, Tenn.
2. 92 years old
3. N.C. Roan County
4. Confederate
5. E-7th Tennessee
6. Farmer
7. Mosie Baker; Saulsbury, Roan co., N.C.; lived at Boliva(r), Hardamen co., Tenn. after 1845; none
8. Safira Coon; Mical Coon and (dont know); Saulsbury, N.C.
9. My grand fathers both came from Germany
10. none
11. no
12. about 100 acres when the war broke out
13. $300.-0
14. log house two rooms with puncheon floors
15. worked on farm plowed an stur? part of the time hoed cleared land etc.
16. worked on farm all kind of farm work. my mother done the cooking carded and spun & wove all cloth for our clothes
17. none
18. yes
10. yes
20. none

BAKER (cont'd.):
21. men who owned slaves did not mingle with those who did not own slaves. they seemed to think themselves better than those who did not own slaves.
22. The slave holder had private schools for his children. All went to the same churches
23. In some there was a friendly feeling but mostly there was not
24. yes
25. no
26. discouraged
27. a Private
28. about 4 months a year 2 in the summer and 2 in the winter
29. about 1½ mile
30. none but subscription schools in a log house with puncheon floor, seats made out of split logs
31. private
32. about 4 months a year
33. no
34. man
35. I enlisted the first year of the war at Bolivar Hardeman county Tenn. in the Confederate army
36. Columbus, Ky.
37. I dont know the first battle I was in was fort Donelson
38. Fort Donelson Tenn.
39. I dont know all the battles I was in. I was in Shilo, Hernando, Cross Roads, Miss. We had very few clothes. Slept on the ground and at times had very little to eat. I went 9 days and had but one biscuit during the time. Was marching all this time. There was at the start 147 in my company at the close there was but 9 of them living.
40. Corinth Miss. after the surrender of Lee.
41. I was at home when Gen. Lee surrendered. Was crippled by a runaway team and sent home
42. farming
43. After the war in 1867 I married Bettie Fulgun, the daughter of Rolf Fulgum. From this union there were 6 children born 4 boys and 2 girls. There is now living 2 boys and one girl. Been farming all the time. Mooved from Hardeman county to Crockett county about 26 years ago. My wife died 35 years ago last Sept. I made a crop myself Do the plowing, hoeing, etc.
44. ----
45. I cant remember but few names of my Company - dont know where the Roster is.
46. Bill Taylor   Boliva(r), Tenn.
    Dr. James Neely   "   "
    Bob Webb   "   "
    Hugh Branch   Alamo, Tenn.
    J.C. Smothers   "   "
    James Baldridge   Bells, Tenn.
    T.J. Evans   Alamo, Tenn
    P.B. Nance   "   "
    T.N. Skelton   "   "

                    BAKER, WILLIAM P.

FORM NO. 2

1. William P. Baker, Gallatin, Tenn.
2. 79? 8 months
3. Sumner co., Tenn.
4. Confederate
5. F - 30th Tenn.
6. a Farmer
7. Isaac W. Baker; Gallatin, Sumner co., Tenn.; Gallatin, Tenn.; a farmer during the war.
8. Mary C. Hines; Judge Pleas Hines and _____: Bolling Green, Ky.
9. ----
10. no property
11. Parents owned 12 or 15
12. They owned about 325 acres

BAKER (cont'd.):
13. about $3000.00
14. a log house 2 rooms
15. worked on the farm plowed and hoed
16. My father was a tinner? by trade and worked on the farm; were cooking, weaving and spinning general house worke
17. They kept 5 or 6 servants
18. it was highly considered and honerable
19. They did
20. most all were engaged at some kind of work
21. They all associated together generally
22. most generaly on equality
23. There was a friendly feeling between them all
24. I think not
25. Were poor oppertunities
26. They were looked upon with some encouragement
27. county mixed school but not in color
28. about seven years off and on
29. about 1½ miles
30. White School
31. Public school
32. From 6 to 9 months
33. Fairly well
34. Sometimes by a man sometimes by a lady
35. in May 1861 at Gallatin, Tenn. in Confederate Army
36. at Red Boiling Springs
37. several months
38. at Fort Donaldson on Cumberland river
39. Went to Camp Buttler Springfield, Illinois and then went to Vicksburg, Miss. I was fairly well fed and clothed. When captured at Fort Donaldson was put aboard of and old stock boat, sent to Camp Buttler Illinois.
40. I was wounded at the fall of Atlanta, Ga. July 22, 1864.
41. ----
42. come home when the war closed and walked on cruches for sevel(several) years
43. I followed farming some times and then I traveled for several years as salesman for the Deering Harvester Co. I was thereafter appointed as custodian and manager of the Tenn. exhibit at the St. Louis Worlds Fair in 1904.
44. Some great men and McMillon governor of Tenn. E.W. Carmack, J.B. Frazier, B_dton? McMillon, col. J.J. Turner all of Tenn.
46. Capt. W.T. Sample   Saundersville, Tenn
    Capt. C.S. Douglass   Gallatin, Tenn
    W.D. Green   El Paso, Texas
    W.J. Mitchell   Cotten Town, Tenn.
    T.D.(S.?) Ellis   Gallatin, Tenn.
    J.K. Miller   "   "
    J.G. McKim?   Hendersville, Tenn.
    Fine Bruce   Station Camp
    Tom Dorris (Davis?)   "   "
46. ----

on extra pages:
Greg's Brigade - after the skirmish we continued our march to Lopper? ford and while in campt there we was ordered to Granado to go on review at that place at time of Jeff Davis was there to review the army and while there we was ordered to Vicksburg and was put on train and proceed by Jackson and Clinton Miss to Vicksburg on our arrival we was ordered to meet the enemy that was landing at Chic__ son Buro? on the 29'dec. 1862. Battle opened at Dalton May 7 fought Resaca 11 & 12 Kingston 14 & 15 Pine Mountain __ Gen Polk killed with cannon ball at time he Gen J. and Gen. ___ were viewing enemys line Kinnasaw Mountain and July 3 & 4th Marietta July __ crossed Chattehoochie River July 12 Gov. (Gen.?) Johnson relieved July 18 Hood place in command then the cutting slashing and killing commenced and I was shot on July 22nd ___ but Maj. Genl Walker was ___ and Maj. Genl. McPherson. There are a few papers I send you hope you got something out of them and if I had any information I can give you will be glad to do so, your friend, W.P. Baker

254

BAKER (cont'd.):
    written on side of paper: Clint Taylor, John Miller and Len Baldwin

BALDRIDGE, WILLIAM T.

FORM NO. 1

1. William T. Baldridge, Martin, Weakley co.
2. 87 years
3. State of Tennessee, Weakley county
4. Weakley county, Tenn.
5. farming
6. farming
7. I had a horse and buggy worth about $200 and about four hundred dollars in money
8. They did not and no member of the Baldridge family ever owned slaves
9. none (see Q. 10)
10. He owned 70 acres of land and enough stock and implements to work it
11. He lived in a log house up to and during the war but built a frame house soon after the war.
12. I worked regularly on the farm, doing kinds necessary. My father and his boys did all the farm work necessary to support his family
13. My father did all kinds of work on the farm, and my mother did her own house keeping, including cooking and as large part of the time spun and wove cloth to make clothes for family.
14. No, they had none at all
15. The man who worked for his living and was honest and upright had the very highest rating, and was highly respected by every body, and no man lost caste on acount of being a working man
16. yes
17. There were none, except as they do now. There were of course some lazy idlers and always will be. They was no class of this kind only individual cases
18. They mingled with equality. There was no aristocrisy
19. They did
20. There was
21. No
22. Yes
23. Encouraged
24. Private country schools
25. about six months
26. about one mile
27. private schools in a small way, between crop - making periods
28. private
29. about 3 months
30. fairly so, during these intervals
31. generally men but sometimes were taught by woman
32. July 1861
33. Company A, 31st Tenn. Infantry
34. To Camp Price and from there to Columbus, Ky. We got there first after the battle of Bellmont.
35. Island No. 10 about month or two
35. We fought next at Corinth, Miss.
37. We went from Corinth to Chattanooga Tennessee going by way of Mobile. We went from Chattanooga to Perryville, Ky. having three or four skirmishes in the way. We faught at Perryville. We went from Perryville, Ky. to Knoxville, Tenn. From Knoxville we went to Murphreesboro, Tenn. at which place we fought the battle of Stone's River From Murfreesboro went to Chattanooga. We engaged in the battle of Chickamauga and Missionary Ridge. Immediately after this I was Mustered? to Ford's Command and remained with him until I was captured and imprisoned at Johnson's Island, where I remained until the war ended. We took the oath, after the war ended and were paroled
38. (see above answer)
39. We were furnished railroad transportation to Union City, Tennessee taking us about four days. We were furnished nothing to eat, by the kindness of a citizen of Sandusky, Ohio we were given about two days rations. Which we made out with until we reach Union City, Tenn.

BALDRIDGE (cont'd.):
40. I worked as a farm laborer one year and married and began farming on my own about 1866 and have been at it ever since. I have lived in the same place (farm) since 1866 to present date
41. I have held no office. I have been a member of the Methodist Church nearly fifty years
42. Josiah Baldridge; cannot give date and place; North Carolina; my father and grandfather were farmers; my father was a Methodist, while my grandfather was a Primative Baptist.
43. Jane Melton; Thomas Melton and (can't remember): in Weakley county, Tenn.
44. My great grandfather Daniel Baldridge served entirely throught the Revolutionary war and was given a section of land for his service, which was located near Raulston in Weakley county, Tennessee. My grandfather, Wm. Baldridge served in the War of 1812. My father and uncle fought the Indians some, but were not otherwise engaged in wars.
45. ----
46. ----   W.T. Baldridge

                          BALDWIN, JAMES WOOD

FORM NO. 2

1. James Wood Baldwin, P.O. Address, Rattan, Oklahoma
2. 85 years old
3. Henry county, Tennessee and moved to Texas when 17 at Henderson Co., Texas
4. Confederate
5. "H" 1st Texas Infantry-1st Regiment
6. Farmer and Stockraiser
7. Lewis Baldwin; Knox co., Tenn.; marryed in Williamson County and moved to Henry County, Tenn.; he moved from there to Arkansas and then to Texas.; was in the War of 1812 and served under Andrew Jackson
8. Elizabeth Click; John Click and Dorcas Click; lived in North Alabama in Jefferson county.
9. My great uncles, Aaron Baldwin and Moses Baldwin were in the Revolutionary War; my grandparents on the Baldwin side came from Scotland; and my mothers parents came from Holland.
10. None owned
11. My father. Lewis Baldwin owned about twelve slaves; I owned none
12. My father owned about half section in Tennessee but sold before war; owned 160 acres in Arkansas during War.
13. His land and stock at the opening of the war was worth about $3000.00
14. Log house with 3 rooms
15. I farmed myself. I plowed, hoed, drove teams and tended stock at the opening of the Civil War.
16. My father was a farmer. He operated a stock farm; plowed; hoed and graded and classed stock. He did much of the work himself but had some help from his slaves and family. My brothers and half brothers helped him on the farm. My mother did part of her house-work, but had some help with slaves; she wove and spun cloth and made all of our every day clothes, flax, cotton and woolen.
17. None outside of their slaves
18. All of this class of work was considered honorable and respectable in our community and most of the white people in my community, ever the large slave holders and land owners did work on the farm together with their own children.
19. Yes. They did this work together with their sons and had the help of their slaves
20. In my community the slave owners, ever the large slave owners, did not hold themselves aloof from the poor and they mingled with them and the poor were considered and respected and mingled in the same society.
22. They did
23. There were friendly and the slave holders in many, many cases were ready to help their poorer neighbors and associated themselves together.

BALDWIN (cont'd.):
24. No, not the fact that a man was not a slave holder, didn't hurt him
    in a political contest; the only draw back to the man who did not have
    slaves would be he might not have as much money with which to make
    his campaign as the others. It was a man's merit that won for him
25. Yes the opportunities for a young man were good. I have known of
    some of the rich men helping young men buy farms by loaning them
    money to buy farms without interest.
26. No they were not discouraged. A young man who was honest and
    virtuous and upright, even though he may be poor and wore ragged
    homespun clothes was looked upon by his friends and even the rich girls
    and boys of the community in exactly the same light as a rich boy.
    Honesty and merit of a young man was what counted in my community
    and the poor ambitious young man had the same chance as the rich.
27. I went to Private schools in a log house
28. I only went to school three months in my life
29. It was three miles
30. This was the only school in my neighborhood; it was not a graded
    school like the present ones, but it gave a good education and
    taught the higher subjects, such as Trigometry and Geometry and etc.
31. Private. And was owned by Prof. J.R. Malone who owned and taught it.
32. It run about ten months in the year.
33. Yes, tolerably regular. The teacher boarded many of the students
    who came from any distance.
34. He was a man
35. We organized a company in Henderson County, Texas. Gov. Sam Houston
    prohibited any troops from going out of the state at this time. But
    we slipped out and chartered a boat at Shreevesport. La. to take us
    to New Orleans where we were mustered in service. We would have
    been arrested by Sam Houston if we were caught trying to leave the
    State, but we slipped out. We were mustered in the service in April
    1861, at New Orleans, La.
36. We were sent to Richmond, Va. We were really not sent, but just went.
37. Just about six weeks
38. First battle of Manasas, at Manasas Junction. Just a few days after
    the battle of Bull Run.
39. From Manasas we went to Dumphries on the Potomac and guarded the
    mouth of Acquire Creek where we spent the winter. The people of the
    country furnished us our clothes; most of them were our own. As a
    whole they good; this winter we were fairly well protected, but
    after that we slept on the ground and were exposed to all kinds of
    weather. We captured a good many dog tents in battles which we used.
    The first year, we were very well fed and drew regular rations consis-
    ting of beef, bacon and good feed, but after the first year we had
    to forage for our eating and ate what we could get, sometimes we
    went without any eating at all for a good while. I was in hospital
    once and captured twice and escaped by jumping from train.
40. I was a scout and got within the Federal lines where I stayed about
    five months and was there when the war ended. I surrendered at
    Frankfort, Kentucky and got my parole there.
41. I went back to middle Tennessee where I had made quite an acquaintance
    during the war and stayed there from May 1865 until November 1865 and
    then went to my home in Texas and went Horseback.
42. I went to farming
43. During the reconstruction and "Carpet Bag" days, I acted as Deputy
    Sheriff in Henderson Co. Texas for 4 years. I resigned and have
    farmed and trucked ever since and am still farming. I came from
    Texas to Oklahoma 1899. I have been and am still a member of the
    Missionary Baptist Church, but am not actively connected with any
    church at this time and do no active church work. I was in every
    battle fought in Virginia up until 1863, to wit: 1st battle of
    Manasas; West Point; Seven Pines; Gaines FArm; Savage Station; White
    Oak Swamp; Malvern Hill. And in Tenn. where I was transferred with
    Hood from Virginia to Tennessee, where I fought in: Chickamaga;
    Houston Olly Creek; Knoxville Tenn. Battle; Atlanta Ga. Battle. I
    cant remember all of the battles as it was all one fight at the last.
    I was ordered by Hood to be a scout and reconoiter and did this on
    horseback. I cut lines of communication, in and around Pulaski,
    Columbia and Murfreesboro.
44. -----

BALDWIN (cont'd.):
45. A.T. Rainey was the first Captain of my Company. He was promoted and made Col. of our Regiment. William Gaston, who now lives in Dallas Texas, was our second Captain. He resigned at Fredericksburg, Va. Bedford Parks was our third Captain and Ike Stephson was our First Lieuteant and R.J. Ro__ was our second Lt. when we were first organized. Amoung the Privates who names I now recall J.E.Hichman (Richman?), H.G. Hickman, Bill Holinsworth, Nathan Hollinsworth, Cole Holinsworth, George Hollinsworth, Jim Tubb, Lark McKinnsie, Jim Evans, John Forster, Bill Foster, Lusk Evans, Tommy Hanks, Brown Hanks, Bob Birdwell, Joe Knight, Bob Rhine, Sam Torrbet, M. Sorge, Bill Gray, Jewett Smith, Bob Tubb.
46. ----

(extra pages):

1

On the 2nd day before the battle of Franklin, while acting as a scout for Gen. Hood, I was directed by him to take twelve men and reconnoiter in the vicinity of Murfreesboro and as near Nashville as I could safely go, for the purpose of locating the enemy and finding out his plans. Of the men who were with me I can now only recall Tom King, Bob Herd, Alf Snell, and a man by the name of Henton. I was instructed after making my tour to report to Gen. Claborne the following morning who would be incamped at Caney Springs. About daylight of the morning before the battle of Franklin we rode into Caney Springs and as we approached it, we discovered that an army was encamped there. Naturally we thought it was Gen. Claborne. However, we soon learned that it was a Yankee outfit. We reconnoitered and located the Marque or headquarters of Gen. Hatch and we diceded to capture the General. We quietly and silently dismounted walked up to the headquarters, disarmed the sentienal, went into the tent and captured the adjutient and his body guard. We then took them out and mounted them on horses which were tied to a corell and carried them to Gen. Hood's headquarters. We also, captured many papers which disclosed their plans and purposes. We met Gen. Hood about fifteen miles from Caney Springs on the road to Columbia. As a part of my reward I captured the parade horse of General Hatch and when we left that section of the country I left the horse with a man by the name of Crisman, who lived near Chapel Hill in Marshall county, Tennessee. After the surrender I came from Kentucky back to Tennessee and Mr. Crisman still had the horse in his possession. He turned the horse over to me and I rode him to Texas.
        (There are many other things that I was connected with during my four years of service about which I might write you but fearing that you may think I am egotistic: and knowing that my personal experiences can be of no value in writing the history of the Confederacy and of Tennessee I will desist from imposing you with them.)

2

During the Civil War I met many of the great men of the War personally some of whom are: I met Gen. Lee personally in 1861 in the winter, at his headquarters near Culpepper Court house in Virginia.
        I met Stonewall Jackson personally at his headquarters I met him frequently.
        I met Forrest, J.A.B. Stuart, Calvary Commander in Va. Joe Wheeler; McGruder.
        I met many of these men by reason of my Scout business and would be ordered from one General to another with dispatches or information which I gathered as a Scout on duty.
        I want to give my opinion as to the soldiers and class of men composing the Confederate Army. I dont believe from what I have read and what I have seen that the chivalry and honesty and upright-ness of the Southern Army was ever equalled by any soldiers or army in the world.
        I think this was shown by the fact that after the war and after they were defeated and came home to a home of ruins and had nothing left they still showed their spunk and chivallry and came around and have made the South the great country it is today.
        I am very interested in your work in preparing a true history of the South and hope to have a copy of the work when it is completed. I haven't told half of my War history and couldn't without writing a

BALDWIN (cont'd.):
    book. I am the father of five boys and one daughter all of whom are
    living and all are big stout boys.
        In 1862, while Gen. Stonewall Jackson had his headquarters near
    Stanton, Va. in the Shenandoah Valley I was on Scout duty. Gen.
    Jackson had been ordered to get in the read of Gen. McClelland. He
    had not communicated his orders to any of his subordinates Generals;
    who were very anxious to know his next move. Gen. Hill and others
    under Gen. Jackson deceided to find out Gen. Jackson's plans and
    Gen. Hill was selected to approach Gen. Jackson and make the inquiries.
    I was in Gen. Jackson's tent when Gen. Hill came in, who saluted Gen.
    Jackson in true military fashion and was in turn saluted by Gen.
    Jackson. Gen. Jackson then asked Gen. Hill his mission whereupon Gen.
    Hill asked what would be the next move. To which Gen. Jackson replied,
    "I do not know". " If my coattails knew I would cut them off." You
    may return to your headquarters and await orders."
        The second day thereafter Gen. Jackson commenced his famous and
    circuituous route to the rear to Gen. McClellan which is not history;
    and which has been recognized by military authorities as one of the
    greatest military marches ever made by an army.
        I refer to the above circumstance for the purpose of illustratting
    Gen. Jackson as I knew him. He took no one into his confidence until
    his plans were completed. I was a scout and in the advanced guard
    from the time we left Shenandoah Valley until he reached the rear of
    McClellan, south of Richmond and I never knew what his intentions
    were; but I obeyed orders with the full assurance that he was
    thouroughly capable of carrying out what ever plans he had made.

                        BALLANFANT, JOSIAH TURNER

FORM NO. 1

1. Josiah Turner Ballanfant, Culleoka, Tenn.
2. 76 yrs. Oct. 1st, 1921
3. Tenn., Maury County
4. Tenn. Maury Co. enlisted in C.S.A.
5. School boy and farmer
6. Farmer and merchant
7. I owned nothing
8. Yes about 8 or 10
9. Yes about 300
10. about $10,000
11. Log house six rooms
12. Went school and did all kinds of work on farm that I was able to do,
    plowing, hoeing, grubing, fencins saturday and during vacations.
13. My Father was a merchant and superintended farm. My Mother super-
    entended all household business and spinning weaving and making
    clothes for family white and black
14. Yes 2 men and 2 women
15. Yes and all that were not doing some kind of work were considered
    lightly
16. Yes
17. None of this kind. All worked phisically able
    (N.B.: the second page of questionnaire is missing with Q.18-33)
34. Camp Cheatham at Springfield, Tenn. then to Camp Trousdale then to
    Bowling Green Ky. then to Russleville Ky. then to Ft. Donaldson
    on Cumberland river
35. about 9? months
36. Ft. Donaldson
37. I went to prison at Camp Douglas (Chicago, Ill.) for 7 mo. exchanged
    at Vicksburg Miss. in Oct. 1862? went Jackson, Miss. - at this place
    was transferred by ____ to 48th Tenn Inftry (Col. Wm. Overhies?) from
    Jackson went Holly Springs Miss thence to Port Hudson, La. - was in
    ____ and in Feb. and 1st May went to Jackson Miss. thence in Big
    Black campaign to rear of Vicksburg thence back to Jackson in battle
    2 days an nights thence to E_tar? prison. We ___ this time we were
    under Brig. Gen. S.R.? Maxey (this Brigade was composed of the 42nd
    and 46th 48th, 49th and 53rd and 58th? Tenn. Regts. and 4th and 30th
    La. and Burwells B____ Texas (Gen. Max__ was since ____ of ___ and

BALLANFANT (cont'd.):
    Gen. W.A. G____was promoted to Brig. Genl. from here were sent to
    Gulf Department?
38. Greenesboro, N.C. in 1865 with Genl. Johnstons army
39. I marched from Greensboro ____ Ashville Tenn. down French Broad River
    and to Strawbery Plains. Flat cars to Chatanooga then ca__ ___ to
    Nashville thence to Culleoka and home got home Friday went to plowing
    Monday morning with yoke of oxen
40. Farming ___ and cultivate 6? acres then commenced teaching school end
    of July and then farming again
41. Taught school about 4 yrs. Farmed balance of ___ and survived?. I
    have followed surveying and farming til present time member of M.E.
    Church 8
42. Charles Allan? Tomlinson; in Ky.; in Maury co. from 8 yrs. of age til
    death at 85 yrs old; too old for the war; was constable and dty
    sheriff of Maury county for 4 yrs.
43. Sallie Daniel Foster; Richard Foster and Betty? Foster; in Maury co.
    Tenn. near Pleasan Grove (now Culleoka, Tenn.)
44. My father's family came from N.C. to Ky. thence to Tenn. My mothers
    family came from Ga. (they were of Irish decent).

(N.B.: the above questions and answers are in different handwriting
from the first part of questionnaire as answered by Mr. Ballanfant.
Perhaps the last section including the father's name as TOMLINSON
belongs to another veteran....cme)

2 extra pages written by Mr. Ballanfant:
"A"- Lieut. Tullis Privates W.B. Sally?, Sam Lee, Jno. Lee, Hes Oden.
James Williams, These were some of the Co. In 1863 in June I was
detailed with many others and formed Capt. J.W. Martins company of
Artilery with Jno. W. Martin Capt. 1st S.S. Sails, 2nd Lt. Joe Mason
and Lt. Hughes. Privates Wes Brown, Frank T. Reid, Chas. Temple,
J.D. Varder, Lemual Zaring, Sam McKay, James Wyatt, James Brigings,
Carvaer (Comissary Seargt.) Wm. Potter (____ Master Sergt.) Clabe
____, ____, Wm. Mathews.
Our command when I joined was in active service and had a special
camp. I was with Gen. Kirby Smith into Ky. this while I was in Cav.?
Col Scott commanding Brig. composed 1st la. Cav. 8?th Tenn. Cav. and
a Ga. regt. commanded by Col. Morisson. I battle of Richmond, Ky.
where I in person captured Gen. Mason? and the command captured Maj.
J____ from here to Covington Ky., Lexington, Ky., Shelbyville and
____ Ky. thence to Greenville Ky. thence to Mur_fordsville? where
the garison surrended thence we came into Tenn. and ____ Tenn. we
became part of Gen. Forests brigade thence to West Tenn. where the
commande took many small garisons? thence back to Midle Tenn. scouting and in battle Thompsons Station thence to N.? Ala. in raid
after Gen. Strait after capture of Strait thence with Army of Tenn.
back to Chicamauga and in that battle thence to Tupelo Miss and then
to W. Tenn captureing many garison ___ also got many recruits and
after wards capturing Ft. Pillow and after these places in June 1864
we were in the battle Brices xroads (crossroads?) and after these
places in June 1864 we were in the battle Brices cross roads and then
in battle of harrisburg Miss where I was seriously wounded in head?
and sent to hospital after getting well I joined Battary again in
last of Sept. 64 in Battle of Sulfur Tressal, Ala. thence along
Tenn. River captureing transports a G_boat (gunboat?) thence to
Johnsonville where we captured more transports and gunbaots and
destroyed large quantities of commissary and quartermasters stores
then joined Gen. Hood in midle Tenn., took part in Battle of Franklin
Tenn. thence to Murphreesboro then joined Gen. Hood on retreat as
w_____ and in battle at Anthoneys hill crossed river at Bain-
bridge Ala going to Varena Miss thence in N Miss skirmishing and
fighting until surrender at Gainsville Ala.
My father: Jno. Ballanfant
Mother: Eliza Turner Ballanfant
Grandparents: Joseph Ballanfant was in War of 1812. Grandmother
Sallie Turner whose father was in Revolutionary war
Since war I on account of trouble of old wounds have been unable to
do manuel labor have done some work in R.R. office but finally had

BALLANFANT (cont'd.):
      to quit that and have done only light work of various kinds Feb. 1922
                     Joe T. Ballanfant

                      BANDY, JAMES HOWARD

FORM NO. 2

1. James Howard Bandy, Trenton, Tenn.
2. 87 years
3. Sumner co., Tenn.
4. Confederate
5. Co. K, 51st Tenn.
6. Farmer
7. Woodford Bandy; Woodford co., Kentucky; emigrated from Ky. and lived
    near Gallatin Tenn.; Esquire and Constable - class leader in M.E.
    Church South
8. Martha Busby; James Howard Busby and Dolly Busby; near Gallatin,
    Sumner co., Tenn.
9. Family came from England and settled in Va. Great Grandfather name
    was George Bandy who was the father of Joseph Wilson Bandy my grand-
    father.
10. Live stock consisting of mules horses cows and hogs. value $600.00
11. My father owned two
12. 80 acres
13. $4000.00
14. Log and frame 4 rooms
15. Did all sorts of farm work such as plowing hoeing and grubbing I also
    when grown taught school in Ill.
16. Father did all kinds of farm work. My mother cooked, washed clothes,
    spun thread and wove cloth in fact made all our clothing
17. none
18. it was
19. they did
20. All white men in my community worked and women too
21. All who owned slaves did not think themselves any better than other
    honest white men
22. They did
23. All were friendly
24. Did not
25. Yes
26. They were encouraged
27. Public and private schools
28. 8 years in public schools and 7 months in private school
29. one mile
30. mainly public schools
31. public
32. 4 to 5 months
33. yes
34. man
35. at Gleason Weakley co., Tenn. in the month of Dec. 1861
36. Henderson, Tenn.
37. 5 months
38. Shilo
39. From Shilo to Tupelo Miss thence to Mobile, Ala. Chattanooga thence
    to Perryville Ky. my second fight - 3rd battle was Peach Tree Creek -
    4th battle was Atlanta fight 5th battle Okalona, Miss. Captured in
    ___ of Atlanta was nine months in prison Camp Chase O.
40. At Camp Chase, O. when the war closed
41. Had free transportation home to nearest town
42. Farming
43. Farmed about 35 years then went into business selling groceries until
    my health gave way since which time I have not been able to do much
    work.
44. ----
45. Capt. Joe Thomason, Geo. Thomason, Pink Word, ___ly Miller, Ten
    Haily, N. Burnett, Henry Burnett, John Hillard (Lillard?), William
    Lillard?, John Jennings, Dolphus Herald?, Geo. Harley, John Harley,

                              261

BANDY (cont'd.):
    John Arnold, L. Arnold, John Dimming, Rob Dimming, Joe Jennings, ____
    Jennings, John Stalcup, John Browney?, Henry Browney?, Tom Starnes?
46. ----

BANISTER, DAVID MONROE

FORM NO. 2

1. David Monroe Banister, Hermitage, Tennessee, Rout 1
2. will be 75 yrs. 15th of June 1922
3. Georgia, Camel (Campbell?) county
4. Confederate soldier
5. Company D, 17th Alabama
6. worked by the day
7. William Banister; dont know; dont know; dont know; raised in Georgia;
    he was in the same company that was that I was
8. Dont know she died when I was 9 mo. old; dont know; dont know; dont
    know
9. Settled in State of Alabama. Dont know anything else about them.
10. I didnt own anything
11. no
12. no
13. Didnt own anything at all
14. lived in log cabin one room
15. Drove a ox team for penitenary Alabama all the plowing I did was with
    oxens
16. My father worked by the day when ever he could get work. Dont know
    anything about my mother
17. no
18. It was considered respectable among the poor class only poor people
    did their own work
19. Only the poor white-slave holders did nothing
20. All that owned slaved did nothing.
21. The slave holders thought them selfs better than the non slave holders
    and did not mix with them.
22. They did not
23. There were not as the slave holder thought him self better
24. I dont remember anything bout that
25. no it was not. The poor people had as poor chance to save anything
26. They were discouraged by slave holders
27. My father paid $1 a month for all the schooling I got
28. about one month, all I learned I learned while I was in the war
29. three miles
30. not very many dont know the names of the schools
31. private
32. I dont remember
33. They did not
34. was a man
35. The year of 1861 month of July Wetumpka, Alabama
36. Mobile, Alabama
37. about 2 years
38. Battle of Shilo
39. I went to penscola after the first battle camped of Mexico Gulf. I
    wasnt engaged in no more battles. We slept on a bunk clothed in gray
    uniform. very little to eat I was in prison in Indanoplis. nothing
    to eat much one loaf of bread ever 24 hrs. a few beans so hungry even
    help eat part of a dog.
40. discharged from prison in the year of 1865.
41. I didnt go back home. I went to Daton, Ohio. I didnt have no home.
    Father was killed in the war.
42. I went to farming
43. Lived in Ohio 11 years from ther to Indiana and stayed there 13 years
    and the remainder in Tennessee. Followed farming ever since the
    close of war. I lost one eye in the battle of Shilo. I was only 15
    years old when I enlisted in the War. Father went and I stood guard
    on penitenary walls before I enlisted in the war.
44. ----

BANISTER (cont'd.):
45. Capt. Hester, Lt. Hull, Lt. Caffy, William Banister, Thomas Ledlow,
    Jones Henkicks, Bulger Ledlow, ___ Roberts, ____ Adkins, Seif Limzy,
    John Peoples.
46. Ben Seaborn   Hermitage, Tenn.
    Kirk Hessey   Hermitage, Tenn.
    James T. Gleaves   Hermitage, Tenn.
    Most of the old soldiers are dead

BARBEE, ROMULUS

FORM NO. 1

1. Romlus Barbee, Statesville, Tennessee
2. 7_ (this number blurred - may be 8)
3. in Wilson county, Tennessee
4. Wilson county St. of Tennessee
5. Farming
6. Black smith
7. No property
8. Father one
9. 15
10. about $1500
11. log house rooms 3
12. All implements of the kind at that day
13. Cooking spining and weaving
14. one until freed
15. yes
16. yes
17. very few they most all worked
18. they did not - they all worked together
19. mingled mixed just they same all to gether
20. no diference
21. one had just as good a how at the office as they other in my community
22. yes he had good chance. most of the young men where I lived was in
    the war and had a hard time
23. incouraged and they helped them
24. county and district
25. off and on for about 15 years
26. 2 miles
27. free and subscription both we had good schools
28. some of each
29. 8 months
30. yes
31. I went to both sex
32. about Jney. (January?) the first 1862
33. Elesson? Shaw and then Bob Wright these main officers; Demps Odum,
    Brit? Odums, Jef Haynes, John Thompson, Yank Thompson, Pake Vantruse,
    Zaid White, Jim Witt, Yergan Tilman, Owen Tilman, Ed Reavs
34. Elexandra, Tennessee
35. 30 minutes
36. tryun?
37. wente from Tennessee to Varginer and from thar to Salt Works Var. -
    thear I was in Battle ____ 12 hours to north Calliner (Carolina?)
    thear in hevey battle thear I was wounded lived very rough in camps
    for days and nights with out any thing to eat an my way home very
    rough part of they (the way) was a foot
38. Washington, Ga. at the close of war
39. Walked from Murfreestown to Cor__ Tennessee 30 nites
40. Blacksmith
41. I have bin a member of Cumberland Church for 30 years. I have bin a
    est___ O____
42. Levy Barbee; comurce, Wilson county, Tenn.; Comerce
43. Polyann Lance; Nettie Lance and Lyle Lee; Commerce
44. My grandfather Joefth (Joseph?) Barbee was born and raised in Tenn.
    Wilson county. was a farmer and a black smith he had slaves they run
    the farm and he run shop worked as long as he lived. owned a big
    farm. that belong to him this is all i know to tell.
                              Romlus Barbee

BARFIELD, M. T.

1. M.T. Barfield, Paris
2. 77 the first day June - R.F.D. #8 Tennessee
3. Green co., North Carolina
4. Green co., N.C.
5. working on the farm
6. Ditching and farming
7. Didn't own any land or property of any kind
8. Didnt own any slaves
9. 20 acres
10. $250.00
11. Log house with two rooms
12. I worked with plow and hoe both
13. Ditching and farming. My mother cooked, spun, wove, clothes and did all kinds of house work
14. No
15. All such work was considered respectable and honorable
16. Yes
17. Rich land owners had other people to do their work
18. some didn't feel themselves any better and some did
19. yes
20. yes generally
21. no
22. not often
23. no
24. small country school
25. 5 months
26. about 3 miles
27. country schools with 2 or 3 months term
28. public
29. 2 or 3 months
30. Some did and some didn't
31. man
32. Sat. before second Sunday in Feb. 1862. Snow Hill, Green Co.
33. Co. C. 67 N.C. regiment. O.J. Tate Capt, John Patrick 1st Lt., J.D. Dixon 2nd Lt., H.E. Stilley 3rd Lt.
34. Went to Camp Shiloh in Eastern N.C.
35. Not very long but don't remember the date
36. Ronoake River
37. Plymouth, Newbern, Kinston, Lost ____ (heavily?), had but few clothes, slept on the ground. little meat and bread. suffered with cold and hunger. some had measles. was in Federal hospital from a serious wound at the close of the war.
38. Kinston, N.C. sometime in April 65
39. walked home, my people were all glad to see me. they had heard that I was killed
40. Farming
41. Farming lived in Tennessee ever since 1871. Baptist.
42. N.B. Barfield; Green co., N.C.; lived always in N.C.; was a private soldier in the Civil War.
43. Clara Rought; Jimmie Rough and (dont remember); N.C.
44. My mothers generations come from England. My fathers generation came from Ireland.

BARKER, JAMES MADISON

1. James Madison Barker, Interstate Building, Bristol, Tenn.
2. 74
3. Sullivan county, Tenn.
4. Confederate
5. B-12th Tenn. Batalion for a short time. Transferred to Capt. Bushking's? Co. of Independent Scouts. Though authorized by the Confederate Government.
6. Farmer

BARKER (cont'd):
7. Joel Nevels? Barker; Washington co., Va.; for 15 years, He was a
   Justice of Peace for 30 yrs. Colonel of a Malicia (Militia?) Regement
   (15 years may imply the time his father was a Colonel - written
   above line...cme)
8. Jamima Kindfuk (Kindrick?) ; ----; ----
9. ----
10. none
11. Four
12. about 200 acres
13. $6000.00
14. First a frame house and afterwards a brick house
15. all kinds of work on the farm
16. My father was a farmer. My mother did all kinds of house hold work
    and spinning and weaving.
17. 4 formerly and 3 later
18. yes
10. yes
20. Most all white men were engaged in some kind of work more so that
    they are noe
21. yes
22. yes
23. yes, a good feeling
24. no
25. yes
26. encouraged
27. subscription schools
28. about six years
29. one mile
30. ----
31. Open to the public, but tuition had to be paid by the parents
32. about six months
33. yes
34. Generally men
35. In June 1863
36. Bulls Gap, Tenn.
37. one month
38. Bulls Gap or Blue Springs
39. Our company was engaged in many skirmishes, but was in battle at
    Russellville, Morristown, Jefferson City (Mossy Creek), Knoxville,
    Strawberry Plains, Lynchburg, Va. Marion, Va. and the last fight was
    at Mooresburg, Hawkins co., Tenn, in which Capt. Bushong was killed
    and half the Co. were killed or wounded among them was myself.
40. At Bristol, Tenn. May 1865
41. ----
42. Farming in summer and in school in winter.
43. After two years on farm I was a clerk in a store at Bristol for
    three years. I then went into a small business, captial $300.00 was
    a merchant until I lost my health in 1889. Then again from 1894 to
    1905, as a wholesale Hardware man in Briston. I was very much inter-
    ested in Public Schools, and was Chairman of the City School Board
    for over 20 years. Resigned this position in 1917. Was a member of
    the State Board of Education for 4 years during which time there
    were four State Normal Schools built. Three for whites and one for
    negroes. The State did not appropriate to purchase sites and contract
    the buildings. I was in the business man connected with the State
    Board of Education and negotiated directly with the authorities of
    a good many towns and cities in order to get land, city and county
    appropriations in order that the buildings might be built.
44. During the Civil War, being a courier for three months I met Gen.
    Mahone, Breckenridge, Hood, Hill, Jones, Vaughan, (Mudwall)Jackson,
45. I think the members of my company are all dead. As far as I know
    except possibly Thomas and John Rogers; Rancy Porter. may be living
    in Texas.
46. William Sullivan   Bristol, Tenn.
    Jame__ P. Rader   "   "
    Elbert Wolfe   Johnson City, Tenn.
    DR. N.M. Reeves   Bristol, Tenn.
    D.F. Bailey   Bristol, Va.
    M.H. Cowan   Bristol, Tenn. R.F.D.

BARKSDALE, HENRY P.

FORM NO. 2

1. Henry P. Barksdale, Milledgeville, Ga.
2. 84 13 of June 1922
3. State of Ga. Warren Co.
4. Confederate
5. Co. E - 9th Tenn., Manneys Bragade Cheatham Division
6. Farmer
7. William B. Barksdale; Warren co., Ga.; lived at Barnett
8. Sylvia Harrell; Chas. Harrell and a (Miss) Boyd; Shelby co., W. Tenn
9. ----
10. Did not own any
11. yes, 35 or 40
12. 6 to 8 hundred
13. It valued 75 to 80 thousand dollars
14. frame house 6 rooms
15. Clerk in a dry goods store in W. Tenn. White men worked better before the war than after.
16. Father was a farmer. Mother's work was raising her children and negro children
17. 4 in house
18. yes
19. yes
20. no
21. they did not
22. yes
23. there was
24. they did
25. good
26. were not
27. country school and college
28. 9 yrs.
29. 1½ miles
30. Pine Grove
31. public
32. 9 mo.
33. yes
34. man
35. Shelby co., W. Tenn.
36. Jackson, Miss.
37. 5 or 6 months
38. Shilo
39. Shilo to Corinth a few mo. then to Chattanooga Tenn. later to Kentucky fought the battle of Perryville left Ky. by way of Cumberland went to Murfreesboro next to Shelbyville 5 or 6 mo. went back in north Ga. fought the battle of Chickamauga next to Dalton, Ga. from there we went to Resaca fought the battle of Resaca.
40. 14 of May 1864 near Resaca, Ga.
41. Several months before I reached home in such a mangled condition
42. teaching school
43. School teacher got along very well since the war. Washington co., Ga. Christian Church attended regularly Poplar Spring. Blanks filled by grand-daughter, Bessie M. Chandler
44. ----
45. ----
46. ----

39. Fought the Battle of Resaca there I lose my right arm and left leg badly mutilated also a wound in left side and that discharged me from the war.

BARNES, ELIJAH C.

FORM NO. 2

1. Elijah C. Barnes, Bluntville, Tenn. Sullivan county
2. 80 years of age 6 day of April 1922

BARNES (cont'd.):
3. Sullivan county, Tenn.
4. Confederate
5. F - 59th Tennessee
6. Farmer
7. William Barnes; Dunlap Creek, Sullivan co., Tenn.; lived at Bakers
   Fall on Halston River; Home Guard in War of '61
8. Rebecca Cross; Elijah Cross and (cant give full name - she was a Cook):
   near Blountville, Tenn.
9. ----
10. Did not own anything
11. none
12. my father owned 60 acres
13. $700.00
14. Log house
15. Farming at home
16. Farming my father did - my mother did all kinds of Domestic work
    cooking spining weaving philinsing flax
17. none
18. yes
19. yes
20. none
21. yes - always sociable
22. yes
23. yes
24. no difference
25. moderate
26. no for there were none to interfear
27. private subscription schools
28. about 2 months in the year
29. 1½ miles
30. subscription schools
31. private
32. about 2½ to 3 months
33. Just tolerable that was owing to how much they had to pay with
34. ----
35. In the latter part of '61 at Bluff City now then Zolacoffer
36. Morristown, Tenn.
37. in the fall of 1862 at Perryville, Ky.
38. above ans. same
39. Came out of Ky. thence Lenor Station Tenn. thence to Vicksburg, Miss.
    surrendered there the 4th of July '62? and paroled and sent home then
    in the fall after the 4 of July was exchanged and sent to the Vally
    of Va. Stanton. then in a fight at Peidmont Va. ordered back to
    Rock Fish Gap from there to Lynchburg thence back to Potomic River
    Arlington Hights thence to back of Washington City trenches then
    back to Winchester Va. Fought several battle there
40. Hillsville, Va.
41. Our trip was bad enough nothing to eat, and no provender for our
    horses to amt. to anything.
42. Digging in the ground to try to make a living
43. Live near Blountville, Tenn. been farming since the war. Held no
    office for the public. I am a Methodist Steward for years.
44. ----
45. Go to pension office in Nashville, Tenn. for reference
46. ----

BARNES, J. W.

FORM NO. 2

1. J.W. Barnes, Troy, Tenn. Obion Co.
2. 76 on the 26 day of June 1922 (26 looks as though it may have been 21)
3. Tennessee Marshall county
4. Confederate
5. Co. D - 4th Tennessee Starnes Regiment
6. Farmer
7. S.F. Barnes; Medium P.O.; Marshall co., Tenn.; lived at Medium; none

267

BARNES (cont'd.):
8. Mary Caldwell Mauldin; Col. Dick Mauldin and (maiden name Johnston);
   Medium, Marshall co., Tenn.
9. Col. Dick Mauldin and wife whose maiden name was Johnston came from
   North Carolina and possibly was of Irish decent. Also Col. Dick
   Mauldin was Colonel in the Mexican War. S.F. Barnes and Mary
   (Caldwell Mauldin) Barnes were also natives of Marshall county,
   Tennessee
10. Did not own anything
11. S.F. Barnes owned one slave
12. 280 acres
13. $3000.00
14. Log House. Two Rooms. One above one below afterward added two rooms.
15. Done most everything a boy could do on a farm
16. Fathers main duty was to see after the farm and have all the work
    done., he being unable most of the time to do manual labor. Mother
    Mary Caldwell Barnes attended all her household duties such as cooking
    in fact every thing connected with house keeping
17. None
18. Honorable and respectable
19. Yes
20. none
21. no
22. yes
23. Friendly as far as I know
24. no
25. Fairly good
26. encouraged
27. Public schools (Primary)
28. Eight years
29. ¼ mile
30. Primary
31. Public
32. from 5 to 8 months
33. Yes
34. mostly
35. Medium Marshall county Tennessee in August 1864
36. First encountered Yankeys in Lawrence and Wayne county then across
    Tennessee river
37. Two weeks
38. Beaver Dam in Hickman county Tenn.
39. Went with Jake Biffel across Tennessee River to Sand Mountains, Ala.
    Were ordered on the Sherman raid through Georgia and South Carolina
    and participated in all the engagements in that campaign under Gen.
    Joe Wheeler. Nothing much to wear and scatly fed and exposure was
    great.
40. At Washington Georgia May 10th 1865
41. Being a cavalry man lost my horse and was compelled to make my trip
    on foot most of the way home and nothing to eat, the country was so
    delapidated no conveniences.
42. Farming
43. Farmed up to 1869 and afterward taken up carpenters trade and follow-
    ed it for about 10 yrs. going to Texas in Jan. 1871 where I remained
    until 1873. Returned to Marshall county, Tennessee in 1873. Worked
    one yr. at the carpenter trade. In 1874 moved to Troy Obion county
    Tennessee and bought a farm in 1876 where I have remained ever since
    and running the farm.
44. ----
45. Capt. Bill Robertson Co.; N.C. Davis, 1st Lt.; Com. Young, 2nd Lt.;
    Ford? Carrouth, 3rd Lt.; Alex. McCurdy, Ord. Sargent; Jim Diser, 2nd
    Sgt.; Privates: Tom Allen, Jack Allen, John Barnes, Geo. Brotherton,
    Geo. Crawford, Tom Dysart, Bob Dysart, Jim Dysart, Lige Davidson,
    Ben Smith, Tobe Smith, Jno. Little, Albert Gentry, Dick Hobbs, Dutch
    Lane, Bill Walker, Fletch Buchanan, Myran Beasley, Frank Sweeney,
    Jiff (Jeff?) Rainey. This is all I can remember. Dont know where
    the Roster cane be found.
46. J.(T.?)R. Inman   Troy, Tenn.
    Jno. Goodman   "   "
    John White   Hornbeak?, Tenn.
    John Cavanaugh   "   "

268

BARNES (cont'd.):
    E.N. Moore   Obion, Tenn.
    Wm. Cunningham   Troy, Tenn.
    Mark Cunningham   Elbridge, Tenn
    Wm. Anderson   Troy, Tenn.
    Dr. F.M. McRill (McRice?) Union City, Tenn
    Bill Massengale   Union City, Tenn.
    Tom Harris   "   "
    Jim Chiles   Obion, Tenn.
    Henry Wilson   "   "
    Alf Moore   "   "
    Jno. Palmer   Union City, Tenn.

                    BARNES, J. W.

FORM NO. 2

1. J.W. Barnes, Antioch, Tenn. RFD #1
2. 79 yrs
3. Williamson co., Tenn.
4. Confederate
5. Co. I 44 Tenn.
6. Carpenter
7. Joseph Barnes; Virginia; Brunswick co., Va.: lived near Nolinsville;
    none
8. Katie Kelly, dont know; dont know; dont know
9. ----
10. None
11. one
12. none
13. none
14. Log house 4 rooms
15. I did all kinds of work that is done on any farm in that day. more
    than half of the work was done by the white men.
16. Father was carpenter. Mother wove spun cook and helped carry on all
    work of house
17. one
18. yes
19. yes
20. some few did
21. some did and some did not
22. some did and some not
23. no
24. I cant say that it did
25. yes
26. no
27. pay school
28. 1 year
29. 2 miles
30. split log
31. publick pay
32. 6 to 8 months
33. yes
34. man
35. I enlisted July 1861 in Davidson county
36. Camp Weekley at Nashville
37. nearly one year
38. Shilo
39. I was in the battle of Mufersburrow (Murfreesboro) Battle Chickanauga
    skirmish battle Mud? River skirmish Battle at Rengole GA Battle Drues
    Bluff was in hospital 3 days from cramp I was in prison at Point
    Lookout Maryland
40. Discharge in prison at Point Lookout Maryland
41. I came 100 miles by boat and the rest of the way to Nashville was by
    rail
42. Farming
43. I went to farming when I came out of the army and have kept it up
    ever since. I am a Missionary Babtist
44. ----

BARNES (cont'd.):
45. Capt. Judge Henry Cook, Ben and John May, Green Moore, John Wright,
    Tom Carper, Pleas Chambers, Geo. Hill, Jim Flippen, Sidney Vaughn,
    Ike Berry, John Moss, John Boyd, Bill Cunningham, John Hoberry, Toose
    Kimes, John and Jim Marshall, Allen Lafouza, Hugh Philips, Jim Hager,
    Jim Shilcut, Loui Hunt, Charlie Boyd, Jim Gant, Harry Mitchell, Sam
    Still, Will Mays
46. Henry Guthrie   Nolinsville, Tenn.
    Jim Guthrie   Antioch, Tenn
    Dick Vernon   "   "
    R.M. Vaughn   Brentwood, Tenn.
    Bud Hubbard   Franklin, Tenn.
    Tom Allison   "   "
    ·Tom Sneed   Antioch, Tenn.
    Tom King   Sta B Flatrock, Nashville, Tenn
    Ben Cook   "   "   "   "

                    BARNES, WILLIAM THOMAS

FORM NO. 1

1. Willim Thomas Barnes, P.O. Median, Tennessee Route No. 1
2. 83 years 9 m. 29.(days?)
3. Lumbirg (Lunenburg) Co., Va.
4. I was living in Madison co. I enlisted in confederacy
5. I was a farmer
6. My father was a farmer
7. I didnt own no land I didnt own no property at all before the war
8. We didnt own no slaves
9. didnt own none
10. My father owned some horses and some cattle. valued at about $400.00
11. four room framed house
12. I plowed howed and done most all kind of farm work
13. My father oversered (Overseered?) most all the time. My mother cooked
    spune wove cloth for the rich people
14. none
15. it was there was lots at sutch work done by white people
16. a good many did
17. some at (of) the rich people was idle some of them worked
18. some of the slave holders did and some didnt
19. thay did not
20. some had friendly feelings and some didnt
21. some did and some didnt
22. a poor man are boy didnt have no opportunities to own a farm
23. thay was discouraged
24. I didnt attend no school as there wasnt no school to attend. - the
    rich class at (of) people harred (hired) thair own teachers
25. didnt go to school
26. about four miles
27. Plesent hill
28. the teachers was hired by the rich but the poor was alowed to go
29. the school went on about four months in the year
30. the poor class of people didnt
31. the teachers was mostly man
32. I enlisted in the confederacy May 1861 at the Presinct 16 district
33. 38 Tennessee regiment company E the members of my company was (this
    is my best reckerlection) 1. Elick Thompson,2. Joe Thompson,3. Harm
    Mullins, 4. P.D. Mason, 5. Plaze Barnes, 6. Jim Cunham(Cunningham?),
    7. L. Mason, 8. John Pouns, 9. Watt Mason, 10. Jim Thompson, 11. Abe
    March, 12. John Thompson, 13. Nute Boone, 14. John Boone, 15. Jim
    Bramblet, 16. John Stanley, 17. P. Rehine?, 18. John Garvy?
34. Two (too) Jackson Tenn.
35. about 10 or 11 months supose
36. East Port Combland (Cumberland) river
37. went to Murphey Tenn. started 6 day fight. Perryville Ky. 10 hours.
    Cumb. Gap 2 hr. Pine MOunting 10 hr. Rockey Face ridge 10 hr. Shilough
    24 hr. I was in the Georgia champaine mostly retreat. faired ruff
    barfooted part of the time. on the ground eny where any eny time.
    we could - we eat eny thing we could get. we was exposed to cold

BARNES (cont'd.):
hungar and disease
38. I was discharged at Greensburogh (Greensboro) N.C. April 1865
39. We was sent to Jonsburogh (Jonesboro?) Tenn. where we got transportation to Johnsville Tenn. we walked from there home. We was furnished
with plenty food cloth was shaby and body lice plentyfull.
40. farming
41. have farmed in Madison county up untill about 1909. when I lost my
eye site and I havent don eny thing since
42. Willim Tomas Barnes; Lunburg, Vo., Va. (probably; William Thomas
Barnes, Lunenburg co., Va.); moved from Lunenburg 1844 to Madison co.
Tenn.; none
43. Rebecka Clark; John Clark and Sallie Clark; in Va.
44. I dont no prackley nothing of my greate grand parents.

(See extra pages below)
37. I inlisted in May 1861. I was in all the engagement that the 38
tennessee Reg. was in during the war. I was wounded sevin times
during the war. I surendered April 1865 at Greensburogh, N.C. I was
the only one ans to the roll call in my company but there was some
come in after the roll call.
33. 19. Wash Wonley, 20. Jim Stanley, 21. John Smith, 22. Ben Auls?,
23. John Codey, 24. Tom Hattaway, 25. Ruff Cocks, 26. Bill Maniard,
27. Jeff Pialet, 28. Grandvile Smith, 29. Ben Lacey, 30. Jim Smith,
31. Frank Smith, 32. John Mathis, 33. Jerry Mathis. I have ans. your
___ usten as to the best of my nolige and rectletions.
Yours truley W. T. Barnes

(N.B.: BARNES, WILLIAM T. Pension No. 5612)

BARNETT, THOMAS ALEXANDER

FORM NO. 1

1. Thomas Alexander Barnett, Cleveland, Tenn. Route 1
2. 88 and 6 months
3. Tenn. McMinn county
4. Tenn. Bradley co., Confederacy
5. farming
6. farming and coopering
7. 120 acres worth 1,000. 2 milk cows 1 wagon and good team horses
besides this I furnished the southern government 3 good horses
regardless of cash dident get any thing for them
8. no sir
9. 160 acres
10. 2 or 3 thousand or more to the best of my judment
11. it was a hewn log house 3 rooms
12. I farmed in general from a boy all my life I plowed began at 10 year
made the crop for eleven my oldest sister Amanda Barnett did the most
of the hoeing had 4 small brothers not old enough
13. my father always farmed and coopered. My mother did the house work
partly and sometimes spin flax my older sisters did a portion of house
work also spin and wove and often would scutch? flax and cut and
sewed we all wore our homemade clothes
14. no sir we all worked from the cradle up
15. it sure was and just lots of it done our neighbors too were more
kind and better co each other those days then msot ___ are now they
ministered to each others needs
16. they did and kept at it untill the war borke out
17. no ones as I can remember every family did their own work no slave
owners in the country round where we lived
18. in some respects those I have seen didnet seem to want to mingle with
others they seemed somewhat? stuck up that is some did
19. to some extent they did
20. there were no slaves owners in our community. John D. Traynor of
Cleveland, Tn. owned slaves also a farm near fathers farm sometimes
he would send out his slaves on the farm a week
21. no sir I coudent see as it did

271

BARNETT (cont'd.):
22. yes they were fairly good many did save up and get started but ___ them selves before the war began
23. I cant say as they concerned themselves either to the best of my knoledge remember that has been a long time and an old man 88 yrs night find ___ how shomething did go off and I want to tell it right
24. just a little district school and very little at that
25. well just cant say but very little learned to read a little and write my name and figure a little
26. between 3/4 and 1 mile
27. there were some more farther away hammond tree school house and the bates school and one at musk rat all I know of in the county
28. public
29. about 3 months
30. the most of them attended pretty regular
31. men always
32. in Oct. or Nov. cant remember definly in the year 62 Cleveland Tenn
33. 4th Ga. George Hughes, Will Airhart, Um_ Bowden, Dave Bearden, Bill Bearden, Jim Cartwright Wisker? Nichols, Jack Dean, Tom__ Cook, Dick Haden, Columbus Coe, Allen Coe, Dick Seaburn, Miles Seaburn, Crabtree Jim Taft Berry Stanton these are all Tennesseans ___ Ed Creekmore and Polk Howl Harry James and one other James man Ga bdg.
34. Sent to Murfreesburogh there were several more I could have named if I had space
35. about a month before the Chickamauga fight I was held out of this on acct of my horses back being so sore
36. the seige of Knoxville was the first regular engagement in a lot of skirmishes I was carried to prison had a very good place to sleep and plenty to eat for awhile but at the last scarcely anything - had very good clothes after I reached prison I dident ___ cold but was powerfully exposed on my way exposed to small pox and other diseases
38. I got out of prison just before the surrender got out on the wounded list and was on my way home ___ reached Kingston Ga at the time of su___ (surrender?)
39. and received my discharge hear well I had many adventurs a to numerus to menten had lots of fun on our way if we hadent we could not have stood it as well as we did I may relate some later
40. I went to farming again and I continued farming just as long as I was able to work. I havent been able to work at all in 25 year. no I never held any office.
41. I never lived in any where out of Tenn. except about 3 year I lived in 5 mile of Cleveland Tenn awhile but for the past 45 year lived here 10 mile of Cleveland
42. William Hazellet Barnett; Knoxville I suppose; Tenn.; I cant say as to this he lived in McMinn where I was born; he did not serve in the war he was not able to work much but farmed what he could
43. Elizabeth Odonald (O'Donald?); have forgot grandfathers name; grandmothers name was Polly but dont remember her sirname
44. My grandparents came from Ireland. My grandfather Barnett fought in the revolutionary war. cant say whether grandfather Odonald did or not. I never heard of them holding any office. our house got burned and old Bible got burned so I cant give much account of their settleng here it was so long ago and most all our families are dead. Just 3 of us boys living. (N.B.: his form was rec'd. Mar. 14, 1922)

(N.B.: BARNETT, THOMAS ALEXANDER Pension No. 4397)

BARRON, JOHN M.

FORM NO. 2

1. John M. Barron, Jonesboro, Tennessee Route No. 12
2. 81
3. Washington county, Tennessee
4. Confederate
5. B-19th Tennessee Rg.
6. Blacksmith
7. Jacob Barron; Jonesboro, Washington co., Tennessee; lived at Douglas Shed

BARRON (cont'd.):
8. Jane Murray; dont know; dont know
9. ----
10. Did not own any
11. Not any
12. About one hundred acres
13. It was valued about four hundred dollars
14. Log house, one room
15. Farming, hoeing, plowing also balcksmith, etc. Did this kind of work about 12 yrs.
16. My father was a blacksmith and the duties of my Mother were cooking, spining, weaving and all kinds of house keeping
17. No
18. It was regarded honorable and also respectable
19. Yes
20. No idleness in my community - all were hard workers
21. No
22. Yes they mingled altogether
23. They were friendly with none slave holders
24. No.
25. Yes, a fair chance
26. They were discouraged
27. Primary, three months in the year
28. About three months
29. About one mile
30. Nothing but Primary Schools
31. Public
32. About three months
33. Yes
34. a Man
35. Jonesboro, May 1861
36. Knoxville, Tennessee
37. about six months
38. Barberville, Ky.
39. From Ky. thru Alabama, Mississippi, Georgia, Northern Florida, South Carolina, North Carolina, Virginia and back to Tennessee. Lived hard, exposed to the cold, hunter and disease. In hospitable with wounded leg.
40. May 1st at Greensburg 1865
41. Started in a wagon and was captured by some Yankee Soldiers and my mules were taken and had to leave wagon and arrived home late on the fifth day.
42. Farming
43. After war I was a farmer, then a blacksmith in Washington County; at Harmony Baptist Church as Deacon; not any office.
44. ----
45. James G. Deadrick, Tom Babston, Dave Byers, Nathan Gregg, Dot Deadrick, Capt. Zed Willet, Company B
46. James Deadrick   Jonesboro, Tenn.
    Tom Babston   Chuckey, Tenn.
    Dot Deadrick   Jonesboro, Tenn.
    James McCloud   "   "
    Hugh Nutherly   "   "
    Sandy Nebeon   "   "
    James Jackson   Dallas, Texas

(N.B.: BARRON, JOHN M. Pension No. 10970)

BARRON, SAMUEL LEE

FORM NO. 1

1. Samuel Lee Barron, Hickory Withe, Fayette county, Tenn.
2. 77 years, 11 mos.
3. York District, South Carolina
4. State of Tennessee, Fayette county
5. Farmer
6. Farmer
7. owned nothing, was a minor and living with father

BARRON (cont'd.):
8. Parents owned about 18 at beginning of war
9. 344 acres
10. $10,000.00 exclusive of slaves
11. First floor log, 2nd floor frame, 6 rooms
12. When I was not in school, did regular work on farm, either with hoe or plow
13. Father did all kinds of farm work; Mother was an invalid.
14. One woman for general housework
15. It was considered respectable, a man who had no profession, and did no work, at all was not looked on very favorably.
16. Yes
17. Almost none
18. No
19. Yes
20. Friendly
21. No
22. Yes
23. Yes
24. Community schools
25. a part of each year for 7 years
26. ¼ mile
27. Oakland, Tenn. 3 mi./ Macon 4 mi./ Somerville, 10 mi/. Hickory Withe, 8 mi.
28. private
29. varied, from 4 to 8 months
30. yes
31. both
32. January 1862, Morning Sun, Shelby Co., Tenn.
33. 38th Tenn., Capt. Wright, M.D.; O.M. Alsup, H.M. Neely, W.F. McFadden, J.H. Oates, J.W. Bondurant, Felix Kirk, Jas. Delauney, Frank Hurt, Dr. Wilson, G.W. Smith, Wm. Hall, J.M. Wilson, J.F. Baker, Jas. Owen
34. Corinth, Miss.
35. Don't remember date, first battle was Perryville, Ky.
36. Perryville, Ky.
37. went to Murfreesboro, engaged in battle there, last one day, defeated I was sent from ther to Atlanta, next to Rome, Ga. there discharged on Oct. 10th, 1863. Fed and clothed very well, but slept on the ground.
38. Was discharged at Rome, Ga. Oct. 10th, 1863
39. I left Rome and went to Missionary Ridge to see my brothers, who were in the line of battle there, from there back to Atlant, thence to lagrange, Tenn. by way of Ala. and Miss.
40. Took up farming after recovering my health sufficiently to do so.
41. Farming; Presbyterian; home Fayette co., Tenn.
42. Thomas Barron; York (then called district), South Carolina; Fayette co., Tenn. (from 1845)
43. Mary Neely Taylor; dont know; dont know
44. ----

(N.B.: BARRON, SAMUEL LEE Pension No. 6487)

BARROW, GEORGE WASHINGTON

FORM NO. 2

1. George Washington Barrow, Madel, Stewart co., Tenn.
2. 79
3. Trigg co., Ky.
4. Confederate
5. Co. D - 50 Tenn.
6. Shoemaker
7. Ervin Barrow; ----; ----; ----; lived at Great Western Tenn. Stewart co.
8. Lyda Eccles Everett; Sidney Everett and ----; Stewart co., Tenn.
9. ----
10. nothing
11. none
12. Father owned 150 acres

274

BARROW (cont'd.):
13. about $400.00
14. Log 2 rooms
15. I worked on the farm plowed hoed and did all kind of work that was done on the farm
16. My father made shoes Mother did house work wove cloth and made our clothes
17. none
18. it was considered honorable
19. yes
20. no most every one worked
21. some seamed to think them selves better
22. they did
23. yes more friendly than now
24. yes
25. yes
26. they we(re) not
27. subscription
28. very little
29. 2 to 4 miles
30. none but subscription
31. private
32. about 3
33. no
34. men
35. Sept. 20th 1861 at Ft. Donalson, Stewart co., Tenn.
36. Stayed at Ft. Donalson until it fell
37. about 4 mo.
38. Ft. Donalson
39. Sent from Ft. Donalson to prison at Camp Douglas, Ill. and stayed 7 mo. next battle I was in was Raymon, Miss., Jackson Miss. Chcomoga, Tunnell Hill and many others at least 16 battles. Scantly clothed and fed. Slept any way I could and exposed every way and in hospital 6 weeks.
40. Camp Chaise, Columbus, Ohio
41. Come to Cincinnati, Ohio by rail, then by boat to Kentucky
42. Farm work
43. I hav worked on the farm every since. I belong to no church. held no office
44. ----
45. John Askew, Ben Allen, Sam Crain, Will Brabston Bill Ball, Jim Bennett, Lou Beasley, Wash Burges, Joe Burges, Bill Wallace, Geo. Wallace, Doss Wallace, Mat Wa-lace, Ed Wallace, Ev Wallace, Nute Wallace, Jim Vinson, Baylor Winson, Josephus Vinson, William Vinson, Stokely Vinston, Tom Vinson, Chas. Saterfield, Jim Wall, Ewing Wyatt, Tom Wyatt, Jim Rushing, Henry Hendon, Jim Summers, Steave Collins, Billie Biggs, Geo. Lewis, Bill Moore, Burt Moore, Lam Larsater, Jim Posh (Pash?), John McDonald (Daniel?), A. Downs, Phillip Rushing, Jim Gamble, Henry Graham
46. John McChriston   Hamlin, Ky.
    Alph Thomas   "   "
    Jim Wall   Big Rock, Tenn.
    Dick McElroy   Dover, Tenn.
    Bob Gorham   Dover, Tenn.

(N.B.: BARROW, GEORGE WASHINGTON Pension No. 14828)

BARROW, W. H.

FORM NO. 1

1. W. H. Barrow, Lebanon, Tenn.
2. W.H. Barrow born in September 12, 1842
3. in Sumner county, Tennessee
4. I was living in Wilson county and went in the confederacy
5. farmer
6. farmer
7. I was only 16 when I left for the servis. I walk to Gallatin 8 miles then on train to the drill field. after drilling a few months I

275

BARROW (cont'd.):
    joined Company K Ban____ in the 18th Tenness. and remain until the close of its war 1865
8. My father had 3 untill the close of the war
9. 125 acres
10. I have the farm - was improved and could haved sold for more than he give
11. He a log cedar house, had an other joing? and some rooms
12. I left home for the war at 16 and did work as a hand on farm. Plowed used hoe all kind of work needed on farm
13. My father did all kind of work needed on his farm. The negro women did the cooking my mother did work needed in the house made cloths for the children
14. he had 3 and at closed of the war they went for themselves
15. yes
16. yes
17. Some did not work, that could help it. many had has and would have them to start to work and then change and see after something that they wish to do
18. I would say no. some would think their was but all to say yes then in a few days all together again
19. Yes. the negro would often meet any man would often take off his hat
20. yes. frenly with each other
21. no
22. yes and often did all they could to make and save some money
23. incourage and said yes for all to do something
24. I did not have a chance to schools untill after the war. I got home in June 65 In September I went school i mile of home 2 teachers 125 pupils and I was 22 and I learned all I could. never went on play ground
25. First not 5 months. after the war, then I went to teaching and taught 3 years
26. one mile
27. mixt boyds and girls
28. both
29. five
30. yes. went and studied
31. I went - 2 men
32. I went to the drill place June 61 near Gallatin. After ____ I joined a Regment confederacy and remain in it until the close
33. The 18 Tennessee, Tom Cox, Jim Soper, Tom Hickson four more I have 10 living
34. After drilling a few months then our Rigment was sent to Boling Green ky. and to work on a hill to keep the Yanks from coming in to Tenn.
35. I will say the last of 61 before any battle
36. I will say Mufresburg (Murfreesboro?) I was sick and sent to Nashville
37. I will say a hard fight we had clothes good tents and had plenty for the first few years. The last year and ½ esd hstf? We went through with Hood on corn from the wagon that we had to parch and on some mill with corn in ther haversack I never seen more men kill than at Franklin, Tenn.
38. After coming in on Hood Rade we 18 Tenn. went near Nashville than sent to Murfreesboro but only stayed one hour then back south and hard time
39. I was discharge at Jackson West Tennessee and come to Nashville, then up the river
40. First went to school 3 months then went to teaching for 4 years this sta___ and Mo. I come back to farming and trade and have done well I am near 80, and home takin good care of myself
41. I have had good time on the farm
42. W.M. Barrow was borned 26 day of September 1805 North Carolina; he was a farmer and worked on the farm
43. Mary An Barrow; Nathan Cartnell and ___, in this county (this may be Cartmell)
44. I am from good family on both sides. I have 6 children and from all ____ we know they will make good citizens. I will now close,
    W.H. Barrow

(N.B.: BARROW, W. H. Pension No. 15887)

BARRY, THOMAS VAN BUREN

FORM NO. 1

1. Thomas Van Buren Barry, Cross Plains, Tenn.
2. 77 - Jan. 28, 1921
3. Tenn. Robertson co.
4. Tenn. Robertson
5. Prizing tobacco, farming and attending school occasionally
6. Tobacco dealer and farmer
7. Being only seventeen I only had one horse valued at $100.00 and one crop of tobacco valued at $50.00
8. yes, two women
9. 160 acres
10. $5,000.00
11. 1½ story log house weather boarded and plastered of 6 rooms
12. I used plows, hoes, mowing blades, cradles and all tools necessary to carry on the farm work. I did all the plowing and the slaves helped hoe.
13. My father worked all the time in tobacco, as prizing, sorting and manufacuring. My mother saw after the house work and did all the spinning, weaving, etc.
14. the two negro slaves were the only servants
15. nearly all the white men in my community did this kind of work, and thought it to be honorable. No man was thought less of by doing this kind of work.
16. Yes
17. All able bodied men in my community did some sort of work.
18. There was no disrespect shown, all were honored and respected.
19. Yes
20. they were friendly and neighborly
21. No
22. Opportunities were not good. Labor was very cheap. Opportunities were good for a man to open a shop or store.
23. I don't think they were discouraged.
24. A two room school. A lady taught the girls in one room and a man taught the boys in the other.
25. I attended about three months each year for ten years.
26. about one mile
27. Only one school which was called the Male and Female Academy at Mitchelville, Tenn.
28. Private
29. about five months
30. Yes
31. Both
32. June 1861, Byrum's Mill, now Handleyton seventeen miles north east of Springfield.
33. 30th Tennessee; Capt. J.L. Jones, J.K. Link, J.T. Caudill, Jerry Byrum, Jack Boyd, Marshal Buring, Laton, K.P., John, Barry, Tom Empson (these last 5 must all be same surname - Empson); Tom, Freeland, J.L. Link (again-comma between what appears to be given names, with last name of Link), J.W. McMillan, William Roney, William Stewart, M. Tolliver, Caly Wilks, B. Wilson, R.H. Dyer, J.H. Jones, D.W. Terrill, Cave Armstrong, Hatcher Burney, George Scruggs, Aaronburg Heiman, D. Mullay, B. Rogers, Smith Dorris, W.D. Freeland, H. Pitt, James Smith, W.H. Armstrong, Hiram Cole
34. Red Boiling Springs
35. 3? months, in Feb. After my enlistment
36. Ft. Donelson
37. I was taken prisoner after 1st battle and sent to Springfield, Ohio. I served seven months and was exchanged at Vicksburg, Miss. I was treated fairly well. Next battle was Chichasaw B____ near Vicksburg. We were victorious, lasted four hours. Next bombardment of Port Hudson, La. 3 hrs. We repulsed them. Raymond, Miss 5 hrs. We retreated being out numbered. Jackson, Miss. 2 days. We lost Chickamauga, 3 days. We won. Missionary Ridge, 6 hrs. we lost. Rocky Face Ridge, 2 days. We won. Mill Creek Gap, 1 day, we repulsed them.
38. Was paroled from Camp Chase, Ohio, on the 4th of May '65.

277

BARRY (cont'd.):
39. We came to Cincinatti on the train the first day. Next day on to
    Louisville. Next day to Franklin, Ky. I paid my own railroad fare
    and other expenses home.
40. Farming
41. Have been engaged in farming ever since, sometimes buying and selling
    tobacco. Have always lived in Robertson co. I am a Methodist.
42. James Barr; North Carolina, Rockingham co.; came to Robertson co. at
    22 and lived here all the time.
43. Margaret Jernigan; william Jermigan and Lucy Tarver Jermigan; Wilson
    co., Tenn.
44. My ancesters on fathers side came from Ireland, settled in Penn.,
    moved to Virginia, one of my ancesters James Barry was a member of
    the Mecklenburg convention. Great great grandfather Jernigan came
    from England, settled in N.C.

(N.B.: BARRY, THOMAS VAN BUREN Pension No. 15820)

BARTLETT, ISAAC ANDERSON

FORM NO. 1

1. Isaac Anderson Bartlett, Concord, Knox county, Tenn. R. 3
2. will be 77 - 5th April 1922
3. Claiborn county, Tenn.
4. Claiborn co., Tenn.
5. Farming
6. Farming
7. did not own land was 16 years old when war commenced
8. no
9. my father died when I was 5 years old
10. my father did not own land only share in his father's land
11. Log 2
12. I plowed and hoed corn and other farm work
13. Farmed - my mother cooked spun and wove cloth
14. none
15. it was
16. they did
17. about all white men worked
18. They did. My grandfather took my mother myself and brother took care
    of us after my father died my grandfather owned good farm but did
    not own slaves
19. they did
20. all got along friendly visited each other
21. I dont think so
22. It was
23. They were never discouraged to my knowledge
24. Free school
25. I dont remember the war kept me out of school four years went about
    8 weeks after war
26. ½ mile
27. Little Sycamore
28. Public
29. three months
30. the most of them did
31. a man
32. I enlisted in the Confederate army in August 1863 we were organized
    as State Gard in Spring of 1863 made up of middle age and old men
    and few? boys joined first
33. first Tenn. Cavelry in Aug. and went in camp at C. Gap. W.A. Black-
    burn, Captain, W.M. Shoemaker 1 Lt., Cling Rice, 2 Lt., Andrew
    Calahan 3 Lt., Thomas Henderson, 1st sgt., Privet: George Colman,
    Prior Lanham, G.R.D. McNiel, Frank McNiel, Robt. Lam?
34. Cumberland Gap, Tenn. when the Federal army came to Cumberland Gap
    we fell back to Jonesvill Va. then went to Bristol
35. I dont remember none (now) the date
36. Kingsport, Tenn.
37. the first Tenn. Cavelry was only confederates at Kingsport time of
    fight was Brigade of Yankes they surrended us got our wagin and few

BARTLETT (cont'd.):

    prisoners we got together (the regment on Reedy Creek) we had 2
    battles at Bluntvill one at Blue Springs Rhea Town one near Rogersville
    we captured 8 hundred prisoners 60 wagon 1000 horses and mules 4
    canons and small arms and etc. I cant remember dates had one ____
    fight at Bristol I was captured near Tagwell (Tazewell?) sent to Rock
    Island prison left Rock Island March 2d 1864 got to Richmond 9th I
    was paroled was not called in servis when the surrender took place I
    came to Tenn. took oath at Cumberland
38. (see above also below question for continuation)
39. Gap I came to Abington Va. on freight train walked from Abigton Va.
    to Pennington Gap Lee co. Va. a man by name of Burges came with me
    his home was in Middle Tenn. He stayed with me at my step father's
    few days went off one morning never seen or heard of since suppose
    he went to Harlin Ky bushwhacker may have killed him
40. Farmed
41. I worked on farm don carpenter work 1884 went in mercantile business
    on small scale owned interest in grist and saw mill
42. Martin Bartlett; Little Sycamore, Claiborn co., Tenn. Dec. 8, 1820;
    lived at Little Sycamore
43. Anna McNiel; John McNiel and Elizabeth (Cambell) McNiel; ----
44. Cant give full names of great grandparants McNiels came from Scotland.
    Bartletts from England. my ansesters settled in North Carlina. My
    grandfather John McNiel was born in Ash county, N.C. 1811. my grand-
    father John Bartlett died before I was born. He was born in North
    Carlina I think that my impresion.

BARY, JAMES LEMUEL

FORM NO. 1

1. James Lemuel Bary, Lebanon, Tenn. Wilson? co.
2. 74 - 11 Months
3. Davidson co., Tenn.
4. Lebanon, Tenn.
5. Had none
6. a Printer
7. Nothing but a horse value 3000.00
8. no
10 Home 3000.00
11. Rock? house 5 rooms
12. too young to work
13. a printer my mother looked after the house and cooking
14. yes one woman
15. yes
16. yes
17. none that I know of
18. yes
19. yes
20. yes
21. I dont think made any difference at that time
22. yes if he would try
23. they were encouraged
24. private
25. about 9 years
26. about 500 yards
27. private and public schools
28. both
29. private about 10 months
30. yes
31. man
32. Confederate in Sept. 1863
33. 4th Tenn. Calvary J.H. Davis(Doris?), J._. Lane, Jack Lester, John
    Ivy, __ Doris, Kirk Bowes, Jim Mlhurson?(this hand writing is terrible)
    Wilt Owenby, H.D. ___, J._. Duke?
34. we went to G____ and I was in the __ all the time as cavary always
    was
35. in skirmish all over the county
36. ----

BARY (cont'd.):
37. were in no real battles in 1864 we were in front? of Shermans march
    ___ ____ as far as Savan (Savannah_ Geo we did not have much to eat
    had a good time in camp when we could ____ ___ __ had very little
    clothing
38. Paroled at Chart N.C. (Charlotte?)
39. we came from Charlotte N.C. horses ____ ____ where stay were taken
    from us and were ____ in train at (to?) Nashville ___
40. Shoemaking
41. Shoe business?, Library ___, Church of Christ
42. Richard? Henry? Bary (this may be spelled Barry also), Nashville,
    Davidson co., Tenn nothing
43. Elizabeth Jane Hayns (Haynes?); ----; ----; Franklin, Tenn.?
44. Had two uncles in Mexican War. James Lemuel Haynes: James Bary(Barry)

(N.B.: BARRY, JAMES LEMUEL Pension No. 15509(&?)

BASHAW, JOSEPH PETER

FORM NO. 1

1. Joseph Peter Bashaw, Mt. Juliet, Tennessee
2. 79 years and 2 months
3. Tennessee Wilson county
4. Tenn. Wilson (Confederate)
5. Farming and going to school
6. Farming and stock raising
7. I was a miner and owned no property
8. yes about 9 or 10
9. 181 acres more or less
10. about 12000
11. It was a hued cedar log hous with 2 rooms and a 8 foot haul between
    and 2 half storys above with gallery running the full length with
    shed room
12. I did all kinds of farm work the negroes did according to ability as
    a boy and went to school most of the time but I plowed, hoed, grubed,
    etc.
13. My father did all kinds of farm work and directed the same my mother
    died before I was two years old
14. I dont just know what you mean by servants we kept the slaves servants
    as busy as was necessary but didn't drive them
15. yeas, and comindable as well
16. yeas
17. none that I know of
18. yes there was no difference honerable men was though as good as any
    man that owned slaves and more than sum of them
19. yes could not tell any difference
20. the very best of feeling no antagonistic feeling what ever
21. not a bit
22. yes and meny times the slave holder would back him with counsel and
    his means (or money)
23. they was encouraged and given the best counsel
24. I sometimes went to what were called free schools and private schools.
    I was going to Mt. Juliet Acadamy when the war came. I left school
    to join the army.
25. a part of 12 years
26. about one mile
27. Mt.Juliet Acadamy
28. Private
29. about ten month private and about 3 months free schools
30. some of them did and sum did not
31. the last school I attended was taught H. H. Merrill a man from New
    York
32. 1861 May 20th at Silver Springs Wilson county, Tennessee
33. Hattons regiment on the 7th Tenn. Co. I - some of the names of (at
    bottom of page - "Since wrighting this answer to no. 33 question I
    have found the roal of company" top of next page - "see accompaning
    sheet question No. 33")

BASHAW (cont'd.):
34. to Camp Trousdal to learn the tackticks in other words learned how to
    drill since writin the answer to this question I have found the roll
    of our company which I send on a different sheet and will number it
    33.
35. about thirteen months
36. Macanixville (Mechanicsville?) the first dayes battle of the 7 days
    battles around Richman (Richmond?) Virginia I was wourded that day
37. The space for answering this question is two limited to answer all
    of them I send one another sheat and mark it No. 36
38. I surendered near Peters Burg Virginia
39. my trip home was uneventful, met with no troble as I was furnished a
    ticket to Nashville and rode the train
40. Farming. I went to school again at Mt. Juliet then I went to Wash-
    ington College, Va. known now as Washington and Lee University in the
    years 1866 and 1867 Lee being its president I did not graduate
    owing to circumstances over which I had no controle. I did not go
    back to school anymore
41. My life after the war has been a private one. I farmed and raised
    stock. I have lived near Mt.Juliet Wilson county I am a Missionary
    Baptist and has been for 52? years
42. James Wesly Bashaw; I think somewhere near Hasili_y (can't make out
    this word), Culpepper co., Virginia. he moved with parents to David-
    son county Tennessee near Nashville.
43. Charlotte Cherry; Ely Cherry and Nancy____; the Stones river bridge
    on the Lebanon pike East side Davidson co.
44. My grandfather Peter Bashaw served as a soldier in the Revolutionary
    war and was under the command of Gen. Washington was at the surender
    of Corn Wallis at Yorktown - my great grandfather James Bashaw came
    from France they were French Hugants settled on the Potomoc river near
    Sum__ Virginia dont know the county - they fled from the persecution
    of the Roman Catholicks to seak a home where they could worship God
    in the open without fear of molestation, in other word "where they
    could worship God under their vine and fig tree (fight?) none to
    molest as make afraid."

Follows are two typed sheets in answer to Q.36:
(1) MY EXPERIENCES IN THE WAR - the first three months were devoted to
drilling and learning the military tactics; then we were sent to
Virginia, but did not get there in time for the first battle of
Manassas; and were then sent to Valley Mountain, from there we were
sent to Cheat Mountain, or near to it on the Huttonsville road, where
we cut the telegraph communications between Huttonsville and Cheat
Mountain,
    Our pickets captured a few prisoners, also killed one man, took
one wounded man; then we came back to Green Brier bridge and stayed
there a few days; then we went to Sewells Mountain to see about
Rosencrans; then we came back to Millsborough, then after a few weeks
we went to Staunton, Virginia; then to Winchester, then to Romy, Va.
then to Bath, then back to Winchester, then to Yorktown, where we
reorganized by electing new company officers.
    There I took the fever and was sent to the hospital at Richmond,
transferred to Lynchburg, Va.; on that account I missed getting in
the Seven Pines battle, but got there in time for the Seven days
battle; I got wounded the first day at Mechanicsville; my next battle
was Cedar Run; next battle was Second Manassas; I was in the first
days fight at the junction on Wednesday, where our brigade (Archers)
fought the enemy that was guarding the junction.
    The fight began just as the sun was rising, lasting until they
were driven back across Bull Run, and then burned the bridge. In
this battle we lost a good many in killed and wounded; we then came
back to the junction, and waited for the depot to burn; then we went
to Centerville; then we went to the old stone bridge; some where near
the battle field of the first battle (that was Thursday); Friday we
held our own, waiting for Longstreet to get through the thoroughfare
gap in the Blue Ridge Mountains.
    On Saturday afternoon, the signal was fired, and "Old Stonewall"
came down the line, with his hat in his hand, and his whole corps
moved forward, and the mail "Ball" opened, and Pope's army stampeeded
and the night came on, and the Second Manassas went down into history,

BASHAW (cont'd.):
as a great defeat of Pope's army.

My feet being badly blistered, owing to wet feet and bad shoes, I was excused from service for several weeks; on that account I missed the Maryland Campaigne; I rejoined the brigade at Martinsburg, Va., from there we started and crossed the Blue Ridge at Browns or Siggs gap, I do not now remember which, and was taken violently sick that night, and next day was sent to Winchester, Va. and from there to Staunton, Va., thence to Richmond, Va., where I lingered for a month, or more, not knowing in which way the scales would turn; but finally got able to go back to the regiment, but too late for the Fredricksburg fight.

My next battle was at Chancellersville, Va., where the much lamented Stonewall Jackson, the great general, was lost to us, and we were in mourning until we started on the march North, on the enemy's territory, and finally reached Gettysburg, Pa., where Archer's brigade brought on the first days fight, and got flanked on the right, where he (Archer) was made prisoner with quite a number of his men and officers.

We rested the second day, but were in the third days battle; I was in that great charge, and was wounded close to the rock fence, but got back without being captured that day, but the next day, while the wounded were being sent back, the Yankee Cavalry run on us, and took 40 to 50 wagons loaded with the wounded, going back to Virginia and I was in one of them, and a prisoner; they carried us to Marsburg, Pa. that night; next morning they took all that could walk, and sent them to prison; those that could not walk, were parolled and left in an old college.

The citizens fed us for about a week, then the Yankees came along and carried us to Philadelphia and after one night, took us to Chester, Pa. to one of their hospitals where we fared just like their soldiers did; We had the very best treatment, fed well and furnished clean underwear once a week, and were required to bathe when we changed clothing. Each ward had a bath room, with hot and cold water, soap and towels. They kept us about six weeks, then sent us back to "Dixie"; I got a furlough until exchanged, which was three months. I had gotten completely well and went back to the army some time in the early winter of 1863.

When spring opened up, we met the enemy May 5th, 1864 in the Wilderness, and had two days battles; then we were in every few days, but not a regular engagement, till we reached Spotsylvania Court House on the 12th of May, 1864; then on and on to Coles Harbor the second time; thence to Petersburgh, there the seige commenced, then the "crater"; after staying in ditches for a week, exposed to mortar fire, hot sun and dog flies in the day time, and rebuilding the breastworks at night, we were relieved to rest up and clean up. We got into trouble down on the Weldon railroad, and had two days battles 19th and 20th of August 1864; and on the 20th, I was captured and carried to Point Lookout Prison, where I took chronic dysentery without treatment, I came near dying, before they sent me to the hospital, where I began to improve a little, but what I got to eat was so scant and bad for a sick boy, I gained no strength.

On the first of November, they sent all the sick in the hospital back to "Dixie" and I was one of those landing at Savannah, Ga. on the 12th of November, 1864, and got another parole furlough of 30 days or until exchanged; after spending the 30 days near Burksville, with one of "Old Virginias" old time hospitality families, I got entirely well again, and then went back to the army at Petersburg on the first day of January 1865, and on the 5th of February 1865, our brigade (Archers) had a hard fought battle, but we did not accomplish any thing, but lost.

It was now looking quite gloomy; General Grant was closing on us, having ten men to Generalds Lee one man; knowing the situation as it really was, no rations, hardly any clothing, hardly any men to cope with the enemy, every body knew that the end was close at hand.

Our men lost heart, and were going home every night, so we had "so called picked men" to guard the picket lines to keep the men from "going to the Yankees" and still they would go.

We all knew that when the campaigen opened up in the spring, General Lee would be compelled to surrender, and the men were very

282

BASHAW (cont'd.):
    badly discouraged, low spirited, they did not care to be killed for
    no purpose, for there was no hope whatever, they were leaving even
    sometimes by whole companies.
        I surrendered near Petersburgh, Virginia on the first day of March
    1865, about nine o'clock A.M.; having accepted General Grant's terms
    of surrender; he agreeing to furnish commutation and transportation
    to Nashville.

                    BASKERVILLE, GEORGE BOOTH

FORM NO. 1

1. George Booth Baskervill(e), Mason, Tenn. R.F.D. No. 2
2. 75 March 29, 1922
2. Fayette county, Tenn.
4. Fayette co., Tenn.
5. a school boy
6. Minister and farmer
7. My father owned 1346 acres of land and between 40 and fifty slaves,
    etc.
8. Yes 40 or 50 I can recall. Land improved sold for 7 to 10 dollars
    per acre
9. 1346
10. you know as well as I
11. six rooms or rather 3 and three half rooms logs weatherboarded
12. I did not work
13. My father sometimes had an overseer sometimes did not. My mother was
    the servant of all of us including the negroes.
14. yes
15. Yes - The teacher I went to was a graduate of a Southern College and
    was killed as a Captain at the head of his company. He told he(us)
    that he worked in the field regularly when he was a boy.
16. no
17. all that were able just as men do now who are able to do so
18. I never knew them to make any difference
19. yes
20. Friendly
21. I was so young I do not know
22. Abundant
23. Were generally assisted. I never when a boy went to schools that some
    poor boy did not go with us from home or one of the family
24. Private
25. From the time I was a little child till I went into the army and after
    the war to college 2 years
26. 1st at home then on 2 miles or four and the last 6 miles - taught by
    all of Va. men
27. Such as I described above. Taught by men who were preparing for
    college later by men who had graduated
28. Private but all went. I recollect hearing there was a fund to pay

29. 10
30. yes
31. man
32. March 1st 1863 near Covington, Tenn. at Mt. Carmel Church. 4 weeks
    before I was 16
33. Co. E 12 Tenn. Cavalry Reuben Burrow Captain. I soon transferred to
    Company F of the same regiment later the 12 Tenn. Cavalry was consol-
    idated with Forrest old regiment. my parole read Co. K. Forest (old)
    regiment. I dont believe (old) was in it. Capt. W.A. Bell? was the
    Captain. Matthews 1st Lt. James Brooks 2nd. F.B. Raglad (Ragland?),
    Jr. was McCall (don't understand this) Will Appleberry, Alonzo
    Gilliam, Thos. Taylor, etc.
34. It was a portion Ranger Regiment
35. In two weeks we were stampeded then we protected N. Miss. under
    Chalmers later Forrest commanded us and we went the rounds south from
    Daleville? Oxford, Miss. Newport, etc. see Forrest's life
36. I dont know if you would call any of them battles tell we went with
    Hood to Nashville and back.

37. We followed Forrest after he took charge of all the cavalry. We slept
    on blankets and covered with them. I don't think I slept in a tent
    as much as a month. In camp one winter we stayed over a month then
    we built sleeping places out of little poles and covered them with
    our oil cloths. We had any kind of clothes, our oil cloths and over
    coats were generally U.S. goods captured. The blue was changed by
    definitely to brown.
38. I was paroled with Forrest Cavalry May 11, 1865
39. We came home on our own horses. I stopped with friends one night -
    the last 40 miles I was alone but ate dinner at a private house in
    Lagrange, Tenn. - a Federal soldier died also
40. Went to College
41. I have preached 54 years. Had a farm my father left me sometimes
    lived on it and then elsewhere that I was pastor - am now farming all
    the time.
42. John Tabb Baskervill; Mecklenburg co., Virginia; this farm 9 miles
    north of Somerville, Tenn. last; he was a minister of the M.E. Church
    South
43. Margaret Payne Malone; Rev. Booth Malone and ____; The Mountain 5
    miles S. of Saulsbury? Town in Mississippi.
44. My parents both were Virginians. Came west first to Middle Tenn. and
    N. Alabama. Married in North Mississippi - lived ____ a few years
    then moved to Fayette co. Tenn. where they spent the remainder of
    their lives.

BASKETT, GIDEON HICKS

FORM NO. 1

1. Gideon Hicks Baskette, 1310 Eastland Ave., Nashville, Tenn.
2. 76 years
3. Tenn., Rutherford county
4. Tenn., Rutherford co. town of Murfreesboro
5. I was a school boy
6. a Physician; resided in Murfreesboro - owned a farm near village of
    Middleton
7. none
8. My father owned I think about 15 slaves
9. about 100 acres
10. about $30,000
11. on the farm a frame two story house. In Murfreesboro, a two story
    brick house, with 10 rooms
12. I was too young to work on the farm. Moved to Murfreesboro with my
    parents in 1850. Afterwards went to school.
13. My father devoted his time to the practice of medicine. My Mother
    was a busy housewife, assisted by her servants.
14. In Murfreesboro they kept a cook and her husband and two children,
    a house maid and a man of all work, negroes.
15. yes
16. The majority of them
17. Comparatively few
18. Respectable slave owners and non-slave owners mingled freely with
    each other. Only professional slave traders, who bought and sold
    slaves for profit were placed on a lower social scale.
19. Yes
20. They were friendly
21. It did not
22. Yes, they were good, considering the then limited lines of occupation
23. They were encouraged
24. The local private schools
25. Eight or nine years
26. About half a mile.
27. Union University - Saule Female College - Barlow's boys school -
    Harris' Boys School & ____ - Bradshaw's School and Davis' Military
    Academy
28. Private
29. Two terms a year - in all about 10 months
30. Yes

BASKETT (cont'd.):
31. Man
32. In November, 1861 at Murfreesboro, Tenn. in Confederate service
33. Forty Fifth Tennessee. I had a muster roll lent have misplaced it.
    Can recall only some of the names - Capt. Addison Mitchell, Capt.
    A. Searcy - both afterwards Colonels. Capt. Richard Sanford?. Lt.
    Lewis Time (Tune?O, Lt. J.W. McFadden, H.(Doc) Barkley, Rufus Haynes,
    Thos. Watkins, Sam'l Mitchell, Lemuel Beard, Wm. Wade, Jas. Green,
    Isaac Cox, Arthur Smith, Goerge Smith, Jas. Holmes, John McDerment,
    James Clark, Wm. James, Drury Crawford, Jas. Black, Dennis? Haywood,
    Tip Randolph, Wm. Alexander, Henry Cowan, Al Tompkins, George Gannaway,
    James Osborn, Cahs. Dement, Andrew Cotton, Cas? Brannon, Joe Sanders,
    Tom Alford, Jesse Adams, Jim Dunnaway, John Parker, etc.
34. To Camp Trousdale, near the village of Mitchelville, just across the
    Kentucky line
35. about 5 months
36. The Battle of Shiloh, also called the battle of Pittsburg Landing
37. Was made Sergeant Major of regiment - engaged in following named
    battles; Shiloh - 2 days; 1st seige of Vicksburg, 3 months; Baton
    Rouge, La. 1 day; Murfreesboro, or Stone's River, 2 days; Missionary
    Ridge, 1 day; Chickamauga, 2 days; Dalton, Ga.; Resacca, 1 day;
    Powder Springs, 1 day; Atlanta, 2½ months; Jonesboro, 1 day; on Hood's
    Raid into Tennessee; 2nd battle at Murfreesboro, 1 day; Pulaski, 1
    day; Savannah, Ga., 2 days; Bentonville, N.C., 1 day; Surrendered at
    Greensboro, N.C. was never taken prisoner. In hospital only one day.
    Endured many hardships in service. Much of time poorly clad, often
    suffered from hunger.
38. On April 30, 1865, at Greensboro, N.C. by the surrender of Gen.
    Joseph E. Johnston's army.
39. The Tennesseans in Johnston's army were placed in command of Brig.
    Gen. J.B. Palmer, without arms and marched by Charlotte and Ashville,
    N.C. to Greenville, Tenn., passing through a hostile country in East
    Tenn. Placed on freight cars at Greenville, under federal guard,
    were being permited to leave the trains when near their respective
    homes.
40. My father having lost heavily by the war, I clerked for a time. After-
    wards became editor of the Murfreesboro News. Then for a short time
    editor Nashville American. Afterwards telegraphis editor Cincinnati
    News then editor Chattanooga Daily. In 1884 became editor in chief
    of Nashville Banner, for 28 years, then editor Nashville Democrat.
    Now Librarian Carnegie Library of Nashville.
41. Have held no public offic, except County School Superintendent. Am a
    Presbyterian, an officer in the church, first a deacon then an elder
    for about 45 years.
42. William Turner Baskette; near Palmyra, Fluvanna co., Virginia; in
    Virginia as a young man, but most of his later life in Murfreesboro
    Tenn.; he served on Gen. Bragg's staff at Murfreesboro as surgeon,
    afterward imprisoned in a northern prison.
43. Melissa Ann Ellis; Hicks Ellis and (don't remember her maiden name);
    in Rutherford county, near Bedford county line.
44. Unfortunately I have no genealogical record of my family. Such record
    if it existed, must have been destroyed during the Civil War. My
    ancestors lived in England, among them perhaps John Basket and Mark
    Basket of London, who were noted as binders and printers of books.
    The old family bibles of my grand-fathers cannot be found.

On extra page - letterhead of the Carnegie Library of Nashville,
G.H. Baskette, Librarian, dated Feb. 24, 1922, addressed to Mr. J.T.
Moore: "My Dear Mr. Moore, I am enclosing my answers to the questions submitted in the form sent me. The questions relating to the
Civil War recall to my mind many incidents and episodes which could
not be compassed in a formal way. Some of these incidents that I
have never seen related in print, have a historic value and if I find
the time I will endeavor to put them in readable shape to be filed
away. With best wishes, Yours very truly, G.H. Baskette." Library
Board: G.H. Baskette, President; M.T. Bryan, Vice-Pres.; C.C. Trabue,
Sec'ty.; Edgar Jones, Treas.; A.E. Howell; T.W. Wreene; J.B. Mason;
Robt. L. Burch; Joes S. Boyd; Garnett N. Morgan.

BASS, J. B.

FORM NO. 2

1. J. B. Bass, Hermitage, Davidson Co.
2. 80 years last January
3. Giles county - 1842
4. Confederate Soldier
5. Company K-3 Tennessee, John C. Brown's Regiment
6. Farmer
7. Maj. John Bass; North Carolina; dont know; he was in the War of 1812, under Andrew Jackson
8. Temperance Ann Sumner; Duke Sumner and (forgotten)
9. ----
10. Land was worth from 30 to 50 $
11. 65
12. 750 acres
13. owned 65 slaves and 750 acres of land
14. frame house 8 rooms
15. went to Collage Bethany Collage picked cotton when school was oute
16. Farmed and in house cooking spining and weaveing
17. 65
18. yes
19. yes
20. Evry boddy worked that was able
21. they all mingled together yes
22. yes
23. yes not antagonist
24. yes
25. yes
26. they were all encouraged
27. private
28. 12 years
29. at one time 3 miles at other ½ mile
30. Presbeterian
31. private and any one that wanted to come
32. about 5 months
33. yes
34. 3 woman and too (2) men
35. May 1861 Drew my gun out of the Capatal at Nashville
36. to Chetam
37. Fort Donaldson
38. Fort Donaldson
39. ----
40. Monrow, North Carolina
41. I had a verry good trip
42. Plowed
43. I went to Texas 1867 married and engaged in farming. I engaged in a battle at Raymond Hines county and was shot down and was captured on the battle field and was recaptured by the Confederate Cavaldry and afterwards came home on a furlow and joined Wheelers Command.
44. ----
45. Lt. E. Hodges, Ike Pulley, A_sker? Cambel

    (N.B.: BASS, JOHN B. Pension No. 15341

BASS, JAMES O.

FORM NO. 2

1. Capt. James O. Bass, Goodlettsville, Tenn.
2. 84 years
3. Wilson County, Tenn.
4. Confederate
5. Co. I, 7th Tenn.
6. Farmer
7. Solomon Bass; Wilson co., Tenn.; lived Laquardo, Wilson co., Tenn; not in war
8. Eliazbeth Parton; Archie Parton and___; Wilson co., Tenn.

BASS (cont'd.):
9. ----
10. none
11. Father owned about 12
12. 335 acres
13. ----
14. Weather boarded log house
15. General farm work - plowing, hoeing and trading
16. Farmer
17. Had slaves
18. .It was
19. yes
20. ----
21. ----
22. yes
23. yes
24. ----
25. yes
26. ----
27. Country school
28. ¼ mile
29. ----
30. ----
31. Public
32. ----
33. ----
34. Man
35. March 1861, Silver Springs, Wilson County
36. Va. (Camp Trousdale first)
37. 6 months
38. in W. Va.
39. There were four of us brothers who enlisted in the army. Two were
    killed on battle field, one died from wounds after the war. I was
    Capt. of Co. I, 7th Tenn. Reg.
40. April 1865, from Federal Prison, Roed Island, Ohio
41. Arrived home June 16, 1865
42. Farming and trading
43. Have lived at Goodlettsville Tenn. since 1867. Belong to Methodist
    Church
44. ----
45. ----
46. J.W. Roscoe   Goodlettsville, Tenn.
    M.L. Roscoe   "   "
    W.L. (this written over might be Dr.?) Dismukes, Goodlettsville, Tenn.
    W.H. Crosswy   Goodlettsville, Tenn.
    J.J. Crosswy (Crossway?)   Denver, Colo.

BASS, WILLIAM JONES

FORM NO. 2

1. William Jones Bass, Kerrville, Shelby co., Tenn.
2. 80 yr
3. Tenn. Shelby co.
4. Confederate
5. B-8 Ark Cavrery
6. farmer
7. Solum (Solomon?) Franklan (Franklin?) Bass; Willson co., Tenn.
8. Sarah Neal Varned
9. had none my father and my mother having dyed befour the war. I have
   recordes by wch to go
10. ----
11. ----
12. ----
13. my parents wer both dead befour the war
14. log
15. plowed hoed pulled fodder tied oats wheat and every other thing
16. my father did all kinds off farm work plowing hoeing cotton oats and

287

BASS (cont'd.):
wheat with cradel my mother cooking spinning weaving cutting and
making cloths
17. ----
18. yess
10. yess
20. ----
21. yess
22. yess
23. they wer friendly
24. I think not
25. yess
26. encorage
27. publick pay school
28. not agate (a great?) much being the oldest boy had to work
29. ----
30. ----
31. private
32. 5 or 6
33. yess
34. man
35. in May 1861 Little Rock Ark.
36. to Pokhintas?, Ark. (Pocahontas?)
37. not untill in 1862 we (transfered?) to Corinth, Miss
38. the big one was Corinth '62
39. I could not state all the fights that we wer from menney
40. Greenvill, N.C. 26 April 1865
41. I came all the way frome ther to Shelby co. Tenn horse back
42. farming
43. I have lived in the second district Shelby county Tenn. since August
the 2 day of 1865 I have served 3 terms as ____crat in the secon civil
districk I belong to the Cumbland Presbyterian (Cumberland?)
44. ----
45. I will (tell) you the ones who wer Tennesseans - Jack Ship_?, George
Canelal?, George Mocum?, ...(this writing is very bad...cme)
46. S.G. Patterson   Kerville, Tenn.
John Willson   Mill_gton, Tenn.
L.A. (J.A.?) McDanel Lucy, Tenn
thoes three are all the old solders living in this neighod.

(N.B.: BASS, WILLIAM JONES Pension No. 14914)

BATES, WILLIAM BRIMAGE

FORM NO. 2

1. William Brimage Bate, ----
2. Deceased - born Oct. 7, 1826-Died 3/9/1905
3. Tennessee - Sumner County
4. Confederate
5. Co. I-2nd Tenn.
6. Farmer - State Inspector
7. James Henry Bate; Birtee Co., North Carolina; lived one mile from
Bledsoe's Lick, now Castolian Springs, Tenn.
8. Amanda Weathered; William Weathered and Patience Dowell; Sumner Co.
near Bldesoe's Lick now Castolian Springs, Tenn.
9. ----
10. About 2400 acres in Texas close to Grandview, as well as about 80
acres in Sumner Co., Tenn.
11. My parents - 25 or 30
12. 240 acres in Sumner Co., Tenn.
13. ----
14. Up to 1840 lived in a log house, when a brick house was built to it
of eight rooms
15. After leaving school he was clerk on a steam-boat plying between
Nashville and New Orleans, from which he went into the Mexican War.
16. Superintended the work of laborers on the farm - Mother's duties were
those of housewife, superintending the work of cooking, spinning and
weaving.

288

BATES (cont'd.):
17. They kept several servants
18. It was
19. Yes
20. Don't know of any now
21. No difference was made
22. They did
23. There was no antagonism
24. Do not know
25. Yes
26. Encouraged
27. Country schools - Law school at Lebanon, Tenn.
28. ----
29. About one mile
30. Two- a female academy at Castalian Springs, Tenn. and a mixed school
    at Rural Academy near the same place
31. Public
32. about 8 months
33. Yes
34. Man
35. In 1861, month of May, at Gallatin, Tenn.
36. Fredericksburg, Va.
37. Very short time
38. Around Fredricksburg, Va.
39. ----
40. At the end of the war at Bentonville, N.C.
41. ----
42. Practice of Law
43. Lawyer in Nashville, Tenn. Twice elected Governor of Tenn and sent
    three times to United States Senate. He joined the Hopewell Baptist
    Church near his old home at Castalian Springs, Tenn. in the latter
    years of his life.
44. ----
45. ----
46. ----

Extra Pages
William Brimage Bate was born Oct. 7, 1826 near what is now Castalian
Springs, Tenn. and spent there his boyhood days. Early in youth he
manifested a bold and adventurous spirit which later characterized
his career as a Confederate soldier. Leaving school he became a
clerk on a steamboat, plying between Nashville and New Orleans, La.
and while in New Orleans he enlisted for the Mexican War, being the
first native Tennesseean to enlist. He served as a private in a La.
Regiment, and when his term of enlistment expired he went with the
Tennesseeans in Cheatham's Regiment. He captured the last flag
captured in the Mexican War. He brought back with him when he
returned from the Mexican War, a Mexican youth, Cedro Posades by name,
whom he kept in his own home and educated and started in life. After
his return to Tennessee, he was elected to the Legislature and after
that studied Law at Lebanon, Tenn. from which school he graduated in
1852, and then made his home at Gallatin. In 1854, he was elected
Attorney General for the Nashville District. In 1861 he entered the
Civil War as a private and was speedily promoted to Captain and then
to Colonel of the Second Tennessee Infantry Regiment. Oct. 3, 1862
he was promoted to Brigadier General. He was severely wounded in the
Battles of Shiloh, Hoover's Gap and Utoy Creek. He had one horse
killed from under him at Shiloh and three in the Battle of Chickamauga.
It is said that his guns were the last guns of the Army of Tennessee
that found echo in battle. After his return to his home in Nashville,
he enjoyed a lucrative practice in the Law; was twice elected
Governor of the State of Tennessee and was sent three times to the
United States Senate, in which capacity he was serving his State when
he died, March 9, 1905. His remains were brought to his native state,
and laid to rest in beautiful Mt. Olivet, Nashville, Tenn.
(There follows this statement, a clear picture of Wm. B. Bate in
Civil War uniform)

(No notation was made as to the person filling in the questionnaire
which was received Oct. 11, 1922)

BATES, ROBERT BAXTER

FORM NO. 1

1. Robert Bates, Bull (Bluff) City, Tenn.
2. 79 the 24 of September 1922
3. Sulivan (Sullivan) Co., Tenn.
4. Sullivan co., Tenn.
5. Farming
6. Farming
7. Father owned 36-¼ acres of land
8. none
9. 36-¼ acres
10. I was verry young and din not give attention to such things
11. log house 5 rooms
12. Did all kind of work that was dine on a farm
13. forked (worked) on the farm mother worked in the house cooked spun wove
14. none
15. Honorable to work
16. yes
17. Very few
18. no much differance where man kept themselves clean and respectable
19. yes
20. yes
21. no
22. not much
23. Som was and some was not
24. the Comon Country school before the war after the war Fall Branch high school
25. About 3 months each year before the war. after the war about 6
26. 2 miles
27. country schools
28. part private and part public
29. 3 or 4
30. yes
31. a man
32. in the yer of 1861. going to the field to hob corn
33. 19 Tenn. Co. G. - But 1st lites company of Va. state ____ under Captain finly and after the battle of Peterburg was transfered to Co. G 19th Tenn.
34. to Va.
35. about 6 months
36. Pitonburg Ky afer which I was trnsfered
37. was in all the but one _ from Chatanooga to Joneboro Ga. __ I was Chakmga (Chickamauga?) I was in the hospittle at Atlanta Ga. I was 121 days under fire from Brezard? lost to Atlanta Ga. them back to Dalton capture fort Nagre? and then on to Franklin thire captured Ky prison at Camp Chase Ohio my experice is to sad for me to write out
38. Camp Chase Ohio Jun 17, 1865
39. taken the oath of allegence as prisoner of war. hospittle Franlin (Franklin?) hospittle Nashville hospittle Lousiville Ky then on to Camp Chase Ohio
40. All for a liveing
41. Hed no office farmed taugh schooll doctored preached worked as marchant
42. Harges Bates; sullivan co.; in the same as farmer
43. Ruth Cox and maried Hages Bates; William Cox and Elizabeth King; Sullivan co. Tenn
44. Robet (Robert) Bates is nu name. I have strickn with paraisis twice cant geve a full hiostory

BATEY, BENJAMIN BLANKS

FORM NO. 2

1. Benjamin Blanks Batey, Christian, RFD 3, Rutherford co., Tenn.
2. I was born Oct. 10th 1838 nearly 84 years of age
3. State of Tennessee Rutherford county

BATEY (cont'd.):
4. Confederate soldier
5. Rutherford Rifles. Co. I, First Tenn. Commanded by Col. George Manney.
   Lastly by Hume R. Fields?. until close of the war making 3 years
   under Fields.
6. Mechnic Farmer and Stock raiser
7. William Gerington Batey; near Brunswick C.H., Brunswick co., Virginia;
   lived near Murfreesboro, Tenn. and died at his home; none to give
8. Elizabeth Sills; Isam Sills and (name not known); lived in the state
   of Virginia I presume in Brunswick county.
9. The information that I can give is that my great grandparents
   imigrated from Ireland at very early date. My grandfatehr Isam Sills
   was a soldier of revolution - any war. My father William Ferington
   Batey did not serve in any of the wars waged in American as he was
   born in the year 1775. And died in December 1850 being nearly 76
   years of age at the time of his death.
10. I did not own land but I owned one man slave and about ($2250.00)
    with value of male slave $4000.00
11. Yes but I cannot give the number owned
12. My parents owned nearly 300 acres
13. I cannot answer the above as my parents were both dead and thir
    property had been divided among their heirs.
14. My parents occupied a framed house two lower and two upper rooms with
    brick chimneys.
15. The certain historians are in error as I know that all boys and many
    young men did farm work before the war. I was taught to work with a
    hoe, and as soon as I was large enough to plough. I went at that
    kind of work. I did all kinds work that our slaves did. I have
    worked late at night with slaves and there is doubt of the fact as I
    know that I did work of all kind both late and early.
16. William Ferington Batey my father was too old to do farm work as far
    back as memory serves - he did work in shop, such as cooperage and
    stocking guns, plows and grain cradles. My mother Elizabeth Sills
    Batey died when I was two weeks old. I knowledge of her. She had
    servants to do all kinds work.
17. Yes they servants but dont how many not having been told by older
    brothers or sisters.
18. All manuel labor as mentioned above was considered respectable and
    honorable. All boys and men applying themselves diligenty to any
    and all kinds of manual labor could at all times find good friends
    wherever they were known.
19. Yes, except such as were too old or such as had plenty of slaves but
    they taught their sons to work
20. I dont think that they were many idlers in a real sence for they
    were busy looking after their farm work and keeping matters in order.
21. They did not in the com. where I brought up. Any one male or female
    that conducted themselves properly were treated in a nice social
    manner
22. Yes. As above any person conduction themselves properly - I dont
    know of any distinction being notised.
23. Yes. Nothing but friendly feeling and a warm hand shaking and how is
    the old woman and the children.
24. I dont remember such a qualification had any effect. People in those
    days tried to help the man whom they believed the best qualified for
    the office.
25. Yes if by practicing strict economy and presing forward doing his
    best having such aims in view.
26. Such as above named were always encouraged and helped forward even
    being helped along in going to school.
27. My first school was primary. My second school was an academy with
    the higher branches taught by graduates of colleges.
28. About six years except that I left school to work on the farm when
    work was needed.
29. About two miles except one fall I walked four miles. That was just
    before the death of my father William Ferington Batey.
30. There were two - one female and one male. The former was in charge
    lady teachers and of about the same grade as the male school
31. The above named schools were for the public but all payed for their
    tuition.
32. Generally about ten months.

BATEY (cont'd.):
33. As well as I rember they were pretty regular
34. My first teacher was a woman. The other teacher were men.
35. The company of which I was a member was organized at Murfreesboro
    Rutherford county Tenn. in the month of April in year 1861. For the
    Confederate service.
36. To Nashville Tenn. and there mustered into service on the first day
    of May 1861 First Tenn. Regt.
37. About five months we run into an ambuscade in the Mts. of West Virginia
    in which there was wounded.
38. The battle of Shilo April 6 & 7, 1862 in which one man was killed
    and one man wounded.
39. To state my experience for four years is too great a task for one of
    my age. After our first battle (Shilo) we fought at Perryville Ky.
    Losing ten killed and seven wounded. Next to battle of M'bor.
    (Murfreesboro?) Tenn and then Chicamauga Ga. then Mission(ary) Ridge
    Tenn. then Marietta Ga. then Atlanta Ga. then to Franklin Tenn. My
    camp life fare is like others. I never was in prison.
40. I was paroled by Genreal Sherman while under the command of General
    Jonston (Johnston) at Greensboro, N.C.
41. On my (way) home I marched a foot to Greerville?, Tenn. then by rail
    home. The Federal guards and soldiers were kind to us not offering
    any insults on account of our failure to gain independence. I still
    appreciate their kindness.
42. On reaching home I engaged in farm work as an hired hand for about 6
    months. The next year I married and engaged in farming for myself.
43. As to a sketch of my life since the close of the war I have worked on
    the farm the greater part of the time. I have worked since at
    carpenters trade when engaged at my farm work and since passing my
    seventy sixth year I have left off all hard labor of any kind. My
    home is near Christian where I have lived since the close of the war
    between the States of North and the South except five years that I
    lived in the counties of White and Van Buren of the state of Tennessee.
    As to my church relations I obeyed the gospel in year 1866 since which
    time I have been identified with the Church of Christ making 56 years
    and if I hold out faith until the end I look for a home where there
    will be no strife nor bloody wars. I have never held office nor have
    I ever asked my friends to vote for me. I have felt that I was
    compent to hold an office neither do I think that my friends regarded
    me as suitable for office.
44. ----
45. William Ledbetter, Capt.; Hardy Murfree, 1st Lt.; Richard F. James,
    2nd Lt.; Charles A. King, 3rd Lt.; Samuel H. Ransom, 4th Lt.; Privates:
    Anderson, B.F.; Anderson, E.W.; Anderson, Jas. L.; Avant, B.W.; Bass,
    A.J.; Batey, B.B.; Batey, J.B.; Batey, W.O.; Beachbord, Wm.; Beesley,
    Jas. M.; Beesley, John; Beesley, N.W.; Beesley, L.J.; Beesley, Wm.;
    Glair, A.H.; Blair, J.L.W.; Back, Adam; Boring, Lonny; Brooks, C.C.;
    Brothers, A.W.; Burrows, T.?(L.?)W.; Carney, L.V.?; Cates, Joseph;
    Clarck, Geo.; Clay, D.D.; Becton, L.W.; Collier, F.W.; Crass, F.H.;
    Crass, Morris; Critchlo, Saml.; Crockett, L.O.; Davis, Samuel; Davis,
    Dony; Dixson, Lewis; Drumwright, W.B.; Dudley, R.A.; Edwards, A.W.;
    Ewing, J.W.; Faris, Jno.; Featherston, Wm.; Fletcher, J.H.; Grigg,
    J.H.; Hall, Jos.; Hallybertton, B.F.; Halloway, J.E.; Haynes, C.C.;
    Haynes, J.E.W.; Henry, J.F.; Hicks, W.H.; Higdon, Johnl Hirshberg,
    Simon; Hodge, S.H.; Hollowell, S.S.; Howse, L.H.; James, Albert;
    Jamison, M.; Jarratt, J.L.; Jetton, Brev.?; Jetton, J.W.; Jones, R.G.;
    Jenkins, J.H.; Jackson, J.W.; Johson, G.W.; Kiney, Thos.; King, J.M.;
    King, J.D.; King, L.M.: Kerr, M.; Lawrence, J.C.; Ledbetter, N.C.;
    Lillard, M.; Leeper, S.C.; Lepper, W.F.; Levy, H.; Loeb, A.; Loeb, M.;
    Love, J.R.; Maberry, Wilson, Manney, D.D.; McLean, A.V.; McLean, C.L.;
    Mitchel, Wm.; Miller, Chas.; Moore, Wm.; Morton, Jas.; Mosby, J.C.;
    Murfree, H.; Murfree, J.B.; Nance, I.N.; Neel, F.E.; Neely, Jno.;
    North, J.M.; North, W.L.; Oden, L.M.; Pearce, L.; Phillips, Jno.;
    Poindexter, Jno.; Ransom, A.C.; Ransom, H.A.; Ross, J.W.; Rucker,
    Robt.; Rutlege, Ples.; Searcy, Wm.; Seward, Mac.?; Shelton, W.D.;
    Sims, B.E.; Sims, N.?H.; Smith, Hue; Smith, B.J.; Smith, Brown; Smith,
    J.D.; Smith, Jno.; Smith, L.H.; Smith, L.J.; Snell, J.L.; Snell, J.L.;
    Snell, L.A.; Snell, F.M.; Sublett, D.D.; Sedberry, Hen.?; Tucker, L.J.:
    Tucker, L.J.; Turner, E.L.; Turner, R.J.; Traylor, W.; Vaughan, E.R.;

BATEY (cont'd.):
   Vaughan, J.A.; Wade, T.?J.; Walter, Geo.; Watts, W.; Wilkinson, G.H.A.?;
   Wilkinson, W.A.; Wheeling, C.E.; White, H.(A?); Wilson, A.; Wilson,
   Thos.
46. ----
   From B.B. Batey, Christian, R#3 Tenn.

BAYLESS, ROBERT R.

FORM NO. 1

1. Robert R. Bayless, Johnson City, Tennessee
2. 71 ys. 7 mths.
3. State of Tenn. Carter County
4. Tenn. Washington Co.
5. Farmer
6. Laborer on farm
7. I did not own property at the beginning of war. I was only 17 years
    of age
8. None
9. My father came in possession
10. (Q. (cont'd.): of 227 acres farm during the war. He did not own
    land previous to that time.
11. Log house - 3 rooms
12. As a boy I worked at home on farm in a general way and worked away
    from home a great deal doing farm labor
13. My father farmed some at home on rented land. He also worked away
    from home for the land lord upon whose property we lived and for
    others also. My Mother had no servants but done her own house work,
    and her spining and weaving. Supplied the clothing for the family
    the same was true in wealthy homes.
14. Kept no servants
15. Most people made a living by farm labor and of course was considered
    honorable
16. Yes there were not many negroes in this part of state.
17. Very few if any. A good many families owned from one to six negroes.
    I only knew two families owning 25 or more negores.
18. No perceptable diference. Slaveholders would hire white men and work
    them with their slaves with their own sons and themselves
19. At church at school and public gatherings slaves and non-slaves
    holders mingled without a diference furthern than good behavior and
    bad behavior would make people differ to-day then the negroes wor-
    shiped with the whites.
20. No perceptible deference on that account
21. Slaves did not help anyone in a political contest
22. Fairly good - not so good as at present when money is plentiful and
    every one any good can have his share
23. There was no disparagement against any young man because of poverty
    but his opportunities were what he himself made of his environments.
24. Public schools - about 3 to 4 months a year during the winter months
25. Something like three years
26. From two to three miles - I did not always attend school at the same
    place as we were renters and moved from one place to another
27. Public schools were all the schools that we had in the country. The
    towns were small, and so was the schools in them. The rich and the
    poor were educated together in the country in the public schools
28. Public - sometimes suplemented by subscriptions and continued in that
    way for two months.
29. From three to four months
30. Yes with anxiety they attended school. Many of them good students
    with poor chances.
31. I went to school to both women and men
32. Enlisted 1862 perhaps in July or August
33. 60th Tenn. Com. Officers J.H. Crouch, Capt.; J.S. Rodgers, 1 Lt.;
    John Taylor, 2 lt.; T.A. Stonecipher, 3 Lt.; Sargeants- 1st Uriah
    Hunt, J.C. Peoples, and John Hughes?; Wm. Speares?, Geo. Ervin,
    Mat___; James Baxter; Geo. brown, Rufus Vaughn, S.B. Winslow; James
    Taylor and others; (Corporals forgotten), Privates- Jos. Archer,
    R.R. Bayless, S.D. Bayless, J.W. Bayless, John Need, Jas. Sealf(Sc?)

293

BAYLESS (cont'd.):
   John Lizenbury, Mathew Yopp?, Joe Campbell, Geo. Hamilton, Geo.
   Hysenger, John Hysinger, Jas. Love, John Harrison, Jas. Porter, Thos.
   Porter, ___ Zimmerman, Jno. Wilson, ___ Harrison, Sam Crawford, 2
   Crawford, Jesse Fulkerson, Jas. Walter, Sam Galloway, Thos. Howard,
   David Howard, Geo. Howard, Sam Hare, Hyrum Mulkey, John Whitlock,
   Henry Husk, Birch Dethridge, Tim Munsey, C.D. Muncy, Geo. Ballon?,
   John Bush
34. Johnson City, Knoxville, Tenn. Montgomery, Ala. Jackson and Vicksburg,
    Miss.
35. perhaps 5 mths.
36. Chickasaw Bayoo and Bluff
37. after Chickasaw Bluff Battle we remained in camp around Vicksburg.
    Drilled and done the duty of soldier lifes in a general way until the
    battle of Big Black river when I was captured on May 17, 1863 was
    taken to prison at Ft. Deleware where I remained until the following
    October and was taken from ther to Pt. Lookout or Pt. Maryland and
    remained there until Feb. 14, 1865 near two years prison life.
38. I was paroled and my ___? had not expired when the surrender come
    in other words I had not been exchanged.
39. I left Pt. Lookout as I now remember Feb. 14, 1864 on Parole came to
    Richmond about the 17th furloughed and came home near Jonesboro Tenn.
    arriving at home on the 23 Feb. 1865. I remained at home between the
    lines until 5 days after the surrender April 13 and took the oath at
    Jonesboro Tenn.
40. Farming has been my single occupation since the war
41. Since the close of the war I have lived three diference places in this
    Washington co. 1st three miles south of Jonesboro for 20 yrs. where
    my people have for seven generations. 2nd 6 miles north and 5 miles
    west of Johnson City where I now live. This is a good town with
    10,000 population and still growing. Senator Gardner and Representa-
    tive Barnes are both from our town Johnson City. I am personally
    acquainted with them both, they are good men though they are Repub-
    licans.
    Co. C. 60th Tenn. Infty. R.R. Bayless

    (N.B.: BAYLESS, ROBERT R. Pension No. 11911(D))

                              BAUGH, WILLIS

FORM NO. 1

1. Willis Baugh, Col. RFD 2, Manchester, Tenn.
2. 79
3. Rutherford co., Tenn.
4. Rutherford
5. Rail Roading
6. Farmer
7. None. All in slavery
8. none
9. none
10. ----
11. Log cabbin, one room
12. great deal of plowing. worked with great deal choped cotton and
    howed corn
13. Shoe maker by trade. worked for his Boss. Mother cooked. She spun
    a great deal
14. ----
15. Verry
16. No. the slaves did all of the work
17. the slaves did it all. the white men just Bossed
18. No. They thought themselves above those that didn't own slaves
19. no did not
20. very often
21. very ofter
22. no wasn't allowed that much freedom.
23. was not
24. none
25. ----

                                  294

BAUGH (cont'd.):
26. no collored school at all
27. white school
28. ----
29. ----
30. the whites did
31. ----
32. Rutherford county, dont know first year of the war
33. the Miller Burg Co.(Meck. Burg.?); Bob Holland, Frank White, Bob
    White, Pomp White, Will White, Clem Gunison, Capt. Newman, Ben Baugh,
    Jack Baugh, Tom White, Bill Benett, Toney Robinson, Wicom? Mankins,
    Fount Nichols
34. to Alabama from Richmond, Va.
35. about 8 months
36. battle of Shiloh
37. fell back Corinth. I was cooking at that time. Next battle at Bools
    Gap about a day or so. we retreated. lived (line?) camp 4 years.
    anything I could get hold of. slept on the ground. pickled meat and
    some times none. like stock. hungry often.
38. at end of war
39. I walked home, took a long land and a hard road
40. Rail roading
41. Rail roading, Coffee co., yes - member of church
42. Clem Malber; lived at Rutherford co.
43. Maranda Baugh; lived at Rutherford co.
44. ----

BAXTER, W. S.

FORM NO. 2

1. W.S. Baxter, Williston, Fayette co., Tenn.
2. 76
3. Fayette co., Tenn. Dist 14
4. I was and am proud of it (Confederate)
5. Co. H, 14 Tenn. Regt. Forest Cavalry
6. Farmer
7. David Smith? Baxter; N. Carolina; (Middle name may be South?) name is
    written over; live near here all his life; none only a good farmer
    and was a Presbitiarn (Presbyterian)
8. Eliza Worthen (this name not clear):lived at this county and state
9. He owned a good farm
10. $5000.00
11. Yes
12. 400 acres
13. $5000.00 and Six thousand
14. log home
15. on the farm
16. He was a farmer and did farming for a living and to make money
17. Yes
18. Yes indeed
19. Yes
20. very few
21. Yes, as a fact they (didn't finish sentence, evidently)
22. Yes, in a general way, we had no clash in this respect
23. No indeed
24. Yes, we did not, make any deference
25. Yes
26. Had every advantage as we have now, but we did not have so many idlers
    as we do not.
27. The old country Dist. school
28. not more then 3 months
29. one mile
30. very few indeed, one or two, other than Dist. school in the county
31. Public
32. 3 months
33. Yes
34. Min, very few women, was imployed those days
35. Nov. 15, 1863, Confederate army

BAXTER (cont'd.):
36. to Como, Miss.
37. Yazoo City, Miss.
38. Yazoo City, Miss.
39. Mostly in Miss. then to Ala. then with Hood, Battle of Franklin
40. Memphis, Tenn.
41. Then we was so near home
42. Farming
43. All my life since the war farming for a living. am now retired.
44. ----
45. John W. Roberts   Wiliston
    Grif (Gip?) McLoi__   Fla
    Henry Lewis   Memphis, Tenn.
    Jon Shaw   Somerville
    Dr. Robertson   "
    Wm. Parirck (Parrish?)   Soldier Home, Ok.
46. W.S. Baxter   Williston, Tenn.

    (N.B.: BAXTER, W.S. Pension No. 15339)

                    BEANER, ANDREW JACKSON
              (this name is BEAVER on 2nd form)

FORM NO. 2
(see data from 2nd form in parentheses)

1. Andrew Jackson Beaner, R 6(4?), Sparta, Tenn.   (A.J. Beaver, Sparta
    Tenn. R#6)
2. 82 yrs (81 years, 8 mo.)
3. Laurence co. Ala   (Larance co., Ala.)
4. Confederate
5. Co. L, 38 Tenn
6. Farmer
7. James B. Beaner; Sparta, White co., Tenn.; lived White county
    (Jas. B. Beaver - Larance co.)
8. Nancy Williams; Dudly Williams and Sarah ___; Ala. (N.C. Williams/
    Avoca, Franklin co, Ala.)
9. ----   (my grandfather and grandmother on fathers side came from
    Doublin, Irland. Settled at Roan Oak, Va.)
10. ----   (did not own land; hogs and cattle valued $200.00)
11. no
12. 80
13. about $2,000.00
14. 1of house 3 rooms
15. farm work plowed and hoed and done all kind of farm work
16. Father worked on farm. and Mother done the cook spinging and weaving
17. None
18. Yes
19. Most all of them did
20. a few had others do their work
21. they treated honorable with respect
22. yes
23. friendly
24. I think not
25. no
26. discouraged
27. Subscription school   (public and free)
28. about 3 months
29. 4 mile
30. i military school
31. public
32. about 1 month
33. about ½ that did not have money to __ basket? (not clear)
34. Both
35. 13 day of June 1861 Anington?, Miss   (Abington, Tenn. June 13, 1861)
36. Memphis Tenn.
37. about 8 months   (something like 12 months)
38. Shilo

                          296

BEANER (cont'd.):
39. I was in 3 battle with cloths no good and grub poor bare footyed part
    of the time slept on the ground in the mud rain and snow (never
    captured; wounded once slightly)
40. Greensboro, N.C. Apr. 26, 1865
41. that was the roughest I every went __ I was a foot and fared badly
42. Blacksmithing
43. Lived in White and work blacksmithing and farming until my health
    failed about 3 year ago and have been a renter every since I have
    been in Whit co. I have been a member of the baptist 60 yr I have
    never held any office
44. ----
45. Capt. E.F. Lee   Columbo, Tenn.
    Lt. Tuck Bland   "   "
    Huston Lovelet?   Lolady St. Miss.
    Jas. Goff   Memphis, Tenn.
    John Goff   "   "
    Jas. Vessels   "   "
    Dick Luna   "   "
    Mike Haps   New Orleans, Lou.
    John McGleson   Memphis, Tenn.
    Henry Davenport   "   "
    Bill Gerly   "   "
    Bill Sumers   Avaca, Ala.
    J.D. Crownocks   "   "
    Bery Crownocks   "   "
    Jas. Crownocks   "   "
    Jake Allen   "   "
    Bob Gray   Wolf Spring, Ala.
    John Gray   "   "   "
    Chas. Smith   Avaca, Ala.
    Mat Young   Jonesboro, Tenn.
    P.O.C. Patman   Raeilgh (Raleigh), N.C.
    Bug Beryman   Wolf Spring, Ala.
    Andy Beryman   "   "   "
    Henry Beryman   "   "   "
46. J.C. Terry   Sparta, Tenn.
    H. Cope   "   "
    W.M. Montgomery   "   "
    W.M. Hoosier   "   "
    W.L. Dibrele   "   "
    Spence Franks   "   "
    ____, Sparkman, E.O.   "   "
    E. Quillin   "   "
    Jas. Huson   "   "
    J.R. Morrison   "   "
    Thos. Young   "   "
    Jas. Cloyd   "   "
    H.C. Clark (C.H.?)   Spencer, Tenn.
    John Goodwin   Sparta, Tenn.
    John Kirby   "   "
    J.F. Knowles   "   "
    Mitchell Martin?   Carthage, Tenn.
    J._. Qualls   Sparta, Tenn.
    Jas. Medlock   "   "
    Lobo Kirby   "   "
    Carol Jones   "   "
    A.J. Beaner   "   "   R. 4
    Hayland Wilhite   "   "
    George Crawford   "   "
    Geo. Davis   "   "
    Bill Chatman   "   "
    Bill Baker   Broad Valley, Tenn.

297

BEARD, RICHARD

1. Richard Beard, Murfreesboro, Tenn.
2. 80
3. Madison county, near Canton, Miss.
4. Confederate
5. I enlisted in Co. H. 7th Tennessee Ing. and served with that until after the Sevend Days battle near Richmond, when I was transfered to Co. E?, 5th Confd.
6. School-teacher for 50 years
7. Richard Beard; Dry Fork, Sumner co., Tenn.; lived at Lebanon, Tenn.; he graduated at Cumberland College, Princeton, Ky. then Professor of Theology, Cumberland University.
8. Cynthia Castleman; Andrew Castleman and Peggy Castleman; lived four miles from Nashville, on Hillsboro Road.
9. My father's father came from near Lynchburg and was a soldier in Col. Lynch's regiment at the Battle of Guilford Court House. My grand-father Castleman was a soldier in the Revolution and received a grant of land, 640 acres, near Nashville. My grandmother Peggy Castleman, was the daughter of Andrew Ewing, probably the most prominent of the early settlers, about Nashville.
10. None
11. Yes-15
12. 180 acres
13. I was quite young at the beginning of the civil war, having been in college all the time to the beginning of the war and paid no attention to values
14. Two story, brick dwelling with eight rooms, the same dwelling now owned and occupied by my brother, E.E. Beard, at Lebanon.
15. I did work on the farm, on Saturdays and during vacations, with the hoe, pulling fodder and assisting in threshing wheat.
16. My father was engaged for 50 years as principal, president and pro-fessor of colleges; first president or principal of Sharon College, near Canton, Miss., then president of Cumberland College, Princeton, Ky. and last professor of Theology, in Cumberland University. My mother was simply housekeeper, no cooking, spinning or weaving.
17. Yes 1 one cook, two house servants and about 12 field hands
18. At Lebanon, there was no such thing as aristocracy, poor as well as rick, generally met on the level. My recollection is that honest labor was considered respectable.
19. Yes
20. Have no idea
21. I think not, expecailly if the nonholding class was any way respect-able
22. Yes, but in those days there was no such public school system that we have now
23. As far as I can remember a kindly friendly feeling existed between them, they lived to a great extent on a footing of equality. No "stuck up" family in the place.
24. I don't think it had any effect one way or the other
25. Yes
26. Encouraged
27. I never went to any school but a college, from the time I was six years of age; never rubbed my back against anything but College (this word is on next live)
28. About 12 years
29. 300 yards
30. Cumberland University and Preparatory school, connected with the University, one Female College and two pay schools, carried on by young ladies
31. Private
32. These school ran for 10 months
33. Yes, I think so
34. Men
35. On May 20th, 1861, I was sworn into the Confederate service, at the Fair Grounds, Nashville, Tenn. and on the night of the 21st, my company was carried in box cars to Camp Trousdale, in Sumner county.

BEARD (cont'd.)
36. Camp Trousdale, and July the 15th, the regiment the 7th Tennessee Inf.
    to which my company belonged was ordered to Virginia
37. I enlisted May 20th, 1861 and was in my first battle, Seven Pines,
    May 31, 1862
38. Seven Pines about five miles from Richmond
39. This battle gave a better conception of Hell than any that I passed
    through afterwards; I passed through a number, but I never experienced
    anything like this first battle; never saw men fall around me as fast
    as they did there. I was wounded three times, almost before I could
    turn around. I was carried to Richmond, to the old Kent hospital,
    reaching there at midnight. The next morn was carried to the home of
    a Mrs. Eckhart, where I stayed until my recovery.
    After recovery, was commissioned 2nd Lieut. and assigned to Company
    B, 5th Confederate Regt. in the West.
    At the battle of Chickamauga, was wounded and on the death of my
    captain, in that battle was commissioned as such in his stead. At the
    battle of Atlanta, July 22nd, 1864 was captured with one half of my
    regiment and sent to Johnsons Island. Was released from prison June
    1st 1865 and I will never fell as happy again until I reach the gates
    of the Eternal City, as I did that bright and beautiful morning in
    June 1865.
    (N.B.: this last answer is written over the spaces for Q. 40-42)
43. Attorney at law, together with a large line of fire insurance. My
    first introduction to Murfreesboro was in the storm and hurricane of
    the battle of the 31st of December 1862, - after the war, I cast my
    lot with her people and have never regretted it. Here I have lived
    and here I expect to die. In the language of Rob Roy, I can say:
    "That the flowers over which I tread while living shall bloom over
    me when I'm dead."
                              Yours very truly, Richard Beard
44. ----

     (N.B.: BEARD, RICHARD Pension No. 16,164

                    BEARD, WILLIAM DAVID

FORM NO. 2

1. William David Beard, Talley, Tenn.
2. Mar. 29, 1922 (80) eighty yrs. old
3. Tennessee, Bedford co.
4. Confederate
5. Co. B-53rd Tenn. Reg.
6. Blacksmith
7. Elijah Beard; don't know; don't know; don't know; Mt. Harmon, Bedford
    co. and south of Lewisburg, Marshall co.; died when I was three yrs.
    old
8. Martha Patton; don't know; don't know; Mt. Harmon (Hasmon?), Bedford
    co., Tenn.
9. Grandfather Beard was private soldier in revolutionary war. Ireland
    is country come from to this country. He left gold ring with his
    wife when he fift (fight?)
10. Lived with mother and two sisters as renter
11. None of any generation
12. Renter all his life and died so
13. ----
14. Log house, two rooms with stick and dirt chimney. In several differ-
    ent houses all have been of same description
15. Pull weeds with older bros. when 4 to 9 yrs. old. from 9 till 1
    month before I was 18 plowed and made a regular hand. Worked many a
    day right among slaves and just the same kind of work as slaves.
16. My father was blacksmith by trade, shoe steers, horses and general
    blacksmith work. He farmed some. My mother weave and spin cotton
    in day-time pick cotton for spinning at night. All general house
    work.
17. None
18. It was considered respectable and honorable in my neighborhood.

BEARD (cont'd.):
19. Slave holders boys did not work any. they would even make a negro slave hand him a drink of water when sittin in house.
20. All white men that had plenty worked very little some poor white men were lazy but had to work
21. Yes. They were all friendly of all classes.
22. Yes. All visited each other and sometimes a negro or two with them.
23. Yes
24. As far as being slave holder made no difference - an honorable man and upright man had more than anything else.
25. No. A renter had no chance to save anything. slave holders were the only men that could make enough moeny to do anything.
26. They could have entered land but they had to go to Nashville to pay entry fees and for this reason poor people took leases and never did have anything a head.
27. Log school building log slabs in the legs for benches
28. 4 days
29. about 3 miles
30. Collins school house. Marshall Academy. Union Academy
31. Public schools
32. two, three and four months in the year
33. some went regular and some had to work and couldnt go
34. Man teacher. never did see a woman teacher when a boy
35. about 1 month before Xmas in 1861. Lewisburg, Marshall co., Tenn. left Mother and two sisters all alone without anyone to support them
36. Camp Weakly 1½ north of Nashville
37. about 3 mos.
38. Ft. Donelson. Fought with double barrel deer shot guns shot 12 buck shot and 1 oz. ball
39. Generals Buckner (Ruckner?) and Pillar (Pillow?) surrendered at Ft. Donelson. From Ft. Donelson to prison. From prison to Ft. Hudson, La. then engaged in building breasworks. Went to Vicksburg and retreated back to Jackson. sent Gonzollee? north of Pensacola as garrison to guard railroads to keep Federals from cutting off supplies. to Missionary Ridge.
40. just before the war ended at Columbia, Maury co., Tenn.
41. Captain Jim Murry (Maury?) give me a sick pass. sick with diarrhora and come on wagon 8 miles and then rode behind cavalry men 4 miles and walked the rest of way home
42. tried to farm but couldnt sick all time with chills. all at home were on starvation but Tom Collins furnished necessities of life.
43. Farm work since war until two years ago and an not able now to do anything much. First lived in a log house rented from Tom Collins and was paid well for my work and married here on Tom Collins' place and from there to widow Rambo place-lived there two years. From there to my father-in-laws place and there 16 years till he died and then I bought a little place at Reed Gap. My mother lived with me all this time and lived on this place 10 years till mother's death and in another year my wife died at that place and three years after my wife died, married second time then lived 11 years at this place then traded for place at Talley about 10 years and then lived on place I now live on still close to Talley.
44. ----
45. Bill Holden, 1st Captain   Lewisburg, Tenn.
    Buck Collins, 1st Lt.   "   "
    Jim Murray, 2nd Lt.   "   "
    Jim Hawkins, 3rd Lt.   "   "
    Billie Patterson, 4th Lt.   "   "
    Porter Bullock   "   "
    Vines Fox   "   "
    Will Roane   "   "
    John Roane   "   "
    Sam Eizley .   "   "
    Gray Edwards   "   "
    Jim Chuk (Cheek?)   "   "
    Joe Beard   "   "
    Hezakiah Chumm?   "   "
    Nimrod Jones   "   "
    Jim Hightower   "   "
    Joe McRady   "   "

300

BEARD (cont'd.):
```
    Lank? McLary             Lewisburg, Tenn.
    John Burkeen?               "        "
    Bazz Dorroty                "        "
    Jack Welch                  "        "
    John Hopwood                "        "
46. Samuel Leonard           Petersburg, Tenn.
    Bill Archer                 "        "
    Wash Cosby                  "        "     RFD
    John Blackwell           Talley, Tenn.
    Jim Pearson                 "        "
    Lynn Twitty              Lewisburg, Tenn.  RFD
    Bob Allen                Belfast, Tenn.
    Tom Armstrong               "        "
    Tom Hazelip              Yell via Lewisburg, Tenn.
    Bob Shaw                 Lewisburg, Tenn.
    Bob? Lune                Spring place, Tenn.
    Bill Bledsoe             Petersburg, Tenn.
    Tom Bledsoe                 "        "
```

(written on extra pages)
39. At missionary Ridge built breast works retreated to Ringold waded
Chickamauga river. fought battles from Missionary ridge to Atlanta
Ga. Made a stand at Atlanta held good for two days lost my Colonel
White from Giles Co. and my brother Samuel Beard and buried in Atlanta
and lost about ½ of co. in Atlanta. retreated from Atlanta to Jones-
boro. Had a battle at Jonesboro - the last battle on this raid.
Left Jonesboro under Hood to Nashville and had battle at Franklin.
Here retreated south and received pass at Columbia. On all this
march waded mud and water without rations. ---------- Special: Lost
brother in Civil War - Samuel Beard; Lost son in World War - Lane
Beard. Now I don't want any more war.

(N.B.: BEARD, WILLIAM D. Pension No. 7552)

BEARD, WILLIAM EDWARD

FORM NO. 2

1. William Edward Beard, Cumberland City, Tennessee
2. 74 years old
3. McNairy county, Tennessee
4. Confederate
5. B-21 Tennessee Cavalry
6. farming
7. Wm. B. Beard; b. in N. Carolina; His father moved to West. Tenn. when
    my father was a boy; Trustee of McNairy county
8. Harriett Ormsby; dont know; dont know; Stewart co., Tennessee
9. Grandfather was Frank Beard. He was in the War of 1812.
10. None
11. None
12. 130
13. $1000
14. log house two rooms
15. plowed and hoed and done general farm work
16. working on a farm. house keeping and carding and spinning and cooking
17. none
18. yes
19. yes
20. none
21. They mingled freely with those who did not own slaves better now than
    did then in general act as if they thought themselves better then the
    latter
22. yes
23. yes, then were friendly toward one another
24. no
25. yes
26. encouraged
27. Public school of the county

301

BEARD (cont'd.):
28. 40 months
29. one half mile
30. a schoolhouse built on the land of a Curbby (does he mean Kirby?) by
    the people of the community.
31. Public
32. 4 months
33. yes
34. man
35. In 1864 at Purdy, McNairy co., Tenn. in the Confederate army
36. Went down on the Tenn. river above Johnsonville, Tenn.
37. 1 mo.
38. Camelsville
39. In the fall of 1864, on our way to Nashville we went to Columbia,
    Tenn. and had a battle there driving the Yankees from there, then
    from there we fought on Duck river, driving the Yankees from there
    then to Spring Hill, Tenn. where we fought some, the Yankees retreat-
    ed to Franklin to which place we followed and engaged in that battle.
40. Was Payroled at Gainsville, Ala. May 10, 1865.
41. Came home horseback
42. Farming
43. Farming in Houston co., Tenn. ever since the war.
44. ----
45. Captain G.W. Carrel, Lieut. Frank Bell, Lieut. W.B. Malone, G.I. Cook,
    T.J. Walker, Tom Malone, Bob Wilson, Jessie Wilson, A.J. Horton, Sam
    White, Gracy Roberson, Charlie Best (Bess?), Jim Stovall, Ben Williams,
    Ben Harris, George Witt, Dennis Macathey, Nute Green, John King, Jim
    Hardison, Allen Hardison, Jim Reckord, _____ Reckord, Billy Snow, Tom
    Reed, Bill Manice, _____ Hiett, Demon Odum, Wiley Odum, Jim English,
    George Baxter, Jim Branch, Basley Ross, Henry Sanders
46. J.A. Halliburton   Cumberland City, Tenn.
    A.J. Blake   Cumberland City, Tenn.
    Columbus McAulay   Erin, Tenn.

    (written on extra page)
39. From Franklin we went to Brentwood, Tenn. driving the Yankees back to
    Nashville, Tenn. we went to Murfreesboro, where we had two battles
    getting defeated in the main fight, when Hood was defeated at
    Nashville and on his retreat to the Tenn. river, we were engaged in
    battle a great deal of the time both day and night. From there we
    crossed the Tenn. river and went to Corinth, Miss. We, Buford's
    Division, were disbanded for twenty days and went home. at the
    expiration of the twenty days we went to Barona, Miss. on the Mobile
    and Ohio railroad, where Gen. Forest reorganized his command, putting
    Bell's Brigade in Jackson's Division. We camped at Barona and West
    Point, Miss. until the last of March 1865 and started to Selma, Ala.
    Forest reached there with part of his command and was defeated, we
    Jacksons Division, were cut off and maneuvered around until the
    surrender.

                    BEASLEY, CHARLES DAVIS (David?)

FORM NO. 1

1. Charles David Beasley, Covington, Tenn.
2. 76 years Nov. 11, 1921
3. State of Georgia, Clark county
4. Cherokee county, Alabama
5. Farmer
6. Farmer
7. I owned no property
8. No slaves
9. 40 acres
10. $500.00
11. Log house with 3 rooms
12. I plowed hoed and done all kinds of farm work
13. My father done all kinds of farm work and my mother cooked, washed,
    spun, wove and made clothes for the family
14. no servants

                              302

BEASLEY (cont'd.):
15. honorable
16. yes
17. All men in the community done their own work
18. Our neighborhood all mingled freely together
19. they did
20. a friendly feeling among all
21. It did not
22. opportunities were good
23. encouraged
24. public school 3 months each year
25. 3 months
26. about 1 mile
27. 3 months public and private school occasionally
28. both
29. 3 months
30. yes
31. men
32. Dec. 29th 1863 at Dalton, Ga.
33. 19th Ala. Inft.; Capt. John Berry, 1st Lt. Jim Leath, 2nd Lt. Bill
    Bell, 3rd Lt. Bill McCullough, Wm. Beesley, Eli Cro_, Andrew Dearing,
    Peter Hartline, Athy. Herman, Wash. Sharp, (may be Noah), John
    Riler,. Frank Weaver, Nick Weaver, Nick Roliter (see John Riler,, this
    may be surname)
34. to Resaca, Ga.
35. about 3 months
36. Resaca, Ga.
37. Hard times, We fell back to Atlanta, fighting almost daily. on the
    28th of July 1864 my regiment was in the hardest battle I was ever
    engaged in, company was all killed or wounded, but 13. I was in a
    hospital about __(blurred) weeks.
38. May 1865 at Kingston, Ga.
39. I walked home about 50 miles
40. Farming
41. I remained in Cherokee county, Ala. about 2 years after the war, then
    moved to Lawrence co., Ala. where I lived for 9 years, then came to
    Tipton co., Tenn. where I have since resided.
42. David Beasley; b. in Virginia; lived in Clark co., Ga.
43. Susan Berger; Charles Berger and Malinda Berger
44. ----

(N.B.: BEASLEY, CHARLES DAVID Pension No. 7499)

BEASLEY, ED. MANEY (Haney)

FORM NO. 1

1. Edward Haney Beasley, Riddleton, Smith co., Tenn.
2. 83 last Sept.
3. Smith co., Tenn.
4. Smith co., Tenn. when I enlisted in Confederacy
5. farming
6. farming
7. I did not own any property of my own
8. They did - about seventeen (17)
9. three hundred acres I think
10. I cant say
11. 4 room frame house
12. plowed houed lots of white men did all sorts of work on farms before
    the war
13. My father was a farmer. My mother did all sorts of housework carding
    spining weaving sewing quilting
14. they did seventeen 17
15. it was
16. they did
17. to not a great extent most all men worked
18. some did and some did not
19. they did with nice honest poor people
20. some was friendly

303

BEASLEY (cont'd.):
21. not many
22. not so good
23. Some encouraged them and some did not
24. Just common schools
25. I dont remember
26. about three hundred yds from home
27. free schools mostly
28. both
29. from 4 to 5 months
30. they did
31. men
32. I enlisted in service of the Confederacy on May 23, 1861 and stayed
    till the war closed 4 years
33. Starn's Regiment Forth Tenn. Cal.
34. Camp Myers?, Oberton co. Tenn.
35. about three mo.
36. Tin? (Jim?) Town, Ky.
37. after the first fight we to Fishing Creek I neber was in prison and
    neber was in a hospital but was wounded several times half starved
    and thinly clad. I was Courier 14 mo. during the war
38. I came home horse back through Chattanooga ober Cumberland Mountain
    was worn out when I got home we joined N.B. Forris (Forest?) there
    one the greatest men ever libed. (he uses b in place of v throughout
    his form)
40. farming
41. engage in farming lived at Union City one year I am a member of the
    Christian Church.
42. McIvr (McIver?) Anderson Beasley; I dont know when he was borned;
    Smith co., Tenn. he was Justice of Peice one term
43. Elizabeth Nixon; ----; ----
44. ----

    (N.B.: BEASLEY, EDWARD HANEY (note the spelling of middle name)
    Pension No. 1851)

                    BEECH, RICHARD THOMAS

FORM NO. 2

1. Richard Tomas Beech, RFD # 1 College Grove, Tenn.
2. Born 1841 Jan. the 20
3. Williamson, Tenn.
4. Confederate
5. 26 Tennessee
6. farmer
7. William Beech; no; no; Virginia
8. Martha Jane Vaughn; Buck Vaughn and Nancy. nance; no (the nance makes
    no sense and is written in small case)
9. ----
10. No
11. no
12. no
13. none
14. log 3 rooms
15. I did all kinds of work on the farm
16. Spinning weaving and all kind - seeding cotton carding
17. no
18. yes
19. yes
20. few
21. most slave owners made no diference
22. yes
23. yes
24. non what ever
25. yes
26. incouraged
27. non
28. ----

                          304

BEECH (cont'd.):
29. ----
30. pay__
31. privat
32. through 44. no answers
45. ----
46. John Ladd, Franklin, R. 1, Tenn.
    J.B. Heithcock (Hathcock?), Franklin, Tenn.

    (N.B.: BEECH, RICHARD T., Pension No. 15212 and 16329/ Widow Pension
    No. 11051)

BEENE, LEMUEL JACKSON

FORM NO. 2

1. Lemuel Jackson Beene, Lodge, Tennessee
2. I am eighty-seven years old (born Aug. 10, 1835)
3. I was born in Tennessee, Marion county
4. I was a Confederate soldier
5. Company A, Fourth Tennessee
6. Farming
7. Obadiah Beene; b. in North Carolina
8. Barbara Heifner; Daniel Heifner and ___ lived on Battle Creek, Marion
    co., Tenn.
9. My grandfather Capt. Robt. Bean (this has been smudged - ink runs;
    difficult to read) fought in the Indian War also in the Revolutionary
    War. He lived in North Carolina. He engaged in the battle of King's
    Mountain. My grandfather, Daniel Heifner, was a German. They first
    settled in North Carolina. For references concerning the war services
    of Robert Beene (my grandfather) see Ramsey's Annals of Tennessee,
    Carnegie Library, Chattanooga,; Capt. Robt. Beene was a brother to
    William Bean, the first settler of Tennessee. (N.B.: this name is
    spelled Bean in early references...cme)
10. I owned eighteen or nineteen hundred acres of land, besides cattle,
    horses, sheep and hogs valued at $5000 approx.
11. I did not own slaves but my father, Obadiah Beene owned about eight
    slaves
12. About 5300 acres
13. My father did in 1840 and his estate had already been distributed
    among his heirs before the war began.
14. My parents occupied a hewed log house consisting of five rooms and
    a hall.
15. I did all kinds of farm work such as plowing, hoeing building fence
    and attending stock.
16. My father was a pioneer of this country. His work consisted of
    clearing land, building fences and home building. My mother kept
    house, did the cooking, spinning, weaving and sewing besides rearing
    and caring for a family of thirteen children.
17. One of the slaves assisted my mother with the cooking. The remainder
    of them worked outside.
18. All kinds of honest toil was considered respectable and honorable
19. Yes
20. In those days there was work for everyone. No one had time to spend
    idly.
21. No distinction was made between honest respectable people regardless
    of their property.
22. They were all on an equality.
23. Up to shortly before the war there seemed to be no antagonism yet
    this feeling appeared with the abolition idea.
24. Not until after slavery was abolished and the negro was enfranchised
    then the non-slave holder was helped.
25. Yes very good
26. This kind of man was encouraged by everyone.
27. There was a short public school (about two months) every year.
28. I went to school about eighteen months altogether.
29. About two miles
30. None except the public school
31. Public

305

BEENE (cont'd.):
32. About two miles
33. Yes
34. The teacher was a man. We had no women teachers in our community.
35. In September, 1862, I enlisted in Captain Bostick's Company in Marion
    county (in the Confederate Army).
36. After enlistment our company was sent to Murfreesboro, Tennessee.
37. About three months
38. The Battle Stone's River
39. I was taken sick while the battle of Stone's River was going on and
    was sent from Shelbyville to a hospital at Rome, Ga. where I stayed
    until September. I then rejoined my company at Chattanooga just
    before the Battle of Chickamauga in which battle I was captured and
    sent to Camp Chase. I stayed there for about four (this evidently
    is continued on extra pages...cme)
40. I took the oath of allegiance after all hopes were lost and was dis-
    charged from prison, in November 1864.
41. After I was released from prison I hired to a man at $1.00 per day to
    help gather his corn so that I might make money to come home on. His
    crop was finished in about a week. I then hired to another man 12
    miles from there. (this, too, is continued...cme)
42. I started to farming when I came home. I would make a crop in the
    summer and teach the public school in the fall.
43. I have spent my life on the same farm on which I was born and reared
    except the time that I would be away from home attending to business.
    I served six years in the Marion County court and one term as sheriff
    of the same county. I joined the Primitive Baptist Church of Sweeden's
    Cove in 1860 of which I have been a member ever since. I retired
    from active business in 1919. I have only missed attending two
    reunions of the Confederate Veterans and I hope to be able to attend
    the one at Richmond this year.
44. ----
45. Beene, J.C.
    Beene, George
    Beene, Robert
    Beene, S.W.
    Birdwell, Ed
    Brewer, Sam
    Smith, Robert
    Hise, James
    Hise, Fayette
    Hargis, Jack
    Thompson, Sam
    Clepper, Tom
    Clepper, Bunk
    Gilliam, Sam
    Smith, Tlias
    Smith, George
    Smith, Wiat
46. Sam Brewer   South Pittsburg, Tenn.
    J.A. Williamson   South Pittsburg, Tenn.
    Sam Bennett   Jasper, Tennessee
    Dan Deakins   Jasper, Tenn.
    Mr. Horned   Jasper, Tenn.
    Crit Hughes   Jasper, Tenn.
    Mr. Myers   Jasper, Tenn.

    (Extra Pages)
9. The name was originally Bean. It was spelled thus until about the
    year 1818 when my father began spelling the name Beene.
    (N.B.: these answers are written on stationary with the letter-head
    of: Beene Stock Farm, C.P. Beene, Proprietor; Successor to L.J.
    Beene; Established in 1818 by Obadiah Beene, Lodge, Tennessee...cme)
39. I was taken sick while the battle of Stone's River was going on and
    was sent from Shelbyville to a hospital at Rome, Georgia where I
    stayed until September. I then rejoined my company at Chattanooga
    just before the battle of Chickamauga in which battle I was captured
    and sent to Camp Chase O. I remained there about four months then
    was sent to Rock Island, Illinois. In camp I was poorly clothed and
    scantily fed since the Confederacy was short of supplies. We had no

306

BEENE (cont'd.):

tents while I was in the camps and we slept on the ground and consequently we were exposed to all kinds of weather. We had plenty of
corn bread all the time and a little meat (sometimes beef and sometimes bacon). In the hospital I had a comfortable bed but the food
was extremely rough for a sick person. But the worst was yet to
come. When I went to prison I was very poorly fed. I almost starved
and froze to death. I stayed there ten months during which time I
was never given any clothes. Each man was allowed one blanket and
was given an allowance of food in the morning consisting of about
half as much meat and bread as an ordinary man would eat at one meal.
This was to last all day. After I was released from prison I was
sent home. The war was nearing a close by this time and I was not
with the army when General Lee surrendered.

41. In this connection I will narrate a little experience that I had
while gathering corn in the country. As soon as I was released from
prison I wrote home for money to be sent to me to come home on. Then
while I was at the farm twelve miles out in the country my money came
to me at Rock Island. When after two weeks of farm work I came to
the Post office to ask for mail the Postmaster asked me what I was
expecting. I told him that I expected a letter containing money for
my trip home. He said that another man whose name was L.J. Beene
(the same as mine), had been there and had gotten the letter and
upon opening it and finding that it contained money had taken it back
to the post office saying that he was sure that the letter was not
for him. I was in such a hurry, to get home, I did not take time to
locate the man and have never seen him, a fact that I have regretted
ever since. After I had bought my ticket home I had only twenty
five cents in money and the same clothes I had worn ever since I
joined the army. I bought light bread with the twenty five cents and
that was all I had to eat on the way from Rock Island to Nashville.
When I got home I had on the same suit of home made jeans clothes that
I wore when I started for I had never drawn a uniform and had worn
the same suit all through the war.

BELL, JOHN WALTER

FORM NO. 1

1. Jno. Walter Bell
2. 82
3. Wayne co., Tenn.
4. Wayne county, Tenn. served in Confederacy
5. Farmer
6. Tanner and farmer
7. 1 horse $125.00
8. Yes - 5
9. 100 acres tillable land
10. $8000.00
11. log house weatherboarded
12. plowed with barshare(?) and bull tongue plows-hoed with eye hoes.
13. Died when I was an infant
14. I cook
15. yes
16. yes
17. To no extent
18. Yes
19. Yes
20. Yes
21. None
22. Yes
23. Encouraged
24. Free
25. 5 yrs.
26. ½ mile
27. Literary to 8th grade
28. Public
29. 3 to 5 months
30. Yes

307

BELL (cont'd.):
31. Man
32. about May 1st 1861 at Waynesboro
33. 1st Tenn. Cavalry; Capt. Biffel, Lt. Burns; Bill Snowden, Andy
    Meredith, Jno. Meredith, Jno. and Jim Arnett, Jim Hanlin, Joe Bailey
34. Mt. Plesant
35. No paticuler engagements scouting principally
36. ----
37. Slept on ground all time. Plenty to eat part of time sometime
    nothing clothing very good exposed to cold weather but in no hospital
    never in prison
38. May '65
39. Very inconvenient from Lack of Transportation and arms for protection
40. Farming
41. Lived in Tenn. & Mo. farmed mostly belong to no church believe in
    Primitive Baptist faith held no office
42. William R. Bell; b. North Carolina; lived Waynesboro, Tenn.; no war
    service except as conscripts't (conscription?) agent; wrote none
43. Adaline Alaxender; Jno. Alaxender and ____; Lawrenceburg
44. ----

BELL, W. T.

FORM NO. 2

1. W.T. Bell, Manchester, Coffee co., Tenn.
2. age 76 yrs
3. Tennessee Coffee county
4. I was a Confederate soldier
5. Co. E, 4 Tenn. Reg. Cavalry
6. a farmer
7. Tom Bell; Coffee co., Tenn.; live near Need More
8. Sarah Crosslin; William and Polley Keel, her maiden name; Beech Grove
9. I cannot satisfactorily answer the last questions
10. I owned about 75 acres at opening of civil war now own about 100 acres
11. the family owned 4 slaves
12. Parents owned about 150 acres
13. about 4 or 5 thousand dollars
14. a double log house
15. I worked on farm used the different farm tools
16. Father done various kind of farm work. Mother done various kinds of
    house and kitchen work.
17. did not
18. the farm work was considered honorable
19. they sure did
20. not many idlers
21. they mixed and mingled very much and friendly
22. they mainley did
23. there was generally friendly feelings
24. I think not
25. very good
26. very much encouraged
27. common free schools
28. about 20 months total
29. from one to 3 miles
30. Chadwick School house and Millersburg
31. Public most generally
32. about 3 months
33. they did
34. mostly man teachers
35. Enlisted in July 1864
36. to Saltworks, Virginia
37. 3 or 4 weeks
38. Salt works Virginia
39. we left Virginia went into North Carolina and on and on and we was
    in many small battles and skirmishes and I was in all my command was
    in
40. I was discharged at Washington, Georgia about 9th day of May 1865.
41. ----

BELL (cont'd.):
42. regular farm work
43. I been farming all the while part time in Rutherford county and part
    in Coffee - never held any office. I belong to the Baptist Church
    at Beechgrove about 40 years
44. Have met Jeff Davis and the General Johnson, etc etc
45. Captain Herbert, Tom Herbert, Mat Web, John Peacock, L. Peacock,
    Billey Fields, John Handcock, Jim Harding, Jim Fulks, Jim Pruitt,
    Joe Childres, Howl Mozley, Jim Fox, J.M. Fox, J.E. Fox, Bill Hoover,
    E.T. Gipson, Bin Mankens, George Pinkard, Jim Newman, Bin Hoover,
    T.N. Gipson, Bob Gipson, Harve Eaton, S.A. Carter, J.R. Shelton,
    Baxter (Vaxter?) Hoover, John Larence, Bob Clemon, Jim Worlk, Jim
    Shelton, Bill Ferrel, Jim Cothern, Joe Holice, Crocet Pearson, Billey
    Lillard, Dave Lillard, Jim Knox, Tom Lambert, Reat Harris, Roley
    Miller, Joe Walkins, Jim Nickles, Fount Nickles, George Drake, Dalies
    Jakups, John Hill, John Shelton, John Huneycutt, John Mayfield,
    Billey Owens, Luna Nowlin, John W. Summers, John Alen Summers, Long
    Jakups, Bin Marlin, Nolin Giles, Bill Blanton, Bob Blanton, Town
    Scrug, Beck Clark
46. Harrison Farriel   Manchester, Tenn.
    Tob Frazier   "   "
    Gilbert Heard   "   "
    Tob Taylor   Hillsbor, Tenn.
    J.R. Shelton   Beechgrove, Tenn.
    Bob Climons   "   "
    Vaxter Hoover   "   "
    Jim Drake   Wartrace, Tenn.

    (N.B.: BELL, W.T. Pension No. 11284)

                        BENNETT, AMBROSE

FORM NO. 1

1. Ambrose Bennett, Flintville, Tenn. R.R. 1
2. 85
3. Tennessee Fate (Fayette?) Co.
4. Tennessee, Lincoln co.
5. farming
6. farming
7. did not own property were renters
8. no
9. ----
10. did not own anything
11. log
12. I plowed with a gopher plow and hoed corn
13. Father plowed with a gopher plow. Mother carded spun and done weaver-
    ing for the family and made our close by hand
14. no
15. yes
16. yes
17. Some white men worked and some did not them that had slaves did not
    work
18. Some slave holder mingle freely with them that did not have slaves
    while others would not
19. most of them did at church and gathering
20. they were friendly
21. mostly did
22. times were not much good then they could not save any money much
23. some time they encouraged them and some time they did not
24. publick
25. about 3 weeks
26. about 2 mile
27. publick
28. public
29. 3 & 4 months
30. yes
31. man
32. 1861 April 2 at Smithland, Tennessee

BENNETT (cont'd.):
33. 1st Tennessee R. Co. H. Capt. Jake Crouse - Charlie Little, Jim Hall,
    Geo. Pickett, John Bennett, Henry Shelton
34. Lynchburg Va. first then went to Richmond Va.
35. little over 12 months
36. Seven Pines Battle
37. I went to the hospital at Richmond Va. 7 days Battle at Richmond cloth
    were then (thin?) and slept 1 blanket to a man beef and biscuit were
    exposed to cold and hunger
38. Saulsberry, N.C.
39. we walked part of our way and beged something to eat on our way we
    walked about 200 mile before we got to the train
40. farming plowering
41. ----
42. Arch Bennett; dont know; Tennessee; lived at Memphis
43. Nancy Taylor; John Taylor and Hulda Haskin; ----
44. ----

(N.B.: BENNETT, AMBROSE Pension No. 2831)

BENNETT, SAMUEL

FORM NO. 1

1. Samuel Bennett, Jasper, Tenn.
2. Seventy-six
3. Tenn. - Sequatchie county
3. Tenn. - Sequatchie county
5. Farmer
6. Farmer
7. All property was in parents name
8. Between 15 and 20
9. Seven Hundred
10. Between forty and forty-five thousand Dollars
11. Frame, with eight rooms
12. General farm work, and trading stock
13. Overseeing the farm and trading stock. Mother looked after the house,
    such as cooking, spinning, and weaving. Made all the clothes for the
    family including shirts, pants, coats, underclothes, socks and etc.
14. Two or three
15. In our community work was considered very honorable, and the man who
    did not toil was look upon as being a no-account.
16. Yes
17. Every(one) who was worth anything or considered as being a respect-
    able person, poor or rich, worked very industriously.
18. Slave holders and non-slave holders mingled very freely and sociably.
    There was no clannishness, nor snobbishness here between these two
    classes, such as I witnessed farther south. All honorable people
    were considered equal rich or poor.
19. Everybody was considered a like and equal.
20. The feeling was very friendly and co-operative.
21. The best man won, slaves or no slaves, rich or poor.
22. Yes, for instance a young man moved in without a nickel, he worked
    hard, saved what he could to educate himself. Some of his friends
    and employees learned of his ambitions, loaned him money to finish
    his education. Made one of the best of preachers and was finally
    promoted to the diplomatic corps
23. They were encouraged to the utmost, the above is a concrete example
24. County grammar school and Van Oldhoff's Acadamey on Lookout Mountain
25. About five years
26. Lived close to grammar school. Stayed in domitory of the academy
27. One county grammar school
28. Public
29. Three and sometimes four
30. Attended regularly as they could
31. Sometimes a man, and at other times a woman.
32. About Sept. 6, 1863 at Dunlap? (This is not clearly written)
33. 4th Tennessee Cavalry, Confederate Army (Smith's); James Ivey, Wm.
    Blakely (Blakesby?), Jno. Kirklin, Abner Barker, Sam Deakins, Jno.

310

BENNETT (cont'd.):
    Fields, Adam Mitchel, Wm. Smith, Gus Smith, Jno. Brown, Marlin Phelps,
    Wm. Phelps, Bob Phelps, Jerry Warren, R.C. Gunter and Capt. Sam
    Gloves
34. On a raid with Gen. Wheeler then middle and east Tennessee, then on
    into Virginia, where we were engaged in our first real battle.
35. Second day after my enlistment, this was a skirmish in the mountains,
    near Dunlap
36. at Saltville, Va.
37. ----
38. Was paroled at Charlotte, N.C. When Gen. Jos. E. Johnson surrendered
    to Gen. Sherman.
39. ----
40. Went to farming the day after I arrived home
41. ----
42. Burel(?) Lasater(?) Bennett; Dunlap, Sequatchie co., Tenn.; lived
    there all his life; He was in the army of Andrew Jackson and fought
    with him in the battle of New Orleans.
43. Elizabeth Lamb; Alexander Lamb and Elizabeth Carmack Lamb; Pikeville,
    Tenn.
44. I know very little concerning my ancesters, except that my fathers
    father came to Tenn. and settled in Sequatchie Valley from North
    Carolina.

    (N.B.: BENNETT, SAMUEL H., Pension No. 12294 and 15584)

BENNETT, WILLIAM JAMES

FORM NO. 2

1. William James Bennett, Bethpage, Tenn. R. #2, Box 93
2. 77 years
3. Tennessee Wilson Co.
4. Confederate
5. Bells company
6. Farmer
7. Jacup (Jacob) Bennett; Wilson Co., Tenn.; lived Wilson co.; died in
    Mex. War in 1846 or 7
8. Adline Gray; James Gray and Elizabeth Adams; Willison (Wilson?) co.,
    Tenn. (may also be Williamson county)
9. ----
10. Nun
11. No
12. Nun
13. Nun
14. log house 4 rooms
15. Plowing hoing and all kinds of farm work cradling in harvest field
    by hand
16. All kind of farme work my Father did. Mother cooking spining and
    weaving and all sort of house work
17. nun
18. yes
19. yes
20. They dun all of thare work
21. no diference betwen them all visiting each other as if thare was no
    slaves
22. yes
23. no diferenc betwen
24. no difference
25. yes
26. encureged by all
27. subscription
28. 24 months
29. 1½ mile
30. subscription
31. privet
32. 3 to 4 months
33. not much
34. men

BENNETT (cont'd.):
35. 1862 Nov. or Dec. Gallatin, Tenn.
36. Lebonen or Stones River
37. First Battle at Hartsville
38. Hartsville
39. never had a tent and was exposed to rain and snow and cold weather
40. at the end of war 1865 was at Camp Cheses (Chase)
41. had to work for money to go home on
42. farming
43. farming summer (Sumner) county Tennessee belong to the Christian
    church no office
44. ----
45. I understand you have all the names I know. Mr. F.G. Durham my
    neighbor said he sent all the names of all I know.
                                 Yours, W.J. Bennett, Bethpage, Tenn. R #2

    (N.B.: BENNETT, WILLIAM JAMES, Pension No. 12625)

                         BENSON, GEORGE W.

FORM NO. 2

1. George W. Benson, Murfreesboro, Tennessee Route 8
2. 76
3. Tennessee Rutherford county
4. Confederate
5. B-23rd
6. Farmer
7. Micaga (Micajah?) Benson; North Carolina; not known; lived near Mur-
    freesboro, Tenn.; none
8. Nancy Rennells; Thomas Rennells and (do not know); lived Marshall co.
    Tenn. when maried afterward Rutherford
9. Not known
10. Nothing of consequence
11. none
12. none
13. none
14. Rented log house 2 rooms
15. General farm work of all kinds that are usually done on a farm
16. Made shoes and tended to farm work in general sutch as plowing plant-
    ing seeding to hay, etc. My mother she did all kinds of house work
    sutch as cooking washing and ironing kniting spining weaving sewing
    and all kinds of house work done for a family
17. none
18. it was
19. yes
20. comparetavely none
21. not a bit
22. yes sir
23. there was
24. not in the least
25. yes if he used his time an tallants in the right direction
26. Encouraged as they wished everybody to do well and make honerable
    living
27. Free schools
28. not a great deal
29. 3 miles
30. free schools
31. public
32. from 3 to 5 months
33. not mutch
34. man
35. Confederate Army; 1861 at Murfreesboro, Tenn.
36. Camp Anderson
37. about 12 months
38. Shilo, Mississippi
39. After the battle I went back to Corinth from there to Coffeeville
    Miss to hospital. The battle lasted about 10 hours we were treated
    very well at hospital. Clothed and fed very scant and exposed to all

312

BENSON (cont'd.):
kinds of weather and not mutch sleep for a poor old Rebel soldier.
40. at Coffeville Mississippi from hospital
41. ----
42. as the Army advanced from Miss. to Perryville, Ky. I came to McMinville
with them and from there I came home
43. I have been engaged in farming. I have lived in Rutherford county
all of my life. My church relations are Methodist Protestant. I
have held no office
44. ----
45. William Lowe, Capt; Asa Lee, 1st Lt.; Levi Todd, 2nd Lt.; Caleb Todd,
3rd Lt.; Garland Anderson, Orderly; John Gun, John G. Arnold, Argile
Benson, Eli Benson, Tom Benson, Jim Benson, George W. Benson, Hurinson
Todd, George Winfrey, Newt Winfrey, Tom Arnold, Rusell Patrick, Aron
Todd, Will Knox, Jim Coleman, Dave Fleming, Ephriam Howland, J. Prator,
Jim Lowe, Calvin Lowe, John Kelton, John Mathews, America Arnold,
Granville Harrold, Billy Harrold, Cambell Sherrill, Jim Burks, Crocket
Burks, Dick McNabb, Dick Lee, Bud Donnell, Jim Donnell, Bob Justice
46. D. Blackman Murray   Readyville R. 1, Tenn.
Frank McKnight   Readyville, Tenn.
Russell Patrick   "   "
Jake McKnight   "   "
George Hatchett   Murfreesboro, R. 8, Tenn.
Epriam Howland   Christian R. 2, Tenn.
J. Prator   Beech Grove R. 2, Tenn.
Louis Hitchcock   "   "   "   "
John T. Kelton   Christiana R. 2, Tenn.
Bob Justice   Murfreesboro, R. 8, Tenn.
Frank Overall   "   "   "
Ben Rankin   "   R. 4,   "
Calvin Carniham   Murfreesboro City, Tenn.
Hugh Hope   "   "   "

BIGGS, ZACK, JR.

FORM NO. 1

1. Zack Biggs, Jr., Trenton, Tennessee
2. Ninety
3. Gibson county, Tennessee
4. Gibson county, Tennessee
5. Practicing medicine
6. Farmer
7. House and lot; one-half interest in drug store; and two slaves and
some stock
8. Yes, six
9. Four hundred acres
10. Both of my parents were dead and estate wound up before beginning of
the war
11. Seven room lof and frame
12. Yes, I worked on the farm doing such work as boys usually do on a farm
13. My father superintended management of his farm and my mother managed
house and superintended cooking, spinning and weaving.
14. Yes they kept several hired men
15. Yes, honest work was considered respectable
16. They did
17. Very few lived lives of idleness
18. They mingled freely
19. Yes
20. Friendly
21. I think not
22. Yes
23. Encouraged
24. Private school
25. About four years
26. one mile
27. Private school - Andrew College in Trenton
28. Private
29. Usually about four months

313

BIGGS (cont'd.):
30. Yes
31. Man
32. Confederacy at Trenton, Tenn. Sept. 1861
33. Col. Brown's Regiment - No. 55; the company to which I belonged was made up of men from Carroll, Gibson and Madison counties. All them going from Gibson county, and dead so far as I know
34. to Columbus, Kentucky
35. Nearly six months
36. ----
37. From Columbus, we were sent to Island No. 10 in the Miss. River, where I developed lung and bowel troubles. As Ass't Surgeon, I was sent in charge of about ten other such men to Memphis and there put these men in hospital. I, myself, was examined by surgeon in charge of hospital there and ordered to Trenton, and from there to Corinth, Miss. When Dr. Lim Caldwell diagnosed my case as consumption and recommended my discharge.
38. at Corinth, Miss.
39. came home on train
40. As soon as I was able I began practicing medicine at Trenton, Tenn.
41. I continued practicing medicine until my health again failed, and my physician advised h__t this I did for several years, then in 1871 went with (into?) wholesale grocery business in Memphis, continued there several years and went back to practicing? - later was in grocery (over)
42. Luke Biggs; near Washington, Beauford co., N.C.; he moved in 1818 to Stewart? Co. staid there until 1820 when he moved to Lebanon? (these town/county names not clear); Gibson county was organized in Luke Bigg's home (see paper attached)
43. Marina Bennett; Bryant Bennett and _____ Watson; Williamston, Martin Co., N.C.
44. Grandfather was Reuben Biggs who moved from N.C. to Gibson co., Tenn. 1820 after staying for years in Stewart Co. Great-grandfather was Kader Biggs who fought in Revolutionary War. Family came from England

(Attached pages as mentioned above)

AT THE HOUSE OF LUKE BIGGS
January Term 1824
State of Tennessee, Gibson County
COURT OF PLEAS AND QUARTER SESSIONS, JANURAY TERM 1824

Be it remembered that in pursuance of the Acts of the General Assembly in such cases made and provided, the following named gentlemen, to wit, William P. Seat, Robert Edmundson, Ollie Blakemore, Benjamin White, Robert Reed, Yarnell Reece, Abner Burgin, John D. Love, William W. Craig, William B.G. Killingworth and Isham F. Davis met at the house of Luke Biggs, the place set apart for holding court in said county on this day, being the 5th day of January 1824, and severally produced a commission from under the hand of William Carroll. Governor of the state of Tennessee, countersigned by the Secretary of State with the great seal therunto annexed, appointing them Justices of the Peace in and for siad county. Whereupon, Bartholomew G. Stewart, Esquire and acting Justice of the Peace in and for the county of Madison, who attended for that purpose, administered to the said gentlemen Justices the necessary oaths, prescribed by the constitution and laws for this State and a court was organized.
Thereupon the court proceeded with the election of a chairman when William P. Seat, Esq., was duly and constitutionally elected, who thereupon took his seat. The court then proceeded to the appointment of constable and to the levying of a tax ect.
The above is an exact copy of the minutes on record book A, page 1 in the office of the County Court Clerk of Gibson County, Tennessee.

(The following is from a newspaper article published in the"Nashville Banner" - date not shown)
TRENTON LOSES NOTABLE CITIZEN (in pencil-1925)
"Dr. Zach Biggs, Son of One of Gibson County's Organizers": Trenton Tenn. Dec. 17-(Special)- Dr. Zach Biggs passed peacefully to his

314

BIGGS (cont'd.):

    abundant reward Wednesday morning at 11 o'clock. His daughter, Mrs.
J.P. Jetton, and only grandson, Albert Biggs, Jr., Memphis, were at
the bedside. His wife died ___ (month cut) 5, 1908, (month appears
to be Dec...cme) and his only son, Albert W. Biggs, nationally known
attorney, died June 9, 1914. Dr. Biggs illness was short; less than
a week had he been confined to his bed. As his whole life was an
exemplary Christian life, so was his passing typical. When taken ill
a few days ago he said, "Daughter, I want to go to sleep right now,
there's so much more in the other world than in this.: During his
long life he had always been most active in church work, and for many,
many years had been treasurer of the Methodist Sunday school. Dr.
Biggs was a surgeon in the Confederate army. He was a Mason with the
highest ideals of the order. The outstanding influence of his life
was his firm faith in God and his active service in church affairs.
He approached the 95th milestone of life with no perceptible abate-
ment of the powers of reasoning or waning of the faculty of memory.
His wholesome interest in affairs, local and national, were as vital
at 94 as in youth. Funeral services were held in the home on High
street this afternoon. His pastor, Dr. Pickens, conducted the
services., assisted by the lifelong friend of Dr. Biggs, Dr. Mahon,
of Brownsville. Dr. Jewell of Dyer and Dr. Jenkins of Lexington,
former pastors, also had parts in the services. Dr. Biggs was born
March 17, 1831, in Gibson county, a little north of Trenton. His
father, Luke Biggs, moved here from North Carolina in 1821, and it
was in the latter's house that Gibson county was organized. In 1823
Gov. Carroll appointed commissioners to perfect the organization of
Gibson county. These commissioners named the first officials of the
county and set the date for the first elections. The first county
court held in Gibson county was held in the home of Luke Biggs. The
appointment were made in the fall of 1823 and the first court was
held in 1824. A few years later Zach Biggs was born in this home and
he had spent his long life in Trenton with exception of five years
when he made his home in Memphis engageing in the cotton business.
He graduated in medicine in the medical department of the University
of Nashville, the forerunner of the Vanderbilt medical school. His
first wife was Tabitha Ellise, whose one child died in infancy. A
few years after her death Dr. Biggs married Miss Julia Raines. Their
two children were Albert W. Biggs, who became a prominent attorney of
Trenton and Memphis, and Miss Latta, who became Mrs. J.P. Jetton of
St. Louis, after her husband's death making her home again with her
father in Trenton.

    (N.B.: in this newspaper clipping, there are some other notices and
articles of some interest, which are here included...cme)
"Paris' First Loose Floor Sale Today" - Paris, Tenn. Dec. 17 -
(Special) - The first sale of tobacco on the Paris loose leaf floor
is being held today, the sale being also the first auction sale of
tobacco ever held in Henry county. There was 100,000 pounds of
tobacco on the floor this morning for the opening. The floor is
operated by C.H. White and Steele Ezell. F.J. Owens is acting as
auctioneer.

    "Marriage Licenses" - Arch Richard and Willie Keith, Arthur Scrivner
and Della DeBow, Robert Woods and Addie Lee Vaughter, Rusus H.
Phillips and Sarah Mai Branch, Robert J. Whitson and Alice Virginia
Smith, Hal Harry Wilber Hill and Agnes Oden.

    (N.B.: BIGGS, ZACK, Pension No. 15554)

BILBREY, FELIX GRUNDY

FORM NO. 1

1. Felix Grundy Bilbrey, Livingston, Tennessee
2. Seventy nine years, last Dec. 10, 1921
3. Tennessee, Overton county
4. Tennessee - Overton county
5. Farmer

BILBREY (cont'd.):
6. Farmer
7. None
8. Not any
9. About two hundred acres
10. valued at about 2500.00
11. Log house - three rooms
12. I used plow, hoe and all sorts of work done on a farm at that time
13. My father run the farm doing most of the work himself with the assist-
    ance of his boys. My mother did spinning, weaving, washing, and all
    kinds of house work, having raised flax, sold to merchants.
14. no
15. All honest work was considered respectable
16. All the best men of our community engaged in all such work to make
    the living
17. none of this kind in my community
18. Alsolutely no difference shown by the slave owners in this repect
19. All went to church and school as one element
20. All best of friends
21. Not one bit, no advantage whatever.
22. By applying himself he could accomplish it in time.
23. The slave holders did not in any way discourage an honest upright
    young man
24. County free schools - using the "old blue back spelling book"
25. would average about three months a year
26. about one mile
27. Roaring river school - Oklona School
28. Both
29. three months
30. yes, while it continued
31. Both
32. yr. 1862 - about May - Livingston - Confederate
33. 8th Tennessee Cavalry. Col. George Dibbrell-Col. Ferd Doughtery-
    General Bedford Forrest.- Capt. Bill Windle Co. A-Cpt. McGinnis-Co. D
    Capt. J___ Barnes-Co. C, Capt. Swairingin-Co. E, Capt. Roberts-Co. F,
    Capt. Bilbrey-Co. G, Capt. Gore-Co. H. McRunnels-Co. __
34. To Neely's Bend, Nashville, Tenn.
35. About two weeks
36. Neely's Bend
37. From Neely's to battle of Nashville, Chicamauga, Franklin, Murfrees-
    boro, Salsbury, at this place we lost most of our men. We were in
    battle at Jacksonville, Trenton, Humbolt, Lexington; we lived in
    tents, and were fed very well on rice, meats, coffee, meal and flour.
    We slept on blankets in tents. Clothing was fairly good. At times
    we suffered some but not serious. I was in hospital at Columbia,
    Tenn. having fever, in prison at Ft. Delaware, one year, we were
    treated very roughly at his place and suffered for food and blankets
    had to up and walk to keep from freezing.
38. In May 1865 at Washington, Ga.
39. We were paid $26.00 in hard money for guarding Jeff Davis to
    Washington, Ga. Took all our horses at Chattanooga, except eleven of
    us and we crossed the river with our horses and we were ordered to
    bring our horses back but we did not heed the orders and rode our
    horses on home, we kept our horses and never were bothered.
40. Farming
41. After war came home, went on farming as before. Was married to
    Emaline Modock (Madock?) in 1871 - we had two sons - Sidney Johnson
    and Ridley L.(?)-Second marriage in 1892 to Sallie Jackson. Have
    served as town Justice of Peace for ten years.
42. William Bilbrey; Overton County, Tenn.; lived in 6th Civil Dist. of
    Overton co. I joined the Methodist Church in 1872 have served as
    Steward of said church for years.
43. Sarah West; Iaasac (Isaac?) West and Polly West; 6th Civil Dist.
    Overton co., Tenn.
44. ----

(Attached copy headed: Tennessee Historical Committee, State Capitol,
Nashville, Tenn.)
Copy of Confederate Discharge of F.G. Bilbrey, Headquarters Depart-
ment of Richmond, March 4, Richmond, Va. Feby. 25, 1865/ not Exc. up

316

BILBREY (cont'd.):
to Mar. 14, J. Patterson, Cap./ in chge. R. Privmas?
Special Orders) In obedience to instructions from Sect. of War, the
following named men (paroled prisoners) are granted leave of indul-
gence for 30 days, unless sooner exchanged at the expiration of which
time, those belonging to commands serving north of the southern
boundry line of North Carolina, and in East Tennessee, will report
immediately to there if exchanged; otherwise, they will report to
Camp of Paroled Prisoners. Richmond, Va. All other paroled prisoners
except those whose commands are serving within the limit above
mentioned, will also report at expiration of their furloughs, to
Camp of Paroled Prisoners, Richmond, Va.
F.G. Bilbrey, Pvt. Co. F-8th Reg. Tenn. Cav. / R.G. Lundry, Capt. /
From Greensboro to Raliegh / P.P. Bardum, Capt. / Cauffer Mar. 4, 1865
/ Rations Cam. for twenty Days / D.G. Mevde, cpmg. / Richmond, Va.
Mar. 5, 1865 fifty dollars-W-pay off. C.I. Barrack / Rations in K__
for two 2 days. Benj. Balis, Qmg. / Quartermaster will furnish
Transportation. By order of Lt. Gen. R.S. Ewell. Jno. Regnamm, Asst.
Adj. Gen./

(Following this is a marvelour photograph of Felix G. Bilbrey in
uniform, written under which is: Pvt. Felix G. Bilbrey - taken at
the age of 18 yrs. in the year of 1861. Overton Co., Tenn. The
photograph is quite clear and in excellent condition...cme)

(N.B.: BILBREY, FELIX G., Pension No. 10049)

BILLINGSLEY, LEE T.

FORM NO. 2

1. Lee T. Billingsley, Pikeville, Tenn. R. #1
2. 78 yrs. Oct. 1921
3. Bledsoe county, Tenn.
4. Confederate
5. Co. F-Second Tenn. Voluntary Cavalry. I have the bade I recieved
   when I enlisted.
6. Farmer
7. John Billingsley; North Carolina; He came to Bledsoe county with his
   bride in 1806 and lived here the rest of his life. He was a member
   of the legislature for several years and Justic of Peace 24 years.
8. Jane Hoodenpile; Philip Hoodenpile and Jane Hoodenpile; near Pikeville. She was my fathers second wife.
9. My Grandfather Samuel Billingsley came from England to North Carolina
   when he was a small boy - he was a captain in the Revolutionery war.
   My grandmother, Mary Billingsley, came from Ireland to N.C. when she
   was about 15 years old. My grandparents were married and reared
   their family in N.C. but came to Bledsoe county in 1809 to be with
   my father.
10. I was a boy when the war began and only owned a little personal
    property
11. My parents owned 40 slaves, 23 males and 17 females. I owned a negro
    boy who was my personal slave.
12. 1500 acres in valley, 7000 acres on mountain
13. My father died in 1856, the property was undivided when the war began
    and managed by my mother. It was valued at $85,000.
14. In 1830 my father finished and moved into a 12 room brick house
15. I did some farm work but not much
16. My father looked after the negros and farm work. He did very little
    if any manual work. Mother saw that each negro woman did her part of
    the work and did it right. Almost all the cloth used was made at home.
    Father raised cotton and owned about 400 sheep. Shoes for the negros
    were made at home.
17. Father kept a manager or an "overseer" too (two?) or the other ser-
    vants were kept
18. For ten or fifteen years just before the war the larger land and
    slave-owners did not regard manual labor as respectable for a gentle-
    man altho the laborer was expected to live in idleness.

BILLINGSLEY (cont'd.):
19. Most of them worked for there were only a few men who owned sufficient property to live without working.
20. There were very few men who were idle all the time. Men who did not have to work on the farm usually were employed in public service.
21. I do not remember whether just not owning slaves caused a man to be treated as an inferior, but I do remember hearing some families referred to as "poor white trash"
22. The more prominent men whether slave holder or not attempted to interest the poor people in school and church
23. With few exceptions I think they were all friendly most of the leading men were interest in church work.
24. I do not think owning slaves would have been a help or a hindrance in this county. Very poor men seldom entered a political contest.
25. The poor young men who really tried was helped and encouraged in every way. I recall several who came to this county with almost nothing and in ten years owned considerable property.
26. I think slave holders encouraged ambitious young men this was and is yet a farming and stock raising community, so about the only way a young man could get along was to rent a farm till he could buy land of his own, or be a stock dealer.
27. Both public and private. The schools here before the war were only run 2 or 3 months each year by the county.
28. About 4 years before the war and 2 years after the war closed at Sequatchie College.
29. 2¼ miles
30. The public school and 2 or 3 months subscription or pay school
31. Both
32. In all about five or six months
33. Some did. Some did not
34. I had both men and women as teachers
35. On June 16, 1861 I was mustered into service in the Confederate Army at Knoxville, Tenn.
36. To Cumberland Gap, Tenn.
37. I do not remember exactly but it was several months before we fought any
38. The first regular battle was at Mill Springs, we were in several small battles or skirmishes before the battle of Mill Springs
39. I was in battles at Fishing Creek, Stubensville, Ky., Murfreesboro, Chickamauga and several other places. Our command was in Kentucky to relieve Morgan and we rode eleven days and nights not stopping longer than two hours at one time. I have eaten raw corn - green pumpkins and most anything else on these raids.
40. At Morgantown, North Carolina, May 1865. We were under Gen. Joe Wheeler. I am sending you his farewell address.
41. I came home horseback down through the mountain of N.C. I did not come straight home at once. Was several months making the trip.
42. Farming. When I reached home the fences had all been burned, the negros all gone except two. The only stock mother had left was a steer.
43. I have been a farmer and stockraiser all my life and have lived in Bledsoe county Most of the time was spent on the farm I returned to from the war. Twelve years ago I moved to my present home about four miles from that farm. I have been a member of the Church of Christ for 45 years. I was Justice of the Peace 12 years and coroner 8 years and now am a Notary Public. I have been married twice. My last wife is still living. I have eleven children.
44. ----
45. Tullos Rangers, known as Company F 2nd Tenn. Cal.: John M . Bridgeman, Capt., James W. Walker, 1st Lt., A.R. Couk (Cook?), 2n. Lt., James W. Fraley, 3rd Lt., Non-Commissioned officers: William Smith, 1st Orderly Serg., W.W. Henson, 2nd O.S., L.T. Billingsley, 3rd O.S., John R. Roberson, 4th O.S., James Dyer, 5th O.S., Maj. P. Swafford, 1st Corp'l., James Abbet, 2nd Cpl., R.W. Brown, 3rd Cpl., J.W. Cunninham - Wagon Master, Anthoney Griffith, bugler,; Private soldiers: James Abbet, James Acuff, J.S. Acuff, Frank Burger, John Austin, Reuben Brown, D.S. Brown, V.A. Beanerett, J.A. Card, Andy Card, G.W. Campbell, James Cain, G.W. Cain, John Carrick, Tim Daviss, Will Couglas, O.P. Durham, H.C. Deatherage, Gav.(?) Eppison, G.W. Ellete, George Frazier, John Frazier, G.A. Findly, C.A. Ford, James Freeman,

BILLINGSLEY (cont'd.):
J.M. Greer, Richard Guess, John Gollihor, A H. Gollihor, T.H. Hinch,
S.P. Henderson, Thomas Hawkins, John Hawkins, W.F. Hutcheson, Wm.
Hatfield, Goins Hatfirld, R.H. Hatfield, W.H. Hatfield, John Hodgkiss,
James Hearn, Wm. Highenbottom, Aaron Hughes, Sam Hughes, Dr. J.A.
Hacker, John Jones, Josh Jentry, John Knight, C.L. Leiws, Thomas
Laster, Houston Lamb, A.J. Larrimore, Thomas Loyd, W.H. McCulley,
J.C. McDowell, James McCunah, G.W. McDonald, John Mitts, James Nale,
P.J. Norwood, T.?(R.)H. Napp, S.B. Panter, Leander Pope, L.L. Pope,
John Pollard, Adam Roberson, Isaac Roberson, G.W. Rogers, Alvin Reid,
Sam Roberson, James Rankin, Reuben Rankin, W.A. Smith, Alfred Swafford,
Thomas Swafford, S.C. Stone, Thaddous Simms, J.R. Smith, James Smith,
Dr. R.A. Stone, W.F. Simmons, W.L. Standifer, L.L. Standifer, James
Scott, Andrew Sherill, Thomas Sherill, John Sherill, Sam Sherill,
I.N. Thomas, G.W. Taylor, Henry Tollett, James A. Walker, G.W. Walker,
A.J. Walker, I.E. Walker, Clay Wimberly, J.C. Worthington, James
Worthington, W. Worthington, S.P. Worthington, W.F. Worthington,
Houston Wheeler, A.D. Williams, James White. Colored or negro
servants for the Company: George Tulloss, James A. Birch, James Ned,
James Taylor, Bird Terry, George Close, Samuel Gallimore. This list
of the Company was printed in a Knoxville paper soon after the close
of the civil war.

46. A.K. Swafford   Pikeville, R. 1, Tenn.
    W.R. Pope   Pikeville, Tenn.
    Bud Wheeler   Pikeville, Tenn.
    L.L. Standifer   Mt. Airy, Tenn.
    Captain W.M. Allen   Dayton, Tenn.
    Frank Knight   Pikeville, Tenn.

Newspaper clipping: WHEELERS FAREWELL ADRESS TO CAVALRY - Original
Copy is Treasured Possession of the Family of Lee Billingsley -
Yellowed with age, worn in two or more parts through constant handling,
one of the proud and treasured possessions of this family of Lee
Billingsley, a gallant soldier of Forest's cavalry, is the farewell
address of General Joe Wheeler to his comrades, issued on April 29,
1865. It was dated at "Headquarters Cavalry Corps" and addressed to
"Gallant Comrades". It follows: "You have fought your fight. Your
task is done. During a fours years struggle you have exhibited
courage, fortitude and devotion. You are the sole victors of more
than two hundred stubbornly contested fights you have participated
in more than a thousand conflicts of arms; You are heroes. You have
done all that human exertions could accomplish. I desire to express
my gratitude for the kind feelings you have seen fit to extend toward
myself and to invoke upon you the blessings of our Heavenly Father,
to whom we must all look in the hour of distress. Brethren in the
cause of freedom, comrades in arms, I bid you farewell.
                     Jo Wheeler"
                     Major General

39. This is a copy of Gen. Joe Wheelers address. If I have not made all
    the questions clear or if there should be any other information I
    could give you please let me do so. I would like to see a good
    history of The Old South and I want to see your book when published.
                     Yours truly, L.T. Billingsley

(N.B.: BILLINGSLEY, LEE T., Pension No. 10718)

                         BING, LEWIS GREEN

FORM NO. 2

1. Lewis Green Bing, Smithville, DeKalb co., Tenn.
2. 84 yrs. 1 mo. 1 day
3. Virginia, Mecklinburg co.
4. Confederate
5. Co. A, 16 Tenn.
6. Farmer
7. Spencer Bing; Mecklenburg co., Va.; lived Mecklinburg;

BING (cont'd.):
8. Elizabeth Johnston; Philip S. Johnston and Patsy Scott; lived Mecklinburg, Va.
9. 1st Phillip S. Johnson (not spelled Johnston) was an architect and
   was a soldier in the Revolutionary war - had two sons who fought in
   the civil war. Their names was viz. Josep (Joseph) E. Johnson
   and Sidney Johnson.
10. I owned a saloone and some property in town worth when I left around
    3000.00.
11. Yes my father owned 10 slaves when we lived in Va.
12. Yes 200 acres (this may be 800 acres - writing not clear)
13. About 10000.00 including slaves and personel
14. it was a frame hous had four rooms
15. My father was a farmer and I worked just as same as the slaves. I
    plowed and hoed and done all kind of farm work six days in the week.
    he was a farmer who counted in his day a verry fine farmer raised
    tobaco corn wheat and oats
16. Father was overseer on the farm. Mother was overseeing the house
    doing lotts of her own work such as weaving cooking making clothes
    and doing house work generaly
17. yes one negro woman
18. yes by people who had money but some people who dident have so much
    counted it a disgrace to work in other words the million air Pospers?
    dident want to work
19. yes the men who wanted to make money
20. I would guess about 2% of the men was idle that is the white men
21. yes the men who did not own slaves who was respectabel the rich people
    associated with them. They dident feel themselves above those
2. yes your wouldent see any diffrence
23. yes you would see no diffrence
24. no then was two parties viz Whig and democrate they held to their
    political belief then as they do now
25. yes
26. Incuraged
27. a common country school and a private school Hill Accadna (Academy)
28. about 3 years
29. about one mile
30. viz Hills Academy and just some district schools
31. We had a private school and a public school
32. about 4 months
33. only fair
34. man
35. I enlisted in Co. A. in May 1861 as Confederate at Smithville DeKalb
    co. Tenn.
36. Estil Springs, Tenn.
37. I cant say exactly but our first engagement was at Paraville Ky
    (Perryville)
38. Paraville, Ky.
39. I experience a hard time. We went to Manassas Va. I was in the
    Manassas fight Va. Murfreesboro Franklin Tenn. Atlanta Ga. Paravil,
    Ky. I was wounded in Paravil, Ky. I lived hard in the latter part
    of the war my clothes was sorry we slept anywhere or any place. Eat
    anything we could get our medical attendence was verry poore
40. I was discharged at Atlants Ga. in May 1865
41. I rode horse back from Atlanta, Ga. to Smithville, Tenn. I had
    nothing to pay my way. I had confederate moeny but it was dead. I
    let my horse eat grass during the day and wauled (walked?) at night
    begin all I eat home
42. farming
43. I have farmed from the time I came home untill a few years ago.
    Farmed untill I got old and unable to work. I never asked the people
    of my co for any office. I have never became a member of any church.
44. ----
45. L.M. Savage, Capt. D., ___ Bailey, 1st Sgt. D., W.C. Cantrell, Sgt.
    D, L.G. Bing, L, Lin Redman, L, Ike McGinnis, John Vanhooser, L.,
    Tom Potter, dead, W.C. Potter, Bill Bing, dead, Jim Bing, dead, Pat
    Cantrell, Jess R. Cantrell, Jim Coges, Dick Cantrell, Bulley Cantrell,
    Jim Cantrell, Will Richardson, Tom Richardson. I cant remember all
    of my Co. My memory is not so good as it once was.
46. ----

BISHOP, JOHN CALVIN

FORM NO. 2

1. John Calvin Bishop, Benton, Polk co., Tenn.
2. 86 years of age
3. South Carolina, Spartenburg co.
4. Confederate
5. Co. C, Gen. Thomas Legion; Steve Whitaker, Captain
6. Farmer
7. Obidiah Bishop; Mount Zion, Spartinburg co., S.C.; lived in Spartenburg
8. Hannah Larence; William Larence and Millie Larence; lived Spartenburg
   S.C.
9. ----
10. two horses and two cows, at the prices then, worth about $150.00
11. No
12. 160 acres
13. $1000
14. a weather borded, two roomed house covered with cedar shingles and
    nailed on with locust pegs
15. Plowed and hoed, both
16. Farmed, only Father. Mother spun and weaved. all the cloth the
    combined family worn.
17. no
18. considered respectable
19. they worked hard, all that did not own slaves
20. not many
21. they did not seem to grade themselves with the man who did not own
    slaves
22. They did not
23. No Sir
24. The candidates who owned slaves hardley ever was elected to any office
25. No sir
26. Discouraged to some extent
27. country school, about three months per year
28. four months in all
29. four miles
30. subscription schools
31. public
32. ----
33. no sir
34. man
35. Haysville Clay county N.C. April 1861
36. to Koker Creeke, N.C.
37. about six months
38. at Zollakoffer, Va.
39. Moved from there to Bristol, Va. From there to Knoxville, Tenn. From
    there to Strawberry Plains, Tenn. and there we had a fight for one
    sollid day. From there to Chattanooga, Tenn. Back to Knoxville to
    Jonesboro, Tenn.
40. I were sent home from the hospital 1864. At Strawberry Plains, Tenn.
41. Walked home, near six days journey
42. I could not work at that time, as my left hand were badlye mangled.
    Three fingers gone at palm of hand
43. After about one year at home I did as best I could in trying to help
    make a living on the farm
44. ----
45. Clint Teetum, Lt.; John Robinson, Lt.; Jace Johnson, Pvt.; Bill Wiggins,
    Lt.; Bob Bird, Or.; Aden Martin, Pvt.; Jessie Schneider, Pvt.; Marion
    Schneider, Pvt.; Bob Bell, Pvt.; Bill Greene, Pvt.; Bill Huskins, Pvt.;
    Ira Robinson, Pvt.; Jim Curtis, Pvt.; Geo. Laudermilk, killed; Martin
    Cross, Sub.; Jim Crews, Pvt.; Bill Fletcher, Pvt.
46. All the old Soldiers I known are dead. Sofare as I now know only:
    Bart Narmon, Benton, Tenn.

(N.B.: BISHOP, JOHN CALVIN, Pension No. 826)

BITTICK, JOHN HOLLAND

FORM NO. 1

1. Mr. Bittick-Rives, Obion co., Tenn.
2. Seventy five years and four months
3. Giles co., Tenn.
4. Just across the river Gibson co.
5. farming
6. Farming and stock raising
7. One horse, briddle and saddle worth I suppose $100.00
8. no
9. sixty acres
10. twelve hundred dollars
11. Four room double log house, two rooms above and two below. Logs nicely hewn. There was a ten foot open hall between rooms
12. I plowed, hawled, hoed, split rails, in fact did any kind of honest labor and was not ashamed neither were our neighbors
13. Father farmed, raised stock and traded considerable in same, expecially buying miles and driving south. Mother did her own house work, carded spun and wove clothing for her family. Also knit our hose.
14. no
15. Those who worked and most of us did, were among the most honerable
16. yes
17. Very few were idle. Large slave holders possible hadn't time to work regularly, but they were less busy for that
18. There was no distinctions made slave holders and non slave holders were friends and neighbors and met and acted as such
19. yes
20. very agreeable
21. no
22. yes
23. Men were just men then as now, some encouraged - some discouraged, while others were neutral
24. Short term subscription schools
25. Not very much and quit school to enlist
26. Three miles
27. Private or subscription schools, while some wealthier families employed Governesses.
28. Private
29. I suppose about three months
30. Yes
31. Man and he believed not in sparing the rod and spoiling his pupils
32. On May 1st 1861 at Toy, Obion co., Tenn.
33. Ninth Tenn. Company H, John Bufor, Capt.; Swanson, 1st Lt.; Stephen Howard, 2nd Lt.; Sim McDonald, 3rd Lt.; Henry W. Head, Orderly Sergt.; Tom Williams, Quarter Master; Names I now recall are Will and L.H. Latimer, Hugh and Dan Bell, Bob Joyner, Dr. Pete Catron, F.B. Taylor, John Cavanough, Dr. F.M. McRee, Dr. C.P. Wyley, Rolley and Dock Crockett, George CArmac, Dr. Richardston, John and Bill Cunningham, Charlie White and others.
34. Union City, Tenn. where we were drilled and later transfered or moved to Columbus, Ky.
35. I think eleven months
36. Shilough (Shiloh) where I was desperately wounded and carried to a hospital in Memphis, Tenn.
37. I had a long serious struggle and I was removed from the hospital by a wealthy man and his wife by the name of Reno and cared for in their home where I finally recovered sufficiently ___ that to rejoin my company, which was then at Chatanooga. I remained with them so far as Sparta, Tenn. where owing to weakness Gen. Buford gave me permission to join the calvery which I did, attaching myself to Colonel Biffle Regiment and from that time to the end we were not idle.
38. ----
39. It was no pleasure trip except at its end
40. FArming and stock raising
41. The last year of the war I married Miss Allice Latimer, purchased a farm five miles west of Union City, Tenn., where we lived, reared and educated six children, three sons and three daughters. I, my wife and children are Cumberland Presbyterian in belief. I have

322

BITTICK (cont'd.):
never held office except at Superintendent of the Capitol under Gov.
J.P. Buchannon.

(On extra pages):
BATTLE? - Dead Angle, Georgia

W. Latimer, Sumner, Texas - Comrads Nelson of Homer, Kentucky give an
account of the battle of Dead Angle. I was a member of the 6th and
9th, consolidated Regiments and was at the battle of Dead Angle. His
version of that deadly conflict is fairly given. He says Dead Angle
is south west of Kenesaw Mountin. I think that Dead Angle is at the
foot of K-S. Mountain and a part of the same. I do not know who
commanded the Federal Troops on that occasion, be he who he may, he
had as brave soldiers as I ever had to stand before during my four
years experience in many hard fought battles of the Civil War. The
federal troops concentrated their forces at the foot of the hill at
turn or elbow of the hill in front of the 1st Tennessee Regiment, Col.
Fields to the most terrifick canonading it was ever my misfortune to
witness, when the canonading ceased the enemy was seen approaching
and very close at hand, then was opened the most destructive close
range fire of musketry I witnessed during the war. The enemy rushed
right up to our works and a flag bearer mounted the works and planted
his collers on them and one of our boys mounted the works and had a
tussle with him for possession, but not as successful as Comrad
Nelson' version give it, he carried them back with him. They made a
gallant assault and had the satisfaction of retiring what was left of
them without making any brake in our line of works. I will mention
a few incidents that has not been mentioned by those writing up Dead
Angle. One of most importance in regard to Col. Field's daring
exploit while the assault was at its closest range which was so close
that the line of breast works was all that seperated the contending
forces. Col. Field mounted the works with drawn sword and cheered
his men to stand the storm, he appeared to forget that the leaden
missles of death was as thick as hail, he was pierced by a minie
ball and rolled into the ditch among his men and work went down the
line that the Col. was slain, but when examination was made a minie
ball had pentrated his fore head at the edgeof the hair and ranged
over the skull and he soon gained consciousness and recovered. Another
incident that I have not forgotten, "don't suppose ever will", just
at the time the assault was raging in its fury Col. Field's Adjt.
came running down the line to the left to the pt. where 6 & 9 was
stationed with orders that 6 & 9 move to the right and fall in behind
his Reg. as they were out of ammunition, we were ordered to move by
the flank and fall in behind his Reg. which was done amid a perfect
shower of lead, but let me say as we went we stooped very low. Another
incident comadore Nelson failed to report accurately Gen. Cheatham at
one of his engagements by flag of truce offered a cessation of
hostilities so the enemy could care for their dead and wounded, they
replied that they would have possession of the field in time to bury
their dead and care for their wounded, but the next evening they asked
for and obtained permission to bury their dead, their wounded many of
them had died before they at attention. The pickets were marked to
half way ground between the contending enemies and when they met the
pickets about forced and stood back to back each facing toward his
own comrades, the federals then scooped holes by each dead body, then
took hold of their clothes and rolled them in and covered them up,
while this was going on was when the boys done their trading and
exchanging coffee, tobacco and canteens. I don't suppose those of us
in the ditches next day after the battle will every forget the scent
arising from their decomposed bodies. Another incident I have not
seen mentioned was the yankee pickets who had cralled (crawled) up
and burrowed himself behind and under the roots of a large tree in
20 steps of our works and picked off several of our soldiers in front
of his hiding place when one of our boys would show himself he was
sure to get lead in his hide and the scamp when he would fire would
crow like a rooster, the boys piled up quite a heap of rocks around
the roots of the tree trying to dislodge him, but all in vain; he
held his position. One other incident and I will give place to the
next old Vet who may be disposed to give his version of Dead Angel

BITTICK (cont'd.):

we were fatigued and worne out with continued watching, resting on
arms in the ditches, we were moved to the left on line of works out
of range of the incessant cannonading it being confined principally
to the Pt. (point) of the angle. We got to our new position and at
once doffed our clothing, spread our blankets in rear of breast works
and lay down to sleep, during the night there was suddenly severe
bombardment from the enemy and bombs bursting over our heads and all
about us and we were ordered to fall in line, we had just gotten
sound asleep and the sudden awakening caused such a panic among our
boys that we could scarcely get inside our fort, the word "fall in
line", was obeyed, some with one leg in their pants the other dangling
nad some pants in hand and others left them altogether, we expected
another assault on our lines, but it never came, a false alarm, but
furnished amusement for the boys for many a day, one telling joke on
the other as to the plight of his clothes, the general opinion being
as bad as if he had been on dress parade.

(On attached note)
Record - Lieutenant, John Holland Bittick, Volunteered for service in
the War between the States in Obion county, Avelanch, 9th Tenn.
Regiment, in April 1861 at the age of twenty one years. He served
as a private with this company until the battle of Shiloh where he
was severely wounded, so bad that altho he rejoined his company he
was never able for Infentry service and was given a forlough by
Colonel Buford to return to his home and recuperate. Soon after he
joined Forest's Cavelry was elected Lieutenant at Pontotock (Pontotoc)
Miss. He served with Forests Cavelery from the time he joined this
branch of the service until the end of hostilities, after which he
returned to Obion county where he married Miss Harriet Alice Patimer.
Both still living, Lieut. Bittick eighty four years of age and Mrs.
Bittick near eighty two.

(N.B.: BITTICK, JOHN HOLLAND, Pension No. 10651)

BLACK, W. W.

FORM NO. 2

1. W.W. Black, Milan Tenn.
2. I was born Mar. 11th 1843 age 79 years
3. Tenn.
4. I was a Confederate soldier
5. Co. B, 1st Ark. Infantry but served all the war East Mississippi
6. My father was rausrd (raised?) on farm
7. Samuel Black; in Greenville Dist., S.C.; when sall (small) boy; S.C.
    came to Tenn.; my father and mother died when I ware child
8. Polly Ross; Daniel Ross and ___
9. My father come Tenn. when small boy from S.C. ansesters Scotch Irish
10. I owned no land I was bound out had no foulks (folks) to live with
11. owned none
12. none
14. bout 3 room log house
15. I worked on farm with sutch tools as we had
16. My mother done all cooking spining weaving and making the cloths we
    wore
17. none
18. was consied (considered) honorable
19. shure did
20. there was no idleness but all worked
21. I saw no diferance the(y) mingled freely
22. I saw no diffrance
23. thare was a frindly feeling
24. I think not
25. If he had will and vim he was
26. they war generally encoureged
27. log house with dirt floore
28. verry little
29. from 1 to 4 miles

BLACK (cont'd.):
30. ----
31. It was verry private
32. ----
33. not mutch
34. man able bodied
35. I enlisted in Confederate at Little Rock Ark. in Feb. 25, 1862
36. to Corinth, Miss.
37. bout 5 weeks
38. Chilo (Shiloh) on 6 and 7 April 1862
39. after the battle Shilo we come back to Corinth. I was taken sick
    wich tiford (typhoid?) pneumonia send to Holly Spring Miss. stayed
    there 4 weeks most of the unconsus (mos of the time unconsicious?)
    but had to leave when I was barely able to set up to more safer
    quarters to Wenona, Miss. an old farmer takened me out home in 2
    weeks
40. I was discharged on the 26th day April 1865 at Greensboroh, N.C. thare
    I was payroled.
41. & paid off the confederate tresure had enough money to pay us boys
    125 one twenty five in silver so I was paid off in full for 4 years
    servis we then march 250 miles across the montains N.C. and East
    Tenn. to Green___ Tenn.
42. I had no home to go two but left my Ark. Regt. at Memphis once 1200(?)
    I left returning 125 the__ we lost men in all the battles but Hood
    had us slauter Franklin
43. I let my co at Memphis-Ragied-louise - thous of us that had no home
    the good women gave us shelter fed us tell we could ___ work and gave
    me a sute clothes they ware not tailor mad but I shur felt dressed
    up so in few days fellow theit had a contrack getting cross ties at
    15¢ tie if I could hire, so I pitched wanted to mak some money though
    not broak still had my 4 years pay 125 so I went getting ties blisered
    my hands they so sore I could not chop but went to driving team
    greased and got hands well so I went back to tie making thare was 25
    men in the camp in few days I was getting 30 ties a day some few days
    would get 40 more than any of 25 men exchp (except?) one negro I
    after words followed the tie business on deferent roads was with Gen.
    Fores (Forest?) in Selmer, Marion and Memphis.
44. ----
45. ----
46. ----

BLACKBURN, JAMES KNOX POLK

FORM NO. 1

1. James Knox Polk Blackburn, Lynnville, P.O., Tennessee
2. 84 years 11 months and 13 days 85 Feb. 20, 1922 (#2 form gives age
    as 74)
3. Tennessee State, Maury county
4. In the state of Texas, Lavaca county
5. Just previous to war student and schoolteacher, teaching assistant
    in Elms(?) Institute, Hallettsville, Texas
6. Farmer and live stock raiser and trader
7. A mare and colt worth about 150 dollars
8. Yes, A man and woman and four or five or six children, cant not
    remember the no. of children
9. About 150 or 200 acres
10. Land about 5000. Herd of cattle about 800(?) work stock and took
    about 600 w___ (wagon wheels?) and & $150 of household goods (this
    last not clear)
11. Frame house with ___ sides ___ (rooms?). Had five rooms I think.
    (N.B.: this handwriting is very difficult to read...cme)
12. As a boy in Maury county Tenn. from 8 years old until about 15 or 16
    years old I plowed hoed planted and reaped as much as any boy I think
    by the side of a negro young man of my fathers and ___ white and
    black.
13. My father did all kinds of farm work until his boys and servants got
    able to relieve him after he bought and frow mules and trade them to
    Selms, Ala. was sold ___ from one to three trips a year. My mother

325

BLACKBURN (cont'd.):
   did all kinds of house work washing weaving spinning etc. having an
   old negro woman ____
14. My parents ____ keeping house with a negro boy only whos parents were
   ____ and
15. yes
16. yes
17. I dont know of any such cases or
18. I never noticed any difference or distinction made between any rich
   and poor and it is a slander in ___ me to say so in the sections
   where I lived in Tenn. and Texas
19. yes
20. were purfectly social and equal
21. no
22. Fairly good at all times I think
23. Encouraged
24. 3 months free schools mostly while in Tenn. My father moved to Texas
   in 1856 when his whole family was with him, and after that I went to
   Alma Institure pay my own way
25. A little every year untill I was about 15 after that I quit ____ with
   a ___ of making my own way
26. one mile
27. in Tenn. mostly public. In texas mostly private
28. both
29. from 3 to 5
30. I think so
31. mostly men
32. 1861 September Houston, Texas (#2 form gives 1 Sept.)
33. 8th Texas Cavalry - Generally called Terry's Texas Rangers
34. We were organized for service in the Virginia army. My company started out as van guard got to Grand Junction Tenn. when an order ____
   us from G___ Junction? and ___ to ____ Ky.
35. about 2½ miles
36. Woodsonville, Ky. where we met the 33rd Indiana Reg. of Infantry. We
   defeated that reg. but lost our Col.
37. After that the reg. soldiered in Ky. from Green___ to Bowling Green
   keeping back any reenforcement from Grant at Fort Donaldson? until
   that fort surrendered after which Gen. Johnson with all his forces
   fell back to the south and our reg with him until he established the
   new base at Corinth, Miss. then soon came on the battle of Shiloh
   for 3 days - two days battle with the infantry artilary and cavalry
   and the 3 day ----
38. Was a prisiner on parole for about a year and in Marshall and Giles
   counties on my crutches part of time reported to regement ____
39. about answers under question 38
40. For a short while merchentazing and then worked on farm raising corn
   and working side by side with 38 hands both ___ ____ ____ plowing
   and hoeing with men
41. FArming chiefly Merchantdizing at two different seasons but kept up
   farming, also lived in Giles county Tennessee 1867. Belong to
   Christian church
42. Edward Rose Blackburn; near Double Springs, Maury co., Tenn.; lived
   in (on) Leepers(?) Creek Tenn. Fayetteville, Middle Creek, Belton,
   Texas; none that I know of
43. Hester Jane Dickey; Samuel Dickey and Elizabeth Dickey I think; King-
   ton South? Carolina and on Dicksons Tenn. (this last not clear)
44. My maternal grandfather I think came to Tenn. with the Frierson(?)
   emigrants he and his wife both buried at Zion Church Maury county
   Tenn. My paternal grandfather to Nashville when a young man and
   helped form that city - His name was Edward Blackburn - His father
   was Robert Blackburn and his father Ephraim Blackburn if I mistake
   not. They were a family from Scotland settled in Va. first. One of
   them Samuel Blackburn was Gen. in war

   (on extra pages): Answer to Q. 41 continued - have been in Tennessee
   legislature 3 times wice ? a member of the house and once a member of
   the senate.

   Deer Col. I will try to ___ this ------. I have furnished ----- ----
   answering as best I can your 44 questions which in ----- ---- my hand

BLACKBURN (cont'd.):

is unsteady and very (my) vision defective and ---- I want to tell you one of my comrades Littlefired by name at Austin Texas gave 25000 to the board of trustees of the Texas ----------
(there continues several hand written pages of notes on his activities during the war. Most of this is very difficult to read.)

Newspaper Clipping: "The Pulaski Citizen, Wednesday, February 9, 1927"
Mrs. Allen Phelps of Pulaski was the guest of Mrs. Thomas Williams, at her home on North Locust street last Thursday - Marshall Gazette.
Dr. Jas K. Blackturn and Hatcher Grigsby of Pulaski were in Lewisburg Tuesday on a business mission. Dr. Blackburn was formerly a highly esteemed citizen of Lewisburg. His father, Capt. J.K. Polk Blackburn, who later had a wide and favorable acquaintance throughout the state, was severely wounded in the battle of Farmington in the Civil War, and was brought to Lewisburg where he remained until his recovery and where he formed many enduring friendships. - Marshall Gazette.

Q. 25 continuation: I entered this institution. I stayed 3 years and taught school one year and returned to institute and remained another year and went from there into civil war in 1861.

Q. 41: Since 1866 (date not legible) have engaged in farming and stock raising continuously with another two years store keeping as a side line - I married 1867 Miss Mackie May Laird of Brick Church, Tenn. Have raised and educated 9 children. One ___ oldest a daughter died of child bed fever leaving an infant who is not 21 years old living in Birmingham, Ala. Two of my sons are practicing physicians one in Pulaski, Tenn. and one in Grand Rapids, Mich. - one daughter married and living in Grand Rapids, Mich. - the other 5(?) boys (could be 4) on the farm and one a druggist in Lynnville, Tenn. One boy a magistrate at Brick Church for 12 years.

BLACKBURN, WILLIAM HENRY

FORM NO. 1

1. William Henry Blackburn, Burns, Dickson co. (Tenn.)
2. 82
3. Tennessee, Dickson co.
4. the same (Confederacy)
5. farming
6. Farmer and Blacksmith
7. 400 acres land that cost about $300.00 on the waters of Turkey Creek
8. Mother owned 7 for about 3 or 4 months before the war broke out.
9. about 300 acres
10. the land was almost worthless, about 30 cents per acre, but slaves were high
11. log house
12. I worked at all kinds of work done on a farm such as plowing, hoeing, grubbins, in fact all the work that is necessary to be done on a farm just the same as the negro slaves.
13. She did all this kind of work, while raising her family as she had not inherited the slaves at that time.
14. just short while all left when war came on
15. yes, and all growing young men worked just as same as the negroes.
16. yes
17. wasn't any of that kind in this community
18. I never knew of any such cases, there were very few slaves and fewer slave owners in this community __ worked of course when they got able they would buy them a negro just like they would a mule instead of owning oxen.
19. yes
20. not in the least antagonistic
21. no
22. yes lots of them did. I did myself
23. sure they were, and any ambitious young man could by hard work and economy become a slave owner himself

327

BLACKBURN (cont'd):
24. we had practically none. a month or two perhaps every year or two when we could secure a teacher
25. about 8 month altogether
26. from one to 4 or five mile
27. Just a private teacher would get up a subscription school occasionally except a month or two each year of free school when a teacher could be had
28. part public and part "subscription" (made up by the neighborhood)
29. 1 to 4
30. when they had them they did
31. usually men (and "plugs" at that) mostly
32. 2nd precinct Dickson Co. Tenn. May 1861
33. 11th Tenn. Gordon's (this name not clear) Reg. memory too poor - expect you already have more of their names than I could give you, My Co. was "K". Capt. F.F. Tidwell.
34. Camp Cheatham, Robertson co.
35. had a little skirmish over at Rock Castle, Ky.. about 8 months after
36. see above
37. Cumb. Gap after several other engagements, was taken prisoner at Marietta, Ga. and carried to Camp Douglas, was treated worse than a dog. Have seen men shot down for gnawing on a bone, when they were starving.
38. Chicago, Ill., Camp Douglas
39. Yankees sent me on train
40. Plowing and cutting bushes
41. farming, never offered for public office
42. Thomas C. Blackburn; near Lebanon, Wilson co., Tenn.; none (He lived at Cross roads)
43. Sarah Anglin (nothing more)
44. came from N. Carolina to Tenn. about time of revolutionary war

(N.B.: BLACKBURN, WILLIAM HENRY, Pension No. 7829)

BLACKWELL, CHARLIE FLEMING (spelled Flemming on form)

FORM NO. 1

1. Charlie Flemming Blackwell, Mulberry, Tenn.
2. I will be 80 yrs old Sept. 20 1922
3. Mulberry, Tenn., Lincoln co.
4. Lincoln co., Tenn.
5. Farming
6. Farming
7. Did not own any land
8. no
9. Did not own any
10. ----
11. Hewed lot house with 5 rooms
12. I hoed, plowed and all other work that was to do on the farm
13. My father did all kind of farm work and my mother did house work and cut and made clothes for the family and for other people
14. one
15. regarded as being all right and honerable
16. yes
17. It was very few but what worked
18. I could not tell any difference between those that owned slaves and the ones that did not own any
19. Yes
20. Friendly feeling
21. No
22. Yes, But boys stayed with their parents until they were 21 yrs. old
23. Encouraged
24. Common free school, which lasted 1 or 2 months in every year
25. about 2 yrs.
26. 3 miles
27. 1 pay school at Mulberry, Tenn. and several free schools scattered around through the county
28. The schools where I attended were Publick schools

328

BLACKWELL (cont'd.):
29. About 3 mo.
30. Yes
31. Men
32. 1861, November at Mulberry, Tenn. Lincoln Co.
33. 41st Tenn. G.W. Alexander, H.H. Alexander, A.P. Street, Geo. Renegar,
    Sant Renegar, Ace Rederick, A.P. Blackwell, Edd Reynolds, Jack David-
    son, Dick Jarred, Sil Sullivan, Berry Sullican, Bill Eslick, Prior
    Buchanan, Presley Dun, Bob Hanaway, John Warren, Daniel Warren, John
    Johnson, Mark Pertum, Captain W.W. James, John Little, H.H. Neice,
    Capt. Loss Little, Henry Morgan and Joe Brock
34. Camp Trousdale
35. about 1 month
36. Fort Donalson
37. The first battle I was in we fought for about 2 day. in snow and
    sleet. I was captured and we were taken prisoners and taken to
    Lafayette, Ind. and put in an old Packong House, we stayed there about
    1 wk. and were taken to Camp Morton, Indianapolis, Ind. stayed there
    7 mo. and 20 da. we were fed very well at first in prison but when
    the soldiers were taken away, and we were guarded by the citizens
    they were afraid of us and sometimes they would shoot through the
    prison. I had the measles at Bowling Green, Ky. and come very near
    dying. we were fed very scant part of the time we had to eat parched
    corn and on the last we were very poorly clothed. I marched from
    Jackson to Yazoo, Miss. bare footed about 100 mi.
38. I was at home sick when the war was closed
39. We had to run out from Nashville, Tenn. When the army fell back I
    came home and was taken sick and was sick when the surrender was made
40. Farming
41. Farming, worked 3 yrs in a cabinet shop, and then went to work in a
    blacksmith shop and worked at the trade 24 yrs. then went out to
    work with my son and worked up until about (no more information)
42. Fleming Gaines Blackwell; Granville, N.C. He lived there until he
    was married and then came to Tenn.
43. Mary Edwards (nothing more)
44. ----

On extra page: Church history - my parents were missionary baptist.
my family were comberland (Cumberland) presbyterians. I joined the
church July 30, 1871 and was maid (made) a elder I hav represented
my church 25 times in Elk presbytary. my son was also a elder hope
to do more

(N.B.: BLACKWELL, CHARLES FLEMING Pension No. 10042 and 11718)

BLACKWELL, THOMAS J.

FORM NO. 2

1. Thomas J. Blackwell, Ripley, Tenn. RR #1
2. 77 past
3. Lauderdale co., Tenn.
4. Confederate
5. Co. C - 31st Miss. Vol. Inf.
6. Doctor
7. Thomas M. Blackwell; North Carolina; Surgeon P.A.C.S.
8. Agnes L. Rice; John P. Rice and Rachel Rowell; Durhamville, Tenn.
9. My grandfather Blackwell was a soldier in the war of 1812, my great
    grandfather Blackwell was a major in Continental of the Revolution.
    my great grandfather Rice was a soldier in Revolution.
10. none
11. yes, he kept only four at home
12. ----
13. about fifteen thousand dollars in cash and securities which destroyed
    by Grierson Cavalry Raid
14. Six room frame
15. I went to school until I was sixteen years old and then went to work
    in drugstore

BLACKWELL (cont'd.):
16. My father practiced medicine. My mother kept house but done work but
    superintend the servants.
17. four
18. Yes, some of the most substantial slave owners made their boys work
    during crop season and sent them to school during fall and winter
19. Yes
20. I was too young to notice such things by my recollection is that a
    very small pr ct were idlers
21. A mans respectibility depended upon his own conduct and not upon the
    number of slaves he owned
22. yes
23. Absolutely friendly
24. Slaves had nothing to do with a mans political connections, some of
    the most rabid secessionist owned no slaves
25. yes
26. They were encouraged and helped
27. Male Academy
28. Four or five terms and but they broken
29. In the town where I lived
30. Male Academy and Female Academy
31. Private
32. Supposed to run six months
33. no
34. Man
35. I was living in Mississippi at the outbreak of the war and I enlisted
    in the call for six thousand volunteers by Gov. Pettus for three
    months emergency service Oct. 1861 and was sent to Bowling Green
    Ky. At the expiration of term the company reorganized and vol. for
    three years or the war in CSA.
36. Mustered into service with CSA Mar. 8, 1862 and sent to Saltino?,
    Miss.
37. Aug. 1862 at Baton Rouge, La.
38. Baton Rouge, La. although we were in the bombardment of Vicksburg by
    the Yankee fleet before that
39. From Baton Rouge we went to Port Hudson and fortified that place and
    was then sent to Holly Springs, Miss. wher Lov__ and Van Dorn were
    moblizing for the attack on Corinth. The regiment I was with didn't
    go with the army but made provost guard and left at Holly Springs.
40. Greensboro, N.C. April 26, 1865
41. Theres not much to tell we retraced the devastated route of Shermans
    advance. But will say that the Federal soldiers treated us with the
    utmost courtesy and kindness.
42. Farming
43. After the surrender I came back to Tennessee and went to work to help
    rebuild the country and redeem it from the blight of Brownlowism and
    affiliated myself with the KKK and continued with them until the
    franchise was given us.
44. ----
45. My company was from Mississippi and the men composing it were from
    South Carolina and Alabama and Virginia. I think I was the only
    Teenessean in it. I have a complete roster of the company and if it
    will be of service to you I can send you a copy if you request it.
    Ther roster will show the casualities of the company and the different
    engagements in which it participated.
46. C.S.O. Rice, Lt. 7th Tenn. Cav., Ripley, Tenn. R. 2
    T.A. Walker, 7th Tenn. Cav., Ripley, Tenn. R. 5
    T.F. Rice, 7th Tenn. Cav., Ripley, Tenn. R. 7
    P.N. Conner, Sr. 7th Tenn. Cav. Ripley, Tenn.
    H.A. Young, Ripley, Tenn.
    Thos. Steele, Sr., Ripley, Tenn.
    G.J. Hutcherson, Ripley, Tenn
    W.B. Drake, Ripley, Tenn. R. 7
    S.M. Roy, Henning, Tenn.
    P.L. Lankford, Henning, Tenn.
    W.H. Fitzpatrick, Henning, Tenn.
    H.P. Dollar, Henning, Tenn.
    J.K.P. Jackson, Ripley, Tenn.

BLAIR, SAMUEL TATE

FORM NO. 2

(N.B.: At top of form: Blank filled out by James T. Blair (son of
soldier), Jefferson City, Mo.
1. Samuel Tate Blair, (Deceased). Died at Springfield, Mo. 3-30-1917
2. 78 yrs. 10 mo. and 26 days at time of death
3. Monroe (now Loudon) county, Tenn.
4. Confederate
5. Company A, Second. Tenn. Cavalry (Prior to Sept. 1 1863) McClungs E.
Tenn. Artillery Ku__ Co. Ashbys regiment after Sept. 1, 1863
6. Cumberland Presbyterian minister and farmer
7. James Blair; near Loudon, Rone co. (now Loudon) Tenn.; lived near
Loudon on farm; Well known in East Tennessee as a minister and reviv-
alist.
8. Jane Gamble Blair; Samuel Blair and Ann Rodgers; Jonesboro, Washington
co., Tenn.
9. Family came from Scotland. Rev. James Blair father was William Blair,
born at Jonesboro, married Sallie Simmons, died near Loudon at Blair
ferry(?). His father was also James Blair and his father John Blair.
Family tradition is that James and John were with Sevier at King's
Mountain.
10. None
11. (Rev. James Blair owned several slaves. Just how many I (James T.B.)
do not know)
12. A large farm near Loudon on Miss.
13. Farm sold for $10,000.00 some years after the war. During rather
hard times. Do not know value of slaves and other property
14. Frame house. (Seemed to me a good house though I saw it only as a
very small child - JTB)
15. My father often told me of working on farm - all sorts of farm work.
His brother did the like. He knew a great deal about farming, as I
discovered when I went to work on farm. JTB
16. ----
17. (None except slaves so far as I know - JTB)
18. (From what my father told me about the work he and his brother did
and from their position in the community, I am sure work was considered respectable - JTB)
19. (Not informed - JTB)
20. ----
21. ----
22. ----
23. ----
24. ----
25. ----
26. ----
27. ----
28. Private school and Euving (Erving?, Ewing?) and Jefferson College
29. ----
30. ----
31. ----
32. ----
33. ----
34. ----
35. Enlisted in Artillery in 1861 in June
36. ----
37. ----
38. Mill Spring, Ky. (Artillery)
39. (The answer to these questions may be found in memoranda to which I
referred in ____ letter - JTB) 1-24-23. On record thought this too
large an order for me. I have my father diaries, kept during the
war and writings since. Their extned is too great for copying. -
JTB)
40. ----
41. ----
42. (Soon started to medical school)
43. Samuel Tate Blair, on his return from the army began the study of law,
for which he had a natural bent. He decided his community needed
physicians more than lawyers and went to Jefferson Medical College.,

331

BLAIR (cont'd.):

Phila., Pennsylvania right after the war. Graduated there and took another course at University of Tenn. Med. College. as I remember it Practiced Medicine at Loudon until 1881. Took active part in politics. Democrat. An orator of considerable ability. Removed to Osborn, Mo. May 1881. Practiced med. there. Was for several years a teacher in Northwestern Medical College, St. Joseph, Mo. Continued live at Osborn until No. 1904 when he removed to Springfield and lived there until his death. He was active in Cumberland Prs. Ch. and after the union(?), the Presbyterian Church. Was a Mason. He never ran for office but was in demand to make speeches for his party in his section, both in Tenn. and in Missouri.

44. ----
45. ----
46. The diaries and roster referred to might be loaned to you if you could personally (Mr. Moore) and absolutely insure their return to me. They contain ____ particulars as to Samuel Tate Blair and many description of battles and camp life. James T. Glair, Jefferson City, Mo. Sup. Ct. Bldg.

BLAKELY, HENRY PINK

FORM NO. 2

1. Henry Pink Blakely, Clinton, S.C. RFD 1
2. 82
3. S.C.
4. Confederate
5. Co. F-14 S.C.V.
6. Farmer and school teacher
7. James F. Blakely; Laurens co., S.C.
8. Mary Lewis Cole
9. ----
10. did not own any
11. my father owned 2
12. 100 (160?) acres
13. cannot tell
14. Log house 2 rooms
15. did all kinds of farm work
16. my father did all kind of farm work and my mother did all kind of house work including spining and weaving
17. none(?)
18. yes
19. yes
20. very few
21. very few did
22. yes
23. all perfectly friendly
24. I think not
25. Money was not made partner(?) easy
26. they were not discouraged
27. country log cabin
28. not much after I was 10 years old about 6 went to 2 months at a time
29. from 2½ to 3 miles
30. just neighborhood country school
31. private
32. from 8 to ten months
33. yes
34. man my father part of the time
35. Aug. 6 (16?) 1861 at Perth old field
36. Lightwood ____ Spring near Columbia, S.C.
37. about 4 months
38. Port Royal Beaufort county S.C. Jan. 1, 1862
39. Went to Virginia in April and our first battle was Gains Mill the next Fraziers Farm the Next Fredericksburg the next Chancellorsville, Fredricksburg again. I lost my right leg below the knee at Gettysburg in 1863 amputated on my birthday 3rd July
40. never was discharged

BLAKELY (cont'd.):
41. Sent to hospital from Gettysburg to Davids Island New York sent to
    City P___t from there then to Petersburg then home
42. farming
43. Farming since lived where born raised Presbyterian never filled any
    office
44. ----
45. Geo. M. Hanna, Crass Hill, S.C. can tell you where ___; I have been
    partielly paralysed for 8 or 19 years and am almost helpless and
    almost deaf eye sight bad I have done the best I could
46. ----
    (N.B.: Rec'd 8-12-1922)

                    BLEDSOE, LOUIS JEFFERSON

FORM NO. 1

1. Louis Jefferson Bledsoe, Fayetteville, Tenn.
2. I will be eighty-two in March
3. Lincoln county, Tenn.
4. Lincoln co., Tenn.
5. Over seeing my daddys farm
6. He owned a big farm but he followed deer and fox hunting.
7. I owned two horses worth about one hundred and fifty dollars each.
8. Dadd owned about twenty Negroes.
9. About four hundred acres.
10. Land, Negroes, stock and everything about thirty thousand.
11. It was a log house of five rooms
12. I worked a little with a plow and a hoe, but most of the time I was
    over seeing on the farm or stilling - making whiskey.
13. Dad didn't do anything but hunt in the barns. Mother stayed in the
    house and helped carry on the house-work such as cooking, spinning,
    weaving and carding.
14. They kept two.
15. It was considered respectable and honerable.
16. The poor class of whites did
17. Not many only the rich class.
18. The slave holders felt a little better and regarded themselves a
    little higher up than the non-slave holder.
19. They did not
20. They were opposed to each other.
21. Sometimes they did.
22. The opportunities were poor.
23. They were encouraged.
24. Private schools
25. about five years
26. about a mile
27. There was just one school in my nieghborhood - it was called the
    neighborhood school.
28. Private
29. About 7 or 8 months
30. They attended pretty regular.
31. Generally a man
32. I enlisted in Sept. 1861 at Smyrney, Tennessee (Smyrna?)
33. 32nd Tenn., Ed Cook was Colonel, Andrew Brown, Ben and Jim Cole,
    Louis Birdsong, Marion Davidson, Al Abanather, Tom Garrison, Bob
    Holland, Captain Bass, John Bass, Fate Nelson, George Adkins, Bill
    Bridgeforth, Lud Estes, Biers Smith, Hugh Smith, Bill Smith, Len
    Smith, all brothers. Tom Dobbins, Jim Higgins, Tom and Wash Thornton,
    John Vance, Pleas McGuire who succeeded Cook as Colonel also my bro.
    Jim Bledsoe.
34. We were sent to Camp Trousdale above Nashville where we staid five or
    six weeks. I took sick and was sent home. Almost all of my command
    was captured at Fort Donelson.
35. Fort Donelson was my companies first engagements, but I was home sick
36. My first battle was at Corinth, Miss.
37. After Corinth my company went to Mobile and came up the Alabama river
    to Montgomery then to Chattanooga and Knoxville. At Knoxville we went
    with Kirby Smith into Kentucky. We won the battle of Richmond but we

                              333

BLEDSOE (cont'd.):
    had to retreat after the battle of Peryville. We came back to Knox-
    ville, Chattanooga and took up winter quarters at Tullahoma. We
    manuvered around over Tennessee and finally retreated to Chattanooga
    where the battle of Chicamauga was fought.
38. I was not discharged, I was turned loose at Columbia by Col. McGuire
    and Capt. Bass.
39. ----
40. I started farming for myself when I arrived home.
41. I have followed farming every since the war.
42. Harvy Madison Bledsoe; in North Carolina; ---
43. Matilda Bufford; Solomon Bufford and ____; ____
44. My parents and grand parents came from North Carolina.

    (extra pages)
37. We won the battle of Chicamauga and then beseiged Chattanooga. After
    about four weeks the battle of Missionary Ridge was fought. We
    retreated from Missionary Ridge into Georgia where we took up winter
    quarters at Dalton. Next spring we manuvered around Dalton and finally
    fell back to Resaca where we had a hard fight. We fought one whole
    day and retreated from there ____. We fell back to New Hope where
    we formed a line but was driven back on to Mariata (Marietta) and
    Atlanta. From Dalton to Atlanta I was in the fighting or in hearing
    of it for 120 days. After Atlanta we started on a flanking movement
    thinking Sherman would follow us. We came back to Tennessee where we
    fought the battle of Franklin and the battle of Nashville. After
    Hood's defeat at Nashville we was ordered to goin (join) his command
    at Columbia. Here I was turned loose to go home and never could get
    out no more for the Yankies.

                        BLEDSOE, T. N.

FORM NO. 2

1. T.N. Bledsoe, Petersburg, Tenn.
2. 79 yrs
3. Lincoln Co., Tenn.
4. Confederate
5. Co. E-41 Tenn.
6. Farmer
7. Thos. H. Bledsoe; born Lincoln Co., Tenn.; lived at Petersburg, Tenn.;
    once a member of Legislature 18_5 of Tenn. from Lincoln, Tenn.
8. Permelia Nelson; James Nelson and Mary Nelson; Petersburg, Tenn.
9. Grandfather Antna Bledsou came from N.C. to Tenn. Lincoln county in
    year 1800. originally he came from England.
10. Didnt have any property
11. Father owned about 10 slaves
12. 500 acres
13. $25,000.00
14. Log house weather boarded and tield (Tiled?) 6 rooms
15. Worked on the farm did any kind of work that the slaves did
16. General farm work besides runing a fraight wagon from Nashville Tenn.
    to Huntsville, Ala. and other points. Mother did general house work
    besides kniting and weaving, spinning for the family.
17. Yes 3 or 4
18. It was regarded as honorable. Every one of the family worked.
19. Yes
20. No one was idle in the whole community.
21. Every one mingled with each other regardless of whether they owned
    slaves
22. Yes
23. They were friendly
24. It made no difference
25. They were
26. They were encouraged at all times
27. Common country schools
28. 4 months a year for 5 ot 6 years
29. ½ mile
30. Bledsoe school, Old Unity school and Hannah's Gap school

BLEDSOE (cont'd.)
31. public subscription school
32. 4 months
33. They did
34. sometimes a man and other times a woman
35. 1861 October Petersburg, Tenn.
36. Camp Trousdale
37. about 5 or 6 months
38. Fort Donelson, Tenn.
39. Captured at Fort Donelson and sent to prison at Camp Chase, Ohio Was exchanged and sent back to Vicksburg, Miss. Our next battle was at Raymond and around Jackson, Miss. Then at Richmond, Ky. I was wounded in this battle. Next at Chickmauga where we fought 3 days and lost the battle to the Yankees.
40. Dalton, Ga.
41. Me and John Cates walked all the way from Dalton, Ga. to Petersburg, Tenn. crossed Tenn. river at Bridgeport, Ala. on 2 logs tied together with a grape vine.
42. Farming
43. I have been farming every since the war up till 10 or 15 years ago. I have never held any office. I am a member of the Church of Christ.
44. ----
45. Capt. Scott of Fayetteville, Tenn.; Capt. Walter S. Heardens?, Tom Harkins, Edd Bearden, Jack Dyer, Cay Dyer, Tom Donner, Jim Bagly, Tandy Lord, Henry Snyly, Jack Snyly, _brad Bilbert, Joe Yawell, Jno. Andrews, Bill Archie, Bill Williamson, Geo. Hamby, John Watkins, Kno. Craig, Willis Foster, Pete Foster. Harrison Stephison, Litt Foster, Tom Pearson.
46. George Hamby   Soldiers Home, Tenn.
    Bill Archie   Petersburg, Tenn.
    Harve Sorells   "   "
    W.L. Shofner   Fayetteville, Tenn.
    Wiley Ellis   "   "
    F.L.? Little   "   "
    Clay Lambert   "   "
    John Firnewalt   "   "
    Lewis Bledsoe   "   "
    W.H. Loving   Petersburg, Tenn.
    These are all I can think of that are living, T.N. Bledsoe, Petersburg, Tenn.

(N.B.: T. N. BLEDSOE, Pension No. 12587)

BLEVINS, W. F.

FORM NO. 1

1. W.F. Blevins, P.O. Dayton, Rhea county, Tenn.
2. 86
3. Meigs county, Tenn.
4. Meigs co., Tenn.
5. Merchandising and farming
6. Farmer
7. No property only my interest in store
8. None
9. about 1300 acres
10. about two thousand dollars
11. a frame 4 room house with one story house porch on each side
12. as a rule farm work
13. Father worked on farm and in griss mill. My mother spun, wove cotton and flax and made clothes for a family of nine and cooked for her family.
14. Servants at intervals.
15. Perfectly honorable by all good citizens were treated a like
16. Yes sir rich and poor worked a like. Plowed and hoed with their negores.
17. Not over two percent of those days
18. no destinction among men of character
19. they certainly did, no destinction

BLEVINS (cont'd.):
20. Their certainly was. their was no animosity in any way
21. no difference was shown in any contest they all voted to gether as
    free men
22. Where a young man had character and industry he could save enough to
    by a small farm
23. All were encouraged to make good citizens of the good classes of men
24. Public schools in our nieghborhood when small and two years at the
    Decatur Academy
25. three years in all
26. about 2½ miles and one three miles we walked
27. the Public schools and Decature Academy
28. usualy private. the Academy was ___ we paid for our subscription(?)
29. about three months
30. fairly good the rest of my teachers was men
31. first to a woman
32. July second at Shilo Church Meigs county Tenn.
33. Company I 5th Tenn. Cavalry. Col. G.W. McKinzie, Lt. W.F. Blevin,
    W.C. Godsy?, Private Jerry Jerry M. McKenie, 1st Lt. Blevins, 3rd Lt.
    Tim ___, Harrison McMillen, Hirem O. Beavers, Pleas Hunter, John
    Blevins.
34. to Chattanooga, reported to Gen. Bragg and arrived (assined) ? to
    Maj. Lews _____(Budlen?) till after Perryville battle in Ky. was on
    Braggs escort from Spart__? at (may be continued on later pages)
35. fought battle of Munsfadville, (Kentuck?)
36. Munnsfordville then Perryville and after the Peryville co___ I went
    to 5th Tenn.
37. the Fifth Tenn was Bragg rear from Perryville to Sickamon? Shoal in
    East Tenn. in many fights in Ky. and east Tenn. along the Gaps in
    east tenn. was the rear guard from Big ___ Gap to Charleston on
    Hawassee, posted pickets on Braggs Right from Orchard Knol to River
    fought Genl. Walden 12 days on road from Ringgold to Tunnell Hill in
    the Chickanauga battle and under fire 120 days from Dalton to Jones-
    boro, Ga. battle of Resaca, Calhoun?, Atlanta, Kensaw, New Hope
    church all around Atlanta
38. At Charlott, N.C. April 26, 1865. Left for home May 4, 1865
39. After we Ashville, one Col. R___ who had 3 or 4 hundred bush wackers,
    Rinkin? lined up his men and demanded? our horses and the 14 officers
    had side arms rode to the front and told Kirk some body would be
    killed if they did not let us pas. they concluded to let us pass.
40. I helped my Mother till I was appointed Clerk and Master. I held
    that office 12 years. Red Law (Read), obtained License but did not
    practice went into the Mercantile Business.
41. I was a merchant for a time in Meigs county. In February 1882 I
    moved to Evansville(?) and sold goods till June 1892 and moved to
    Dayten (Dayton?)
42. James Blevins 1805 (must be birth date);in Sulivan county Tennessee;
    lived in Meigs county and died at age of 48 years; he was a Justice
    of the Peace in Meigs co.
43. Ruth Rockholt; Frank Rockholt and (I dont know her)
44. I never knew any of my grandfather and father were English men and
    his wife Irish and my mother was Scotch descent
                          W.F. Blevins,
                          Dayton, Tenn. Jan'y 3rd, 1922

    (N.B.: W. F. BLEVINS, Pension No. 7111)

                    BODENHAMER, DAVID SHIRES MYERS

    (Filled 2 forms)

FORM NO. 2

1. David Shires Myers Bodenhamer, 5632 Miller Avenue, Vickery Place,
    Dallas, Texas
2. Oct. 1, 1924. I am in my 81 st year of age, born Feb. 2, 1844.
3. Tennessee, Giles county
4. Confederate

                              336

BODENHAMER (cont'd.):
5. Company H-32nd Tennessee. Col Ed Cooke, Gen. John C. Brown's Brigade, Gen. A.P. Stewart's Division, Gen. Hardee's Corp., Army of Tennessee
6. Farmer and Justice of Peace
7. David Bodenhamer; July 15, 1798; Mecklenburg co., North Carolina; lived at Bodenham, Giles co., Tenn. having come early in 19th century from N.C.; he did no war service, never wrote no books, lived a simple farmers life, a ruling elder in the C.P. Church until his death in 1887, May 12, 89 years old
8. Cynthia Wood Reed; Robert Reed and Betsy (Myers) Reed; lived at Bodenham, Giles co., Tenn. after coming from Mecklenburg, N.C.
9. My grandfather Bodenhamer was a man of fine brain and high culture and came from overseas to the Scotch-Irish settlement in North Carolina which became Mecklenburg county. I knew three generations of the Reeds. They were a pious people. Many of them preachers, elders and deacons in the Mt. Moriah Cumberland Presbyterian Church. Before 1874 about 25 preachers had gone out from this church (cont'd. under Question 46)
10. As a farmer's boy who was largely engaged in work on the farm I did not own any land or other property at the beginning of the war as then I was only a small boy of 17 years.
11. My parents had two small families of slaves about 12 or 15 in number counting men women and children.
12. Five hundred
13. About $30,000 which continually decreased in value until 1878 when it sold for $10,000. Receiving a small interest in this estate I had a little house and lot for the first (time) but soon lost in on account of changes in 1902 the College moved and our house and lots was left behind and we have not had a home since.
14. The first log house one room was destroyed by fire, another one room log house later two room frame building one story one with a stack chimney between the two, later was added a little distance to SW was added another one room log house for a kitchen and this was joined by a covered porch to the first log house the living room
15. When a boy only 8 years old I made a regular hand on the farm hoeing, plowing, harvesting, gathering corn, picking cotton, felling trees, spliting rails, building fences, all kinds of work connected with a farmer's life and going to school when not needed on the farm. The hardest work I had when a small boy was to go to mill some times 4 miles away on horse-back with a full sack of corn or wheat which could not be well balanced. I would set on the smaller end, try to keep it balanced but the heavy end continued to gain until the sack would fall off and I had to wait for some one to come who had the strength to life the sack and put it back on the horse.
16. My father did all kinds of work on the farm when he was not otherwise engaged; harvesting, pulling corn, picking cotton, etc. He had a black smith shop in which he made and sharpened his plows and all implements or utensils needed on his farm. He also had carpenter tools with which he did all building (cont'd. under Q. 46)
17. About 8 of the negroes were large enough to work on the farm. Some of the females who had (cont'd under Q. 45)
18. Yes surely in a high degree as far as my knowledge which was limited to a very small circle including Bodeham, Mt. Moriah Camp Ground, Rural Hill, Cherry Hill and Slates Springs Academy, all of Giles co.
19. Yes as far as I was able to see and know.
20. I knew none within the small circle of my limited acquaintances who were idle and having others do their work.
21. As far as I could see and know they did and I saw no evidence or thing that they felt themselves better than non slaveholders.
22. Yes! It seemed clear to me that they did at the schools and meetings at Mt. Moriah Rural Hill, ___ale Mills and public gatherins attended.
23. There was clearly and surely a friendly feeling in my community of small slave holders. I know not how it was in communities where there were large slave holders.
24. It did not. At least I have never known an instance in which the candidates winning was due to owning slaves but always due to some other influence.
25. Yes! but his success in reaching the goal was conditioned upon his ability, health, and thrift as well as the price of the farm and the kind of business he desired to enter or capital required to establish

BODENHAMER (cont'd.):
    his business.
26. They were encouraged in the small circle of my community where the
    slave holders were small, but I had no first hand knowledge of
    communities where the slave holders were large so I do not know. It
    might be either yes or no.
27. In my earliest years, "Old Field" school in which the teacher ruled
    with a rod or beech or hickory switch.
28. From age 6 to 15, 3 to 5 months each yr. the length of the school
    year depending upon the teacher and the time I could be spared from
    the farm.
29. One mi. to the fartherest, 4 mi. When a boy less than ten yrs. old
    I walked or trotted to a school 4 mi. from home later I went to a
    school 4 mi. away and had be there at sunrise and was held until
    sundown so had to run going and coming.
30. They were all private schools. One teacher doing all the teaching
    from ABC to Gramer and arithmetic. There were frequent changes of
    teachers in the few years that I attended these schools. I had about
    a dozen different teachers reciting to some a few months (cont'd. with
    Q. 31)
31. (We had no public schools) - to other more, depending upon the teachers
    length of term 3 mo. to 5 mo. There were few school houses in the
    community. The church houses were free to the teachers. One school
    I remember was taught in a vacant store house. The boys and girls
    played together.
32. Three to five months except in special cases when a teacher was
    prepared to give more advanced work, he lengthened the term to give
    aspiring students the benefit of his knowledge.
33. Usually, except those who on account of poverty could go to school
    only when not needed at home.
34. Of the dozen or more teachers I had, I recall only one woman. She was
    the loveliest, best teacher I had.
35. Soon after the ordinance of secession from the Federal Union by
    Tennessee, May 2nd, 1861. Companies were formed by volunteers from
    Giles county and the adjoining counties of Maury and Lawrence. We
    had public meetings and drills and did not go to camps until Oct. 7th.
36. To the Fair Grounds, Nashville and later to Camp Trousdale near
    Mitchellsville Station, Tenn.
37. About five months during which we had some training for the duties of
    the soldiers life.
38. Fort Donelson, where after 4 days had fighting we were completely
    surrounded, and captured and sent to prison in Indiana.
39. After the battle of Fort Donelson we were sent to prison in Indiana,
    first at Lafayette where we suffered severly from disease, moved to
    Camp Morton, Indianapolis, ___ usually faring well and remaining there
    until Aug. 27, 1862., then we were sent to Vicksburg, exchanged and
    sent back to the army of Tenn. We were in all the battles from
    Murfreesboro to Atlanta (cont'd. under Q. 45)
40. Having received a severe wound in the foot that disabled me, I was on
    furlough in Miss. when the Confederate armies surrendered and dis-
    banded.
41. Being on furlough with relatives in Miss. when the Confederate armies
    surrendered it was a simple thing to get bridle, saddle and horse, go
    on horseback to the river, cross by ferry boat and soon find my way
    home.
42. I began to reach and study in the best schools in the county and in
    Sept. 1867 entered Cumberland Univ., Lebanon, graduating in College
    Sept. in class of 1870, in Theology in 1874 receiving the degrees of
    A.B.A.   B.D. and later Ph. D and C.E.
43. After the preparation for active service already mentioned, I spent
    two years as Principal of the Classical Preparatory of Cumberland
    University, three years as Principal and Professor of Loudon High
    School, Loudon, E. Tenn., 5(?) yrs. in charge of my home church Mt.
    Moriah, Giles co., Tenn. coming to Texas in 1883. I was a member of
    the faculty of Trinity University 31 years, 19 years at the old
    location Tehuacana and 12 years at the new location, Waxahachie.
    Retiring from above service T.U. in 1914. I became emeritus professor
    of mathematics, making my connection with T.U. 41 years while my
    active after graduating was 44 yrs. Since retiring I have spent much
    time gardening and service in yard and house. This work has been

BODENHAMER (cont'd.):
    continued to some extent to the present but now the greater part of
    my work is in the house. The degree Ph. D and CE were received after
    entering Trinity University.
44. The answer to this question is in the package sent some weeks before
    Sept. 27, 1924.
45. I do not know where the roster can be found. All that I could get
    are given on other questionnaire. There are rosters in the Dallas
    Public Library of the 3rd Tenn. regt. and other regts. of hoods
    Brigade

    (extra pages)
17. regular work in the house. Sometimes worked in the field when most
    needed there, then we all white and black, male and female worked
    together on the farm. My parents had everything needed and desired
    on a farm, horses and mules for every needed work, milk cows provid-
    ing an abundance of milk and butter; cattle, hogs, chickens, turkeys,
    ducks furnishing a variety of choice meats, with many especially hogs
    for the market, with sheep for wool, and geese for feathers, gardens
    with berries in abundance, home made goods and etc. everything except
    coffee and sugar. The old time brown sugars which wer bought once a
    year in large sacks of tow.
39. Chickamauga, our greatest battle lasted two days. The Confederates
    won the victory but lost heavily. The Ga. campaign was almost a
    constant battle with pickets, sharphooters and batteries from Dalton
    to Atlanta with several general engagements each lasting a few hours,
    and our loss usually heavy. Sometimes we fared well in camp, our
    comfort and fare depending upon the weather and the social condition
    of the vicinity. Our usual fare was hard bread and beef or bacon.
    We suffered hunger and cold on long forced marches in cold, rainy
    weather, wading through deep mud to the knees and streams of water
    up to waist. We slept on blankets, two or three in groups. Sometimes
    in the open around fires or in beds of snow. At first we had home
    made clothes, grey jeans suits, later such as we could get. My
    experience in hospital was severe, bitter and sorely distressing
    beyoond the power of words to tell.
46. There is a large camp of Confederate veterans here. No Tennesseans.
    In vain I tried to get from them P.O. addresses. Probably you might
    get some addresses by writing to Adj. Blair, Sterling Price Camp of
    Confederate Veterans, Court House, Dallas, Texas. I found six Tenn.
    veterans at Waxahachie and requested the Adj. to send names and
    addresses to you. If you failed to receive them you may get them by
    writing to Adj. Marchbanks, Hinnie? Davis Camp of Confederate Veterans,
    Waxahachie, Texas.
9.   Among the preachers were, my mother's uncle, Rev. Carson P. Reed, who
    preached many years at the Mt. Moriah Camp Grounds, Giles co., Tenn.
    and Rev. Wiley Reed, my mother's cousin, pastor of the First Cumber-
    land Presbyterian Church, Nashville, Tenn. at the opening of the war
    between the states, when he became an officer in the Confederate
    army and fell leading a charge in the battle of Shiloh in which the
    great General Albert Sidney Johnston was killed. My grand father
    Robert Reed was born in 1779 and was the oldest of a family of 12
    children, 9 boys and three girls. His father, my great grandfather
    was born in 1759 and died in 1817. The Reed ancestors were Scotch
    Irish and came from overseas to this country settling with the Ulster
    Presbyterians in what became Mecklenburg county, N.C.
16. and repairing needed. My mother was the house keeper, directing and
    doing partly the work of cooking, spinning, weaving and making clothes.
    She was seemingly a tireless worker. She gave tasks to her helpers,
    rising early and working willingly and diligently with her own hands.
    "She layeth her hands to the distaff and her hands hold the spindle"
    and the "hum of industry in her home and in the kitchen garden,
    poultry yard and cow lot there is busy work. She extended her hand
    to the poor." :The Sabbath is kept sacred by the Bible is first in
    her home." The law of kindness is on her tongue.: Her children rise
    up and call her blessed." Prov. 31: 26,28.
    (N.B.:   There is an extra page for form with Q.'s 45 and 46 attached)
45. I don't know where the roster of my Company can be had. I suppose
    you have the rosters of Regts. of Gen. John C. Brown's Brigade. If
    not you can get them from the Dallas Library, Dallas, Texas.

BODENHAMER (cont'd.):
Jan. 22, 1863 I was appointed Sergeant Major of the 32d Tenn.
Regt. The following are names of men who were members of this Regt.:
Killed in Battle Chickamauga: Wm. D. Brady (Braly?) and Logan Johnson;
Died in Hospital at Lafayette, Ind.: John J. M. Foust, W.F. Lauder-
dale, Stephen J. Martin, Jas. C. Maults, John H. McMasters; Died in
Hospital at Indianapolis: James M. Hardy and Thomas J. Kind and at
St. Louis - Lt. John M.J. Lee.; Killed at Ft. Donelson: Alonzo
Pillolow (Pillow?) and at Kenneesaw Mt.: Samuel RAndolph; The
following names are recalled: Major Wm. Brownlow, Thos. Ezell, Lt.
G.W. Hammonds, (perhaps this is G.H.), Wm. Johnson, Lt. Col. W.P.
Moore, G.W. Pierce, Stephen W. Rutledge, T.W. Smith.
        This is list of casualties in the regt. in the battle of Jonesboro
given by Alonzo A. Wilkinson a member of the Regt.: Killed - Col.
Ed C. Cook, Adj. Irwin, Sgt. Alexander, James (I. or J.) Baker,
W.W. Bugert, H.H. Hollinwender, W.R. Smith; Wounded - J.K. Alsup,
R.J. Brunson, L.K. Bradley, J.P. Cammel, Lt. C.L. Coffey, Thomas
Dobbins, Capt. Deavenport, G.L. Gibbs, S.F. Hale, J.F. Hannah, H.C.
Neil, T.J. Noah, Thomas Little, Billy Pulin, Marsailes Rasbell, Lt.
Reasons, G.W. Mclenden, C.A. Shields, J.E. Smith, Capt. Sumners, Capt.
C.G. Tucker, J.R. Warren.
46. There is a large Camp of Confederate veterans in Dallas, I went to
    see the Adjutant and sent him two letters asking for the P. O.
    addresses of the members of the Camp but got no work from him.
    Seeking aid from the Confederate Veterans, Nashville and the Confed-
    erate historian of Texas was in vain. Many months ago I asked Adju-
    tant Marchbanks, Confederate Camp, Waxahachie to send you list with
    P. O. addresses of the living Veterans of the Camp. He found six and
    I suppose that he sent you names and addresses accordingly.
        I am not at all satisfied with what I have done, but all things
    considered, I have done the best I was able to do. If I had been set
    to the task forty years ago, I could have made the work complete with
    one tenth of the time and labor. When the Confederate armies surrend-
    ered and the war was over, I turned my back upon the past and set my
    face like a flint toward the goal of my ambition. After 50 years of
    activity in the work of character building the memory of the war
    records had faded.
        Thank you for your courtesy and kindness and holding you in grate-
    ful remembrance, I am sincerely and cordially,
                                        David Shires Myers Bodenhamer,
                                        5632 Miller, Dallas, Texas
                                        August 5, 1924

    (N.B.: from second form)
5. Co. H., 32nd Tennessee. which was organized at Camp Trousdale in Oct.
    1861 after which I was appointed Sergeant Major. I had close rela-
    tions to all the companies in the Regt.
9. Among the preachers were Rev. Carson P. Reed, Pulaski, Tenn. who
    preached many years at the camp meetings at Mt. Moriah Church, Giles
    co., Tenn. and his son, Wiley Reed, pastor of First C. P. Church,
    Nashville, Tenn. at opening of Civil War.
13. About $20,000 a large part of which was lost in the war.
14. The first was a one room log house, later a small frame building two
    rooms, was added. My parents lived a very simple farm life.
    (Rest of questions answered approximately the same, with few additions
    researcher may wish to read for themselves...cme)
39. Time and space would fail to tell of the exposure to the severe cold
    of midwinter at Fort Donelson while exposed to heavy firing from
    field guns and gunboats of the deep distress of being surrounded and
    captured. I would be a long tedious story to tell of our grief and
    pain on our way to prison in Indiana and of the long wearisome months
    in prison away from home and loved ones. At Camp Lafayette we suffer-
    ed much but the citizens received us kindly and when removed to Camp
    Morton we found rest, comfort and freedom from the suffering and
    horrors of war.
40. In August 1864, in front of Atlanta, Ga. I received a severe wound
    in the foot ......

BODENHAMER (cont'd.):
(On attached pages Mr. Bodenhamer writes of his ancestors...cme)
Genealogical Date - THE ANCESTORS OF DAVID SHIRES MYERS BODENHAMER:
5632 Miller Avenue, Dallas, Texas:
(The following notes are largely taken from the histories of the
pioneers of Tennessee and the South West and from Vols. I and II of
"The Building of the Nations" found in the Dallas Public Library,
Dallas, Texas):
The Ulster Presbyterians or Scotch-Irish had a passion for whole
freedom. They were a liberty loving people serious religious of the
Moses stamp, of domestic instincts, of straight forward simplicity.
They were strong men, shrewd, bold and zealous to the death for an
ideal. They kept the Sabbath. They contended for their own form of
worship and for their civil rights. Many of them were well educated,
specially their preachers. They were taught to read at an early age.
No person was admitted to the privileges of the Church who did not
understand and approve the constitution and discipline of the Presbyterian Church. They were versed in the basal teachings of the Bible
and the writing of their great preachers. They were democratic and
largely had found refuge from persecution. The famous Presbyterian
minister, Rev. Alexander Craighead was persecuted in Va. for preaching
democratic doctrines and was forced to flee for refuge to North
Carolina. The Scotch-Irish being deeply religious, respected and most
sacredly guarded their religious liberty.
The immigrants from beyond the sea who came to American by
Charleston were Sctoch-Irish and found a home in the settlement in
North Carolina which became known as Mecklenburg county. It is claim-
ed that the Scotch-Irish were the first to declare for American
Independence. A declaration is said to have been drawn up and signed
in Mecklenburg county, N.C. May 20 (26?), 1775. Often I heard my
father, David Bodenhamer, Say that he came to Tennessee about the year
1808, from Mecklenburg county, N.C. and my cousin, Mrs. Alice (Reed)
Knox told me that she often heard her father, my uncle, my mother's
brother, say that his ancestors were Scotch-Irish. So it seems clear
to me that my grandfather, Robt. Reed and my grandmother, Betsy
(Myers) Reed, probably at the same time and moved by similar impulses,
came with my father and my uncle, Henry Shires Bodenhamer to Tennessee
from Mecklenburg county, N.C. or the Bodenhamer, Reed, Shires and
Myers families, all came to Tennessee from Mecklenburg co., N.C. and
are Presbyterian Scotch-Irish descent. My grandfather Robert Reed
was born in 1779 and was one of a family of 12 children - 9 boys and
3 girls. He was the oldest of the children. His father, my grandfather, who married Margaret Carson, was born in 1757 and died in 1817.
The Reed ancestors were Scotch-Irish and came over to this country,
settling first in Mecklenburg co., N.C. thence coming to Tennessee
about 1808. My grandfather Bodenhamer was a man of fine mind and
high culture and of Scotch-Irish descent.

(Extra Page)
"The original copy was so defaced, that I make this a true copy": H'd
quarters 32d Tenn. Regt. Camp near Wartrace, Jan. 22, 1863 - Special
Order) - This is to certify that David S. Bodenhamer, Private of Co.
H. 32nd Tenn. Regiment has this day been appointed Sergeant Major of
the 32nd Tenn. Regiment and is ordered to enter upon the duties of
said office this day and this shall be his warrant of said appointment.
By order of: Ed. C. Cook, Col. 32nd Tenn.
Regt.

BOLES, G. R.

FORM NO. 1

1. G.R. Boles, Sparta, Tenn.
2. 72 (73?)
3. Fentress co., Tenn.
4. White co., Tenn.
5. I was on the farm with my father plowing, howing, reeping, mowing....
6. a farmer and raising of cattle and hoges

BOLES (cont'd.):
7. i had some hoges an cattle worth a bout five hundred dollar and when
the federal army took it all so i was left with oute anney thing
8. no slaves
9. 150 acres
10. a boute 2 thousand dollar
11. partley loge and fraime hade 5 rooms
12. i don all kinds of farm work from the ho handle to the handle of the
mowing ___ and the handle of a pitch fork
13. my father don farm work my mother she had her cotan and flax she spunn
and wove cloth she had her flax whell and spun flax thread and made
___ clothes and all kinds of clothes
14. no servants
15. it was respectable an onrable young men ___ dide not engage in some
kinds of ___ was not respected. the fact is that all young men that
did not have .... (This old gentleman had terrible handwriting)
16. all white men was during ther parte of work that it toke to ___ ___
of the country
17. all white men had to have some sort of busnus to _____ the white man
work as same as slave
18. ther was no diference in the non slav holder and the slave holder
the thing was the respectability
19. i colde not tell aney diffrence in slave holder and none slave holders
20. ther was good feeling between both slave holders and not in - it was
the character
21. the was two political parties and all held to ther parteys regardeless
of slave or no slave
22. it was good
23. they was incuraged by slave holders
24. both public and subscription
25. i do not rember
26. a boute one half mile
27. both kinds
28. bothe private public
29. a boute three months
30. veri much so
31. some time a man an some times a woman
33. 8 ten. cavelry comanded bey _. G. Dibrell.
34. i donot remember
35. i do not remember
36. i think it was ____ on cumberland river
37. after the first battle i dont remember where we went after the first
battle i do not remember how long they lasted was in every battle
that my command was in i remember how they went the first battle we
got beat all the rest of the battles we won in camp we had no tents
and took the weather as it come and sometimes we had something to eat
and was not well clothed
38. i surendered at washington, georgia on the 12 day of may
39. we left washington ga for home and when we got to chatinooga they took
our horses an we come home a foote an when i gote hom i found a
widowed mother and three sisters and one brother which was discharged
at Corinth, Miss.
40. farm work
41. come home and was in a bad shape i was not able to do hard work so i
went to farming the best i colde (could) to make a living for my
mother so i stayed with my mother un till 1880 i maried an we don the
best could - i am to day suffering from disease i contacted in prison
an not able to do anney thing my church relation is cumberland pres-
beterin i have not held anney publick offis.

(4 extra sheets attached - #37):
37. i was in ever battle that the command was in i was in carters creek
pike on in the fite upon we run the yankes back and held? St Clouds
hill we drove the yanks back to carters creek and on the nolans vill
pike we drove them back in ___ at colag (College?) grove .... they
left franklin for nashvill i was in the raid.... the first yankee we
come up with after we crossed tennessee river was at coton grove an
they ____ as soon as we com on them and the next place was humbolt
we drove them from ther the next place was gasdon as we routed them

342

BOLES (cont'd.):

ther an then went to a stocade eight miles from Jackson? and they run
down a train load of men when our caissons opened fire on them they
run back to get out of danger the next place was parkers crossroads
an had a hard fite and the comand that we foute surendered an a rein-
forsment came a grater then we had an we broke throu their line of
battle an come ....cliften (Clifton?) and croste the tenness
river an don some fiting a cros the river on ---then to florance
alabama stayde there a whil an had a small scrap then back to tennsse
and then to charnooga an then back to sparta white co. and we had a
fite on the calf killer river near the mouth of wilcat creek and we
sent them back to marinvil(?) an in a short time they came back an
i was on the......................i forgot the raid to Clarksvill
the worst time we ever seen it rained an raise the river on we could
not cross the river an then turned cold and we had nothing to eat for
four days and we come back to spring hill i was in prison
twenty months and was sent south on the sick list they sent south
such as was considered totally disable to do anney thing.
i got richmon the first of march an went to a small station near
Rollie an stayed ther untill the arme left Rollie and i struck out
for my comande an went with them to washington Ga. and was in the
surender.

33. Lybun Wells, A. Christin, Martin Eldrege, Doude Stevens, Nick stevens,
John Stevens, Dock Taylor, Jhon (John) Dyobrt, Jhon (John) Markram,
Carrel Richeson, Jack Sells, Henry Killman, Dave Killman, Hiram
Patrice (Patrick?), John Lee, Fede Lee, Hamilton Brown, George Speck,
Fayete White, Frank Parton(? This may be Poston), Lewis Parton or
Poston, Zedock Parton or Poston, John Harrigon?, Henry Harrigon?,
W.W. Windle, A.L. Windle, Harry Windle, Milt Oakley, Earric (Eric)
Cox, Gorge (George) Hill, James Anderson, James Ford, Rubin _teram,
Gorge Gayhart, Jake Cochran, Clay Garrete, A. Jackson, Joe Howard,
Burge? Howard

BOND, J. H.

FORM NO. 2

1. J.H. Bond, 119 Ala. St. Bristol
2. Eighty
3. Sullivan co., Tenn.
4. yes (Confederate)
5. Com. F-59 Tenn. Regt.
6. Farming
7. James Bond; Sullivan co., Tenn.; lived or near blountvill county seat
   ....
8. Elizabeth Stokes; Jacob Stokes -----
9. the family record is not convient
10. non
11. one
12. two hundred
13. bout three thousand dollars
14. log 8 rooms
15. worked on farm general farm work
16. thru 44 missing
45. ----
46. E.C. Barnes, Casy Malone, Wilson Cresler (Blountville, Tenn._ ---bing
    flats? ____Wiliam (William?) Hall, Dock Harismon - Silver cole Tenn.
    David Dracke (Drake?), William; Jacob Wedner (Weaver?) Piney Flats,
    Tenn., W.W. Davis, Bristol, Tenn.

BONDURANT, BENJAMIN T.

FORM NO. 2

1. Benjamin T. (L.?) Bondurant, Sharon, WEakely co., Tenn.
2. 75 years old
3. Weakley co., Tenn.

343

BONDURANT (cont'd.):
4. Confederate
5. Co. I, 20th Tenn. Cav. In Feb. 1865 the 19th (Newsoms Regt.) and the
   20th (Russell's) regt. were consolidated and I was put in Co. E, under
   Capt. Tom Gay(?)
6. Farmer and County Court Clerk
7. Churchell P. Bondurant; b. in Ky.; lived; Dresden, Weakley co., Tenn.
   at time of death; was Co. Court Clerk at time of death in 1853.
8. Mary E. Etheridge; Thomas Etheridge and Elizabeth Harvy (?); lived
   ten miles west of Dresden in Weakley co., Tenn.
9. My grandfather Benj. Bondurant and wife (Sarah Moseley) moved from
   Buckinham co. Va. to Ky.; from Ky. to Dresden Tenn. about 1821. My
   grandfather Etheridge moved from Currituck co., N.C. to Weakley co.
   Tenn. in 1833; my great grandfather Thomas Harvy came to Tenn. with
   his daughter died here, was a soldier in the revolutionary war and is
   the only one burried in Weakley co. that I know of
10. I as a minor was the owner of 120 acres of land and four slaves at the
    beginning of the war.
11. My parents owned 8 slaves   and 120 acres land
12. 120
13. My parents had both been dead; father 9 years and mother 5 years when
    the war commenced.
14. log house 4 rooms
15. I worked at farm jobs when not in school, but was in school when
    there was school
16. My father ran his farm with his slaves and was Co. Court Clerk at time
    of his death when I was five years of age. My mother was house keeper
    and superintended the house work by the slaves
17. Yes the women slaves cooked, washed, spun, weaved and cleaned the
    house
18. Yes, no man or woman was looked down on because they did honest work
    for a living
19. Yes, unless they owned sufficient slaves to be independant of work
20. None, but such as owned sufficient property to keep them from it and
    not of of them (not many of them)
21. Every body was on an equality socially
22. yes
23. all friendly and on equality socially
24. No. if any difference was in faver of the non slave holder
25. yes. people encouraged such young men
26. encouraged and helped
27. the common country schools
28. from seven to sixteen years
29. about three (3) miles, but I boarded away from home and attanded
    school some
30. only the oridnary county schools houses mostly log
31. private. I never attended fall (full.) school but 3 months and that
    was the only one ever taught in my community
32. about 8 to 10
33. yes
34. I went to both, but generally a man
35. I left home the 27th day of Nov. 1863 but was not sworne in until the
    first of Dec. 1863, near Newbern, Dyer co., Tenn. in the Confederate
    service.
36. We went from Newbern to Moulton, Ala. to get some guns that had been
    deposited there by Gen. Bell
37. about 3 months
38. in Ocalona, Miss.
39. After the Ocalona battle, we went on a raid to Paducah, Ky. we then
    wer furloughed to go home for about 20 days, after that my brigade
    (Bells) was on the Fort Pillow raid I was absent on detail when the
    Fort Pillow raid) after that we went back to Miss. then the Brice
    Cross road fight in June then the Harrisburg fight in July, then the
    fight north of Oxford and the raid on Memphis in Aug.
40. I was paroled at Gainsville, Ala. the 12th of May 1865.
41. It took 10 days hard riding to get home where I arrived on the 22d
    of May 1865.
42. worked on farm 1865 and 66
43. In 1867 I began reading medicine in 1869 I was graduated from the old
    Medical college of Nashville, Tenn. and practiced medicine nine years,

BONDURANT (cont'd.):
   then run for Trustee of Weakley co. was elected and held the office
   two terms (4 years) then farmed three or four years, then held the
   office of store keeper, weigher and guager in custom house in Memphis
   Tenn. for 5 months, resigned, returned home and lived on farm for
   sometime, then held office of Postmaster at Sharon, Tenn. for 12 years,
   resigned and have not been doing much since for 12 years.
44. ----
45. ----
46. ----

   (N.B.: BONDURANT, BENJ. T. Pension No. 16355)

                        BOOKER, THOMAS

FORM NO. 2

1. Thomas Booker, Elmwood, Tenn.
2. 77 years
3. Wilson county, Tenn.
4. Confederate soldier
5. Company G, 28 Tennessee
6. farmer
7. Elias Booker; b. Kain Creek, Wilson co., Tenn.
8. Martha Jain (Jane?) Dugless (Dougless?); Mr. Dugless and (dont know):
    Smith Co., Tenn.
9. My grandfather was raised in Wilson county and was a miller
10. I did not own anything but a horse
11. no
12. about 40 acres
13. it wasant worth but little it wasant cleared about $140 as near as I
    know
14. a log house 1 room
15. I plowed with a yoke of steers
16. My father worked on the farm and my mother spun and cooked and weaved
    all
17. no
18. yes
19. some did and some did not the colard men done the most
20. about one thurd I think
21. no they thaught there selves better then the poor men
22. no they did not mingle
23. there was not a frindley feeling to ward each other
24. no they did not help any
25. yes I think so
26. discouraged by slave holders
27. I went to the county school on bad days that I could not work
28. about a year
29. about one mile
30. just the county school
31. public
32. about 3 months
33. some did and some did not the poor boys had to work
34. old man
35. at Murfreeboro
36. Stateville, Tenn.
37. 5 or 6 months
38. Myrfreeboro
39. after the first battle, I went to Stateville, Tennessee that was the
    only battle I had typhoid feaver and one of my legs swolen up and I
    garded the Batry and my leg is still sore with a bad sore on it I had
    no food much and slept cold
40. I was discharged at Tulihoma
41. I wrode a horse home and was 4 days on the road not able to wride
    eather
42. I was not able to work for over a year with my leg. I never hav been
    able to work since then but little
43. I have not been able to work but little never had no education to hold
    no office of any kind. Me and my father and grandfather belonged to

                              345

BOOKER (cont'd.):
      the Sothern Medithis Church
44. ----
45. B--d Clark was the Captain (this may also be B--d Clark Cunningham)
    I will tell you about my ____ ____......(may be "brother Sam Booker")
    he fought through the war I guess he must (went?) this writing is
    difficult to read...cme: (to the best of my ability, here is the
    basis of his information:)...the brother was shot or wounded on the
    battle field, left for dead, and Thomas went looking for his brother,
    found him and...the rest is almost impossible to read); Thomas was
    evidently injured in the leg, as he makes some mention of a "sore or
    some such" still bothering him; he raised nine children and then not
    able to work; then he tells of all the names he can remember in his
    company: Mat Ford, Bill___, Tom Lanford?, (may be Lambert), _____,
    Anson Lambert, James ___, Mat Jones, (rest is too blurred)

BORING, PETER

FORM NO. 1

1. Peter H. Boring, Jonesboro, Tenn. R. 10 Box 52
2. 74
3. Tenn. Washington co.
4. Tenn. Washington co.
5. Day labor on farm
6. Doctor
7. none
8. none
9. 130
10. about $3500.00
11. Framed house with 6 rooms
12. done general farm work
13. Father had large practice devoted his time to profession. My mother
    did all the house work in addition spun wove cut out and made cloth-
    ing for a family of nine children with but little hired help.
14. occasionally some hired help both male and female
15. yes
16. yes
17. as a general rule they energetic and industrious
18. Every body that was respectable was considered on an equality
19. yes
20. Friendly feeling a stranger at public gatherins could not distinguish
    any difference
21. none
22. yes
23. encouraged
24. Public and subscription
25. about 10 years. sometimes 2 or 3 months in the year
26. 2 miles
27. none but above mentioned
28. both
29. from 3 to 5 months
30. very irregular all had to work when wanted on the farm
31. both
32. in the Confederate Army Aug. 8th 1864
33. Capt. Wm. Fry's Scouts, Vaugn's Brigade, none living to my knowledge
34. Western N.C.
35. about 2 months
36. At a battle of several engagements between Morristown and Bristol
37. The only battle of much importance was in Dec. 1864 at Marion, Va. we
    had after the battle an extremely cold spell we was at Mt. Airy Va.
    thinly clad with nothing to eat except corn parched on cob for
    several days and no tents to sleep in with but little or no ____. I
    never was sick while in the service
38. April 1864
39. I scouted home most of way after night. The enemy was mistreating
    many comrades after they had surrendered and laid down their arms
40. farming

346

BORING (cont'd.):
41. I have been a farmer all my life except 6 years I was in the merchan-
    dise (mercantile) business.
42. Dr. Isaac Boring; b. Boons Creek, Washington co., Tenn.; where he was
    born and raised (and lived); none
43. Nancy A. Yoakley; Peter Yoakley and Rachel Canoles; near Bluntville,
    Tenn.
44. My grandparents on my fathers side were German and on mothers side
    Irish.

    (N.B.: BORING, PETER H. (not BONNING)

                        BOSTICK, BERRY RICE

FORM NO. 2

1. Berry Rice Bostick, Dechare (Decherd, Tenn.)
2. 79
3. Franklin co. Tenn.
4. I was a confederate soldier
5. Co. H., 4th Ark. Regt. transferd to Morgans Cavely Co. H. 3d Kentucky
6. farmer
7. Little Berry Bostick; b. South Carolina; lived near Winchester, Tenn.;
    died before the war between the states.
8. Sophia Graham; dont remember; her parents came - lived in South
    Carolina.
9. My parents died when I was young and I have no record of them
10. none
11. 5 slaves
12. 100 acres
13. $500.00
14. Log house 4 rooms
15. Farm Work
16. My father farmed. My mother done the house work and made the cloths
    for the family
17. none
18. I was henerable those that did not work and try to make a henerable
    living was very little thought of
19. ----
20. not more than 5%
21. the(y) did think as much of those that did not own slaves as those
    that did
22. ----
23. frendly
24. did not
25. by industry and economy he could
26. they were incouraged and the slave holders was ready and willing to
    help them
27. Free schools as a rule
28. about 2 years
29. about 2 miles
30. what was known as free schools
31. Public as a rule
32. about 3 months
33. as a rule they did
34. both
35. 1861, 26th of August in Montgomery co., Ark. transferd to Morgans
    Cavely (cavalry) 1863.
36. Misouri that was when I was in the 3 Ark. Regiment
37. ----
38. Elkhorn battle in Misouri
39. We went from the first battle back to Ark. went in winter quarter
    our fare was much though we made the best of it. we could and was
    ready to lay(?) them again when called upon. Af. going with Gen.
    Morgan on his raid in Ohio was captured in 1863 and remained in
    prison in Ill.
40. Paroled the 2 of March 1865 at Camp Douglass and went from (there)
    to Richmond, Va.
41. We would ride when we could but had walk most of the time and got

BOSTICK (cont'd.):
rations as best we could and not much of that.
42. Farming
43. I have engaged in farming and stock raising and trading have made very good living have a good comfortable home. My health has given a way am not able to leave my room am just waiting for the last roll call as the most my comrades has answered.
44. (written in space of Q. 43) I cant call to mind all of them. I was personally acquainted Col. Pete Turny, Col. Albert S. Marks(?), and most of the leading men in our county mixed with them when convenient.
45. Privates: I have the roster of Co. H 3 Kenty Regt. 2nd Brigade Morgans Cavelry: W.O. Henderson, Henry Bryant, Bery Bostick, Forest Bostick, Tom Doil, Jo_ Dotson, George F___, John Featherson, Will ___, Robt. ___, Fideler (Fielder?) Helm, E. Johnson, Dick Lyle, Dave L__, Lafayett Mosly, Elija Mills, Jake Madock, Dick McGee, Americus Oaks, John Quarles, Rose, Blake Ryan, Dock Stovall, B__ Tyler, Dick Williams, J.D. Wilforce, Tim Burger, Joe Barton, Joe Baily, Jim Barton, Albert Bostick, Amos Crockett, Gordan Duncan, John Fisher, John Hensill, Shey Gorman, Joe Grizard, Will Grizard, Harry Herenden, Tim Herenden, Ed Jones, Bud Keller, John Lyle, G.T. Morgan, John A. Metter?, Tim Morrow, George McGee, Jim Neel, Pat. O'Conner, Alexander Rutherford, Robt. Rutherford, --- Shelton, Joe Shackelford, Dick Tyler, Jack Williams, Robt. Williamson, G.A. Good. Names of Officers: Capt. Ike B. Baker, 1 Lt. D.G. Burdan, 1 Lt. W. Evans, 3 Lt. Frank Justice, 1 Sgt. ___ Whitaker, 2 Sgt. Sam Sanders, 3 Sgt. E. Carter, 4 Sgt. Hugh Trabue, Corp. Marshall ___, Cpl. Ben. Waters, Cpl. Will Claude, Cpl. Tim Borders.
46. Alex Usry   Decherd, Tenn.
    Henry Holt   "   "
    J.P. Kinsley   "   "
    Dare Coble   "   "

(N.B.: BOSTICK, BERRY Pension No. 15833)

BOURNE, EDW.

(Attached is sheet: letter dated - Nov. 30, 1922: on EDWARD BOURNE AND COMPANY, 36 Southern Express Bldg., Insurance and Bonds, Memphis, Tenn. - est. Feb. 12, 1883)
Letter to Mr. J.T. Moore, re-Personal History and War (1861-65) Experience.
Mr. Bourne sent by registered mail a large collection of data and requests that Mr. Moore "not throw it in the waste basket if he can't use it, but to return to him". He states that it took too much time and work to get it up, to throw it away, and then, one of my children might be glad to have it. He also states that he had drawn two flags and a shield on the title page, with the coat of arms or seal of the State of Tennessee; plus the battle flag of Cleburne's Division, which was also the battle flag of Hardee's Corps. "The flags (not to show that I could draw a little) but for historic reasons. The flags on the title page, are those under which TENNESSEE has had ___ being and the ones under which I have served as a soldier. The one of the last page is rarely, if ever, shown in pictures of Confederate battle flags, though it was borne by as brave and gallant body of Confederate soldiers as ever fired a gun. Therefore I think it should be rescued from oblivion. If it was, as I think, the battle flags of Hardee's Corps, it was also borne by Cheatham's and Bate's Divisions, which together with Cleburne's former said Corps, and old Tennessee surely had a big interest in it, for many of her sons poured out their life blood in defence of it and died under its waiving folds."
                Yours for dear old TENNESSEE
                     Edward Bourne (his signature should be
                                                    seen)

Title: Life of Edward Bourne, Brig. Gen'l., N.G.S.T., Retired, of Memphis, Tenn. and Ramifications pertaining therto. by Him.

BOURNE (cont'd.):
FORM NO. 1

1. Edward Bourne, Residence, 705 Tate AVe. and Office, 408 American
   Railway Express Bldg., Memphis, Tenn.
2. On my last birthday, June 23, 1922, I was (76) seventy six years old
3. Tenn., Shelby county and City of Memphis
4. See Sheet No. 1, attached.
5. Going to school and office boy in my fathers office.
6. He was a partner in several mercantile firms at different times, but
   when the war came, he was in the Steam Boat Agency business.
7. (Here, Mr. Bourne crosses out "you" and writes in "He" discussing his
   father): Did not own any property, except cash and negotiable assests.
   After arriving at Montgomery, Ala. he invested in sugar and cotton,
   all of which was destroyed by order of the authorities when a raid
   by the Federal Cavalry was expected at Montgomery, near the end of
   the war.
8. My father owned one, a man, who nearly killed another negro, because
   he thought he reflected upon my father in a remark he made.
9. None that I know of, rented.
10. Don't know.
11. Frame, about six rooms
12. Lived in the city most all my life, know nothing about plowing. Just
    after the war, engaged in the Steamboat and Railroad Agency, business
    with my father. The claim of certain historians is all "rot".
13. Office and outside work necessary to this business. Worked for
    himself. Mother stayed at home, kept house and raised her children.
    Always had several servants to help her. No special work done about
    the house other than the usual housekeeping duties. No spinning
    and weaving.
14. Yes, differed at times, usually two or three.
15. Never heard it spoken of otherwise.
16. Some did
17. Don't recollect, our family associated with the best people, among
    which there were doubtless a number that did not have to work.
18. I was only about fifteen years old when the war came, but I do not
    recall that any distinction was made on that account.
19. As far as I know they did. I noticed nothing to the contrary.
20. I think the feeling was friendly, at least, it so appeared to me.
21. I think not
22. Yes, I believe the general dispostion of the people was to help such
    a one.
23. I believe they were encouraged.
24. About six months, the (public) city high school, the rest of my
    schooling was in private, or pay schools, and the Germantown (Tenn.)
    Military Institure.
25. About eight years or more.
26. a few city blocks
27. (Public) City schools and a number of private schools.
28. Both
29. About ten (10). We usually had vacation during July and August.
30. Yes
31. With one exception, a man.
32. See Sheet #1, Question 32.
33. When I joined it, it was the 3rd Confederate Inft., just before the
    close of the war, the regiments of Gen. (?) Brigade were consolidated
    into one regment known as the 1st Ark. Consolidated and our regiment
    became Co. "K", - See Sheet 2.
34. To fight the enemy in front of Dalton, Ga. but their first fight
    was at Mundfordville, Ky. (or Tenn.) (N.B.: this is in the state of
    Kentucky.)
35. Don't recall exactly, but it was not many weeks.
36. My first contact with the enemy was on the skirmish line in front of
    Dalton, Ga. after we broke up winter quarters.
37. See Sheet #3 attached.
38. Greensboro, N.C., May 2nd, 1865, when Gen'l. Goseph E. Johnston, the
    grandest and best general of them all, surrendered.
39. Walked most of the way and road on top of box cars the balance to
    LaGrange, Ga. where my father and family had gone from Montgomery,
    Ala. several months before. We (our family) came home to Memphis by

BOURNE (cont'd.):
   steamboat and railroad.
40. Steamboat Agency business, then Railroad Agency and last, Insurance Agency.
41. See Sheet #4 - attached.
42. James Treadwell Bourne; Arrondale, Mass. now Kennebunk, Ma.; state of Mass. now Maine, Sep. 24, 1812; lived at: Kennebunk and Bangor, Me., Portsmouth, N.H., Boston, Mass., Cincinnatti, Ohio, moved to Memphis, Tenn. 1840, where he lived except during the war, until he died Sept. 3rd, 1883. He was collector of Customs at port of W___ during President Filmore's administration and during the war, commissioner for the Confederate government to appraise steam vessels.
43. Martha Tucker Freeland; John Freeland and Hepzibah (Adams) Freeland; lived at Salem and other places in Mass. and Portsmouth, N.H. Mother died Mar 2_ (blurred may be 23 or 28), 1899, on her 86th year, being born June 2nd, 1813.
44. See Sheet #5 attached.

   Sheet 1:
   Ans. to Q. 4: Memphis, Tenn. has always been my home. After it was captured by the Federals, June 6th, 1862, which naval battle I witnessed from the bluffs of said city, our family refugeed to Lounds (Lowndes) co., Miss. near Columbus, and then in a few months thereafter, to Montgomery, Ala. A short while after we arrived at the latter place, I got a position as shipping clerk, in the George W. Wilson & Co.'s warehouse at Selma, Ala.; at which place the Confederate government had one of their largest arsenals, and all of the freight for said arsenal, to and from the river, was handled by and through said warehouse. I remained in said postion a few months, after which I was one of the clerks on the Steamer "Jeff. Davis", Captain Willis O'Bannon, Master, which was practically a government transport, and ran the Alabama river between Montgomery and Mobile, Ala. After filling this position on the steamer "Jeff Davis" and steamer "Virginia", the latter being the boat used in place of the former, during low water, several months, upon learning my brother had been promoted to a captaincy and having a promise from my father, that when he did, he would let me go to the army, I resigned, much against the wishes of the other officers of sd. boat, went to Montgomery, where my father fitted me out for the army, and then from there to Dalton, Ga. where I enlisted for the war in the Confederate army.
   The Wilson Warehouse kept a large flatboat on the river at the foot of their incline, where they put the freight to be shipped and the freight they received from the steam boats. The shipping clerk had charge of the loading and unloading of sd. flatboat, often there were hundreds of tons on it being shipped and as many being received, on and from a boat and it was a hard thing to handle the freight so as to avoid sinking the flatboat. I was only 16 years old at that time, which fact should be considered, when I left the employment of Wilson & Co. and received the following compliment from Mr. George Wilson, the senior partner of the firm, when he was bidding me goodby. He said, Ed, I am sorry to see you go...you are the only clerk we ever had that did not sink one or more flatboats in the same space of time you have been with us.

   Ans. to Q. 32: In the winter of 1863-4, when the Army of Tennessee was in winter quarters at Dalton, Ga., I enlisted, but I was so anxious to get into the army, having made three unsuccessful attempts previously, I did not impress my mind with the month or day. To the best of my recollection, Gen. Braxton Bragg was still in command and our regiment the 3rd Confederate Inft., was still consolidated with the 5th Confederate Inft. and in Polk's Brigade, and soon after, Gen. Joseph E. Johnston, the greatest general of them all, succeeded Gen. Bragg in command of the army. Our regiment was separated from the 5th Confederate, Polk's Brigade broken up and our regiment put into Govan's Brigade. I enlisted in "The Young Guard", a company from Memphis, Tenn. For additional information as to said company, see Sheet #2 and Lindsey's Military Annals of Tenn., pages 599 to 602. I drilled with the "Young Guards" when they were organizing and drilling to go into the war and wanted to enlist then, but was refused on account of my youth, again when they were in camp at Columbus, Ky.,

350

BOURNE (cont'd.):
I went to them and tried to enlist, and after being with them a week
or so, was sent home for the same reason. My next effort to get into
the service was an attempt to join Co. "A", 7th Tenn. Cavalry, but my
father getting wind of it, captured me and prevented the accomplish-
ment of my ofject. So when I finally got his permission to join the
army, I did not stand upon the order of my going, but went at once to
"The Young Guard" and enlisted as said before, without giving thought
of the month or day.

Sheet 1:
Q. 33: A partial Roster (writing this paper from memory in 1922
nearly 57 years after the war of 1861-1865, many names have been
forgotten, therefore omitted) of: "The Young Guards", organized at
Memphis, Tenn. and went from there to take part in the war of 1861-65,
between the states, for camp of organization at Jackson Tenn. in May
1861.
Officers: (When the company left Memphis for the camp at Jackson,
Tenn.) - Commissioned: John Frazer Cameron, Capt. (Afterwards Lieut.
Colonel)
John Baine, 1st Lieut. (At Jackson, Tenn., was appointed adjutant of
    the 15th Tenn. Inft.)
William Freeland Bourne, wnd Lieut. (At Jackson, Tenn., promoted to
    1st Lt., and later to Capt. Co. "A", 3rd Conf. Inft. and killed
    July 22, 1864 on the third line of the enemies breast works,
    while leading the right wing of his regiment in a charge he being
    at the time, second in command of the rgt. The writer, with the
    help of Sgt. Pixley, buried him on the battlefield near where he
    fell.)
Otis Hazel Smith: Junior 2nd Lieut. (At Jackson, Tenn. was promoted
    to 2nd Lt. and was killed at Calhoun, Ga., in 1863, accidently,
    when the command was moving by rail.)
None-Commissioned:
Jerome Wilson, 1st Sgt. (At Jackson, Tenn., promoted to Junior 2nd
    Lt. and afterwards promoted to Capt. and Aide-de-Camp.)
Bob Harney, 2nd Sgt. (At Jackson, Tenn. promoted to 1st Sgt. and later
    killed in battle)
Hunsden Cary, 3rd Sgt. (At Jackson, Tenn. promoted to 2nd Sgt., and
    later to 1st Sgt. and still later to Junior 2nd Lt. and assigned
    to an Arkansas Co. of the regiment, commanded by Capt. Tom Newton.
    At the battle of Shiloh, he was seriously wounded, and honorably
    discharged from the service.)
John F. Lovin, was a Sgt. (Probably the 4th. Later he was promoted
    to 1st Lt.)
Patrick S. Powers, was a Sgt. (Probably the 5th. Later lost his right
    arm in the battle of Shiloh, and honorably discharged from the
    service.)
William Thomas, was a Corp. (The company left Memphis with a full
    compliment of non-commissioned officers, but the others I can not
    recall and they are enrolled below as privates.)
Privates:
H.W. Brookshire; Ed. C. Brookshire (later 1st Sgt.); Sam Bernhard;
William G. Bridges; Barney B. Blue (afterwards promoted to Capt. and
Aide-de-Camp); ____ Blair; Edward Bourne; George Dent; ____ Dowdy;
Joseph Elliott; William Frazier; ____ Farley; ____ Fitzsimmons; Louis
Ferguson; Charles Harrison (killed in battle of Shiloh); John Hendy;
John H. Jarnigan (later 3rd Sgt. and afterwards Capt. A.Q.M.); ____
Kelly; ____ Lenox; Ab. Mathews; Henry Moore; Patsy McGann; ____
McHenry (later made 1st Sgt.); Andy O'Harra; Tony Powers; William
Puckett; Steve Perpingnam; W. Allie Redford (later Ordinance Sgt.);
John Rohr; George Rohr; ____ Schaeffer; Robert Shipley (later Color
Sgt.-killed at battle of Spring Hill, Tenn.); Ed. Sassaman; John
Scaggs; "Big" Shea; "Little" Shea; Israel P. Startzer; Charles Slover;
Frank Smith; ____ Tanner; Fred Taft; ____ Williams.
Q. 34 (lengthy recital of war experiences. Mentions death of his
brother William Freeland Bourne; also lengthy remarks on "The Young
Guard".)
His parole is dated: greensboro, N.C., May 2nd, 1865 and signed by
F.S. Howell, Col. C.S.A. Commanding, and W.L. Hembert, Lt. and A.D.C.,
U.S.A., Special Commissioner.

BOURNE (cont'd.):
    Sheet 4:
    Ans. to Q. 41: My Life Since the War of 1861-1865: HOME LIFE:
    Memphis, Tenn. has been my home. For about eight years I lived
with my father and mother. March 11, 1869, I married Miss Jennie
Garth McGarvey, 3rd daughter of John William Alexander McGarvey and
Virginia Catherine McGarvey (nee Miss Virginia Catherine Cross), at
her uncle, Capt. Louis Garth's residence, "Mount Aventine", near
Trenton, Todd county, Ky. and brought her to Memphis, Tenn. immediately after the ceremony, where we have resided ever since. Sometime in
1873, we left my father's house and set up housekeeping for ourselves.
We rented the three different houses we lived in until 1888, when we
moved into our present home, a two story, metal roof, frame house of
nine rooms, not counting bath and store rooms, porches and halls,
which we built (I give this detail description of our house, because
in the questionnaire you ask a description of the kind of house my
father lived in at the beginning of the war.)
    My wife was born and raised in Hopkinsville, Christian co., Ky.,
April 4, 1847 and that was her home until 1866 or 1867 when her
father moved his family to Memphis, Tenn. In 1867 her father moved
to Crittendon co., Ark, but only lived there a few months. I met her
for the first time while she was living there. Comparatively soon
after our marriage she became converted to Christianity and joined
the Central Baptist Church, Memphis, of which church I was then and
am still a member. In fact I helped organize sd. church in Dec. 1865
an am now the only member of it that did so. My wife has been a
faithful member of our church to this day and in a quiet retiring way,
has done more or less Christian work.
    God has been good to use and blest us greatly. He has not only
bountifully fed, clothed and housed us, but in addition has given us
five good children, three boys and two girls, viz-Edward, Jr. May
Belle, Martha Virginia, Alexander and Louis McGarvey. All of our
children were born and reared in Memphis, Tenn. Our first child,
Edward Jr. was born May 31, 1870 and he married June 5, 1905 at
Shelbyville, Tenn. Miss Rowena Ewing Eakin, 3rd daughter of Capt.
Spencer Eakin and Milbrey Ewing Eakin (nee Miss Milbrey Ewing). The
latter was a sister-in-law of Col. Henry Watterson, who for years was
publisher of the Courier Journal, of Louisville, Ky. Edward, Jr. and
his wife have been blest with three daughters, all born in New Orleans,
La., viz-Milbrey Eakin, born Dec. 13, 1907, and Virginia McGarvey
and Rowena Eakin, twins, born Feb. 3, 1912. As he was living in New
Orleans, when he married, he took his bride there and lived there
until about three years ago, when he became ass't. manager of the
Southern Department of the North British and Mercantile Insurance
Company and moved to New York City, where he and his family have
resided ever since. He joined the Central Baptist Church, Memphis,
Tenn. while a boy and has lived a faithful, consistent christian life
to this day. While living in Memphis, he was for some time a member
of the finance committee and Financial Secretary of said church. His
wife and oldest daughter are members of the Christian Church and the
youngest daughter, Virginia McGarvey, probably will be soon, as she
is religiously inclined. The other twin daughter died a few days
after her birth. Our second child, May Belle, was born May 22, 1872.
She was a beautiful little blue eyed blond girl, but God only loaned
her to us for a few months and took her home to him. She died June
26, 1873. Our third child, Martha Virginia, was born July 15, 1874.
In her early girlhood, she was converted and joined the Central
Baptist Church, Memphis, she has been faithful to the Master and for
some years has been very active in the church and sunday school work,
both locally and in other Southern states. She is frequently called
upon to visit towns and cities, and teach in training schools the
Junior Department Work of the Sunday schools, also takes an active
part in Baptist Womens' conventions and missionary societies. She
has never married, lived at home with us. She is not only a great
comfort to us, but her happy jovial dispostion adds greatly to our
happiness and like sunshine, she despels all gloom. Our fourth child,
Alexander, was born Feb. 5, 1877. He also joined the same Baptist
church in his early boyhood and was a faithful church and sunday
school member to the day of his death, July 26, 1894. He was large
for his age, a fine looking handsome and very popular boy, beloved

352

BOURNE (cont'd.):

by all who knew him. Mothers of his boy companions, used to say, "if my boy is with Alexander Bourne, it is all right, I am not worried about him." He was a manly boy loved foot ball and other out door games and was a leader among his companions. Our fifth child, Louis McGarvey, was born Nov. 23, 1884, also joined the same Baptist church in his early boyhood and has been a faithful, consistant member, taking considerable interest in the work of the church and some in the sunday school work. He was Secretary of the Finance Committee and Financial Secretary of the Church, for number of years, up to about two years ago, when he went to Dallas, Texas, to live. While a member of the Central Baptist Church, the church elected him a deacon and the Gaston Ave. Baptist Church, Dallas, of which he is now a member to elect him to the same high office, but he declined both honors. However, he is a teacher in the sunday school of that church. Like the children mentioned before, he has been a very affectionate, thoughful and dutiful son to us. June 25, 1913, he was married at Memphis, Tenn. to Miss Susan Gertrude McKay, only daughter of Luther McKay and Gertrude Hull McKay (nee Miss Gerturde Hull), of the same city. God has blest their union with two daughters, Gertrude Martha, born at Memphis, Tenn., June 16, 1919 and Beverly born at Dallas, Texas, Sept. 1, 1921. His wife is a member of the Christian Church. When he first went to Dallas, April 1920, he was manager of the Dallas office of Alexander Eccles & Co., a large Liverpoor, Eng., firm of cotton buyers. Oct. 1, 1921, he was made a partner of said firm and one of its American representatives. He was connected with the firm for several years prior to his going to Dallas, as Ass't. Manager of their Memphis office. He is considered a fine business man by the cotton men of Memphis and greatly respected for his integrity, upright dealings and exemplary character, by all who know him. Neither of my sons were soldiers in the world war, the oldest beyond the draft age and the youngest, just came within the age of the last draft, but was not drafted. But, I have no doubt, both would have volunteered as soon as war was declared, had not both of them had families dependant upon them, as both are patriotic. How could they be otherwise with such a patriotic mother and grand mother, viz-during the war of 1861-65, my wife was in a house, the one we were married in, when it was shelled by the Federals and several shells fell in the yard and exploded near the house. And again at her home in Hopkinsville, Ky., when a small force of Confederates cavalry were suprised there and forced to retreat, they passed through her father's yard, fighting as they retreated, trying to find a ford to a deep creek, that was cutting off their escape and my wife, then a young girl, with her sisters, guided them to the ford, all the time being under fire from the Federals. One of the Confederates being wounded and falling off his horse near their house during the time, was carried into their home and nursed and cared for until he was well enough to be moved, when the Federals sent him to prison. My wife took his pistol, crawled under the house and hid it, showing by her acts both courage and patriotism. My mother, when she was biddin me goodbye, when I was leaving home to join the army, said to me, "Edward I hate to see you go, because you are too young, but, as you are going, I want to say this to you, never come back unless you come with honor", then she kissed me and I left. Although my mother was born and raised in New England, she was a staunch Confederate and gave her boys to fight for the Confederacy, cheerfully, one of which sleeps in a hallowed grave upon the battle field.

In the fall of 1869, my wife's father, mother and sister, Miss Lucy Alexander McGarvy, came to live with us, and when we moved in to our new home, fall of 1888, my father having died prior thereto, my mother also came to make home with us. The first two and the last one mentioned, lived with us until they died and my sister-in-law, is still making her home with us. Mr. McGarvey died March 1883, his wife, March 11, 1900 and my mother March 28, 1899. Notwithstanding there were so many inlaws living under the same roof so many years and belonging to different Christian denominations, one presbyterian, two episcopalians, five baptists and one not a member of any church, it was a happy family. My dear little wife, God bless her, was the "doctor" or "Balance wheel" that kept harmony.

BOURNE (cont'd.):
    Self and family remained in Memphis through the great yellow
fever epidemics of 1873 and 1878 and probably would have through the
one of 1879, but I was in the railroad business at the time and was
ordered out of the city by the Gen'l. Manager. In the epidemic of
1878, two of our children, Edward Jr. and Alexander, also my brother,
Jason, our negro cook and a white hand on the place were all sick
with the fever. The last two died and the first three had very
severe cases. I hope I will never again have to go through with the
terrible experience we had to face in the epidemic of 1878, words
can not describe it.

RELIGIOUS LIFE (Including briefly, as a preface, before the war.):
My mother being a member of the First Presbyterian Church of Memphis,
Tenn. when I was a baby, I was christened in said church. I think
the Rev. Dr. Coons, was the pastor then. Up to about the age of
twelve years, I attended a Presbyterian church and sunday school.
About 1857 or 1858, an Episcopal minister, the Rev. Dr. Shetky, who
was fond of and had a great influence over children, came to Memphis,
organized Grace Episcopal Church and became its first rector. He made
a personal canvas for children for the Sunday school. A number of my
young companions decided to join and I followed them. For the next
four years, or about that time, I attended that church and sunday
school. During my boyhood up to the war of 1861-65, I had a very
unfavorable opinion of the Baptists and Methodists churches, sometimes
voicing the opinion, that they were only fit for negroes. This
opinion was bassed upon the fact that most every negro, if not all at
that time, were either Baptists or Methodists. Besides, I had never
been in a white Baptist church, or ever saw a baptism as practiced
by them. I had witnessed a number of negro baptisms by emersion, but
only as a sort of a circus, for in most cases, they were very rediculous and anything but impressive, and were always out doors in a
pond or the river. In some cases their baptisms were really disgusting to me. While my father and mother were refugeeing in Montgomery,
Ala. and during my few months of residence there, I became acquainted
with and fond of a girl whose mother was a member of and attended the
First Baptist Church of that city. While I lived there I attended
the Presbyterian Church where my parents attended, but the two
churches were not far apart and ours let out a little earlier than
the Baptist church did, so it was my custom to hurry down to it and
when said young lady came out, to meet her and escort her to her home.
On one occasion, when I arrived at the baptist church, a number of
people came out, but the young lady failed to appear. A number of
the private carriages remained. I asked one of the drivers, if church
was out and he told me it was not, they were going to have baptism.
Not having ever witnessed a white Baptist baptism and wishing to see
the young lady, I went to meet I decided to go in and see the baptism.
An usher met me at the door and conducted me to a good seat on the
south side of the church. The minister, I.T. Ticiner, was beginning
a discourse upon baptism, during which he read a number of passages
on baptism from the Bible. I was very much interested and impressed
with the scripture and his remarks thereon. At the close of which,
Dr. Tichiner (N.B.: notice different spelling...cme) retired to the
dressing room, the deacons removed the pulpit from the rostrum and
uncovered the baptismal pool, which was almost under where the pulpit
had stood. When ready, Dr. Tichiner came out, knocked at the door
of the lady's dressing room and a beautiful girl, unknown to me this
day, came forth dressed in pure white, with her long golden hair
hanging down her back. He walked with her to the steps leading down
into the pool from the south side, took her by the hand and helped
her down into the water, repeating an appropriate verse of scripture,
as they decended to the south. Then in the name of the Father, Son
and Holy Ghost, put her under water, thus picturing a burial, then
raised her from the watery grave, which pictured the resurrection.
She came up out of the water smiling and as she mounted the steps,
looking upward the sun shown upon her and water, as it fell from her
dripping garments, looked like drops of gold. Her ascension from the
watery grave, most beautifully pictured the glorious resurrection.
I, involuntarily, thought the Baptists have surely got them all on
baptism. (N.B.: here once again Mr. Bourne gets rather "lengthy"

                                    354

BOURNE (cont'd.):
   in prose. Much of which is not herein noted...cme) ....joined the
   Baptist church in LaGrange, Ga. just after the war on his way home.
   In December 1865, about 125, according to my recollection, there may
   have been less, members of the First Baptist Church, Memphis, including myself, withdrew from said church and together with a number of
   members from Beale St. Baptist Church, Memphis, who were without a
   pastor, organized the Central Baptist Church of Memphis and its sunday school. I am the only original member of that church known to
   be living today....I was appointed a teacher and for over 56 yrs.
   have been either a teacher or officer in it.; 2 yrs. ass't. Supt. and
   2 yrs. Supt. of Same; served 4 yrs. as a clerk, 20 yrs. as treasurer
   and many years on its finance committee, active deacon and trustee.;
   was chairman of the board of deacons; now am Associate Deacon and
   Sec/Treas. Board of Trustees. Supt. of its Mission sunday school for
   a number of yrs.; attended many years ago, at Jackson, Tenn. the
   first meeting of the West Tennessee Baptist Sunday School Convention-
   Bro. R.G. Craig, first president; Mr. Bourne was elected president
   over the 2nd, 3rd, and 4th conventions; elected as 5th convention
   president but declined; appointed by Big Hatchie Association as
   chairman of committee to organize a county Baptist Sunday School
   Convention (Shelby, Tenn.): presided through 5 conventions and was
   elected pres. for 6th convention but declined; etc.

BUSINESS LIFE:
   In 1865, soon after returning to Memphis, Tenn. my father and I
   formed a co-partnership under the firm name of James T. Bourne & Co.
   to do a steam boat agency business and continued the same until the
   early part of 1870; his father was appointed Memphis agent of the
   Star Union Fast Freight Line (owned and controlled by Pennsylvania
   Central R.R.) and son held postion of bookkeeper and chief clerk;
   after that company (James T. Bourne & Co.) was dissolved, his father
   resigned as agent/agency of the Star Union Line, succeeded in that
   position by Alfred G. Tuther; the younger Bourne continued to work
   for that company; held that position until 1875 (8 years); resigned
   to accept the Memphis agency of the Canada Southern Fast Freight Line
   (one of the New York Central R.R. lines) and held that position for
   4 yrs. until early 1880; then occupied himself with temporary jobs
   of various kinds; the first of which was in the office of the chairman of Shelby County Court (as accountant) and second, same type of
   position for a Building and Loan Company or Association; Feb. 12,
   1883, was appointed local agent for Commercial Fire Insurance Co.
   of New York which company had just entered the state (Tenn.) for
   business; he joined the Memphis Board of Underwriters, associated
   himself with C.B. Bryan under firm name of Edward Bourne & Co.
   (N.B.: there is a great deal more on his business life for interested
   researches...cme)

POLITICAL LIFE - ....his father was a Whig; after the war becoming
a Democrat; continued so until his death; Mr. Bourne of this sketch
is a Democrat, etc.

SOCIAL LIFE - His father was a prominent Mason and Odd Fellow and
other fraternal organizations; he is a non-drinker; belonged to an
organization called the Mathian Association (church organization):
was connected with the Confederate Historical Association in this
city, which is also Camp 28, United Confederate Veterans and Bivouack
18, Confederate Soldiers of Tennessee (Gen. George W. Gordon was
once it's president;, etc.

MILITARY LIFE - (Since and before the war, excepting army): mentions
his deep interest in the military from early boy-hood; attended a
military school; mentions reunion of "Chickasaw Guards" in 1894
including James E. Beasley, confederate veteran; (will not include
all the data on these next pages, but abstract the names only; for
further research in this written material, researcher should read
micro-film...cme): Capt. William W. Carnes (graduate of Naval
Academy at Annapolis, Md.); also the brother of above - Gen. Sam
Carnes; members of above organization - Wm. W. Carnes, Keller Anderson, James Dinkins, Edward Bourne, Jr.; mentions Brig. Gen'l. A.R.

BOURNE (cont'd.):
Taylor; Edward Landstreet; Mr. Bourne offered his services for the
Spanish-American War but was declined; and again with war on Germany,
his services were declines;, etc.

REMARKS ON ANCESTRY - Ans. to Q. 44:
My father, James Treadwell Bourne (see answer to Q. 42) was the
only child of Benjamin Bourne and his first wife, Mary Treadwell
Bourne (grandfather Bourne married three times, his second wife being
Clarrisa Warren, daughter of Dr. Warren, a surgeon in the American
Rev. Army and neice of Gen. Warren, who fell at the battle of Bunker-
hill, near Boston, Mass. By her he had two sons, Jason Langdon and
George Franklin. His third wife was Narcissa Sewall, by whom he had
no children. The latter was a member of the prominent Sewall family
of Maine. Grand-father Benjamin Bourne was the first son of his
father, John Bourne, III. Great-grandfather, John Bourne, III was the
first sone of his father, John Bourne, Jr. and the latter, was the
first son of his father, John Bourne. All of them lived in that part
of Massachusetts, which in 1820 was made in to the state of Maine.
Either John Bourne, Jr. or his father commanded a Colony company in
the war against the French; they were all ship builders and owned
ship-yards at either Bangor or Kennebunk, Me. The family came from
England soon after the arrival of the Mayflower and located in
Massachusetts. Grandfather Benjamin had several brothers and two
sisters, their names, to the best of my recollection, were Thomas,
Israel, Charles and Edward E., there may have been other brothers and
sisters, Olive and Julia. They were probably not born in that order.
Edward E. Bourne was judge of one of the courts of his county, a
member of the legislature of the state of Maine, and president of the
maine Historical Society. He wrote a book, a history of the BOURNE
FAMILY, which he published for the family. I expected to get a copy,
but was disappointed. I saw a copy of it however, and made a cursory
examination of it. He was married and had at least one child, Edward
E., Jr. and I think more. I was named for uncle Edward, but my father
did not favor middle names, so in naming me, left the middle name out.
His sisters Olive and Julia, were both married and I think each and
a number of children, but I do no recall to whom they were married
and have no information as to their children. It is more than prob-
able grandfather's other brothers married and had families, but
information regarding them is sadly limited to the above record. My
uncle, Jason Langdon Bourne, was a soldier in the Aroostook (Aroo-
stock?) War and died some years later with consumption brought on by
exposure, etc. while serving in sd. war. He married Sarah Hukil,
by whom he had one daughter, Clarrissa Warren, the latter never
married and died some years ago. I think he also had a son, but may
be mistaken as to that. My uncle George Franklin Bourne, was 1st Lt.
and then Capt. of Co. B, 4th Maine, U.S.A., in the Civil War. He was
wounded and captured by the Confederates in a battle before Richmond,
Va. and died of his wounds in a Confederate hospital at that place.
He was a devoted follower of Christ. Peace to his ashes, I believe
and trust we will meet on the other shore, ...; we did not hear of
this until some years after said war, all communication between my
grandfather's family and my father's being discontinued during and
for some years after the close of the war.) My father was born at
Arondale, Mass., now Kennebunk, Maine, September 24, 1812. Moved
his family from Cincinnati, Ohio, to Memphis, Tenn. in 1840 and died
at the latter place Sept. 3, 1883. He took quite an active part in
business and in everything that was for the best interest of our city;
a prominent Mason and Odd Fellow and numerous fraternal organizations;
Whig before the war and Democrat after and until his death; never
became a member of any church but for some years was a regular attendant at the Lauderdale St. Presbyterian Church; my father married my
mother, Martha Tucker Freeland, at Portsmouth, N.H., Nov. 24, 1833.

My Mother: (see answers to Q. 43):
was the fourth daughter and sixth child of John Freeland and his
wife, Hepzibah Adams Freeland, was born at Salem, Mass., June 2, 1813;
she died at Memphis, Tenn., Mar. 28, 1899; was a faithful and consistent Christian; was a member from girlhood of the Presbyterian church;
constant reader of the Bible; very patriotic, brave and fearless in

BOURNE, (cont'd.):
danger; affectionate and devoted mother; dutiful and loving wife;
she had four brothers and sisters, all of whom were born in Salem,
Essex co., Mass. of which I will speak later. Mother's father, John
Freeland was born in Boston, Mass., Dec. 29, 1779; we have no record
of his parents or their ancestors; he was a United States naval
architect at Portsmouth, N.H. navy yard; died at West Newton, Mass.,
Sept. 21, 1866; was probably married at Beverly, Mass., on Nov 14,
1802.
    Mother's mother, Hepzibah Adams Freeland, was born at Beverly,
Essex co., Mass., Nov. 11, 1780, second daughter and fourth child of
Daniel and Hepzibah Bachelder Adams, who married Mar. 14, 1773; she
was a direct descendant of John Bachelder who was born in 1610; he
married Elizabeth Herrick, both died in 1675; my grandmother,
Hepzibah Adams Freeland, died at West Newton, Mass., April 20, 1866;
her mother my great-grandmother, Hepzibah Bachelder Adams, was the
daughter of Josiah and Mary Leach Bachelder. Children of Daniel and
Hepzibah Bachelder Adams:
1. Josiah B. Adams, b. Oct. 27, 1774, died at sea.
2. Daniel Adams, Jr., b. Oct 5, 1776, married Hezibah _____.
3. Mary Leach Adams, b. Oct 11, 1778, married Bery Blanchard.
4. Hepzibah Adams, b. Nov. 11, 1780, married John Freeland, Nov.
    14, 1802.
5. Samuel Adams, b. Oct. 10, 1782, married Sallie Sugden, Feb 2,
    1806.
6. John Adams, b. Apr. 11, 1787, died at sea.
7. Emily Adams, b. Oct. 3, 1789, married Eben Eveleth Oct 27, 1808.
8. Lucy Adams, b. Feb. 27, 1892, married Eben Berry, Dec. 5, 1825,
    died Feb. 8, 1858.
Children of Daniel and Hepzibah (___) Adams, Jr.:
1. Hepzibah Adams, b. Feb. 22, 1801, died young.
2. Elizabeth Adams, b. May 7, 1802.
3. Hepzibah Adams, b. Nov. 15, 1804.
4. Josiah B. Adams, b. Sept. 3, 1807.
5. Sally Jordan Adams, b. Aug. 24, 1809.

Children of John and Hepzibah (Adams) Freeland:
1. John Freeland, Jr., b. Aug. 25, 1803, died at sea, May 29, 1824.
2. Josiah Adams Freeland, b. May 29, 1805, died at Calcutta, Oct. 25,
    1852.
3. Elizabeth Baker Freeland, b. Mar. 30, 1807, married Francis B.
    Dennis, Sept. 5, 1830, died about 1898.
4. Harriet Corbin Freeland, b. July 6, 1809, never married, died at
    Portsmouth, N.H. Sept. 5, 1836.
5. Caroline Bachelder Freeland, born. Nov. 18, 1811, married Clement
    Jewett, Jan. 5, 1842, died since the war of 1861-65.
6. Martha Tucker Freeland, b. June 2, 1813, married James Treadwell
    Bourne, Nov. 24, 1833; died at Memphis, Tenn. Mar. 28, 1899.
7. Marie Eloise Freeland, b. Feb. 26, 1815, married George William
    Rice, Sept. 11, 1840, died since the Civil War.
8. William Washington Freeland, b. Mar. 7, 1817, died at Manilla,
    P.I., Aug. 30, 1838.
9. Joseph Henry Sheebon Freeland, B. Jan. 16, 1822, married Francis
    Jane Shannon, June 19, 1845, who died May 15, 1850, and he
    married (2) Adeline Issabelle Woodhouse, June 22, 1852. He died
    at New York City, Mar. 25, 1912.

Children of Samuel and Sallie (Sugden) Adams:
1. Marry Ann Sugden Adams, b. Feb. 21, 1809, married William S.
    Leach
3. Luch Sugden Adams, b. Dec. 10, 1811.
4. Sally Adams, b. Apr. 3, 1815, d. June 7, 1841.
5. Hannah Chapman Adams, b. Apr. 20, 1819.
6. John Adams, B. Sept. 10, 1822
2. (N.B.: this birth out of place)
    Louise K. Adams, b. in 1810, married (2nd wife), Alvah Woodbery;
    he died Feb. 4, 1852, aged 40 yrs. 11 mos. She died Apr. 26, 1863,
    aged 58 yrs. 3 mos. They left a son, Alvah Woodbery, Jr., living
    in Beverly, Mass. in 1905, the other children are all dead and
    left no descendants.

BOURNE (cont'd.):
Children of Eben and Lucy (Adams) Berry:
They had four sons, all dead.

Children of Francis B. and Elizabeth Baker (Freeland) Dennis:
1. Francis B. Dennis, Jr., I think there were more, but my record
   stops there.

Children of Clement and Caroline Bachelder (Freeland) Jewett:
1. Birtie Jewett, died young
2. Edward Mortimer Jewett, married, had a family and died, but my
   information is very limited.

Children of James T. and Martha Tucker (Freeland) Bourne:
1. Martha Elizabeth Bourne, b. at Portsmouth, N.H., Dec. 6, 1834,
   died young.
2. James Treadwell Bourne, Jr., b. at Boston, Mass., Oct. 22, 1836,
   died young.
3. William Freeland Bourne, b. at Cincinnatti, Ohio, Apr. 14, 1840,
   was killed in battle in front of Atlants, Ga., July 22, 1864;
   never married.
4. Edward Bourne, b. at Memphis, Tenn. June 23, 1846, married Jennie
   Garth McGarvey, Mar. 11, 1869.
5. John Freeland Bourne, b. Memphis, Tenn. Dec. 29, 1848, died young.
6. Jason Langdon Bourne, b. Memphis, Tenn. Feb. 29, 1852, married
   Maggie S. Shepherd, Dec. 6, 1880, died Jan. 28, 1905.
7. Charles Bourne, b. Sept. 4, 1853, Memphis, Tenn., married Belle
   Garrett, dau. of Kenneth and Martha Louise Patrick Garrett and
   grand daughter of J.M. Patrick, Dec. 20, 1877.
8. Alice May Bourne, b. Memphis, Tenn., Jan. 29, 1858, died young.

Children of George W. and Marie Eloise (Freeland) Rice:
1. Marie Eloise Rice, b. Dec. 9, 1847, died young.
2. Elizabeth St. George Rice, b. Jan. 16, 1849, married Dr. (Fred?)
   Thayer of West Newton, Mass.; had no children; died Sept. 1920.
3. George Alexander Rice, b. Jan. 2, 1854; supposed to be still
   living.

Children of Joseph H.S. and Adaline Isabelle (Woodhouse) Freeland:
1. Caroline Jewett Freeland, b. July 9, 1857, d. Jan. 4, 1861.
2. Lillian Issabelle Freeland, b. Dec. 11, 1858, d. Aug. 11, 1861.
3. Annie E. Freeland, b. ----; married John Franklin Whelan, June 11,
   1878 at Philadelphia, Penn.; died Oct. 30, 1921.
4. William Henry Freeland, b. -----; married Grace Beatrice Anderson,
   Mar. 31, 1891; at Honey Brook, Pa.; dead
5. Frances J. Freeland, b. ----; married Ralph T. Hills, Aug. 26,
   1899, at Hartford, Conn.

Children of Edward and Jennie Garth McGarvey Bourne:
1. Edward Bourne, Jr., b. May 31, 1870, married Rowena Ewing Eakin,
   June 5, 1905, at Shelbyville, Tenn.
2. May Belle Bourne, b. Memphis, Tenn. May 22, 1872, died June 26,
   1873.
3. Martha Virginia Bourne, b. Memphis July 15, 1874.
4. Alexander Bourne, b. Feb. 5, 1877, d. July 26, 1894.
5. Louis McGarvey Bourne, b. Nov. 23, 1884, married Susan Gertrude
   McKay at Memphis, Tenn., June 25, 1913.

Children of Jason Langdon and Maggie E. (Shepherd) Bourne:
1. Jason Langdon Bourne, Jr., b. Memphis, Tenn., Oct. __, 1888,
   married Bertha May Green.
2. Eloise Bourne, b. Memphis, Tenn., Jan. 2, 1882, married Frank
   Wendell Truesdall, he died. She then married Shelby Murray.
3. Mary Treadwell Bourne, b. Memphis, Tenn., May 30, 1885, died at
   same place, July 30, 1888.
4. Jennie Irwin Bourne, b. Memphis, Tenn., May 1, 1892, died Aug.
   1892.

Children of Charles and Belle (Garrett) Bourne:
1. Carrie Harris Bourne, B. Memphis, Tenn., Jan. 2, 1879, married

BOURNE (cont'd.):
Eugene R. Hurst, of Beaver, Pa., at Memphis, Tenn., Apr. 20. 1909.
2. Charles Bourne, Jr., b. Memphis, Tenn. Feb. 5, 1881, married Ida Lee Sledge, June 7, 1905, Memphis, Tenn.

Children of John F. and Annie E. (Freeland) Whelan:
1. Frank Henry Whelan, b. (about 22 yrs. old in 1905.)
2. Annie Lillian Whelan (about 10 yrs. old in 1905.)

Children of Willian H. and Grace Beatrice (Anderson) Freeland:
1. Grace Beatrice Freeland, (about 13 yrs. old in 1905.)
2. Mildred A. Isabelle Freeland, (about 10 yrs. old in 1905.)

Children of Edward and Rowena Ewing (Eakin) Bourne, Jr.:
1. Milbrey Eakin Bourne, b. Shelbyville, Tenn., Dec. 13, 1907.
2. Virginia McGarvey Bourne, b. New Orleans, La. Feb. 3, 1912.
3. Rowena Eakin Bourne, b. New Orleans, La. Feb. 3, 1912; last two twins. and Rowena Eakin Bourne died young.

Children of Louis M. and Susan Gerturde (McKay) Bourne:
1. Gerturde Martha Bourne, b. Memphis, Tenn., June 16, 1919.
2. Beverly Bourne, b. Dallas, Texas Sept. 1, 1921.

Children of Charles and Ida Lee (Sledge) Bourne, Jr.:
1. Carolyn Bourne, b. Memphis, Tenn., Nov. 28, 1906.

Children of Frank W. and Eloise (Bourne) Truesdell:
1. Frank Clifton Truesdell, b. 1905 perhaps in April.
2. Harry James Truesdell, b. ab. Oct. 1907.

Children of Shelby and Eloise (Bourne) (Truesdell) Murray:
1. Andrew Paul Murray, b. ab. Apr. 1916.
2. Mary Louise Murray, b. ab. Apr. 1918.

Children of Jason and Bertha May (Green) Bourne, Jr.:
1. Jason Langdon Bourne III, dead.
2. Ansalem Abner Bourne, dead
3. Arthur James Bourne, b. ab. Apr. 1914.
4. Leroy Wilson Bourne, dead
5. Russell Lee Bourne, b. ab. Sept. 1921.

My wife's father, John William Alexander McGarvey, was the only (son) of Alexander and Isabelle (Moore) McGarvey, born at Hopkinsville, Ky. Dec. 1, 1822. His father was born in Ireland and came from County Donegal to this country. His mother was born at Lexington, Va., the daughter of John and Jane Steele Moore. John Moore, her father, was the son of William Moore of Va. After the death of my wife's grandfather, Alexander McGarvey, his widow married James T. Miller, who was born in Kentucky. They has several children. They moved to Bloomington, Ill. where they lived many years and died. My wife's father lived in Hopkinsville, Ky. up to the breaking out of the Civil War when he joined the confederate army and fought to the end. He was a member of Morgan's command and a faithful soldier. After the war he moved his family to Memphis, Tenn. A year or two after, moved to Crittendon co., Ark. where he farmed for a time; on his entire family becoming sick, moved back to Memphis, where he lived and died; was in merchandising; died at my home, Mar. 31, 1883. My wife's mother, Virginia Catherine Cross McGarvey, was the first dau. of George and Virginia Garth Cross. She was born in Todd co., Ky. near Trenton, Jan. 15, 1824; married John William Alexander McGarvey, at home of bride's step-father, Col. Benj. Reeves, near Trenton, Todd co., Ky.; she died at my home in Memphis, Mar. 11, 1900. member of Grace Episcopal Church of Memphis; her mother's parents were Thomas and Catherine Waite Garth, of Virginia.

Children of John and Jane Steele More, who were married in 1785 (the former was b. Feb. 22, 1764 and the latter, Nov. 10, 1767)
1. William, b. Nov. 11, 1786.
2. Thomas, b. Oct. 11, 1788.
3. James, b. Feb. 1, 1791.

BOURNE (cont'd.):
4. Issabella, b. Jan. 15, 1793, m. Alexander McGarvey, 4/20/18.
5. John S., b. Nov. 20, 1776 (should be 1796?).
6. Andrew F., b. Mar. 8. 1799.
7. Jane S., b. Sept. 15, 1901.
8. Robert, b. July 1, 1804.
9. Margaret A., b. Oct. 4, 1807.
10. Virginia J., b. Apr. 19, 1810.
11. Mary L., b. Oct. 19, 1812.

Children of George and Virginia Garth Cross:
1. John, b. ----; married Sallie Davis.
2. Virginia Catherine, b. Jan. 15, 1824, married John William Alexander McGarvey.
3. Lucy T., b. ---, married Louis G. Garth.
4. Georgia Ann, b. ---; married John Hardin Wood.
5. Martha, b. ----; married Jesse Cole Dickinson.

Children of Benj. and Virginia Garth Cross Reeves:
1. Missouri, married John Ainslie.
2. Eugenia, married Martin Griffin.
3. Crittenden, married Louise Dickinson, she died and he married Martha McElvanie.

Children of J.W.A. and Virginia C. McGarvey:
1. Issabella, b. Nov. 14, 1843; m. Dr. Henry W. Peter.
2. Lucy Alexander, b. Mar. 25, 1845.
3. Jennie Garth, b. Apr. 4, 1847, m. Edward Bourne, Mar. 11, 1869.
4. Louis, b. ----; died at Memphis, Tenn., Mar. 1872.

Children of Dr. Henry W. and Issabella McGarvey Peter:
1. Henry W., Jr., b. Mar. 19, 1868, Married twice.
2. Louis, b. ab. two yrs. later, and died in babyhood.

Also included in Mr. Bourne's manuscript material is the Battle Flag (drawing) of Cleburne's Division of Hardee's Corps, Army of Tenn. C.S.A.
    "Flag was about 50 in. square, of light blue with a 2½ in. border of white, (all around it) and about a 10 in. white ball in the centre. As an honorable distinction, every regiment that captured a batter was permitted to place crossed cannons in the white ball. I believe every regiment in the Division had them on their flag. I know sure, 3rd. Confederate Inft. did. I am not certain, but think it probable, this flag was also the battle flag of Hardee's Corps." (signed) E.B.

BOWDEN, ROBERT LUCIUS

FORM NO. 1

1. Robert Lucius Bowden
2. 82 and 7 months
3. Marshal-Lewisburg
4. in Marshall county I volunteered I was refuse on account of my health
5. was in undertaking business
6. my father died when I was a small boy 9 or 10 yrs old - Mother raised a large family; we farmed for a living.
7. I owned 5 negroes and 30 acres of land value $5000.
8. 18
9. 400 acres these land ware divided (among) children
10. land & negroes and cattle and other property I would say about 25,000.
11. large frame of 6 rooms
12. I work on farm athe happiest days of my life we all white and black worked together on the farm; white men hired to my mother and work with us
13. Mother superintended all work; she wove the cloth; negro women spinning; mother would make cloth, cut and make all our clothes; she had black cook but my sister help in the kitchen and house.
14. yes 18
15. it was - a good many white hired out to plow and drive teams

BOWDEN (cont'd.):
16. they did
17. there were very few as I remember
18. they did though it some times hapened like does now some that envied others on acount povity and riches on will never be any other ____ so long as world hold on
19. They did - a hav known my father to take negroes and us white boys to help nabors who were sick or behind help them up
20. they were
21. not that I remember
22. yes a good many did it.
23. I never new of a cace of the slave holder discouraging any one from tring help himself
24. wee had free schoole and pay school I atneded boath
25. (8?) years
26. my first waas 2 miles
27. free and apy those who ware able sent there children two an acadamy and apied their tuition
28. free school were publie
29. 3 months sometimes 4
30. they did
31. boath men and wimmen
32. I do not remember the dates but place was Lewisburg - Confederate
33. I served with 3 Regiment, 17, 22 (33?), 3, (N.B.: have no idea what this means) transfered to other first with 17 until battle Murfreesboro then 3d the battle Chickamuga then with 3 Tenn. untill we come in Tenn. (war? come in Tenn.?) in ____ _____ Col. (C).?) --- when Hood went out
34. To Camp Harris from there to Camp Trousdale
35. I do not remember dates Fishing Creek, Wild cut was our first battle there six of m company kiled in that fight
36. Murfreesboro
37. I was in the battle of Murfersboro and Hovers gap, Rocky face, Ga. Chickamauga Mission Ridge Rasacca; we ware poorely cloathed and fed wee would draw rations for one day I could eat it all at one meal trust fa___ in providence for next meal. for want of beading (bedding?) bitter coald weather wee would build a big fire sit around telling yarns until fire burn down then wee would throw the hot ashes over the ground then dig it up and ____ I spread one blanket on the ground all but one of men lye down then blanket over them then he would pile some tops over them then they would let him root up in middle of men
38. I was not discharged I was in bead for nearly a year of Hood came into Tenn.
39. My trip home was with Hood he did the best he could - crossing Sand Mountain our ration was a ear of corn sometime a feller would draw a rotton ear - it was good by to sorgum crops for wee lefft nothing but the root and fooder was let
40. Carpentering
41. hav held the office of corner for 39 years I farmed and worked at carpentering and I am a presbytearien (Presbyterian) in faith all I had was negroes they went two the yanks and took everything they could with them
42. James Miles Bowden; in Murray county, Tenn.; he moved to Marshall and magestrate up to his death which was before war (Maury co., Tenn.)
43. An Harriet Allison; James Allison and Mildred Whitfield; Belfast, Beadford co. (Bedford co., Tenn.)
44. ----

BOWDEN, JEFFERSON

FORM NO. 1

1. Doctor Jefferson Bowden, Martin, Tenn. (N.B.; this may be first name and not a title)
2. 79
3. Henry co., Tenn.
4. Henry co., Tenn.
5. Farmer

BOWDEN (cont'd.):
6. Merchant and farmer
7. I owned no property of any kind when I went to war.
8. did not
9. I think about 100 acres
10. I owned no property and cannot tell you value of property owned by my father
11. two story frame
12. the different kinds of farm work
13. My father ____ after his farm and spend most of his time in store; duties of my mother was housekeeper
14. did not
15. yes considered honorable and honest and respectable
16. yes sir they did
17. very few idlers in the county most men worked
18. yes they did - slave holders did not fell any better than those were not slave holders
19. yes sir they mingled together as though not slave holders
20. they were friendly to each other
21. did not help him in any way to win votes
22. good as far as I knew for any industrious young man
23. as far as I knew they were encouraged
24. just common county school
25. I cannot answer this question. my schooling was very limited
26. in my little home town Cottage Grmr.
27. none but good common school in the little towns and through the country
28. Private
29. about 9 or 19 months I think
30. as far as I remember they did
31. Both male and female teachers
32. Confederacy - 20(?) May 1861
33. 5th Tenn. Infantry
34. Humboldt, Tenn. next Union City, Tenn. next to Columbus, Ky.
35. I don't remember just how long
36. at Columbus, Ky.
37. from Columbus we went to Island No. 10 Mo. where we had little fighting, then to Hickman, Ky. on down the river.
38. at home - I was at home when our army surrendered
39. ----
40. Farming
41. I have lived ____ since the Civil War in Henry and Weakley county, in the mercantile business and traveling salesman.
42. Robt. D. Bowden; Rally (Raleigh?), Wake co., N.C.; lived at Cottage Grove(?), Henry co., Tenn.; nothing of the kind to report.
43. Eliza Jane Goode; ----; ----
44. nothing new to sat at present

BOY, ADAM ALFRED

FORM NO. 2

1. Adam Alfred Boy, Church Hill, Tenn.
2. 77
3. county of Sullivan (State) of Tenn.
4. Confederate
5. Co. B-4th Tenn.
6. Farmer
7. John Riston (Boy); Sullivan co., Tenn.; lived Sullivan co., Tenn.; he served in Rev. War
8. Magaret (Lathan); Jim Latham and Margret Latham; Washington co., Va.
9. ----
10. no land, one horse valued at $120.00 (one hundred and fifty dollars)
11. no
12. 80 acres
13. $5000.00
14. log house 4 rooms
15. worked on farm plowed and hoed and any thing that was necessary

BOY (cont'd.):
16. Father farmed. Mother general house work cooking spining weaving and sewing by hand
17. none
18. yes
19. yes
20. done own work at larg extent
21. mingled freely with those who didi not own slaves
22. yes
23. friendly
24. no nothing about contest
25. yes
26. no
27. free country school
28. one ur.
29. 2 mi.
30. Boy School House
31. public
32. 3 mo.
33. no
34. woman
35. 1864 at Bristol, Tenn.
36. to Georgia
37. 2 mo.
38. forget
39. went in to camps after first battle (Macon, Ga.) one battle 2½ hr. but fiew wounded - clothed bad- slept on ground - bread and meat and a part of time nothing - lay our and take the weather as it were - two or 3 day nothing to eat - disease rhumatism - was not in hos. or prison.
40. discharged at close of war in state of South Carolina
41. on coming home I rode horse back and was on the road five days from South Carolina to Sullivan co., Tenn. and only ate one meal on the way - was very dificult trip.
42. Farming
43, Since Civil war have farmed principal all of my time engaged in no other business lived in Tenn. Joined Methodist South (Southern) held no office
44. ----

BOYA, CHARLES WASHINGTON

FORM NO. 2

(N.B.: This name may be BOYD...cme)
1. Charles Washington Boya (Boyd), Franklin, Tenn. RR #3
2. 79 Dec. 15, 1922
3. Tenn. - Williamson
4. Confederate
5. Co. I - 44th Tenn.
6. Farmer
7. William A. Boya (or Boyd): Ireland; lived near Franklin
8. Christine (Christina?) H. Wall; Edmond Wall and ____; lived near Franklin
9. ----
10. I was not of age
11. 7
12. 570
13. 25,000 dollar
14. Part log and part frame
15. worked on farm when not going to school
16. Looking after the house, cooking, spinning, weaving and making clothes for family and slave
17. 7
18. yes
19. yes
20. none
21. yes
22. yes

BOYA (cont'd.):
23. kindly
24. no
25. yes
26. encouraged and helped financially if necessary
27. Pay school in neighborhood
28. about 5 years
29. about 1 mile
30. neighborhood school
31. semi-private
32. about 8
33. yes
34. both
35. at Estelle Springs in Nov. 1862
36. to Murfreesboro
37. about 6 weeks
38. Murfreesboro
39. I was in all engagements from Murfreesboro to Chickamauga. Was sent
    to East Tenn. under Longstreet and was captured at Louden and sent to
    prison at Rock Island. Was sent from ther to Richmond, Va. in March
    1865. Was furloughed from there and paroled.
40. at Jackson, Miss. in May 1865
41. ----
42. Farming
43. upon the death of my Father I inherited a small farm upon which I have
    lived until now. Am still living upon it with a married daughter.
    Raised a large family of children who are now scattered.
44. ----
45. ----
46. ----

BOYD, WILLIAM TOWNES

FORM NO. 2

1. William Townes Boyd, Covington, Tipton county, Tennessee
2. 78 - will be 79 January 20, 1923
3. Mecklenburg county, Virginia
4. Confederate
5. Company A - 3rd Virginia Cavalry - afterwards transferred to First
    Company, Richmond Houitzers(?)
6. Merchant and planter
7. Francis Walker Boyd; Mecklenburg co., Virginia; lived at Boydton,
    county seat of Mecklenburg co., Va.; he was a colonel of Militia and
    a member of the Virginia Legislature.
8. Isabella Hopkins Townes; William Townes and Lucy Maclin Townes;
    Occonachee, Mecklenburg county, Virginia
9. The above named William Townes, my maternal grandfather, for whom I
    was named, was a soldier in 1812. He was also a member of the Virgin-
    ia Legislature.
10. I was of age in the spring of 1865 and my portion of my father's
    estate was not given to me until the slaves were set free.
11. Yes - 30 or 40
12. My father owned about 1600 acres
13. $60,000.
14. large frame house with 8 large rooms and many closets, and basement
    rooms, greenhouses, etc.
15. I did not have to work as I was continually at school and college
    until I went into the army.
16. My father died when I was six years old, and I only know that he was
    a successful merchant and large planter. My mother was one of the
    most famous housekeepers in southside Virginia. She did no manual
    labor except sewing and knitting.
17. Yes, for or five
18. Yes, it was respectable, but as I was raised with rich people, they
    did not do any heavy work.
19. Some of them did. The rich people did not.
20. Very few. If they did not work with their hands, they had many other
    important duties to perform.

BOYD (cont'd.):
21. If people were educated, genteel and well behaved, it made no diff-
    erence whether they owned slaves or not.
22. Yes
23. They were friendly
24. No
25. I do not think so
26. They were encouraged
27. Country schools and then college
28. 12 years
29. Mile and half or two miles
30. Just ordinary county school usually in a log cabin. There were no
    free schools.
31. There was no free school. Every child had to pay tuition.
32. As I remember about 9 months
33. yes
34. Man
35. August 1862, somewhere in Culpeper county, Virginia in Fitz Lee's
    Confederate Cavalry.
36. We were then on our way to Maryland where the battle of Sharpsburg
    was fought.
37. We had frequent skirmishes, but fought the first battle at Boonsboro,
    Maryland.
38. Boonsboro, Maryland.
39. I was at Chancellorsville and Gettysburg, but the cavalry took only a
    minor part in these great battles. The Confederate rations were very
    meager, though the quality generally good enough. They did not issue
    any clothes that I remember, except cotton shirts. (I never was in
    a hospital or prison.)
40. At Farmville, Virginia, April 1865
41. I walked home in company with a cousin of mine about 60 miles
42. I was editor of a county newspaper for about 20 years.
43. I lived at my old home in Virginia until November 1878 when I moved
    to Warranton, North Carolina. I left there for Tennessee in Sept.
    1880, and I have lived in Tennessee 42 years. I was editor of a news-
    paper in Covington, Tenn. until about 1900. I was clerk and master
    of the Chancery Court from 1897 to December 1909.
44. ----
45. ----
46. ----

BOZE, WILLIAM CARROLL

FORM NO. 2

1. William Carroll Boze, Elmwood, Smith co., Tenn.
2. 84 yrs.
3. Tennessee - Smith co.
4. Confederate
5. Co. B-7th Tenn.
6. Farmer
7. Elijah Boze; Bluff Creek, Smith co., Tenn.; lived at Bluff Creek
8. Nancy Paty; John Paty and ____; lived at Bluff Creek.
9. John Paty was killed in War of 1812
10. ----
11. Three
12. 150
13. ----
14. log house 6 rooms
15. worked on farm
16. father farmed - mother cooking sewing spinning and weaving
17. Three
18. Yes
19. Yes
20. ----
21. They had great respect for the respectable honerable men in their
    community, yet you could tell they lived in a different atmosphere.
22. no
23. no

BOZE (cont'd.):
24. ----
25. yes
26. encouraged
27. ----
28. ----
29. ----
30. ----
31. ----
32. ----
33. ----
34. ----
35. Early in 1861
36. After brief drills at Camp Trousdale we were ordered to Virginia but got there too late to participate in battle at Manassas.
37. ----
38. Our first regular engagement was battle of Seven Pines
39. ----
40. Lynchburg or within 6 miles of it.
41. I went to Winchester hoping to get paroled and free transportation home, but were denied the latter, unless I took the oath, this I refused to do and had to walk home, reaching there about the middle of Aug. 1865.
42. Carpenter
43. Worked at Carpenters trade 2 yrs. then went into the mercantile business at Chestnut Mound - lived near Elmwood since close of war - member of Baptist church - was in the mercantile business for 18 yrs. and accumilated considerable wealth at the end of that time - lost everything by fire - having had three disastrous ones with no insurance. Not only lost my property but my health. The only thing left me was a small farm, on which I spent my remaining years.
44. ----
45. ----
46. ----

(N.B.: WILLIAM CARROLL BOZE Pension No. 14734)

BRADFORD, JOHN

FORM NO. 2

1. John Bradford, Belleview, Tenn.
2. Eighty one years 4 months
3. Tennessee, Davidson county
4. Confederate soldier
5. Old Hickory Guards, 20 Tenn. Regiment
6. Farmer
7. Frederick Bradford; b. Virginia; lived Belleview, Davidson co., Tenn.
8. Elizabeth Virginia DeMoss; Abraham DeMoss and Elizabeth (Newsom) DeMoss; lived Belleview, Tenn.
9. ----
10. ----
11. Yes they had 50 or 60 negroes, men, wemen and children
12. 500 acres
13. At that time negroes sold for from $300 to $1500 according to their age and qualifications.
14. Log house with two rooms
15. General farm work.
16. Farmed, my mother was a general house wife
17. Yes about 50
18. We all had to work to support our negroes. Such work was considered honorable.
19. They did
20. The white men were the hard workers, having to provide for the slaves.
21. Yes and no
22. Yes
23. Yes
24. No. Men that had negroes did not want any of these little offices.
25. ----

BRADFORD (cont'd.):
26. Encouraged
27. Pay school
28. five or six years
29. about 1 mile
30. There were no schools only one where the teacher was paid by the community.
31. Private
32. five or six months
33. yes
34. Man
35. 1861, 19 day of May
36. Camp Trousdale
37. in Feb. after we enlisted in May.
38. Battle of Fishing Creek
39. In hospital as (at?) Numan(?) Ga. I was in the battles of: Battle of Battonrouge, La. (Baton Rouge, La.); Hoovers Gap, Mursfreesboro, Tenn. Campaign through Ga. Franklin, Tenn. and Nashville, Tenn. Chickamauga, Tenn. in Prison a camp Chase, Ohio.
40. Greenville, Tennessee in April 1865
41. Reached home May 5, 1865
42. all kinds of farm work
43. ----
44. ----
45. John Allen, Tom H. Sneed, W.F. Porch, John Proch, Tom Frazier, John Frazier, William Frazier, Ed. Bradford, Silas Greer, John Greer, Jim Hight, Mat Canada, Bill Williams, Ab Turner, Wallice Evans, Henry Wolf, John Newsom, Jim Newsom, Baily P. Harrison, John Russell, Jack Pentacost, Sam Cathey, Jim Brady, Pat Waldrum, Valentine Higgins, Buck Shute, Bapt? Ewen-the captain of this company was William Foster.
46. Dr. W.T. Porch   Waverly, Tenn.
    Mr. Nath Morris   Franklin, Tenn.
    Joe Smith   "   "
    Pack Short   "   "
    Tom H. Sneed   Brentwood, Tenn. R. 2
    Tom Whitfield   Franklin, Tenn.
    Jim Cooper   Nashville, Tenn.

(N.B.: BRADFORD, JOHN Pension No. 15993)

BRADLEY, ANDREW JACKSON

FORM NO. 2

1. Andrew Jackson Bradley, Dixon Springs, Tenn.
2, 82, born April 20, 1840
3. Smith county, Tenn.
4. Confederate
5. Co. B-7th Tenn. Reg.
6. Physician
7. James S. Bradley; Dixon Springs, Smith co., Tenn.; lived at Dixon Springs, Tenn.; Federals ran him from home and he went to Va. and helped the wounded on the battlefields.
8. Nancy P. Bradley; John Bradley (Colonel) and ___; he came from Va. and settled on a section of land here.
9. My ancestors all came from Va. to Tenn. I cannot trace beyond that. An uncle, William Bradley, fought in the Mexican War of 1812.
10. None
11. My father, James S. Bradley, owned 14 slaves
12. 400
13. $20,000
14. Log house with an L, 4 rooms
15. I worked on the farm. I plowed, hoed, etc. along with the slaves. I worked more regularly than that after the war.
16. My father was a physician and my mother did all kinds of house work such as cooking, weaving, spinning, etc. We had 10 acres in cotton every year to make up into clothes, besides we kept about a hundred sheep.
17. None except the slaves

BRADLEY (cont'd.):
18. Yes, everybody on an equality in this respect.
19. Yes
20. There were none that I can recall
21. They respected each other. Everybody who was able to buy slaves owned them.
22. Yes
23. The slave holder and none slave holder were friendly towards each other, at all times. No antagonism.
24. No, no difference whether he owned slaves or not
25. Yes, by hard work and saving
26. Encouraged
27. Common country schools
28. About 3 years altogether
29. About a mile or mile and half.
30. Common country schools
31. Public
32. About 6 months
33. Yes, even grown girls
34. Men altogether
35. In the Confederacy, in May in 1861, at Camp Trousdale, near Gallatin, Tenn.
36. We started to Manassas and went to Va. The battle was fought before we reached there.
37. About 12 months, however we did some skirmishing before then.
38. Seven Pines
39. I fought in the battle of the Wilderness where Jackson was killed, I also fought around Richmond, at Gettysburg and surrendered with Lee at Appomattox, and came home after that and made a crop. I was sometimes fed good, though more often not so good. I was clothed very well but exposed to very much cold. I was captured at Gettysburg and carried to Ft. Deleware where I stayed 10 months. I received very bad treatment at Ft. Delaware. I finally escaped and went back to my regiment.
40. ----
41. I walked to Chattanooga, took the railroad tracks. I came to Nashville by train, then on home by conveyance.
42. Farm work. Made a crop the same year I returned. I reached home sometime in May.
43. I have lived at Dixon Springs all my life and engaged in active farming until a few years ago. I have been a member of the Methodist Church.
44. The greatest men I ever met were Robt. E. Lee and Stonewall Jackson.
45. Billy Boze   Elmwood, Tenn.
    Dr. Knight   Chestnut Mound, Tenn.
46. ----

(N.B.: BRADLEY, ANDREW JACKSON Pension No. 14126 & 15427)

BRADLEY, J. W.

FORM NO. 1

1. (he did not fill this part of form with his name)
2. was born March 3d 1840
3. Sumner county Tennessee
4. Sumner county Tenn.
5. Farming
6. Farming
7. I was poor own no property
8. none
9. 220
10. $1100
11. 2 log houses one with upstairs
12. I help my father make a crop every year raising corn and tobacco
13. Father farmed it until the crop was finish then he work at the carpenters trade as (and) got out rail road timbers from (for) the L & N R.R. Mother was a woman of the old type-she cooked, washed, miled cows, wove, spin her wool into thred and wove it into coverlets

BRADLEY (cont'd.):
14. none
15. very honorable
16. they did
17. there was some few spent their time in drinking and _____ two day out of each week all work and look after their interest with pleasure
18. not even one ------- few only associated with slave holders of their equals
19. Some did and some did not
20. There was some who thought themselves better than the non slave holders
21. the slave seem to have no bearing in a political contest
22. the poor young man had a poor chance to save any money - wages 25 to 40 per day (that is in cents) and very dificult to get a job.
23. The slave holder never gave the poor young man but little encouragement
24. We had a log house very open and a 3 months school taught by some lady and (or) gentlemen and we had 75¢ public funds and rest our parents paid
25. about 7 months
26. 2 miles
27. one fall it would be at the John D. White school house next fall at the Esq. John Raney school house.
28. all went that wanted to
29. 2½ to 3 months
30. no
31. sometimes a lady and again a gentlemen
32. 17 day of May 1861
33. Company B - 30 Tenn. Vols. Col. John W. _____ was our first Col. J.J. Turner 2nd Col. Abner Baskerville, A.C. Dobbins, David Combs, W.T. McGlothlin, C. McClothling, Andy McClothin, Ellis Harper, Scotch Moye, Jackson Bradley, John Bradley, W.W. (H.W.?) (A.W.?) Bradley, John Hiram Bradley, Tobe Anderson, ___ Legg, W.D.? Sands, S.F. Sands, Jack Sands, James Harp and J.L. Woodall and myself the only ones living.
34. Red Boiling Springs, Macon co., Tenn. then to Fort Donaldson (Donelson) Tenn. there we was captured and caried Camp Butler Illinois.
35. 15 day of Feby. 1862
36. Battle of Fort Donaldson, Tenn. (Donelson)
37. we was carried to Camp Butler Ills. suffered great deal with cold 50 percent of our regiment had pneumonia and several of us died we remain there until the _____ September next September....16 of our company taken oath and came home and 16 had died in this time the remainder was exchanged at Vicksburg, Miss we next engage the Federal Army above Vicksburg at Chickasaw Gap? defeating them. badly taken ____ Jackson? went to ....
38. Camp Morton Ind.
39. all of us who was paroled remain north of the Ohio River until the war was over but due ____ he left us and went home
40. I taken a contract to work in the timber under(?) ____ M. Wilson
41. I have been a farmer all my life except while in the war I have been a member of the M.E. Church for 56 years
42. Jessee Bradley; b. Feby. 29, 1815; Sumner co., Tenn.; lived near Fountain Head, Tenn
43. Mary Kirby; Capt. T.? Kirby and Jinie Kirby; near Fountain Head, Tenn.
44. Grandfather Laurence Kirby came from Ky. near Bowling Green and grand mother came from Virginia her father and mother was Wm. Woodall and Judah Woodall. Father was a son of Joshua Bradley and wife and both of my great grand fathers lived in Sumner co. nearly all their life. Wm. Woodall and William Hall their names. Grandfather Hall died near Boonville, Ind.

(extra page Q. 37): went to Port Hudson, La. from ther to Jackson, Miss. we had many battles in and around Jackson on the 12 Day of May 1863 was one of our worse battles we fought 6000 Federals nearly all day with 1300 men loosing many of best men Col. McD___k was killed just as we made the first charge our regiment and the 10th Tennessee was consolidated. I had been captured the month previous by the 22nd Moses Regiment and parole but continued in service until Sept. when I had malarial fever and was left on the evacuation of Jackson, Miss. I got somewhere near Brandon, Miss and was recaptured would have been

BRADLEY (cont'd.):

release on my parole at Vicksburg there came an order for the Federals
to leave at once I was put on a boat and kept there for several days
then I was sent to Camp Morton Ind. and remain until September 1864
when me and several others was paroled to remain north of the Ohio
River and to report every 70 days to the Commander of Camp Morton who
was Col. A.A. Stephens. I had a bad case of chronic diarrhea. I
suppose they thought they would throw? me out to die but I luckily
found a friend who contributed to wants and necesities.

BRADLEY, THOMAS EDWARD

FORM NO. 1

1. Thomas Edward Bradley, Lebanon, Wilson county, Tenn.
2. I was born Nov. 8, 1837. I am in my 85 year
3. was borned in Smith co., Tenn.
4. was living in Smith co., Tenn.
5. I was in Hotel business on the corner of Cedar and Cherry St. Nashville, Tenn. sold out to take part in war.
6. He was a farmer and trader
7. Had interest in hotel sold out to take part in the war-loaned my
   money to James Shed of Coffy co. who was in the set(?) at the time
   after the war he bank rupted mi note - he was one man that I wante
   to kill if I had the chance
8. My father owned negroes 25 or 30
9. Four or Five hundred acres
10. his land was worth $100 an acre negros $1000 each
11. It was brick with six or eight rooms, that my grand father build of
    after the battle of New Orleans and lived (homestead) in it tilled he
    died my father being youngest boy agreed...
12. My father had 4 boys and we worked plow hoe with the negros on farm.
    we all engaged in the war and was shot up badly in all the battles
    from Murfreesboro to Atlanta when Gen. Hood took command followd back
    Franklin Tenn and went out with him one ___ at Franklin went Lee army
    in battle Petersburg ___ ___ Lee.
13. my father looked after the farm. my mother looked after her family
    and house hold duties kept negro girl help in house - help cook to
    cook for family and negros some ran the loom some machine card and
    spun while the men work in the field one followed Hood on and surrend-
    ered with Johnson.
14. ----
15. all work was regarded as honest and honorable
16. the majority did
17. verry few men but what did honest employment
18. All men whether slave holder or not were on an equal footing with
    slave holder and well thought of and mingled at church and all gather-
    ing. I have said nothing of the Georgia Campaign from Dalton to
    Atlanta at Kenisaw mountains on bob Taylor left and sat on his left
    ___ over. (N.B.: this old gentleman's mind seems to wander some;
    gets off the subject)
19. Cheatham Hardee and Polk stood on breast work first shell went over
    the next shell got him when Johnson was crosing ___ I disrember
    Armstrong was ordered to dismount and charge McPhersons artilery he
    told the (N.B.: all this and the following is written in where
    Questions 18 through 23 should be answered)--------he carry the colors
    I thought a very ford went down through flames smok Taylors co. lost
    bout fifteen men the next day they ___ heavy for 14 day high it raned
    on us Taylor his Comp our on gunpow (he also put Harris out in front
    Brewer with me after some time Harris came back refused to stay I
    went with (him) soon I heard a ___ bust but I got back found federal
    stradle Brewer choking it all I c___ to keep them boys from killing
    him I just as well stop I could wite month and then tell nothing
    I could draw furlow swap horses boy never drew money well when Hood
    left Tenn. boy Taylor told me that he had a brother in the Virginia
    army he had applied for transfer to his company his name Alf Taylor
    offered me transfer to any Tenn company would select
21. it did not
22. ----

BRADLEY (cont'd.):
23. they wer encouraged
24. comon country school which slave holder and noneslave holder all attended
25. I went to school 20 months
26. sometime we walked 3 mile some time 1½ mile
27. from tim to tim they imporve
28. private
29. from 3 to 5 months
30. yes
31. men
32. Captain William Burford and myself rased (raised) a Company at Dixon Spring of 106 men when Isham G. Harris made his first call for volunteers.
33. ---Burford and myself rased a company at Dixon Spring Smith co., Tenn. organised Burford was made Captain I was made first Lutenant of the company we went to Nashville was sworn it to state servis by Gen. Pickett sent Camp Trousdale in a day or so I - company came Jackson co. I company from Overton 2 Lincoln co 2 Beford 1 marshall which made ten companys forming regament we were named 8th and Alf Fulton Col William Moore Lt. Col. and put in Gen. D.S. Donelson brigade in or so Col. John Savage regament cam down from the mountains and was numbered 16 that composed Donelson brigade we were rush to Va. lon with Gen. Andersons brigade which (this continues on through several spaces for answers to other questions and becomes more and more confusing; have not taken time to abstract all his ramblings)
41. they paroled me footed home found military governor disfranchised negros given franchised So I confess Christ got behind old becks bul toung plow and went to work.
42. Hugh Holland Bradley; Dixon Spring, Smith co.; (makes comment "you may have to have interpreter to read this arm broken my wife sick in bed hasent walked in 24 years hip brok...."
43. Martha Jane Dillon; William Dillon was in the Revolutionary war at 14 years old; came from Prince Edward Virginia the dates I dont know Bibles distroyd
44. James Bradley was revolutionary soldier and turned his old fling lock musket over to the government when I entered civil war James Bradley came from buncom co north carolina in 17 hundred entered 2000 acres land old grand and deed at my father death Bible and record carried Kentuck we trace to be found father died in 1866 many thing I could relate it was the charge that Armstrng made with Pinson ___ that save Gen. Forest artilery at Murfreesboro after the battle of Franklin
I send my parole long hoping that I may get pension before...

(N.B.: BRADLEY, THOMAS EDWARD Pension No. 15899)

BRADSHER, STEPHEN GARRETT

FORM NO. 1

1. Stephen Garrett Bradsher, Oakland, Tennessee
2. 80 yr
3. North Carolina, Person Co.
4. Tennessee, Fayette Co.
5. Farming
6. Farming
7. He own a very good farm. The value about $1500
8. Two slaves yes
9. 224
10. 1500
11. Log house two rooms
12. I work with a plow hoe
13. My father work on farm. My mother work was cooking spining and weaving
14. Yes two
15. Yes
16. The majority of the people work
17. The majority of the people work.

371

BRADSHER (cont'd.):
18. Yes. They were all very sociable
19. All went to church and school to geather
20. There were all very sociable togeather
21. ----
22. Opportunities were good for any man to save up to buy him a farm.
23. Encouraged
24. We attended log cabin school
25. Four months at a time
26. Two and ½ miles
27. Garrison School
28. Private
29. Six months
30. Yes
31. Both
32. 1862 March Clofton, Tipton Co.
33. 7 Tennessee Cavalry. W.M. Bradsher, W.F. Yancey, John Hilliard, Tomie Hilliard, Charles Jordon
34. We were sent to Trenton, Tennessee
35. About three months
36. Old Laman, Miss.
37. In March 1862 I enlisted with Capt. Russel at Clofton, Tipton county after the first battle we went to Holly Spring, Miss. Corinth Battle ½ day we were repusle and we fell back Ripley Miss. we fare pretty good while in camp very good clothes slept on ground over with the sky Beef and bread to eat. We didn't suffer for cold or hunger. I was in hospital at Laurdale Spring, Ala.
38. April 1865 Gainsville, Ala.
39. We came home alright.
40. Farming
41. Farming. Fayette co., Tenn. Method. Church
42. R.H. Brasher; North Carolina; Person co., N.C.; Rock Burrow (no state)
43. Elizebeth Bradsher; John Bradsher and -----
44. My grandparents came from England. First county was Person.

(N.B.: BRADSHER, STEPHEN GARRETT Pension No. 8458)

BRANSFORD, A. T.

FORM NO. 1

1. A.T. Bransford, Westmoreland, Tennessee Route 1
2. seventy eight. 78
3. Smith County, Tennessee
4. Smith County Tennessee Confederate
5. Agriculture
6. Agriculturing
7. Owned nothing but my cloths.
8. Not any
9. Between 75 and 100 acres
10. Something like $650.00 I suppose for land was cheap.
11. Old log house with two rooms. one down stairs and one up stairs.
12. I ploughed, hoed or did any kind of work there was to do, barefooted and in rags at that.
13. Anything to be done on the farm father worked same as a slave while mother kepted house spun, wove and made all of our cloths at home
14. Not any
15. Respected and honored indeed a man who made his living by the sweat of his brow was highly honored. Those who dident were no.
16. All white men who had farms worked if they had slaves or dident
17. We had some loafers while we had some who depended on their father, father-in-law or some one else for their living.
18. The majority respected the poor man if he was a gentleman while there was some who owned a number of slaves felt somewhat important kindly like the present time.
19. They did
20. They were all friendly as a rule.
21. No they did not recognize the slaves only they voted for the one that needed it worse if they thought him capable.

BRANSFORD (cont'd.):
22. Not to a great extent a poor young man did not have as many favorable
    opportunities to start a business of his own as now adays
23. They were discouraged.
24. Country school with an old log house with no floor, and seats of
    split timber on wooden legs and holes cut in the walls for windows
25. Not over one year
26. About 500 yds.
27. Primary schools. We had good Sunday Schools but had them out in
    groves in the woods.
28. Private
29. 3 or 4 months not never over five months
30. Not much
31. I have gone to both
32. Fall of 1862 at Dixon Springs, in Smith county, Tennessee
33. 30th Tennessee Company G; Harve Hesson, James Taylor, Robert Shouldrs,
    William Day, James Merryman, This is a precious few to remember but
    it's been as (so) long and I was just a boy I cannot remember any
    more.
34. After enlisting in the 30th Regiment we were sent to Fort Donelson
    where we fought a battle.
35. Do not remember just how long, but we were captured there and carried
    to Camp Butler, Ill. and put in prison 7 months.
36. Fort Donelson
37. After getting out of prison what was left went to Vicksburg, Miss.
    there in that state we came in contact with several skirmishes, Yazoo
    City, Battle of Chickamauga and Chatanooga, then went back to Atlanta
    Ga. meeting many different skirmishes. Camp life very disagreeable
    short rations, exposure to all sorts of diseases, rest and sleep
    seldom, sleeping on a blanket or naked ground with a rock pillow.
38. I lost my arm at Decatur, Alabama and stayed in hospital about 3 days
39. After coming out of the hospital I went on an empty wagon pulled by
    four mules to West Point, Mississippi there I struck the Mobile and
    Ohio Railroad wich (which) carried me to Mobile, Alabama. I stayed
    there a few days and crossed....
40. Being without education or money I started to school after finishing
    went to teaching. My education was paid for by my wealthy friends
    of my home neighborhood.
41. After teaching two years I married we lived together 53 years and
    now left alone I have held county offices and engaged in the farm
42. W.L. Bransford; Dixon Springs, Smith co., Tenn; there a no. of years
    and died in Macon co.
43. Mary J. Ballenger; Richard Ballenger and (cant recall); Macon co. at
    her death
44. ----

(Extra Pages)
37. Beginning with Atlanta Ga. Had some hard fighting around Atlanta.
    Our army left Atlanta and started for Shiloh after a march of several
    days and nights we reached Decatur, Alabama and rested for the night.
    At sunrise next morning the enemy discovered our campfire and began
    firing us with their cannon. The second shot got my right and the
    right legs of two of my comrades.
39. the Bay and boarded the train for Lynchberg, Va. stopped before
    getting there having learned that Sherman had cut the South into
    after spending two nights there I met with an old gentleman by the
    name of Jessie Brown, after learning my condition he carried me to
    his home where I stayed until the war closed. On my way home a kind
    red headed lady gave me 10 one dollar bills. I reached home with
    $2.00 June 1st, 1865. Next day I was 21 yrs. old.

(N.B.: BRANSFORD, A.T. Pension No. 1473)

BRANTLEY, SOLOMON NORMAN

FORM NO. 2

1. Solomon Norman Brantley, Halls, Tenn. Route 2
2. 75 yrs. old

BRANTLEY (cont'd.):
3. Haywood county, Tenn.
4. Confederate soldier
5. Company L, 7th Reg. Forrests Command
6. Farmer
7. Augustus Brantley, b. Bertee co., North Carolina
8. Martha Elizabeth White; Solomon White and Barbra White; Bertee co., North Carolina
9. ----
10. None
11. My father owned 5 slaves
12. 320 acres
13. About $16,000 dollars
14. Frame house 4 rooms 2 Halls Frong and back porch
15. General farm work. I was an expert with a hoe. We cut wheat with a cradle. Tramped it out with horses and cleaned same with a fan by hand.
16. My Father run the farm. My Mother run the house and was Boss over the negro women who done the cooking spinning and weaving.
17. 5
18. It was considered honorable
19. Yes Sir
20. None that I know of
21. We all associated with one another
22. Yes Sir
23. All friendly
24. No
25. Yes Sir
26. Encouraged
27. Country school
28. I quit school at the age of 16 yrs. and enlisted in the Confederate army
29. about 2 miles
30. Allen's School and Spring Hill School, both in Haywood co., Tenn.
31. Private
32. Six months in year
33. Yes Sir
34. Man
35. Brownsville, Tenn. Oct. the 1st 1863
36. Oxford, Miss.
37. about 6 months
38. Tishamingo Creek, Miss.
39. Our Adjutant General Pope was killed in this battle at Tishamingo Creek. His home was in Memphis, Tenn. I was standing near him when he was killed. We had a fine time in general camp. We had a battle at Harrisburg, Miss.
40. Gainsville, Alabama, May 1865
41. Had a jolly good time wasent scared at all. Dident have to do picket duty or shoot at Yankees.
42. Building up what the Yankees tore down on my fathers farm.
43. Farming - Have lived in Tenn. all my life. I am a member of the Baptist Church.
44. ----
45. Gen. N.B. Forrest, Col. Bill Duckworth and Capt. Aleck Duckworth (brothers); Lt. Chas. Tollivar, wnd Lt. Will Pugh, 3rd Lt. Will Weatherspoon; Privates: John Herring, J.H. White, R.D. White, T. Sutton, A. Rainey, T. Owens, W. Lynn, Tom Cobb, Sim Cobb, John Cobb, Jim Costello, Hardy Jones, Billy Scott, Ed Tollivar, John Thomas, Albert Thomas, Running Trailor, Sam Taylor, Jim Hopkins, Sam Hopkins, Henry Sangster, Ed Rooks, Geo. Rooks, John Duckworth, Bob Grover, Dick Grover, Dick Hotchkiss, Luther Coleman, Tom Nelson, Joe Clay, Hugh Branch, Ben Hughes, Bill Hughes, Bill Powell. This is about all the Old Boys I can remember just now, but I want to say that Forrests Command was a fighting Piece of Machinery as you will find out in the letter I am going to write you when Gen. Sturgess and his Co. of Negroes came out from Memphis to capture Forrest and his men.
46. J.W. Dunnivant   Halls, Tenn. Route 2
    Mr. Goins   "   "   "
    Billie Duttan   "   "   "

BRANTLEY (cont'd.):
    Joe Wright   Halls, Tenn. Route 2
    T. Sutton   Gates, Tenn.
    Tom Green   Ripley, Tenn.
    Tom Stelle   "   "
    Capt. Hutcherson   "   "
    P.N. Connor   "   "
    Jim Langley   Curve, Tenn.
    Bill Langley   "   "
This is all the Old Veterans I know that is living.

(Following are extra pages written by Mr. Brantley)
    I will relate to you the battle of Tishamingo Creek, Miss. May 15th
1864 as I saw it. Gen. Sturgess with 8000 men black and white came
doen from Memphis, Tenn. to find Gen. Forrest and his men and when
Sturgess found Forrest and got him stirred up we went on them like a
nest of hornets. Forrest had 3000 men. Sturgess and his men had
formed a line on top of a hill in the woods. Forrests men when given
orders to charge had to cross a field in open view of the enemy and
we kept on going and the enemy was so excited that they was shooting
to high and cannon balls and bombs was flying over our heads singing
like bumble bees. In the midst of the battle Gen. Forrest with 60
men flanked Gen. Sturgess on the left wing scattering his company of
negroes to the fore winds of the earth. and that is when we had some
fun. We captured all of the artillery medical wagons and ambulance
and forage wagons. We run them all the way from the field of battle
to Ripley, Miss. a distance of 60 miles. We capture white prisoners
all along but no negro prisoners were taken. The negroes throwed
their guns down and then their coats and last of all their shoes and
run back towards Memphis much faster than when they come out to meet
us and I venture to say that if any of those negroes are living today
they will tell you that they dident even have time to start a crap
game in Miss. This battle was fought about 4 hours before we got
the enemy stampeded. Our losses in battle were very light while the
enemy lost very near everything with heavy loss of life. I should
say about 5000 Yankees were killed and a few prisoners taken. I was
detailed to guard a Federal doctor that we captured, but have forgotten his name. I know he had a very fine gold watch which I could
have taken but wouldent do it and if he is living I would like for
him to write to me. as I know he recollects the incident that happened to him later on I never robbed a prisoner under no circumstances
as I never thought it was right. Hoping this may be of some benefit
to you in the near future, I beg to remain, Sincerely yours in Peace,
                              S.N. Brantley, Halls, Tenn. Rt. 2
P.S. Please publish this letter in the Lauderdale Co. Enterprise
at Ripley, Tenn.

                    BRAWNER, JOHN N.

FORM NO. 2

1. John H. Brawner, Gleason, Tenn.
2. 79
3. Weakley co., Tenn.
4. Confederate
5. Co. E-Col. Chester's Reg.
6. Farmer
7. William F. Brawner; Weakley co., Tenn.; lived near Gleason, Tenn. was
    a Confederate soldier.
8. Rena Russell; Aaron Russell and (don't know); near Gleason, Tenn.
9. ----
10. None
11. No
12. 200
13. $2,000
14. Log house with three rooms
15. Father plowed, hoed, cleared land and done all the work that is usual
    to a farmer.

BRAWNER (cont'd.):
16. Father plowed, hoed, cleared land and done all the work that is usual
    to a farmer. My Mother done all the house work, done her own spinning
    and weaving and the family sewing.
17. no
18. yes, people who did not work were not respected
19. yes
20. Nothing of the kind was in our community
21. Some people who owned slaves felt themselves better than other people.
    but that was an exception as most of the slaves holders were good
    neighbors and associated with non slave holders.
22. All mingle together and there was no distinction.
23. Friendly
24. Slave holders appeared to support each other, but it was not a politi-
    cal issue.
25. Yes
26. No, they did not discouraged the boys.
27. small country school
28. about three months
29. two miles
30. Green hill primary school
31. both
32. about 6 months
33. yes
34. man
35. 1860, October, Henderson, Tenn.
36. Corinth, Miss.
37. in April 1861
38. Shiloh
39. Went back to Corinth, and was in battle there. We had plenty to eat
    when in camp, and fared pretty well. I was in a hospital at Lagrange,
    Tenn. was there about two months, was pretty badly crowded but other-
    wise well treated was in prison at Louisville, Ky. was captured at
    Atlanta, Ga. at Peach Tree Creek and stayed in prison at Louisville,
    Ky. about three months. I was well treated in prison, took the oath
    of Allegiance and was discharged at the close of the war.
40. I was discharged from Louisville, Ky.
41. I road on the train part of the way, and walked a part of the way and
    arrived home in Oct. 1864.
42. Farming
43. I have engaged in farming since the civil war.
44. ----
45. T. Haley, J.H. Bandy, John Jenkins, Dr. A.D. Cutler and Dr. Burnett,
    Capt. Joe Thomason, Wylie Miller, Col. Chester, Major Randell.
46. T. Haley   Gleason, Tenn.
    J.H. Bandy   Trenton, Tenn.
    B.W. Dunlap   McKenzie, Tenn.
    S.W. Dunlap   "   "
    A.F. Montgomery   "   "
    Polk Alexander   Gleason, Tenn.

    (N.B.: BRAWNER, JOHN H. Pension No. 11488)

                        BRAY, J. F.

FORM NO. 1

1. J.F. Bray, Henderson, Tenn.
2. 83 in July
3. Tennessee, Marshall county
4. Madison county, Tenn.
5. Farmer
6. Farmer
7. Some lotes in Henderson value $1000.00
8. Parents did 12
9. Father owned about 1200 a.
10. $20,000.----
11. Log house 2 story 9 room
12. Plowing and doing (driving?) team and work at gin mill.

BRAY (cont'd.):
13. Farm work - mother house keeper
14. Yes 1
15. Yes
16. Yes
17. Very few
18. Yes
19. Yes
20. Yes
21. All worked togather
22. Yes
23. Encouraged
24. Subscription school
25. 3 years
26. 1 mile
27. Subscription school
28. Private
29. 10 mo.
30. Yes
31. Man
32. Out from Henderson Co. F, 6th Tenn. Inft. May 1861
33. 6th Tenn. Capt. J.F. Newsom, Lt. Robt. Arnold, L.W.M. Bray, Lt. Jim
    Boyd, _.D.M. Spencer, Sel Conner, Lige Davis, Bell Davis, Jerome
    Harris, Low Williams, Dave Williams, Jim Williams, Kit Williams, John
    Williams, Joe Smith, Tom Smith
34. Union City, Columbus, Ky. and New Madrid, Mo.
35. about 11 mo.
36. Shilo, Apr. 6-7, 1862
37. ----
38. May 1865 Augusta, Ga.
39. ----
40. In mercantile business
41. ----
42. Elijah Bray; Chatham co., N.C.; came to Tenn. 1837
43. Elizabeth Patterson; Jim Patterson and ___; Orange co., N.C.
44. ----

(Extra pages - Letter head: J.F. Bray, Dealer in Staple and Fancy
Groceries, Henderson, Tennessee)
37. from Shiloh we went to Perryville Ky. back to Murfreesboro then to
    Choanooga (Chattanooga) Chicamauga Missionery Ridge then the campaign
    from Rocky Face Ridge Ga. to Loveday Station in 100 days battle in
    Cheatham Division was in all the battles that the army was in of course
    we had a hard time but complaining seldom heard by men that had pride
    for home and country never in hospital not any serious wound.
39. walked and rode on train to Nashville down Cumberland river to Paducah,
    Ky. then up Tenn. River to Saltillo, Tenn. then walked home the 30
    miles.
41. sold good in Henderson from 1865 to 1870 went Texas stayed four years
    on farm. from there to Henderson, Tenn. farmed for 30 years being in
    meat and grocery business until 2 year ago health failed had to quit.

(N.B.: BRAY, J. F. Pension No. 10536)

BREWER, J. A.

FORM NO. 2

1. J.A. Brewer, Sneedville, Tenn.
2. Eighty four years old
3. Hancock Tenn
4. Confederate soldier
5. Co. D-29 temm
6. farmer
7. Martial Brewer; Sneedville, Tenn.; Hancock co., Tenn.; Sneedville,
   Hancock co., Tenn. a justice of the Peace and also a County Court
   Clerk
8. Sarah lite (perhaps Light?) -----
9. ----

377

BREWER (cont'd.):
10. With about $500 hundred (worth about)
11. none
12. six hundred acres
13. ten thousand dollars
14. log with two rooms and a kitchen
15. awl kinds of farm work in them dayes plowed with old bull tong
    (toungue/tongue) plows and hoed corn and maid rails and fenced and
    cleared land
16. farmed and black smithed. mother spun and wove cloth made garments
    and ___ to cloath her famley of nine children
17. 2 servants
18. yes lawling plowing and kinds of work
19. yes
20. awl men and women worked
21. awl comon
22. yes
23. awl comon
24. he would help him
25. yes
26. no
27. free schools 2 and 3 months in a year at that time
28. 2 or 3 months in year till was sixteen years of age
29. one mile
30. free schools
31. public schools
32. 2 or 3 months
33. yes
34. men
35. in the Confederate in the year of 1861
36. Greenville(?), Tenn.
37. about 3 months
38. Wilecat, Ky.
39. went (out of state) (Cant state just where i went) the second battle
    it might have bin fishing creek battle Perryville Ky Murfreesboro
    Tenn Corinth Miss. Chicago Tenn I lost my arm in a skirmish in
    Resaca Ga. and were in the hospitale one year and was not able to
    help myself for nine months time
40. at Knoxville Tenn
41. I came on the train to Rusellville Tenn a part (about) 30 miles from
    home and walked the rest of the way home it tuck me 4½ days to walk
    home for I was so weak I couldnt walk
42. farming
43. farming and ___ my church is Primitive Baptist my mind is week til
    I cant think of lots of things has past of ---- I am 84 yrs old and
    about blind.
44. ----
45. ----
46. John Fletcher   Rose Hill, Va.
    Tom Greer   Mulbery Gap, Tenn.
    Cart Whit   Yavier(?), Va.

    (N.B.: BREWER, J.A. Pension No. 454)

                    BRIDGMAN, MATHEW N.

FORM NO. 2

1. Mathew N. Bridgman, Bristol, Tennessee
2. Eighty nine years old
3. Washington county, Virginia
4. Confederate
5. Co. E-63 Virginia
6. Farmer
7. (Same as mine) Mathew N. Bridgman; East Va.; Bedford co., Virginia;
   near Abingdon, Va.; never held any office. Had no education.
8. Mary Collins; Gilson Collins and (don't know); all in Washington Co.,
   Va.

BRIDGMAN (cont'd.):
9. Had two uncles in Revolution war - old mans memory bad - says one was Joshua Bridman. (Bridgman?)
10. No property
11. No - had life interest in ten acres of land given him.
12. only the ten acres
13. had no property excelp life interest of my father in 10 acres
14. Hued log house
15. Farm work plowed and hoed corn worked all his life, in _ardetts(?) largely and does some gardning now.
16. worked on the farm
17. no servants poor man
18. sensible people respected honest toilers
19. with exception of rich men which men worked same as now
20. very few idle
21. men of character were respected by rich and poor
22. received kind treatment at all classes
24. not many slave holders held office
25. as a rule they had a good chance where they were educated. my father had no education and I had but little what I got was in the army
26. as a rule they encouraged them hired them as overseers and tobacco pedlers and other work many poor boys become land owners
27. only went to school a month had work to live
28. only month
29. half mile pay school and father not able to pay
30. pay school only
31. private
32. about 2-6 months or longer some times
33. most ____ the children attended a few winter months
34. ----
35. Enlisted think it was in May 1861 under Campbell Dunn
36. first Camp Jacks to ____ returned to West Virginia near White Sulpher (word may be drill)
37. about a year
38. went to Kanoy? Salt works in several skirmishes - memory seems bad. (N.B.: the person filling in the form for the old gentleman inserts these bits of information...cme)
39. His memery is so bad cant give an intelligent (answer) was wounded he says near Richmond about the close of the war and was so disabled he got a discharge
40. Discharged in Richmond Spring of 1865 just before the surrender
41. come on the train
42. went back to the farm
43. He has lived in Bristol, Tenn. and around the(re) in the neighborhood. Has made his living largly by working gardens but for his pension he could not made his living.
44. His health is very bad and his memory is very scattering.
45. Capt. Dunn. 1st Lt. Jim Carmack, Bill Rush, Andy Ruch, Dav Rush, Bill Brigman, (oldest brother), Dan (Dav?) Brigman, John and John Brigman - all his brothers and all dead. (N.B.: the Bridgman name is spelled Brigman on this form)
46. He is incompetent to give any names - you had better get this information from some of the Camps.

BRIGGS, WILLIAM HERSCHEL

FORM NO. 2

1. W. (William) H. (Herschel) Briggs, Greenbrier, Robertson co., Tenn.
2. 82 years
3. Robertson county, Tenn.
4. Confederate
5. Captain Mayes - (Co. D. 53rd Tenn.)
6. Farmer
7. John Briggs; Oxford, N.C.; moved here, Greenbrier, Tenn. 1837
8. Francis (Frances) Jackson; Ezecial (Ezekiel) Jackson and Elizabeth Oakley; Oxford, N.C.
9. ----
10. did not

BRIGGS (cont'd.):
11. one man
12. about 300 acres
13. 1750.00
14. log house 2 rooms
15. yes I worked regularly on the...using plow, hoe or any other work
    that came to hand
16. father did general farm work, mother did general house work spining
    weaving and made all out clothing
17. one man slave
18. any of the general work was considered honorable
19. yes
20. not nearly so many idlers as now
21. they did not fell any better
22. yes
23. yes
24. no
25. yes
26. encouraged
27. common free school
28. about three years
29. 1½ miles
30. common free schools
31. public
32. 3 months
33. yes
34. man
35. Sept. 1, 1863 Whites Creek, Tenn.
36. battle at Whites Creek next day and I was taken prisoner
37. next day
38. Whites Creek near Nashville Tenn.
39. I was taken prisoner sent to Nashville and left there for thirty days
40. General Ewing sent me home from Murfreesboro
41. ----
42. Farming
43. I have been farming near Greenbrier, Tenn. am a member of the Mission-
    ary Baptist church. I have held no office.
44. ----
45. Tom Black, Barry Hulsey, William Harrison
46. W.M. Fryer   Gre_b_, Tenn. (may be Greenbrier)
    A.L.P. Williams   "   "
    J.T. Hinkle   "   "

(N.B.: BRIGGS, W. H. Pension No. 14077)

BRIGGS, WILLIAM JACKSON

FORM NO. 2

1. William Jackson Briggs, Union City, Obion co., Tenn.
2. near 77 years
3. Hickman county, Tenn.
4. Confederate
5. Company B - Wheeler's Command (6th Tenn. Cav.)
6. Farmer and blacksmith
7. James G. Briggs; Hickman co., Tenn.; Centreville where died in 1900;
    he was magistrate at one time
8. Angelina Stanes (this name is not clear; Jackson and Ceailee Stanes;
    in Hickman county Tenn until death
9. ----
10. no
11. no
12. about 100 acres
13. about $3000.00
14. two log houses joined
15. plowed every year and done all other farm work
16. father worked on farm and in the blacksmith shop - mother done her
    own work spun wove sewed washed and cooked on fire place - she was
    the mother of 13 children I think she done more work than any woman

380

BRIGGS (cont'd.):
     I ever saw
17. no
18. yes
19. yes
20. none
21. yes
22. yes
23. fredly (friendly)
24. no
25. yes
26. encouged (encouraged)
27. we had very poor schools
28. I supose all together about 2 years
29. about ½ mile the first one then about 2 miles the next
30. verry common and sorry teachers
31. Public
32. about three
33. no
34. both
35. Centrevill, Hickman county
36. on scout duty
37. dont recollect
38. ft. donelson
39. was not in prison caught measels at camp murry Nash. Tenn. went home
40. was not discharged
41. never got back to my command after Hood raid
42. farming
43. farmed for several years then run blacksmith sevrel years then sold
     goods for some time I retired 12 or 14 years ago I am a Methodist
     a widowere wife been dead nearly 6 years
44. ----
45. dont know of but one living I think he is crazy
46. H.M. Mcnee (McNee?)
     D.L. Craver
     J.H. Stell
     G.W. Pehbus
     L.R. Clanch
     J.T.? Mabry
     Joe Nailling
     C.B. White
     Joe Davis
     H.M. Oliver
     T.J. Harris
     W.J. Ma_tens?, J.H. Palmer and W.J. Briggs; all of Union City, Tenn.

                        BRINGHURST, EDW. S.

FORM NO. 2

1. Edward S. Bringhurst
2. Born June 10th 1842
3. Tenn. Montgomery county
4. Confederate
5. Co. H, 14th Tenn. Infantry
6. Carriage Mfr.
7. Wm. R. Bringhurst; German Town, Philada. co., Penn.; Clarksville,
     Tenn. about 60 years; he was Mayor of Clarksville two or three times.
8. Julia Hulings; ___ Hulings and ___; Harrisburg, Penna.
9. My father and mother came to Clarksville, Tenn. - Philada. Penna.
     about 1825.
10. Owned a good house with three acres land
11. My parents never owned a slave
12. Three acres
13. about $3000
14. Good eight room house
15. I was born and raised in town. Was at school when the war started.
16. My father was a carriage mfr.
17. Yes usually two

                                381

BRINGHURST (cont'd.):
18. Yes. It all depended upon the man himself as to how he stood in the community where he lived.
19. Some others did not
20. I do not know. Not many.
21. I dont know
22. Owning slaves or not had nothing to do with a mans standing socially
23. ----
24. no
25. Yes about the same as now
26. Slave holding had nothing to do with it
27. Male School. Stewart College, Clarksville, Tenn. I was at school about 8 years
28. ----
29. about a quarter of a mile
30. I dont remember
31. They were public, but not free
32. Ten months
33. They did
34. They were men
35. I enlisted as a private soldier in Apr. 1861 in Clarksville, Tenn. in Co. H., 14th Tenn. Regiment (Confederate) Infantry.
36. We were sent to Va. under Gen'l Lee.
37. about four months
38. The battle of Cheat Mountain, W. Va. Aug. 1861
39. The next battle that we engaged in Williamsburg, Va. 1862 and practically all of the battles that followed to the end of the war.
40. At Appomattox, Va. under Gen. Lee
41. I had a devil of a time getting home. It would take too long to tell you. I was from Apr. to Sept. making the trip.
42. Carriage making
43. I haven't time to write an auto-biography. My life has been a very busy one.
44. I am not a historian.
45. The roster of the Co. I was in is at Clarksville, Tenn.
46. I have not lived in Tenn. for many years and have been unable to keep in touch with the survivors of the command to which I belonged. I am sure that the most of them have crossed the river.

                            Sincerely yours, E.S. Bringhurst
                            Ex, Private Co. H 14th.
                            Tenn. Regt. C.S.C
Apr. 7th 1922   Gulfport, Miss.
My ancestors all who are now alive live in Phlada. Penna. We have known very much of them.

                    BRITTAIN, THOMAS C.

FORM NO. 2

1. Thomas C. Brittain, Collage Grove, Tenn.
2. 78 yrs. Mah (March?) 27, '22
3. Marshal co., Tenn.
4. Confederate
5. Co. B 14 Tenn. Calvary
6. Farmer
7. Joseph F. Brittain; North Carolina; farm on (near) Chapel Hill (Tenn?); magistrate (?) of County Court
8. Mary Ann (Williams) Brittain; Larry Williams and Allison (no notation whether this is given name or surname...cme); Chapel Hill, Ten.
9. Joseph F. Brittain and Mary Ann Brittain was rased in Marshall coty, Tenn. (county_?)
10. no land
11. 10 slaves
12. 200 acres
13. 10,000.00
14. 6 rooms log house
15. all kinds of work on farm
16. All kinds of work done in house keeping
17. Yes Ten (10)

BRITTAIN (cont'd.):
18. respectable and honest I had an old negro man fer my Boss
19. Yes
20. The white men did more work then than they do now
21. thar was not mcu difference in the ones that owned slave than the ones
    that did not
22. they mingle as one in ___
23. thar was a frinly feeling in all
24. all the same
25. to the young man that work his chances was good to own land
26. encurged
27. at first log cabin shool at (it gradulay got better
28. at (about) 3 yrs.
29. one mile
30. log cabin Forguson (Ferguson?) Corner than Chapel Hill Tenn
31. both privet and publick
32. from 3 to 6 months
33. just tolable
34. both
35. enlist in fall 1862 in Confederat
36. Spring Hill
37. not long
38. Spring Hill and Morfreesboro (Murfreesboro)
39. went to Columbia to Morrisborrow then went south and in est Tenn was
    in calvary was going nerly all the time did without somthing to eat
    at Murfreborrow untill I lost my a__te_ (?) had a pritty hard time
    step on my horse lost (lots) of the time (this may have been slep on
    my horse) rashins (rations) was scarce lots of the time
40. Ga.
41. had a hard trip
42. Farming
43. I farmed and traveled manfactors tobacco movement lived in Columbia
    then on farm not able to do nothing now
44. ----
45. M.M. Swaim, James Swaim, James Ferguson, John Nevels?, Wat Neveles?,
    Robt. Wilson, J.G. Hobart, C__Hawkins, W.C. Hakins, Pi__ Hawkins,
    Joseph Rily, Robt. Nolin, Marsh Gates, R.H. Brittain, Mitch Gan -
    Federal came to us; Chick More, Bud More, Bob _rberry, Rovt. Brown,
    W.C. More. Lots of others we had 100 in our camp.
46. T.C. Brittain   Collage Grove, Tenn.
    J.G. Hubbard   Franklin, Tenn
    Thos. T_11 ?   "   "
    Anderson Wilson   Collage Grove, Tenn.
    Thos. Wilson   "   "   "
    Gil Terner   Chapel Hill, Tenn.
    Scot Noris   Lewisburg, Tenn.
    Robt. Haly   Collage Grove, Tenn.
    Coatney and Cal__ Harderson   Franklin, Tenn.
    I could give lots more but I thank this in enought I ___ pary good
    blessing on all of us that is living whitch is with _____ I have just
    attend Gipsy Smith m__ and felling good, Yours, in g_____
                                        T.C. Brittain

                    BROADAWAY, JESSE E.

FORM NO. 1

1. Jesse E. Broadaway, Fayetteville, Tennessee RFD No. 1
2. 78 yrs
3. Tennessee Lincoln County
4. Tennessee Lincoln County
5. Farmer
6. Farmer
7. owned no property
8. Did not
9. Dont know father before I could recollect
10. Dont know
11. Log house 4 rooms
12. Ploughed and other kind work incident to farm life

BROADAWAY (cont'd.):
13. Farmer. My mother did housekeeping cookins spinning weaving etc.
14. Kept none
15. It certainly was
16. They did
17. Most of them worked very few idle
18. Mingled freely together slave owners were kind and generous to all
19. They surely did
20. Friendly allways
21. Dont think so
22. I think so
23. Encouraged
24. Common Schools
25. Two or three months
26. about two miles
27. Common free schools
28. Public
29. 2 or 3 months
30. Some did and some did not
31. A man
32. 1861 dont remember Oak Hill Lincoln Co.
33. 8th Geo. W. Higgins, Captain, W.C. Griswell, David Sullivan, E.S.N. Bobo, Joe G. Carrigan, M.C. Shook, T.L. Williamson, Francis wells, M.C. Cotton, W.B.M. Kenzie (McKenzie?), M.L. (S.?) Dollins, T.H. Clark, J.R. Ashley, Jim Armstrong
34. Camp Harris
35. No regular battle for about (forgot to fill in time limit) had several skirmishes previously
36. Perryville, Kentucky
37. From Perryville to Murfreesboro drilled etc. Wounded and imprisoned pretty rough cmap life - poorly clothed slept on the ground on a blanket usually - corn-corn bread - my experience exceedinly rough
38. Turn? out of prison
39. Came on train part of way walked about twenty miles nearly starved.
40. Farming
41. Farming all together about 4 miles north of Fayetteville Tenn. Old Primitive Church.
42. Jno. Green Broadaway; near Fayetteville, Lincoln co., Tenn.; near Fayetteville; died long before the war.
43. Elizabeth Boaz; Thos. Boaz and Fannie Boaz; near Fayetteville, Tenn.
44. Cant furnish this information.

   (N.B.: BROADWAY (BROADAWAY), JESSE E. Pension No. 5848)

                         BROOKS, JOE C.

FORM NO. 2

1. Joe C. Brooks, Michie, Tenn. McNairy co.,
2. 81 years and four months
3. McNairy co., Tenn.
4. Confederate
5. Co. I, 154 ser_?
6. farmer
7. Aaron T. Brooks (dont know county), Tenn.; lived in Carrol co., Mississippi at his death
8. Narsissis Ann (Harris); William Harris and (dont know); Columbia, Murry co., Tenn. (Maury co.)
9. My grandfather James Brooks served in the War of 1812. he was a private soldier.
10. ----
11. My grandfather James Brooks owned two slaves
12. ----
13. ----
14. framed house two rooms. I was five years old when my father Aaron Brooks died.
15. plowed hoed and all kinds of farm work
16. all kinds of farm work. Mother done all kinds of house work spinning and weaving sewing by hand also wove rugs and carpets

                              384

BROOKS (cont'd.):
17. no servants
18. it was the hard enerjetic people was the respected ones
19. yes
20. very few
21. very few
22. aparantly
23. all neighbors
24. very few
25. no emposibale for a young man to own land
26. encouraged
27. common country schools
28. one year
29. one half mile
30. country schools
31. public
32. two
33. yes
34. men
35. in May 3rd 1861 at Purdy, McNairy co., Tenn.
36. Fort Wright at Randolph on the Mississippi river.
37. ----
38. across the Mississippi river from Columbus, Kentucky
39. Shiloh Tenn. to Corinth Miss - I was in the Shiloh battle two days.
    Richmond Kentucky one day and night. My clothes was good part of the
    time. I slept on bunk and ground part of time. My health was bad
    the last two years.
40. April 1865 Corinth, Miss.
41. I walked
42. Farming as soons I was strong enough
43. I married Aug. 16th 1865 to Mary Jane Kerr, have lived in McNairy co.,
    Tenn. since I was five years old. Ihave lived in Tenn. all my life
    but dureing the war and three years as a child.
44. ----
45. John Adams, Dick Beard, Wiley Burks, Tom Burks, Tom Barlow, Henry
    Barlow, Dan Burton, Tom Baker, Tom Bowers, Ike Bowers, John Browning,
    Bill Burkhead, Jim Brooks, Joe Brooks, John Bagsby, J.K. Burns, Walter
    S. Condon, Henry Cunningham, Billie Bunningham, Alexander Cleghorn,
    Clay Chambers, Alphonso Cross, Capt., John Cross, sec. lieu., A.M.
    Cobey, first lieu., Bob Cates, Robt.Cobb, Fletcher Cobb, Geo. Church-
    well, Ned Dicus, John Dunn, Tom Derien, Pole Derien, John East, Tom
    Estes, Troy Erwin, Dave Framer, Marion Fisk, Dave Gill, Ben Gill,
    Noell Gulf (Gull?)(Gill?), Straw Gill, John Gibson, Bill Gibson, Bill
    Holbrooks, John Huddleston, Henry Holderfield, Milfred Hendris, Harom
    Hankins, D.P. Hogue, Frank Howell, John Howell, Mat Hailey, John
    Ho_man, J.N. Jeans, Fed Jeans, Sisero Jeans, Tom Jones, H.H. Jones,
    Jessie Jones, John Knotts, A.J. Lunsford, John Monroe, Dave McKensie,
    Jim McKenzy, Hugh McAllen, John Miller, Dick McGoughey, Riley McGee,
    Moody McGee, John McWait, John McNull, Fost Moore, Carrol Moore, Jim
    Ownes, George Owens, Dave Price, John D. Page, Jim Ray, Buck Ray,
    Sam Ray, John Ray, Hugh M. Ray, Bill Ray, W.S. Ray, Jim Rains, Wes
    Rains?, Josh Roller, E.D. Roberts, Bob Stewart
46. Benton Kendrick   Stantonsville, Tenn.
    Bob Michie   "   "
    Green Hendrix   "   "
    Mat McKenzy   "   "
    Buck Poindexter   Pittsburg ldg(?), Tenn. (landing?)
    Bob Webb   Hamburg, Tenn.

    (Ques. 45 cont'd.)
    Zone Sulivan, Ned Sanders, Bill Smallwood, Poke Smith, Dick Turner,
    Bill Turner, Frank Tanner, Dick Tanner, Tom Tilman, Monroe Wardlow,
    John Waller, Jack Wilkerson, Dick Wilkerson, Charley Wharton, Bill
    Wharton, Caleb Wharton, Dick Wharton, Jim Wiseman, Tom Wagoner.

    (N.B.: BROOKS, JOE C. Pension No. 4313 (could also be 4303 - not
    clearly written)

FORM NO. 2

1. B.R. Brown, Shouns, Tenn.
2. will be 81, 4th Aug. 1922
3. North Carolina, Ashe co.
4. Confederate
5. Co. A-65th Regt. (6th Cav.) was first Co. "F", 7th Bat. N.C. Cavalry but when the 5th and 7th Battalions were made the 6th Cav. was made Co. "A".
6. Farmer
7. James Brown; Three Forks Church, Ashe co., N. Carolina; lived at the place of birth till 1848 when he moved to Tenn.; he held no office except Major of Militia.
8. Harriet N. Farthing; Rev. Wm. W. Farthing and Mary W. Farthing; Beaver Dam, Ashe co., N. Carolina
9. My grandfather was Joseph Brown and paternal grandmother was Anna Haigles and both came to Western N.C. from the Pedee country in N.C. My grandfather Farthing came to Ashe co., from Person or Wake co., N.C. My maternal grandmother was daughter of _____ Halliburton also of Person or Wake co., N.C. (N.B.: he does not know given name of "grandmother" Halliburton.)
10. Was school boy owned only such stock as country boys owned "horses, etc.:
11. yes, 6
12. 6 or 8 hundred acres
13. I suppose about fifteen to twenty thousand
14. Frame house 6 rooms
15. I did nay kind of work required on the farm "attending school in winter".
16. My father worked on the farm when at Home. He was a live stock dealer "in part" - my mother did cooking, spinning, weaving and general housekeeping could and did do anything necessary in her home, besides tending her children (ten in all)
17. Only the 6 negroes but hired by the day or month when needed
18. There was no question of respectability of work of any kind
19. yes
20. There were some who did not work more or less and those who had farms were busier than those who had no lands.
21. Yes. There was no thought so far as known of any claim to superiority by slave owners.
22. yes, the negores belonged to the same churches with the whites
23. Answered above
24. no
25. Yes. White wages were cheap land was also cheap and any young man could get all the land he wished and good time to pay for it and besides there was land he could get from the state.
26. Always encouraged
27. Free school and usually a subscription school was held after the free school ended.
28. I went to the free school from 6 years till I was 18 years old, every winter
29. 1 mile. I attended Boons Creek Academy 1860 and was in school at home when the war commenced.
30. Free and subscription
31. Public and private
32. From 3 to 5 or 6 months
33. some did. some did not
34. man
35. I enlisted in Co. D, 1st N.C. Cavalry at Asheville on the 19th August 1861. "Confederate Army"
36. After a few weeks at Asheville we went to Ridgway in Warren co. 60 miles n. of Raleigh
37. After drilling at Ridgeway till Oct. 61 we went to Centerville and army? of Northern Va.
38. 26th Nov. 1861 at Vienna? on the Alexander and Leasburg R.R. with the 3rd Tenn. Cavalry.
39. We were in Gen. J.E.B. Stuarts Brigade and did picket duty towards Washington till March 1862 when we were sent to Eastern N.C. "after

BROWN (cont'd.):
the fall of Newbern" but went back to Richmond (and we made a
disastrious charge at Willis Church on sunday), Fraziers Farm Monday
and Malvern Hill Tuesday.
40. at Wakefield about 20 miles from Raleigh where Gen. L.S. Baker sent
flag of truce to Gen. Sherman after he and Gen. Johnston had agreed
on terms for the surrender of Johnston's army. We flanked Shermans
army and came away without anything of interest happening.
41. (the above answer takes this space)
42. Odd jobs till 66 when I helped make a crop on the Uankin river in
Caldwell (Coldwell?) co. N.C.
43. I was elected 2nd Lt. in Co. D 1st N.C. Cav. April 1862 and served
with that Co. till 13th Sept. 1862 when I was wounded at Middletown,
Md. (check this spelling...cme) and before I was fully well made up
the Co. I commanded till we disbanded at Ridgway, N.C. (after Lee's
surrender) by Gen. Baker's permission and all who chose to go with
him to make an effort to reach Johnston army, we were on the Lower
Roan__ from the time Oct. 1864 when the gunboat Albermarle was blown
up till the end. I married September 1864 and came (day they surrender) to Lenoir where my wife was keeping house for her sisters and
mine to attend Davenport College. I went to Helton, Ashe co., N.C.
Oct. 66, and sold goods 3 yrs. lived on a small farm I bought till
the winter of 1873, when account of the death of Jacob Waynes (Haynes?)
my wife's father, I came back to Johnson co. (to help pay up court
costs and damages for being "Southern in sentiment.")
44. ----
(On extra pages: letter head - MAYMEAD FARM - B.R. Brown, Purebred
Shorthorn and Stock Cattle, Shouns, Tenn. - June 8th 1922 to Mr.
J.T. Moore, Nashville, Tenn.) Sir - I have answered the questions
in the enclosed questionaire the best I could. My brother, S.J.
Brown and myself served with the 1st N.C. Cavalry in Va. and N.
Carolina were in all the engagements of the command including the
battles of 1862 below Richmond, was with the army in Md. where I was
wounded in a cavalry fight at Middletown 13th Sept. 1862. I organized
the Co. "F" 7th N.C. Ca. - ("A" 6th Regt.) cav. and he was made 2nd
Lt. and came to us in spring 1862.
Arrested conscripts and fought bushwhackers till May 1862 then
went to Pegram's Brigade in Ky. In the latter part of the summer we
followed Sanders Raiders to Lenoirs and to New Market when they
destroyed the R.R. bridge at Strawberry Plains we went to Big Creek
Gap and scouted into Ky. and picked in the gaps of the Cumberland
mountains till the campaign commenced that ended in the battle of
Chickamauga where Lt. Brown was wounded - were in the fight at
Philadelphia when Morrison with part of the Pegram Brigade and Gen.
Dibbrell captured several hundred of Wolford's men.
We stayed in the Sweet? Water Valley till the seige of Knoxville
when we were driven out by Wilder coming before Sherman for relief
of Knoxville.
Went to Eastern North Carolina at Kinston till Oct. 1864 when we
went to the Roanoak (Co. "A") to keep watch towards Plymouth a post
we held till Lee surrendered. I came back to Johnson co., Winter
1873 and have been trying to farm ever since. We had to get the farm
out of the Freedmans Bureau which with damage costs ets. took about
ten years to accomplish. I never was excused from duty from being
sick and never had a furlough except to get married Sept. 1864 and
not at home again till the end. We were paroled 20th April 1865.
Some of the best friends I have had were "Federal soldiers" and
had no trouble with anybody when I came back.
I trust you will succeed in good History of the Confederate
Soldiers of Tenn.
If I can be of any service to you in anyway let me know. Very
truly,   B.R. Brown, Ex Capt. Co. "A"
Men who surrendered with me? T.?H. Sotherland, H.T. Grand, Dan'l
Wagner, D.W.B. Mash?, Benj. Shull, Wm. Johnson, D.J. Farthing, J.K.
Farthing, Isaac Hays, S.J. Brown, Lt.
45. B.R. Brown, Capt. Co. A, 6th N.C. Cav., D.B. Dougherty, 1st Lt.,
W.P. Thomas, 2nd lt., S.J. Brown, 2nd Lt.; I.N. McQuoron?, O.S.,
J.N. Duff, O.S., J.S. Mash, Regt. 2 M Sergt., D.G. Tilley, 2M Sergt.,
Wm. Hodges, Sergt. D.B. Wagnr, Sgt., P.S. Grand, Sgt., Jas. Grover,

BROWN (cont'd.):
Sgt., Emmet McEwen, Corp., Wilborn Greer, Corp., Wm. Elrod, Corp.,
Jno. R. McQuoron, Corp., W.C. Mash, Corp., Privates: Thomas Arnold,
D.W. Bradley, Jno. Bamyor_ner(?), Wm. Bush (Buss?), J.P. Blair,
M.S. Brown, Wm. Brown, Jas. Copenhaver, __ Crouch, E.H. Dougherty,
Eugene Dickson, John Ellison, Jas. Fain, Madison Forn, D.J. Farthing,
J.K. Farthing, Hiram Gragg, W.T. (H.?T.), J.T. Grand, D.S., Lem Green,
Ham Gammon, Com., George Gammon, Louis Glover, Isaac Hayes, Jo. Horton,
Jno. Houston, Hugh Hagaman, Jno. Houston, Jno. Jackson, Wm. Johnson,
Patrick Johnson, Thos. Johnson, Joseph Johnson, Wm. Leffter, Jno.
Lunsford, Nat Wm. Morrison, D.W.B. Mash, V.B. Mash, Jas. H. Mash,
H.P. Mash, Orville Marchand, P.G. Moore, Jo. McGuire, Sidney Norton,
Jno. Noff, Danl. Osborn, Jno. Parker, Jas. Parker, Thos. Potter, Dave
Randle, Larkin Rose (Rush?) (Ruse?), Alf, Roberts, Tom Roberts,
Wm. Roberts, Geo. Robinson, Jno. Robinson, Jas. Robinson, G.H. Shepard,
Jas. Smith, Jno. Smith, Dave Sotherland, Jack Sa__, Benj. Shull,
Columbus Teague, Jas. Toster, Robt. Toster, Nell Warren, Fr__ Waren,
Martin Warren, Danl Wagner, David Wagner, Jo. Wagner, John Walsh, Wm.
Walsh, Pinkney Wapli__, Bartlet Wood, Albert Wilson, E. Yelverton.
46. Members of Co. "A" alive: Hiram Gragg, Colfax Wash.; W.C. Mash,
Colfax, Wash.; Benj. Shull, Coos co., Oregon; H. Sotherland, Creston,
N.C.; John Barton, W. Jefferson, N.C.; John Robinson, Ba__y, N.C.:
.N. Horton, Vilas, N.C.; Jas. Blair, Elizabethton, Tenn.; Tom Arnold,
Doude(?), Tenn.; Geo. Robinson, Texas; J.K. Farthing, Patterson, N.C.
Confederate Soldiers living in Johnson co., Tenn.) F.P. Cu_teo?,
Butler, Tenn.; Lindsay Jennings, Shouns, Tenn.; D.C. Davis, Trade,
Tenn.; Geo. Cable, R.D., Butler, Tenn.; Marion Millsaps, R.D., Butler
Tenn.

BROWN, GEORGE WASHINGTON

FORM NO. 2

1. George Washington Brown, 600 B. Street, Lenoir City, Tennessee
2. I was born Mary 27, 1822
3. McMinn county, Tennessee
4. Confederate
5. Lanier Dragoons (Cavalry), 3rd Regiment
6. Furniture and Coffin manufacturer
7. Aaron Brooks Brown; b. Decaure co., (he thinks), Tenn.; lived Athens,
Tenn.; designed furniture and coffins. On account of religious
belief would not serve in Army.
8. Lucinda Crawford; John Crawford and......; Athens, Tenn.
9. ----
10. ----
11. On account of father's religious belief he did not own slaves. My
mother kept one personal attendant.
12. 700 acres
13. Father died about the time the Civil War broke out. I went away and
when I returned from the war almost everything in the way of tangible
property was gone. Father lost $15,000 in cash when the Athens Bank
failed.
14. Father and I boarded at the Mayo Hotel in Athens. Mother died when
I was six months old and he never married again. (Father kept a
family on a farm to take care of me when I was a small boy)
15. I spent my boyhood days helping on the farm and hunting, fishing, and
trapping. I did not have to work, and I was just like all other boys
who have everything they wish, not so fond of it. (When I was about
four years old I was out playing and an old Indian kidnapped me. His
name was Falling. He was very kind to me and I learned to love him
very much. Father offered a reward of $900 and Uncle Abraham found
me after about 12 or 14 months. I was so fond of the old Indian and
begged so hard for him that father put him on one of his farms so
that I could be near him. I learned the Indian language and we had
wonderful times together hunting and fishing.
16. My father designed and directed the making of all kinds of furniture,
cabinets and coffins.
17. On account of religious belief father kept none; mother kept a personal servent, but no more because she honored father's religion.

388

BROWN (cont'd.):
18. Honest Toil was considered as very respectable; it was the man who had nothing and "loafed" who was looked down upon.
19. The poor white boys worked and a few of the wealthier boys.
20. The men who idled were arrested under the Vagabond Act and made to work. I knew one man, John Henderson, who was bid off at 6½¢ and put to work by the buyer; afterwards he bought his freedom, later bought a farm for $15,000. He would often laught about being sold for 6½¢. I was about eighteen at that time.
21. Men were not looked down upon for not owing slaves, but they were looked down upon for laziness and for not trying to accumlate anything. My father was a land owner and he was industrious, consequently he was highly respected.
22. They did.
23. A man was not more highly respected just because he owned slaves. My father was a non-slave owner and he mixed and mingled freely with slave owners. It was the lazy fellow whose habits were not above those of the negro who was not respected.
24. I do not think so, the people looked to the man and his platform. Of course, if a man was for freeing the negros without compensating the owners he did not stand much chance.
25. The opportunities were very good if a poor man was industrious.
26. They were encouraged.
27. I attended one free school in Athens, but father kept me in private school as long as I would stay.
28. I attended several private schools and one free school for about six months, but I was so fond of the country that I did not stay in school as long as father wished me to stay.
29. There was a free school in Athens.
30. Athens free school and private schools.
31. ----
32. ----
33. Yes
34. Man
35. In 1861 I enlisted in the service of the confederacy. I was not in favor of seccession but I wished to go with my State.
36. Knox county, then to Knetucky
37. ----
38. Mills Springs battle (Fishing Creek)
39. My grandfather, Aaron Brown, lived to be over eighty. He served in the Revolutionary War but I do not know in what capacity. He fell and totally disabled himself about ten years before his death, and his wife, Naoma Brown, supported the family by baking and selling ginger cakes and cider. In addition to keeping the family out of the proceeds from her ginger cakes and cider, Grandmother Brown bought a farm for which she paid $800. (The same farm in that section of the country today would be worth about $100,000) When grandmother's children were grown she adopted another little girl to raise. This little girl found her dead in bed one morning. As grandmother weighed 300 pounds, it was decided she had smothered to death. I was very small at that time, I suppose seven or eight, but I remember that all the country attended her funeral. I have been told that on account of her industry she was held in very high esteem in her community. She was a member of the Presbyterian Church. She was over ninety at the time of her death. To the union of Aaron and Naoma Brown there were born the following children; Brooks, Abraham, Joseph, Jess, Sarah and Naoma. Brooks Brown (my father) was a furniture and coffin manufacturer; Uncle Abraham Brown was a wagoner, hauling produce of all kinds from Tennessee to Georgis; Uncle Joseph was a printer; Uncle Jess assisted my grandmother Brown in selling her cakes and cider; Aunt Sarah was a painter. An English publisher came to the country and persuaded Uncle Joe and Aunt Sarah to return to England with him. Aunt Sarah's salary was $1500 besides extra money she received for her paintings. I remember that my great-grandfather and great-grandmother Babb (Grandmother Brown's parents) lived in a small log house. They owned a small farm of about fifty acres. They both lived over one hundred years. I have heard it said that great-grandmother Babb lived 116 years. She was a very small woman. Grandmother Brown ofter carried her in her arms and called her baby. I remember that I as a child was not very fond of

389

BROWN (cont'd.):
    my great-grandfather Babb because he once tapped me over the head
with an axe handle. I had slipped his axe out and gapped it. The
name of Mother's father was John Crawford of Athens, Tenn. He owned
more land than any other man in Athens at that time; he also owned
the largest dry goods store in Athens; he also owned five houses and
lots and nine slaves. Usually a good strong negro man was worth
$800; a good negro woman, $600, however, Grandfather Crawford paid
$1500 for his blacksmith negro.
40. I was discharged at Camp Morton in 1864.
41. I was sick and worn out in health. I was too anxious to reach home
    and family to take note of many things that happened on my trip.
42. Farming
43. After the war I farmed until I was eighty years of age. I lived in
    Loudon county, Tenn. Since that time I have lived in Lenoir City,
    Tenn.
44. ----
45. ----
46. ----

    (N.B.: Following this questionnaire are two newspaper articles, one
a picture of Mr. Brown at age of nearly 104 and material concerning
his obituary...cme)

    "GEORGE WASHINGTON BROWN DIES AT AGE OF NEARLY 104' CAPTURED BY
INDIANS ONCE, DROVE A STAGE COACH" (Special to the Knoxville Sentinel)
Lenoir City, Jan. 4 - (no year): "George Washington Brown, who would
have been 104 years old March 27, died this morning at 5:45 o'clock
at his home here. Mr. Brown has an unusually interesting life history,
which includes his capture by Indians when a boy, living with them
and learning their secret of scoutcraft, driving a stagecoach in
East Tennessee during the pioneer days, then in the Civil war serving
as dispatch boy and as private in the ranks for two and one-half
years during which time he had thrilling experiences. The beloved
centenarian was born at Athens, Tenn., McMinn county, March 27, 1822.
His father, Brooks Brown, who was well known in McMinn county, died
in 1862. His mother, Lucinda Crawford before her marriage to Mr.
Brown, died when Mr. Brown was only six months old and he was reared
by his grandmother and an aunt.
    "Captured by Indians"-At the age of 6 years while playing near a creek
where his aunt had gone to do the family washing he strayed away and
was found by an Indian who took him to his wigwam, where he remained
for twelve months. The indians treated him very kindly and taught
him to shoot with bow and arrow and to kill game with as great pro-
ficiency and (continued, but rest of article missing)

    "LENOIR CITY'S OLDEST CITIZEN, 100 YEARS OLD ON MARCH 27"-(Lenoir City
News)-George Washington Brown, Lenoir City's oldest inhabitant, will
if he lived until the 27th of this month (and apparently is in the
best of health) celebrate his 100th birthday on that date. (Gives
his birth date which matches other article, and the same information
concerning the Indians, his mother's death, etc.) This article states
"his uncle offered a large reward" - Mr. Brown raised a family of 17
children; was married twice, 9 children by his first wife, who was
Miss Mary Thompson before her marriage to Mr. Brown. Two of these
children, Mrs. Kitty Bailus and Mrs. Laura Bradwell, are still living.
In 1879, after the death of his wife, he again married, this time to
Miss Anna Hawkins, and by her had 8 children, of whom the following
are still living: Hugh M. Brown, of Knoxville; Mrs. Elvira Plemmons,
of North Carolina; Miss Rena Brown, of Washington, D.C.; Mrs. Dava
Duncan, of Nelsonville, O.; C. Edgar Brown, of Decatur, Ala. and John
Brown, of this city....on October 7, 1863 he was captured by the
Federal troops and taken to Camp Morton, Ind. where he remained till
close of the war. He receives a state pension of $20 a month for his
services.....After the war he was a mail carrier, later going into
business for himself; lived in Lenoir City for over 20 years; appears
to be in good health and spirits for a man of his advanced age; talks
readily and entertainingly; he had a boyhood scuffle with a companion
on account of his tenacity to his political faith, he being a democrat
and the companion a Whig. Later he knocked this fellow down with a

BROWN (cont'd.):
stick and stabbed him with a knife. This was, he said, the only time
he ever remembered swearing, remarking to a friend who tried to stop
him from cutting the boy "I'll kill the whole d___ family if they
don't leave me alone."

BROWN, HIRAM RIEMES

FORM NO. 2

1. Hiram Rieves (note difference in spelling as to file folder tag...cme)
    Brown, Union City, Tenn. Rt. 2
2. will be 77 the 2nd day of Oct. '22
3. Tenn. Obion (co.)
4. a Confederate soldier
5. Co. K - 2nd Tenn. Cavalry Gen. Nathan Bedford Forrest Command
6. a farmer
7. John Milles Brown; Chester co., S.C.; lived Troy, Tenn. on a farm
8. Jane Rieves; Hiram Rieves and Margret Rieves; who lived near Troy,
    Tenn.
9. my ancesters come from Ireland from county Down near county Antram
10. none
11. none
12. about 100 acres
13. land was cheap at that time
14. it was a log house had 2 rooms
15. I did all kinds of work I folered (followed) Old Beck when I was 10
    years old
16. he don all kinds of farm work. my Mother cooked, washed, spun and
    wove all our ware but wee had plenty to eat my Father settled in Tenn.
    in the year of '35.
17. none
18. it shorley was and the kids worked too and no whiskey a lowed in my
    neighborhood
19. tha all worked
20. their was non
21. tha did not
22. ----
23. tha did make any diferance
24. non what ever
25. well I will say their was
26. tha was encouraged
27. comon country school
28. about 4 months evry winter
29. a bout half mile
30. Hors(e) Shoo (Shoe) Bend with punchion floor and cab board door with
    a log sawed out behind to put __ a writing desk. Our seates was
    small poplars split open and holes board in and legs put in som short
    and som log to fit any lenth of leg in a -------
31. (Q. 30 answer cont'd.)" --- ---- backs and the teacher used a good
    kickery and kept the ____.
31. all private
32. about 4 or 5 months
33. did not miss a day only from sickness
34. mostley men
35. I left home Oct. 1862 the day I was 17 years old. I enlisted at
    Diersburge, Tenn.
36. to Island 10 on Missipy River
37. about one month
38. Island 10
39. well I could not tell all the battles I was in I was in all the
    engagements with Forrest from the time he came in to west Tenn. until
    the war was over.
40. April 1865 at Gainsville, Ala.
41. I lost my horse and rode in a box car to Corinth, Miss. and walked
    the balance of the way
42. got between the plow handles
43. I went to school 1 yr. after the war 1868 I maried in the year of
    1870 and went to farming and raising childron my wife has bin dead

BROWN (cont'd.):
    20 years never maried any more have 3 childron living now in this
    state. I and one sister lives together on the farm and have plenty
    to eat well I will close I go too all the Reunions, Yours truly
                                H. R. Brown
44. ----
45. ----
46. ----

    (N.B.: BROWN, HIRAM R. Pension No. 13120)

                            BROWN, ISAAC

FORM NO. 2

1. Isaac (he spells it Isacc) Brown, Route One, Dayton, Tenn.
2. Seventy nine - Eighty October 23rd 1922
3. Meigs county, was raised in Rhea county.
4. Confederate soldier
5. Co. D: 19 Col. Cummings afterwards, Col. F.M. Walker
6. Carpenter and farmer
7. Jessee S. Brown; athen, McMinn co., Tenn; lived at Athens; no war
    service or office holder.
8. Mary Allison Brown; Peter Allison and Jesse Brown (Evidently he was
    confused here - as this is his father's name) - no name shown for
    wife of Peter Allison; lived Athens, Tenn.
9. Was original from Virginia. My grandmother was a Sharp and was Scotch
    Irish.
10. a horse and wagon
11. no
12. had no real astate
13. not over six hundred dollers
14. hewed log home two rooms and cook room
15. farm work of all kinds
16. Farm and carpenter work
17. none
18. verry honorable and respectable
19. they did
20. no. boddy all respectable people worked one who would not work was
    not respected
21. Their was no social distinction all respectable men was same
22. Their was no diffence in honest labor
23. Their was no diffence in public society gatherings
24. no difference
25. Their was no difference so he was honest and worked
26. They was encouraged. I was going to school when the war came up
    tring (trying) to make something out of my self.
27. One term at Washington College on Acadame(?) and one subscription
    school
28. about ten months
29. Father boarded at Rev. A.T.? Eusty(?) and my teacher was Professer
    Duke
30. none
31. The Washington Academy which was built in 1856.
32. nine months
33. yes Sir
34. A man, Professer Duke and old uncle Ralph Locke
35. At Washington, Rhea county in Capt. W.E. Calvillry (Cavalry?) --- in
    May 1861
36. to Knoxville, Tenn.
37. did service at Big Creek Gap and Cumberland Gap
38. Fishing Creek where our Brigadier General F.K. Zolicover (Zollicoffer)
    was killed
39. Ordered to Fort Pillow in Donaldson and they surrendered before we
    reached their from ther to Shilow or Coranth(Corinth) the battles
    lasted two days, lost about 9 killed, had crocker and bacon most of
    the time, our clothes was verry comin (common) slept on ground, we
    was exposed to cold and hunger. I was wounded at in hospital for a
    short time was never in prison (he doesn't say where he was wounded)

                                392

BROWN (cont'd.):
40. at Scharliet (Charlotte), N.C. in the battle we fought captured their
    ____ and got their ____ stocked
41. we walked down the French Broad to Greenville Tenn. and was given
    transportation to Chattanooga Tenn. and walked and began our way to
    Washington, Rhea co., Tenn.
42. went to farming
43. I have farmed all my life was engaged in the mercuntile business about
    three yrs. farmed mostly on rented land.
44. ----
45. Out of 114 Rank and file, Isaacc Brown was orderly sergt. of Co. D.
    and when Johnston consolidated the company out captain Ware was made
    captain and the new organization made me orderly sergeant. I was
    left in command of Co. D at Chickamauga when Capt. Grover and Lieut-
    enant Dabrille was wounded I beged Lt. Col. B.F. Moore (ordered) not
    to put me in command of Co. D. he ordered me to take command and if
    any man offered to drop out to shoot him. we was in Gen. Frank
    Chetums ____ at Stone River and Gen. Breckenridge Division at Murfree-
    sboro and lost our Capt. J.G. Frazier? and that fearful charge that
    Gen. J.C. Breckenridge made on Gen. Bragg right out of the 114 men
    rank and file their is four men, Isaac Brown, W.P. Thomison, Hoyal
    Hale and N.P. Frazier now living. Hoyal Hale is in the west the
    other three live in Rhea county. I have seen Gen. Sidney Johnston,
    Gen. J.E. Johnston, Gen. Pat ____, Gen. Jo Wheeler, Gen. J.C. Brown,
    Gen. W.M. Bety?, Gen. Forrest, in fact all of the western generals.
    Gen. J.C. Breckenridge was the finest --- Gen. W.Y.C. Hunes? the
    best dressed man and little Jo Wheeler the smallest and sorryest
    looking men. I seen C. Harris, Andy Johnson and W.G. Brownlow and
    ---- most of the politicians of the early sixty.
46. Isaac Brown   Dayton, Tenn.
    Isaac Broyles   Sprg. City, Tenn.
    ---- Files   "   "   "
    John ----   "   "   "
    J.L. McPherson   "   "   "
    H.D.W. Ferguson   "   "   "
    N.P. Fracier   Evensville, Tenn.
    I.J. Roberson   "   "
    A.L. Larner   Dayton, Va.
    W.F. Blecins   Dayton, Tenn.
    W. . Thomson   "   "
    A. King   "   "
    E.N. Ganaway   "   "
    Asa Johnston   "   "
    Dr. G.W. Brewn   Georgia
    W.G. Allen   Tenn.
    A.L. Hicks   Munro, Tenn.
    A. Elrod (Flerd?)   Graysville, Tenn.
    The above all I can recollect. I am your frend and ready to answer
    anything you may ask I am called Ike Brown for short. I sign my
    name, Isaac Brown, Rt. one Dayton, Tenn.

                        BROWN, JAMES AMOS

FORM NO. 2

1. James Amos Brown, Church Hill, Hawkins co., Tenn.
2. I am now seventy eight years old
3. Tenn., Hawkins co.
4. Confederate soldier
5. Co. D-63rd Tenn. Infantry
6. a farmer
7. Ephraim Brown; Wytheville, Wythe co., Virginia; lived Rotherwood,
    Hawkins co., Tenn.
8. Elizabeth Hoggard; James Hoggard and Elizabeth Hoggard; lived Jones-
    borough, Washington co., Tenn.
9. My grandfather, Michael Brown, came from Holland to American shortly
    after the Revolutionary War and settled in Pennsylvania. My grand-
    father, James Hoggard, emigrated from Scotland to American. My grand-
    mother, whose maiden name was Elizabeth Wright, came from Ireland.

                              393

BROWN (cont'd.):
10. I did not own any property
11. Did not own any slaves
12. two hundred and fifty dollare
14. Brick house, seven rooms
15. I did all kinds of farm work, such as all farmer boys engaged in at that time; such as plowing, hoeing and mowing.
16. My father did all kinds of farm work, such as was necessary to keep up a farm. My mother did all of the house work, such as cooking, washing, milking, churning, etc. She also spun and wove cloth for our summer and winter clothing, also for bedding.
17. They did not keep servants.
18. It was all honest work, was considered that way, in my community.
19.. They did.
20. There were none or comparitively none - not so much idleness as at the present time.
21. The slave holders whom I knew, did not think themselves better than non-slave holders
22. I think they did
23. They were friendly
24. It did not
25. They were good
26. They were encouraged
27. Common school when small. Two high schools at Rotherwood and Kingsport, Tenn.
28. about five sessions
29. One and a half miles
30. A subscription school, which continued about three months
31. Private
32. about three months
33. They did
34. a man
35. I enlisted in the service of the Confederacy in June 1862 at Strawberry Plains, Tennessee
36. Knoxville, Tennessee
37, I do not remember
38. at Chickamauga, near Chattanooga, Tenn.
39. The 63rd Tennessee Infantry was used to guard bridges between Bridgeport, Alabama and Bristol, Va., before the battle at Chicamauga. After the battle, we were transfered to Lee's army, at Richmond, Va. I was in a battle at Walthall, Va. was in a skirmish every day from the first of May 1864 until the 16th which was the battle of Drurys Bluff in which I was wounded.
40. I surrendered to Sheridan's Cavalry at Lynchburg, Va.
41. I walked from Lynchburg, Va. to Wytheville, Va. from Wytheville to Bristol on the train then walked from Bristol, a distance of thirty three miles, to my home.
42. Farming and carpenter work.
43. I have lived the balance of my life in Hawkins co., Tenn. near the place where I was born. I have been a member of the M.E. Church South for sixty two years, also a member of Clay Lodge 386 F. & A.M. of Church Hill, Tenn. for about fifty four years; during this time I was elected Master, two years in succession.
44. ----
45. Frank A. Moses, Joseph Lyle, George Patton, Sam Lynn, W.A. Brown, Lt. John L. Wilson, Hugh Hackney, Will Henderson, Fred A. Ault, Joseph Walker, Joseph Arrington, Lt. James Carter, Alfred Carter, Abe Tipton, George Williams, George Whatenbarger, George Welch, James Land, Sergeant ____ Morrell, Thomas Morrell, Sergeant _____ Kelsy.
46. Thomas Loyd   Church Hill, Tenn.
    John L. Walters   "   "   "
    Toad Walters   "   "   "
    William Vineyard   "   "   "
    James Kelly   "   "   "
    John Lee   "   "   "
    Elijah Sams   Surgoinsville, Tenn.
    Joseph Lyle   Johnson City, Tenn.

(N.B.: BROWN, JAMES AMOS Pension No. 1010)

394

BROWN, JAMES P.

FORM NO. 1

1. James P. Brown, Sparta, Tennessee
2. 71 years old
3. Tenn. White county
4. White co., Tenn.
5. White co., Tenn. a farmer
6. farmer
7. owned one little colt 27$ I paid for it and work
8. No
9. did not own land
10. some two or three hundred dollars in stock
11. I was a log house
12. General farm work
13. Father worked in the farm as a hire land; Mother done the house work
    weaved and done the cooking washing iron etc. general house work
    (N.B.; probably means his father was a "hire-hand".
14. No
15. It was considered respectable and honerable
16. Yes
17. The white men generally all done their part there was no idleness in
    my neighborhood
18. They mintled freely with those who did not own slaves
19. They did
20. There was a friendly feeling among them.
21. It did not
22. It was
23. They were
24. Common school I only went 10 months
25. about 10 months
26. about two mile
27. White Seminary
28. Private
29. about 6 months
30. Yes
31. Man
32. 1863 dont remember what month
33. 1st Tennessee Batallion - S.V. McClennans(?), Milton Fisk, Clark
    Meeks, Howard Ally, Jos. Vincent, Jack Swody(?), Bob Ja__id
34. Camp Weakley near Nashville
35. Not long we went to Fort Donelson from Camp Weakley
36. Fort Donelson
37. We was captured at Fort Donelson and carried to Camp Morton in
    Indiana, stayed in prison 7 months, after this I was transfered to
    S. S. Stantens Regt. lived hard in camp. We had very common diet.
    Some times nothing. We were exposed to cold, very poor clothing, was
    badly exposed while in prison and had nothing scarcely to eat.
38. I got sick at Tullahoma and Col. Stanten gave me a furlough to come
    home and I came and was in bed 18 months.
39. I hired a man-old man Cole-give him $18 to haul me home after I was
    furloughed.
40. Farm work
41. I have been farming since the war doing general farm work. I have
    56 acres land.
42. ----
43. ----
44. ----

(N.B.: BROWN, JAMES P. Pension No. 12207)

BROWN, JESSE C.

FORM NO. 1

1. Jesse C. Brown, Cookville, Tenn. RFD 5 Box 67
2. I was born January the 23, 1843 I am 79 years
3. near Bunkhill(?) in White county, Tennessee

BROWN (cont'd.):
4. I was in county Putman(?) Tenn. when I enlisted in the confederate
    army
5. farming
6. farming
7. ----
8. no
9. 220
10. about one thousen ($1000) dollers
11. Log including kitchen which was not connected with the maine building
    four
12. I plowed hoed made rails built fence cleared land and other work as
    need.   I did not know of any men but worked.
13. My father done all kinds of farm work.   My mother done all kinds
    housework such as cooking washing spining tread (thread) weaving in
    cloth and that is not all she had several girls and she put them to
    work too
14. no
15. it was considered all right
16. they did
17. I did know of any able boded (bodied) men lofing
18. so far as new (knew) there was no discrimation betwen slave holders
    and non slave holder if honest
19. They did so far I new
20. so far I new was no anagoinnam (antagonism) between them all honest
    people to be respected.
21. not so far new (not so far as I knew)
22. it was god so far as I new of corse was but a boy and my acqutance
    very limited
23. encouraged to go ahead and make thing of themself
24. my chance for schooling very poore nothing but the publick which
    lasted two or three month in the year
25. not over two month for a year
26. about one mile
27. noth(ing) but the public there was no privat school in our community
28. Public
29. from two to three month
30. so far as I new
31. a man
32. I enlist in the confederat army in July 1861 in Putnam county Tennessee
33. It the twety fifth (25th) Tennessee regiment - Captain Abe Ford, first
    Lt. S.J. Johson, second Lt. Sherd Horn, privats - Sol Jonson, Sam
    Johnson, William Jackson, Levie Jackson, William Emry, Wesley Englen,
    Sam Randolph, John Blaylock, John Hord, Aron Brooks, Leonard Willhite,
    J.R. Wilson, William Hugins, Joe Phifer, William Phifer, Rodric Poe,
    John Smith, Frey Smith, Tom (JOHN?) Tabors, Noah Tabors, William
    Vest, James Welsh
34. We were first sent to Camps near Livingston(?) near Overton county
    Tennessee for while then to Old Monrow in the same county then
    shortly in company the 28 we tuck a march thrugh Kantuckey.
35. about six months
36. Fishing Creak (Creek) Kanetucky (Kentucky) the result was we got
    badly defeted
37. My war record as a fiter is not very brilant one we were (went) to
    Murfesburogh (Murfreesboro) Tenn. on to Tupelow (Tupelo) Miss. and
    there remind untill some time the summer when Brage (Bragg) taken up
    his ____ Kantuckey we sent the vicinity Chattooga (Chattanooga) Tenn.
    the regiment folerd on after him my helth gave way and I was left at
    Chattanooga then sent to Knoxville Tenn. hering our regiment was
    ____ Levington (Lexington?) I was sent it
38. I was with Genrel Leass (Lee's) army when he serenderd at Appomax
    (Appomattox) court house and discharged there
39. I was a long way from home with money or anything to eat and to wal
    to Knoxville Tenn. we then got on a car and rode to Decherd Tenn we
    had to walk the reminder of the way about 75 miles the sitizens fed
    us
40. I made my way to my fhather and went to farming on his farm
41. Farming has been my vocation ever sence I have lived in Putnam White
    and Franklin countys Tennessee ever sence.

BROWN (cont'd.):
42. Joshua Brown; 1802 in Buncomb co. North Carolina; his father Benjamon
    Brown moved to White
43. Jane Howerd (Howard?); William Howred (Howard?); ----
44. I know but little about my ancesters except I heard father Joshua
    Brown say that my granfather Benjamin Brown was in the Revolution war.
    All I know about my granmother is that maiden (name) was Martha
    Howard, daughter of William and his wife Mary Howard.

    (extra page Q. 37)
    with three others on to join but when we got had been order on so I
    had reminded tell futher orders. But as soon as I learned they got
    back in midel Tennessee I got three recruits joind in time take in
    the battel of Marfesburough I was ther I was captured at Drures Bluff
    on the sixteenth of may 1864 carried Elmira Vey (Va.?) (should be
    New York) exchain the folowing February and taken in the last fiting
    around Richmon and Petersberg Vergina.

                    BROWN, JOHN WILLIAM

FORM NO. 2

1. John William Brown, Westmoreland, Tenn. RFD No. 3-Box 88
2. 81 years 29 days
3. tennessee Sumer (Sumner)
4. confederate
5. Co. F -20
6. Farmer
7. James Brown; Garretts Creek, Sumner co., Tenn.; none
8. Marry Tuttle; Peter Tuttle and Betsey Tuttle; (no one?) (N.B.:
    evidently means he does not know)
9. grandfather came from Scotland to Virginia
10. dident own no property
11. not any
12. two hundred
13. $1600
14. log 2 rooms
15. plowed and hoed worked hard try did hoe and plow
16. farmed done house work spun and wove cloth
17. none
18. it sure was
19. they did
20. a few leading lives of idleness
21. codnot see no diference
22. they did mingle to geather
23. did not
24. ----
25. i think there were
26. they couraged
27. subscription school
28. one year
29. one mile and a half
30. subscription school
31. private
32. three to four months
33. not regular
34. man
35. in fall of 1862 in Oct. Murfsbur (Murfreesboro) confederate
36. (not readable)
37. three months
38. Stones River
39. i were wounded the 3 day of battle losted one week i live bad in
    camp medium clothed slept toliby mear vlour bread exposed bad to cold
    bad to hungry disease in horsepital at Murfreesboro bad
40. got furlow home after i were wounded
41. walked part of the (way) rode part
42. farming
43. i have lived a cival Christor. life since the war farming Sumner co
    tenn. general Babtis church no office

BROWN (cont'd.):
44. ----
45. Dave Brown, Morron Brown, Jim Brown, John Brown, Wick Doss, Martin
    Doss, Hord Culwell, Dave Culwell, Charlie Sinons (Simons?), Bob
    Hones (Hanes?), Smith Hoges, John Wooders, Dick Hoges, Jack Hoges,
    Sam Anderson, Frank Anderson, Wid Morris, John Morris, Bob Morris,
    Jim Coats, Dick Clark, Jack Carter, Buck Carter, Sandy Escue, Sam
    Epison, Jim Durham, Frank Durham, Miles Durham, James Key, Bill Roy,
    Var Dolton, Jessie Rippy, Sid Rippy, Bill Perry, John Perry, Bob
    Hilbern, Henry Willerford, Green Willerford
46. Wick Doss   Westmoreland Tenn. R. ten
    Will David   unknown
    Tom Harris   Westmoreland   tenn
    Henry Fykes   "   R. 3   "
    Buck Stone   "   "
    Jim Jackson   "   "
    Jim Malone   Gallatin   "
    Capton Dugloss (Captain) "   "
    Tom Elis   "   "
    Jim Brown
    John Brown   Westmoreland R 3 Box 88 Tenn
    Capton Davis (Captain) unknown
    Names of Officers: Col. Tom Smith, Lt. Col. Lavander, Major Clay-
    brooks, Brig. Gen. Preston, Died com. John C. Brackinridge, Albert S.
    Johnston, Braxton Bragg, Longstreet, General Williams Bates.

    (N.B.: BROWN, JOHN W. Pension No. 9144 or 9145 the last number has
    the five written over it)

    (2nd form also filled)

1. John W. Brown, Gallatin(?) (this ? was written by someone)
2. 74 yrs.
3. Sumner co., Tenn.
4. Sumner co., Tenn.
5. farming
6. farmer
7. no property or land
8. no
9. 200 acres
10. about $1500
11. log house 3 rooms
12. plowed and did a good deal of work with hoe
13. Father plowed hoed and all kinds of farm work. Mother cooked did
    spining weaving
14. yes one
15. yes
16. yes
17. no idleness all worked
18. No class distinction whatever
19. Yes
20. Friendly
21. No
22. Yes
23. Encouraged
24. Subscription schols log school houses
25. unable to state schools were so irregular
26. 1½ miles
27. Subscription schools altogether
28. Private
29. 3 mo.
30. No
31. Men
32. Sept. 1862 Murfreesboro, Tenn.
33. 20th Tenn. Col. Tom Smith, Capt. Davis. Lt. Ray and Durham Morgon,
    Hardy Caldwell, Geo. Roy, Bill Roy, John Key, John Morris, Sid Rippy,
    Jess Rippy, Henry Weathford, Frank Durham, Will Rippy, Jerry Troutt,
    Jim Brown, David Brown
34. Remained at Murfreesboro
35. about 2 mo.

BROWN (cont'd.):
36. Murfreesboro, Tenn.
37. Got wounded at battle of Murfreesboro, sent to hospital at Murfrees-
    boro (or Murfreeston) stayed there about 6 days furloughed from
    hospital to Bedford co., furloughed from Bedford co. home
38. no discharge came home on furlough
39. came round at port of Cumberland Mts. afoot about one week reaching
    home
40. unable to work for 4 years after war entered farming on small scale
    afterwards
41. Own a small farm and been farming since I got able from the war.
    Until a few years ago when my health got bad and have not done any-
    thing. In Sumner co. close to where I was born and raised. I belong
    to Gen. Baptist Church. Held no offices at all.
42. ----
43. ----
44. ----

BROWN, RIDLEY SHADRICK

FORM NO. 2

1. Ridly Shadrick Brown, North Chattanooga, Tenn. (Note difference in
   spelling of first name)
2. I will be 84 years old the 12 day of May 1922
3. Tennessee, Bedford co., Tenn.
4. Confederate
5. Co. F-17
6. Farmer
7. George Washing(ton?) Brown; borned Bedford co., Tenn.; lived near
   Shelbyville, Bedford co., Tenn.
8. Nancy M. Winn; Ridly B. Winn and ____; near Shelbyville, Bedford
   county
9. ----
10. Horses and mules and wagons
11. my Parents and (owned) 5 or 6 slaves
12. my parents owd one hundred (and 50?) acres
13. ----
14. 6 it. Log 2. Sorry chink on dobd(?) wetherbord. chimby at each
    end of rooms one ____ 18 by 26 ft. with 8 ft. fire place and kitchen
    cooked on ____
15. as a boy i plowed and hode and all kins of farm work my father cold
    at 4: o'c in the morning i went to the stable feed curred horse fore
    work i done the same kind of work our negros did and eat the same
    kind grub they did but not at the same table
16. my father farmed traded in horses and mules and had teams doing
    publick halling mother looked after all of her house work such carding
    rols carding bats for wuilts then wove and made our every day close
17. Mother had cook and nurse the children and the negro wer all servants

18. it was and a young man are boy that did not work he was shund by all
    clases
19. they did
20. none only a few old topers that went to town everday and came hom at
    nite tank up
21. in most of cases you could tell whitch was the slave holder
22. they wer on a ewual at most places some time a giddy girl would make
    the mistake
23. there was vary frendly ofter the vary first young man mary in the
    welthest famby
24. i never new any contest any thing of that sort it is he a dimercrat
    or a whig all thin being eaquel we vot dimercrat or whit
25. it was not the opertunities fore school was bad free scool 6 or 8
    weaks in the year
26. they were varry of recieved in couragedement and help from the slave
    holder
27. my school was vary limited
28. ----
29. about 2 mils

399

BROWN (cont'd.):
30. free school 6 to 8 weak
31. ----
32. ----
33. ----
34. man
35. in April 1861 at Chapel hill, Marshall co., Tenn.
36. Camp Harris near Estel Springs
37. ----
38. wild cat Kentucky
39. after the wild car fite the comand felback i was taken sick and with
    tifod and new mony (Typhoid and penumonia) fever i was in hosputle
    10 weaks came home and went to inky(?) miss. not being able to do
    duty sent me off with the forge thain to orteasion(?) station.
40. i was capturd near larrence burg soon after the fite at nashvill
    taken near lewisburg tenn.
41. it was smooth i met mrs. Jams Gambril She
42. ----
43. first to bild up the torn down plases on the farme fenses stables
    and such like on the farme then quit farme and went to the carpenters
    trad and in 1881 (or 1889 this number not clear) i moved to Chatta-
    nooga where i hav bin ever sence my health fadde (failed) me severl
    years ago and i git no pension they say you took the oath before
    the surender as to my church I belong to best church in the world the
    M.E. Church South if i didnot beleve it was would join the won i
    bleaved was
44. well while quite young of meating President Polk my father pres___
    was the polits (politest?) man living one inst some one sed President
    Pole (sic) you this you htat your ___ to niger ___ (not much sense
    here, but perhaps someone else can decipher it)
45. (This answer makes little sense, and the writing and spelling is
    very difficult to read, but here is the basis of his answer): dont
    allow any body to be more polite than I am that was my first intro-
    duction to Demockerson (Democracy?) and Andrew Jonston he fore ___
    years during the war but come back when we was ___ and then was govner
    Harris he carred the school funds of Tenn. and ___ then back and
    turned over to those that was in power then and was elected to the
    U.S. Sennet and dide in the servis then come the gallant Edward W.
    Carmack the herow of ___ and one of the most ___ men the state
    ever prodused as a riter as a bub___ as a congresman as U.S. Senerter.
46. ----

    (Extra pages)
40. the oath and went home i think it was some time in January 1865 i got
    home i found fencis all destroid my Father had bin ill treated one
    time hung up by the neck and was cut down by a lutenant ho (who)
    hapened up at the time.
42. was first to bild fencis git in a few oats was thecould have something
    to fead our horses then a small corn crop then some coten use the hoe
    then in march my Father dide (died) i had three brothers at home big
    enough to work and we did well in our crop our coton was fine and it
    a big pris (price) and it gave us mony by neseares (necessaries) of
    life in Sept. a brother that caputred jus before close came home i
    marred me a wife the 20 of December 1865. 6 children. 4 boys. 2
    girls. 22 grandchildren and 2 grate grand children.

    ------if you see fit publish any of theas rambling remark if not
    return to waste basket, R.S. Brown

    (N.B.: BROWN, RIDLEY SHADRICK Pension No. 12617 and 15534)

                        BROWN, RUSSELL LASETOR

FORM NO. 1

1. Russell Lasetor Brown, Palmer, Tenn.
2. I was born in 1842 and I am going on 80 years
3. Warren co., Tenn.
4. I was living in Grundy co., Tenn.

BROWN (cont'd.):
5. Farming
6. He was a farmer and a preacher. he belong to the M.E. Church S.
7. I did not owned land or any thing les when the war came up
8. no we did (not) owned any
9. my father owned 200 acres
10. I cant say what my Father was worth, but very little as every thing was very cheap then.
11. My father lived in a long house only one room of course whad? kitchen house little distance from the other house (Note- probably means "log" house and kitchen house at a distance)
12. We plowed with Bultung plow that was about all the kind plows we had before the war and we hoed the corn every time it was plowed.
13. My father farmed and preached some and taught some schools. my mother tended to the house work and would card cotton and spin thread and have cloth made of it. She never wove any.
14. My father never kept any servants.
15. All such work as plowing and hauling and the like was considered respectable and honorable.
16. the white men engaged in most any kind of work that was to do.
17. most every boddy worked in the country that was able to work as far as I know
18. Slave oners here did not think them selvs better than other men that did not own slaves. They would all meet a publick places you could tell no diference
19. Slave holders and non slave holders all seamed to be on an equal footing
20. I think there was a friendly feeling betwen the slave holder and the non slave holders in this community.
21. if any thing of this kind ever happened in this country I never herd of it
22. we had some nice honorable industorous young men in the country, but very few ever saved a nough money to go into business
23. I dont think poor honest industrous young men were discouraged by slave holders
24. I went to free schools we would have about 3 months school every year but would hardley ever get to go till the school was out would half to quit for foder pulling
25. I never got as much as six months in all. I ever got.
26. It was about 3 miles to our nearest school house
27. we would have free schools and once in a while a subscription would starte up but I was never able to go to a subscription school
28. the school ware public
29. the schools would run about 3 months in the year
30. all the children attended regulary
31. our school teacher a man
32. I enlisted in the Confederate in May 1861 at Irvin College, Tenn.
33. Our regiment ware the 16th Tenn. Colonel John H. Savage, Comander. H.L. Medows, John Akeman, L.H. Sims, James Parks, George Parks, W.G. Etter, George Etter, Rison Etter, Wm. Etter, James Etter, Robert Safley, James Jones, Adran Anglin, Tip Anglen, Marion Perry, John Brown, J.V. Brown, William Womac, Lond Ware.
34. we were sent first to Allazana(?) that is between Tulahoma and Dechards. and staid there quite a while and drilled.
35. I cant say how long it was after our enlistment til our co. ware engaged in battle it was in N.W. Virginia
36. The first regular ingagement that I went in was at Peraville, Ky.
37. Our Regt. ment first went to Alazona at Sona then went to Camp Trousdale 50 or 60 miles belowe Nashville then we went to Charleston Tenn from there we went to S. Carolina from there we went to Corinth Miss. from there we went to Virginia the first battle our regt was in was at Cheat Mountain. I was not in the battle I was sick down with fever. We went to Ky. our Regt. ware in the Peraville fite. I think it was one one hundred and ninty nine men we lost in our Regt. me and my brother both got wounded. I got shot through the left hip. My brother, J.V. Brown got shot in the leg. We were both captured. I had a long spell of fever while I was there. I was down from in Oct. till February. Then we are exchanged at Richmon, Va. I was in the battle at Franklen and the battle at Nashville. I was not discharged after the Franklen fite My feet were bleeding we got back

BROWN (cont'd.):
      near Columbia. I left the army and came home. I was more than a
      week after I left the army till I got to Shelbyvill a Yankee bought
      me a pair of shoes (N.B.: this answer continues through spaces for
      ques. 37 through 40)
41. After I came home and the war closed, I went to farming. I never held
      any office. I belong to M.E. Church South.
42. William Santford Brown; near McMinnville, Warren co., Tenn.; my father
      was not in the war, he was elected Regestor for the Co. several times.
43. Nancy Dykes; Isham Dyles and Pruda Shoat.
44. I dont know what country my great gran parants come from. my gran
      father Brown came from North Carolina. my gran father Dykes came
      from Virginia.

                              BROWN, STEPHEN J.

FORM NO. 2

1. Stephen J. Brown - died; (typed in: Shouns, Johnson Co.)
2. was born August 11, 1843
3. (Ashe) now Watauga Co., N.C.
4. Confederate
5. Co. "D" 1st N.C. Cav. from July 1861 till March 1863, then Co. F, 7th
      Bat. N.C. Cav. - the 5th and 7th Battalions "joined" M'ch 6th N.C.
      Cav. Sept. 1863.
6. Farmer. Born Oct. 1811
7. Jos. Brown; South Fork, New River, "Ashe" now Watauga co.,N. Carolina;
      his birth place till 1848 when he came to Tenn.; was over age for
      military duty but served with Home Guard.
8. Harriet Farthing (on the Confederate Side); Wm. Farthing and Mary W.
      Curton (Curlon?); Beaver Dam, Ashe co., N.C.
9. ----
10. was boy under 18 when entering the confederate army
11. yes (5)
12. 100 acres improved in all 6 or 700 acres.
13. about thirty thousand
14. two story frame 6 rooms
15. Did any kind of farm work in summer and attended free and subscription
      school in winter.
16. He worked on the farm at anything necessary and was a dealer in live
      stock. Mother did anything from general housekeeping to spinning,
      weaving, etc.
17. None except negroes who worked with the whites to do any work on the
      farm.
18. There was no question as to the respectability of honest toil and
      white and black worked together.
19. Yes
20. There was none who did not some kind of work
21. Yes. No. The Negroes rather looked down on poor white trash who
      wouldnt work and were not respectable.
22. Yes
23. Yes there was antagonism.
24. No. There was no question as to whether a man owned or did not own
      slaves. The slaves belonged to the same churchs as their owners.
25. If a young man was aspiring and had ability he had as a chance as
      any one.
26. Always encouraged
27. Districk school and after the war was over attended Academy at Lenoir
      N.C.
28. From 3 to 6 months from 6 years till he joined the Confederate army.
29. one half mile
30. None except the free schools and subscription schools
31. Public and private "that is" those who subscribed to the subscription
      were the patrons.
32. From 5 to 6 months sometimes supplemented by 2 or 3 months subscription
33. some did, others did not
34. Always men
35. He enlisted in Co. D-1st N.C. Cavalry 15(17?) July 1861 at Ashville,
      N.C. Confederate Army.

                                    402

BROWN (cont.d):
36. First at Ashville, then in camp of instruction at Ridgeway, North Carolina
37. about 4 months
38. Cavalry fight near Viena with the 3rd Penn. Cav.
39. The 1st N.C. Cavalry under Col. Robert Ransom and Gen. Jeb Stuart was on the picket lines towards Washington till the army fell back to Warrenton, Va. when the Regt. was sent to Eastern N.C. came back and was in the 7 days battle below Richmond. Was down with a severe case of inflammatory rheumatism.
40. 20th April 1865 at Wakefield, N.C. He was a private in the 1st Cav. but 2nd Lt. in the 6th(?)
41. There was nothing of interest in the trip to Lenoir, N.C. his fathers family having refugeed to Caldwell Co. on acct. of bushwhackers and robbers.
42. Went to school and afterward studied law under his Col. G.N. Folk(?)
43. He was awhile with the engineers locating the line of R.R. between the head of the road to Ashville and for awhile with Crawford and Huliy(?) Salisbury, N.C. Was married in 1874 and came back to Johnson Co., Tenn. in 1875.
44. ----
45. B.R. Brown, Capt.; D.B. Dougherty, 1st Lt.; W.P. Thomas, 2nd Lt.; S.J. Brown 1-2 Lt.; I.N. McQuo__, O.C.; J.N. Duff, O.S.; J.S. Mash, Reg. 2 M.C.; D.B. Tilley, Sergt.; W.M. Hodges, Sgt.; D.B. Wagner, Sgt.; P.S. Grand, Sgt.; Jas. Groves, Sgt.; Ernest McEwen, Corp.; Wilborn Greer, Cpl.; Wm. Elrod, Cpl.; Jno. R. McQuown, Cpl. W.C. Mash, Cpl.; Thomas Arnold, D.B. Bradley, John Bumjordans (this name is never clear); Wm. Bass, Jas. Blair, M.S. Brown, Wm. Brown, Jas. Cofonhams(?), _____ Crouch, E.H. Dougherty, Eugene Dickson, Jno. Ellison, J._. Forn, (probably Farm), Madison Farn, D.J. Farthing, J.K. Farthing, Hiram Gragg, H.T. Grant, J.T. Grant, Daniel Green, Hamilton Gammon, Geo. Gammon, Luna Glover, Isaac Hayes, J.W. Horton, John Houston, Hugh Hagaman, Jno. Jackson, Wm. Johnson, Tom Johnson, Patrick Johnson, Joseph Johnson, Wm. Leffler, Jno. Lunsford, Nat Morrison, D.W.B. Mash, V.B. Mash, Jas. H. Mash, H.P. Mash, Orville Moreland, C.G. Moore, Joseph McGuquire(McQuire?), Jno. Naff, Jno. Parker, Jas. Parker, David Randall, Sidney Norton, Tom Porter, Alf Roberts, Geo. Robinson, Jno. Robinson, Jos. Robinson, Geo. H. Robinson, Jno. H. Shoun, Jas. Smith, John Smith, David Sutherland, T.H. Sutherland, Jack Sands, Benj. Shull, Hiram Squir, N.H. Shipley, Jno. Shepard, Isaiah Shepard, Wm. Shepard, Geo. D. Taylor, Ja_ Tester, Robert (?) Tester, Neil Warren, Fred Warren, Martin Warren, Danl. Wagner, David Wagner, Jo. Wagner, Pinkney, Wuslick(?), Albert Wilson, Jno. Welsh, Wm. Wheeler(?), Fhed (Thad?) Yelverton, Columbus Teauge(?)
46. D.M.S. Brown   Winchester, Ky.
    Jas. Blair   Elizabethton, Tenn.
    Thom. Arnold   Trade, Tenn.
    Thos. Sutherland   Creston, N.C.
    Jno. Parker   West Jefferson, N.C.
    Jas. (Jos.) Parker   Colfax, Wash.
    Hiram Gragg   "   "
    Benj. Shull   Coos co., Oregon
    John Robinson   Buoy(?), N.C.
    J.W. Horton   Vilas, N.C.
    J.K.(?) Farthing   Patterson, N.C.
    Geo. Robinson   "Texas"
    B.R. Brown   Shouns, Tenn.
    Lindsey Jennings   "   "   (name may be reversed unable to
                                          tell from list)
    D.C. Davis   Trade Tenn.
    F.P. Carter   Butler, Tenn.

                         BROWN, THOMAS

FORM NO. 2

1. Thomas Brown, Stanton
2. Eighty years six months
3. Washington co., Tenn.

403

BROWN (cont'd.):
4. Confederate soldier
5. Co. A - _ Regiment
6. farmer
7. William Brown, B. Washington co., Tenn.; two old for to be in the war
8. Raichel Cloure; William Clour and Lizy Cloure.
9. ----
10. father owned a hundred sixty acres land worth about one hundred
    dollars
11. none
12. 160 acres
13. 1 thousand
14. a log house with three rooms
15. farming both plowing and howing white men done all their work them
    days. as for my part I plowed hoed mowed cradle and bound wheat in
    fact done all kinds of work done on farm work.
16. my father did but farm, my mother done all kinds of work that was
    done in a house cook spun wove sew in fact don all kinds of work
    done in a house
17. no servants at all
18. it was every body work them days
19. they did
20. they were none every body work them days
21. they did not they was but few slaves in the county I live at that
    time I could see any difernce in slave holders and non slave holders
22. they surly did
23. their surly was at that day and time
24. he did
25. they was at that time their was
26. they was not
27. the elemtry spelling book
28. we only had three month school them days
29. the school house was three hundred yards from fathers house
30. the elemetry
31. publick
32. three month
33. yes they sure did
34. a man
35. I inlisted in sixty two I disrember the month and date
36. to Vickburg Miss
37. about four months was in January
38. the Chicksaw byo fight that the jineral ingagement dind last but one
    day then we staid in camps at Vicksburg till sometime in May then we
    was ordered to Champion hill to meet Grant we had a little skrimish
    and then fell to Big Black river there was captured. (N.B.: this
    answer runs over into Ques. 39.)
40. I was in prison at Fort Delaware they had so many prisoners they dind
    hav room for them so paroled all the sick and wonded and sent a cross
    the waters to Petersburg Va. I was in the hospital about two weeks
    then went to Richmond Va. from there sent us home till we was exchange
    for I went back to farming (N.B.: these answers fill in spaces for
    Ques. 41 and 42.)
43. when I got home and got able I went back to the farm having been
    farming all my life at the close of the war I live in carter co east
    Tennessee up till 73 then I move to fayet (Fayette) co west tenn
    hav been living since making coten and corn and doing all kinds of
    farm work all my life
44. ----
45. ----
46. I will giv the names of Co. A - postofis (Post Office) Clar Branch
    Tenn William Effler, John Ellfer, Gavan Laming, M.H. Laming, Jim
    Brown, Charly Bean, Gorge Title, Will Clous, J.O. Cloure (both these
    men may be Cloure), Thomas Tilson, Vince Tapp, Thad Tapp, Jim Debport,
    Samson Conn, Sturt Nelson, Nute Bab, Henry Bab, Colib Bab, Samson
    Coon, Stuart Nelson, Bownbon Adkins, FRank Blair was my captain, Bill
    Kile my lutent, Sturt Nelson first Sargent, I have met Nat Taylor,
    Bob Taylor, A. Taylor our present gov., Thomas Nelson, Landon Hanes,
    Been with them deal, heard them speak.

BROYLES, ISAAC N.

FORM NO. 1

1. Isaac N. Broyles, R.F.D. No. 1, Spring City, Rhea county, Tennessee
2. Age 78 years
3. Rhea county, Tenn.
4. I was living near Rhea Springs, Rhea county, Tenn. where I now live.
5. Farmer
6. Farmer, school teacher and County Officer
7. We owned 178 acres of land worth at that time, from 5 to 10 dollars
    an acre
8. No
9. Our land was owned in common.
10. ----
11. Log house
12. Plowed, Hoed, Grubed, Chope timber, and all work done on farmes.
13. Mother did and superintended all the work done in and about the house,
    which was preparing and cooking meals, milking cows, caring for the
    milk productions, carding and spinning flax, wool, cotton, etc.
    Knitting socks - stocking and weaving cloth for sheets and other bed
    furnishings. and clothing for the family. Father was a Justice of
    the Peace. He taught schools in the fall and made a crop in Spring
    and summer.
14. no.
15. Yes, more so than the ways of many who made a living in other ways
16. Yes, all the better class
17. There was about 5 percent including merchants, lawyers, doctors, the
    majority of slave holders, preachers, school teachers and live stock
    traders work or had work carried on.
18. There was no preference shone in any way for the slave holders by
    the leading citizenship.
19. Yes
20. They were frindley, neighberly and I never hered of any diferances
    between people on the account of slavery.
21. No
22. Yes
23. A greater part of them did
24. We had about 3 months schools in the fall and winter
25. ----
26. 1 to 2 miles
27. Dr. T.K. Muncy's at Rhea Springs, Prof. Bailey at Mars Hill, Dr.
    Pyott at Washington, and others.
28. Both
29. From 3 to 5 months
30. Yes
31. Both
32. 1862. October. at Rhea Springs, Rhea co., Tenn.
33. First Tenn. Cav. Comanded by James E. Carter, Capt. Burton, Leuty.
    and G.B. Keys.
34. I joined the command at Kingston, Tenn.
35. I do not remember but the first battle I was in was at Murfreysborough,
    Tenn.
36. Mufforsborough
37. I cannot remember, all, but we made several raids in to Kentucky and
    was for some time in East Tennessee, we were at the seige of Knoxville
    and were at two engagements at Morristown, Bulls Gap, Blue Springs
    under Gen. Williams, and many other smaller fights. we were dismount-
    ed at Abington Va. and sent to Peadmont with Gen. Wm. E. Jones who
    was killed May 5th 1864 I was wounded and left on the battle field
    the same day and when I got able for duty I returned to my command
38. At Kingston, Ga. May 12th 1865. I was paroled came and took hold of
    the plow handles the next day after I got home.
39. ----
40. ----
41. I came home and went to work clearing land and making crops, and have
    been at the same work ever since and at the same place.
42. Daniel Broyles; Jonesborro, Washington co., Tenn.; lived afterwards
    near Rhea Springs

BROYLES (cont'd.):
43. Hariet Ann Newell; ---- and Mary Peters, was her maden name; lived at Rhea county, Tenn.
44. My grandfather, whose name was Daniel Broyles, came from Germany to Mayerland (Maryland) and from there to Washington county, Tennessee and from there to Athens, Tennessee where he served for many years as Circuit Court Clk.

BRUCE, A. M.

FORM NO. 2

1. A. M. Bruce, Cumberland Gap
2. 79 years lacking 9 days (form was filled out March 28. 1922)
3. Was born Campbell co., Tenn.
4. Confederate
5. Co. D - Capt. Owens - 2nd Tenn. Cav.; "the young man says coward from that king turned and knocked him to his knees 3 times when he rose he came with vengance 7_ from 4 ____ "
6. He was a southern Methdist preacher
7. William Bruce; Wythe co., Va. he made his living by farming and left the knife stick ing in his shoulder (N.B.: I presume this last quotation belongs with the above...cme)
   ...he was a local elder in the M.E. Church South he married than most
8. Cynthy Ann Maupin; Amos Maupin and Sallee Ayres; Well Spring, Tenn. he died about the close of the war (age 93? - this is not clear)
9. The Bruces came from Scotland and settled Va. I think in Albemarle. My grandfather said he was a decendant of Bruce-King scots. My grand mother was Irish. Grand F. Maupin was of English descent. I think they settled in Nodaway county Va. grand Mother Maupin was of French descent. grandfather found her about Cytheand(?) Ky., married and brought her to Tenn. she died about the year 55. (Cynthiana, Ky.?)
10. I owned nothing before the war. I had a horse I aimed to ride into service in 62 but some clever rogue took one night.
11. My grandfather Maupin gave my mother a negro girl when she married. She grew.
12. about 75 or 100 acres of valley land
13. 150 Mountain side...I guess they ____ four or five thosand dollars worth of
14. It was a frame two rooms below one above with an old log kitchen standing close the SE corner
15. Well so far as work is concerned I never liked it any too well but I always had to do my part or have a limbing. I made a hand at the plow at 12 years of age and was small and weakly at that and when it came to hoeing I generally had the cleanest row if it was not quite so long
16. My father did most any kind of work on the farm. He managed to make a good living and clear two or three hondred dollars a year. Mother did all kinds of house work such as carding, spinning, knitting, ironing, making clothes for us children whom there (were) 9 and 7 are still living. She died in 1900.
17. None except the negro girl I spoke. They generally hired __ several days work through crop time
18. In my neighborhood every body who was able worked on the farm and thought it no disgrace those who had the most generally worked the hardest so as to add something to their belongings.
19. As a general thing white men did the principal part of the work that was done.
20. Now you have struck me a hard blow. for I have never found that class I gues they lived some other neighborhood.
21. Another question hard to answer, though so far as I remember there was but little difference in their respectability, though I am looking at it through a poor mans eyes.
22. It has been so long since a way back yonder before the war I can hardly remember though I think there was little inequality among them.
23. If there was any hardness among them I dont remember at all they seemed willing to live and let live.

BRUCE (cont'd.):
24. That was before I took any part in politics so can not give you much light on the subject but presume it little to do with winning the election so he was an honest man.
25. one who had the energy could make a good living if he would apply himself to business and stick to it long enough.
26. I never heard of one discouraging a young man in trying to make something of himself
27. Just the common free schools, principally when I was small I went to a little subscription school or two
28. about 2½ or 3 years altogether
29. one and one half miles
30. Just the public schools and they were poorly attended most of the time.
31. answered
32. from 5 to 7 months
33. When the weather good they attended tolerably well
34. I went two or three months woman the rest of the time I wint to men
35. I enlisted on April 1863 as soon as I was suffering (sufficiently recovered) from typhoid fever. we were in combat Knoxville some time gathering recruits and absentees together.
36. We were sent across the Cumber(land) mountains our about Monticello Ky. (?)
37. About two months I guess we were camping at a little place called Stubinsville, Ky.
38. the enemy came across the Camber (Cumberland?) river to try our strength we fell back two or three miles
39. before engaging them then they fell back to a black jack grove there is when I saw my first dead Yankee. We had two or three men wounded our Colonels horse was shot through the thigh and in a few minutes he was shot through the head (heel?) so we retired from the field and pretty soon came back to Tennessee we stayed in the vicinity Knoxville till Morgan
40. made his rade into Ohio. When we (N.B.: here he leaves off with his report of his war activities, which ran over into the spaces for Q. 39 and 49)...I was never discharged.....Q. 39-40 cont'd: we were sent in to Ky. to relive (relieve) him
41. ....when the end came I was on a thirty days furlough in Va. among my fathers people so did not come home for a year after the war. I was a little afraid ti might not be right healthy up here in these mountains ___
42. I went to work on the farm am still with it but dont expect to stay here long I am about worn our but I hope theres a better day coming.
43. in the year 67 I hired to a man to work on the farm when that was out I went back to my fathers farm and made two or three crops in the year 70 - drove a team through to the lone star state (Texas) came back and have been in Tenn. ever since except a few hours at a time in 1880 I bought a small poor rocky farm and am still with it farming has been my chief occupasion all my life never held any office except I was P.M. (Post Master) at Oldtown a country post office on the Star route as to my church relations I feel sorry I cannot give a better record I made a profession of faith in the year 1868 and joined the M.C. Church South under the ministry of Rev. W.B. Lyds and Rev. John Freeman a good old Baptist devine but have gone to their reward and I am expecting to go soon. my chief regret is that I have not done more for the cause of my heavenly master but by the grace of God I am what I am and I hope to gain admitance in to that rest prepared for the faithful.
44. ----
45. a few years ago I could count 60 so you see I am loosing out, it looks strange(?) a man will forget
    Capt. Bill Owens, 1st Lt. Moore, 2nd Lt. B.A. Crosier, 3rd Lt. John McMahon, Orderly Sgt. W.M. Ellis, Mess Sgt. Jeff A. Nash, Ordinance, John D. Marts, 1st Cpl. Sam Stepens, 3rd Cpl. Melvin McBee, Privates Warren Dyer, Calvin Dyer when heard of were in Greenville Tenn., John W. Nichols when last seen was standing on the wharf at Ft. Deleware March 2nd '65, B.F. Petree, Cicero Petree, Sam Alexander, Billy Smith, Bob Smith, Sterling Smith, Thomas Smith, Sterling Smith, Jr., Wm. Smith, Henry Maupin, Joe Stepens, Johnican Bunch, Bo__ Bunch, Bill Cleveland, Bill Lenard, Callaway, Calvin Sulivan, Squire Sulivan,

407

BRUCE (cont'd.):
    Caloway Kelly, T.N. Kelly, Sam Jud Greer, /Sulivan/
    Joe Greer, W.B. McNew, Nin Beeler, Bob Fields, Bussell, Calibos,
    Barnett (Haze), Bill Rogers, Bill Epps, "What carries him along -
    Legs": Jack Legg, George Legg, Ad Legg, Will Legg - norisy; Will
    Legg - dumgy (these last two notations not clear and make little
    sense) Charlie Linard.
46. L. Owsley - Co. B 2nd Tenn. - Middlesboro, Kentucky
    James Veal   Middlesboro, Ky.
    George Willburn   -------
    George Hibert   Arthur, Tenn.
    Jim Haze   "   "   (we are getting scarce)

    .....in these parts so will devote the remainder of my space to a
    little reminisisence to begin I was born April 1843 that fall my
    father moved to Mo. stayed one year then moved back to Tenn. on the
    way politics were runing so they said Polk and Clay were runing for
    president they men would come riding by and hollor hurah Clay and I
    would stick my head out and say huray for Polk the Polk men would
    stain their wagon covers and the Clay men used clay, enough unless
    it was (I was?) little. We started on our March through Big Creek
    Gap about what time I dont remember the time it was I never kept any
    diary sufficent to say we marched nearly all night and went into
    Williamsburg the next day then from there Loudon Ky from there Rich-
    mond where I got me a new gun and from to Winchester without sleep
    or any thing to eat from there we fell to Irvin from there we took
    west ward by course and came in to lancas the next day where some of
    my (us?) were taken in and sent to Camp Chase and stayed there 7
    months. New Years day 64 was the coldest day I ever experienced I
    I remember going to well to ____ camp bottle of water and as I was
    carrying to the camp it would slap our and roll along on balls of
    ice, about the 2nd of March we started to Ft. Deleware where I came
    near starving to death my hip bones cut through and I was not sick
    wither could eat all I could get was hungry as when I got done eating
    then I was when I begun, but one of the worst things I witnessed was
    a young man steal a middle aged men ------------------his pay the
    young man had been follow ing around with a knife and came in the
    barracks started to climb on the bunk 1st (N.B.: none of this is
    very clear).
    (On extra page) Mr. J.T. Moore, Nashville, Teknessee, "For the want
    of something better I am using your letter to write a little rhyme -
    "If it is not too late/ I would be glad to state? To save a little
    time"
    In speaking of the great men I have met I would say we have never
    been away from home enough to meet many though I have seen a few whom
    were good men they are the ones whom I count great will give names of
    a few, T.(?) R. Catlet of my boy hood days, A.J. Frazier in my riper
    years, J.B. Little, W.B. Lyda, W.C. Graves add others..."And not Mr.
    Trotwood More/Since my head is getting sore/ And I can think of noth-
    ing to write/ I will lay down my pen/ and say amen/ and bid you a
    long good night"...
    A.M. Bruce

    (N.B.: On the front of the letter from Mr. Moore, Mr. Bruce add this
    "I guess this is only just fit for the waste basket but would be glad
    to know what became of the young man who killed King. I could give
    his name if thought it the thing to do." A.M. Bruce)

    (N.B.: BRUCE, A. M. Pension No. 14162)

                        BRUCE, JOHN HARDIMAN

FORM NO. 2

1. John Hardiman Bruce, Rutherford
2. 80 years 6 months
3. Tenn. Marshel co.
4. Confederate
5. Co. C-17 Calvary

                                408

BRUCE
6. Blacksmith
7. John Pennington Bruce; b. North Carolina; none
8. Elizabeth Prear Burnes; John Burnes and Mary Cunningham; ----
9. dont know
10. 1 horse $40.00
11. 1 - Tonenie Bruce
12. 40
13. $1500.00
14. Log - 4 rooms
15. plowed to a great extent. Worked with hoe, cut grain with sythe blade.
    Mowed hay with mowing blade. Taken the hay up with wood fork.
16. Father was a blacksmith, mother done the cooking and house work. She
    spun and wove all of our cloths.
17. did not
18. yes indeed
19. yes
20. every body worked
21. all on an equal
22. they did
23. yes
24. no difference
25. no opportunities
26. The slave holders encouraged the poor boy in our community
27. free
28. two years
29. 1½ mile
30. 1 free school
31. public
32. 3 months
33. yes
34. men and women
35. In the year 1861 month of Apr. at Chapel Hill in the confederacy
36. Estell Springs, Tenn.
37. 12 months as well as I can remember
38. Crow Creek
39. I had a hard time the most of the time sometimes I had plenty to eat,
    and again I didnt anything to eat for 3 days and nights especly whin
    I was on my way to prison, some time I had to sleep out in the snow,
    most of my cloths came from home
40. May 1864 at Flornce (Florence) Ala.
41. I rode a bay mare home and was glad to get the to (there too?)
42. Farm work
43. I have been on the farm every since the civil war and have made a
    living thank the Lord. I have spent the most of my time in William-
    son Co. My church relation is Premeth Babdas (Primitive Baptist)
44. ----
45. John Biggers, Jim & George & Ballaam Ezell, John & Can & Jim Bickman,
    S.A. Smith, Willie Vaughn, Red. Jones.
46. Tom Wilson   Eaglevill, Tenn.
    W.H. Grahame   Franklin, Tenn.
    Frank Smith   Allisona, Tenn.
    S.A. Smith   "   "
    . H. Moseley   "   "
    Gill Turner   Chapel Hill, Tenn.

    (extra pages)
39. I was in hospital or in a little log bar that was used for a hospital.
    I was down with typhoid fever. I got good attincion while I was sick.
    I was first put in prison at Lowsville (Louisville/Lewisville) Ky.
    and was treated might bad (excuse me) I was in the battle at Franklin
    Tenn and all so at Murfreesboro, Tenn. and I got out with out a
    scratch.

FORM NO. 2

1. John I. Bruce, Whiteville, Tenn.
2. 79 years
3. State Tenn. - Madison Co.
4. Confederate
5. Sneed envencible - 9th Tenn. Reg.
6. Farming
7. George Bruce; unknown; unknown
8. Emeline Adams; Isac Adams; unknown; Fayette co., Tenn.
9. My grandparents came from Scotland
10. dident own any
11. no
12. dident own any
13. unknown
14. log house two rooms
15. Farm work, plow and hoe and any other work necessary
16. General farm work. She done general house work such as cooking, weaving, spinning and making cloth
17. none
18. Respectable and honorable
19. Yes the majority
20. Probably one Fourth
21. considered their selves superior
22. yes
23. yes
24. yes
25. yes
26. encouraged
27. common country school
28. 18 months
29. 1½ miles
30. common country school
31. Public
32. 8 months
33. yes
34. man generally
35. enlisted in Fayette co., Tenn. 1861
36. Union City, Tenn.
37. 12 months
38. Belmont
39. next battle was Shilo after the Shilo battle was sick in hospital several weeks, then I was sent the army of Chattanooga, we started from Tennessee through Kentucky and had a battle at Perryville Kentucky lasted one day then started on the retreat through Kentucky back to Tennessee
40. ----
41. ----
42. Farming
43. continued farming - belong to the Methodist church
44. ----
45. J.M. Bullock, Turner Buffalo, Captain Irby, William Irby, Londey Irby, Tazzel Wolf, James Walls, Oney Walls, Bob Bullock, Jim Sanders, Tom Coffee, forgot the remainder of the names
46. ----

BRUMMITT, JOHN HENRY

FORM NO. 1

1. John Henry Brummitt, Martin, Tenn. R. 6
2. 78 yrs
3. State of N.C. - Granville county
4. State of N.C. - Granville county
5. farming
6. farming
7. had none

BRUMMITT (cont'd.):
8. father did. owned 4 slaves
9. father owned 199 acres
10. about 8 or 19 thousands dollars
11. framed house 3 rooms and plastered
12. I did all farm work with the negroes same as they did
13. father did farm work all the time made a good hand himself. mother
cooked spun and wove did house work in general
14. no special servants
15. yes as much so as it is today
16. they did
17. not many in my community was idle
18. not as a general thing of course there was some few that thought them
selves better but not many
19. no difference that way all the same
20. yes as a general thing they were
21. I was no difference in political contest
22. yes all he had to do was to work and try
23. I never heard the questions brought up I saw no difference
24. free school public
25. not over 3 years
26. 2 quarters of a mile
27. just free schools no high schools in the country as they have now
28. free school public
29. from 3 to 5 months
30. most of them did. girls did most. boys had to work could not go as
much
31. generally a man
32. I enlisted in 1861 in May at Rawleigh, N.C.
33. 44th regiment, Eurah Cutts, Sam Hughes, Steve Knott, Bill Ellis,
Gardner Hayes, William Sherron, Luiecol (Luiecoe?) Sherron, Dose Beck,
Elijah Coley, Mose Garner, Henry O. Bryant, Thomas J. Bryant, Bill
Eastridge, Rom Eastridge, John Stanly, Aron Emery, Jim Emery, Bruce
Emery, Ruffan Buckhannon, Jim Sanderfer, Elic Monegue, Jim Coply,
John Nevels, Burton Nevels, Joe Cash, Henry Bryant, Apps Norwood.
34. from Oxford to Rawleigh
35. about 6 weeks
36. Swifts Mill
37. I went to Petersberg camped there and drilled awhile. I engaged in
a battle 2½ miles east of Petersberg. Lasted 1 hour and half the
whole Co. was made prisoners except a few. Battle at Gains Mill,
lasted ½ day or more, The confederates whipped - battle of the Wilderness lasted 2 days confederates whipped and held the field. Spotsylvania Court House lasted 2 or more days confederates whipped and
held the field, battle of Cold Harbor lasted 2 days confederates
whipped.
38. I was discharged by having a parole in my pocket was carried to
Point Lookout from near Petersberg. I was captured near Petersburg
27 of Oct. 1864.
39. they carried me from Point Lookout to Acon's landing where I was met
by our men and taken to Richmond and paroled. My brigade was in the
battle of Gettesburg. I lived in camp common. clothed common.
slept on ground or blanket. eat hard tacks and bacon. exposed to
cold very much.
40. farming
41. I have engaged in farming all the time and lived in Granville co. 3
years after the war and then moved to West Tenn. in Weakly co., have
been here since.
42. Wesely Brummitt; six mile south Oxford, Granville co., N.C.: lived
isx mile south of Oxford.
43. Marth E. Bobbitt; John Bobbitt and Peggy Stone; in Granville co.
44. John Bobbitt came from England this is as far back as I can remember
I cant get the perticulars of my great grand parents

(N.B.: BRUMMITT, JOHN HENRY Pension No. 9148)

(on attached page):
Mar. 14, 1922, Martin, Tenn. R. 6 - Mr. Moore, Kind Sir,
I have filled out the paper the very best I can I cannot remember
it all just as it come exactly. I was taken prisoner 27th day of

411

BRUMMETT (cont'd.):
   Oct. 1864 and kept in prison 5 months guarded by negros had been out
   of prison about 1 month or little over when Lee surrendered. Had not
   been exchanged so could not go back in army until I was exchanged and
   Lee surrendered and that is the way I came out of the army. Well
   close hoping this information will be a benefit to you, Yours respt.,
   J.H. Brummitt.

BRUNSON, ROBERT JACKSON

FORM NO. 1

1. Robert Jackson Brunson, Pulaski, R. 5, Tenn.
2. I will be 80 yrs old Apr. 18/22
3. Giles co., Tenn.
4. Giles co., Tenn.
5. a farmers boy going to school
6. black smith, wood workman & farmer
7. ----
8. My parents owned 14 slaves
9. 540 acres
10. $25,000.00
11. log house of 3 rooms weather boarded and ceiled with upstairs
12. I did all kind of work a boy could do and worked with the negors on
    the farm
13. Father worked in the blacksmith and wood shop and mother with the help
    of the negros did the spinning and weaving, all the clothes and shoes
    were made at home.
14. 2 in the house-cook and house girl
15. it was.
16. they did
17. to a very small extent all most all worked
18. They all mingled to gather there was no distinction at church or at
    home
19. yes
20. They were friendly
21. No, it did not
22. Yes, his opportunities were just as good as any ones
23. The slaveholders encouraged and helped the poor young men to make
    something of themselves.
24. We had only subscription in the country and these that were not able
    to pay went free the teacher did not charge them.
25. Some every year for 11 years perhaps 3 months a year
26. about 2½ miles
27. None but subscription schools
28. Public subscriptions
29. from 3 to ten months
30. yes
31. Some times both man and his would frequently teach together (man and
    his wife?)
32. August 1861 in the Confederacy at Pulaski, Tennessee
33. 32 and 5 Tenn. (see ---- ----)
34. Camp Trousdale
35. About 5 months
36. Shelton(?) Hi-1, Miss. May 28. 1862
37. Was in 22 battles in which the Regt. was engaged. Have notes maid on
    the field of battle. Went half clothed and fed for 3 year and 8 mo.
    Sleeping 3 together on the ground on 1 blanket or 2 blankets over us.
    But am to old and blind to write. I dont care to part with my notes.
    I have 6 or more papers published '61-2-3. Have an old knap sack
    with everything in it just as it was the day I was wounded, also have
    the old bloody shirt.
38. Wounded Dec. 6/64 and given a unlimited furlow (was barefooted with
    rags tide on my feat and it was snowing.)
39. Brought home in a buggy by my father from Franklin Tenn. whare I had
    lane in Fathers(?) house for 5 days with out my wounds being treat,
    contracted pneumonia.
40. Farming

BRUNSON (cont'd.):
41. Have lived on the same farm all my life was elder in C. P. Church member of Ku Klux Klan. I have the original robe worn by me.
42. Abdallah Brunson; Augusta, Ga.; he came to Giles co., Tenn from near Huntsville, Ala.
43. Darcus Steele; Robert Steele and Martha Star Stelle; York co., S.C.
44. See History of Steele Family by Dr. M.?C. Steele

(BRUNSON, ROBERT JACKSON Pension No. 16170)

BRYAN, THOMAS LEDBETTER

FORM NO. 1

1. Thomas Ledbetter Bryan, Summitville, Coffee co., Tennessee
2. Seventy-eight
3. Tennessee. Coffee co.
4. Tennessee. Coffee co.
5. Farming
6. Farming
7. ----
8. Four
9. about two hundred acres
10. Three thousand or four thousand dollars - land at that time was from $5.00 to $10.00 an acres
11. Log house four rooms
12. Farm work. All the family worked. The four negro children not being old enough to work and their mammy cooked.
13. My father tended to the planting and sowing of the grain and was always busy. and when the war broke out made a regular hand in the field. The negro woman did the cooking, my sisters did the spinning. My step-mother helped with all the houseowrk.
14. not any
15. It was considered respectable and honorable
16. yes sir
17. There was very few that depended on others to do their work.
18. They certainly did. No they did not show in any way that they felt themselves better than the ones that did not own slaves
19. yes
20. always - no
21. no
22. about the same as now, not many different thing to work at then as now, mostly farm work here.
23. encouraged
24. free schools
25. about 3 months in a year and until the war broke out
26. one half mile
27. common free school
28. public
29. 3 months
30. yes
31. man
32. 1861, July, Manchester
33. 4th Tennessee Cavalry - Liberty Duncan, Tom and Jim and Cornelius Martin, Brooks Haggard, Capt. Reid Holmes, Fate Vandygriff, Lee Hickerson, Dan Anderson, Jasper Umbarger (Vanbarger?), George W. Haris, Jim Oldsfield, By Rhea
34. to guard a bridge on this side of Chattanooga
35. about two or three months was in battle pretty regular after the first fight
36. dont remember
37. was through Tenn., Ga., Ala., S.C. was wounded and sent to Charlotte, N.C. to the hospital was there about 6 or 8 weeks, clothed very well, sometimes we had plenty to eat and at times nothing at all. Slept good, but sometimes in water when we ___ waked up, had bread meat and crackers to eat --- exposed to cold all through the winters, was treated well in the hospital, never was captured.
38. At the end of the war was paroled at some place in Ga.

BRYAN (cont'd.):
39. ----
40. farm work, everything was high after the war
41. was at home 3 or 4 years then went to California, there worked on a
    farm, stayed twenty years, came back and married and have lived here
    every since.
42. John Bryan; (no other information on his father)
43. Neely McGuire; (no other information)
44. I cant remember and dont know who has the old Bible.

(BRYAN, THOMAS LEDBETTER Pension No. 2060)

BRYANT, JOHN DAVID

FORM NO. 1

1. John David Bryant, Lincoln county, Kelso, Tennessee R.F.D. 2
2. Eighty two years past 82
3. Tennessee Bedford county
4. I was living in the Lincoln co., Tenn. when enlist Confedarcy
5. I was a farmer when a boy but latter on I became a man I was a
   railroader with section crew
6. he was a farmer but was a scree maker (screw?) for gin presses and
   all so a leather tanner and a driver.
7. I did not own any land but I had some stock, such as horses and mules
   and hogs, and corn that was worth something like seven hundred dollars
   and when I enlisted to go to the war I just left my stock and all with
   father and that was the last of stock corn and bacon, never redeemed
   anything.
8. had one slave, was very old and he died before the war.
9. owned fifty acres
10. I would say land and house and everything would amount to as mutch as
    a $1000.00
11. he lived and a big log house with two rooms with puntion floors hued
    out with ax for we had no saw mills any where near us at that time.
12. I plowed with old wooden made board plow and bull tung plow and hoed
    with homade hoe did all most all the farming that we did that way but
    we made plenty of corn and wheat that way, some few rich men would
    not work
13. My father work as a tanner most of the time he did not farm very much
    we was a ____ and he was a jin scrue maker - he would take a white
    oak tree, 30 in. in diameter 30 ft. lond (long.) and cut the scrues
    and tops for the jiners and mother did her own cooking spinning and
    weaveding for the hold (whole) family and father made shoes for his
    nabors and many things
14. we did not have any
15. most all in this part thought it was honorable to work but some that
    owned slaves taught their sons and daughters not to work, but most
    everybody thought it was all wright to work
16. yes most did, and (but?) as I said their was some that did not work
17. those that owned a good many slaves like to lead idle lives but the
    poor could (class) of men had to work at something.
18. we all seamed to be sociable with those who owned slaves but some
    thought them selves better than others but mighty few was that way
    that I ever new of
19. in most all cases they did that I no of
20. we never did have any trouble with them of corse those that owned
    slaves was suposed to be ritch and we thought them that way but they
    was all ways good to the poor white people as far as I can say
21. I can not say as the one that owned slaves had any better chance in
    any political contest than the one that did not owne slaves
22. no there was not any (very) mutch chance far a poor to make enuff to
    buy a farm but they could enter this land from the government as fer
    buying any thing they did not get enuff pay to buy any thing, six
    dollars per man was big pay
23. you and all ought to no that us(?) __ and if any men could stay at
    home and work for $25 or $30 per day that was not very mutch incour-
    agement for any body but we could not do any better
24. I attend free school about three months per year but we had to quit

414

BRYANT (cont'd.):
to pull foffer and about two months for year was all I every went to
school had old blue back speller book.
25. I never went to school 12 months all told. I just learned to read
and write a little and that was all
26. something like two miles
27. free school but they had a pay school for some few months in the
winter
28. was public
29. three month in the year
30. yes untill fodder pulling time then we all had to stop to help
31. was a man
32. I joined Oct. or November 1861 confederate army at Flintville, Tenn.
33. Col. McClan___ Comapny A, Capt. Stiles 44 Tenn., A.F. Seaten, N.M.
Jenkins, R.L.(P?) Lackey, Bill Lackey, John M. Dickens, Sam Nix,
Temple Taylor, John H. Taylor, Benj. Fam__n, Jack Fanning?, Noe
Cooper, Jeff Lenard, Davie Jean, Wilt Jean, ----; ----; Jim Luttel,
Jim Still, Jim Bryant, Jim Riley, Sa__ Pickett, W.T. Taylor, Wes
Woodall, Dr. Tripp, Dr. Noblet, Geo. McNee, Dick Webb.
34. We were sent to Camp Trousdale tenn 50 miles from Nashville we staid
their about 4 days, we went from there to Bolen Green, Ky. then to
Nashville there 5 weeks then to Columbus there 5 day we had order to
come home
35. something like six months
36. Shiloh was the first battle was the April 6, 1862
37. we give the yanks a good whiping the first day but they give it to us
the next day and we retreated from Shiloh back to weat(?) Miss. I
was detailed as nurse in the hospital. I was in the hospital six
months when I left the hospital I ---- we went to Mobile Ala. from
Mobile to Atlanta, Ga. from Atlanta to Chooniga (Chattanooga?) Tenn.
in cars then I was fetch to help load 500 wagons with provisions
to carry to Ky. then we went from Chattanooga to Ky.
38. I was discharge at Point Lookout, M.D. (Md.) June 24, 1865
39. I got in ___ and to Washington D.C. from there ___ from Louisville,
Ky. from there Nashville from the Dechard, Tenn. by rail from there
to home afoot the best way I could get there. I arived home the
fourth day July 1865.
40. I first began to make barlles (barrels) and then I got married soon
after got home and I settle down here and I have been living here
every since practly at the same place with all the ups and down that
any body could have.
41. I have work in timber and cleared land was was a merchant for 2 years
but have work hard all the time, --------- untill I got to old to
work.
42. William Robert Bryant; North Carolina, ; dont know; he moved to Tenn.
when he was a boy; I no as good as nothing of my father young days,
or his people
43. Her was Eliza Hick; Edman HIck and (dont know); Buck Horn Tover(?),
Ala.
44. my grand father came to this country from Ireland and that is as far
as I no of my people.

(attached sheet)
41. after I got so I could not work I filled out application for pension
and they gave me a pinchen for a few years then they cut me off said
I had enuf to live without it. So that is they way if is with some.
I have been a member of Christ Church for more than 50 years. I am
living and _____ my self ____ live with my son Walter Bryant and his
wife. I ------- and ad more but I dont think it nesery, to do it.
34. to Fayetteville, Lincoln, we staid at ------ about a week until the
army came through we got with the army near Fayetteville and we marched through the country to Athens, Ala. from there to Decater, Ala. we
got on the train we went 40 or 50 mi. west, then we got off the train
and sturck camp from there Creant(?) Miss. we camped there about 2
weeks then was where we drew our first gun and we drilled there ----
few days from there wer went to the battle of Shiloh.
37. we marched across Woldnut (Walnut?) Ridge and one of my partner taken
sick, and I was detailed to wait on him, we staid there 5 days then
we staid with a untion man where we was treated all right then we
started f___ to catch the army we went along down the _____ to

BRYANT (cont'd.):

McMinnville and we staid all night we cought up with a soldier riding and leading two horses he let us ride with him until we came up with the army. we came up with tht army at Greenrive, Ky. from there to ---- Ky. from there to Camp Dick Roberson came through Cumberland Gap to Knoxville Tenn. from Knoxville to Chattanooga Tenn. we marched to Allasen__ to Shelberville, Tenn. and from there we camp at Stones river or near Murfreesboro until the battle taken place the battle was next day year 1862. there I had my right hand man by the name of Jack Fanning was shot down and killed. this (then) we retreated back to Tullahome, Tenn. we staid there the rest of the winter. I was detailed to ___ service until they retreated for there I was at Decatur? Tenn. when the union solder brunged the (burned the) town. I went from there to Dalton, Ga. then we brought on the battle Chickamauga, which I was captured in the first days of battle. I had my left hand man shot down there. I was captured in the little field near a spring - I had got lost from the rest and the Uank had me cut off from the rest. They cep (kept) us all night near the battle lines. They taken us to Chatanooga from there to Stevenson, Ala. we boarded train to Nashville, Tenn. I was carreid from theire to Camp Douglas near Chicago, Ill. I was there in prison nearly two years. After most two year they sent me on exchange to Baltimore, Md. to Point Look Out prison and their I received my discharge.

(BRYANT, JOHN DAVID Pension No. 11557)

BRYANT, R. A.

FORM NO. 2

1. R.A. Bryant, Huntingdon, Tenn.
2. 83 yrs. 5 months
3. Carroll co., Tenn.
4. Confederate
5. Co. H. - 55th
6. Farmer
7. Alfred Bryant; Spartanburg, S.C.; lived at Huntingdon, Tenn. a number of years; he served as sheriff, J. P. and Constable.
8. Polly Stone; Aaron Stone and ----; in Carroll co., Tenn.
9. ----
10. ----
11. two
12. 162 acres
13. about $5000
14. a framed house with 4 rooms
15. I worked at any thing necessary to run a farm
16. He worked at all kind of jobs necessary about a farm. My mother did all the work the house.
17. ----
18. It was considered honorable
19. They did
20. But very few
21. ----
22. They did
23. There was a frendly feeling
24. It did not
25. There nothing hinder him succeeding
26. They were encouraged
27. Not much of any kind
28. not over twelve months
29. ½ mile
30. ----
31. both
32. 3 months
33. no
34. man
35. Enlisted in Confederate army at Trenton, Tenn.
36. to Columbus, Ky.
37. 3 months

416

BRYANT (cont'd.):
38. Island 10 on Miss. river
39. were captured at Island 10 April 8, 62. I was engaged in several
    other battles notably Port Hudson, Jackson, Miss., 22nd and 2 th July
    Atlanta 1864 Franklin, Tenn. Nov. 3rd 1864 Nashville (Dec. 15/16/61)
40. Johnson Island about 25th June 1864
41. The good women of Cincinnati brought us something to eat on the boat
    and were preparing to spread it out when a Yanke capt. came on board
    kick the baskets in the river cursed the women and left us hungrey.
    (N.B.: This answer is written in spaces for Q. 41, 42 and 43.)
44. ----
45. ----
46. Army life was very rought corn bread and tough beef and half enough
    of that. Clothing of the very coarset (coarsest) I have seen men
    marching barefooted over the frozen ground, sleeping on the grcund
    with one blanker. P.S. You will excuse this badly gotten up document.
    I getting old. My memory is bad. All of which is respectfully
    Submitted, R.A. Bryant

                       BRYANT, WYLIE RICHARD

FORM NO. 2

1. Wylie Richard Bryant, Arlington, Tenn.
2. 78 years
3. N.C., Colwell Co.
4. Confederate
5. Co. B - 26th 1st Tenn.
6. Farmer
7. Charlie Bryant; Lanore, Colwell co., N.C.; lived at same place; none
8. Martha Bryant; ----
9. All facts pertaining to grand parents and great grand parents was my
    great grand parents came from Ireland and settled in Colwell co., N.C.
    and served through Revolutionary War and grand parents I never learn-
    ed.
10. none
11. no
12. 500 acres
13. According to value of things then about $2000
14. log house 4 rooms
15. worked on farm did considerable work with plow and also hoe and made
    harness and shoes
16. Father was a farmer and harness maker. My mother did the regular
    work such as cooking, spinning, weaving, sewing, washing, ironing,
    milking, churning, scrubing and worked in field when needed.
17. none
18. yes
19. yes
20. very few
21. some few did not but very few
22. the majority
23. There were no quarrels among them
24. about equal
25. yes
26. Nothing but the rich had the opportunity to go to school
27. public school
28. about 1 month
29. 5 miles
30. none but the public school
31. public
32. 3 months
33. some did and some had to work
34. man
35. In the year 1861, 5th Mo. In Johnson Co., Tenn.
36. Knoxville
37. about 6 mo.
38. Fort Donelson
39. The 1st battle I was in was at Fort Donelson and was captured and 7
    mos. in prison treated very nice then was exchanged next battle

BRYANT (cont'd.):
    Murfreesboro, Missionary Ridge, Lookout Mt., battle Chickamauga at
    Franklin at Nashville seige at Atlanta slightly wounded by shell had
    plenty to eat and wear and good place to sleep at beginning near the
    close had nothing.
40. Discharged in N.C. in 1865
41. Rode a mule 300 miles home in six days, begged feed for my mule an
    old lady baked me some bread that lasted me home I slept on the
    ground by my mule.
42. Farming
43. I married in about a year after I came home and lived there about 6
    yrs. moved to Washington co., Tenn. moved then to Fayette co. then to
    Shelby co. Professed religion while in the army then after the war
    joined the Missionary Baptist church.
44. ----
45. Dont remember them.
46. Mr. Joe Harrell   Arlington Tenn.
    Mr. C. Rhodes   Brunswick, Tenn.
    Mr. W.L. Thompson   Kerrville, Tenn.
    Mr. John Sink   Kerrville, Tenn.
    Mr. Jessie Willias   Brighton, Tenn.
    Mr. Jim Rhodes   Kerville, Tenn.

    (N.B.: BRYANT, WYLIE RICHARD Pension No. 6815)

                        BUCHANAN, CLAUDIUS

FORM NO. 2

1. Claudius Buchanan, Ravenscroft, Tenn.
2. 79
3. Williamson co., Tenn.
4. Confederate
5. Co. D - 20th Reg.
6. Farmer
7. Joseph Buchanan; Williamson co., Tenn.; lived in Williamson co.; ----
8. Martha Edmiston; John Edmiston and ____; lived in Davidson co.
9. Family came from Kippen in Scotland to Coldrain in Ireland then to
    Virginia
10. a horse
11. Parents owned three grown negros and about six children
12. 500 acres
13. ----
14. Frame house with seven rooms
15. I made a hand with the negros doing exactly the same work they did
16. Regular farm work and regular duties of a housekeeper - cooking,
    spinning and weaving were all done.
17. Yes. The slaves I've mentioned before
18. As far as I knew it was considered honorable.
19. With about one exception.
20. I don't remember but one case of this kind.
21. I was too young to notice such things.
22. I was too young to notice such things.
23. I was too young to notice such things.
24. I was too young to notice such things.
25. Yes, as well as I can remember they were
26. Don't remember that they took any stock in it one way or the other.
27. a 9 mo. school
28. ----
29. 1½ miles
30. ----
31. private
32. about 9
33. yes
34. man
35. In Confederate army at College Grove, Tenn. was sworn in 27th of May
    1861
36. Camp Trousdale
37. ----

                              418

BUCHANAN (cont'd.):
38. Barboursville, Ky.
39. Battle of Shiloh - 6 and 7th of April, 1862. Wounded in battle of
    Murfreesboro Jan. 2, 1863. In prison at Rock Island, Illinois for
    15 months. Helped eat a dog and several rats.
40. Paroled at Richmond, Va. a short time before Lee's surrender.
41. Reached home in Williamson co. soon after Lincoln's assassination.
42. Farming
43. Always a farmer - lived always in Williamson co. till last two years
    which I have spent in White co., Tenn. Worshipful Master of Marshall
    Lodge 372 F. and A. M. for a number of years.
44. ----
45. Roster of Co. and Regiment can be found in McMurrys History of 20th
    Tennessee Regiment. Call on Dr. Deering G. Roberts for History.
46. Nearly all confederate Veterans I know belong to Troop A, Co. B and
    Troop C, of Nashville, Forrests Cavalry.

                        BUCKNER, DANIEL L.

FORM NO. 2

1. Daniel L. Buckner, Huntland, Tenn.
2. 76 yrs.
3. Tenn., McMinn co.
4. Confederate
5. Co. H., 43rd Tenn. commanded by Col. James Gillaspie all through the
    war
6. Dentist
7. James Buckner; near Athens, McMinn co., Tenn.; lived at Riceville 7
    miles west of Athens, Tenn.; was sheriff of McMinn county in his early
    days.
8. Susan Stephenson; Alexander Stephenson and ----; 7 or 9 miles east of
    Athens, Tenn.
9. At an early day the Buckner family came from Scotland and settled in
    easter Virginia and we branched out from there and that is about all
    I know about them.
10. I owned nothing
11. Seven
12. 220
13. about ten thousand dollars
14. A log house with framed addition with 4 rooms and basement.
15. I worked some on the farm but spent more of my time with my father in
    the dental office.
16. My father was a mill wright in his early days. Built a good many
    mills then took up dentistry. My mother did all kinds of house work
    including spinning, weaving, etc.
17. Owned seven but did not use them as servants about the house.
18. Labor was considered honorable in my community
19. The white men worked as much or more than the slaves in my community
20. I believe less than 5 pr cent
21. A few that owned a large no. of slaves seemed to think they were
    better than the poor man
22. As well as I remember they did
23. about the same as between the rich and the poor of the present day
24. I dont believe the owner of negros had any advantage on that account,
    the man of merit got the votes
25. Just as good or better than at this time
26. They were encouraged
27. Public
28. about 8 or 10 months
29. about two miles
30. One little log house of Mouse Creek known as the Wassom Schoolhouse
    and one near Riceville known as the Riceville Academy and I attended
    that 3 or 4 months
31. public
32. am not sure but think it run about 5 or 6 months in the year
33. pretty regular there seemed to be considerable interest in schools at
    that time
34. a man

BUCKNER (cont'd.):
35. In the fall of 1862 dont remember the date. Joined or enlisted at
    Knoxville, Tenn.
36. in to Kentucky on Braggs raid
37. about 19 days or two weeks
38. at Perryville, Ky.
39. We came back off Braggs raid to Knoxville and soon we were sent to
    Vicksburg, Miss. did considerable fighting out from Vicksburg out the
    big black river. Then went in to Vicksburg and were beseiged for
    three months surrendered on 4 of July.
40. At Washington, Georgia on the 9 day of May 1865. The agreement under
    which we
41. were paroled allowed us our horses and the officers their side arms
    to guard us back through the mountains and we reached home the 17 day
    of May 65
42. Dentistry
43. After my return home from the war I railroded two years for the East
    Tenn. and Virginia R.R. from Knoxville to Bristol, in March 1868 I
    came to Middle Tenn., Franklin co. commensed the practice of dentistry
    and have bin with and worked for the same people for 54 years. I feel
    that I have a good friendship here and would love to serve the same
    people as much longer if the Lords willing and would give me the
    strenght to do so.
44. ----
45. The roster has been lost for many years and cannot recall many of them,
    only about two that I think are now living.
    Those living are: Jecz. (Jessie?) Gwinn, Mike Millsap, Richard Grisson,
    Thos. Grisson, Carles (Charles?) Riggins, Silus Riggins, Thomas Tarter,
    James Liner (Limes?), Phillip Dake, Robt Friar, Robt. Office, J.T.
    Funk, (note: Gwinn lived at Dayton, Tenn. and Millsap at Lunchburg,
    Tenn.)
46. James Stiles   Winchester, Tenn.
    Jo Huddleston   "   "
    Nathan Martin   "   "
    R.G. Smith   "   "
    Charley Hatfield   "   "
    David Coble   Decherd, Tenn.
    Sanford Smith   Lexia, Tenn.
    Robt. Templeton   Flintville, Tenn.
    Toke Smith   Lexia, Tenn.
    H.R. Moore   Huntland, Tenn.
    S.M. Alexander   Winchester, Tenn.
    Mat McDowell   "   "
    Thos. Modeny   Decherd, Tenn.
    Alexander Torter (Tarter?) Winchester, Tenn.

                     BUFFAT, AUGUSTUS GUS

FORM NO. 1

1. Augustus Gus Buffat, Knoxville, Tennessee R. #6
2. 79
3. Canton Vau Switzerland (N.B.; "Canton" is one of the so called states
    of Switzerland, or what we would call states; the one mentioned here
    is actually Vaud, whose capital is Lausanne...cme)
4. Tennessee, county of Knox
5. Farming
6. Farming
7. None
8. None
9. 300 acres
10. about $7000.00
11. Half log house and half frame house, 6 rooms
12. I plowed, hoed and done every thing that had to be done on a farm
13. My father helped farm. My mother helped to the house work.
14. None
15. Yes
16. Yes
17. Very few

                            420

BUFFAT (cont'd.):

18. We associated with people who owned slaves and were treated respect-
    ably.
19. yes
20. no
21. yes
22. yes
23. no
24. Country schools
25. In Switzerland I went to school 3 yrs. in U.S. 7 years
26. ½ mile
27. Public school
28. Public
29. Some years one month never exceeded 3 months
30. Yes
31. Men
32. I enlisted the Confederacy Oct. 1861
33. Company C, 37 Tenn. Inf.; First Captain Stephen Cock after his death
    Capt. James Long, Lt. Dave McClellen, 2nd Lt. Ben Long, Color Bearer
    Richard Huffmaster, Pvt's: J.D. Sloan, Jess Rice, John Cox, Frank
    Belcher, Harve Mathis, Geo. Mathis.
34. Sent Jefferson, Cock and Greene county to arrest an organization of
    men who were to distroy the East Tenn. and Va. R.R. thereby cutting
    off the supplies of the Confederacy.
35. First battle was Mill Springs, Ky.
36. Byrd and Sanders attack on Knoxville, June 18, 1863
37. Went to Nashville awaiting orders to go to Carthage to rejoin the
    regment. Next battle Chickamauga it lasted 2 days, 19 & 20 Sept.
    1863. We drove the Federals in to Chattanooga. Came around to E.
    Tenn. and stayed wit the 1st Tenn. Cav. throu different skirmishes in
    one of which we captured the 2nd Tenn. mounted U.S. 4 miles east of
    Rogersville, Also a battery 7th Ind.
38. Tyners Sta. Sept. 1862 on acct. disability but continued with the
    army when I was able to due duty.
39. I was captured on my way home to get new clothing Feb. 1864. May 1865
    went to N.Y. Sept. came back south.
40. Working for N.C and St.L R.R. untill 1867 then went in the lumber
    business untill 1876 then went to Texas in 1877 worked in a machine
    shop returned to Tenn. Dec. 1877. Last 41 yrs. been connected with
    the zink mining interest in Tenn. as Supt. of mines.
41. ----
42. P.F. Buffat; Warren, Canton Vau, Switzerland; lived Agle, Canton Vau
    where he taught school; he wrote school books.
43. Sylvia Taux; Frank Taux and (cannot remember); Agle, Canton Vau,
    Switzerland.

    (on attached sheet)
37. Then came down with dispatcher from Gen. Ranson to Gen. Longstreet
    who was beseiging Knoxville. From there I went to Marietta, Ga. with
    the quartermasters Dept. which we turned over in Atlanta to another
    dept. Left Atlanta Jan. 1st came back up to Va. then down to the
    Confederate forces in East Tenn. Was in a raid that drove the
    Federals accross the river at Strawberry Planes sunk the pontoon as
    their ordinance and other supplies were crossing it. Some eight or
    10 wagons were sunk into 15 foot of water, few days after we made a
    raid within three miles of Knoxville, captured a few prisoners from
    the 22nd Wis. Inf. who through their guns and ran. 1863 and 1864 we
    used no tents, some times bare footed and often two days without any-
    thing to eat. I was captured some time the latter part of Feb. 1864.
    kept in prison 2 weeks took the oath was released and went North.

    (N.B.: BUFFAT, AUGUSTUS GUS Pension No. 13588)

                        BULLEN, SAM D.

FORM NO. 1

1. Sam D. Bullen, Greeneville, Tenn. RFD 1#
2. Seventy seven

BULLEN (cont'd.):
3. Tenn., Greene co.
4. Greene co., Tenn. Confederate
5. Working on farm
6. Farmer
7. Did not own any property
8. My father owned five slaves
9. one hundred and forty acres
10. posibly about 1200 dollars (not including slaves)
11. Hued log house containing five rooms
12. I did general farm work such as plowing, hoeing, hauling, etc.
13. My father done general farm work with the negros and my mother done all kinds of house work such as cooking, washing, ironing, spining, weaving, etc.
14. no
15. all kinds of honest work was considered honorable
16. yes
17. none at all
18. There was no difference made or no disctinction between the two classes.
19. They certainly did and the slave holders took their slaves to such places
20. There was a frindly feeling between so as I could tell
21. The fact that one party owned slaves did not cut any figure so far as I could tell
22. not very good
23. There wer encouraged as much by slave holders as they were by non slave holders
24. Subscription school for which I paid (or my father did) one dollar per month, also Tuscu__ (Tusculum) College.
25. about 3 months per year for about 8 years
26. 1½ miles
27. Those mentioned above
28. Private and publick
29. about 3 months
30. yes
31. men
32. the latter part of 1862 but dont remember the month
33. 12th Tennessee Cavalry Co. B 12th Batalion; Lloyd Bullen, Joe Bullen, George Bullen, Dave Ross, John Cavendy?, Alex Walker, George Wootner?, John Johnson, Bob Brannan, Bob Woolins (this may be same as above), George Cavinder.
34. I enlisted in Greene co. and remained there
35. Just a few days
36. Rhea Town
37. I went into Virginia then back to Tenn. engaged in battle at Bluff City then at Rogersville, where we were victorious and captured 947 prisoners was in Tenn. and Virginia throughout the war. was poorly clothed, poorly fed, went hungry a great deal, of the time, was captured at front and was kept at Knoxville for 3 months then sent to Camp Chase, Ohio where I remained a prisoner for 8 months.
38. was discharged in April 1865 at Newburn, Va.
39. I rode my horse from Newburn to Mt. Airy, N.C. thence home through the mountains was four or five days making the trip
40. farming with the exception of 3 years when I was guard at the state prison at Tracy City under Bob Taylors administration. Have been laid up with theumatism for 15 years and am helpless now.
42. Lee Bullen; Greene co., Tenn.; lived 3 miles from Greeneville; was wagon master, hauling for the Confederate army.
43. Nancy Gass; John Gass and Jennie Gass; lived in Greene county
44. My grandfather Joe Bullen came from New England and lived in Greene county the remainder of his life. My grandmother Jennie Bullen was Jennie Ross borne in Greene co. My grandfather on my mothers side John Gass came from Ireland and lived in Greene county until his death.

(N.B.: BULLEN, SAM D. Pension No. 3479)

BUNCH, FRANCIS MARION

FORM NO. 1

1. Francis Marion Bunch, Pulaski, Giles co., Tenn.
2. Seventy four (74)
3. Tenn., Giles county
4. Tenn. Giles co.
5. Clerk for my father
6. Overseer then miller in mercantile business when war began
7. I owned nothing myself. My father owned considerable town property
8. none
9. town property and about 100 acres land
10. about ten thousand dollars
11. frame with five rooms
12. I done all kind of work required around a water power sash saw and griss mill
13. My father done all kind of manual labor. He made several trips to New Orleans and (on) flat boats from Pulaski with cotton. Mother was cook done spinning weaving and all of the washing for six children.
14. none
15. no one doubted it being respectable and honerable
16. yes
17. Everybody worked but little idleness. Of course some hired men usually taken the front row with men hired house raising and log rolling swapped work
18. mingled freely - everybody was on a level no one thought themselves better than any body else
19. they did
20. frendly feeling existed so far as i can remember
21. It did not that I know of
22. yes
23. encouraged
24. mixed
25. five or 6 years
26. ½ mile
27. Giles College, same sight (site) as Pulaski High School now
28. private
29. Ten (10)
30. yes
31. Part time woman and mostly a man
32. 1861 Sixteenth day May Pulaski, Giles co., Tenn.
33. Third 3rd Tenn. infantry, J.C. Brown 1st Col.; I enclose names of my Company on another paper. I was orderly Sergent and have my roll call book now in my possession
34. Camp Cheatham, Rob. Co., Tenn.
35. May 16, 1861 to Feb. 12, 1862 at Ft. Donelson
36. Fort Donelson
37. From Donelson to Camp Douglas, Chicago, Ill. we were there 7 months. was exchanged at Vicksburg, Miss. in Sept. 1862. Regt. was reorganized at Jackson in Sept. I was made O. Sergent. In battle at Raymond, Jackson was at bombardment Port Hudson, La. when Faragut had such a narrow escape when his vessel was set on fire. we were all through north - at Chicamauga, Mission Ridge, Resaca, New Hope church
38. I was never discharged was captured on Hoods retreat in Jany. 1865 taken the oath in place of going to prison again and I knew it was all over.
39. brought here by Yankey guard taken oath at home
40. carpenter on bridge gang of M & C now Southern R.R.
41. I have been engaged in the mercanteel business most of the time groceries, hardware, butcher. Presbyterian Church. I am now Justice of the Peace.
    Other battles not mentioned above, Chicasaw Bayou, Miss., Atlanta Jonesboro, Ga., Marietta, Ga. Powder Spring, Ga. served 4 yrs in the army in every battle the regt. was engaged wounded at Raymond Miss. never missed roll call but once. never in hospital never paid as much as $25. doctor bill for myself in my life.

FORM NO. 1

1. Robert Lee Burks, Livingston, Tenn.
2. 73 years and 8 months Jan. 12, 1922
3. Tenn., Rutherford co.
4. Tenn., Rutherford co.
5. doing errands for my mother
6. Hotell propriator
7. no no
8. yes, my father owned slaves, dont know how many
9. my father owned land at time of my birth and was a failure (?) at Rutherford co, Tenn.
10. dont know my father was broken up at that time
11. lived in a rented hotell building at Shelbyville, Tenn.
12. did all sort of farm work from 12 to 16 year old which was from 1860 to 1864
13. have stated above my father occupation and my mother did all sorts of work pertaining to house keeping at that time cooking, spining weaving, cutting, making, etc. etc
14. never after leaving hotell
15. it was by every person
16. they did
17. a very small number lived idle
18. there was no difference made in society
19. they certainly did
20. they were perfectly friendly
21. I never observed any difference
22. there were
23. encouraged
24. common school when primary grades were taught
25. about four or five years
26. from ½ to 2½ mile
27. cant name them
28. public
29. from 5 to 10 months
30. yes
31. both
32. 1864 July near Millerburg, Rutherford county
33. 4th Tenn. Cavelry (Starnes) Capt. W.A. Hillard, John Leacock, John Hancock, W.G. Dillard, Jim Knox, Bill Feilds, Bob Clemmon, Jim Fulk, Jim Fox, Mat Webb, J.M. Fox, J.E. Fox, Tom Lee
34. I enlisted during Wheeler Raid into Tenn. in 1864
35. 2 or 3 months afterward
36. Saltville, Va.
37. after the battle of Saltville we went into north Ga. and fought all battles from Atlanta to Savanna, Ga. and from there around near the coast to Bentonville, N.C. we were poorly clothed and poorly fed but fought like heros.
38. at Washington, Ga.
39. I left my horse with a comrade and took a freight to Atlanta walked from Atlanta to Dalton got a freight from Dalton after staying in Dalton 2 days got a freight to Chattanooga stayed in rail yard one day and night and then to Fosterville on freight on home.
40. farming
41. farming afterwards practicing medicine then pharmacy then dealer in real estate
42. Willis Burks; near Beechgrove (then) Bedford co., Tenn.; lived same place; was a sone of Sam Burks a soldier of the American Revolution
43. Lucinda Blakely; James Blakely and Katy Blakely; near Millersburg, Rutherford co., Tenn.
44. My grandfather Sam Burks came from S.C. was a pensioner of the Govt. from the Revolutionary war while in Tenn. and afterwards from Mo.(?) until his death which was probably some where from 1840 to 1850 A.D. The family came from Ireland first settled in (N.?) Carolina then at South Carolina.   R.L. Burks

(N.B.: BURKS, ROBERT LEE Pension No. 14614)

BURNLEY, W. D.

(N.B.: written on side of form is "According to his mothers old Bible")

1. W.D. Burnley, Westmoreland, Tenn. RFD 3
2. He is 73 years old the 20 of April
3. ----
4. ----
5. W.D. Burnley is not able to asn. no quistions as he has been sick
   under the Dr. every since July and it would be imposible for him to
   ans. eny quistions and was as his friends dont expect him to be able
   eny more and if you could just see him uy would not expect eny ans.
   from him.

   Nothing is filled in on the form

   (N.B.: BURNLEY, WM. D. Pension No. 7184)

BUSLY (BUSBY?), JACK

FORM NO. 2

1. Mr. Jack Busly, Corinth, Miss.
2. 81
3. Tennessee the State, Macnery (McNairy) county
4. I was Confederate soldier
5. Company E-26 Mississippi
6. my father was a farmer
7. Cager Busly (Busby?); born in South Carolina; Fairfield District;
   lived Linger (Tinger?), Tennessee; he was a Justice of the Peace
8. Bodicy (Rodicy?) Barns before marriage; John Barns and (do not know);
   South Carolina then to Corinth, Miss in 1876 (could this date be
   incorrect?)
9. Grandfather was revolutionary war man. He came from England. Grandmother came from Ireland. They first settled in South Carolina there
   he raised a family of 8 boys and 2 girls. He was a farmer.
10. I had no property I was only 17. Her proper (theri?) was near Corinth,
    Miss. valued at $1000
11. no slaves
12. parents owned 160 acres
13. The 160 acres was valued about $1000
14. They lived in a frame house. Only 4 rooms
15. I farmed when I was a boy. I used plow and hoe, I plowed 1 acres a
    day
16. Father farmed. Mother cooked, carded, and spun she wove and made
    cloth, milled and house clean
17. none at all
18. This was honorable and respectable to men. Because this made them
    an honest living
19. All were engaged in such work
20. All were busy and had no one to work for them
21. Those who owned slaves near us did seem better than us. We all ranked
    in same class
22. All went to same school and churches, mingled together and had jolly
    times
23. All were friendly and economical toward each other.
24. no they did not do that
25. yes, all opportunities were good in our neighborhood
26. They were all encouraged by the small number of slave holders
27. I attend a country school
28. I went 5 years to school
29. 3 miles was nearest
30. only 1 country school where you were taught to read and write a little
31. The school was public school
32. 3 months in 1 year
33. no they did not
34. a man was the teacher
35. in 1861, March 1, Corinth, Miss. Yes I enlisted as a Confederate
    soldier

BUSLY/BUSBY (cont'd.):
36. at Boland Green, Kentucky
37. 11 months
38. Fort Doloson (Donelson) Tennessee
39. After 1 battle I went in prison Indonaplis, Indiana. I steward in
    the hospital. I was captured by federals. Then to Vicksburg, Miss.
    Federalist-none; Confederates-none; clothed scarce, slept on a
    blanket on the ground. 1 pint meal per day. Exposed to weather.
40. Point Lookout, Maryland
41. Ship was bloun away, arrived in Mobile, Ala. on another ship. Aug.
    27, 1865. No one was drouned but several died after. Did not have
    hardly anything to eat. Started from New York - 2 months to come
    home.
42. I worked at a steam mill. Work was not so hard. Worked all day
    until 10 o'clock of a night.
43. After civil war I was 21 year of age. I married in 1867 at Corinth,
    Miss. Here wife and me lived for a no. of years and raised a family
    of 4 girls and 3 boys. I was farming there. My children all
    married but 1. Then I moved to toun and began the occupation of a
    grocier store. Stayed in business about 3 months. Then I followed
    night watching and weavers manufacture in Corinth. By this time 4
    of my children died and also my wife. Then I lived with my relatives
    for a while. Then I moved with my son and night watch in the summer.
    I never held an office. I am a Bebtis (Baptist) member. Go to church
    often. 81 and look as young as ever.
44. ----
45. Will tell you all I can remember: Col. A.E. Reynolds, Lt. Col. Martin
    Boon, Capt. Jim Sharp, Quarter Master L.M. Henerson; J.M. Pickens,
    Jack Jones, Billie Jones, John Larue, R.M. Springer, Poke Cashing,
    Henery Smith, Jim Woods, Nat Busly, Jack Busly.
46. Nash? Bigim   Leada, Miss.
    Mr. Burns   Corinth, Miss.
    Mr. Dalton   "   "
    Mr. Coon Vanaduvar   "   "
    Proffesor Harris   "   "
    Mr. Murphy   "   "
    Mike Powell   "   "

BUTLER, THOMAS JEFFERSON

FORM NO. 1

1. Tomas Jefferson Buttler, Whittwell (Whitwell), Tenn.
2. 78 in Sept. 1922
3. Coffee co., Tenn.
4. Coffee co., Tenn.
5. Farming
6. Farming
7. did not owne any property
8. did not own any
9. 230 acres
10. $3500.00
11. Log house 4 rooms
12. plowing hoeing any kind of farm work
13. plowing hoeing all of farm work. Mother cooked spun and weaved cloth
    to cloth(e) the family
14. no
15. yes
16. yes
17. all worked
18. I never noticed any difference
19. yes
20. friendly
21. no
22. yes fairly good
23. no disencouragement
24. public 3 or 4 months per year
25. 2 years
26. 1 mile

BUTLER (cont'd.):
27. 7 away at Manchester Tenn
28. public
29. 3 month
30. yes
31. man
32. Beach Grove, Tenn. in confederacy May 1861
33. 17 Tenn. James Armstrong, Capt. , James Govel, Tom Waterson, Sam
    Rabon, The? Martin, Bill Jenkins, Wes? Haggard, Luther Haggard, John
    Stevens
34. Bowin Green (Bowling Green) Ky
35. 6 months
36. Rock Castle, Ky.
37. to Va. back to Ky. had battle Mill Springs Ky. (to Tenn. Murfreesboro
    battle), to Va. with Long St. (Longstreet) and surrender with Lee at
    Appamottox - all day in at Mursboro (Murfreesboro?) - sorry clothed
    usually. 2 blanket slept on ground with out ---- ---- part of time
    poorly fed
38. Attamatox (Appomatox) Va.
39. by R.R. War Trace, Tenn.
40. Farming
41. Farmer and rock mason in Bedford co., near Wartrace and whitwell,
    Tenn.
42. David Butler; Coffee, Tenn.; lived at Beach Grove.
43. ---- Adams; John Adams and (she was Hickman); Man------ (Manchester?)
    Tenn.
44. Grandfather Peter Butler came from N.C. Mothers father John Adams
    Ireland to Manchester, Tenn.

BUTTS, MELMON MARION

FORM NO. 1

1. Melmon Marion Butts, 1114 South High Street (no city shown)
2. 78 yrs. 8 mo.
3. Maury co., Tenn.
4. Maury co., Tenn.
5. Farmer
6. Farmer
7. Did not own any
8. Father own one negro woman some time before the beginning of the war
9. Did not own land
10. ----
11. Log house two story four rooms two on first story and two on second
    story
12. I practically worked on farm all the time plowed hoed grubed cut
    wood hauled and all other kinds of farm work
13. My father did all kinds of work theres to do on farm altho he was to
    old to do very much phisical labor when the war started. My mother
    did all the work with the assistance of my two sisters cooking for
    the family did all the spinning weaving sewing and made all the
    clothes for the family
14. no
15. It was quite honorable most white people did all of it
16. yes
17. ten per cent had enough slaves that they didn't have to manual labor
    but didn't live lived of idlesness
18. not very many had that attitude everbody was very sociable
19. yes
20. all were sociable and very friendly feeling existed would help each
    other all possible in any
21. no local politics didn't play very big part
22. yes
23. they were encouraged
24. country district school
25. fifteen months
26. two to five miles
27. two or three district schools in a radius of five or six miles
28. public

427

BUTTS (cont'd.):
29. from three to six months
30. yes
31. both
32. September 1861
33. Maury Artillery - Capt. R.R. Ross, Lt. Mat Sparkman, Lt. Felix Cook,
    Lt. Sig? Thompson, Sam Walker Orderly Sargeant, E.P. Alexander, Even
    Alexander, A.J. Alexander, W.W. and O.P. Hite, Dick Hite, Jim Bruce,
    Pink Fitzgerald, Green Jack, Tom Dodson, Jno. Dodson, Raliegh Dodson,
    Ann? Waters, Bob Waters, Henry Waters, Bird Waters, Jim Shaw, Tom
    Pigg, Poke Pigg, Dan Pigg, Sam Jones, Jim Jones, Henry Jones, Bid
    Beverly Jones, David Jones, Ane Charter, Marion Dockley, Nevels
    Dockley, Hame Hutcherson, Bud Hutcherson, J.N.B. Johnson, Abe Fitz-
    gerald, Bryant Escew, Tom? Headscuff, Andrew West, Bill West, Frank
    Allen, Poke Godwins, Tom Moore, Frank Smith, Harrison Robinson, Jno.
    -Sam-Jim-Bill Wooley, Jno. and Jerry Miller, Dan Dickus, Tho. Skelley,
    Bill Hood, Monroe Hood, Lige Watson, Lt. Watt Cook, John Goad?, Jim
    Goad?, Geo. Notgears?, John Cumming, Joe Macrady
34. Hopkinville, Ky.
35. Three months
36. Fort Donelson, Tenn.
37. To Chicago as prisoner. Stayed there seven months was fed very well
    exchanged at Vicksburg Miss. went from there to Jackson Miss. stayed
    there two months from there Thangabato (_____) La. there one week
    from there to Clinton La. about thirty miles camped there two months
    from there to Port Hudson La. about re miles then hard times began
    built fortification bressworks magazines ___ Had anything to eat we
    could get sugar and molasses seige began we were fighting for 48 days
    and nights captured on 8 July 1863
38. Camp Morton, Ind. May 20th 1865
39. Rode a freight from Indianapolis Ind. to Louisville Ky set us across
    the river on a boat. Took another freight to Nashville Tenn. took
    a freight to Cuters? Creek Station there I bid them goodbye.
40. farming
41. Lived on a farm until 1888 moved to Columbia, Tenn. her since. member
    of Christian Church. Police fire or six years constable
42. Thomas P. Butts; Georgia; do not know; from Georgia to Maury co. Tenn.
    Tenn.
43. Diana Lee. (no other information)
44. ----

    (on attached sheet - headed "Louisville & Nashville Railroad Co.")
37. was caried to Camp Morton, Ind. I remained until the war ended on
    May 1865. My treatment at Camp Morton was bad. No wholesome food -
    expose to cold weather some froze to death - went hungry and about
    half naked - had lice and mites - which was very troublesome -
    officers and guards treated us very bad - punishment unnecessary.

    (N.B.: BUTTS, MELMON MARION Pension No. 12261)

                          BYNUM, E. J.

FORM NO. 2

1. E.J. Bynam, Daylight Rt. 2, Tennessee
2. 81 yrs
3. Tennessee, Cannon County
4. Confederate
5. Co. E- 4th Calvary; Brigade Commander-Horton; Div. Commander-Joseph
   Wheeler; Capt. Nichols, Compy-commander
6. Farmer
7. Redmon Bynum; Bradyville; Cannon co., Tenn.; lived at Bradyville.
8. Jane Joy; dau. of ____ Joy and ____; lived Cannon county, near
   Bradyville, Tenn.
9. Grandfather on father side came from North Carolina
10. not any
11. no
12. 100 acres
13. $1500.00

BYNUM (cont'd.):
14. Log house, one room
15. worked on farm, plowed with bull-tongue plow and did hoe work
16. Father worked on farm. Mother did cooking, spinning and other general house work.
17. none
18. work on farm then was considered honorable and respectable
19. all white men worked
20. all men did their own work
21. not any distinction made
22. mingled freely with each other and all ways showed a lending hand toward each other
23. Friendly feeling
24. The fact that men owned slaves, and men that didnt own slaves, did not have any bearing in political contest.
25. Opportunities then were good for all young men.
26. Encouraged
27. Private school, usually three months a year
28. ----
29. about 5 miles
30. private schools
31. private
32. Two to three months
33. when not engaged in any work.
34. ----
35. September 30th, 1862. Cannon county, near Bradyville
36. Perryville, Ky.
37. about 8 days
38. Perryville
39. From Perryville went thru East Tennessee to Knoxville, got cut off from supplies and did without eats 3 days and nights and rations we got was meat and bread without season. Next fight at Murfreesboro and then at Chickamauga, Ga.
40. April last at Charlotte, N.C.
41. Had no means when discharged and but few clothes-made the trip by pieces - got home the best I could.
42. farming
43. Since the Civil War I settled on farm and have engaged in such work since. Member of Methodist Church. Received in church at Daniel's Church, Cannon Co. 5th Dist. present membership at Cross-Roads, Cannon Co. near Short Mountain. Principally lived in Cannon and Warren Counties.
44. Personally acquainted with General R.E. Lee, Joseph E. Johnson, Joseph Wheeler, Nathan B. Forest, John Savage.
45. Willie fowler, Ord. Sgt.; Tom Yates, Pvt.; Boss and Kern? Yates, Pvt.; Bob Williams, Pvt.; Jay Cooper, Pvt.; Tommy Ing?, Pvt.; Tom Roberts, Pvt.; Dock, Bill and James Taylor, Pvt.; John Arnold, Pvt.; Willy Gray, Pvt.; Poke? Segley (Segler?), Pvt.; John Willy (Wilber?), James and Jesse Jernigan, Pvts.
46. James Hollis   Daylight Rt. 2, Tenn.
    John Purser   Smithville, Tenn.
    Jay W_lling   McMinnville, Tenn.
    Bill _ell   "   "
    Manse Smallman   "   "

BYRD, JAMES JORDAN

FORM NO. 2

1. James Jordan Byrd, Linden, Tenn.
2. 82 years
3. Tennessee, Williamson Co.
4. Confederate
5. Co. B-54 Alabama
6. Carpenter
7. H.L. Byrd; South Carolina; Dont know; lived Williamson, Murray and Marshall Counties; Private in Mexican War under Higgins of Athens, Ala. also private in Civil War.

BYRD (cont'd.):
8. Susan Crane; dau. of Thomas and Mattie Crane; lived South Carolina, town dont know.
9. ----
10. none
11. no
12. none
13. none
14. Log house
15. General farm work
16. Carpenter
17. no
18. Honorable
19. yes
20. Generally industrious
21. All very social
22. yes
23. Friendly
24. Nothing considered except qualification
25. Some
26. Encouraged
27. Public Schools
28. Six months
29. Mile
30. Dont know
31. Public
32. Three
33. Yes
34. Man
35. Capitol. Nashville July 4, 1861
36. Randolph county, Virginia
37. Five months
38. Huntersville, Virginia
39. after first Battle was sent to Montney? Va., Reedsville, Bakers Creek, Miss., Jackson, Miss. and several minor battles.
40. Montgomery, Ala. June 1 "65"
41. train less than half way and rest of way walked.
42. General farm work till year 1887. Public works.
43. General County Collector. County Corornor. Deputy Trustee, County Jailer many years.
44. ----
45. Capt. C.B. Rasler, Athens, Ala.; Lt. Williamson, Don't know; Jim Turettine(?), Athens, Ala.; Privates: Blake Byrd, Bethesda, Williamson Co.; Francis Marion(?) Byrd, Columbia, Tenn.; L.M. Byrd, Thompson Station, Tenn.; H.L. Byrd, Linden, Tenn.; Jeff Bradshaw, Athens, Ala.
46. Dr. J.N. Black   Linden, Tenn.
    N.B. Strickland   "   "
    E.L. Humm(?)   "   "
    Joe Warren   Lobelville, Tenn.

BYRNE, GEORGE DALLAS

FORM NO. 2

1. George Dallas Byrne, Monterey(?), Tenn.
2. 77 yrs. and 10 months
3. Jackson, Tenn.
4. Confederate
5. Co. K-17 Tenn.
6. Farmer
7. Laurence Byrne; Kingston, Rone co., Tenn.; lived Middle Tenn.; Glove maker and Postmaster.
8. Sarah Carlisle; dau. of Simon Carlisle and ___
9. Simon Carlisle (my grandfather) was a pioneer Methodist Preacher. A young (man) for spite sliped a piston (pistol) in his sadle bags while he was at diner, soon after he left the young man said the preacher had stole his piston (pistol). The young man made a full confession on his death bed.
10. none

430

BYRNE (cont'd.):
11. no
12. None
13. $500.00
14. Log
15. All kinds farm work
16. Raising sheep and cotton, spinning, weaving, cooking, washing
17. no
18. All together
19. They did
20. Very few
21. could tell but little diference
22. They did
23. Friendly
24. Mad(e) no diference
25. Good
26. Encouraged
27. Public
28. Six or eight month all told
29. Two and half mile
30. None but public
31. Public
32. Two or three
33. Not very
34. Man
35. July 1863 near Shelbyville, Tenn.   (Confederate)
36. Remained in Bedford Co. sometime
37. 3 or 4 months
38. Murfresboro
39. Wounded at Murfresboro sent to Rome Georga. Got back to my co at
    Tullahoma was in the battle at Hooves (Hoover's) Gap and Chickmaga
    (Chickamauga).
40. Was sent from Knoxville over the montain for horses. got cut off
    never got back
41. Sliped thrugh Federel lines walk by night slept by day and begd for
    bread.
42. Farming
43. For a start I got married worked on the farm made a Methodist
    preacher. Joined the Tennessee Conference. Traveled all over middl
    Tennessee and settled at Monterey, Tenn.
44. ----

    (N.B.: BYRNE, GEORGE DALLAS Pension No. 12248)

                         BYRNE, JAMES POLK

FORM NO. 1

1. James Polk Byrne, 913-20th Avenue South Nashville, Tenn.
2. 79 last birth day - April 23, 1920
3. Jackson County, Tennessee
4. Putnam County, Tennessee C.S.A.
5. Farmer
6. Farmer
7. None
8. No
9. 100 acres
10. About $500
11. Log house - four rooms
12. Hoed, plowed, split rails, built fences, cleared land and all other
    kind of work usily don on a farm
13. Father did not work on the farm on account of physical inability.
    Mother and sisters cooked, washed, ironed, spun cotton and wool on
    an old time spining wheel, made cotton and wool cloth on a hand
    loom.
14. No
15. Yes
16. Yes
17. None

                              431

BYRNE (cont'd.):
18. No
19. Yes
20. Yes 0 no antagonistic feeling existed
21. No
22. No
23. Neither
24. Public known at that time District or free school
25. about 12 months
26. one to two miles
27. none but free schools
28. Public
29. one to three
30. Yes
31. a man
32. June 1861 at Granville, Tennessee
33. S.B. McDearman, Wade W. Cowan, R.B. Montgomery, G.W. McDonald, Matt
    Montgomery, J.D. McKinley, George McKinley, T.J. Lee, J.M. Lee,
    Moss Sadler, Wm. Lewis, Jas. Maurier, Dent Parkerson, John Fuqua,
    Pink Stanton, G.W. Stanton, Jno. Swan, Absalom Bryant, Wm. Wyatt,
    Jesse (Jason?) Bearley, John Apple, James P. Byrne, R.C.? Byrne,
    G.D. Byrne, Marion Young
34. Camp Trousdale
35. Seven months
36. Fishing Creek
37. Marched to Iuka, Miss. Battle of Shiloh. Company camped and drilled
    at Tupelo, Miss. from there to Mobile, Ala. on train. by boat to
    Montgomery, Ala. by rail via Atlanta to Chattanooga, marched over
    the mountins Sand Shoals, crossed the Cumberland River thence
    Munfordsville where we captured a lot of yankees on to Bardstown(?)
    through eastern Ky. to Cumberland Gap, in the battle of Perryville,
    Murfreesboro and Chickamauga.
38. June 9, 1865 at Fort Delaware, Del.
39. Went up the Delaware Bay to Philadelphia on steam tugs(?) By rail
    to Nashville, Tenn. Had one dollar in green back bought 15¢ worth
    of cheese and 10¢ worth of crackers in Philadelphia, which was all I
    had to eat on the trip to Nashville, where I arrived June 11, 1865
40. Clerking
41. Engaged in mercantile business for 30 years. Member of the City
    Council 11 consecutive years. Was president of the Council 4 yrs.
    City Recorder 5 yrs. Deputy Registor 12 years.
42. Laurence Byrne; Mecklenburg co., North Carolina
43. Sarah Carlisle; Rev. Simon Carlisle and ____ Tate; near Granville,
    Tenn.
    (Signed: J.P. Byrne, Lieut. Co. K., 17th Tenn. Infty. C.S.A.)

(N.B.: BYRNE, JAMES POLK Pension No. 15490)

FEDERAL SOLDIERS

Prepared by
Dorothy Sewell Peters
Fort Worth, Tx.

A man, Jesse 21
Abernathy, Co. ...143
  Press 92
Acra, John 33
Acuff, Joel 14
  Joel A. 1
  John D. 2
Adair, George W. 2
  G. W. 4
  Isac 2,3
  James David 3
  J. D. 1
  Mary 35
Adams, George 105
  James 46
  Mary 30
  Whig 48
Adamson, C. E. 57
Adkinson, Gails (?) 129
Aged, Jess 35
Agee, Kerry 76
  Wm. 76
Ailey, Arnold 116
  Harrison 116
  Huston 90
Akins, Rafel 107
Alen, D. S. N. 68
Alexander, Andrew J. 21
  Joseph 14
Aliger, Adam 51
Allen, Arch 104
  B. B. 97
  Chambles 66
  D. B. 97
  House 52
  James 50
  Joe 52
  John 52,90,116
  W. 65
Allison, Robert M. 4
  Thomas 4
  Uriah S. 4,37
  William 37
Allister, Z. T. 21
Ambrose, Mash.(?) 10
Amey, H. 97
Anderson, George 5
  George R. 33
  G. W. 97
  Harris 52
  J. 97
  James 7
  John 7,50
  John Fain 4,7
  John R. 7
  J. R. 7
  Lem 78
  Martin 98
  R. E. 6
  Samuel 5,7
  S. H. 7
  William 6,7,50
Andie, Moore (Andie Moore?)
  90
Andrews, Henry 47
Angel, Geo. 103
  James P. 103
  S. F. 103
Archer, Isaac 21
  John 19
Aric, Capt....14
Arnel, James 55
Arnes, Sigh 131
Ary, Wm. 70

Ashford, John 57
Ashly, Bene 68
Asker, Felder 21
Aslinger, Bill 24
Atchley, Jessie 54
  W. D. 54,81
Atchly, William D. 8
Attlee, Ewin 65
Ausbin, William 14
Awls, Bill 23

Babb, Abner 21
  A. F. 95
  Isaac Eweuan 8
  Landen F. 21
  Landon 28
  William Landon 8
Backsley, Jno. 135
Bacon, C. N. 149
Badget, Mrs. Timey (Tinney?)
  67
Badgett, Jo. 103
Bageal, John 98
Baily, H. J. 96
Baine, Patrick A./O. 21
Baker, Benjamin 145
  Capt....143
  Daniel 135
  Dav 140
  Jake 90
  John 107
  John L. 21
Balch, Hartwell 18
Baldan, Nathan 129
Bales, Harry 9
  Harvey 135
  Jonathan 9
  L. R. 10
Ball, Bill 52
Ballard, Anthony 21
Ballew, Thomas 62
Banch, Joe 54
Bandy, Lt....47
  Wes 80
  Wesley 17
Banks, Nathaniel P. 25
Banster,....122
Barbee, Jno. 76
Barberson, William 78
Bard, John H. 14
Bardell, John 37
Bardetl, Martin 37
Barger, Jim 78
  Johan 33
Barkley, John Henry 6
Barnard, Joseph A. 33
Barnet, Nute 84
Barnett,....143
  John Wilson 10
  William Hazelett 10
Barnhart, Conrad 116
  Elizabeth 116
  Evasoul 116
Barnheart, Jake 125
Barns, Elexander 145
  Robert 145
Barrett, G. L. 97
Bartholomew, Milt 48
Bartlett, Cap. 131
Baston, Add 125
Batman, Green 15
Battles, W. F. 153
Baxter, Chaly L. 21
Beard, Joe 35

Beard, cont'd:
  J. A. 96
Beaver, Andy 79
Beckidite, Lem 78
Beirns(?), Giorg 122
Bell, ...102
  Maud W. 150 ·
  Robert 64
Bellers, Andres J. 33
Benedict, Anna 123
Benkert, E. G. 97
Bennet, Sam 23
Bennett, Benjamin F. 11
  Liza An 12
Bentlea, ...46
Berket, Bill 48
  Frank 48
Berks, ...46
Bewley, Anthony 13
  Jacob Murphy 13
  Josiah B. 13
  Philip Meroney 13
Bibb, Lun 139
  Tom 139
Bill, Jim 17
Bird, James 34
  Jesse 4
  J. H. 1
  Jim 24,54
  Nancy 4
  Robert K. 4
  Simon 81
Birdwell, Albert 14
Bishop, John 103
  Nancy Ann 70
  Sallie 70
Bissell, John 98
Bittle, George 50
Bivins, Joe 55
  William M. 50
Bixler, ...46
Black, I. M. (Dr.) 70
  J. N. 125
  Major...55
Blackburn, J. H. 42
  Joe 57
Blackwell, Sam 52
Blair, William C. 15,16
Blake, Bill 54
  E. D. 6
Blalock, William 129
Blankenship, Ace 41
  David 16
  M. 17
  Sam 41
  Samuel S. M. 16
  S. S. M. 136
Blazor, George 34,54,81
Blevens, Ganes 129
  John 129
  Lewis 129
Blevins, Gerge 68
Bloodworth, Ruth 125
Boatman, Green 107
  Henry 69
  Kazih 69
  Nancy 69
Boddie, Grandma 121
Bogle, Chloer 59
Bohanan, Jim 87
Boing, David C. 21
Boles, Harvey 121
  Jess 21
Bolgalvy,...122

CONFEDERATE VETERANS